READINGS IN ANTHROPOLOGY

Volume II

Readings in Cultural Anthropology

Also by Morton H. Fried

Fabric of Chinese Society

Morton H. Fried

READINGS IN

ANTHROPOLOGY

Volume II

Readings in Cultural Anthropology

Thomas Y. Crowell Company · New York · Established 1834

Designed by Laurel Wagner

Cover design by Ingrid Fraenckel

Manufactured in the United States of America by the Vail-Ballou Press, Inc., Binghamton, N.Y.

Library of Congress Catalog Card Number 59-6441

Introductory Note

THIS VOLUME contains 38 articles devoted to various aspects of cultural anthropology. They define the subject and present concrete examples of the work which is carried out, both descriptive and analytical, in the field and in the analysis of the structure and content of culture. This book is the continuation of Volume I—*Readings in Physical Anthropology, Linguistics and Archeology.*

The selections are uneven. They differ in degree of detail, in complexity of analysis, in the facility of their authors' pens. Some guide to the main point or points made in each article will be found in the editor's statement which precedes it. Those who read this book in conjunction with a course in anthropology will be guided by their instructor. A few technical remarks, however, may make the reading of this book easier and more enjoyable.

Though the articles proceed in an order sensible to the editor, many other alternative organizations are possible and one does not have to examine the materials sequentially. A certain amount of cross referencing has been done in the prefatory statements. References are, e.g., to II:32—meaning selection No. 32 in this volume, which is the second of two. Articles in the first volume are referred to, for example, as No. I:1, etc.

A glossary of unfamiliar terms will be found at the end of this book as well as a table showing the correspondence between the selections in these pages and the organization of the presently available text books in anthropology. In the contest between the desire to include as many selections as possible and the obvious limitations of space, one important compromise was made: the extensive footnoting, particularly bibliographical, of most of these articles was deleted. Students who wish to pursue a subject further are urged to look up the original selection and examine its bibliography.

Contents

Cultural Anthropology

WITH linguistics and archeology treated in the first volume as aspects of cultural anthropology, the heading here may appear redundant and confusing. The use of the phrase "cultural anthropology" to designate the study of culture exclusive of archeological and linguistic specializations is conventional in the United States, and for this reason it appears above. Elsewhere, as in Great Britain, the phrase is steadfastly avoided, "social anthropology" being preferred. The two fields thus delimited are generally congruent, but their distinct names reflect a significant difference in their contents if not their methods. To some extent the difference is reminiscent of (but basically unlike) the distinction between cultural anthropology and sociology. (The reader who is puzzled over this particular difference might begin clarifying the matter by comparing the table of contents of this volume with that of the Schuler, Gibson, Fiero and Brookover *Outside Readings in Sociology*.) Briefly, where cultural anthropology retains a very broad view, studying social organization in larger cultural contexts, social anthropology tends to concentrate on the structure and functioning of particular human societies with a consequent de-emphasis of other aspects of culture.

The breadth of view of American cultural anthropology has encouraged the development of various new types of research, some requiring skills developed in other disciplines. Community studies borrow heavily from sociology and culture-personality research leans upon psychological and psychiatric methods.

Though it is sometimes said that anthropological interest in modern complex societies is a recent development, both Tylor and Morgan, not to mention other outstanding nineteenth-century anthropologists, had vital interests in the complex societies of their time. It is true, however, that whereas nineteenth century sociology concentrated on European society, the contemporary anthropology was largely devoted to studies of aboriginal cultures and speculation about the evolution of culture.

The shrinking of the globe through revolutions in transportation also threatened to extinguish ethnography, the study of particular cultures, since fewer and fewer cultures remained untouched by trade, money or machinery. One of the first reactions of the ethnographers was to concentrate on the old people; working intensively with them it was possible to recall and record something of those cultures which a generation before had been thriving and now were altered and feeble. Soon, however, it was realized that the meeting of two cultures with subsequent changes in one or both was itself a most important thing to study. With acculturation studies also came research in non-primitive communities—plantations, peasant villages, Chinese towns and Yankee industrial cities. Regardless of changes in the theory or methods of cultural (and social) anthropology, field work remains the main source of data and a prime requirement in the developing careers of fledgling anthropologists.

First among the problems of cultural anthropology is the definition of its subject (No. II:1). Immediately after comes the necessity of dividing it into manageable portions (No. II:2) and establishing the methods by which the subject shall be worked (Nos. II:3–5). Beyond this point various directions might be followed. We have chosen a topical sequence which is based upon a trisection of culture into primary institutional sectors: technological, sociological and ideological. These are preceded, however, by a consideration of the interaction of the physical environment and culture (Nos. II:6 and II:7) and followed by an equally brief treatment of themes in the culture/personality field (Nos. II:33–35).

A. Culture and Its Study

1. THE SCIENCE OF CULTURE *

Twenty-eight pages of Kroeber and Kluckhohn's *Culture: A Critical Review of Concepts and Definitions* (1952) are devoted to a listing of definitions of culture. Notable, however, is the authors' statement that the basic anthropological meaning of the word is that which was given by Edward Tylor in 1871 and which is reprinted below. Common to all anthropological definitions of culture is the notion that it includes all symbolically learned patterns of behavior, not simply those which are chic, or highly valued, or associated with the arts or with civilization. Tylor did more than establish the anthropological meaning of culture. He took his place with those who insisted that human behavior was a kind of natural phenomenon, caused and regular, which could be subjected to objective study and analysis with hope of the ultimate discovery or formulation of laws of cultural process and evolution. The matter rests in controversy. Tylor's views live on (see Nos. I:3, I:35 and II:9) but there is strong opposition (see No. II:29).

Culture or Civilization, taken in its wide ethnographic sense, is that complex whole which includes knowledge, belief, art, morals, law, custom, and any other capabilities and habits acquired by man as a member of society. The condition of culture among the various societies

* Edward B. Tylor, "The Science of Culture," Chapter 1 of *Primitive Culture* (London: John Murray & Co., 1871, 2 vols.), pp. 1–25. Reprinted by permission of the publisher.

Sir Edward Burnett Tylor (1832–1917) held the first chair of anthropology established at the University of Oxford. While his experience of exotic cultures was limited of mankind, in so far as it is capable of being investigated on general principles, is a subject apt for the study of laws of human thought and action. On the one hand, the uniformity which so largely pervades civilization may be ascribed, in great measure, to the uniform action of uniform causes: while on the other hand its various grades may be regarded as stages of development or evolution, each the outcome of previous history, and about to do its proper part in shaping the history of the future. To the investigation of these two great principles in several departments of ethnography, with especial consideration of the civilization of the lower tribes as related to the civilization of the higher nations, the present volumes are devoted.

Our modern investigators in the sciences of inorganic nature are foremost to recognize, both within and without their special fields of work, the unity of nature, the fixity of its laws, the definite sequence of cause and effect through which every fact depends on what has gone before it, and acts upon what is to come after it. They grasp firmly the Pythagorean doctrine of pervading order in the universal Kosmos. They affirm, with Aristotle, that nature is not full of incoherent episodes, like a bad tragedy. They agree with Leibnitz in what he calls 'my axiom, that nature never acts by leaps (la nature n'agit jamais par saut),' as well as in his 'great principle, commonly little employed, that nothing happens without sufficient reason.' Nor again, in studying the structure and habits of plants and animals, or in investigating the lower functions even of man, are these leading ideas unacknowledged. But when we come to talk of the higher processes of human feeling and action, of thought and language, knowledge and art, a change appears in the prevalent tone of opinion. The world at large is scarcely prepared to accept the general study of human life as a branch of natural science, and to carry out, in a large sense, the poet's injunction to 'Account for moral as for natural things.' To many educated minds there seems something presumptuous and repulsive in the view that the history of mankind is part and parcel of the history of nature, that our thoughts, wills, and actions accord with laws as definite as those which govern the motion of waves, the combination of acids and bases, and the growth of plants and animals.

The main reasons of this state of the popular judgment are not far to seek. There are many who would willingly accept a science of history if placed before them with substantial definiteness of principle and evi-

---

to a visit to Mexico (1856) and later (1884) to the Southwestern United States, where he visited Pueblo Indians, he had an experimental, research view of anthropology which is manifest in his writings. His contributions to anthropology are numerous and varied, ranging from specific studies in the diffusion of traits to a theory of the origin of religion. Among his books are *Researches into the Early History of Mankind* (1865), *Primitive Culture* (1871) and *Anthropology* (1881).

dence, but who not unreasonably reject the systems offered to them, as falling too far short of a scientific standard. Through resistance such as this, real knowledge always sooner or later makes its way, while the habit of opposition to novelty does such excellent service against the invasions of speculative dogmatism, that we may sometimes even wish it were stronger than it is. But other obstacles to the investigation of laws of human nature arise from considerations of metaphysics and theology. The popular notion of free human will involves not only freedom to act in accordance with motive, but also a power of breaking loose from continuity and acting without cause,—a combination which may be roughly illustrated by the simile of a balance sometimes acting in the usual way, but also possessed of the faculty of turning by itself without or against its weights. This view of an anomalous action of the will, which it need hardly be said is incompatible with scientific argument, subsists as an opinion patent or latent in men's minds, and strongly affecting their theoretic views of history, though it is not, as a rule, brought prominently forward in systematic reasoning. Indeed the definition of human will, as strictly according with motive, is the only possible scientific basis in such enquiries. Happily, it is not needful to add here yet another to the list of dissertations on supernatural intervention and natural causation, on liberty, predestination, and accountability. We may hasten to escape from the regions of transcendental philosophy and theology, to start on a more hopeful journey over more practicable ground. None will deny that, as each man knows by the evidence of his own consciousness, definite and natural cause does, to a great extent, determine human action. Then, keeping aside from considerations of extra-natural interference and causeless spontaneity, let us take this admitted existence of natural cause and effect as our standing-ground, and travel on it so far as it will bear us. It is on this same basis that physical science pursues, with ever-increasing success, its quest of laws of nature. Nor need this restriction hamper the scientific study of human life, in which the real difficulties are the practical ones of enormous complexity of evidence, and imperfection of methods of observation.

Now it appears that this view of human will and conduct as subject to definite law, is indeed recognised and acted upon by the very people who oppose it when stated in the abstract as a general principle, and who then complain that it annihilates man's free will, destroys his sense of personal responsibility, and degrades him to a soulless machine. He who will say these things will nevertheless pass much of his own life in studying the motives which lead to human action, seeking to attain his wishes through them, framing in his mind theories of personal character, reckoning what are likely to be the effects of new combinations, and giving to his reasoning the crowning character of true scientific enquiry, by taking it for granted that in so far as his calculation turns out wrong, either his evidence must have been false or incomplete, or his judgment upon it unsound. Such a one will sum up the experience of years spent in complex relations with society, by declaring his persuasion that there is a reason for everything in life, and that where events look unaccountable, the rule is to wait and watch in hope that the key to the problem may some day be found. This man's observation may have been as narrow as his inferences are crude and prejudiced, but nevertheless he has been an inductive philosopher 'more than forty years without knowing it.' He has practically acknowledged definite laws of human thought and action, and has simply thrown out of account in his own studies of life the whole fabric of motiveless will and uncaused spontaneity. It is assumed here that they should be just so thrown out of account in wider studies, and that the true philosophy of history lies in extending and improving the methods of the plain people who form their judgments upon facts, and check them upon new facts. Whether the doctrine be wholly or but partly true, it accepts the very condition under which we search for new knowledge in the lessons of experience, and in a word the whole course of our rational life is based upon it.

'One event is always the son of another, and we must never forget the parentage,' was a remark made by a Bechuana chief to Casalis the African missionary. Thus at all times historians, so far as they have aimed at being more than mere chroniclers, have done their best to show not merely succession, but connexion, among the events upon their record. Moreover, they have striven to elicit general principles of human action, and by these to explain particular events, stating expressly or taking tacitly for granted the existence of a philosophy of history. Should any one deny the possibility of thus establishing historical laws, the answer is ready with which Boswell in such a case turned on Johnson: 'Then, sir, you would reduce all history to no better than an almanack.' That nevertheless the labours of so many eminent thinkers should have as yet brought history only to the threshold of science, need cause no wonder to those who consider the bewildering complexity of the problems which come before the general historian. The evidence from which he is to draw his conclusions is at once so multifarious and so doubtful, that a full and distinct view of its bearing on a particular question is hardly to be attained, and thus the temptation becomes all but irresistible to garble it in support of some rough and ready theory of the course of events. The philosophy of history at large, explaining the past and predicting the future phenomena of man's life in the world by reference to general laws, is in fact a subject with which, in the present state of knowledge, even genius aided by wide research seems but hardly able to cope. Yet there are departments of it which, though difficult enough, seem comparatively accessible. If the field of enquiry be narrowed from History as a whole to that branch of it which is here called Culture, the history, not of tribes or nations, but of the condition of knowledge, religion, art, custom, and the like among them, the task of investigation proves to lie within far more moderate compass. We suffer still from the same kind of difficulties which beset the wider argument, but they are much diminished. The evidence is no longer so wildly heterogeneous, but may be more simply classified and compared, while the power of getting rid of extraneous matter, and treating each issue on its own proper set of facts, makes close reasoning on the whole more available than in general history. This may appear from a brief preliminary examination of the problem, how the phenomena of Culture may be classified and arranged, stage by stage, in a probable order of evolution.

Surveyed in a broad view, the character and habit of mankind at once display that similarity and consistency of phenomena which led the Italian proverb-maker to declare that 'all the world is one country,' 'tutto il mondo è paese.' To general likeness in human nature on the one hand, and to general likeness in the circumstances of life on the other, this similarity and consistency may no doubt be traced, and they may be studied with especial fitness in comparing races near the same grade of civilization. Little respect need be had in such comparisons for date in history or for place on the map; the ancient Swiss lake-dweller may be set beside the mediæval Aztec, and the Ojibwa of North America beside the Zulu of South Africa. As Dr. Johnson contemptuously said when he had read about Patagonians and South Sea Islanders in Hawkesworth's Voyages, 'one set of savages is like another.' How true a generalization this really is, any Ethnological Museum may show. Examine for instance the edged and pointed instruments in such a collection; the inventory includes hatchet, adze, chisel, knife, saw, scraper, awl, needle, spear and arrow-head, and of these most or all belong with only differences of detail to races the most various. So it is with savage occupations; the wood-chopping, fishing with net and line, shooting and spearing game, fire-making, cooking, twisting cord and plaiting baskets, repeat themselves with wonderful uniformity in the museum shelves which illustrate the life of the lower races from Kamchatka to Tierra del Fuego, and from Dahome to Hawaii. Even when it comes to comparing barbarous hordes with civilized nations, the consideration thrusts itself upon our minds, how far item after item of the life of the lower races passes into analogous proceedings of the higher, in forms not too far changed to be recognized, and sometimes hardly changed at all. Look at the modern European peasant using his hatchet and his hoe, see his food boiling or roasting over the log-fire, observe the exact place which beer holds in his calculation of happiness, hear his tale of the ghost in the nearest haunted house,

and of the farmer's niece who was bewitched with knots in her inside
till she fell into fits and died. If we choose out in this way things which
have altered little in a long course of centuries, we may draw a picture
where there shall be scarce a hand's breadth difference between an English ploughman and a negro of Central Africa. These pages will be so
crowded with evidence of such correspondence among mankind, that
there is no need to dwell upon its details here, but it may be used at
once to override a problem which would complicate the argument,
namely, the question of race. For the present purpose it appears both
possible and desirable to eliminate considerations of hereditary varieties
or races of man, and to treat mankind as homogeneous in nature, though
placed in different grades of civilization. The details of the enquiry will,
I think, prove that stages of culture may be compared without taking
into account how far tribes who use the same implement, follow the
same custom, or believe the same myth, may differ in their bodily configuration and the colour of their skin and hair.

A first step in the study of civilization is to dissect it into details, and
to classify these in their proper groups. Thus, in examining weapons, they
are to be classed under spear, club, sling, bow and arrow, and so forth;
among textile arts are to be ranged matting, netting, and several grades
of making and weaving threads; myths are divided under such headings
as myths of sunrise and sunset, eclipse-myths, earthquake-myths, local
myths which account for the names of places by some fanciful tale, epo-
nymic myths which account for the parentage of a tribe by turning its
name into the name of an imaginary ancestor; under rites and ceremonies
occur such practices as the various kinds of sacrifice to the ghosts of the
dead and to other spiritual beings, the turning to the east in worship, the
purification of ceremonial or moral uncleanness by means of water or
fire. Such are a few miscellaneous examples from a list of hundreds, and
the ethnographer's business is to classify such details with a view to
making out their distribution in geography and history, and the relations
which exist among them. What this task is like, may be almost perfectly
illustrated by comparing these details of culture with the species of plants
and animals as studied by the naturalist. To the ethnographer the bow and
arrow is a species, the habit of flattening children's skulls is a species, the
practice of reckoning numbers by tens is a species. The geographical distribution of these things, and their transmission from region to region,
have to be studied as the naturalist studies the geography of his botanical
and zoological species. Just as certain plants and animals are peculiar to
certain districts, so it is with such instruments as the Australian boomer-
ang, the Polynesian stick-and-groove for fire-making, the tiny bow and
arrow used as a lancet or phleme by tribes about the Isthmus of Panama,
and in like manner with many an art, myth, or custom, found isolated in

a particular field. Just as the catalogue of all the species of plants and animals of a district represents its Flora and Fauna, so the list of all the items of the general life of a people represents that whole which we call its culture. And just as distant regions so often produce vegetables and animals which are analogous, though by no means identical, so it is with the details of the civilization of their inhabitants. How good a working analogy there really is between the diffusion of plants and animals and the diffusion of civilization, comes well into view when we notice how far the same causes have produced both at once. In district after district, the same causes which have introduced the cultivated plants and domesticated animals of civilization, have brought in with them a corresponding art and knowledge. The course of events which carried horses and wheat to America carried with them the use of the gun and the iron hatchet, while in return the whole world received not only maize, potatoes, and turkeys, but the habit of tobacco-smoking and the sailor's hammock.

It is a matter worthy of consideration, that the accounts of similar phenomena of culture, recurring in different parts of the world, actually supply incidental proof of their own authenticity. Some years since, a question which brings out this point was put to me by a great historian —'How can a statement as to customs, myths, beliefs, &c., of a savage tribe be treated as evidence where it depends on the testimony of some traveller or missionary, who may be a superficial observer, more or less ignorant of the native language, a careless retailer of unsifted talk, a man prejudiced or even wilfully deceitful?' This question is, indeed, one which every ethnographer ought to keep clearly and constantly before his mind. Of course he is bound to use his best judgment as to the trustworthiness of all authors he quotes, and if possible to obtain several accounts to certify each point in each locality. But it is over and above these measures of precaution that the test of recurrence comes in. If two independent visitors to different countries, say a mediæval Mohammedan in Tartary and a modern Englishman in Dahome, or a Jesuit missionary in Brazil and a Wesleyan in the Fiji Islands, agree in describing some analogous art or rite or myth among the people they have visited, it becomes difficult or impossible to set down such correspondence to accident or wilful fraud. A story by a bushranger in Australia may, perhaps, be objected to as a mistake or an invention, but did a Methodist minister in Guinea conspire with him to cheat the public by telling the same story there? The possibility of intentional or unintentional mystification is often barred by such a state of things as that a similar statement is made in two remote lands, by two witnesses, of whom A lived a century before B, and B appears never to have heard of A. How distant are the countries, how wide apart the dates, how different the creeds and char-

acters of the observers, in the catalogue of facts of civilization, needs no
farther showing to any one who will even glance at the footnotes of the
present work. And the more odd the statement, the less likely that several
people in several places should have made it wrongly. This being so, it
seems reasonable to judge that the statements are in the main truly given,
and that their close and regular coincidence is due to the cropping up of
similar facts in various districts of culture. Now the most important facts
of ethnography are vouched for in this way. Experience leads the student
after a while to expect and find that the phenomena of culture, as resulting from widely-acting similar causes, should recur again and again in
the world. He even mistrusts isolated statements to which he knows of
no parallel elsewhere, and waits for their genuineness to be shown by
corresponding accounts from the other side of the earth, or the other
end of history. So strong, indeed, is this means of authentication, that the
ethnographer in his library may sometimes presume to decide, not only
whether a particular explorer is a shrewd, honest observer, but also
whether what he reports is comfortable to the general rules of civilization. 'Non quis, sed quid.'

To turn from the distribution of culture in different countries, to its
diffusion within these countries. The quality of mankind which tends most
to make the systematic study of civilization possible, is that remarkable
tacit consensus or agreement which so far induces whole populations to
unite in the use of the same language, to follow the same religion and
customary law, to settle down to the same general level of art and knowledge. It is this state of things which makes it so far possible to ignore
exceptional facts and to describe nations by a sort of general average.
It is this state of things which makes it so far possible to represent immense masses of details by a few typical facts, while, these once settled,
new cases recorded by new observers simply fall into their places to
prove the soundness of the classification. There is found to be such regularity in the composition of societies of men, that we can drop individual
differences out of sight, and thus can generalize on the arts and opinions
of whole nations, just as, when looking down upon an army from a hill,
we forget the individual soldier, whom, in fact, we can scarce distinguish
in the mass, while we see each regiment as an organized body, spreading
or concentrating, moving in advance or in retreat. In some branches of
the study of social laws it is now possible to call in the aid of statistics,
and to set apart special actions of large mixed communities of men by
means of taxgatherers' schedules, or the tables of the insurance office.
Among modern arguments on the laws of human action, none have had
a deeper effect than generalizations such as those of M. Quetelet, on the
regularity, not only of such matters as average stature and the annual
rates of birth and death, but of the recurrence, year after year, of such

obscure and seemingly incalculable products of national life as the numbers of murders and suicides, and the proportion of the very weapons of crime. Other striking cases are the annual regularity of persons killed accidentally in the London streets, and of undirected letters dropped into post-office letter-boxes. But in examining the culture of the lower races, far from having at command the measured arithmetical facts of modern statistics, we may have to judge of the condition of tribes from the imperfect accounts supplied by travellers or missionaries, or even to reason upon relics of prehistoric races of whose very names and languages we are hopelessly ignorant. Now these may seem at the first glance sadly indefinite and unpromising materials for scientific enquiry. But in fact they are neither indefinite nor unpromising, but give evidence that is good and definite so far as it goes. They are data which, for the distinct way in which they severally denote the condition of the tribe they belong to, will actually bear comparison with the statistician's returns. The fact is that a stone arrow-head, a carved club, an idol, a grave-mound where slaves and property have been buried for the use of the dead, an account of a sorcerer's rites in making rain, a table of numerals, the conjugation of a verb, are things which each express the state of a people as to one particular point of culture, as truly as the tabulated numbers of deaths by poison, and of chests of tea imported, express in a different way other partial results of the general life of a whole community.

That a whole nation should have a special dress, special tools and weapons, special laws of marriage and property, special moral and religious doctrines, is a remarkable fact, which we notice so little because we have lived all our lives in the midst of it. It is with such general qualities of organized bodies of men that ethnography has especially to deal. Yet, while generalizing on the culture of a tribe or nation, and setting aside the peculiarities of the individuals composing it as unimportant to the main result, we must be careful not to forget what makes up this main result. There are people so intent on the separate life of individuals that they cannot grasp a notion of the action of a community as a whole —such an observer, incapable of a wide view of society, is aptly described in the saying that he 'cannot see the forest for the trees.' But, on the other hand, the philosopher may be so intent upon his general laws of society as to neglect the individual actors of whom that society is made up, and of him it may be said that he cannot see the trees for the forest. We know how arts, customs, and ideas are shaped among ourselves by the combined actions of many individuals, of which actions both motive and effect often come quite distinctly within our view. The history of an invention, an opinion, a ceremony, is a history of suggestion and modification, encouragement and opposition, personal gain and party prejudice, and the individuals concerned act each according to his own motives, as determined by his character and circumstances. Thus sometimes we watch individuals acting for their own ends with little thought of their effect on society at large, and sometimes we have to study movements of national life as a whole, where the individuals co-operating in them are utterly beyond our observation. But seeing that collective social action is the mere resultant of many individual actions, it is clear that these two methods of enquiry, if rightly followed, must be absolutely consistent.

In studying both the recurrence of special habits or ideas in several districts, and their prevalence within each district, there come before us ever-reiterated proofs of regular causation producing the phenomena of human life, and of laws of maintenance and diffusion according to which these phenomena settle into permanent standard conditions of society, at definite stages of culture. But, while giving full importance to the evidence bearing on these standard conditions of society, let us be careful to avoid a pitfall which may entrap the unwary student. Of course the opinions and habits belonging in common to masses of mankind are to a great extent the results of sound judgment and practical wisdom. But to a great extent it is not so. That many numerous societies of men should have believed in the influence of the evil eye and the existence of a firmament, should have sacrificed slaves and goods to the ghosts of the departed, should have handed down traditions of giants slaying monsters and men turning into beasts—all this is ground for holding that such ideas were indeed produced in men's minds by efficient causes, but it is not ground for holding that the rites in question are profitable, the beliefs sound, and the history authentic. This may seem at the first glance a truism, but, in fact, it is the denial of a fallacy which deeply affects the minds of all but a small critical minority of mankind. Popularly, what everybody says must be true, what everybody does must be right—'Quod ubique, quod semper, quod ab omnibus creditum est, hoc est vere proprieque Catholicum'—and so forth. There are various topics, especially in history, law, philosophy, and theology, where even the educated people we live among can hardly be brought to see that the cause why men do hold an opinion, or practise a custom, is by no means necessarily a reason why they ought to do so. Now collections of ethnographic evidence bringing so prominently into view the agreement of immense multitudes of men as to certain traditions, beliefs, and usages, are peculiarly liable to be thus improperly used in direct defence of these institutions themselves, even old barbaric nations being polled to maintain their opinions against what are called modern ideas. As it has more than once happened to myself to find my collections of traditions and beliefs thus set up to prove their own objective truth, without proper examination of the grounds on which they were actually

received, I take this occasion of remarking that the same line of argument will serve equally well to demonstrate, by the strong and wide
consent of nations, that the earth is flat, and nightmare the visit of a
demon.

It being shown that the details of Culture are capable of being classified
in a great number of ethnographic groups of arts, beliefs, customs, and
the rest, the consideration comes next how far the facts arranged in these
groups are produced by evolution from one another. It need hardly be
pointed out that the groups in question, though held together each by
a common character, are by no means accurately defined. To take up
again the natural history illustration, it may be said that they are species
which tend to run widely into varieties. And when it comes to the question what relations some of these groups bear to others, it is plain that the
student of the habits of mankind has a great advantage over the student
of the species of plants and animals. Among naturalists it is an open question whether a theory of development from species to species is a record
of transitions which actually took place, or a mere ideal scheme serviceable in the classification of species whose origin was really independent.
But among ethnographers there is no such question as to the possibility
of species of implements or habits or beliefs being developed one out of
another, for development in Culture is recognized by our most familiar
knowledge. Mechanical invention supplies apt examples of the kind of
development which affects civilization at large. In the history of fire-arms,
the clumsy wheel-lock, in which a notched steel wheel revolved by means
of a spring against a piece of pyrites till a spark caught the priming, led
to the invention of the more serviceable flint-lock, of which a few still
hang in the kitchens of our farm-houses for the boys to shoot small
birds with at Christmas; the flint-lock in time passed by modification into the percussion-lock, which is just now changing its old-
fashioned arrangement to be adapted from muzzle-loading to breech-
loading. The mediæval astrolabe passed into the quadrant, now discarded
in its turn by the seaman, who uses the more delicate sextant, and so it
is through the history of one art and instrument after another. Such examples of progression are known to us as direct history, but so thoroughly
is this notion of development at home in our minds, that by means of it
we reconstruct lost history without scruple, trusting to general knowledge
of the principles of human thought and action as a guide in putting the
facts in their proper order. Whether chronicle speaks or is silent on the
point, no one comparing a long-bow and a cross-bow would doubt that
the cross-bow was a development arising from the simpler instrument.
So among the fire-drills for igniting by friction, it seems clear on the face
of the matter that the drill worked by a cord or bow is a later improvement
on the clumsier primitive instrument twirled between the hands. That

instructive class of specimens which antiquaries sometimes discover, bronze celts modelled on the heavy type of the stone hatchet, are scarcely explicable except as first steps in the transition from the Stone Age to the Bronze Age, to be followed soon by the next stage of progress, in which it is discovered that the new material is suited to a handier and less wasteful pattern. And thus, in the other branches of our history, there will come again and again into view series of facts which may be consistently arranged as having followed one another in a particular order of development, but which will hardly bear being turned round and made to follow in reversed order. Such for instance are the facts I have here brought forward in a chapter on the Art of Counting, which tend to prove that as to this point of culture at least, savage tribes reached their position by learning and not by unlearning, by elevation from a lower rather than by degradation from a higher state.

Among evidence aiding us to trace the course which the civilization of the world has actually followed, is that great class of facts to denote which I have found it convenient to introduce the term 'survivals.' These are processes, customs, opinions, and so forth, which have been carried on by force of habit into a new state of society different from that in which they had their original home, and they thus remain as proofs and examples of an older condition of culture out of which a newer has been evolved. Thus, I know an old Somersetshire woman whose hand-loom dates from the time before the introduction of the 'flying shuttle,' which new-fangled appliance she has never even learnt to use, and I have seen her throw her shuttle from hand to hand in true classic fashion; this old woman is not a century behind her times, but she is a case of survival. Such examples often lead us back to the habits of hundreds and even thousands of years ago. The ordeal of the Key and Bible, still in use, is a survival; the Midsummer bonfire is a survival; the Breton peasants' All Souls' supper for the spirits of the dead is a survival. The simple keeping up of ancient habits is only one part of the transition from old into new and changing times. The serious business of ancient society may be seen to sink into the sport of later generations, and its serious belief to linger on in nursery folk-lore, while superseded habits of old-world life may be modified into new-world forms still powerful for good and evil. Sometimes old thoughts and practices will burst out afresh, to the amazement of a world that thought them long since dead or dying; here survival passes into revival, as has lately happened in so remarkable a way in the history of modern spiritualism, a subject full of instruction from the ethnographer's point of view. The study of the principles of survival has, indeed, no small practical importance, for most of what we call superstition is included within survival, and in this way lies open to the attack of its deadliest enemy, a reasonable explanation. Insignificant, moreover, as multitudes of the facts of survival are in themselves, their study is so effective for tracing the course of the historical development through which alone it is possible to understand their meaning, that it becomes a vital point of ethnographic research to gain the clearest possible insight into their nature. This importance must justify the detail here devoted to an examination of survival, on the evidence of such games, popular sayings, customs, superstitions, and the like, as may serve well to bring into view the manner of its operation.

Progress, degradation, survival, revival, modification, are all modes of the connexion that binds together the complex network of civilization. It needs but a glance into the trivial details of our own daily life to set us thinking how far we are really its originators, and how far but the transmitters and modifiers of the results of long past ages. Looking round the rooms we live in, we may try here how far he who only knows his own time can be capable of rightly comprehending even that. Here is the 'honeysuckle' of Assyria, there the fleur-de-lis of Anjou, a cornice with a Greek border runs round the ceiling, the style of Louis XIV. and its parent the Renaissance share the looking-glass between them. Transformed, shifted, or mutilated, such elements of art still carry their history plainly stamped upon them; and if the history yet farther behind is less easy to read, we are not to say that because we cannot clearly discern it there is therefore no history there. It is thus even with the fashion of the clothes men wear. The ridiculous little tails of the German postilion's coat show of themselves how they came to dwindle to such absurd rudiments; but the English clergyman's bands no longer so convey their history to the eye, and look unaccountable enough till one has seen the intermediate stages through which they came down from the more serviceable wide collars, such as Milton wears in his portrait, and which gave their name to the 'band-box' they used to be kept in. In fact, the books of costume, showing how one garment grew or shrank by gradual stages and passed into another, illustrate with much force and clearness the nature of the change and growth, revival and decay, which go on from year to year in more important matters of life. In books, again, we see each writer not for and by himself, but occupying his proper place in history; we look through each philosopher, mathematician, chemist, poet, into the background of his education,— through Leibnitz into Descartes, through Dalton into Priestley, through Milton into Homer. The study of language has, perhaps, done more than any other in removing from our view of human thought and action the ideas of chance and arbitrary invention, and in substituting for them a theory of development by the co-operation of individual men, through processes ever reasonable and intelligible where the facts are fully known.

Rudimentary as the science of culture still is, the symptoms are becoming very strong that even what seem its most spontaneous and motiveless phenomena will, nevertheless, be shown to come within the range of distinct cause and effect as certainly as the facts of mechanics. What would be popularly thought more indefinite and uncontrolled than the products of the imagination in myths and fables? Yet any systematic investigation of mythology, on the basis of a wide collection of evidence, will show plainly enough in such efforts of fancy at once a development from stage to stage, and a production of uniformity of result from uniformity of cause. Here, as elsewhere, causeless spontaneity is seen to recede farther and farther into shelter within the dark precincts of ignorance; like chance, that still holds its place among the vulgar as a real cause of events otherwise unaccountable, while to educated men it has long consciously meant nothing but this ignorance itself. It is only when men fail to see the line of connexion in events, that they are prone to fall upon the notions of arbitrary impulses, causeless freaks, chance and nonsense and indefinite unaccountability. If childish games, purposeless customs, absurd superstitions, are set down as spontaneous because no one can say exactly how they came to be, the assertion may remind us of the like effect that the eccentric habits of the wild rice-plant had on the philosophy of a Red Indian tribe, otherwise disposed to see in the harmony of nature the effects of one controlling personal will. The Great Spirit, said these Sioux theologians, made all things except the wild rice; but the wild rice came by chance.

'Man,' said Wilhelm von Humboldt, 'ever connects on from what lies at hand (der Mensch knüpft immer an Vorhandenes an).' The notion of the continuity of civilization contained in this maxim is no barren philosophic principle, but is at once made practical by the consideration that they who wish to understand their own lives ought to know the stages through which their opinions and habits have become what they are. Auguste Comte scarcely overstated the necessity of this study of development when he declared at the beginning of his 'Positive Philosophy' that 'no conception can be understood except through its history,' and his phrase will bear extension to culture at large. To expect to look modern life in the face and comprehend it by mere inspection, is a philosophy whose weakness can easily be tested. Imagine any one explaining the trivial saying, 'a little bird told me,' without knowing of the old belief in the language of birds and beasts, to which Dr. Dasent, in the introduction to the Norse Tales, so reasonably traces its origin. Attempts to explain by the light of reason things which want the light of history to show their meaning, may be instanced from Blackstone's Commentaries. To Blackstone's mind, the very right of the commoner to turn his beast out to graze on the common, finds its origin and explanation in the feudal system.

'For, when lords of manors granted out parcels of land to tenants, for services either done or to be done, these tenants could not plough or manure the land without beasts; these beasts could not be sustained without pasture; and pasture could not be had but in the lord's wastes, and on the uninclosed fallow grounds of themselves and the other tenants. The law therefore annexed this right of common, as inseparably incident, to the grant of the lands; and this was the original of common appendant,' &c. Now though there is nothing irrational in this explanation, it does not agree at all with the Teutonic land-law which prevailed in England long before the Norman Conquest, and of which the remains have never wholly disappeared. In the old village-community even the arable land, lying in the great common fields which may still be traced in our country, had not yet passed into separate property, while the pasturage in the fallows and stubbles and on the waste belonged to the householders in common. Since those days, the change from communal to individual ownership has mostly transformed this old-world system, but the right which the peasant enjoys of pasturing his cattle on the common still remains, not as a concession to feudal tenants, but as possessed by the commoners before the lord ever claimed the ownership of the waste. It is always unsafe to detach a custom from its hold on past events, treating it as an isolated fact to be simply disposed of by some plausible explanation.

In carrying on the great task of rational ethnography, the investigation of the causes which have produced the phenomena of culture, and of the laws to which they are subordinate, it is desirable to work out as systematically as possible a scheme of evolution of this culture along its many lines. In the following chapter, on the Development of Culture, an attempt is made to sketch a theoretical course of civilization among mankind, such as appears on the whole most accordant with the evidence. By comparing the various stages of civilization among races known to history, with the aid of archæological inference from the remains of prehistoric tribes, it seems possible to judge in a rough way of an early general condition of man, which from our point of view is to be regarded as a primitive condition, whatever yet earlier state may in reality have lain behind it. This hypothetical primitive condition corresponds in a considerable degree to that of modern savage tribes, who, in spite of their difference and distance, have in common certain elements of civilization, which seem remains of an early state of the human race at large. If this hypothesis be true, then, notwithstanding the continual interference of degeneration, the main tendency of culture from primæval up to modern times has been from savagery towards civilization. On the problem of this relation of savage to civilized life, almost every one of the thousands of facts discussed in the succeeding chapters has its direct bearing. Survival in Culture, placing all along the course of advancing civilization way-marks full of meaning to those who can decipher their signs, even now sets up in our midst primæval monuments of barbaric thought and life. Its investigation tells strongly in favour of the view that the European may find among the Greenlanders or Maoris many a trait for reconstructing the picture of his own primitive ancestors. Next comes the problem of the Origin of Language. Obscure as many parts of this problem still remain, its clearer positions lie open to the investigation whether speech took its origin among mankind in the savage state, and the result of the enquiry is that consistently with all known evidence, this may have been the case. From the examination of the Art of Counting a far more definite consequence is shown. It may be confidently asserted, that not only is this important art found in a rudimentary state among savage tribes, but that satisfactory evidence proves numeration to have been developed by rational invention from this low stage up to that in which we ourselves possess it. The examination of Mythology contained in the first volume, is for the most part made from a special point of view, on evidence collected for a special purpose, that of tracing the relation between the myths of savage tribes and their analogues among more civilized nations. The issue of such enquiry goes far to prove that the earliest myth-maker arose and flourished among savage hordes, setting on foot an art which his more cultured successors would carry on, till its results came to be fossilized in superstition, mistaken for history, shaped and draped in poetry, or cast aside as lying folly.

Nowhere, perhaps, are broad views of historical development more needed than in the study of religion. Notwithstanding all that has been written to make the world acquainted with the lower theologies, the popular ideas of their place in history and their relation to the faiths of higher nations are still of the mediæval type. It is wonderful to contrast some missionary journals with Max Müller's Essays, and to set the unappreciating hatred and ridicule that is lavished by narrow hostile zeal on Brahmanism, Buddhism, Zoroastrianism, besides the catholic sympathy with which deep and wide knowledge can survey those ancient and noble phases of man's religious consciousness; nor, because the religions of savage tribes may be rude and primitive compared with the great Asiatic systems, do they lie too low for interest and even for respect. The question really lies between understanding and misunderstanding them. Few who will give their minds to master the general principles of savage religion will ever again think it ridiculous, or the knowledge of it superfluous to the rest of mankind. Far from its beliefs and practices being a rubbish-heap of miscellaneous folly, they are consistent and logical in so high a degree as to begin, as soon as even roughly classified, to display the principles of their formation and development; and these principles prove to be essentially rational, though working in a mental condition of intense and inveterate ignorance. It is with a sense of attempting an investigation which bears very closely on the current theology of our own day, that I have set myself to examine systematically, among the lower races, the development of Animism; that is to say, the doctrine of souls and other spiritual beings in general. More than half of the present work is occupied with a mass of evidence from all regions of the world, displaying the nature and meaning of this great element of the Philosophy of Religion, and tracing its transmission, expansion, restriction, modification, along the course of history into the midst of our own modern thought. Nor are the questions of small practical moment which have to be raised in a similar attempt to trace the development of certain prominent Rites and Ceremonies—customs so full of instruction as to the inmost powers of religion, whose outward expression and practical result they are.

In these investigations, however, made rather from an ethnographic than a theological point of view, there has seemed little need of entering into direct controversial argument, which indeed I have taken pains to avoid as far as possible. The connexion which runs through religion, from its rudest forms up to the status of an enlightened Christianity, may be conveniently treated of with little recourse to dogmatic theology. The rites of sacrifice and purification may be studied in their stages of development without entering into questions of their authority and value, nor does an examination of the successive phases of the world's belief in a future life demand a discussion of the arguments adduced for or against the doctrine itself. The ethnographic results may then be left as materials for professed theologians, and it will not perhaps be long before evidence so fraught with meaning shall take its legitimate place. To fall back once again on the analogy of natural history, the time may soon come when it will be thought as unreasonable for a scientific student of theology not to have a competent acquaintance with the principles of the religions of the lower races, as for a physiologist to look with the contempt of past centuries on evidence derived from the lower forms of life, deeming the structure of mere invertebrate creatures matter unworthy of his philosophic study.

Not merely as a matter of curious research, but as an important practical guide to the understanding of the present and the shaping of the future, the investigation into the origin and early development of civilization must be pushed on zealously. Every possible avenue of knowledge must be explored, every door tried to see if it is open. No kind of evidence need be left untouched on the score of remoteness or complexity, of minuteness or triviality. The tendency of modern enquiry is more and more towards the conclusion that if law is anywhere, it is everywhere. To despair of what a conscientious collection and study of facts may lead to, and to declare any problem insoluble because difficult and far off, is distinctly to be on the wrong side in science; and he who will choose a hopeless task may set himself to discover the limits of discovery. One remembers Comte starting in his account of astronomy with a remark on the necessary limitation of our knowledge of the stars: we conceive, he tells us, the possibility of determining their form, distance, size, and movement, whilst we should never by any method be able to study their chemical composition, their mineralogical structure, &c. Had the philosopher lived to see the application of spectrum analysis to this very problem, his proclamation of the dispiriting doctrine of necessary ignorance would perhaps have been recanted in favour of a more hopeful view. And it seems to be with the philosophy of remote human life somewhat as with the study of the nature of the celestial bodies. The processes to be made out in the early stages of our mental evolution lie distant from us in time as the stars lie distant from us in space, but the laws of the universe are not limited with the direct observation of our senses. There is vast material to be used in our enquiry; many workers are now busied in bringing this material into shape, though little may have yet been done in proportion to what remains to do; and already it seems not too much to say that the vague outlines of a philosophy of primæval history are beginning to come within our view.

2. THE CONTENT OF CULTURE AND THE UNIVERSAL PATTERN *

To deal with culture there must be ways of reducing the whole nebulous range of phenomena implied by the term to some kind of categorical order. A number of concepts have been used for this purpose; two of the most fundamental are culture trait and culture complex, and from these flow others, such as culture area, culture type and culture core.

Beyond the attempt to define units of culture analogous to basic units in the physical sciences, is the effort which seeks to discover kinds of activities which must go on in every culture. The selection below includes an early approach to the question. Though suggestive, the view it contains of universals has been severely criticized and altered. In general, we are much more sensitive now to the question of whether such categories really apply to alien cultures or whether they simply project our culture's categories where they do not belong. More specifically, some of Wissler's categories are clearly non-universal; furthermore, the categories are on several different levels of abstraction. Even so, the Wissler article helps us to come to grips more readily with the huge universe of cultural phenomena.

THE CULTURE TRAIT

The field-worker in anthropology begins his study of tribal cul-ture by concentrating upon one or two points. Thus, he may set out to see how fire is kindled, observing that it is made by boring one stick into another, but that these simple looking implements are fashioned according

* Clark Wissler, *Man and Culture* (New York: Thomas Y. Crowell Co., 1923), pp. 50–71, 73–77. Reprinted by permission of the publisher.

The author (1870–1947) was Curator of the Department of Anthropology of the to a specific pattern and that the procedure is likewise fixed as in any handicraft. Yet, it is not enough to say that fire is kindled by wood friction; the individuality of the implements and the accompanying procedures must be recorded and representative objects collected. Thus, the fire-making implement, accompanied by photographs and field notes, becomes the objective record of a unit of observation. Such is, for practical record of a unit of observation. Such is, for practical purposes at least, a unit of the tribal culture and is spoken of as a *trait*. This term is also applied to mannerisms and to concepts of whatever kind. Thus the custom of a man marrying his wife's sisters may be observed and, if so, is set down as a trait of the tribal culture. It follows then that a tribal culture is characterized by the enumeration of its observable traits and that the culture of one tribe is distinguished from that of another by differences in these traits. So it was that in a preceding chapter we gained our first notion of what culture is by calling attention to striking contrasts in the traits of Eskimo culture. In any event, the individuality of a tribal culture will be manifest in its most unique traits.

The preceding paragraph may convey the impression that the chief concern of anthropology is to discover queer customs and to note the differences between the respective groups of humanity. While it cannot be denied that anthropological literature is unduly weighted with the enumeration of differences and that the writings of explorers emphasize the curious and unique, to the exclusion of the commonplace, yet the history of anthropology shows clearly that progress in the study of culture has been substantial only in so far as the enumeration of tribal traits has approximated completeness. In fact, it was not until many tribal cultures had been worked out completely that the problems of culture took shape. In short, then, a culture is not to be comprehended until the list of its traits approaches completeness.

THE CULTURE COMPLEX

We are now confronted with a more serious problem. If we mean by *trait* a unit in the tribal culture, then we must discover the nature and characteristics of this unit. When potatoes are shoveled into a bushel measure, we may correctly speak of them as a bushel of potatoes, by which we imply that each potato is a complete and independent unit

---

American Museum of Natural History from 1907 until his retirement in 1942 and in 1937 was elected Dean of the entire scientific staff of that institution. He was also a Professor of Anthropology at Yale. In his early career Wissler did field work among the Blackfoot and Sioux. Among his books are *The American Indian* (1917, and still in print), *Man and Culture* (1923), *An Introduction to Social Anthropology* (1929) and *Indian Cavalcade* (1938).

in itself. Some students of culture seem to have regarded traits as similar independent units, to be scooped up in the tribal measure and dealt with as a mere collection. Yet, when one carefully scrutinizes a trait, he finds, not a clear-cut unit, but a kind of complex. For example, the Ojibway Indians in the vicinity of Lake Superior were observed to use wild rice for food and this was correctly set down as a trait of their culture. Yet, each member of the tribe did not snatch his rice food directly from the plant as do the birds, but received it as the end of a cycle of activities in which he, as an individual, played a varying part. Thus, though the plant is wild, some care was given the plots where it grew; later, the plants were tied in bunches to discourage rice-eating birds, then the rice was gathered, cured, hulled, winnowed, stored, cooked, and eaten. Incidentally, some of it was exchanged and some given away. The many processes involved required techniques of various complexities and special appliances. But that is not all, for intimately bound up in the whole are property rights, labor obligations, etiquette, methods of keeping time, and a number of special religious observances, prohibitions, and taboos. It is thus plain that if we arrive at an adequate notion of the wild rice trait, we must see it as a complex of many processes, all of which bear a functional relation to the end to be achieved. The name usually given to such a chain of activities is the *trait-complex*, or in this instance, the *wild rice complex*.

Some of the best known trait-complexes are, head hunting, totemism, couvade, tobacco, maize, wheat, dog traction, the horse, use of milk, the wheel, exogamy, sun worship, and blood sacrifice. The reader can elaborate the list according to his experience with the subject. While it is true that the term *complex* is not always used in this connection, it is implied, for the significance and interest of these topics arise from the fact that they are the head-lines for important culture trait-complexes, in the main, typical of the whole content of culture.

THE CULTURE TYPE

At the outset, we spoke of our own culture as belonging to the Euro-American type because, by the comparative method, we discovered that the cultures of some tribal, or national, units were very much alike in trait content. In other words, we find it convenient to ignore political boundaries and to classify the cultures of the world according to their content; for as we have shown, what are essentially the same trait-complexes may be found in a number of cultures. The milking of cows, for example, the milk-butter-cheese complex, is found in Euro-American cultures and a number of Asiatic cultures, but strange to say, some of the latter have a cattle-complex that excludes the use of milk. Many Negro peoples of Africa use milk, but so little are some of them addicted to butter and cheese that they may be said to have a mere milk complex. As in the preceding chapter, where we imagined ourselves traveling through the contiguous habitats of cultures, we can readily check out the variations in trait-complexes, common among a number of cultures, and reach an objective estimate of the degree to which they approach identity.

This brings us to a question of technique. All such questions are bothersome and should be kept out of sight as much as possible; but as the success of any scientific procedure rests upon the precision and impersonal nature of its technique, a few remarks upon the subject must be endured. The fact is that the trait-complex is a variable and must therefore be treated as any other variable. Two families within the tribe may differ somewhat in the practice of a given trait, but this variation is usually negligible as a deviation from the tribal norm, the approximate form in which the trait most frequently manifests itself. So again when we compare the trait norms from different tribal cultures, variations may be expected, but these will be easily recognized as mere deviations around a central idea. Perhaps this can be made clear by noting an example from the material cultures of certain American Indians. Between the Mississippi and the Rocky Mountains may be found a distinct pattern of female attire. Yet, each tribe has its variants and in turn the individuals within a tribe show deviations from the tribal style. Each kind of variation can, however, be easily recognized and the tribal styles determined, thus justifying the assumption of a common trait in these tribal cultures. The patterns in themselves also show what we mean by variation of a trait. To complete the picture, imagine this group of tribes surrounded by other clusters of tribal patterns varying around distinctive types. Though the above illustration is quite material, we could cite many social and religious traits with the same kinds of variability, indicating that we are dealing with a phenomenon that is constant and verifiable.

If now we regard cultures as units, we find them also comparable as variable phenomena, for though absolute identity in tribal cultures is not to be expected, some of them are easily recognizable as mere variants of the same culture form. Thus, we find not only a garment pattern distributed among the Indian tribes of this area, but a great many other trait-complexes as well. So if we select at random one of these tribal cultures and, taking up its trait-complexes one by one, follow out their distributions, we meet with the same kind of uniformity as in the case of costume, from which we conclude that we are dealing with a type of culture readily recognizable and definable. Variations around this type will consist in the variations of the trait-complexes themselves, as well as in the absences of certain traits. What we mean is that two tribal cultures may differ chiefly in that two or three trait-complexes are peculiar to one of them. So the incidental absence of a trait here, and the occasional excess of one there, are expected variations around the type. Hence, by type of culture we mean a norm, or standard form, of tribal culture readily distinguishable from others.

THE CULTURE AREA

Our definition of the culture type should be understood as a method of classification by which cultures themselves can be grouped, but the culture type has its geography, since it appears that a trait-complex is not to be found scattered at random up and down a continent, but localized, or in clusters. From what has gone before, it follows that the segregation of cultures of the same type will form a geographical area, characterized by the type. Anthropological research in the New World has revealed a number of these areas. For example, as stated in an earlier chapter, the United States and Canada comprise nine areas as follows: the Plains, Plateau, California, North Pacific Coast, Eskimo, Mackenzie, Eastern Woodland, Southeastern, and Southwestern areas. We observe, for one thing, that the names used to designate these areas are geographical and, to a certain extent, characterize the territories covered, the significance of which we shall consider later. Further, each area embraces a large number of tribal units and consequently an equal number of tribal cultures; but these many tribal cultures belong to one type, so that the culture area defines the range of the culture type. For South America, our data are less complete, but yet sufficient to reveal similar areas. Turning to the Old World, we find little in the literature concerning culture areas, since it is chiefly the American school that has taken up this investigation; or rather, it was in the synthetic treatment of New World data that these areas were discovered. One may, therefore, inquire if such areas are peculiar to the New World. That they are not is apparent when one scans the data for Central and South Africa, where, though no one has yet attempted to mark out the culture types, it is plain that clusters of a similar kind do exist. Again among the wilder peoples of Asia, we meet with the same suggestions, and so we might continue until the whole of the known world was plotted according to tribal cultures. To avoid confusion, we have passed over the so-called civilized nations as well as the extinct cultures, but it can be shown that even among them we have definable culture areas. We must conclude, therefore, that the culture area is universal, or that we are dealing with one or more constants and it is to the discovery of these constants that our search is directed.

It will readily appear that the tribal units in a culture area are distinguishable as marginal and central and from hints in the preceding pages, we may anticipate corresponding differences in their cultures. Now the fact is that the drawing of precise boundaries to the range of a culture type is beset by the difficulties inherent in all variable phenomena, for it will sometimes prove difficult to decide to which of two or more culture areas a given marginal tribe belongs. Thus, if we take any aboriginal area in America, and tabulate the tribal distribution of traits, we find that those upon the margins lack some of the trait-complexes common to the central group of tribes. However, it does not follow that these marginal tribes possess a lesser number of trait-complexes, because they manifest additional traits not found at the center and whose true home is in the adjoining culture area. In other words, the tribal cultures lying at the boundary between two distinct culture areas are mixtures, or markedly divergent from the respective culture types. Again, the trait-complexes, as previously noted, will appear on the margins in attenuated form, that is, they will have lost many of the elements they possess at the center. So if we seek the type specimen of tribal culture, we must look to the geographical center of the area.

To define one of these areas satisfactorily, then, one must proceed by a suitable statistical method and tabulate the trait-complexes for the successive tribes. With this list before him, he will have little difficulty in fixing a satisfactory boundary to the area, for it matters little to which of the two adjoining areas the most marginal tribal culture is assigned. In fact, some of these intermediate tribal cultures may contain an equal number of trait-complexes from the two adjoining centers. Hence, though the phenomena we deal with are complex and variable, they can be dealt with empirically, reduced to statements of sufficient exactness, consistently classified, and their geographical distribution plotted.

Moreover, what one may suspect is, that the culture area merely defines the coincidence in trait-complex distribution, and that, to understand the case fully, one must observe the distribution of individual complexes. Perhaps the simplest examples of such distributions are to be found in the data for extinct cultures, since for these we have as a basis for interpretation only the surviving artifact and its distribution. Our ignorance of the original tribe and the variability of the complex relieves us of all the above complications. As an example we may cite the distribution of certain types of curious stone ornaments found in the United States. No one yet knows the uses of these primitive works of art, nor the tribal groups to which they belonged, but when their distribution is plotted we discover that there was, on the level of some past culture horizon, an area for these ornaments, and since these are all that seem to have been preserved for us, we may further suspect that they are the remnants of a long extinct culture type. Thus, the center of each distribution falls in the same locality, it being understood that each form covers the entire area included by its boundary. So all the forms will be found in the central area, but in the immediate surrounding zone the number will be three, in the next two, and in the outermost zone, but one. No doubt, if we could turn back the hands of the clock and peep in upon this ancient culture area, we would note a full complement of perishable trait-complexes, among the tribal groups occupying the country bounded by the innermost circle of Moorehead's map, which tended to fade away in the outer zones and at last to disappear altogether; or more correctly stated, were displaced by other trait-complexes. That this distribution of stone ornaments is not a unique case can be shown by other archaeological data, for instance the distribution of pottery styles in southwestern United States, where we find successive zones. In this case the archaeologist, Nelson, discovered that, as one traveled outward from a center in the upper Rio Grande Valley, taking note of the potsherds scattered about on the ground, the several styles of decorating pottery disappeared one by one. He was thus able to define a number of consecutive zones, in the smaller of which all the styles were found. So, as in the case of stone ornaments, we find traits tending to concentrate in a center of distribution. These inspiring triumphs of sound method in archaeological research serve to bring home to us the homely truth that the curious stone objects and contemptible potsherds, scattered over the land, are like skeletal remains of dead cultures, which whenever re-articulated, will reveal the outlines of the living forms.

One of the most striking characteristics of the zone-like distributions we have just noted, is their circular character. Considering the variable nature of the phenomena, their regularity is remarkable. However, we must not expect that the boundaries to all culture areas will closely approximate circles, for since culture lives upon the land, it must adjust itself to the topography and to other geographical features. The shapes of the areas are therefore various and their boundaries irregular; a range of mountains here, a desert there, a lake between, etc., will dent or otherwise distort the lines that define trait distributions. Yet, the form is always discernible, for no matter how elongated and twisted the lines may appear, they still remind one of concentric circles. The culture area, then, expresses a principle of trait-complex distribution to the elucidation of which we shall return later.

THE CULTURE CENTER

In the introductory chapter reference was made to culture centers, the implication being that such were the sources from which sprang new cultures. This may be correct, but we must not take it for granted. Our observations so far produce facts of distribution only, but, when confronted with such an all-prevailing type of distribution as we found in the culture area, interpretations automatically come to mind. For example, Moorehead's diagram suggests that the several patterns of stone ornaments first appeared in the central section and spread thence outward in all directions. If so, then the central part of the culture area may be regarded as the point of dispersal, or the center of influence. Our problem, then, is to prove or disprove the correctness of this assumption, or to find evidence to support the inference that trait-complexes do move in this way. Fortunately, we find such proof from an unexpected quarter. In the pottery distribution noted, Nelson discovered that the radii of distribution varied as the time. Thus, the traits confined to the small central section were of recent origin, while those reaching the outer zones were the oldest. This he was able to prove absolutely since at the center he found stratified deposits, one style of pottery above the other, the time-relations for which were obvious. There can thus be no doubt whatever as to the order in which these different pottery traits came into existence. But this sequence in the vertical section, as it were, is also the horizontal sequence, or the sequence of distribution.

It follows, then, that in this case, the center of the area was not only the point of dispersal, but the point of origin, in the usual acceptance of that term. Further, though we have as yet no stratigraphic check upon Moorehead's distribution scheme, there is good reason to believe that the same relation holds. We can go even farther afield and refer to certain researches of which Lowie's study of Plains Indian societies is typical. This author shows clearly that the center of dispersal for these trait-complexes is in the heart of the area, and while it is not possible to demonstrate their time-relations, in so satisfactory a way as for Nelson's pottery, we find precisely the same kind of distribution. We are therefore justified in assuming that the true culture area is a succession of distribution zones encircling a nucleus and that this center is the point of dispersal from which trait-complexes are diffused.

THE ADHESION OF TRAIT-COMPLEXES

A review of the preceding sections indicates that each trait-complex has a continuous distribution radiating from a center. This can be set down as one of the basic, verifiable characteristics of culture traits. Further, we observed that these trait-complex centers often coincided, resulting in an accumulation of traits in a circumscribed territory, to which we gave the name *culture area*. These two things should not be confused; the former is an expression of culture processes, whereas the latter appears to be a mere accumulation in a locality. One of our problems, therefore, is to discover the nature of this accumulative association of traits. Since we found tribal cultures to be such collections of traits, and classified these cultures by the traits they have in common, the question arises as to the nature of a culture. Is it a mere accidental conglomeration, or is there some functional relation between the several trait-complexes? Thus, when we enumerate the trait-complexes manifested by a tribal unit and speak of them collectively as a culture, we are merely asserting that we conceive them to be related one to the other only in that they pertain to the same tribal unit; so, unless we find some basis for their association other than mere presence in a group, these trait-complexes are without functional relations to each other. In our discussion of the trait-complex, we found its components associated because they had logical and functional relations, necessary or assumed so by the tribe, as the case may be. In the wild rice complex, for example, a sequence of processes was necessary to produce the food ready for eating. Yet, while it is obvious that rice could not be served unless it was gathered, it is not at all clear that this process must be accompanied by specific ceremonies. Apparently these could be dispensed with without disturbing the remainder of the complex. It appears, therefore, that while some traits in the complex are indispensable, others are not. A review of any trait will make this clear, as for example, the milk complex; some cultures know butter and cheese; some have all but these traits; some milk cows, others goats, camels, horses, or reindeer. Again, maize is now cultivated in Europe and America; in the former, it is used for feeding cattle and horses, but in America it is also a popular human food. In Africa kaffir corn is a great staple, but in America it is fed to live-stock. So, in general, if one follows out the full distribution of a trait-complex, he meets with an attenuation as he leaves its center.

The situation becomes somewhat clearer when we take up a few trait-complexes with superimposed distributions. Thus, a very widely distributed trait-complex is tailored skin clothing, which is, or was, continuously spread from northern Europe, across Asia into America, as far as Labrador. It barely touched the United States and did not reach far down into Europe and Asia. Even the Greeks were content with a rectangular sheet draped over one shoulder. Now it so happens that dog traction, that is, the drawing of sledges by dogs, has also about the same range. If one asks concerning the cause for the coincidence of these two trait-complexes, there comes into mind an environmental relation, since snow and cold are favorable to each, though perhaps not to the same degree. Yet, if we choose complexes of different ranges, the environmental factor is not discernible; for instance, maize was cultivated by the New World aborigines from Chile on the south to the St. Lawrence on the north, the center of dispersal falling somewhere in Middle America. Pottery also seems to center in the same place and has a continuous distribution approximating that for maize. So we find again a coincidence, but here the range takes us across the torrid zone and into both of the temperate zones. Further, we find both semi-arid and relatively humid regions covered by these trait-complexes. Hence, we cannot say that the environment is the determinant. That the environment plays a part, we shall see later, but that it causes trait-complexes to be coincident cannot be maintained. Continuing our inquiry, then, we observe that in the Old World also there seems to be some correspondence between the ranges for pottery and those for agriculture, but the situation is complicated by the presence of several types of agriculture, on the one hand, and incomplete data for the early distribution of pottery on the other. Yet, in general, it appears that when we consider maize and the Old World cereal complexes, their distributions tend to be coincident with the respective pottery complexes. What then, is the nature of this relation?

Returning to more specific cases, no reason appears why pottery is necessary to maize culture or the reverse. The Californians, for example, successfully cooked similar foods in baskets by dropping in hot stones and on the other hand, maize bread required nothing in the way of a cooking vessel. The most likely explanation, therefore, is that the maize and pottery complexes were evolved in the same center and at about the same time, spreading outward in the universal manner. Their coincidence is then in the nature of an historical event. Presumably had pottery made its appearance later, its distribution at the discovery of America would have been much more restricted than that for maize. We do in fact find many complexes having the same center as maize but more restricted. So it is the time element that contributes to the association of trait-complexes and accounts for their coincidence. The events that led to their time-relations, or the history of the case, is necessary to a full understanding of the phenomenon. As we shall see later, this is what anthropologists mean by historical explanations for culture.

It appears, then, that the association of trait-complexes is due to causes wholly external to themselves, a subject to which we shall return under another head. One of our problems, then, is to observe what complexes are associated. This is a matter that can be approached by the methods of empirical science. The first attempt of this kind was made by Tylor in 1888, by correlating trait distributions, one with the other. Thus, if one wrote at the head of a column the name of a trait-complex, say maize, and at the head of another, pottery, he could then take up the names of the tribes in order, writing them under each head when the trait in question was present. As we have stated, the result would be that many of the names in the first column would also appear in the second. If this were merely a matter of accident, each tribal name would have an even

chance of falling in the second column; but if the correspondences between the two columns were found to be greater than could be allowed
for accident, then we must seek another explanation. Tylor first tried
this method out with specific social traits, such as the many curious rules
and prohibitions governing the social intercourse of men and women.
Thus among some cultures the son-in-law must not look upon the face of
his wife's mother, much less speak to her. First, Tylor made an inventory
of the cultures in which the custom is found, and out of some 359 cultures
listed, found it in thirty-six. He then followed through the same lists the
custom of the son-in-law to reside with the parents of the wife, finding
that in fourteen cultures, the husband not only lived permanently with
his wife's parents, but also kept out of their sight. A mere chance relation
would account for about half as many cases. The point is, then, that the
number of times the custom of avoiding the wife's mother is found in a
culture, where it is the rule for the husband to reside at the home of the
wife's parents, is twice as great as it should be were it merely a matter
of chance. In this manner Tylor tried out a large number of marriage and
social customs, finding that their coincidences, or their presence in a
culture, was something more than an accident. To such associations of
trait-complexes Tylor gave the name *adhesions* and a very good name it
is; for limiting its meaning to the "state of sticking to one another," when
brought into contact under favorable conditions, we have an adequate
characteristic of the phenomenon.

So to discover *adhesions* one must proceed to work out the distributions of complexes among the successive tribal cultures and then correlate these distributions. In this way one may discover what trait-complexes are associated. Practically everyone who seriously studies the
distribution of culture phenomena uses this method, but the quality of
the work depends upon its precision. Recently, a notable research was
undertaken by Hobhouse and his associates to discover what adhesions
prevailed for food gathering and other material trait-complexes on the
one hand, as against the complexes of government, justice, family,
warfare, social rank, cannibalism, infanticide, human sacrifice, and
property on the other. A great deal has been written on these subjects, but so far no one had taken the trouble to tabulate the traits for
the representative tribal cultures of the world and thus be able to make
exact statements. Tylor's work, however, deals with what is essentially
one large trait-complex, viz., marriage. Thus, as we have noted, he finds
that in far too many cases to be accounted for by mere chance, there is
an *adhesion* between the custom of the husband going to live with his
wife's parents and his avoidance of his mother-in-law, and suspects that
one accounts for the other. This may be the true explanation, but, if so,
it is merely a relation like that between hulling wild rice and eating it,

or one of the logical sequential relations within a complex, as previously noted. Hobhouse has, on the other hand, classified some six hundred tribal cultures, according to their food trait-complexes, under such heads as Lower Hunters, Higher Hunters, Dependent Hunters, Agriculture I, Pastoral I, Agriculture II, Pastoral II, and Agriculture III, and then tabulated the frequency of occurrence for such trait-complexes as the Chief's Power, Purchase of the Bride, Polygamy, Rank of Wealth, Slavery, etc. From this method it appears that whereas bride purchase does not tend to adhere to hunting it does to agriculture. In like manner, these authors find that polygamy and pastoral traits show a maximum adherence one to the other, as do human sacrifices with agriculture, infanticide with hunting, wife-lending with hunting, etc. Among negative, or equally balanced adhesions, mention may be made of the two forms of descent, matrilinear and patrilinear, each of which adheres about equally to a number of other traits. What appears, then, is that, as interpreted by Hobhouse, certain trait-complexes all the world over tend to adhere to hunting complexes, others to pastoral, and still others to agricultural complexes.

Two aspects of the case should be noted. First, the economic rating of the tribal cultures studied is somewhat arbitrary; second, due account is not taken of the geographical distribution. Taking these up in order, the distinction between hunting and agricultural complexes is obvious, so the above-noted adhesions are valid in so far as they are based upon these differences. Yet, what we should like to see are attempts to correlate specific trait-complexes. Hobhouse had in hand the data for this, but seldom used them. One exception is where he shows an adhesion between nobles and slaves; even in simple tribal groups these two trait-complexes show adhesion. Yet, is not this a mere logical complementary relation? On the other hand, can as much be said for the relation between human sacrifices and agriculture? It is true that a logical relation between the idea of propitiating germination and fruitful harvest on the one hand, and the sacrificing of blood, on the other, has been maintained, but the case is weak. Certainly the relation is not like that between nobles and slaves, or between hulling rice and eating it.

Further, if the geographical distribution of the cases cited by Hobhouse be considered, they are seen to comprise two tribal clusters, the Malay Archipelago and Central Africa. The authors could have strengthened their case by data from the central maize area in the New World, for the Aztec, Maya, and Andeans are notorious for the number and monstrosity of their human sacrifices. In each of these areas, however, the sacrifices takes special ritualistic forms and so must be considered as more or less distinct. In the case of Mexico and the Andes, we know that the New World type of sacrifice is distributed concentrically, a form we have shown to be characteristic of trait-complexes in general. To be more specific, then, we should say that one type of sacrifice complex adheres to maize (New World), another to rice (Malay Archipelago), and still another to kaffir corn (Africa). This presents the matter in a different light than to say that generalized agriculture and generalized human sacrifice show a tendency to adhere. It also brings us back again to the distribution type, for when two or more complexes arise in a center at about the same time, they set out upon their distribution simultaneously and so stick together for at least the greater part of the way. Technically we speak of this coincidence as adhesion.

We could, if necessary, take up the other adhesions noted and account for them now as mere logical, necessary relations, or again, as historic coincidences. But something yet remains: why do so many trait-complexes occur in agricultural areas and not among hunters? This we shall take up later, for the answer lies outside the trait-complex involved. In short, a tribal culture is a collection of trait-complexes, developed and acquired in the course of tribal life; so the association of one with the other can be fully accounted for when we learn the events that brought them into these relations.

THE UNIVERSAL PATTERN

In the opening chapters we met with good reasons for suspecting that cultures are very much alike in their structure and behavior, and after our discovery of the units, or elements, of the phenomenon, found at least one fundamental form common to all these elements. We found, further, that trait-complexes tend to adhere, suggesting that they are linked in some way, though we found such linking to be for the most part independent of factors inherent in the traits themselves. If we shift our point of regard from the several trait-complexes to the tribal cultures as wholes, we note that notwithstanding these cultures fall into types, a certain similarity holds throughout. We have just seen that all trait-complexes have much in common as well as a common fundamental structure. So as one might say, the aggregates of similar things will themselves be similar; but since trait-complexes vary in kind, and, as we have seen, cultures are distinguishable by the trait-complexes, they have or have not, it follows that cultures differ in their content. Yet, familiarity with cultures soon reveals something we have so far ignored, viz., that after all a tribal culture has a plan or pattern. If we should liken trait-complexes to building materials, then the plan of the house to be built of them would correspond to the pattern of a culture.

Such recognition of culture patterns is not contradictory to what we have observed to be true of the materials that make up these cultures. We are already aware that trait-complexes travel, or spread, and that

THE CULTURE SCHEME

1. Speech
   Languages, writing systems, etc.
2. Material Traits
   a. Food habits
   b. Shelter
   c. Transportation and travel
   d. Dress
   e. Utensils, tools, etc.
   f. Weapons
   g. Occupations and industries
3. Art. Carving, painting, drawing, music, etc.
4. Mythology and Scientific Knowledge
5. Religious Practices
   a. Ritualistic forms
   b. Treatment of the sick
   c. Treatment of the dead
6. Family and Social Systems
   a. The forms of marriage
   b. Methods of reckoning relationship
   c. Inheritance
   d. Social control
   e. Sports and games
7. Property
   a. Real and personal
   b. Standards of value and exchange
   c. Trade
8. Government
   a. Political forms
   b. Judicial and legal procedures
9. War

they often do this in the company of others, so it was necessary to examine into this relation. What we found is again comparable to what we find in building materials; if bricks are chosen for the walls, then mortar and other elements of the complex follow, but we may choose the same kind of roof our neighbor puts upon a cement house, or any other kind of roof. No doubt this is obvious when we think of houses, but many good people forget it when they set out to deal with matters of culture. But to return to our subject, the plans for houses all call for walls, roofs, floors, and numerous other things, so what about patterns for culture?

In the first place, students of cultures find that the same general outline will fit all of them; thus, we say the facts of culture may be comprehended under nine heads as in the accompanying table; viz., Speech, Material Traits, Art, Mythology, Religion, Social Systems, Property, Government, and War. This outline can be greatly elaborated, if the reader gives his constructive imagination full play. It is, however, full enough for our purposes.

Now, if we take up our own culture and fit the details into this scheme, we see how readily they fall under these heads. So do the old cultures of Rome, Greece, etc. But these and our own are so intimately connected in origin that we should suspect the pattern of one to fit all. On the other hand, there are lowly, simple, crude peoples, like the Australians, who are said to have no culture. If we take literally many of the statements made by contemptuous writers on the subject, this would end the matter; but the facts are otherwise, for turning to the literature of the subject and taking first the main headings in our outline, we find all represented in the supposedly simple life of the Australian. Thus, even among very primitive peoples there are cultures which readily fall under the heads enumerated above.

Now someone may object, on the ground that even though this be true, the content under each head is so meager as to be contemptible and remind us that the Australian, for instance, went without clothes of any kind, and that, here at once, our pattern fails to fit. Yes, it is true that the Australian was not over-burdened with clothing, but it is not true that he was devoid of *dress*, or that he did not put great store upon it. Ornaments there were in considerable numbers and the septum of the nose was often pierced to carry a wooden button, a practice analogous to the ear-piercing of our own people. In short, he had something to place under this head. If, again, we are told that so crude a savage could have no religion, the answer is not far to seek. Go to a library, take down the books of Spencer and Gillen, there you will find a complex of religious practices that almost defies understanding. Again, when you turn to Australian marriage and relationship systems, you will be more bewildered. The fact is that the whole round of life with the Australian is held in a net of practices so intricate that there is little room for anything else. So the content of his culture is far from negligible and conforms closely to the general pattern we have sketched. But we need go no further; the reader's imagination can call up sufficient details of other cultures to see that the scheme will fit all the cultures known to history.

So far we have dealt with categories of classification rather than with concrete trait-complexes, but, when passed in review, we find many of these complexes identical for all cultures. Thus, all the historic cultures, however primitive, knew fire. They also knew its value in the preparation of food. In every case they knew, or formerly knew, how to chip stone. The principle of the knife was known and the fundamental idea of the drill. Likewise, the art of twisting string, or the making of cord; as to weaving, there was not one that did not understand the fundamental step. The fact that some of them went no further is not to the point. Still other technical processes could be enumerated, but the reader can add to the list at his leisure. The point is that there are certain groups of technical traits that belong to all cultures. We can go even farther, for there were common beliefs. The belief in a soul or spiritual counterpart of some kind, that defies death, is universal. Again, the idea that evil fortune can be avoided by the strict observance of formulated prohibitions, or taboos, as they are often called, is equally so.

These illustrations are sufficient. We see that not only are the historic cultures, from the most primitive to our own, built upon one general pattern, but in some instances the materials are identical. And though we have dealt with historic cultures, we now know that the same is true of the late paleolithic cultures, for they had fire, chipped stones, drew remarkable pictures, modeled in clay, and buried with their dead objects for the future use of the spirit. Incomplete though this picture of their life must remain, we may be sure that since it fits our one pattern at so many points, it will at the others as well. However, the present value of this concept consists in its emphasis on the fundamental similarities between cultures, whereas we are apt to overstress the objective differences. It is this fundamental similarity which we express by the term pattern, or skeleton of culture. It is true that the skeleton of culture we have offered is a generalized one and so not a stern reality, and yet, it is as real as the osseous skeletal pattern for man as a whole —both abstract generalizations based upon objective data. Further, no one denies that this bodily pattern is part of a more comprehensive pattern for mammals as a whole; and in just the same way, one must admit that the culture pattern expresses the fundamental lines of the evolution of the phenomenon itself.

Now we have, as it were, set up a few categories which, taken together, seem to cover the entire range of culture content. Thus, under speech we may include language, sign-talk, gesture, and all forms of writing, and so far as we now see, something under this category will be found in every culture. Yet, the several tribal cultures will differ in the kinds and number of trait-complexes falling under this head. If we turn to art, the facts are similar, and so on through the series. Nor need we trouble ourselves with the question as to whether culture was always laid out in this way, for that would lead us off into a search for other patterns, a problem to come later. Moreover, the pattern we have sketched here is the human pattern, the justification for that term resting upon usage, for by man is usually meant a mammal that possesses a culture conforming to this pattern.

It appears, then, that for the different cultures these categories show a wide range in content. Further, since under each category we find the familiar trait-complexes, all more or less interlocking, we may properly speak of the pattern as made up of *culture complexes:* speech, art, religion, etc. Again, what happens in the evolution of culture is an elaboration and enrichment of these complexes, a process which we sometimes speak of as progress. We can now comprehend why it is practically impossible to draw satisfactory distinctions between primitive and higher cultures, other than that they differ in complexity, or richness of content. It looks as if, after all, man's activities were deeply channelized, for though we have among us dreamers who fancy a time when the whole language complex, for example, will be transcended and thought speak to thought direct, yet so far there are no indications but that if the unexpected happened, the mechanism employed would still rest upon language or pictures, as have all known traits in the speech complex. The very existence of a universal pattern implies a fair degree of rigidity in limitations and asserts that every culture is predestined to keep within these bounds. No doubt this will come as a shock to many and arouse the resentment that all feel toward limitations to personal freedom; nor is it particularly stimulating to realize that these limitations, marked out ages and ages ago, seem to have held fast and firm through all the centuries to this very hour, for what signs are there to encourage the belief that the bars will be lowered! Still, the outlook is not so forbidding as it seems, for within the bounds of the pattern are spaces for tremendous expansion. It is in fact the wonderful flexibility of the culture pattern that makes it nature's masterpiece.

CULTURE COMPLEXES

We may now inquire as to the significance of the nine topical heads in the foregoing outline of the pattern. As we have said, they are conventional and arbitrary, and yet they are the results of experience, for everyone who draws up a scheme to cover the culture of a people will arrive at similar divisions; so there must be some basis to these topical heads. Moreover, when critically examined, we see them as basic concepts of human activity. For example, the term *war* stands for something instantly recognized, nor can an anthropologist conceive of any existing culture, however primitive, in which the idea is not equally definite. All languages that have been recorded have a term corresponding to the word we use. It is, of course, obvious that there will be some difference of opinion as to the absolute scope of such a concept, but if one notes that the dispute is always between the concepts as formulated, the suspicion arises that the specific trait-complex in question is mixed, or overlaps other traits, an aspect of the phenomenon we shall revert to later. Yet, in the main, the nine heads in our outline do express the fundamental and embracing concepts in culture. The simplicity of the classification invites objection from those who are fond of contemplating the complexity and largeness of human affairs, for they will say that no such simple scheme can in any way serve as a statement of culture. But such assertions merely dodge the issue, for in everyday affairs we ourselves deal with the problems of the hour in similar broad concepts and do it effectively. Further, there is a reality underlying each of these concepts, even though not immediately apparent. And as to complexity, we recognized that at the outset, finding that culture comprises trait-complexes, and these meshed, or felted, under culture complexes, which is the name we have given to these divisions of the pattern scheme.

These complexes are conceived to be also entangled into a whole, known as the tribal culture. This should make it clear that the simplicity of the scheme is only apparent, but that on the other hand, there is a unity in culture as expressed by the basic concepts.

3. AMONG THE SIRIONO,
NOMADS OF THE LONG BOW *

Fieldwork remains central in cultural anthropology. Basic data come not
from laboratories but from living cultures. An anthropologist goes to live
in another culture. He settles down amidst unfamiliar surroundings and,
if he is successful, his status slowly changes from clumsy alien to friendly
stranger. Ideally, he speaks or will learn to speak the local language
but inevitably he will rely on certain people more than others as teachers,
interpreters, or informants. To some extent, the anthropologist lives like
his hosts, as well as among them. This is quite variable, depending on the
culture, the personality of the fieldworker and the situation itself. In any
event, the fieldworker participates in activities as well as he is able and
as far as he is permitted. He observes whatever he can of the endless series
of events and the tangle of relationships which surround him. He maps,
questions, records, photographs, jokes, mourns, and gets drunk at local
blowouts. Sometimes he gets sick because he may be exposed to hazardous
sanitary conditions. So often does this occur in fieldwork that one
distinguished anthropologist, Elman R. Service, recently dedicated a book
to anthropological field workers—persons who are otherwise intelligent
and literate but who refuse to acknowledge the germ theory of disease.
Though the following excerpt from an ethnographic monograph reveals
some of the difficulties which may be encountered in fieldwork, it also
indicates the thinking and preparation that precede the choice of a
particular locale or culture for study.

* Allan R. Holmberg, *Nomads of the Long Bow* (Washington, D.C.: Smithsonian
Institution, Institute of Social Anthropology, Public. No. 10, 1950), pp. 1–4. Reprinted by permission of the author and publishers.
 The author (b. 1909) is Professor of Anthropology at Cornell. He has done fieldwork
in Bolivia and Peru under varying conditions and has special interest in the field of
applied anthropology. Professor Holmberg is now preparing a much more extensive
treatment of the Siriono than appears in *Nomads of the Long Bow*.

As I CONTINUED my anthropological studies, it became more and more apparent to me, as to others, that a science of culture and behavior was most apt to arise from the application of techniques, methods, and approaches of several scientific disciplines concerned with human behavior—particularly social anthropology, sociology, psychology, and psychoanalysis—to specific problems. Consequently, in casting around for a subject on which to carry out field work, I began to search for one that would be especially adaptable to cross-disciplinary treatment.

While studying at the Institute of Human Relations, I became keenly aware of the significant role played by such basic drives as hunger, thirst, pain, and sex, in forming, instilling, and changing habits. Because of the difficulty of studying human behavior under laboratory conditions, our knowledge about the processes of learning has been derived largely from experimental studies of animals. However, the procedure, successfully employed in psychological experimentation, of depriving animals of food suggested that it might be possible to gain further insight into the relationship between the principles of learning and cultural forms and processes by studying a group of perennially hungry human beings. It was logical to assume that where the conditions of a sparse and insecure food supply exist in human society the frustrations and anxieties centering around the drive of hunger should have significant repercussions on behavior and on cultural forms themselves. Hence, I took as my general problem the investigation of the relation between the economic aspect and other aspects of culture in a society functioning under conditions of a sparse and insecure food supply. More specifically, the problem resolved itself into determining, if possible, the effect of a more or less constant frustration of the hunger drive on such cultural forms as diet, food taboos, eating habits, dreams, antagonisms, magic, religion, and sex relations, and upon such cultural processes as integration, mobility, socialization, education, and change.

In our own society there are many individuals who suffer from lack of food, but one rarely finds hunger as a group phenomenon. For this reason a primitive society, the Siriono of eastern Bolivia, was chosen for study. The Siriono were selected for several reasons. In the first place, they were reported to be seminomadic and to suffer from lack of food. In the second place, they were known to be a functioning society. In the third place, the conditions for study among them seemed favorable, since it was possible to make contact with the primitive bands roaming in the forest through an Indian school which had been established by the Bolivian Government in 1937 for those Siriono who had come out of the forest and abandoned aboriginal life.

I left for Bolivia on September 28, 1940, and arrived in the field on November 28, 1940. Between November 28, 1940, and May 17, 1941, I worked with informants of various bands of Siriono who had been gathered together in a Bolivian Government Indian school at Casarabe, a kind of mixed village of Indians and Bolivians, situated about 40 miles east of Trinidad, capital of the Department of the Beni. At the time of my stay this so-called school had a population of about 325 Indians.

Following my residence in Casarabe, where I became grounded in the Indian language and those aspects of the aboriginal culture that still persisted there, I left in May 1941, to join a band of about 60 Siriono who were living under somewhat more primitive conditions near the Rio Blanco on a cocáo plantation, called Chiquiguani, which was at that time a kind of branch of the above-mentioned school. Upon arriving at Chiquiguani, however, I found that as a result of altercations with the Bolivians, the Indians had dispersed into the forest, and so I encountered no people with whom to work. Consequently, I returned to a ranch near the village of El Carmen. There I was fortunate in meeting an American cattle rancher, Frederick Park Richards, since deceased, who had resided in the area for many years and who had a number of Siriono living on his farm and cattle ranch. Through him I was presented to a Bolivian, Luis Silva Sánchez, a first-rate bushman and explorer for the aforementioned school, who offered to be my companion and who stayed with me during most of the time that I lived and wandered with the Siriono. In company with Silva I set out in search of the Indians who had dispersed into the forest. After about 10 days they were located, and they agreed to settle on the banks of the Rio Blanco, about 2 or 3 days' journey up the river by canoe from the village of El Carmen, at a place which we founded and named Tibaera, the Indian word for assaí palm, the site being so designated because of the abundance of this tree found there. I spent from July 15 to August 28, 1941, at Tibaera, continuing my general cultural and linguistic studies, but under what I regarded as unsatisfactory conditions, since I had previously laid my plans and devoted my energies to acquiring techniques for observing a group of Siriono who had had little or no previous contact. Consequently, I suggested to Silva that we go in search of other Indians. Finally, on August 28, 1941, I set out from Tibaera, in company with Silva and parts of two extended families of Indians (21 people in all), traveling east and south through the raw bush in the general direction of the Franciscan Missions of Guarayos,

where we were told by the Indians that we might locate another band
who had had little or no previous contact. After 8 days of rough travel,
much of which involved passing through swamps and through an area
which had long been abandoned by the Siriono, we joyously arrived
at a section of high ground containing relatively recent remains of a
Siriono camp site. My Indian companions told me that this site had
been occupied by a small number of Indians who had come there in
quest of calabashes about three "moons" earlier.

Inspired by the hope of soon locating a primitive band, we silenced
our guns and lived by hunting with the bow and arrow so as not to
frighten any Indians that might be within earshot of a gun. We followed the rude trails which had been made by the Indians about 3
months earlier, and after passing many abandoned huts, each one newer
than the last, we finally arrived at midday on the eleventh day of march
just outside of a village. On the advice of our Indian companions, Silva
and I removed most of our clothes, so as not to be too conspicuous in
the otherwise naked party—I at least had quite a tan—and leaving
behind our guns and all supplies except a couple of baskets of roast
peccary meat, which we were saving as a peace gesture, we sandwiched
ourselves in between our Indian guides and made a hasty entrance into
the communal hut. The occupants, who were enjoying a midday siesta,
were so taken by surprise that we were able to start talking to them in
their own language before they could grasp their weapons or flee.
Moreover, as their interest almost immediately settled on the baskets
of peccary meat, we felt secure within a few moments' time and sent
back for the rest of our supplies.

Once having established contact with such a group, I had intended
to settle down or wander with them for several months, or until I could
complete my studies. I was forced, however, to abandon this plan when,
after being with them for a day or two, I came down with an infection
in my eyes of such gravity that I was almost blinded. Fearing that
this infection would spread to a point that might cause the loss of my
sight, and since I carried no medicines with which to heal it, I decided to set out for the Franciscan Missions of the Guarayos, about 8
days' distance on foot, the nearest point at which aid could be obtained.
Before leaving, however, I consulted with the chief of this new group
(his name was Ačíba-eóko or Long-arm) and told him that I planned
to return and study the manner of life of his people. In the meantime,
the Indians in our original party, knowing of my plan, had already convinced the chief and other members of his band to return with them to
the Rio Blanco and settle down for a while at Tibaera, a plan which
suited me perfectly. Consequently, in the company of four Indians
of this new band and Silva, I traveled on foot to Yaguarú, Guarayos.

After about 2 weeks of fine treatment at the hands of the civilian administrator, Don Francisco Materna, and the equally hospitable Franciscan fathers and nuns, I was able to rejoin the band, and we slowly returned to Tibaera, arriving there on October 11, 1941.

Besides what studies I was able to make of this band while roaming with them during part of September and October, 1941, I continued to live with them at Tibaera, except for occasional periods of 10 days' or 2 weeks' absence for purposes of curing myself of one tropical malady or another or of refreshing my mental state, until March 1942, when my studies were terminated by news that the United States had become involved in war 3 months previously.

As can be readily inferred from the account given above of my contacts with the Siriono, they were studied under three different conditions: first, for about 4 months, while they were living at Casarabe under conditions of acculturation and forced labor; second, for about 2 months, while they were wandering under aboriginal conditions in the forest; finally, for about 6 months, while they were living at Tibaera, where aboriginal conditions had not appreciably changed except for the introduction of more agriculture and some iron tools. During the course of my work, I made a complete ethnological survey of the culture, only part of which can be published here, although my attention was focused primarily on the problem of the sparse and insecure food supply and its relation to the culture. As my knowledge of the language and culture increased, I was constantly formulating, testing, and reformulating hypotheses with respect to this problem.

Since Siriono society is a functioning one, three fundamental methods of gathering field data were employed: (1) the use of informants, (2) the recording of observations, and (3) the conducting of experiments. The first two methods were followed throughout the course of the work. Experiments, such as the introduction of food plants and animals, were performed during the latter part of the study, although the extensive use of this method was limited by the termination of the research.

The application of the above field methods was facilitated by the use of various techniques of which the following were the principal ones: (1) the use of the language of the people studied and (2) the participation of the ethnographer in the cultural life of the tribe.

When possible, data were recorded on the spot in an ethnographic journal, which was supplemented by a record of personal experiences while in the field. As the group was small, everyone was used as an informant, and since most of the activities of the Siriono center in but one hut, data on the behavior patterns of almost everyone could be recorded. No paid informants were used, although gifts such as bush knives and beads were given. No Siriono was a willing informant; little information was volunteered, and some was consciously withheld. Had it not been for the fact that I possessed a shotgun and medicines, life with the Indians would have been impossible. By contributing to the food supply and curing the sick, I became enough of an asset to them to be tolerated for the period of my residence.

At the time of leaving the field (I had not finished my studies) I did not feel satisfied that I had gained a profound insight into Siriono culture. True, I had studied the language to the extent that I could carry on a fairly lively conversation with the Indians, but the time spent in satisfying my own basic needs—acquiring enough food to eat, avoiding the omnipresent insect pests, trying to keep a fresh shift of clothes, reducing those mental anxieties that accompany solitude in a hostile world, and obtaining sufficient rest in a fatiguing climate where one is active most of the day—often physically prevented me from keeping as full a record of native life as I might have kept had I been observing more sedentary informants under less trying conditions. However, if I have contributed something to an understanding of these elusive but rapidly disappearing Indians, I shall feel more than satisfied.

4. SOME PSYCHOLOGICAL TECHNIQUES
AND OBJECTIVES IN ANTHROPOLOGY *

When the anthropologist is settled in the field there are certain
procedures which he follows and a number of theoretical precautions
which he must exercise. In part he must know himself, for the
anthropologist is no less the product of a culture than any other member
of society. The preconceptions and biases carried into the field are not
overly troublesome if they are recognized and brought into the open. If
they remain in concealment, they may blur the ethnographer's vision
without his being aware of it. Other perils beset the ethnographer. How
reliable are his informants? How good is his knowledge of the language?
How representative of the culture are the events and relationships he
observes? The author of this selection is an experienced field worker,
though some of her most important work was done
after she wrote this article.

1. TRENDS TOWARD PSYCHOLOGY

T HE BIAS of American field work has been in the direction of those
descriptive ethnographies which give a type picture of culture. However,
a general change in the character of scientific thought during the last
decades has made itself felt in pure ethnographic descriptions. Even

* Cora DuBois, "Some Psychological Objectives and Techniques in Ethnography,"
The Journal of Social Psychology, 8 (1937), pp. 285–300. Reprinted by permission
of the author and publisher.

The author (b. 1903) is Professor of Anthropology at Harvard University. A specialist in cultures of Southeast Asia, she has been an advisor to the United States Department of State. Among her books are *People of Alor* (1944) and *Social Forces in
Southeast Asia* (1949). At the time she wrote the article here reproduced, Dr. Dubois
was involved in extensive fieldwork among the Indians of northern California.

where interest still lies primarily in the generalized type picture, a recognition of type as a measure of central tendency in a range of material is coming more and more to the fore. The specific application of statistics to cultural anthropology is still in a very questionable infancy, but the whole system of thought implicit in the normal distribution curve has permeated both the social and experimental sciences. It represents a change from the nineteenth century cause and effect to the twentieth century probability philosophy of thought. In ethnography, the departure from naive type descriptions has come from a number of sources and has expressed itself in various forms. Some of the devices used in this departure are merely incidental to the usual formal presentations. Names of informants are given. Direct quotations have been introduced more generally. Contradictory data are indicated. Discrepancies between theory and practice are noted. Anecdotal material is used more freely. All of these devices serve to stress the individual as a variant in the type picture of culture. Simultaneously, with the growing interest in the range of material and the individual who represents that range, the influence of the case history approach has made itself felt. In those social sciences which employ the case history technique, there are always specifically minded individuals who object to departure from this raw material. In anthropology these individuals are the ones who have stressed biographical and autobiographical material. Radin was one of the first to emphasize this type of data. A few younger field workers are following in his footsteps. Given anthropology as a point of departure, we see that the specifically minded person has drifted toward psychology where he feels he can deal with the least common denominator or, as he expresses it, the ultimate reality in the realm of culture. Such analytic and specific ultimates are, of course, only relative to the point of departure. A trait psychologist certainly would never consider a biography or case history the least common denominator.

Another recent trend in anthropology is the relationship between culture and personality. This is an approach which lies half way between the purely psychological and the social.

Closely allied to the growing stress upon the individual has been an interest in unformalized aspects of cultural behavior. This has varied from reports on unconscious motor habits in Spier's excellent monographs to the psychologically weighted interpretations of Margaret Mead.

It is interesting that the revolt against formal ethnographic descriptions should lead so variously into the psychological field and that the study of the individual and unformalized cultural behavior have become field objectives in themselves. Naturally there has been a variety of other developments in anthropology which, however, need not be discussed at this point. Nor do I wish to imply that all anthropologists whose concern lies with the specificity of material, have turned to psychology.

Any attempt to sketch in a few sentences some recent psychological emphases in anthropology must of necessity be superficial. They have been suggested because they indicate the need not only for new field techniques but also for refinements of the old. One cannot approach new and perhaps more delicate material without sharpening one's tools.

Cultural anthropologists have been markedly inarticulate about field techniques. The subject is one which should be discussed by a person of long and varied experience. That capable field workers have rarely expressed themselves in print in no way indicates that the matter is unimportant. The provisions made by the American Laboratory of Anthropology for introducing students to their first field work under the supervision of a seasoned ethnographer, may represent a tacit admission that there are transmissible skills. Yet oddly enough there has been no discussion of what skills the novice may hope to absorb through his contacts with an experienced worker.

2. PERSONALITY FACTORS OF THE FIELD WORKER

Most anthropologists have been sent into the field for the first time without instructions. They have been told simply to collect the ethnography of a particular group. Presumably the risk of biased reports are minimal under such circumstances. Yet it is also true that every individual's material is sifted through his own personality, not only in the informants he chooses but also in the material he emphasizes. Some ethnographers have difficulty in collecting obscene myths or sex practices. Others concentrate on details of material culture at the expense of social organization. These are faults of omission rather than commission. They are soon recognized and to some extent they may be compensated for. However, the distortions which arise from deep seated personality biases are less easy to cope with. There is always the danger that an ethnographer may discover his own temperament in every culture he studies. Evidence in that direction is not entirely lacking. Problems also may be selected and solved in terms of temperamental biases. When a person goes into the field with a specific problem in mind, the conscious omissions are allowed *ab initio*. Criticism of a field worker for material he has not collected when he set out with a definitely limited problem is out of place, particularly since descriptive data can never be considered complete. But in such cases the unconscious faults of commission, the temptation to see a priori that material, and only that material, which points an answer, becomes acute. Field workers who have gone out with such definite problems in mind have not escaped the suspicion of their colleagues when they have returned with equally definite answers. On the other hand, if anthropology is ever to be anything but an antiquarian interest, a sense of problem must exist and it is too dismally true that it is a rare problem which can be solved by culling the contents of descriptive ethnographies.

Radin has often said that every ethnography should be prefaced by a personality sketch of the writer. The idea is actually being experimented with in the University of Cambridge. I am under the impression that at least one field report is about to appear preceded by a personality sketch of the ethnographer which is based on a battery of tests taken at the National Institute of Industrial Psychology under C. S. Myers.

Closely allied to this matter is the suggestion made by E. J. Lindgren that a field worker should select groups which are temperamentally compatible to him. Basic to the point of view that field work should be pursued in a congenial milieu is the assumption that an ethnographer should identify himself with the culture he is studying. So far as I know, no American anthropologist undertakes field work with such considerations consciously in mind. Yet the belief that one should identify oneself with a particular group and participate as far as possible in the deeper aspects of its life, is not absent. The opinion has been expressed that particularly for the study of unformalized aspects of culture, it is desirable to share as far as possible in the affect content of the community. Whether such an identification is possible can be ascertained only by the honest self-examination of those who profess to such abilities. It is perhaps not unfair, however, to demand of such field workers that their objectivity should balance their identifications. If such an empathic technique is employed, psychoanalysis would seem a prerequisite form of training.

However, in how far a field worker should try to identify with a culture and its participants might be debated. Participation, inevitably clumsy at its best, may make the ethnographer even more enigmatic than usual to informants. With that may go loss of confidence. Also participation may involve one in local factions to the detriment of a complete and balanced picture. There may also be the possibility of securing better material when the informant considers the ethnographer a completely foreign and extraneous person devoid of the emotional connotations attached to their cultural behavior. On a somewhat more superficial level, one wonders for instance whether Gusinde as a spectator might not have secured just as adequate material on the initiation rites of the Ona as he did by being a participant. There are merits on both sides which might profitably be discussed.

3. PRELIMINARY CONTACTS WITH INFORMANTS

Once an area for work has been selected there are still the many and varied devices necessary to make one's preliminary contacts with potential informants. The social worker is in a position of assisting a client. The psychiatrist's aid is definitely solicited by a patient. In other words, the person being interviewed is on the whole, by the very nature of his status, in a more or less cooperative mood. He comes hoping to secure advantages from the contact. Where social research is being carried out through surveys, an appeal can generally be made to local pride, as in the Middletown study, or to oblique advantages as in a minimum budget or health survey. Obviously no such appeals and no such preliminary relationships can be established by the anthropologist. The situation is largely unmotivated for the aboriginal.

It is customary, at least in North America, to pay informants for the time they give the field worker. Under these circumstances it is often possible to enlist the assistance of informants even though they are at first at a loss to understand the purpose of the ethnographer. Of course great variation is found among informants and cultural groups in the appeal which money makes in enlisting cooperation. I should hazard the guess that the appeal is in direct ratio to the disintegration of the culture. In North America where Indians have from necessity gone over to a money economy and yet where opportunities for them to earn it are usually rare, this method has distinct value as a preliminary entrée. An ethnographer who has funds to collect museum specimens has an entering wedge of considerable value, for not only does the purchase of specimens establish contacts on a comprehensible basis, but if sales are negotiated the person interviewed is favorably disposed by receiving a sum of money. Of course, if the field worker's primary object is to collect specimens cheaply, he may reverse the process and attempt first to establish friendly relations. In conversation with anthropologists any number of devices for securing preliminary contacts are mentioned. When the ethnographer is young enough he may be able to account for his presence and interest by speaking of his work as school lessons and thereby throw himself on the informant's amiability. Or he may declare an interest in the history of the tribe and appeal to the informant's pride in possessing such knowledge. The efficacy of such devices is not only limited but on the whole exists only where a culture is well on the way to disintegration. One anthropologist tells of making his first contacts by walking past a row of tepees while he was absorbed in weaving string figures which were a favorite game in that tribe. Exchanging myths and distributing abalone shells have both been used in the pueblos with success. Collecting vocabularies or learning the language are often preliminary approaches. Hired "boys" or interpreters may be used to greatly facilitate early contacts. These devices are understood to be simply means of introduction and represent obstacles with which the usual investigator in social research has fewer difficulties than the anthropologist. The ingenuity of the ethnographer and the nature of the culture must dictate procedure. No generalizations are possible except that patience, tact and good nature are prerequisite. Unless motivated by considerable zeal or hardened by long experience, a diffident person may find these first obstacles almost insurmountable.

4. LINGUISTIC FACTORS

Language problems in field work are many and varied. They range from the most advantageous choice of interpreter through the question of text material to the learning of aboriginal languages. Each one of these three points will be discussed in turn.

In almost all cases where English can be used as a medium of communication, the necessity of acquiring a vocabulary sufficiently limited and colloquial and yet sufficiently flexible to convey impressions foreign to the informant's usual conversation in English, is a very real problem. Often an interpreter is necessary. In such instances naturally the greatest discretion must be used in selecting the proper person. An interpreter should be (a) accurate, (b) acceptable to the older and more conservative portion of the population, (c) willing to serve the ethnographer and his interests, and (d) passive and unobtrusive in his role of mediator between the ethnographer and the informant. Much can be done in a relatively short time in training an interpreter. A course which seldom fails with an intelligent and cooperative person is to appeal to him as a fellow ethnologist and to make him feel a responsibility for the elucidation of the problems which have been explained to him. In short, he must be induced to identify himself with the ethnographer's work. Very often such a person will collect material of his own accord when the ethnographer is not present. I am convinced that when an interpreter is necessary, a large measure of success will depend upon a judicious choice. Often of course, the protracted services of a single individual are not available. In such cases, a younger relative of the informant who knows both languages can often be secured. Where the ethnographer must make his own preliminary contacts with an informant, it may be best to permit the native to suggest the interpreter who will be acceptable. Here one may sacrifice excellence in the interpreter for the sake of *entente* between the three persons involved.

It has long been a dogma that data secured in text are more accurate than those secured in English. Therefore a great body of text material has been collected and published for its content rather than for purely linguistic purposes. However, to my knowledge the dogma has never been thoroughly tested. In a paper written by Demetracopoulou and myself an inconclusive examination of this premise was made incidental to a study of change in myth forms. To do this it was necessary to weigh language as a possible variable. Myths told by a bilingual informant first in English and then in his native tongue were compared. Also myths recorded simultaneously in text and translation furnished by a trained interpreter were examined. The differences in all cases were so slight as to be negligible. Upon further reflection it seems at least plausible that thoroughly accurate material may be secured in English. Obviously a translation is necessary if data are to be used. The question then resolves itself into who shall be the translator. Either the informant, the interpreter or the ethnographer must assume responsibility for a translation. The informant may quite possibly have an inadequate knowledge of English, but this is balanced by the fact that the ethnographer almost surely has an incomplete command of the native tongue. If the ethnographer attempts a translation there is the further drawback that it has been sifted through the mind of a person to whom the culture is at best only partially known. If the ethnographer uses an interpreter to assist him in the translation of a text obviously there is less danger of linguistic distortion, but in that case at least two personalities have interposed themselves between the original material and the translation which reaches the reader. My point is simply that it may be desirable wherever possible to have an informant give his own translation. In such instances it may be a work of supererogation to record the material first in text. I am not convinced that this viewpoint is necessarily correct. It might be desirable to have the whole question of text vs. English data checked by careful and specific studies. The proponents of textual data are usually those who have steeped themselves in the culture of a particular tribe. It is possible that they have confused their thorough knowledge of the culture with the value of text material per se. Obviously these comments are completely out of place for an area where bilinguality does not exist among the aborigines.

This leads us into still a third attitude concerning language, i.e., that a speaking knowledge of the native tongue is prerequisite. No one would deny the desirability of such a claim, but its feasibility is open to question. There are some ethnographers who have claimed that in a span of weeks or even days they have acquired sufficient command of a native language to permit field work in some of the more subtle and elusive aspects of culture. It is difficult for the Americanist to comprehend that a language can be learned as quickly as has been claimed, or ever thoroughly enough to secure penetrating material. Lowie has more than once expressed this doubt in print. The counterclaim hinges upon what constitutes knowing a language. The opinion has been expressed that affect, gesture and vocabulary are the essentials, rather than a grasp of the complexities of grammatical structure. It is stated further that understanding a native language is different from elaborate self-expression in that medium. Lastly of course, there are real differences in linguistic ability and in the complexity of languages. These counterclaims all have certain validity but they are not reassuring when the ethnographer professes to secure subtle material with so blunt an instrument.

5. INTERVIEWING TECHNIQUES

Those social sciences, applied or theoretic, which depend upon interviewing for their raw material, have recently been taking cognizance of techniques in approaching clients, patients, or subjects as the case may be. In non-functioning cultures, the ethnographer also depends largely for his information upon the success of his approach as an interviewer. In functioning cultures observation may be substituted to some extent for interviewing, but even in such cases it is doubtful whether it can be entirely dismissed as a valuable tool. This is particularly true if the historic changes which have occurred during the last three or four generations are of any interest to the investigator.

There is a tendency to appraise anthropologists as successful or unsuccessful field workers. That appraisal may rest on a variety of factors —a sense of problem, resourcefulness, persistence, thoroughness—but it rests also upon skill in gaining rapport with informants. Ethnographic results are inevitably affected by the relationship of the field worker to the informant and the reader is entitled to some indication of that relationship as a guide to the material presented. Interviewing will probably always remain primarily an art but this does not mean that awareness of rapport and relationship should be ignored. By a thorough awareness of his techniques, the individual field worker should develop greater range, flexibility and control in handling human material. Even in the arts, articulateness and awareness in techniques are not necessarily handicaps. In those social disciplines which profess to be sciences, they become obligatory.

There are two major types of interviewing which can be used with informants, the active and the passive. In active interviewing material is secured largely by direct questioning and by indicating the material desired. In passive interviewing the informant is allowed to bring out material as he chooses in a modified type of free association. It may not be necessary to stress that whether the interviewing technique is passive or active, it should be envisaged as a dynamic device, a working tool whose control is the responsibility of the ethnographer. The informant, the culture or the aim of a particular piece of research will determine the choice of interviewing technique. For formal, tabular and certain descriptive material the active technique may prove the most economical tool. But even in such cases sympathetic rapport is basic to accuracy and detail.

In addition, an active interviewing technique must often be used where the material desired would seem less suited to the procedure. Informants are sometimes consistently resistive. The most difficult type of resistance to overcome is engendered by complete lack of interest in describing native life. Certain groups like those of the Great Basin are reputed to be uninterested in giving information and incapable of coherent accounts. Where such cultural patterns exist the skill and particularly the time of the ethnographer are put to a severe test.

Also there are certain cultures where the resistance of informants is based on a definite policy of secretiveness and conscious hostility toward the whites. Here it would appear that data are procurable only through cajolery and pressure—often of an economic type. Perhaps the clearest expression of that type of approach is contained in Fortune's *Omaha Secret Societies*. Obviously material secured only through pressure on the informants is not ideal, nor must the conditions of work be conducive to a convincing and penetrating understanding of the culture. Where it has been used, an overt statement to that effect is owed the reader. White's *Pueblo of Santo Domingo* is a case in which an honest statement of difficulties and procedure prefaced the material. It would be desirable to have such statements more often and in greater detail. In this connection there is no need to emphasize that the informant should be thoroughly assured of the ethnographer's discretion in imparting the source of his information, particularly to other tribesmen. The ethnographer owes the informant the same security which the lawyer offers his client or the doctor his patient. The extent of care to be exercised often exceeds anticipation, even when the information may be on some subject as devoid of emotional content as house types. The point of view just expressed is not necessarily accepted by all field workers. I have heard ethnographers state that they make a point of exploiting individual hostilities to procure information and that the results are successful. Quite apart from the ethics of the situation, one's skill in handling such situations must be a determinant in this matter.

Even in areas where resistance is not the rule, pressure may seem indicated in breaking down the reticence of certain individuals. There are of course many degrees of directness. One may threaten, bribe, or exploit hostilities. Or one may assume a knowledge of certain information considered by the informant to be secret. In this fashion the informant

may be either startled into conversation or else feel absolved from responsibility and proceed with a clear conscience.

Another consideration affecting interviewing techniques grows out
of the so-called topical approach. Ordinarily field work is with one more
or less homogeneous group and covers a considerable period of time.
In such cases all the more desirable field techniques may be applicable.
Sometimes, however, the ethnographer is concerned with a particular
topic. He is occupied with securing data only on one subject in a number
of ethnic groups. In the topical problem where subtle and unformalized
material is desirable, difficulties are greatly magnified. Time and funds
seldom permit the slow building up of confidence which is essential to
procuring such material and at the same time the choice of informants
and interpreters can never be so careful. Under such circumstances it
may be necessary to use an active interviewing technique in some of its
less attractive aspects. Furthermore, the curtailment of time presents a
real dilemma in determining how far one should direct discussion. When
a complete description of tribal life is one's objective, almost any gossip
or garrulousness on the part of the informant has some value. In the
topical approach this is not the case and the ethnographer must weigh
constantly his desire for relevant information against the injury to rapport which too much active interviewing and directing might produce.

All the tactics which I have just mentioned may well prove traumatic
to the informant and if such direct approaches are to be made at all,
they should be used only as a last resort. I believe that it is of the greatest
importance that an informant never be urged to relate material whose
telling he will subsequently regret. It may even be desirable to evince no
interest in certain matters of considerable importance until the informant
is willing to discuss them at length. This attitude is really the basis of
passive interviewing. That such precautions are not always employed,
would doubtless surprise the psychiatrist, but after all it must be borne
in mind that the ethnologist has neither humanitarian nor therapeutic
interests to serve. However, in their own self-interest, discretion seems
indicated. Any direct attack upon reticences may do real harm not only
to the rapport between the informant and the ethnographer, but also to
the work of future ethnographers. Whenever an individual has been
pushed beyond his own desire to speak, there may follow a strong reaction which leaves him more guarded than ever. When one is dealing with
tribal fragments, this may mean a serious and permanent loss. There
exists a sole survivor of a strategically located Californian group who
refuses to serve as an informant because of just such a traumatic experience. The data which he alone knows, are now permanently and need-
lessly lost. Quite apart from any ethical regard for the informant as a

human being the field worker has obligations toward ethnographers who may subsequently interview the same person.

The passive technique of interviewing is usually applicable and always desirable where the aim of the ethnographer is to secure subtle religious, social or psychological material. Patience, regularity of interviews over a prolonged period, indirectness of approach, the differences between earlier and later interviews, are all points in which the anthropologist may learn from the psychoanalyst. Receptivity on the part of the ethnographer to the affective content of the material imparted is indubitably valuable. He must be able to shuffle off the thinking habits of his own culture and participate sympathetically in those of his informant. For instance, I believe that in order to interview a shaman effectively, the ethnographer must be able to think, at least temporarily, in terms of the reality of supernatural manifestations. This is, of course, quite different from the identification with a congenial cultural milieu mentioned earlier. Also, whenever possible, the field worker must be prepared to avoid inadvertent references to affect-laden subjects. Formal work in anthropology probably does much in preparation for such attitudes.

A factor enters in the use of the passive technique which does not ordinarily occur in psychiatric interviews. The psychiatrist, by the very nature of his therapeutic object and the cooperativeness of a patient who has gone so far as to seek his assistance, is almost automatically the directing and leading component in the interview relationship, even though the passive technique is used and even though the patient may at times resent the situation and try to alter it. The ethnographer, however, neither has his assistance solicited nor is he offering therapy. He is rather in the position of an apprentice who is being introduced into the intricacies of an unfamiliar pattern. In appearance at least, therefore, the ethnographer who uses the passive technique will be forced to yield control of the interview to the informant. Primitive people are so consistently relegated in their contacts with Europeans to a status of inferiority, that an informant may easily slip into an attitude of overcompensation in the friendly relationship offered by the ethnographer. Such overcompensations may manifest themselves in domineering, demanding and inconsiderate requests which make further work difficult. On such occasions increases in pay are often asked. It is unfortunate if an unskillful handling of rapport makes it necessary to abandon a useful informant.

The logical consideration which springs from the preceding paragraphs is the psychoanalytic concept of transference. If by transference is meant simply "a confidence and personal regard," then it becomes a *sine qua non* of good field work. There is of course the possibility that the ethnographer may himself secure one of these mild transferences to the informant. I can see no disadvantage to such a situation. I wonder if ethnographers who speak of identifying with a culture have not some such experience in mind and have failed to distinguish between the individual and the culture he bears? If on the other hand, transference is given the more extreme and accurate interpretation, then the situation becomes more difficult to control. I have in mind at least four cases in which marked transferences occurred and were sufficiently badly handled to interfere with field work. It would be interesting to learn from persons experienced in the transference situation some of the devices for handling it most effectively.

Despite many difficulties peculiar to the ethnographic interview—and I have mentioned only a few—there are also many advantageous factors. It has been suggested that the more disintegrated a culture is, the more communicative informants become concerning moribund or extinct life habits. This is probably true in the majority of cases and may be explained in part by the diminished affect of the old culture as well as by a certain nostalgic pleasure in reminiscences. In illiterate groups it is often customary for the old men to instruct the young in tribal lore. In a disintegrating or rapidly changing society, the old person may find that the young ones are not interested in a store of accumulated experience which is no longer relevant. At this point the ethnographer may step in as a substitute in the life of the older person. Similarly, bed ridden or blind natives are often highly satisfactory informants. Having been cut off from normal social life, they not only have time to review their past but they are also pleased at the ego outlet which is ordinarily denied them. Or again, it is possible that certain informants are able to explain their old life more clearly because they have had the advantage of experiencing a contrasting culture. The sophistication of some natives in regard to the arbitrary nature of social structures far exceeds that of many western Europeans who have not had the advantage of an object lesson in comparative culture. Another factor which may facilitate the gathering of ethnographic material has already been suggested. It is the flattery of being interviewed and befriended by a representative of a "superior race" and the pleasure derived by an informant from talking about his culture to a sympathetic member of that group. In addition I believe that it is a matter of general experience that many informants heartily enjoy talking once their confidence has been gained. Most people enjoy talking about their culture as they do about themselves. Those who most sublimate their personal ego into their culture make the best informants. When they meet an ethnographer who has a sympathetic and sincere attitude toward their culture, they frequently become expansive. All these factors apply largely to disintegrating societies. They compensate to some extent for the observations which can be made in a functioning group.

6. NUMBER OF INFORMANTS

The number of informants interviewed is a practical problem faced by every field worker. The matter of objectives suggested in the first part of this paper enters into the question, as does also the statistical concept of sampling.

Circumstances may determine the answer quite apart from objectives. There is an ethnographer who had only one capable informant left in a particular tribe. He spent one summer exhausting all possible information from that person and felt it was profitable for him to return the following year to get the same material in text in order to add whatever nuances that might yield. The results, which still await publication, should be interesting from several methodological points of view.

Where the individual as such is the object of the ethnographer's interest, he must answer the question: How much time and money can justifiably be spent in dealing with a single person and in securing the diminishing returns involved in such a procedure? If one is concerned solely with psychology, presumably any amount of time and money is justified, since cultural data and the concept of the norm become subsidiary to the interest in the individual as such. However, if one is primarily interested in the social sciences the question is not so easily solved.

If the relationship of culture to personality is also the objective, it will affect the number of informants chosen for study. In such problems prolonged concentration on a few individuals is more than legitimate. However, the ethnographer should guard both himself and the reader from cultural generalizations based alone on such limited material.

On the other hand, if the field worker is concerned with norms, in how far can he accurately portray and interpret the more subtle aspects of culture without devoting time and effort to intimate relationships with many typical and atypical personalities? Even where unformalized or psychological material is not the objective, how far can a single informant, however gifted, be considered to give a representative picture of formal procedure? Pater Schmidt, for instance, has definitely defended the point of view that one intelligent individual is better able to describe the tribal ideology than several mediocre persons. He has been willing to venture many pages of interpretation upon the account of such an Indian from a northern Californian tribe. Yet subsequent field work showed that this individual, although highly capable, was quite aberrant to the tribal norm. The willingness to accept one individual as representative implies two problems. One is the degree to which range in a social group is necessary to establish a norm. The other is the discrepancy between practice and theory. Undoubtedly the ideal or formal structure of an institution is desirable material. Yet even here a single informant does not necessarily give a reliable description. The degree to which actual practice approximates the ideal is equally important from both the psychological and the social viewpoint. For such a picture many informants are essential. If the norm, on the one hand, and the relationship between theory and practice, on the other hand, are of any concern to a particular worker, he cannot be satisfied with material from only a few persons however reliable they may be. The range of psycho-sociological material is so great and the curve so low, that the sample must be a large one. So far ethnologists have not taken these questions under serious or systematic consideration. No categorical answer presents itself but the matter should not be overlooked in the course of field descriptions.

I have attempted to suggest some of the reasons for growing interest in psychology within the field of anthropology. As a concomitant to that interest, former techniques must be sharpened even where purely cultural interests still predominate. Where interests in psychology predominate, new and more sensitive procedures will have to be considered. None of the techniques discussed in this paper are hypothetical. The "good" and the "bad" have all been used presumably with some modicum of success. However, the time is past when we can be satisfied with such modica and it is essential that techniques keep pace with expanding objectives.

5. THE ANTHROPOLOGICAL
APPROACH IN SOCIAL SCIENCE *

Important as field work is, the utilization of data rather than its procurement poses the most vexing problems of anthropology. Though the discipline has experienced periods in which primary emphasis was placed upon description, the current has usually been in favor of the formulation of general statements concerning the nature of culture and regularities in its structure and development.

The article which follows discusses the goals and fruits of anthropological analysis but also points out some of its trials and tribulations. The reader will note the rapidity with which attention is focussed on social structure and may correctly conclude that the author is a social (rather than cultural) anthropologist.

WHEN you did me the honour of inviting me to preside over the Anthropological Section at this first post-war meeting of the British Association and I considered the subject on which it would be most appropriate to address you, I decided, for a number of reasons, that it would be desirable to attempt some indication of the rôle of Anthropology in the development of Social Science. Some of the most substan-

* Daryll Forde, "The Anthropological Approach in Social Science," *The Advancement of Science,* Vol. IV, No. 15 (1947), pp. 213–224. Reprinted with the permission of the author and the publisher.
The author (b. 1902) is Director of the International African Institute and Professor of Anthropology, University College, London. While his major fieldwork in recent years has been in Africa, especially in Nigeria, he has carried out research in two American Indian cultures, the Yuma and the Hopi. Editor of the *Ethnographic Survey of Africa,* Professor Forde has personally contributed several numbers to this series. He is also known as the author of *Habitat, Economy and Society* (1934, et. seq.), the editor (with Radcliffe-Brown) of *African Systems of Kinship and Marriage* (1950) and *Studies in the Cosmological Ideas and Values of African Peoples* (1954).

tial of recent contributions in Anthropology lie in the sociological sphere; but the cessation of conferences during the years of war and, in particular, the interruption of the annual meetings of the British Association, which have provided so valuable a forum for the exposition and exchange of ideas among workers in the various specialist fields of science, have been unfavourable to any assessment of the extent and significance of progress in Social Anthropology. Still more important, perhaps, the British Association itself has recognised, in the creation of a special division for the Social and International Relations of Science, both the need for studying the relations of scientific advance to social problems and for the scientific study of society itself. It seemed to me, therefore, timely to attempt to present some account of the Anthropological approach in Social Science. Obviously in a short address it is only possible to sketch some broad outlines and to present a few illustrations, but I hope it may prove useful to indicate, however briefly, the relation of sociological problems to anthropological studies and the ways in which anthropological methods and concepts have been developed in the attack on them.

As a study of the collective characters and activities of mankind, Anthropology has by tradition been diverse both in its approaches and in the variety of its problems. On the one hand, it has been directed towards the understanding of the physical diversity of mankind. This is the approach of evolutionary biology with its concern for the evidence of the occurrence and causes of the evolution and diversification of human varieties. At the same time, it has sought to discover and understand the cultural diversity of mankind and to unravel the vicissitudes of cultural development of human groups. In this field there is first the direct interest in the actual cultural history of mankind comparable to the palæontological and taxonomic interests in the biological sphere. But the attempts to evaluate the various factors which account for the particular features in any given culture and of cultural change through time have inevitably led to inquiry into fundamental and universal processes which, operating at variable intensities and in differing combinations in particular situations, account for the actual character of particular cultures.

At the same time, the comparative study of diverse cultures and of their biological and environmental contexts affords the means whereby the existence and operation of particular factors may be determined. In other words, the variety of human cultures affords a laboratory in which, through the comparison of differing forms and their contexts, particular processes can at least in part be isolated for study. This last is the more strictly scientific or analytic approach with some aspects of which I shall be mainly concerned to-day.

The term science is often loosely employed with a wide variety of meanings and, while there is no opportunity to-day to consider the matter at any length, it is necessary to recall both the essential character and objectives of scientific study and their relation to other modes of knowledge. Science, properly speaking, is a mode of investigation directed towards the discovery of processes of universal application with regard to a relevant field of phenomena. Its method is essentially analytical, it seeks to disclose the properties or attributes of classes of phenomena and the causal relations between them. These it formulates by means of definitions and rules which embody these properties and their interconnections. Everyone is familiar with such rules or laws in connection with the elementary principles of physics or chemistry that are part of general education, but the relevance of this mode of analysis is frequently ignored or misunderstood when human actions are involved. In consequence, the implications, which are of fundamental importance, for any science of society, are often lost sight of. Of these, the most important is firstly that a particular scientific analysis does not seek to account at one and the same time for all the characteristics of any concrete situation or a series of such situations. Selected properties are isolated for study in relation to others that may be found to be functionally interdependent with them.

In human affairs the direct and comprehensive interest in the concrete situation, whether it be a general pattern of social organisation, certain forms of beliefs and ritual practices, or a technique whereby artifacts are produced and employed, leads to provisional explanation in terms of integrated description. That is to say, a very wide range of known conditions and processes are reviewed and their contribution as determinants of the concrete situation is qualitatively expressed. This is the essence of the historical approach to understanding, an approach which, contrary to common misconception, does not mean an approach merely in terms of time or an explanation in terms of chronology. Time and the measure of its lapse by means of chronology is significant in history because it is one of the coordinates of the phenomenal world, but space is of equal significance and the expression of spatial relations are equally prominent.

But what it is fundamentally important to stress here is that integrated descriptions of this kind are dependent on science. In the first place, no statement of this kind, that is, no explanatory account of how things come to be as they are in a given field of space-time, is possible without postulating and employing for explanatory purposes certain properties and rules of relations already assumed to be applicable to the phenomena in question.

Thus an account of a particular political organisation such as an African chiefdom or the British constitution at any phase of its development involves, in fact, assumptions concerning rules or uniformities applicable to the political relations exhibited by man in society. It may, for example, be assumed that the scale of political organisation is dependent on such factors as the physical and technical facilities for intercommunication and that changes in the latter will tend to changes in political scale. It may similarly be postulated that interests arising from occupational activities within the economic framework of a society will be reflected in its internal political structure such that increases in the economic power of any section of the community as a result of technological changes or the reduction of earlier restraints will tend to be accompanied by changes in political structures whereby the interest of that section secures an increment of political authority. The point to observe is that descriptive studies of particular social conditions or developments, whether they be what are commonly regarded as historical studies treating social and cultural developments over considerable periods of time, or ethnographic descriptions of very limited time depth, and whether they be wide in the range of activities and institutions considered, embrace a great deal of the life of a people, or whether they be confined to the portrayal of a particular institution, depend always for the interpretation of the particular events and their interrelations on the assumed validity of manifold general principles assumed to underly the social behaviour of man. In fact, historical or descriptive studies are a species of applied science. Just as the various branches of engineering depend on the postulated uniformities of physical sciences, and modern medicine depends for diagnosis and therapy on the application of the concepts and principles of biological sciences, such as physiology and biochemistry, so the analysis and description of particular cultural situations presuppose principles concerning human behaviour. Not a line of human history could be written without such assumptions. Some body of theory concerning the cultural behaviour of man is implicit in every attempt at integrated description of the activities of human groups. The theories and the concepts which they employ may be vaguely formulated, they may not be explicitly stated, but conceptually they are of the same kind as those of natural science. The fact that they may be vague, that their verification is weak, that they may even be shown to be fallacious, or that when they are made explicit they appear to be part of common knowledge, is irrelevant to their status in this respect.

I should call attention here to another point of fundamental importance, namely, that practical activity in human affairs, the formulation of policies, the practice of administration and individual conduct in society similarly involve hypotheses of social action. The politician's estimate of the attitudes of his constituents or of the public at large to some particular measure of legislation; the action of a leader in directing a team, the estimate formed of the capacity, worthiness or usefulness of an individual in connection with an activity, all these in large part depend on what we commonly refer to as experience and judgment. But experience and judgment in practical affairs are the expression of hypotheses concerning regularities and interrelations in human behaviour, in other words, of theories concerning the social nature of man.

Here it may be objected that it is preposterous to raise to the level of scientific theories the vague, half conscious and all too fallible assumptions implicit in practical judgments. But this is to misconceive the nature of scientific theory. A scientific theory is, as I have already emphasised, a hypothesis, the most satisfactory hypothesis available at a given time from the points of view of verification and comprehensiveness, concerning the properties of certain natural phenomena and their interrelations. The theories or laws of physics and chemistry differ in degree, in degree of explicitness, precision and verification, but not in kind, from hypotheses concerning processes in human society. This difference in degree may be and often is enormous, and the reasons are not far to seek. As we pass from inorganic to organic, and from organic to social phenomena, the complexity and variability of the phenomena and of the factors involved in determining their properties, as well as the extent to which these can be isolated for examination and the difficulties of securing observation under requisite and known varieties of circumstance, are all greatly multiplied. Where as in the study of the social relations of man, the variable factors that in combination determine any section of the pattern are so manifold it is not surprising that hypotheses are, as compared with those in physical science, crude or limited in reference and are so much more difficult of verification and precise expression.

But such hypotheses are a condition of logical thought about social life, and since belief and action in this field are, as a consequence of man's self consciousness, paramount human interest, their formulation and critical examination are of unique importance. Current among every people there are hypotheses as to the processes controlling their cultural activities and their social relations. Everywhere these theories are factors in their explanations of the events that befall them as a community and of their judgments as to the practical courses they should pursue. We have lived in a period when crude and demonstrably fallacious hypotheses ascribing unalterable biological foundations for unverified cultural aptitudes and social tendencies to particular peoples have been accepted as official doctrines of a powerful state. The so-called 'racial theories' of Nazi Germany were hypotheses concerning alleged factors in the social process which were accepted by millions and provided a foundation for historical explanations and the acceptance of political actions which have devastated Europe and impoverished the world. That these particular hypotheses, like hundreds of other sociological myths that have strewn the pages of historical and political writings at all periods, could be shown to be fallacious, does not affect the fact that the particular cultural and social conditions in which men find themselves are interpreted, and indeed can only have meaning, in terms of theories of society.

From this follows the paramount importance of the endeavour to subject social phenomena to the inductive analysis and the critical testing of hypothesis which are the canons of science. That this is a task of very great difficulty where the data are so complex, and the variables so numerous and so difficult to isolate, where the investigators themselves are inevitably entities in a social system, and so especially liable to emotional attachments, is not to be denied. But it is here that the anthropological approach can perhaps claim some merit as one conducive to a detached attitude to social theories affecting one's own group and period. For the anthropological tradition has in the first place emphasised the need to consider particular problems within a framework embracing the human species as a whole. Whether it be economic organisation, religious belief and practice, or political institutions, the anthropologist eschews hypotheses of special creation concerning particular human qualities of vice or virtue, or of the divine providence of ethnocentric deities. Thus a practice such as shamanism, whereby phenomena of psychic dissociation are interpreted as spirit possession and utilised according to a set pattern in the alleviation of social crises, is not approached by the anthropologist on the assumption that peculiar and occult powers are the special qualities of certain peoples, scattered through the world. Every instance provides material towards determining, by analysis of each and comparison among them, the range of conditions in which these phenomena of dissociation are stimulated and institutionalised.

Similarly, the occurrence of slavery in many societies is not ascribed to the especial brutality and cupidity of particular groups within the human race. A comparison of forms and contexts shows that the degrees of subjection established with legal sanctions and social approval range from the mildest of enforced adoption to the maintenance of slave gangs devoid of social status. We are dealing not with a single thing—'slavery' —nor with a single process due to a simple cause, but with a wide range of social phenomena which have certain formal criteria in common, and are resultants of a number of concomitant factors operating at exceptional intensities in particular societies. Comparative study of the social character and context of subjection reveal, as Siegel has recently shown, that there is effective economic or political inducement to the enforced control of human beings of extraneous social origin over only a limited range of technological and ecological conditions. Still more limited and distinct from one another are the characteristics of the several contexts in which there is inducement to such variants as pawning, enforced adoption of captives, domestic servitude, and chattel slavery. Chattel slavery in the Classical World, in the New World plantations, and the indigenous slave colonies of some West African societies were responses to facilities for comparatively large-scale production and commercial exchange where manual labour was a scarce and limiting factor. Very different are the social character and economic conditions of agrarian serfdom in self-subsistent local communities, whether of Medieval Europe or of chiefdoms in East Africa and the Sudan, where the division of labour is slight and the units of surplus output are small and dispersed. Other forms of subjection do not seek economic advantage. The domestic servitude of captives practised by many peoples in Africa and the New World are rather dependent on the tendency to assimilate the captive and increase the numbers of the kin or local group for its political aggrandisement within the wider community.

I have given these brief illustrations to show that for the anthropologist, the customs, beliefs and patterns of intercourse among a particular people are but one picture in the vast gallery of the ever-changing cultural activity of Man. In the study of any aspect of a particular culture he seeks in the first place to delineate its character, its qualities and interconnections. But he is also challenged to dissect from it the operation at particular intensities determined by both the bio-physical and the wider cultural context, the multifarious processes that are the universal determinants of culture and social organisation.

Secondly, it may be claimed that Anthropology has, in its concentration of attention on the cultures of non-European peoples, been less liable to emotional distortion in its approach to description and analysis. Although exceptions could no doubt be cited, the anthropologist, in his appraisals of cultures and social systems, has been comparatively free from the passions underlying historical apology or of the polemics of social struggle. He has remained substantially outside the society which he has studied; its values have not permeated his own to the detriment of accurate observation and recording. Indeed, his very difficulties in securing and presenting reliable data, and in discovering coherence among them, spring in large measure from his lack of prior attachment. He may grope uncertainly for the determinants of the social phenomena he observes, he may be baffled to analyse in adequate categories the ideas and customary actions he encounters, but he is at least assisted by his detachment in distinguishing between observable event and indigenous rationalisation.

The anthropological outlook with regard to social science may therefore be said to be characterised by two complementary approaches. On the one hand, it seeks to determine the structure of social relations among any given people in terms of a comprehensive observation of their cultural norms. While it may be necessary for practical reasons or in the pursuit of some particular problem to concentrate on some aspect of the culture or of social relations, particular institutions are not divorced from the total cultural context, nor is the social structure described and analysed only in terms of the ideal patterns or vitiated by acceptance of the rationalisations of the people themselves. In short, the anthropological aim is to determine and interpret social systems in terms of comprehensive ethnographic data.

On the other hand, the anthropologist views any given society as one exemplification of general processes whereby aggregates of the human species cohere in response to the physical condition of their habitat and to their psycho-physiological drives as organisms. His analysis of any one community is informed by the need to present data that are significant and accurate for subsequent comparative studies. And in these comparative studies he seeks through the detection of concomitant variations both within the social structure and between it and the external environment or the organic conditions of the population, to isolate abstract but recurrent properties inherent in a range of concrete behaviour whose functional dependence on other properties of the social system or on bio-physical determinants may then be determined.

It is necessary to recall here, however, the very wide range of processes that are involved in determining the collective activities of any group of people. The physiological and psychological qualities of individuals are variable, and so in the aggregate will be those of any given groups, and both general and special characteristics in this field are significant determinants. The understanding of the significance for culture of physiological and psychological processes and of their variable incidence is obviously dependent on the advances made in these sciences by their own methods. This is but an instance of the familiar interdependence between different fields of science, but is deserving of emphasis. Every branch of science makes assumptions and employs concepts the validity of which depends on the findings of sciences at more basic levels. And it is important to remember that any analysis of culture makes physiological and psychological assumptions and that in cultural studies there emerge problems which depend for solution on investigations in those fields. Secondly, the conditions of the habitat and of all the natural resources which are drawn upon in the life of individual and group will affect the modes of activity in that life. But the effects of the psycho-physiological and environmental ingredients in the immensely complex equation are also secondarily modified at any time by an existing cultural pattern, so that one may have to reckon with differences in their short and long run effects in view of cultural inertia. Furthermore, within the cultural field, different sectors or categories such as technology, economics, political organisation and cultural values are interdependent in the sense that changes in any one will have effects on the others, while each is sensitive in varying measure to changes in the external world.

This approach to social analysis owes an immense debt to Herbert Spencer, who insisted not only on comprehensive analysis of all the factors involved in the determination of a particular social situation, but also emphasised and illustrated the importance of comparative methods for the elucidation of the factors and the abstract formulation of processes underlying the concrete behaviour of man in Society. Spencer also stressed the great value of data from small-scale societies in which the totality of the system could more readily be grasped and analysed. His addiction to the use of ethnographic evidence from 'primitive' or small-scale societies has often been criticised by later sociologists who have seen it as a wasteful or irrelevant deflection of attention from the data and problems of modern industrial societies. But Spencer appreciated, as did Durkheim, Hobhouse, Sumner, and others whom he so strongly influenced, that for the discovery of underlying process by comparative methods, it was necessary not only to consider a wide range of social forms and contexts, but also to begin analysis with material that is comparatively simple from the structural point of view.

It is, of course, necessary to distinguish between Spencer's conceptual framework and the details of his methods and use of ethnographic data. The first as set out in the opening chapters of his *Principles of Sociology* can hardly be bettered to-day as a comprehensive statement of the scope of social science and of the general connections between the physical, biological and cultural phenomena involved in its study. He formulated with admirable comprehensiveness the scientific validity and methodological importance of empirical study of social morphology and social function, and of the comparative method for isolating and estimating the effects of the various factors determining particular features of morphology and function.

On the other hand, his actual procedures in investigation, dominated as he was by the desire not merely to demonstrate the validity of an evolutionary hypothesis, but to establish the actual course of the social evolution of mankind, suffered from grave defects which vitiated social theory and much of the work in Anthropology itself for many years. By introducing *a priori* stages of evolution which captivated the imagination and diverted the attention of anthropologists for two generations, he substituted for the comparative study of actual societies which he advocated in principle, the formulation of hypothetical social conditions in imaginary primeval societies which could be considered plausible starting-points for processes of unilineal evolution by which the more complex historic societies have emerged. This was particularly glaring in his treatment of marriage and the domestic family, where attention was focused not on the need for exact study of the morphology and function of the marital group, but on a vain endeavour to substantiate from defective ethnographic data a purely speculative evolution from promiscuity through polyandry and polygyny and marriage by capture to the monogamous family of 'higher' civilisations. A further defect, which sprang in part from this *a priori* bias, allowed him to be comparatively well satisfied with the sketchiest ethnographic material. Although, as has been said, he provided in his theoretical framework of sociology an admirable conspectus of the character and mutual intérdependence of the many factors contributing to the determination of social form and emphasised the need for their consideration, both in attempting to understand any given society and in accounting for the differences among them, he failed to stress the need for intensive and specialist investigation of societies comparable to the morphological and physiological studies of the biologists in order to obtain the data which would make such analysis possible.

Thus, although Spencer fully appreciated the importance of comparative study on the widest scale in order to determine generalisations of validity for all human societies and, in consequence, made great use of ethnographic evidence and devoted much energy to promoting the compilation of a corpus of ethnographic data for the express use of his successors, it was not he, but those who were later compelled to undertake the task of demolishing *a priori* evolutionary dogmas, who demonstrated the importance of the meticulous examination of the particular forms of social life in order to determine morphology and functional relations in any given society. It is to the pioneers of intensive ethnographical field work, to Cushing, Bourke, Boas, Kroeber and Lowie in the United States, and to Rivers, Radcliffe-Brown and Malinowski in this country that we owe the development of more exact methods of investigation and analysis, whereby the nature of the forms and the essential character of the processes and their conditions can be adequately presented for the comparative study which Spencer so rightly saw was indispensable both for a scientific theory of society and for explanation of the occurrence and interconnections of the specific features of social structure in any particular society.

By way of illustration of the manner in which detailed and comprehensive ethnographic investigations and the comparative studies which these render possible have advanced our understanding of the determinants of social structure, I will consider briefly some aspects of the character and rôle of kin groups in social organisation. The tendency for rights and status in any community to be transmitted to succeeding generations on the basis of kinship is a fairly obvious function of paréntage and can be shown to affect succession in all human societies. But one of the problems which confront any students of the rôle of kinship in social organisation is the great variation in the extent to which this tendency gives rise to corporate groups of kinsfolk within and between which a great part of the social life is organised. The ethnography of a sufficient number of societies of different type is now known with enough precision to make possible not only preliminary determination of the variable relations of such groups to the wider social framework, but also for analysis of the functional dependence of their development and decline on more fundamental cultural variables.

Where, as a result of limiting conditions of the habitat and of the techniques for essential production, the stability and density of population is low, we find a class of societies exemplified by such peoples as the Andamanese, Eskimo and the aborigines of the Great Basin of Western North America, in which the local community is a small unstable aggregate of domestic families, a dozen or less in number, which has equally unformalised relations with neighbouring communities sufficient only to maintain cultural homogeneity as expressed in language, techniques, cosmology and ritual. Detailed and systematic analysis of the social structure of such communities as, for example, that of Radcliffe-Brown on the Andamanese, of Boas, Rasmussen and others on the Central Eskimo, and of Lowie, Kelly and Steward and others among the Basin Shoshoneans, has shown that the normal sentiments of solidarity and mutual obligation between parent and child and between siblings, which are generated by prolonged interaction in the domestic unit, are clearly manifest. The usual extensions through secondary links to collateral kin underlie the prominence of kinship links in maintaining cohesion between the component families of the local group and in determining the inter-group movements of particular individuals and families.

But the poverty of the habitat, the rudimentary character of productive techniques, or the combination of both, so severely limit the scale and stability of both separate settlements and of the wider community, that the tendency for the permanent attachment of a regulated body of persons to an aggregate of fixed resources has little opportunity for expression. The establishment of specific rules for the transmission of collective and individual rights in the control and exploitation of resources is likewise inhibited. The food supply in any locality, whether it be a harvest of pinyon nuts or wild grass seeds, among the Paiute or the seal population at winter and spring hunting grounds, and the caribou herd migrating through an inland valley among the Central Eskimo, is so unpredictable or so widely scattered that the tendency for particular kinsfolk in any generation to form coherent exclusive groups is frustrated by the opportunism enforced on the individual and the household by the ecological situation. Systematic organisation through rules governing the residence of families, the affiliation of individuals to groups and succession to status or economic rights in accordance with descent, is lacking because the ties latent in parentage and siblinghood are prevented from formalised expression in the social organisation.

Where the combination of available resources and exploitive techniques reach higher levels, the stability and size of local groups and the regularity of interaction among them all tend to increase. In such societies, the fundamental tendency to transmit rights and status from parent to child and for them to be shared among siblings of one or other sex, has wider scope. In combination with the equally fundamental dichotomy of the sexes in economic and political rôles, this leads to the emergence of more stable groupings of kin according to a principle of unilineal affiliation. Thus groups of unilineal kin may collectively identify themselves both practically and symbolically with tracts of territory they occupy, exploit and seek to defend, and place high value on their condition of mutual obligation and their internal coherence with reference to outsiders.

There is no lack of well documented demonstration of the process whereby the individual on reaching maturity in many such societies derives from one or other parent, and sometimes severally from both, membership in a unilineal group of kin with rights of residence, and participation in its collective life. This includes, in particular, a share in the exploitation of resources controlled by the group to which the parent belongs, and the enjoyment of that status in the wider community which may be associated with the group as a persistent segment of society.

But the scale and degree of formalisation of groupings based on unilineal grouping of kin is highly variable. Equally variable according to the complexity of the culture, is the degree to which the various elements of social status and of rights and obligations are specialised and distinguished one from another. In some societies unilineal succession and the sphere of operation of groups of unilineal kin may be restricted to limited sectors of the social process. The transmission of particular rights such as residence, the use of specific resources, the ownership of movable goods, the assumption of honorific titles or the practice of magic, may be divorced from one another and some only subject to rôles of unilineal inheritance. Indeed the duality of parentage and the differentiation in the procreative, domestic and economic rôles of males and females sets up opposed tendencies to patrilineal and matrilineal transmission and grouping. Limitation of space makes it impossible to inquire here into the significance of the growing evidence for the persistence and importance for social structure of both tendencies. It is clear, however, that while one line of descent often confines the other to unformalised and inter-personal spheres, and once established tends to pervade the social structure, it is nevertheless more common than was formerly supposed for both to receive formal expression over different fields of social organisation.

To return, however, to less complex situations; in some instances a simple relation is obvious between collective control and organisation by a group of men of tracts of hunting, fishing or farming territory, and the transmission of membership in that group to their sons, a situation well exemplified on a small scale by the family hunting territories of the Algonkian studied by Speck, and by the dominance of patrilineal continuity in membership of the winter camp groups among the Blackfoot described by Wissler. Transmission in the opposite sense by women to their daughters is also recorded in rudimentary form as, for example, among some Australian aborigines in Queensland, where rights to the exploitation of wild yam patches are transmitted matrilineally among women.

I recall and illustrate these well-known tendencies not because I wish to suggest that there is a simple and always readily discernible relation of immediate cause and effect between current modes of food production and division of labour on the one hand, and kin-group organisation on the other. On the contrary, uneven change and cultural inertia may give rise to discordance between them which can persist for considerable periods. I wish to suggest only that when a comparatively low threshold of stability and density of settlement is reached, tendencies for unilineal transmission of both individual and collective rights, giving rise to the formation of unilineal kin groups, emerge spontaneously from the conditions of the economy in consequence of the operation of two general processes—parent-child succession and the sex division of responsibility for the provision of economic needs. Incipient organisations of this type may, as in the case of the patrilineages discovered by Gifford among the Miwok and other peoples of Central and Southern California, receive little or no formal recognition or expression in social symbolism.

The elucidation of factors tending to produce both unilineal transmission of rights and status and groups of unilineally related kin are, however, but the starting-point of any interpretation of the wider phenomena of clan organisation. It has already been recalled that, below a certain level of scale and stability, this type of organisation does not emerge. Moreover, as has been said, any comparative survey shows that the scale, the degree of formalisation and the functional importance of organisation is highly variable. There is a great diversity in the numerical strength of major unilineal groups, in the number of such groups in the community, as well as the degree to which the major groups are segmented into sub-divisions in a descending order. Thus, a few hundred people in a single Hopi Pueblo may be divided among nearly a dozen matriclans, each counting only some twenty adult males. But each is a fully corporate and exclusive group with regard to house sites and farming land and a distinctive segment in the organisation of the community for ritual purposes. At the other extreme, the major unilineal groups among some African peoples, such as the Akan peoples of the Gold Coast or the Baganda and the Nuer, may each run into more than a thousand members. Even small localised clans, the majority of whose members are in frequent and direct interaction, are commonly found on investigation to be seg-mented into component lineages consisting of kinsmen descended from one ancestor, only three or four generations back. Thus the Hopi clans are aggregates of still smaller lineages, and both ritual prerogatives and authority within the clan as a whole inhere in one on grounds of tradi-tional seniority. Where major unilineal groups of larger scale occur, it is found not only that there often is segmentation at a series of levels, but that with respect to the transmission of rights and duties, the more specific the claim or obligation, the narrower the segment involved. Even admittedly inadequate material on the Iroquois makes it clear that the basic unit of economic, political and ritual organisation was not the large non-territorial and exogamous matriclan, but their component unnamed matrilineages, certain of which had established rights of nomination to clan and tribal offices.

Fortes' recent analysis of lineage structure within the clan organisation of the Tallensi has demonstrated in detail both the extent of this seg-mentation and its functional relations to succession and the organisation of effective groups for both practical activity and ritual. It has also con-firmed Evans-Pritchard's finding that lineage segmentation, as studied by him among the Nuer, is a function of opposition of sub-groups within a wider unity.

Intensive field studies, in which the formal concepts of social organisa-tion employed by the people themselves have been analysed in relation to the actual composition of groups as revealed by genealogical and census data over a sufficient sample, have also shown how the proliferat-ing unilineal kinship ties, which are being continually created afresh with each parent-child sequence, tend on the one hand to produce segmenta-tion of sibling groups and on the other hand permit a wider social cohesion among the spread of collateral kin.

The dispersed clans commonly found in large ethnic groups do not consist of an undifferentiated aggregate, in which, for any purpose, one clansman is socially identical with another. The members are not dis-persed as individuals, but in small lineages, the descendants of a common grandparent or great-grandparent. These minor lineages, not the individuals, are the essential units within a dispersed clan. Thus, Dr. Richards reports that the dispersed matriclans of the Bemba are made up of 'houses,' each comprising the direct descendants of a recent ancestress three or four, or, at most, five generations from the active adults, and that it is within the 'house' that the unilineal transmission of status, rights and duties is normally confined, whether it be the inheritance of goods, the succession to a chiefship or ritual office, or the fulfilment of an obligation. Similar small lineages of close kin are also shown to be the essential units of social continuity and the vehicles of social replacement within the dispersed patriclans of the Nuer. The same essential functions have been found to attach to small lineages of three to five generations in depth as part of the unilineal structure of larger clans as a result of recent studies among the Ibo and the Yakö in S.E. Nigeria, and the Ashanti in the Gold Coast. In seeking to understand the significance of unilineal organisation, it is on this unit that attention should be focused; for this is the group which, in the frequent and direct interaction of its living members, in the strength of the sentiment of common descent from a clearly remembered ancestor and in the uniformity of numerical strength, is common to so many and otherwise various social systems. It is a body of persons linked by siblingship or parallel cousinhood up to the third degree, which appears to represent a recurrent adjustment to the scale of co-operation and mutual aid elicited under stable conditions of small-scale production.

Having found that what may be termed the basic lineage, with a depth of three to five generations from living adults to the apical ancestor, is so widespread a feature of unilineal kinship organisation, we are in a position to consider groupings more extensive and variable in scale in terms of their relation to this basic unit. In some societies, of which the Hopi and the Yakö may be cited as examples, the wider unilineal organisation consists of simple aggregates of a few such lineages. But there are also societies in which a considerably more elaborate structural relation between the basic lineages is maintained in terms of real or alleged genealogical links. A number of basic lineages which rank as distinct and opposed groups in one social context are in another merged as a single group in opposition to one or more similar groups of this order which are likewise segmented with regard to more particular rights and duties. And this process of aggregation in balanced opposition is found to hold through further stages, being effective in some cases right up to the total membership of a large clan. In other words, the aggregate of clan membership is found to be successively segmented with regard to action and sentiment into a series of groups of decreasing genealogical depth so that one can, as does Fortes, speak of maximal, major, minor and

minimal lineages among the members of each of which a sense of solidarity is evoked in particular situations. This relativity in lineage structure
within large clans has been reported by Evans-Pritchard for the Nuer
and by Fortes for the Tallensi, and a similar structure can be inferred
from less systematic data for the Ibo and the Ashanti. It will doubtless
be revealed in the future as a distinctive feature of the social organisation of other peoples in which there are descent groups of large scale.

What are the factors which determine the extent to which lineage
organisation, which is confined in some instances to what may be called
the basic lineage of siblings and close cousins, is elaborated into larger
groups of varying kinship span and corresponding genealogical depth?
This is obviously a large problem which involves consideration of many
aspects of the social structure but a preliminary consideration suggests
that one significant factor derives from the scale and degree of autonomy of the territorial groups or local communities. Among the
Yakö of S.E. Nigeria, there is a strong tradition of compact settlement
and an equally strong sentiment of village autonomy. Confining ourselves
on this occasion to the patrilineal organisation of the Yakö, we find that
the patriclan is a compact unit with regard to both residence and land
holding. It stands as a unit as opposed to all other patriclans in the
village community in the maintenance of an established share in the
resources of the territory just as the village asserts its autonomy with
respect to other villages. But the patriclan as a whole numbering 100 or
more adult males commonly reaches a size considerably too great for
the co-operative organisation of labour and for the maintenance of intimate quasi-domestic relations between its members. Genealogical and
other data reveal that the patriclans have undergone continuous and
complex internal processes of fission and accretion as well as expanding
with increases in the number of descendants in successive generations.
So that, although territorially, juridically and ritually the patriclan is a
close-knit corporation under the leadership of its head, it subdivides
in the sphere of transmission of particular individual rights and in the
field of economic co-operation into a series of lineages which have been
derived both from fission between more remote groups of patrikin with
the expansion of the group, and from the accretion of outsiders whose
descendants have acquired status of clan members by continued residence
and informal adoption.

With compact settlement in autonomous communities, there is restriction on the increase in the size of the clans and of the number of its
component basic lineages. When crises of internal dissension or pressure
of population becomes too great for the continued territorial unity of a
clan, the structure provides only the opportunity for a complete break.
Among the Yakö a dissident fraction, be it a newly dividing segment
of a lineage or one or more already established lineages, removes to an-

other settlement area and abrogates its former ties of patrilineal kinship. The clans and lineages of the Hopi bear a similar structure relation both among themselves and to the autonomous pueblos or compact villages of which they form part. Fission with continued inter-segmentary relationship is possible within clan and lineage inside the pueblo, but the continuance of wider group solidarity between segments separated by migration to other pueblos, which conflicts with the economic, ritual and political autonomy of the village unit, is inhibited.

Among the Nuer, the Tallensi and the Ibo, on the other hand, the pattern of settlement does not yield such sharp territorial segregation. In the case of the Nuer, it changes seasonally with the migration from wet-season villages to dry-season camps in which the men of a minor lineage or even of an individual household may move according to their particular needs and inclinations, so that people of one village commonly scatter to several dry-season camps to stay among new neighbours. Furthermore, the wet-season settlement pattern grading through ever more inclusive groups from homestead, through hamlet and village to district and tribal section, does not involve any sharp cleavage within which a more or less closed organisation, whether for economic, ritual or, still more important, political purposes, would tend to crystallise. The most persistent factor in Nuer settlement appears to be the tendency for close patrilineal male kin to remain together, a tendency which as Evans-Pritchard has shown, is buttressed by dominance of sentiments concerning the use and transfer of cattle in Nuer cultural values.

It appears, however, that the various tribes differ significantly in the scale of their clan organisation and in the political relations based thereon, in close relation to the extent to which the physical conditions enforce frequent and large-scale dispersal. In the better-watered western areas, where it is possible for village communities to maintain considerable isolation in the dry season as well as in the wet, tribes and their component clans are small, while among the Luo and other eastern tribes the increasing scale of both kin group and political organisation, which results in much larger tribal units with a more extensive internal segmentation, is related to severe seasonal scarcity of pasturage which compels extensive movements and temporary dispersion and intermingling of households and lineages from widely separated wet-season villages. The Nuer settlement pattern crystallises round the basic lineage of close and co-resident male patrikin which appears to be the essential nucleus; but the exigencies of seasonal migration and past opportunities for territorial expansion with numerical growth, have permitted a proliferation of growing lineages over wide areas to form large clans which in their growth and territorial expansion have segmented many times. These have, however, in response to the continued contacts resulting from seasonal mobility and co-operation in cattle tending and raiding, maintained sentiments of solidarity over a very wide span and in terms of a genealogically very remote common ancestry. At the same time isolated, stable and autonomous village communities are lacking. The economy of combined cattle rearing and grain growing in the particular physical conditions of alternating swamp and semi-desert neither requires nor induces close and persistent attachment to fixed sites, while migration has brought into territorial proximity on favourable wet-season farming sites, sub-lineages of very diverse origin, including dependent groups from conquered tribes. In consequence we have a pattern in which any village or locality is composed of an aggregate of lineages of diverse origin. The members of the lineage and clan which can sustain a tradition of earliest settlement in the locality has the prestige of moral ownership and of precedence over segments of the other clans which have come to settle in the area, and a position of leadership in the external or political relations of the village, district or tribal section. This non-correspondence between the composition of the territorial units of Nuer society and that of wider kinship groupings is clearly dependent on the continual dispersal and territorial intermingling of the latter in response to economic exigencies in a hazardous environment.

A structurally parallel proliferation and segmentation of kin groups under conditions of relatively free territorial expansion has been observed among a number of Ibo tribes, particularly those of the north and west. It is not possible to point to any ecological factors which would account for the sharp antithesis that they present when compared with their semi-Bantu neighbours to the east, but north-eastern Ibo tribes such as the Ikwe and Ezza are as strongly wedded to dispersed settlement in scattered hamlets as are the Yakö to concentration in compact villages. They have, moreover, in the recent past, as the wider kinship affiliations and the traditions of migration of kin groups show, expanded by the continual throwing out of new homesteads and hamlets into unoccupied forest or into the territories of less resistant neighbours. And among these Ibo, as among the Nuer, there has in consequence been a wide proliferation of expanding unilineal kin groups. The basic patrilineage of three to five generations in depth from a single ancestor is the co-residential nucleus which normally coincides with a hamlet. The wider locality within which local economic exchange, earth cult rituals and men's societies are organised, characteristically includes a series of such lineages themselves forming a single wider lineage in relation to others of the same order that are dominant in adjacent localities. These together may in turn comprise a single major lineage in which the ancestor priest of the traditionally senior sub-lineage is the ritual leader, who wields sanctions for offences against the community at large, and focuses the unity of the lineage as a whole in opposition to threat or injury from without. Here, again, the vicissitudes of territorial expansion and differential growth have led to the territorial intermingling of lineages of different origin, some of which, although having collective rights on behalf of their members to agricultural land and equal rights to unappropriated resources in the territory as a whole, are inferior in prestige and are dependent in ritual status to those which claim the first occupation of the area.

It would appear, therefore, that once social cohesion and continuity is established between close unilineal kin, the system is capable of wide proliferation through collateral kinship links in the same sense, and may form the framework of a territorial and political organisation of considerable size. Some Nuer tribes are said to number over 30,000 and the Ikwe and Ezza Ibo are of the same order. The conditions for extensive proliferation of unilineal kin and the formation of large segmented clans appear to be the maintenance of social continuity over a widening series of territorial entities, a condition which requires both considerable physical mobility and facilities for continued territorial expansion. This tendency is inhibited on the other hand by strong development of exclusiveness and self-sufficiency within local settlements and by physical or human barriers to expansion. Obviously a wide variety of factors, including physical conditions, the level of technique, opportunities for exchange, pre-existing cultural values and the political pressure of external groups, are all capable of affecting the degree to which such local isolation may be established and maintained. Where any combination of factors promotes the increase of population from a small nucleus and permits a concomitant territorial expansion, with the maintenance of cohesion through sufficient interaction between the members of the derivative communities as they hive off, the establishment of a ramifying system of unilineal kinship groups is to be expected, and under favourable conditions such a system can form the basis of a political organisation of considerable scale and complexity. Two considerable and famous political confederations, the League of Iroquois and the Ashanti Federation are instances of very extensive political organisation on this basis.

But the effective organisation of unilineal kin is, on the other hand, known to be of very limited range or of minor importance in many societies of considerable scale, including those with more advanced techniques and higher degree of economic specialisation. Lowie and others have pointed out that clan organisation tends to be absent both in the simplest and the most complex forms of social structure. We have already suggested that a threshold of stability and numerical strength must be reached before this type of organisation can emerge at the lower level. What are the factors that tend to diminish it at the other end of the scale? This again is obviously a problem that cannot be briefly handled, and space prevents its adequate consideration here. But among the processes already well recognised as inhibiting or curtailing any extensive development of a segmentary system of balanced unilineal groups as the framework of political and other organised relations, is of course the establishment of centralised political authority. When through the impact of one social system upon another, or through internal technological or other forms of cultural change, some fraction of the aggregate is in a position to dominate and control the organisation of the rest through any combination of physical coercion, economic control and social prestige, the opportunity for organising such authority on centralising administrative and military principles tends to produce a vertical organisation with specialisation of economic and political functions. Social status of both persons and groups then derives primarily from position in the resulting hierarchy and no longer on membership of a graduated series of equal and opposite groups of kin. In such situations territorial and status interests become paramount at the expense of solidarity with remote kin, so that sentiments and group organisation which embody the former tend to extinguish the coherence of widely extended unilineal groups, and to relegate kinship ties to secondary principles of affiliation within the class and territorial structure. The Bemba, among whom the large dispersed clans display little or no sense of solidarity and the basic matrilineage is alone a coherent and self-conscious group, appear to illustrate a comparatively early stage in the atrophy of a wider system of unilineal grouping with the establishment of political centralisation.

Baldly stated in this manner, this hypothesis of the effects of political centralisation and economic specialisation on the rôle of unilineal kinship in social organisation is subject to many qualifications, but it appears consistent with the broad contrasts in the social recognition and structural importance accorded to these ties that are to be found between unilineally segmented societies and those in which a centralised system of government has been established. Some of the fundamental differences in political structure between segmentary and centralised societies have been analysed with great penetration by Fortes and Evans-Pritchard, who have also considered the demographic and cultural concomitants of the two types. But these raise further problems which cannot be pursued on this occasion. I have sought only to illustrate in this brief and necessarily incomplete consideration of the processes and factors involved in the development of unilineal kin groups, the scientific value of ethnographic data secured by thorough field investigation and the importance of analytical and comparative methods in attempting to reach understanding in scientific terms of any problems of social structure and process. These are tasks and methods which have been emphasised and cultivated in Anthropology and are essential features of its approach to the development of Social Science.

B. Geography and Culture

WE KNOW that Aristotle regarded climate and terrain as important features in conditioning human character and behavior; we suspect that thinkers before his time were attracted by the idea. Few hypotheses have the rational impact of geographical determinism which states that culture is shaped by the environment which surrounds it. Yet simplistic ideas linking geography to culture may be swiftly eliminated. To the anthropologist, necessity is *not* the necessary mother of invention: the native population of Tierra del Fuego shivered for centuries in the cold Antarctic blasts that swept across the Straits of Magellan, yet their culture developed no article of clothing more comforting than the cloak. We know also that the presence of resources fundamental to certain kinds of productive systems need not kindle the beginnings of such systems. Many factors determine the use of readily available resources and, indeed, influence a culture's definition of a resource. Most important, perhaps, is the level of technological development in the previous history of resource utilization: thus, the Mesabi iron range of Minnesota, where ore can be extracted by simple digging, was the former habitat of such American Indian tribes as the Menominee and Winnebago. These people never smelted iron, despite its availability; curiously, they used a few iron tools which were made, not from iron ores, but from meteoric iron treated as stone.

The cultural geographers have coined the term "possibilism," to describe the permissive relations between habitat and culture. Some anthropologists would go further, though they are cautious: the histories of both anthropology and geography include episodes of disasterous attempts to seek a geographical solution to riddles of culture.

The concept of ecology, which has already been encountered in the first volume (see No. I:5), has been borrowed from the biological sciences and

79

given a distinct role in the science of culture. An ecological approach differs from geographical determinism in making the relationships of environment and culture and their drive toward equilibrium paramount, whereas geographical determinism invokes the simple formula: environment → culture. Few, if any, competent anthropologists work in the latter tradition but there are many who are much attracted by cultural ecology.

6. THE CONCEPT AND METHOD
OF CULTURAL ECOLOGY *

A tide swept through the sciences in the nineteenth and early twentieth
century and eroded one of the basic concepts of the past, the idea of simple
causal relationships, the immediate and sole dependence of a thing or
event upon a particular prior thing or event. This sweeping theoretical
change did not wipe out determinism but conditioned scientists to look
for multi-faceted relationships and fields of interactivity on
all levels of analysis.

Geography and anthropology also felt the effects of this shift. Nowhere
was this more apparent than in the analysis of the ties between specific
physical environments and the cultures associated with them. Eschewing
simple geographical determinism, students from both disciplines
converged on an approach which stresses mutuality and the establishment
of states of equilibrium which may be upset by unilateral alterations of
either environment or culture. Called "cultural ecology," the implications
of this approach are given general treatment in the selection which follows.

OBJECTIVES IN ECOLOGICAL STUDIES

Aт тне risk of adding further confusion to an already obscure
term, this chapter undertakes to develop the concept of ecology in relation to human beings as an heuristic device for understanding the effect
of environment upon culture. In order to distinguish the present purpose
and method from those implied in the concepts of biological, human,
and social ecology, the term *cultural ecology* is used. Since cultural ecol-

* Julian H. Steward, "The Concept and Method of Cultural Ecology," *Theory of Culture Change* (Urbana: University of Illinois Press, 1954), pp. 30–42. Reprinted by permission of the author and publisher.

ogy is not generally understood, it is necessary to begin by showing
wherein it differs from the other concepts of ecology and then to demonstrate how it must supplement the usual historical approach of anthropology in order to determine the creative processes involved in the adaptation of culture to its environment.

The principal meaning of ecology is "adaptation to environment."
Since the time of Darwin, environment has been conceived as the total
web of life wherein all plant and animal species interact with one another
and with physical features in a particular unit of territory. According to
Webster, the biological meaning of ecology is "the mutual relations between organisms and their environment." The concept of adaptive interaction is used to explain the origin of new genotypes in evolution; to
explain phenotypical variations; and to describe the web of life itself in
terms of competition, succession, climaxes, gradients, and other auxiliary
concepts.

Although initially employed with reference to biotic assemblages, the
concept of ecology has naturally been extended to include human beings
since they are part of the web of life in most parts of the world. Man
enters the ecological scene, however, not merely as another organism
which is related to other organisms in terms of his physical characteristics.
He introduces the super-organic factor of culture, which also affects and
is affected by the total web of life. What to do about this cultural factor
in ecological studies has raised many methodological difficulties, as most
human and social ecologists have recognized. The principal difficulty
lies in the lack of clarity as to the purpose of using the concept of ecology.
The interaction of physical, biological, and cultural features within a
locale or unit of territory is usually the ultimate objective of study.
Human or social ecology is regarded as a subdiscipline of its own right
and not as means to some further scientific end. Essentially descriptive,
the analysis lacks the clear objectives of biology, which has used ecology
heuristically to explain several kinds of biological phenomena. If human or social ecology is considered an operational tool rather than an
end in itself, two quite different objectives are suggested: first, an
understanding of the organic functions and genetic variations of man
as a purely biological species; second, a determination of how culture
is affected by its adaptation to environment. Each requires its own concepts and methods.

The first, or biological objective, involves several somewhat different
problems, all of which, however, must view man in the web of life.
Since man is a domesticated animal, he is affected physically by all his
cultural activities. The evolution of the Hominidae is closely related to
the emergence of culture, while the appearance of *Homo sapiens* is

probably more the result of cultural causes than of physical causes. The use of tools, fire, shelter, clothing, new foods, and other material adjuncts of existence were obviously important in evolution, but social customs should not be overlooked. Social groups as determined by marriage customs as well as by economic activities in particular environments have undoubtedly been crucial in the differentiations of local populations and may even have contributed to the emergence of varieties and subraces of men.

The problem of explaining man's cultural behavior is of a different order than that of explaining his biological evolution. Cultural patterns are not genetically derived and, therefore, cannot be analyzed in the same way as organic features. Although social ecologists are paying more and more attention to culture in their enquiries, an explanation of culture per se has not, so far as I can see, become their major objective. Culture has merely acquired greater emphasis as one of many features of the local web of life, and the tools of analysis are still predominantly borrowed from biology. Since one of the principal concepts of biological ecology is the community—the assemblage of plants and animals which interact within a locality—social or human ecology emphasizes the human community as the unit of study. But "community" is a very general and meaningless abstraction. If it is conceived in cultural terms, it may have many different characteristics depending upon the purpose for which it is defined. The tendency, however, has been to conceive of human and biological communities in terms of the biological concepts of competition, succession, territorial organization, migration, gradients, and the like. All of these derived fundamentally from the fact that underlying biological ecology is a relentless and raw struggle for existence both within and between species—a competition which is ultimately determined by the genetic potentials for adaptation and survival in particular biotic-environmental situations. Biological co-operation, such as in many forms of symbiosis, is strictly auxiliary to survival of the species.

Human beings do not react to the web of life solely through their genetically-derived organic equipment. Culture, rather than genetic potential for adaptation, accommodation, and survival, explains the nature of human societies. Moreover, the web of life of any local human society may extend far beyond the immediate physical environment and biotic assemblage. In states, nations, and empires, the nature of the local group is determined by these larger institutions no less than by its local adaptations. Competition of one sort or another may be present, but it is always culturally determined and as often as not co-operation rather than competition may be prescribed. If, therefore, the nature of human communities is the objective of analysis, explanations will be found through use of cultural historical concepts and methods rather than biological concepts, although, as we shall show, historical methods alone are insufficient.

Many writers on social or human ecology have sensed the need to distinguish between biological and cultural phenomena and methods, but they have not yet drawn clear distinctions. Thus, Hollingshead recognizes a difference between an "ecological order [which] is primarily rooted in competition" and "social organization [which] has evolved out of communication." This attempt to conceptualize competition as a category wholly distinct from other aspects of culturally determined behavior is, of course, artificial. Bates, a human biologist, recognizes the importance of culture in determining the nature of communities, but he does not make clear whether he would use human ecology to explain the range of man's biological adaptation under environmental-cultural situations or whether he is interested in man's culture. The so-called Chicago school of Park, Burgess, and their followers were also primarily interested in communities of human beings, especially urban communities. Their methodology as applied to Chicago and other cities treat the components of each as if they were genetically determined species. In analyzing the zoning of a modern city, such categories as retail businesses, wholesale houses, manufacturing firms, and residences of various kinds, and even such additional features as rate of delinquency, are considered as if each were a biological species in competition with one another for zones within the urban area. Such studies are extremely enlightening as descriptive analysis of spacial distributions of kinds of activities within a modern Euro-American city. They do not, however, necessarily throw any light on world-wide ecological urban adaptations, for in other cultures and periods city zoning followed very different culturally prescribed principles. For example, most of the cities of ancient civilizations were rather carefully planned by a central authority for defensive, administrative, and religious functions. Free enterprise, which might have allowed competition for zones between the institutions and subsocieties arising from these functions, was precluded by the culture.

A fundamental scientific problem is involved in these different meanings attached to ecology. Is the objective to find universal laws or processes, or is it to explain special phenomena? In biology, the law of evolution and the auxiliary principles of ecology are applicable to all webs of life regardless of the species and physical environments involved. In social science studies, there is a similar effort to discover universal processes of cultural change. But such processes cannot be conceptualized in biological terms. The social science problem of explaining the origin of unlike behavior patterns found among different societies of the human species is very different from the problems of biological evolution. Analyzing environmental adaptations to show how new cultural patterns arise is a very different matter than seeking universal similarities in such adaptation. Until the processes of cultural ecology are understood in the many particulars exemplified by different cultures in different parts of the world a formulation of universal processes will be impossible.

Hawley, who has given the most recent and comprehensive statement of social ecology, takes cultural phenomena into account far more than his predecessors. He states that man reacts to the web of life as a cultural animal rather than as a biological species. "Each acquisition of a new technique or a new use for an old technique, regardless of the source of its origin, alters man's relations with the organisms about him and changes his position in the biotic community." But, preoccupied with the totality of phenomena within the locale and apparently with a search for universal relationships, Hawley makes the local community the focus of interest. The kinds of generalizations which might be found are indicated by the statement: "If we had sufficient knowledge of a preliterate peoples to enable us to compare the structure of residence groups arranged in order of size from smallest to largest, we should undoubtedly observe the same phenomena—each increment in size is accompanied by an advance in the complexity of organization." This is the kind of self-evident generalization made by the unilinear evolutionists: cultural progress is manifest in increasing populations, internal specialization, over-all state controls, and other general features.

Hawley is uncertain in his position regarding the effect of environmental adaptations on culture. He states: "The weight of evidence forces the conclusion that the physical environment exerts but a permissive and limiting effect," but he also says that "each habitat not only permits but to a certain extent necessitates a distinctive mode of life." The first statement closely conforms with the widely accepted anthropological position that historical factors are more important than environmental factors, which may be permissive or prohibitive of culture change but are never causative. The second is nearer to the thesis of this paper that cultural ecological adaptations constitute creative processes.

CULTURE, HISTORY AND ENVIRONMENT

While the human and social ecologists have seemingly sought universal ecological principles and relegated culture in its local varieties to a secondary place, anthropologists have been so preoccupied with culture and its history that they have accorded environment only a negligible role. Owing in part to reaction against the "environmental determinists," such as Huntington and Semple, and in part to cumulative evidence that any culture increases in complexity to a large extent because of diffused practices, the orthodox view now holds that history, rather than adaptive processes, explains culture. Since historical "explanations" of culture employ the culture area concept, there is an apparent contradiction. The culture area is a construct of behavioral uniformities which occur within an area of environmental uniformities. It is assumed that cultural and natural areas are generally coterminous because the culture represents an adjustment to the particular environment. It is assumed further, however, that various different patterns may exist in any natural area and that unlike cultures may exist in similar environments.

The cultural-historical approach is, however, also one of relativism. Since cultural differences are not directly attributable to environmental differences and most certainly not to organic or racial differences, they are merely said to represent divergences in cultural history, to reflect tendencies of societies to develop in unlike ways. Such tendencies are not explained. A distinctive pattern develops, it is said, and henceforth is the primary determinant of whether innovations are accepted. Environment is relegated to a purely secondary and passive role. It is considered prohibitive or permissive, but not creative. It allows man to carry on some kinds of activities and it prevents others. The origins of these activities are pushed back to a remote point in time or space, but they are not explained. This view has been best expressed by Forde, who writes:

Neither the world distributions of the various economies, nor their development and relative importance among the particular peoples, can be regarded as simple functions of physical conditions and natural resources. Between the physical environment and human activity there is always a middle term, a collection of specific objectives and values, a body of knowledge and belief: in other words, a cultural pattern. That the culture itself is not static, that it is adaptable and modifiable in relation to physical conditions, must not be allowed to obscure the fact that adaptation proceeds by discoveries and inventions which are themselves in no sense inevitable and which are, in any individual community, nearly all of them acquisitions or impositions from without. The peoples of whole continents have failed to make discoveries that might at first blush seem obvious. Equally important are the restrictions placed by social patterns and religious concepts on the utilization of certain resources or on adaptations to physical conditions.

The habitat at one and the same time circumscribes and affords scope for cultural development in relation to the pre-existing equipment and tendency of a particular society, and to any new concepts and equipment that may reach it from without.

But if geographical determinism fails to account for the existence and dis-

tribution of economies, economic determinism is equally inadequate in accounting for the social and political organizations, the religious beliefs and the psychological attitudes which may be found in the cultures based on those
economies. Indeed, the economy may owe as much to the social and ritual
pattern as does the character of society to the economy. The possession of
particular methods of hunting or cultivating, of certain cultivated plants or
domestic animals, in no wise defines the pattern of society. Again, there is
interaction and on a new plane. As physical conditions may limit the possibilities
of the economy, so the economy may in turn be a limiting or stimulating factor
in relation to the size, density and stability of human settlement, and to the
scale of the social and political unit. But it is only one such factor, and advantage
may not be taken of the opportunities it affords. The tenure and transmission
of land and other property, the development and relations of social classes,
the nature of government, the religious and ceremonial life—all these are parts
of a social superstructure, the development of which is conditioned not only by
the foundations of habitat and economy, but by complex interactions within its
own fabric and by external contacts, often largely indifferent to both the physical
background and to the basic economy alike.

CULTURAL ECOLOGY

Cultural ecology differs from human and social ecology in seeking to
explain the origin of particular cultural features and patterns which
characterize different areas rather than to derive general principles applicable to any cultural-environmental situation. It differs from the
relativistic and neo-evolutionist conceptions of culture history in that
it introduces the local environment as the extracultural factor in the fruitless assumption that culture comes from culture. Thus, cultural ecology
presents both a problem and a method. The problem is to ascertain
whether the adjustments of human societies to their environments require
particular modes of behavior or whether they permit latitude for a
certain range of possible behavior patterns. Phrased in this way, the
problem also distinguishes cultural ecology from "environmental determinism" and its related theory "economic determinism" which are generally understood to contain their conclusions within the problem.

The problem of cultural ecology must be further qualified, however,
through use of a supplementary conception of culture. According to the
holistic view, all aspects of culture are functionally interdependent upon
one another. The degree and kind of interdependency, however, are not
the same with all features. Elsewhere, I have offered the concept of
cultural core—the constellation of features which are most closely related
to subsistence activities and economic arrangements. The core includes
such social, political, and religious patterns as are empirically determined
to be closely connected with these arrangements. Innumerable other

features may have great potential variability because they are less strongly tied to the core. These latter, or secondary features, are determined to a greater extent by purely cultural-historical factors—by random innovations or by diffusion—and they give the appearance of outward distinctiveness to cultures with similar cores. Cultural ecology pays primary attention to those features which empirical analysis shows to be most closely involved in the utilization of environment in culturally prescribed ways.

The expression "culturally prescribed ways" must be taken with caution, for its anthropological usage is frequently "loaded." The normative concept, which views culture as a system of mutually reinforcing practices backed by a set of attitudes and values, seems to regard all human behavior as so completely determined by culture that environmental adaptations have no effect. It considers that the entire pattern of technology, land use, land tenure, and social features derive entirely from culture. Classical illustrations of the primacy of cultural attitudes over common sense are that the Chinese do not drink milk nor the Eskimo eat seals in summer.

Cultures do, of course, tend to perpetuate themselves, and change may be slow for such reasons as those cited. But over the millennia cultures in different environments have changed tremendously, and these changes are basically traceable to new adaptations required by changing technology and productive arrangements. Despite occasional cultural barriers, the useful arts have spread extremely widely, and the instances in which they have not been accepted because of pre-existing cultural patterns are insignificant. In pre-agricultural times, which comprised perhaps 99 per cent of cultural history, technical devices for hunting, gathering, and fishing seem to have diffused largely to the limits of their usefulness. Clubs, spears, traps, bows, fire, containers, nets, and many other cultural features spread across many areas, and some of them throughout the world. Later, domesticated plants and animals also spread very rapidly within their environmental limits, being stopped only by formidable ocean barriers.

Whether or not new technologies are valuable is, however, a function of the society's cultural level as well as of environmental potentials. All pre-agricultural societies found hunting and gathering techniques useful. Within the geographical limits of herding and farming, these techniques were adopted. More advanced techniques, such as metallurgy, were acceptable only if certain pre-conditions, such as stable population, leisure time, and internal specialization were present. These conditions could develop only from the cultural ecological adaptations of an agricultural society.

The concept of cultural ecology, however, is less concerned with the origin and diffusion of technologies than with the fact that they may be used differently and entail different social arrangements in each environment. The environment is not only permissive or prohibitive with respect to these techologies, but special local features may require social adaptations which have far-reaching consequences. Thus, societies equipped with bows, spears, surrounds, chutes, brush-burning, deadfalls, pitfalls, and other hunting devices may differ among themselves because of the nature of the terrain and fauna. If the principal game exists in large herds, such as herds of bison or caribou, there is advantage in co-operative hunting, and considerable numbers of peoples may remain together throughout the year. If, however, the game is nonmigratory, occurring in small and scattered groups, it is better hunted by small groups of men who know their territory well. In each case, the cultural repertory of hunting devices may be about the same, but in the first case the society will consist of multifamily or multilineage groups, as among the Athabaskans and Algonkians of Canada and probably the pre-horse Plains bison hunters, and in the second case it will probably consist of localized patrilineal lineages or bands, as among the Bushmen, Congo Negritoes, Australians, Tasmanians, Fuegians, and others. These latter groups consisting of patrilineal bands are similar, as a matter of fact, not because their total environments are similar—the Bushmen, Australians, and southern Californians live in deserts, the Negritoes in rain forests, and the Fuegians in a cold, rainy area—but because the nature of the game and therefore of their subsistence problem is the same in each case.

Other societies having about the same technological equipment may exhibit other social patterns because the environments differ to the extent that the cultural adaptations must be different. For example, the Eskimo use bows, spears, traps, containers and other widespread technological devices, but, owing to the limited occurrence of fish and sea mammals, their population is so sparse and co-operative hunting is so relatively unrewarding that they are usually dispersed in family groups. For a different but equally compelling reason the Nevada Shoshoni were also fragmented into family groups. In the latter case, the scarcity of game and the predominance of seeds as the subsistence basis greatly restricted economic co-operation and required dispersal of the society into fairly independent family groups.

In the examples of the primitive hunting, gathering, and fishing societies, it is easy to show that if the local environment is to be exploited by means of the culturally-derived techniques, there are limitations upon the size and social composition of the groups involved. When agricultural techniques are introduced, man is partially freed from the exigencies of hunting and gathering, and it becomes possible for considerable aggregates of people to live together. Larger aggregates, made possible by increased population and settled communities, provide a higher level of sociocultural integration, the nature of which is determined by the local type of sociocultural integration. [See No. II:23.]

The adaptative processes we have described are properly designated ecological. But attention is directed not simply to the human community as part of the total web of life but to such cultural features as are affected by the adaptations. This in turn requires that primary attention be paid only to relevant environmental features rather than to the web of life for its own sake. Only those features to which the local culture ascribes importance need be considered.

THE METHOD OF CULTURAL ECOLOGY

Although the concept of environmental adaptation underlies all cultural ecology, the procedures must take into account the complexity and level of the culture. It makes a great deal of difference whether a community consists of hunters and gatherers who subsist independently by their own efforts or whether it is an outpost of a wealthy nation, which exploits local mineral wealth and is sustained by railroads, ships, or airplanes. In advanced societies, the nature of the culture core will be determined by a complex technology and by productive arrangements which themselves have a long cultural history.

Three fundamental procedures of cultural ecology are as follows:

First, the interrelationship of exploitative or productive technology and environment must be analyzed. This technology includes a considerable part of what is often called "material culture," but all features may not be of equal importance. In primitive societies, subsistence devices are basic: weapons and instruments for hunting and fishing; containers for gathering and storing food; transportational devices used on land and water; sources of water and fuel; and, in some environments, means of counteracting excessive cold (clothing and housing) or heat. In more developed societies, agriculture and herding techniques and manufacturing of crucial implements must be considered. In an industrial world, capital and credit arrangements, trade systems and the like are crucial. Socially-derived needs—special tastes in foods, more ample housing and clothing, and a great variety of appurtenances to living— become increasingly important in the productive arrangement as culture develops; and yet these originally were probably more often effects of basic adaptations than causes.

Relevant environmental features depend upon the culture. The simpler cultures are more directly conditioned by the environment than advanced ones. In general, climate, topography, soils, hydrography, vegetational cover, and fauna are crucial, but some features may be more important than others. The spacing of water holes in the desert may be vital to a nomadic seed-gathering people, the habits of game will affect the way hunting is done, and the kinds and seasons of fish runs will determine the habits of riverine and coastal tribes.

Second, the behavior patterns involved in the exploitation of a particular area by means of a particular technology must be analyzed. Some subsistence patterns impose very narrow limits on the general mode of life of the people, while others allow considerable latitude. The gathering of wild vegetable products is usually done by women who work alone or in small groups. Nothing is gained by co-operation and in fact women come into competition with one another. Seed-gatherers, therefore, tend to fragment into small groups unless their resources are very abundant. Hunting, on the other hand, may be either an individual or a collective project, and the nature of hunting societies is determined by culturally prescribed devices for collective hunting as well as by the species. When surrounds, grass-firing, corrals, chutes, and other co-operative methods are employed, the take per man may be much greater than what a lone hunter could bag. Similarly, if circumstances permit, fishing may be done by groups of men using dams, weirs, traps, and nets as well as by individuals.

The use of these more complex and frequently co-operative techniques, however, depends not only upon cultural history—i.e., invention and diffusion—which makes the methods available but upon the environment and its flora and fauna. Deer cannot be hunted advantageously by surrounds, whereas antelope and bison may best be hunted in this way. Slash-and-burn farming in tropical rain forests requires comparatively little co-operation in that a few men clear the land after which their wives plant and cultivate the crops. Dry farming may or may not be co-operative; and irrigation farming may run the gamut of enterprises of ever-increasing size based on collective construction of waterworks.

The exploitative patterns not only depend upon the habits concerned in the direct production of food and of goods but upon facilities for transporting the people to the source of supply or the goods to the people. Watercraft have been a major factor in permitting the growth of settlements beyond what would have been possible for a foot people. Among all nomads, the horse has had an almost revolutionary effect in promoting the growth of large bands.

The third procedure is to ascertain the extent to which the behavior patterns entailed in exploiting the environment affect other aspects of culture. Although technology and environment prescribe that certain things must be done in certain ways if they are to be done at all, the extent to which these activities are functionally tied to other aspects of culture is a purely empirical problem. I have shown elsewhere that the occurrence of patrilineal bands among certain hunting peoples and of fragmented families among the Western Shoshoni is closely determined by their subsistence activities, whereas the Carrier Indians are known to have changed from a composite hunting band to a society based upon moieties and inherited statuses without any change in the nature of subsistence. In the irrigation areas of early civilizations the sequence of sociopolitical forms or cultural cores seems to have been very similar despite variation in many outward details or secondary features of these cultures. If it can be established that the productive arrangements permit great latitude in the sociocultural type, then historical influences may explain the particular type found. The problem is the same in considering modern industrial civilizations. The question is whether industrialization allows such latitude that political democracy, communism, state socialism, and perhaps other forms are equally possible, so that strong historical influences, such as diffused ideology—e.g., propaganda—may supplant one type with another, or whether each type represents an adaptation which is specific to the area.

The third procedure requires a genuinely holistic approach, for if such factors as demography, settlement pattern, kinship structures, land tenure, land use, and other key cultural features are considered separately, their interrelationships to one another and to the environment cannot be grasped. Land use by means of a given technology permits a certain population density. The clustering of this population will depend partly upon where resources occur and upon transportational devices. The composition of these clusters will be a function of their size, of the nature of subsistence activities, and of cultural-historical factors. The ownership of land or resources will reflect subsistence activities on the one hand and the composition of the group on the other. Warfare may be related to the complex of factors just mentioned. In some cases, it may arise out of competition for resources and have a national character. Even when fought for individual honors or religious purposes, it may serve to nucleate settlements in a way that must be related to subsistence activities.

THE METHODOLOGICAL PLACE OF CULTURAL ECOLOGY

Cultural ecology has been described as a methodological tool for ascertaining how the adaptation of a culture to its environment may entail certain changes. In a larger sense, the problem is to determine whether similar adjustments occur in similar environments. Since in any given environment, culture may develop through a succession of very unlike periods, it is sometimes pointed out that environment, the constant, obviously has no relationship to cultural type. This difficulty disappears, however, if the level of sociocultural integration represented by each period is taken into account. Cultural types therefore, must be conceived as constellations of core features which arise out of environmental adaptations and which represent similar levels of integration.

Cultural diffusion, of course, always operates, but in view of the seeming importance of ecological adaptations its role in explaining culture has been greatly overestimated. The extent to which the large variety of world cultures can be systematized in categories of types and explained through cross-cultural regularities of developmental process is purely an empirical matter. Hunches arising out of comparative studies suggest that there are many regularities which can be formulated in terms of similar levels and similar adaptations.

7. THE THEORY OF
ORIENTAL SOCIETY *

Two contrasting views of the origin of agriculture presented earlier in the first volume (Nos. I:28–32) actually represent facets of a single problem in the relation of the development of culture to its environmental matrix. There are several other classic problems of similar stature but few are more intriguing or so relevant to the present as that which is presented below.

Stripped to essentials, the theory of Oriental society maintains that agricultural systems are of two kinds: one requires the construction of an irrigation and drainage system, the other operates with available rainfall and has no pressing problem of floods. The hypothesis states that the former system tends to generate great and repressive institutions of government and thereby imputes a much more than permissive function to environment. Since a variety of non-environmental factors, technological, sociological and ideological, enter into the theory, it seems

* Karl A. Wittfogel, "Die Theorie der orientalischen Gesellschaft," *Zeitschrift für Sozialforschung* VII (1938), pp. 90–122. The version which appears here was made from a translation by the Far Eastern and Russian Institute of the University of Washington and completely revised for this book in February, 1959, by Dr. Wittfogel. Reprinted with the permission of the author, publisher, and translator.

The author (b. 1896) is Director of the Chinese History Project and Professor of Chinese History at the University of Washington. For over thirty years he has made extensive researches into the comparative history of institutions. While he has not undertaken anthropological fieldwork, Wittfogel has been much influenced by anthropology just as he has had an influence on aspects of anthropological theory. Presently completing an institutional analysis of Chinese communism, Wittfogel is the co-author (with Chia-shêng Fêng) of *The History of Chinese Society: Liao* (1949). Among his other books is the recent definitive statement of his position, *Oriental Despotism* (1957).

properly classed with cultural ecology.

The concept of Oriental society as a distinct type arose at the end of the 18th century and was a contribution of the so-called classical economists. It was created because these economists could not comprehend the economies of ancient Egypt and Mesopotamia, or contemporary China and India on the basis of their understanding of Greece and Rome or of Europe under feudalism or capitalism. Treated by Marx, the idea passed to the sociologist Max Weber, then to the author of the next selection who has given the theory its most extensive treatment. Though called "Oriental," the theory has been applied to the New World, particularly to the pre-Conquest civilizations of the Andes. Archeologists have been attracted to the theory but most of them have been cautious and continue to reserve judgement.

Dr. Wittfogel also insists that contemporary international politics can be understood only in the light of his theory. Here, even more than in its implications for the past, there is great controversy. Nothing like general acceptance is yet accorded the theory in any of its implications but its sheer intellectual weight and juxtaposition of cultural and environmental factors command our attention.

ABSTRACT

THE ARTICLE starts with a clarification of the economic importance of certain material elements which underlie the agricultural labor process—land and water. Artificial irrigation has the significance of a primary determining factor, for, by requiring relatively intense forms of labor, it excludes slave labor as an essential element. The true "oriental" form of production first arises when waterworks must be undertaken on a larger scale (for purposes of protection and irrigation). On a lower level of technical development, the state then acquires a specific economic function: public works and astronomy. A differentiated form of society comes into being; at its base are the peasants, either bound to the village or—later—free; the upper ranks comprise the autocratic sovereign and an administrative, religious, and military bureaucracy. The pure oriental type in its simple form is exemplified by the old Inca society before its destruction. The higher form (with the development of inner contradictions) was attained by India, Babylonia, Assyria, Egypt, China, among others. The "compact" hydraulic type, e.g. Babylonia, displays a different form of crisis from the "loose" hydraulic type of China. In the latter, the agricultural crisis is conditioned by extensive mobilization of arable land and by the cooperation of commercial capitalists with the centrifugal upper strata of society. Quasi-feudal or pseudo-feudal traits may be operative in creating a crisis, as in India or China, but they are not the basis of the society, which is different from feudalism in its system of production, social organization, and state. Japan is feudal, or more correctly, "Asiatic"-feudal.

The analysis of the organization of the productive forces makes it possible to explain the stagnation of the oriental agricultural society from the particular, centralized structure of the system of production based on irrigation. This is in contrast to the decentralized nonirrigational agriculture of feudal society, which did not hinder the development of towns and of an industrial capitalism fostered by late feudal absolutism.

"The Theory of Oriental Society" constitutes an attempt to describe both the western and eastern worlds as sectors of one human society, which includes stagnation as well as development as movements of the total historical process.

1. THE PROBLEM

Theoretical concern with the complex of China and its Oriental background needs no detailed justification in the year 1938. The world of historical practise has become small. The intimate connection between the eastern and western segments of human society is shown most directly by the Sino-Japanese War and its repercussions on the remaining centers of historical activity. The scientific analysis of China, which for ten or fifteen years might have seemed either romantic or at all events peripheral, now returns towards the center and becomes a demand of objective necessity.

Ad hoc analyses show themselves quickly as inadequate, particularly if they are not presented as the result of previous thorough preparation. Critical theory teaches that an actual historical phenomenon becomes understandable only if it is taken in its full historical and spatial perspective. The laws of movement within Chinese society only reveal themselves truly if they are developed genetically. The same is true of the neighboring complex of Japan, concerning which we must know whether it is structurally similar to China or different, before we can truly comprehend the peculiar forms of its historic activity. Thus problem leads to problem. Have we, in the case of China, to deal with a social type like that of the western lands, or have we not? If not, what are its distinguishing features? Are there present, in the structure of this state, basic peculiarities corresponding to the (perhaps present) socio-economic peculiarities, which support or correct the general theory of the state, or show it in a new light? Or yet again: if the analysis is to be socio-genetic, at what level is such an analysis to start? The great French historians of the early nineteenth century conceived history as the movements of socially distinguished strata (classes). Critical theory, not satisfied with this, posed the question of the structural principle of all such social formations and conflicts.

From the envisioning of such a basic analysis of history to its realization is a long way. Numerous attempts show at least the extraordinary difficulty of the problem, if they do not indeed demonstrate something more negative: its insolubility. Perhaps, when one postulates the methods of production during an epoch as the first problem of analysis, one has set himself too much to do. Should one perhaps consider history, as did those great Frenchmen, mainly as social history—that is, a history of social movements with introductory remarks on their economic background and with careful simultaneous analysis of political and social phenomena, whose origin may be considered sufficiently explained thereby? Comparative consideration of the scientific historiography of the past decades shows that, apart from the crude forms of a mechanical *Geschichtsökonomismus* ("economic interpretation of history"), scientific analysis has by preference used just such a socio-historical method.

The investigation of a complex like the Chinese, so "new" from the theoretical standpoint and to which a meaningful tradition has not yet been attached, might help to clarify the basic methodological problem. More: if a basic consideration of Oriental and Occidental social development discloses specific basic movement—patterns of the "East" (whatever that may be), then possibly a new point of departure for the methodology of investigating "Western" developments may result. And finally: if material analysis of the eastern world finds out by the best known historical steps that it is not a separately progressive but rather a stationary social complex, there arise out of such an insight some essential conclusions for our conception of social history in general. This conception must then obviously include and explain not only developments but also a historically extremely significant variation: stagnation.

2. EXPERIMENT IN ONE FUNDAMENTAL ANALYSIS

A. *Artificial irrigation as a specifying factor in agricultural production.* The social phenomena which we are studying develop at a stage of history below that of capitalistic industry and above that of primitive agrarianism. The latter, in its various manifestations, forms the point of departure. But this point of departure must already have been passed before a specific form of work and life can arise.

The agricultural process of production sets in motion, on the objective level where material analysis commences, two elements in combination: land and water. Differences in the type and productivity of the land, the soil, determine to a large extent the settled social stage of the resultant labor-process; they lead, however, only to variations, not to a fundamentally divergent pattern of the labor-process. This effect proceeds from the second of the chief factors in the means of work—from water. Water gives to the soil and to the plants contained therein as in a vessel, the moisture without which no transfer of nutritive elements into the plant organism and no metabolism of this organism can occur. It also carries with it dissolved organic and, above all, inorganic substances which are required for the nourishment of the plants. The type of climate here comes into play. Apart from the factor of temperature, which affects various stages of agrarian development in various ways, differentiating and limiting them, the factor of rain, caused by the movements of the wind, is decisive. Rain-water may moisten the soil in a timely and quantitatively sufficient manner, or it may not. In the former case the agricultural labor-process can proceed without additional irrigation, while in all other cases agriculture is either completely impossible or can only succeed by means of the planned application of water through socially working men— i.e., by means of artificial irrigation.

Several basic possibilities thus present themselves. The specifying factor in all cases other than the first is the presence or absence of river or of ground-water—i.e., of rain-water which "originates" outside the area in question and then enters this area. (See Table 1).

The table below offers the specifying types of the water situation in a manner newly defined according to our categories. Of course these facts have not been exactly represented in the maps of physical or economic geography, and yet the agrarian-economic categories which we are trying to analyze can be recognized without difficulty in their spatial arrangement on good maps of climate and vegetation. It is indeed to be borne in mind that the factors we have treated indicate merely the possibility of a corresponding nomadic or agricultural development, not yet its reality. In order for a primitive social organism to proceed towards agriculture or cattle-raising, certain natural pre-conditions (apart from the activity of the people and the means of work at their disposal) are necessary—above all, in socially simple conditions, the physical existence of a reproductive flora and fauna. Failure to fulfill these conditions either leads, as in the case of Australia, to stagnation on the level of food-

TABLE 1

Variations of the Water-Situation			Rain for Specific Agricultural Types		Rivers, Ground-Water, etc.		Tendency to—
			Timeliness	Sufficiency	Present?	The Task:	
A	1	a	+	++	a +	a 1 Drainage, Protection a 2 —	Patterns of Water-Control
		b			b —	b —	
	2		+	+		Insignificant	Rainfall agriculture. In case of temporary nomadism, transition to rainfall agriculture plus cattle-raising.
	3	a	+	+	a —		
		b	+	+—	b +	Transition to B 1 a	
B	1	a	+	— But enough for Pasture	a +	Supplementary Irrigation	Irrigation Agriculture
		b			b —		Nomadism
	2	a	—	+	a +	Irrigation for the Sake of Insurance	Irrigation Agriculture
		b			b —		Nomadism
	3	a	—	— But enough for Pasture	a — +	Irrigation to Make Agriculture Possible	Irrigation Agriculture
		b			b —		Nomadism
C		a	—	—— No Rain at All	a +	Irrigation to Make Agriculture Possible	Irrigation Agriculture
		b			b —	Desert!	

The sign + means: Sufficient or present in considerable quantity
"   ++   "   Present in excess
"   —   "   Present only in slight, insufficient quantity
"   ——   "   Not present at all

gathering, or, as in the case of America, prepares a one-sided agricultural, not pastoral, development. Socially active man creates this form of his history, just like any other form, yet the actuality of his history on each achieved phase of his social production is determined by the pattern of the natural productive forces that can be realized at the moment.

Our table makes one thing immediately clear: just as food-gathering societies originate and exist under very different conditions, so do the societies that cultivate plants and animals. Apart from extreme forms (the desert C b and the super-abundant variant of A 1 a), the water-situations fall into three chief types: the case A 2 with its marginal forms I b and 3 a and b (Rain-agriculture); the case B 1 a, 2 a, 3 a, and C a (Irrigation agriculture); and the case B 1 b, 2 b, and 3 b (nomadism), whereby the last two types remarkably enough grow in the main out of similar situations, which will only be varied by a substantial factor (presence or absence of river- or ground-water). The relations of the theoretical categories reflect adequately the relations of the real conditions. The two forms of production are found indeed regularly as the two sides of a related natural basis. Specific social features in the relations between these two production organisms, the mechanism of the economy in the border territories, invasions, the so-called nomad dynasties, the phenomenon of the Great Wall, receive their scientific explanation here from the structure of their productive forces. The great nomadic societies developed in Africa and Asia on the borders of agrarian societies with irrigated agriculture, on which they inflicted from outside effective sociological, military, and political disturbing factors. On the other hand, the nomad areas (B 1 b, 2 b, and 3 b) also border on agrarian lands of Type A 2 and 3, and on more primitive and early feudal agrarian organisms (A 1 without facilities for water control), as in Central Africa. In each case a truly scientific analysis must take into account the already-established categories for the clarification of the entire socio-economic mechanism.

If the "B . . . b"-variant (nomadism) lies outside the sphere of agricultural production, then the water-situation within it is split into two basic types: A and B . . . a plus C a, i.e., into areas where agriculture may be carried on by means of the quantity of water "naturally" furnished by rain, and areas where this is not the case. In the second case it is sometimes possible to find agriculture in the lower forms (more or less A 3 b) set up at first in the hinterland of the still untamable rivers. Agriculture only attains higher productivity when its practitioners manage to make good the water-deficit by furnishing supplementary water: i.e., by artificial irrigation. The new agrarian technique thereby achieved may be in the beginning an act of necessity, which makes agriculturally poor areas for the first time yield any crop at all. But very soon the new productive method is generalized and now concerned not only with the

creation and insurance of a single harvest, but also with the intensifica-
tion of this harvest and often with its multiplication. Socially working
man has found access to a new "nature-machine," whose appropriate
application in some circumstances may lead to a garden-like intensifica-
tion of agriculture such as areas given to rainfall agriculture do not
know—at least, not to any considerable degree.

The differentiation of productive powers on the side of nature develops
necessarily, as soon as Man brings it about concretely in his work-process,
a corresponding differentiation of the socially-conditioned means of
work, as well as of animal and human working forces. The more intensive the work-process becomes in the matter of irrigation, the smaller
becomes the soil-surface necessary to the reproduction of the immediate
producers and the less rewarding becomes the use of work-animals. On
the other hand, the more the system of rainfall agriculture extends, the
more necessary become effective working tools in order to mobilize the
powers of the soil, and the more desirable becomes the use of work-animals
(oxen, horses) able to pull these effective implements over the wide
fields. In areas of irrigation agriculture, suitably primitive tools will
suffice, with a whole arsenal of very refined installations for irrigation
often supplementing them. In regions of rainfall agriculture, a more
highly developed plow and plow-animals come completely into the foreground, while facilities for irrigation are naturally lacking.

The peculiarity of irrigation-economy expresses itself indeed not only
in the special formation of tools and such items. Here, since the success
and failure of production depend in the highest degree upon the care-
fulness of the laborer, a specific type of labor force turns out to be essentially unsuitable: the full slave, without property or family. We have
already treated this point in earlier systematic analysis, and further studies
in the field of Oriental social economy have confirmed us in this view.
There were, to be sure, house-slaves in abundance in the zone of irrigation
agriculture, but the slave played an altogether peripheral role in the
process of agricultural production. Insofar as he entered it at all, he appeared always, as in handicrafts, in circumstances which mitigated his
status as a slave and offered him real incentives to qualified activity. The
different position of slaves in late Rome and the "Orient" is thus explained
by its material basis. And at the same time the peculiar development of
late Rome is similarly explained. As the slave system decayed in consequence of the lack of opportunity to import unfree persons from the
border territories, there resulted a reaction on the natural economy of
Western Rome—i.e., on the sector of the state whose agrarian economy
was centered about slavery. Eastern Rome, which likewise was affected,
managed to maintain itself more or less on a higher economic stage by
the production of simple merchandise, and by towns and trade capitalism.

For the chief areas of the East—Egypt, Syria, and Asia Minor—rely essentially on artificial irrigation. The immediate producers were not as a rule slaves, but peasants of the most diverse types.

B. *The general pattern of waterworks as a second specifying factor.* The presence or absence of artificial irrigation lends a very definite coloring to the productive powers of agriculture. Yet the qualitative factor alone is not enough. The irrigation water may be of purely local origin. Then the reservoirs may be either individually or locally managed, and no further need for supplementary labor arises. But perhaps the water must be tamed on a larger scale. Streams are to be dyked, reservoirs are to be built, canals are to be dug. Then the great task of waterworks arises, with which at this stage neither the techniques of individuals nor those of local groups are able to cope. In this case the task of water-regulation must be carried out socially, either through a state already established by some other means or through separate groups which unite and become independent through these and other such tasks and so, attaining economic and political power, set themselves up as states.

Another factor enters into this: time keeping. The farming year is throughout determined by the rhythm of the seasons, and a knowledge of this rhythm is everywhere important. But only when the beginning and ending of the rains, the rise and fall of the rivers, becomes vitally important, does the need for a relatively precise calendar arise as an immanent problem of the production-process. In general, where a leading group concentrates in its hands the control of the waters, we find this group and the state which stands behind it as well, in direct or indirect control of astronomy. Thus two new types of productive forces are found which give to the state functions which in other agrarian societies it did not have to fulfill. In the basic strata of an extensive rainfall agriculture, there are only certain military, juridical, and religious functions which are carried out by special ruling groups. The state growing out of this includes a multitude of individual landlords, who finally set up a feudal and hierarchical order, but only in a loose and federal manner. No central economic function gives the state such a decisive preponderance that it can suppress the rebellious feudal lords and make itself absolute in its position. Even if, at the beginning of capitalistic development, the absolute monarch raises himself above the bourgeoisie and the feudal lords, playing the one against the other, he still cannot completely sweep away the old lords of the manor and divert the surplus of the peasant production which hitherto flowed into the granaries of the feudal lords, into his own treasury.

It is quite otherwise in an irrigation society, in which the control of the waters is carried on socially—i.e., at this stage, by the state. The bureaucratic-priestly-military hierarchy which appears as the state is either from the beginning the sole master of the peasants' fate—in other words, of the peasant's production and its fruits—or it becomes so in the end, with the growing significance of its double economic function (water-works plus astronomy), by conquering, expropriating, transforming, replacing a feudal landed aristocracy which possibly existed in the economic hinterland of the rivers.

We bring together the results of our considerations so far, in a table which indicates how the various types of productive-power structure lead to different patterns of social-political type. We add Variant III (the society with a slave economy) to Type II (feudalism); they only show higher features than I and II in one aspect, that of local work-organization, while otherwise they show an extremely low development of material and personal productive powers. The other two types are of universal scope; the society with a slave economy, on the other hand, has found but one full expression, in the Greco-Roman world. They rely upon rain-agriculture as does the feudal agrarian order, out of whose seed-forms they probably grew in particular historical circumstances. A perhaps unique situation in the Mediterranean permitted the concentration of a patriarchal agrarian predatory state, to which the enfeebled condition of the Oriental states offered a rich booty. As soon as the state had reached the limits possible to its communications and military techniques, the productive structure, which was only able to reproduce itself by the continual addition of cheap slave labor from the border regions, quickly decayed. The extraordinary world-historical significance which the culture of this epoch has gained for the history of mankind entitles us, in spite of the uniqueness of Type III, to place it beside Forms I and II, by whose side it always goes as a theoretically interesting variant.

A specific totality of essential productive powers is gathered together in a specific manner of production, which corresponds to a specific social condition and an appropriate political order. We designate Type I as Oriental society, not simply because it appeared exclusively in the Orient, but because it appeared there in its most powerful form and because the word "Orient" recalls specific circumstances of soil and, above all, climate, which were indeed of decisive significance for the genesis of this social-economic formation.

Variant II a, which developed most spectacularly in Japan may be counted, by reason of its basis in irrigation, as an Orientally colored form of the feudal society, a fact which can be expressed terminologically by the designation of Oriental feudalism. Following historical traditions, we designate the means of production in Type I as Asiatic means of production, the circumstances of production growing out of them as Oriental society, and the state which expresses this society as Oriental absolutism or—in order to emphasize the peculiar strength of this type of state—as Oriental despotism.

With the establishment of these terms we have concluded the first section of our analysis, which lays bare the essential structure of the social organism we are considering. The phenomenon shows a number of features which do not appear to accord with the basic structure. The continuation of the analysis has to determine whether these apparent contradictions are only of a subjective kind or whether they express objective contradictions which may be scientifically explained.

C. *The problem of social and state order*

1. THE SIMPLE FORM. The first question that should be answered concerns the character of the ruling class. Economically we see the same stratum of the population which dominates either over the totality or at all events over the decisive mass of the most important media of production (Land and Water). The mass of the national surplus product accordingly falls into their hands. Is there such a class in Oriental society, and what is it like?

In order to clarify the basic relations, we must start with a purely Oriental society. Apart from the early forms of Indian society, the Inca state offers a particularly clear picture for this. The peasantry, organized into clans (*Ayllus*) reproduced their own existence by means of collectively regulated agriculture. The surplus production of this very strictly controlled commandeered labor went to the state, which applied it both to the reproduction of the material machinery of the state and to the maintenance of the court, the administrative officers, priests, and the military —i.e., officialdom in its diverse categories. The situation here is completely transparent. The sovereign and his bureaucracy exercise material control over the totality of the cultivated lands, and consequently the surplus production engendered by these lands falls to the ruling class organized as the state. A peculiar form of the relationship between ruling class and state-bureaucracy-plus-court emerges: they are identical. The natural revenue of the land-bound peasantry's labor is paid directly to the ruling bureaucracy. The revenue here is like a tax. A primitive class-arrangement of a classical transparency obtains. The kin group persists and cultivates the soil in partnership, just as the old Indian community, which has partially continued into modern times, knew collective ways of tilling the communal fields.

2. THE DEVELOPED ORIENTAL SOCIETY. As soon as one has acquainted oneself with the specific peculiarity of the Oriental state (the ruling class = the sovereign and the bureaucracy), the problem seems to offer no essential difficulty. In fact, things are not that simple. In few areas of

TABLE 2

Methods of Production

Powers of Production					I	II a	II b	III
Agriculture	The Work	Medium	nature		+ Fruitfulness of the soil	+	+ (no water except rain)	+
					+ Water for irrigation	–	–	–
			Conditions set up by society		– Apparatus for irrigation	+	Tools and + work-animals	–
	Labor	Organi-zation	Qualification		+	+	+| –	–
			Local		+ Eventually in two stages / –	+| –	+| –	+
			Territorial		+	–	–	–
		Astronomy			+	(+)	–	–
Essential social conditions					Village-bound or free peasants. Absolute sovereign and bureaucracy (scribes, priests, administrative officials, officers)	Serfs, feudal lords		Slaves, slave-holders
Character of the State					Centralized absolute bureaucratic state	De-centralized feudal state		Slave-holding state
General designation					"The Orient"	"Oriental" Feudalism	Feudalism / True	Antiquity

Social Science is the condition of theory so confused as here. Certain phenomena of the Oriental world, which in their visible form during the 18th and 19th centuries and in the accounts of Oriental historical science appeared just as importantly meaningful as the picture we have just drawn, are the cause of this. Private property has extended to the countryside. The village community has decayed in many cases, and new social classes have arisen; apart from the private landowners of bureaucratic origin, above all the little and big merchants who as profit-makers and in part even as landowners bring completely new features into the picture which at first was so simple. Can theory explain this change, or is not Oriental society rather dissolved by it and transformed into another kind of social formation?

A great part of the prevailing confusion can be explained by the fact that the original conception of Oriental society occurred in a period— before and shortly after the middle of the 19th century—when neither the social history of Egypt and Babylon nor that of India and China had been handled by modern means. Meanwhile, in the last decade, the documents of the great early Asiatic cultures have been deciphered in great quantity and applied to the unveiling of every land's social history. Especially great steps have lately been made in research into the social history of China. China's thousand-year-old historiography transmitted to the present age a uniquely rich and coherent material for history, which now will be made available with the methods of critical analysis to the social scientists of China and, one may hope, to those of the rest of the world. If one adds the results of the researches carried on in the last decade to the realm of theoretical consideration, it is shown that through the new facts the conception of Oriental society is not shaken or destroyed, but that it is on the contrary deepened, strengthened, and made more specific.

The disintegration of the simple Oriental society may take place from two sides, but basically the dual phenomenon may be reduced to one basic cause. The powers of production grow. Metal implements for agriculture (above all, iron agricultural tools), as well as the development of the technique of irrigation and, in addition, in a certain degree the application of draft animals make the results of tillage much more productive and, at the same time, make individual farming more profitable than the old forms of communal cultivation. Artisanship and also certain branches of industry grow at the same time, together with the greater industrial needs of agriculture and the state-economy. The "free" individual peasant who buys and sells on the market, arises, so that in the end everything, including his individual land-property, can become merchandise.

On the other side, and in varying degrees, the merchant arises as the agent of the growing circulation. Trade—and some industry—and even money-lending capital is to develop out of this, to some degree in Egypt, to a high degree in Mesopotamia, and quite highly in India and especially China. They attract to themselves a part of the revenue in the form of profit. Private property in land carries with it a further consequence: If the farmer is free to sell his land, then others are free to acquire it. Large private land-holdings appear, occasionally in the hands of the new commercial capitalists, often in the hands of the members of the old upper class, who can obtain the ownership of land not only by purchase but also by gifts from the ruler or by retaining service-land. The social-economic order has become much more flexible. But are its bases thereby abolished?

In Pharaonic Egypt, the influence of commercial capital appears to have been particularly slight. Also in Babylon trade and money-lending remained in the hands of the ruling classes, namely those of the priesthood, the "temple." The phenomenon of a land-owning merchant class appears much more extremely in China. In all cases, however, the mass of the free peasants remains a "public sector" paying taxes and service to the state and its bureaucracy. The key economic positions remain therefore in the hands of the office-holding bureaucracy which controls the greatest part of the surplus work and produce of the farmer. Whatever the new legal forms may be—there may be many—the bureaucracy remains by far the greatest landowner, bringing together in its own hands the greatest proportion of the surplus production and the forced labor. The levies on trade- and money-lending-capital—which by the way may take very diverse forms —and on the private great landowners, who pay less taxes as they grow more powerful, weaken the central power, complicate and contradict the action of the Oriental despotism, though they do not abolish its specific character.

At the end of the development, we therefore find dissolved and still-undissolved village communities, partly unified in a social complex as in India. We find the power of disposition over the farm work and farm production in the hands of the state bureaucracy, in the hands of private officials and officers, of priests (temples), and also in certain circumstances of great merchants. The simple Oriental society has, in consequence of the development of the basic powers of production, transformed itself into the developed Oriental society.

3. MILITARY AND CIVIL FUNCTIONS OF THE DOMINANT BUREAUCRACY. Heretofore we have described the upper classes in the simple and the developed Oriental society as if they were at the same time military and civil. This description is not wrong, but it needs more exact definition. We see before us such societies as Babylon and China, where apparently administrative officials and priests or officials with priestly functions stand at the peak of the social pyramid, while in India the

priesthood had to share its power with the warrior caste. In Assyria, the military element even steps clearly into the foreground. Does not this change in the type of the ruling class indicate at the same time a difference in the social-economic substance?

The difference we have noticed is indeed significant, but not in the way an outsider might expect. An officer finds himself economically on the same level as a priest or an administrative official. Both social categories live on revenue in kind or money, which the state has taken from the peasants in the form of taxes, especially the land-tax, and which is distributed, via the state-treasury, to its bureaucracy. The officer, therefore, although professionally resembling the feudal knight, is economically far from him, but close to the civil official. His relationship to the mass of the farm population is, in the case of the Orient, indirect, impersonal and temporary, while in the case of the knights it bears a direct, personal, concrete, and permanent character.

The difference in the two groups of officials, therefore, does not lie in their economic positions, but in the significance of their day-to-day functions. This is conditioned in a far-reaching way by the international situation, in which a given Oriental complex exists. If the complex in question is surrounded by powerful states, then the external military functions are of first importance beside the internal political repressive and economic tasks (police, justice, public works). The civil bureaucracy does not disappear. This would be impossible, since it forms an integrating part of the social organism. But in its activity in some circumstances it will not only be supplemented but even overshadowed by the functions of the military bureaucracy, in the event that the latter must fulfill protective tasks of great importance and duration. In Assyria this was apparently almost always the case, while at the same time the typically "Oriental" features (waterworks, administration, etc.) were relatively limited. In India several great waterworks-complexes were centered around a number of isolated river-systems, so that the antagonistic political conditions and the corresponding large-scale military tasks always arose anew. A complete victory of the military or secular elements, which found a potent weapon in Buddha's anti-Brahman teaching, thus became impossible. Even in the realm of Asoka, Buddhism, which had reached the height of its power, could still not fully displace the ideas of the Brahman priestly caste. Finally Buddhism was completely defeated, and an interesting balance of power between the priesthood and the warrior caste, the Brahmans and the Kshatriyas, came about—a social balance which the functional duality between the two upper groups of the Indian Oriental upper class plainly expressed.

China's social structure accommodates itself without difficulty to the principles we have indicated. A variant of situation A 1 a 1 (too much summer-water in the periodically rising loess-rivers, insufficient rain at the right time) enforced the adoption of local irrigation, but above all water-control measures on the grand scale. In the time of Confucius (about 500 B.C.) the management of waterworks had already taken on the character of a long-perfected, legendarily revealed, heroic accomplishment.

The first epoch of unified empire (221 B.C. to 220 A.D.) left many military tasks undone. It established the civil element and its particular ideology, Confucianism, in a solid and programmatical manner. Only Central and South China were actually not assimilated. The push into the southern areas disrupted the temporarily unified state order. In the Period of Disruption (221–589) we find military accomplishments again attaining high social prestige. The T'ang era (618–906) mourned the decline of the knightly customs. What had happened? After the building of the Grand Canal under the Sui dynasty (589–618), which, by means of an artificial Nile, combined China's two great stream-valleys in an economic-political unity, after the establishment of the examination system, after the reorganization of all-important branches of political life, the civilian element ruled supreme in the reunified country. The literary Oriental officialdom (and Confucianism) pushed the warrior officials (and Buddhism) into the background. Conqueror nations such as the Mongols and the Manchus were able to proclaim once more temporarily the supremacy of the military virtues. In vain. The world "within the four oceans," Greater China, had grown together into a rather loose but dynamic unity. Even in the shadow of the conqueror peoples the Chinese representatives of Oriental bureaucracy, the Confucian officials occupied the supreme positions in the Chinese hierarchy of social prestige.

4. AGRARIAN AND STATE CRISES IN ORIENTAL SOCIETY. In a simple Oriental society agrarian crises are mainly the result of too much or too little water. Large-scale catastrophes of flood or drought, endangering the physical existence of great populated regions, drive the victims of flood and hunger to mass emigration and uproar. The crisis in such a case still bears an immediate natural character. At this stage the subjective factor of a good or bad government—maintenance or disrepair of the waterworks—plays an especially great role for the economy of the country.

The mechanism of crisis becomes very involved if Oriental society with its productive powers develops its property-based conflicts. This can occur essentially in two ways, according to the two basic forms of the developed Oriental society. The agricultural production may be closely concentrated about the life-giving irrigation system; or this system may bear a loose, uneven, dispersed character. The second type is very clearly represented by China, which in this sense may serve as an example of a specific variant of Oriental society (as its B-form). Inner crises occur in both cases, but in case B they take on especially violent forms.

The development of productive powers allows generally an extension of the basic complex over a larger region. With the extension of the dominant economic area, the ruling bureaucracy grows in number and function. In case the original area retains its political superiority, it can successfully prevent the growth of outside rival groups. In Pharaonic Egypt the merchant class is insignificant. India's trade develops more strongly than the Egyptian, but even here the bureaucratic central power blocks each threatening development of the merchants and money-lenders. The weakening results accordingly, not from the outside, but from an internal conflict of the ruling bureaucracy itself.

The origin of the internal conflict can be of two kinds. The machinery of the state may more or less effectively prevent the steady acquisition of peasant lands by centrifugal elements of the bureaucracy; but, since the means of communication often are imperfectly developed, it cannot prevent—in consequence of the great territorial extension of the developed Oriental state—the relative independence of its territorial organs (satraps, governors, tax-controllers, and district officials). With the increasing appropriation of the locally collected land tax by the local bureaucracy, the power of the local officialdom increases. The consequence is either a shrinkage in income of the central power or, if this income remains constant, an intensified oppression of the peasant masses, from which the additional local appropriations must be extracted by added local pressure. In the first case, the possibility of financing public works is materially damaged. In the second case the excessive abuse of the peasantry by the "grinding bureaucracy"—excessive from the standpoint of the traditional average—strikes vitally at the personal foundation of the public works. In both cases with the weakening of public works the productivity of agriculture shrinks and thereby the very foundation of political power within the state in question. The tendency towards disorder and uprising grows. In case the neighboring nomadic societies have then reached a point of relative concentration and high aggressive striking power, the decadent irrigation state can be easily overrun by nomadic conquerors. If the outside cause is lacking, then the cataclysm follows as soon as the internal disintegration is far enough advanced. Either way, however, it is an inner crisis-mechanism which loosens up the Oriental social structure and prepares it for civil war or for defeat from the outside.

A variation of the just-described cases is the concentration of land in the hands of individual members of the ruling bureaucracy, who exert excessive military, priestly, or administrative power. The temple may get much land and pay little or no taxes. High local officials acquire land as special gifts or as regular pay, and this assignment, considered as temporary, may develop into a permanent possession in consequence of economic-political conditions. As the income of the central power weakens, it is unable to fulfill its specific Oriental task in the process of agricultural production. At the end of the Old Kingdom in Egypt, before the invasion of the Hyksos, before the ascent of the Ammon priesthood, and before the coming of Alexander the Great, the central power seems to have been weakened in this fashion.

These cases show a great many varieties, but they all belong to the same basic type. Every time the crisis develops out of the conflicts of Oriental bureaucracy, which permits beside itself either no or only peripheral economic elements. The B-Type, China, in consequence of the essentially looser form of the basic irrigation system, has prepared a favorable soil not only for the training of centrifugal elements in the ruling bureaucracy but also for the growth of influential non-bureaucratic elements. A higher mobilization of land ownership was technically possible, was economically desirable from the standpoint of the tax-levying bureaucracy, and was therefore officially established. The function of a commercial bourgeoisie could only be exercised partially and imperfectly by the state bureaucracy. The cycle therefore had to assume a particularly complicated form.

The "public sector" (formed by the free peasants) at the beginning of a new epoch surpasses the "private sector" (great landholders and tenants), since the collapse of the old regime destroyed countless peasants and many landlords and laid waste large stretches of farming land. A farm policy which distributes land, seed, and tools and which keeps taxes low brings the landless elements back to the villages. The peasantry grows. The crop grows. The taxes grow. The power of the state grows, which increases its initial efforts to build canals and dykes. However, the upswing carries within it the seed of its own downfall. With the growing well-being of the villages and the state, the profit of the merchants and the income of the officials also grow. The accumulated liquid capital tends to change into an immobile form, into land. The private sector expands and therewith that portion of the peasantry which is fully taxed. The active or retired landowning officials and the mighty merchant landlords pay little tax. With growing extension of the private sector the public income decreases. The effectiveness of the state to carry out its economic functions is decreased. It gives less to the farmers but takes more from them. Taxes rise and with them—*circulus vitiosus*—the tendency of the free farmers to flee from the open into the private sector, i.e., to transfer their land to a private landowner (possibly also a monastery) and in this way to escape from the tax-collector. At the same time with the decay of the waterworks, the pressure rises even in the private sector. Peasant uprisings, initially local, take on larger dimensions. The internally weakened regime, whose centrifugal elements form a destructive block of interests with the merchant landowners and eventually even simple landowners, becomes ever less secure in its power, more cynical in its morals, more cruel in its taxation. An uprising, led by uncompromising elements of the old upper class, or a nomadic invasion, or a combination of both, accomplishes what the weakness of the economic sphere has thoroughly prepared: the fall of the dynasty, on whose ruins the leader of the victorious movement newly establishes himself with a reform program, as the absolute chief of a rejuvenated, though basically unaltered, Oriental despotism.

5. WHY NO INDEPENDENT DEVELOPMENT TOWARDS INDUSTRIAL CAPITALISM? The discovery of a crisis-mechanism, which runs in the form of a vicious circle, involves another principle which shows only a particular side of the same process: the agrarian and political crises moved in a vicious circle and not in a steadily increasing spiral. The social-economic system reproduces itself instead of developing. Why?

The Orient has applied a specific type of nature- and culture-conditioned productive power (irrigation-water, facilities for irrigation, intensive manual labor) which played little or no rôle in the agriculture of the West. Thus in the Oriental zone a higher productivity of agricultural work is reached than in the West. This result is based on public works of great magnitude. While in the West managerial and intellectual centers of agrarian order were not needed, in the Orient they become a *conditio sine qua non* for the simple reproduction of the agricultural life. The political center in the Orient becomes economically more important and politically more powerful because—in contrast to the feudal world—in one way or another it has a direct bearing on the activities of the peasants. The Oriental state and its representatives thus arrogate to themselves the bulk of the land revenue, whereas Western (and Japanese) absolutism conceded a great part of the land rent to the feudal lords.

In the West the transition to capitalism occurred in cities, which knew how to make themselves independent by a chain of more or less political aggressive movements. The surplus from handicraft and commercial activity remained in the hands of the bourgeois class, under whose control it grew. The accumulation of capital was thus possible politically as well as economically; the surplus was not taxed away, confiscated, or taken away as a pseudo-loan. The industrial productive powers could be developed as well, without negatively touching the agricultural hinterland, in whose urban centers the new development took place; and the absolute central power had to encourage industrial progress all the more eagerly, since here, in contrast to the feudally-controlled villages, it expected additional income and power for the court and its administration.

Quite different in the "Orient." The city centers here dominated the economic reproduction either of decisive parts or of the whole agricultural life. Anyone who, for the purpose of gaining bourgeois freedom, drove the central power from the cities, upset the nerve centers of the agricultural hinterland. Obviously then, the position of the Oriental administrative city is a different one, not only in the sense of the immediate production techniques. It is so likewise in regard to the distribution of surplus products. Occupying the social-economic center and either destroying or decisively limiting the existence of feudal revenue-getters, Oriental absolutism gains supreme power also over the city's production. The wretched artisans of the Orient and the proud and independent artisans of the West are the product of different developments, in the course of which one side is kept at a bare minimum by taxes, etc., while the other side learns to defend its interests in powerful guild cities.

The development of Western industrial capitalism accordingly occurred because there a peculiarly decentralized structure of the agricultural productive power permitted—economically, sociologically and politically—the commencement of capital-accumulation, while the centralized structure of the highly productive Oriental agrarian order worked in the opposite direction, namely towards the reproduction of the existing order, towards its stagnation.

Despite any cyclic collapses, Asiatic society, insofar as it was not physically destroyed from outside, could therefore re-establish itself in principle after the worst disaster. The classical type of a society which tenaciously reproduces itself, a stationary society, is created.

C. Economic Anthropology

Economics is the study of the production, distribution and consumption of goods and services. From the point of view of anthropology, economic studies have three primary facets: the description of the tools and techniques of production, the designation of the particular means and level of subsistence, and the analysis of social relationships which involve the movement of goods and services. The selections which follow treat of each of these things and one of them (No. II:9) deals with the relation of technology to the evolution of culture.

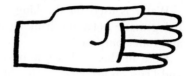

8. SIUAI TECHNOLOGY *

Sporadic tool use is reported for a variety of animals but man everywhere, and for as long as we have knowledge of him, depends upon implements in order to survive. In a sense, the basic formula of cultural ecology rests upon two variables—physical environment and the tools and methods used to exploit that environment. As universal as language, technology plays a critical role in the determination of other aspects of culture. Put another way, it is necessary to understand the technology of a culture in order to comprehend its other aspects.

"Siuai" is the name of a people who live in southern Bougainville in the Solomon Islands. In 1938–39, Dr. Oliver lived in Siuai villages and made extensive observations of the culture. What follows is his description of Siuai technology from a recent monograph which describes the culture as a whole.

T HE SIUAI utilize only a small proportion of the vast number of distinguishable items found in their environment, but even so, their raw materials inventory numbers into the hundreds. Here are some of those items most commonly used.

They make use of soil for agriculture; red and black clay for pottery manufacture; white clay and red ocher for paints, cosmetics, and magic. Large boulders serve as shrines, grindstones, and anvils, small stones are used as hammers. They no longer manufacture or use stone axes and adzes but many natives remember using them, and scores are still being kept for eventual sale to whites.

* Douglas L. Oliver, A Solomon Island Society (Cambridge: Harvard University Press, 1955), pp. 11–35. Reprinted by permission of the author and the Trustees of Harvard University. The author (b. 1913) is Associate Professor of Anthropology at Harvard University. Specializing in Oceanic and Melanesian ethnology, he is also the author of The Pacific Islands (1952) and Studies in the Anthropology of Bougainville (1949).

Water is used for drinking, cooking, and bathing—a sharp distinction being made between drinking-water streams and those used for bathing and toilet purposes.

Here in this rank wilderness, where fence and house posts take root and keep on growing, native life is heavily dependent on plants. Besides the items grown for food (taro, yam, sweet potato, plantain, sago, coconut, almond, sugar cane, and many more), numerous other plants are collected in the forest for eating (leaves, ferns, flower buds, mushrooms, funguses, etc.). The natives mix areca nut and pepper catkin with lime for their betel-chewing mixture, and are inveterate smokers of their home-grown tobacco. All their houses are made of wood, held together with plant fibers and thatched with leaves. Most containers are of leaves, plant fibers, and coconut shells; all their furniture, most of their weapons and many of their tools and musical instruments are made of wood. Aside from recently acquired calico loincloths, all their clothing is made of leaves or bark. Most dyes, oils, adhesives, and many body ornaments come from plants or plant products; and their pharmacopoeia, too, is largely vegetable.

Animals and animal products are not nearly so extensively or variously utilized. The Siuai eat the flesh, heart, blood, and liver of pigs, and use pigs' long bones for tools and tusks for bracelets, but they ignore pig bristle and hide. They also capture opossums and eat their flesh and organs but discard hair and hide. They capture and eat tree-rats and eels but reject house rats, snakes, and lizards. Now and then they shoot or net flying foxes and some kinds of birds, but make little effort to exploit the forests' many other resources in edible flying things. They occasionally eat grubs and certain kinds of spiders and ants.

They engage in desultory attempts to catch the fish and prawns living in their creeks, and they travel to distant southern beaches to collect shells for making tools and lime, but do not trouble with fishing while there.

It appears then that the Siuai get most of their raw materials from plants; compared with such peoples as the Arunta or Pacific atoll-dwellers, they have not begun to utilize fully the other kinds of materials found around them.

Some of this selectivity may be because of the kinds of tools they possess or lack. Their native cutting tools consist of bamboo and shell knives, and stone adzes and axes. The stone adzes and axes have now been replaced by steel axes, machetes, hatchets, and adze blades, but large flat bivalve shells are still used for peeling things like taro; and bamboo knives, kept sharp by removing slivers, continue to be used in some cutting operations. Heavy steel axes are scarce and have not yet supplanted the small steel ax- and adze-hafted blades traded from the

Germans twenty-five years ago. The all-purpose cutting tool owned by nearly every youth and man is a ten- to twelve-inch machete; these knives are almost like appendages, as they are carried continually and used for purposes as varied as paring finger nails and felling trees. The casual rubbing against boulders they receive does not keep them very sharp, but it is difficult to imagine what this generation of Siuai natives would do without them. A new kind of tool among the recent imports is the small pocketknife now carried (but not in pockets!) by many men and used for carving with more precision than they found possible with native tools. There is no sex bar to use of cutting tools but in general the heavier ones, including steel, are wielded by males.

Bone is also used for tools. Small pointed bones are employed to pierce shells and to split fibers for weaving; a sharpened pig's femur is used for splitting areca nuts as well as for separating coconut meat from its shell. Scraping is done with sharp-edged bivalves; shredding with tooth-edged ones. Stone tools used to be polished and sharpened by grinding against boulders. Hammering is done with fist-sized pebbles; digging with pointed sticks. A rough-surfaced leaf is employed for smoothing wooden surfaces and an oily nut for polishing them.

All these tools are used to make end-products or other implements and hence might appropriately be named primary tools. Some end-products, to be sure, are made without tools: an effective umbrella is produced simply by ripping off a large banana leaf and holding it over the head, and an adequate container can be quickly made from a coconut frond entirely by hand. In a number of instances, moreover, tools are devised on the spot: a handful of leaves is the most common brushing and wiping implement, and saplings are used as levers and carrying poles. Most end-products, however, require the use of primary tools in their manufacture; rather than list all end-products here according to their component raw materials or their process of manufacture, it will serve our purposes better to consider them in due course in connection with the kinds of activity for which they are used.

The Siuai are frugal and skillful in their utilization of fire; they use it rather like a precision tool, keeping it in narrow bounds and applying it specifically. Except for cremations and pottery-baking, one rarely sees a large blaze; even trash-burning fires in the gardens are kept within narrow bounds. Cooking fires are small, houses are kept warm and mosquito-free at night by a continual smolder of radially arranged sticks rather than by a lively blaze: as one informant expressed it, "one can get *nearer* to a small fire." Nor is the hearth a focal point; natives do not sit facing it. (One of the most difficult adaptations I had to make was to sit through long, cold, and pitch-black night wakes or dances with no fire save a smoking ash bed to light pipes from, and able to distinguish my mat-black companions only by their voices.) On the other hand, fire is used to fell trees; to straighten bamboo arrows; to harden digging-sticks, spears, and other tool points; to ring-bark trees; to preserve food and dry tobacco; to incise designs on objects and scarify skins; to soften fibers; to burn lime for betel-chewing; and to perform numerous other operations. A careful householder keeps a smolder going continually, and if it does go out, secures a live coal from a neighbor. Natives can and sometimes do make fire, by the plow method, but it is considered a long and strenuous job, and I have seen individuals give up in exhaustion and disgust before obtaining a spark. The few boxes of inferior trade-store matches that drift in from the coast are quickly used up. When traveling, natives carry a lighted chunk of wood or a bundle of smoldering twigs bound together with fibers.

CONTAINERS

The Siuai possess a wide variety of containers and carrying methods and show considerable ingenuity in devising new ones. Clay pots, which are used for cooking, all have the same general round-bottomed, wide-mouthed shape, but vary in size from about eight inches in diameter and ten inches in height to eighteen inches in diameter and forty inches in height, the latter being used at club-houses for feasts. The best pottery clay is located in northeast Siuai which is the center of pot-making. Pots are manufactured by molding short strips of coil onto a hand-molded bowl-shaped base. A small wooden paddle is now and then used to thin and smooth the sides but most of the shaping is done by hands alone, kept wet by frequent dipping into a coconut-shell bowl full of water. The pot is fired in an open blaze, and this completes the process—no glazing, no painting, and only occasionally a few incised lines for decoration. Cracking is frequent during firing and the life of a pot is short. Nowadays every cook tries to obtain a more durable pot of iron from the coastal trade-store, but so far only about one household in ten owns one.

Green vegetables are often steamed in bamboo containers, and water is carried and stored in bamboo as well as in coconut-shell bottles stoppered with leaves. Coconut shell also is used to make bowls, cups, and ladles. Gourds sometimes serve as liquid containers but their principal use is for carrying betel-chewing lime. Food-mashing pestles are made of wood and have pointed bases to allow them to stand up in the ground; mortars are also of wood, as are some types of bowls and trays. But for every one of all these other kinds of containers found in any household there will be two or three baskets or woven trays. Basketry containers range widely in size, shape, and technique, from enormous five-foot-long coil-woven trays used for feasts to the tiny purses carried in men's net bags. Some of these take several days to make and require rare fibers, but a usable basket or tray can be improvised in a few minutes out of the wealth of leaves and common fibers always within reach. An examination of the photographs in this [Oliver's] book will indicate the extensive and varied uses these Siuai make of plant-fiber weaving. In some cases a specific kind of container and a concrete use are fixedly linked, for example, the large satchels made by women and used by them to carry potatoes and taro corms; while in other instances one use will be served by a number of different kinds of containers, with fashions continually changing. When we first arrived in Siuai the place had the appearance of a pouch factory; nearly every man and youth was making a soft and finely woven pouch, about eight inches long by five wide, to be carried in their net bags. Whenever natives stopped chopping wood or eating or mixing betel, out would come the partly finished baskets from their net bags—reminiscent of a group of American women knitting in wartime. If one Siuai put his handiwork down for a few moments to do something else, as likely as not an unengaged companion would pick it up and weave a few rows. Latter on the fashion in carrying bags changed and men went back to larger and cruder pouches which were carried by means of a shoulder strap.

Because of the wide variety of weaving materials and the uses made of dyes—indigenous vegetable dyes and trade-store imports—Siuai natives have wide scope for devising new forms and for imitating alien ones, and they are particularly receptive to innovations coming from the islands to the south.

Net containers are less varied in form and use, the chief one being the shoulder-strap bag carried or rather *worn* by nearly every male with anything to carry. In these bags one invariably finds a small gourd filled with lime, a few areca nuts, a leaf packet of pepper catkins, a piercing tool fashioned from a pig's femur, a bamboo box full of tobacco leaf, a packet or two of magical ingredients, and, perhaps, a few spans of shell money. Australian shillings have holes through the center, thoughtfully coined in this form by a practical-minded government, and are ordinarily carried —on the infrequent occasions when they are carried—strung onto a cord which is passed through a pierced ear-lobe.

Woman's principal carrying device is a tumpline strap fashioned of bark fiber; in this she places her pouches of taro or potatoes, leaf packets of greens or relishes, her cape, firewood, betel mixture, and anything else, all usually topped by a small child. Bent over as she usually is with such burdens, her digging stick serves as a useful staff to help her up and down slippery paths. Men do not like to encumber themselves with burdens, and when they do have to transport heavy loads they attach them to a pole carried across one shoulder.

SETTLEMENTS

A bird's-eye view of Siuai would reveal islands of cleared or scrub-over-grown land surrounded by a sea of dense forest growth. In these clearings the Siuai natives dwell and work, only occasionally penetrating the surrounding forests to hunt or to journey to another settlement.

Aboriginal settlements consist of small, one- to nine-house hamlets scattered about the scrub. When the Australian Administration began to bring this region under control during the early 1920's, it was part of the policy of patrolling officers to consolidate smaller hamlets into larger villages in order to simplify control, improve public health, and "bring about friendlier relations among the natives."

These villages—"lines" the Siuai call them—are usually located on top of interfluvial ridges, near springs (for drinking water) and large streams (for bathing and sanitation). A few villages are located directly on the sandy banks of streams to avoid the continual climbing back and forth to water, although natives recognize the hazard of this kind of location because of the danger from floods.

Each married man is required by the Administration to own a house in a village and these houses are usually built on piles—the officials' theory being that pile dwellings are healthier. Every village is kept clean of weeds and rubbish, and is surrounded by a sturdy fence designed to keep out pigs. There are from ten to twenty-five houses in each village, the average number of houses to a village in northeast Siuai being thirteen.

In nearly every case the Siuai have retained their older-type hamlet settlements so that now most households possess two houses each—one in the village and one in the hamlet. The hamlet or bush houses—"pig-food" (*hurupao*), they are aptly called—are generally built directly on the ground.

Hamlet houses are generally built nearer streams—at stream level, in many instances. Usually these hamlet houses are off the main paths and shielded from village clearings by trees.

Some natives reside in their hamlet houses all the time and keep their village houses in repair merely to satisfy Administration requirements. Others divide their time between village and hamlet houses. Still others eat and sleep in their village dwellings and retire to the hamlet houses only to feed the pigs and secure privacy.

Besides village and hamlet houses, there are other kinds of structures found in Siuai settlements. The most important of these are the men's club-houses (*kaposo*), where men meet together to gossip, beat slit gongs, and hold feasts. Generally, most club-houses are built beside important paths—a significant contrast to villages, which are usually separated from main paths by screens of vegetation, and in even sharper contrast to hamlets, which are completely hidden away.

In many settlements there are work-sheds (*aurui*), small replicas of club-houses but without slit gongs. Pottery-making takes place in the work-shed, which is also a center for gossip; women are not barred from it as they are from club-houses.

Finally, there are the *pari*, smaller sheds hastily constructed in the gardens to serve as shelters against rain and midday sun, and sometimes, when the garden is far away from home, as a place for sleeping.

In spite of the lack of good fishing and suitable gardening land, and the presence of mosquito-ridden swamps and crocodile-infested lagoons along the southwestern Bougainville coast, there formerly were several Siuai settlements there. This is attested by traditions of the natives themselves and by accounts of Europeans who visited this region in the early twentieth century and shortly before. At that time there was a lively trade between Mono and Alu Islanders and the Buin Plainsmen; and whole communities of trade middlemen settled along the coast. When Bougainville was severed politically from Alu and Mono and brought into the Territory of New Guinea, a customs barrier was interposed between the Territory and the Solomon Islands Protectorate and as a result native trade between Bougainville and Alu-Mono ceased. Consequently most of the coastal settlements of the Siuai were deserted, and the inhabitants moved inland to healthier, more productive land. In 1939 the last community on the Siuai coast withdrew three miles inland and built a new village at a place called Morokintu ("Flying-fox-Creek").

The area of land actually under cultivation in Siuai at any one time is not great but by constant rotation very extensive tracts are kept permanently cleared of large timber. Of course, clumps of virgin forest remain scattered through the "cleared" areas, and secondary growth is allowed to grow to considerable size before again being cut away for gardens; but in contrast with the majestic rain forests, the "cleared" secondary-growth areas are like open fields.

Besides utilizing land for cultivating the staple taro and sweet potato crops, Siuai natives plant groves of coconut and areca-nut palms. And they hunt in the forests, fish in the streams, and clear paths between settlements. Hunting and fishing activities do not transform the landscape; I have no record of any natural area set aside solely for hunting, nor did I discover that the periodic damming of rivers for fish drives had any permanent effect on the course of the rivers.

Pathways vary greatly in width: from faint trails through regions of secondary growth to eight-foot-wide roads—highways, actually—along which the Administration officials travel during their periodic census and tax-collecting expeditions. But width is no indication of the amount of traffic—the beautifully repaired "Government Road" might remain untraveled for days on end, whereas the tiny track leading from village to spring will be in constant use. Real transformation of the landscape by roads has occurred in only those places where rival leaders have vied with one another to see who could clear the widest roadway.

SHELTER, CLOTHING, AND GROOMING

Protection against sun and rain appears to be a determining factor affecting when and how the Siuai erect shelters. They are not indulging in poesy when they speak of the *angry* (*iro*) sun; despite their bushy coiffures and black skins they are subject to mild sunstroke and burning. Hence they behave perfectly rationally and try to stay out of the midday sun. Rain they also avoid, and with good reason. Light showers are not disliked, but these usually give way to stinging, drenching, and chilling downpours which set them to shivering and, they believe, help bring on sickness. Consequently, on starting to work on a new garden site one of the first things they do is to build the sun and rain shelter already mentioned. This is usually a lean-to based against the fence or a simple four-posted shed, both types being thatched with sheets of sago leaves. When men spend several days in the forests hunting for opossum they usually build a rough lean-to covered with big leaves as protection against drenching, the sun being no hazard there.

Additional physical factors enter into the construction of dwellings. It is considered essential that houses be tight and sturdy enough to keep out cold night air and hungry pigs. (In former times of feuding it was also essential for walls to be sufficiently thick to ward off the arrows and spears of enemies.) Besides these physical factors there are other considerations which affect the forms of dwellings; these include the desire for privacy and need for space. Size requirements vary greatly, depending upon the numbers to be housed and the ambitions of the household head; on the other hand, what we might call *aesthetic* considerations play little part in house construction.

Some dwellings are on piles, others are built directly on the ground; still others combine both features by extending forward the verandah overhand of a pile-built house and by walling-in the whole structure. Materials and techniques are standardized but no two dwellings are of exactly the same size and form. The illustrations show more clearly than words what dwellings are like, but it will be helpful to list a few structural principles. The frame is nearly always made of peeled but otherwise unshaped poles of medium-hard wood. The roof is supported by posts thrust directly into the ground; in a pile-dwelling the raised floor rests on a separate set of posts and is only weakly attached to the roof supports. There is very little shaping of timbers to make fitted joints except at the tops of the ridge posts, which are occasionally gouged out to support the ridgepole. Rattan is used for all tying and binding. The floors of pile houses are made of split but otherwise unshaped lengths of tough areca-like palm. The lower parts of some walls are made of horizontal timbers, otherwise both walls and roofs are made by overlapping sheets of sago leaf. These sheets are as important to the Siuai as shingles used to be to a Cape Codder; they are the building cover par excellence and a supply of them is usually kept on hand for repairs or for trade. Industrious men and women can often be seen constructing them when they have nothing more pressing to do. They are made with sago or nipa palm leaves folded over and fastened to a double or triple span long lath.

The open-sided work-sheds are somewhat larger than most ground dwellings but structurally similar except for lack of walls. These huts serve the purpose of workshops; people sit in them to manufacture pottery and large baskets and to restring shell money. Also similar in structure but usually much larger and more elaborately built are the men's club-houses found near every settlement. In these, the rattan lashings may be neater, the roofs thicker, and some attention paid to decorative detail; but even including these structures Siuai architecture is makeshift and unadorned according to some Melanesian standards. On the other hand, their buildings do constitute fairly satisfactory adjustments to the southern Bougainville environment. They protect from sun and shed rain admirably. The open-sided structures, which are usually occupied only during daylight, permit free air circulation and are cool on the hottest of days. The hamlet dwellings, which are built directly on the ground, effectively close out cold, and smoldering fires keep them dry and mosquito-proof—although a less-hardened mortal might prefer to be chilled and bitten rather than be suffocated in the smoky atmosphere. Moreover, these dwellings keep hungry pigs away from infants and provide an impenetrable screen for privacy.

The pile dwellings, which the Administration has encouraged natives to build in the villages, may be more sanitary from some points of view, but they are much more drafty.

There is adaptive efficiency even in the flimsiness of Siuai buildings. Although the sedentary life of the natives makes permanency feasible, the readily available building materials and the climate limit narrowly the durability of anything they build. Termites and rot dissolve most frames within a decade, and the average roof has to be renewed after three or four years. Why, therefore, invest extra effort in strengthening and embellishing structures which in any case cannot endure?

In the matter of adjusting their own bodies to the environment the Siuai have been less successful. Nowadays every native past five or six years old wears a span-length of trade-store calico wrapped around the waist and reaching below the knees. For males this is the only garment, but women carry a kind of short, hooded cape (*soroma*), made by sewing together strips of specially cured palm leaves. This they use as rain-cape, sun-shade, and sitting mat. Some men wear fine conical hats (*ohkuna* or *iropira*) made of dried pandanus leaves, or rough cylinder-shaped ones (*kukutu*) made of wild banana leaves; physically speaking, both these hair coverings are of more nuisance than value because of low-roofed houses and narrow, tangled trails. The women's capes, and the ready availability of leaf umbrellas, provide protection from rain, but otherwise natives are fully exposed to mosquitoes, to cold and, in the case of males, to sun. Before the days of calico most men went completely naked throughout life except for a bark-fiber belt (*kurumira*) for carrying knives, and females donned a small pubic apron only upon marriage. There is, of course, a credit side to nudity in a wet tropical setting; except directly in the sun, exposed bodies are cooler and dry more quickly after drenchings. And in this sense, on rainy days and cool nights calico is likely to be damp, and may be a health hazard.

Infants are bathed in cold water poured out of coconut-shell containers, while all other natives past toddler age bathe in streams. Coconut oil is rubbed over the skin to make it glisten, and bamboo combs are used to untangle the frizzly hair and leave it bushy. Some men remove face hair with small bivalve shell depilators; those with heavier beards let them grow or occasionally shave them with trade-store blades. Delousing is a familiar scene wherever natives congregate.

Careful grooming is linked with age. People lavish tender care upon infants and toddlers—bathing, oiling, combing, and delousing them; but children past that stage are left for days covered with dust and ashes before being taken to the stream and forced to bathe. Natives again show interest in grooming themselves when sexual activity begins, and this fastidiousness continues until shortly after marriage, when most men and women revert to the comfortable squalor of childhood except on festive occasions.

Red ocher and white riverine clay are used for body paints. Young dandies trim their mops of hair into many shapes and sometimes bleach it with lime or trade-store peroxide; others use lamp soot to color their hair a more uniform black. Women wear plaited fiber arm bands around the biceps, men wear theirs higher up. Both men and women wear nose plugs, ear plugs, *sieruma* bracelets, and *kesi* pendants made of tridacna shell; and on special occasions they deck themselves out with shell or dog-tooth necklaces, feathers, flowers, and scented leaves. Scar patterns are made on the body by cutting or burning and rubbing ash into the wounds.

The Siuai use innumerable materials and techniques for dealing with bodily ailments, and while most of these depend upon magic for effectiveness there are also several of a more or less rational kind, including purges, emetics, unguents, and poultices. Surgery is rarely practiced, and then only for lancing boils or removing splinters, but bone-setting without surgery is in lively demand during the season when males climb the high almond trees to collect nuts.

AGRICULTURE

More than half of an adult Siuai's working hours are taken up with food—with producing, collecting, processing, and consuming it. This is an average, for women spend about ten hours daily at it and men generally much less. These natives eat a wide variety of comestibles; but when one of them speaks of "food" (*pao*) he is usually referring to taro. In month-long records I kept of meals eaten by representative households taro constituted some 80 per cent by weight of everything eaten. Informants told of having eaten a few "wild" taro during straitened times, otherwise all taro consumed is grown in their gardens.

Taro gardens are laid out on well-drained terrain where the soil is deep and free of sand. Another technical requirement is that gardens be located in areas of secondary growth; I did not see a single instance of primary forest being cleared for gardens. Natives say that it is too difficult even with metal axes to cut down and remove the huge trees; but there are other reasons why new gardens are located on old garden sites.

Taro gardens are laid out in patches fenced in to keep out pigs. These patches are rectangular and a single patch varies from one to five thousand square yards in area. Very rarely does one see isolated patches; they are generally arranged in sequence, as shown in Figure 1. Taro is ready for harvesting after about four months' growth, and planting is a continuous process without perceptible seasonal differences in growth and yield. Added to this is the fact that the Siuai do not know how to preserve taro and hence must consume it within a few days after harvesting it. As soon as the plants are harvested from a matured garden the corms are cut off just below the stalks, for eating, and the stalks are replanted in another site after their leaves have begun to rot. The gardener's ideal is to have several contiguous patches in various stages of growth. Figure 1 illustrates the technique. Patch A is completely harvested and over-grown with reeds and small trees; most of its fence timbers have already been used for firewood and those remaining are scattered and rotting. Patch B has been completely harvested of taro and now contains only a few banana and plantain trees still in bearing. Patch C contains growing taro some of which is ready for harvest. Patch D contains unripe taro in various stages of growth. Patch E has been wholly prepared for planting and contains a few plots of new taro shoots. Patch F is in process of being cleared and fenced; some trees have been felled and split for fence timbers, others have been laid on the ground to mark off plots, while still others have been strip-barked and left standing. The remaining plant rubbish is being piled and burned and the ashes scattered over the patch to enrich the soil.

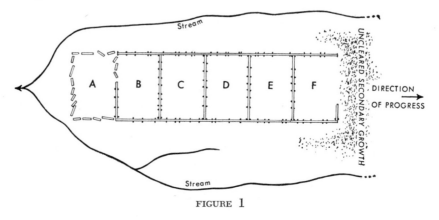

FIGURE 1

While Patch F is being cleared and fenced most efforts will be concentrated upon finishing that job; but on all other days the workers spend most of their time weeding and removing insects from Patches C and D. On all gardening days, however, before returning home a few plants are harvested from Patch C and their stalks piled up in Patch E ready for planting within the next day or so. Then natives load up with firewood by dismembering the fences or chopping up the dried trees left standing in Patch B.

Ideally this sequence will be continued as long as there is any suitable land adjoining the existing patches, and until an old patch is ready for reclaiming and planting. In hilly northeast Siuai, where suitable land is limited to the long and rather narrow interfluvial ridges, gardeners attempt to extend the patch-sequence in one direction until the old end-patch is ready for replanting (Fig. 2A). On more level terrain of central and southern Siuai the sequence follows a different pattern (Fig. 2B). In either case, natives judge that a place has lain fallow long enough when the trees on it are of a convenient size for fence-building (an interim of about six years). Their judgment might be a rationalization based upon convenience: it involves much less effort to clear land after six years than it does after three or seven or eight or more because there will be neither jungle undergrowth nor overlarge timbers to deal with, nor will there be a necessity for finding fence wood elsewhere. On the other hand, the natives' conception of the period of soil-replenishment might be empirically arrived at (I recorded several reports of crop failure due —according to informants—to gardeners not allowing land to remain idle long enough). Probably both of these factors are behind the native theory.

FIGURE 2

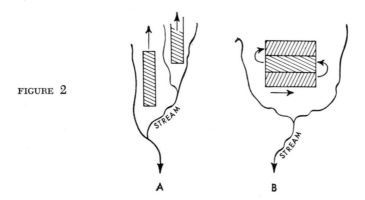

A   B

The *ideal* technique, in the northeast region, is to progress in one direction for about six years and then return to the starting point and begin again. For such a process each family would require a continuous strip of fertile land about 100 feet wide and about ¼ mile long. A mapping survey of northeast Siuai indicated that such an ideal is seldom realized. Some kind of barrier—either another household's garden or an effective natural or cultural boundary—usually gets in the way.

What sometimes happens is that each household has three or four gardens, as in Figure 3.

FIGURE 3

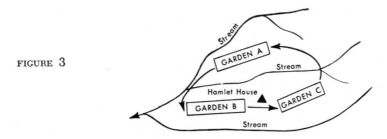

Garden A has been deserted for three or four years; it will be replanted when Garden C is completely cultivated.

Garden B is partly harvested (at the southwest), and there is a stand of ripe taro at the northeastern end.

Garden C is being cleared and fenced in now; the gardeners plant the stalks from Garden B in the southern end of Garden C.

Firewood is collected from the southwestern end of Garden B.

I spent many days in Siuai taro patches and became deeply impressed with the rhythmic efficiency of sequence-gardening. Given their implements—ax, machete, wooden rake, and digging stick—it would be difficult to devise a more efficient procedure which would also satisfy the need for strong fences. A steel-bladed hoe would probably speed up weeding, but more complex tools and chemical insecticides would not be feasible in terms of the present economy. I learned to appreciate the labor-saving economy of sequence-gardening particularly after watching the preparation of a patch out of sequence. It happened, as it not infrequently does, that a patch was prepared at an isolated site covered with jungle past the customary growth stage. Many of the larger trees on the site had to be felled and laboriously dragged clear of the patch to avoid shading the garden excessively, and many of the fence posts and some of the horizontal fence timbers had to be brought from elsewhere since trees of the proper size were not to be found on the site. Fence building in any case is hard work, but when heavy timbers must be carried long distances it is back-breaking, and natives so regard it. Nor do they risk failure by attempting to replant prematurely an old garden site; the thorny tangle of vines and bushes is difficult to clear and the resulting taro crop is likely to be anemic.

Fences vary in height and in thickness according to the location of the garden. Those bordering much-traveled paths are made high enough to block out the stares of strangers; those within a few hundred yards of bush-houses have to be built unusually thick and sturdy to withstand hungry domestic pigs—wild pigs being smaller and easier to fence out. It would therefore appear easier for men, who build the fences, to locate gardens farther away from settlements to permit easier fence construction. However, women have much to say about the location of gardens, and they try to avoid walking over-long distances laden, as they usually are, with crushing loads of firewood. Other factors affecting garden location will be described later on.

The taro patch is divided into plots (*nopu*) two spans wide by nine spans long (10 by 45 feet), with pathways left clear along the fences and between every two or three plots (Figure 4). These plots are marked off with logs laid on the ground, and have a number of functions. All the taro in any one plot (an average of 102 plants) is at very nearly the same stage of growth, and on the rare occasions when taro is sold the sale unit is the plot-full, which therefore provides a convenient and fairly uniform unit. Furthermore when pigs break into a patch and root up the growing plants the number of plots molested supplies a basis for indemnification —although an additional tort payment is nearly always assessed. Sociological purposes are also served by the plot layout; and I am tempted to point out—although it was never rationalized to me in these terms— that delineating plots with logs cut when clearing a patch saves having to drag the logs clear of the planting.

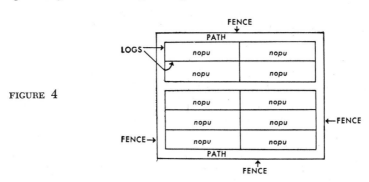

FIGURE 4

Taro occupies so prominent a place in Siuai life that one might appropriately go on for pages describing the numerous varieties grown; the exact details of planting, weeding, and harvesting; the high value placed upon it as *the* vegetable food; the feelings of deprivation natives express when they must go without it; the frequency with which it enters into conversation; the numerous metaphors for it and its use in ritual; etc. Some of this will be reported in later chapters; but rather than burden the reader with a long technical account, however justified that may be by the importance of the topic, I merely ask him to remember that Siuai natives spend more hours growing taro than in any other enterprise, that the plant comprises 80 per cent of their diet, and that it is the basis of their subsistence economy generally. If that is forgotten during consideration of more dramatic activities, then true perspective on Siuai life will have been lost.

In most taro patches natives also grow some tobacco, a dozen or so plantain and banana plants, and several yam and gourd vines trained up along the fences. Now and then one comes across a patch containing a few stalks of maize, some tomatoes, and a bush of tiny red peppers which are used as condiments. Few Siuai have yet acquired tastes for the recently introduced maize and tomatoes. Yams sometimes reach lengths of three and four feet and are pointed out as curiosities, but no special effort is made to produce or display them; because of their coarse, fibrous texture they are not rated highly as a food. Being easily roasted however they, along with plantains, are occasionally cooked and eaten as snacks by natives working in the gardens or lazing in the club-houses.

Sweet potatoes are second only to taro in Siuai diets. As their native name, *peteita*, indicates, they are of recent introduction, assertedly from Alu, but their use is expanding and even during our short stay potato acreages increased. Older people express some contempt for them, calling them pap: "children's food; not solid, strength-giving food like taro." In fact, they figure importantly only in the diets of households with mission-trained members. As a food crop sweet potatoes have several advantages: they will grow on sandy soil unsuited to taro, they require little care after planting, and they produce a higher yield per area. On the other hand they are more tempting to pigs and require sturdier fences than taro gardens do; it is said that pigs will exert greater effort to break into a sweet potato garden. Consequently natives do not waste labor by planting taro and potato in the same enclosure; in fact, they usually locate potato gardens in flood-plain valleys far away from settlements. Here, out of reach of domestic pigs, there is less danger of marauding; and if the gardener wishes to take the extra precaution of building a fence he has only to build on the landward side of a creek bend (Figure 5). Furthermore natives claim that the sandy alluvial soil is ideal for sweet potatoes.

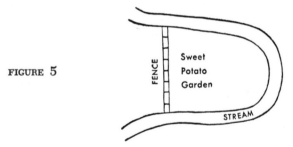

FIGURE 5

No Siuai meal is complete without a few slivers of coconut meat or a portion of coconut oil poured over the vegetables. For special feast dishes it is indispensable—being shredded and baked with sago or mixed with boiled taro, or used to "grease" food generally, and in other ways. But far more important is the coconut's everyday use as a light repast or thirst-quencher; except for water and broth it is a Siuai's only drink. One of the compensations for anthropologizing in coconut-land is the drink of cool, slightly sweet, tangy liquid from an unripe coconut; it is not only superbly refreshing but nutritious and energy-producing. For a combination meal and drink the Siuai prefer a nut in which meat has begun to form; after cracking it and allowing the liquid to guzzle down their throats they separate the two halves and scrape out slivers of soft meat. For a more solid snack they obtain a completely dry nut and eat not only the half-inch-thick layer of meat but the spongy kernel as well. There are no sex-bound restrictions on collecting coconuts, but young boys are the ones usually sent scurrying up a palm for them. When climbing a high palm they slip a short loop of light rope around both insteps and, using that to grip the trunk, pull themselves upward with their hands by means of short hops. Coconut are husked by jabbing them against a pointed stick stuck into the ground. Nut shredders are made of a shell or metal saw-toothed shredding blade attached to a wooden frame.

It is quite possible that some coconut palms might have "escaped" from cultivation and grown wild in parts of southern Bougainville; most of those we saw were clearly derived from native planting. If a few old palms are found standing in the wilderness, a little more searching or inquiry will establish that the place was formerly a settlement. Most palms are found near dwellings or immediately around club-houses, and show that not much thought has been given to spacing; but here and there one sees small and orderly groves. Indications are that new plantings are on the increase—stimulated partly by the Administration prescript that ten palms be planted for every newborn child, and partly by the ideas acquired at whites' plantations. There is no cash-income trade in coconuts—the only potential purchaser being a Chinese trader located on the coast one day's walk away; but judging by the frequency with which ambitious natives have to taboo their groves to accumulate nuts for feasts there is still an unfulfilled subsistence need for coconuts.

The breadfruit season lasts from early May to the middle of June and while it is in progress natives roast the fruit and eat it as a staple. It rots so quickly that it is usually eaten on the same day picked. Siuai distinguish between a large and a small variety, and prefer the latter. Most households own a few breadfruit trees and the fruit is eaten with evident enjoyment during the first few days of the season; soon however the novelty wears off and natives return to their favorite, taro. Informants tell of certain trees having been purposefully planted in past years, but I did not learn of any new plantings during our stay.

Canarium almonds leave a deeper impress on Siuai life. When they ripen, in late July and August, even garden work is forsaken for a few days to allow time for collecting nuts and extracting the kernels. Almond trees grow to heights of 100 feet or more and the nuts cluster on the outermost branches, with the result that picking them is a hazardous undertaking. Poles and ropes are used to climb the long distance to the first limbs, and then natives have to edge out to the branch ends to cut or twist loose the clusters of nuts. Now and then someone will fall, and this occasionally proves fatal.

The skill required and the danger involved add a zest to almond collecting which these usually phlegmatic natives seem to enjoy. Numbers of them will gather around a tree and yelp with admiration when a climber breaks off and drops a cluster from a topmost limb.

The kernel of a ripe canarium almond is about the size and shape of the Jordan almond. It is covered with a hard shell encased in a purplish fleshy hull. (Pigeons often eat the hull and discard the rest, littering the ground with the nuts which natives then collect.) Kernels are extracted by holding the nut on one stone and cracking it open with another. Then the kernels are either eaten whole and raw or mashed in a mortar and added to sago and taro puddings, or they may be smoked and packed away in bamboo or leaf containers for future eating or trade.

The seasonal growth of almonds, which constitute an indispensable ingredient for most special feast delicacies, results in the holding of most feasts in the months immediately succeeding nut-ripening. There is nothing inevitable about this feast cycling since properly smoked nuts will last a full year or more, but it is customary to consume the nuts within a few months after picking.

The Siuai seldom plant almond trees. They carefully avoid injuring them when clearing jungle, and build small protective fences around young trees, but the long interval between planting and fruiting appears to discourage systematic cultivation. Men will however plant a new tree to replace an old one that has to be cut to make way for a Government road.

Compared with the vast areas of sago palms found in New Guinea, the few small groves scattered around the marshy places of southern Bougainville appear quite insignificant. Nevertheless, these antediluvian, giant fern-like plants do have a number of important uses for the Siuai. The starch obtained from the pith of the trunk is a substitute food staple, fronds are the principal thatching material, the broad bases of branches are used as troughs, and rotting palm stumps crawl with choice edible grubs. Sago flour is obtained by felling the palm, stripping off its outer hull, shredding the pithy center, and washing out its starch into a wooden standing-trough. A bamboo-edged adze is the shredding tool; one of the tree's own branch bases and its vegetable matting serve as washing-trough and strainer. After starch has settled in the standing-trough the water is drained off and the flour packed into cylindrical-shaped leaf containers for storage.

I could not learn whether the Siuai purposely plant sago palms, and suspect not, but I have seen them erect a crude fence around a new plant to protect it from being crushed by pigs crowding around to devour grubs and gleanings of sour sago in old stumps.

During periods of mourning, when the Siuai forego gardening, or during times of continuous rainfall, when they do not like to go to their garden because of the danger of crossing swollen creeks or the difficulty of walking along slippery paths or the cold discomfort of working in wet and mud, they reluctantly fall back upon sago for their staple; otherwise they reserve that food for their travels because of the ease of carrying and roasting it.

COLLECTING, HUNTING, AND FISHING

In addition to the plants the Siuai grow or encourage to grow for food, they collect *hari* nuts, and many kinds of edible leaves, nuts, ferns, mushrooms, and fungi from the forest. Some of these wild foods are ordinary fare, others have special uses: for example, one kind of wild yam is a rare delicacy; "pig's-wife" fern is eaten only with pork; the leaf of the *surasia* tree is a delicacy used in invalids' broth. All such foods are used as relishes—not being "solid" like taro; they constitute only a small proportion (about 2 per cent by weight) of any ordinary meal.

When food staples become scarce as a result of crop failure and sago shortage, natives ward off starvation by collecting "wild" sago, wild yams, and wild taro, but such times are infrequent and only one such "Big Hunger" was recalled by my informants, who attributed it to a prolonged drought.

Salty condiments are used extensively and are considered indispensable for the domestic meal. Natives nearer the coast make a salt by evaporating salt water; those farther inland utilize the ashes of several plants. Salt ash is kept on the smoke rack over the hearth to increase its pungency.

Collecting edible insects is only an incidental activity—if natives see them they may try to catch them; there are no special implements involved. In addition to the sago grubs, which are regarded as a delicacy, the Siuai like to eat beetles, white ants—large and small—and certain kinds of spiders.

Hunting is less haphazard. Hunting for wild pigs is in fact a serious undertaking requiring skill, persistence, and some courage. Many Siuai take sporting pleasure in hunting, even though the booty is usually small. Wild pigs and opossums are the chief quarries, but natives will shoot at tree-rats, flying foxes, and birds if they see them reasonably close.

In southern Siuai natives may go for a year or more without eating wild pig, and during my fifteen-week residence in one northern village only two wild pigs were killed by my neighbors. In villages bordering the unbroken rain forests, however, pigs are hunted more frequently and successfully, and some residents keep packs of starving dogs for the purpose. One native I knew spent about a fifth of his working time in hunting and managed to bring in a pig or two a month.

The customary hunting method is for one man to start off with dogs and roam through the forest until the dogs find and run down an animal which is then killed by a long throwing spear made of hard limbum palm with either a plain fire-hardened point or a point of razor-sharp bamboo. (The more elaborate bone-pointed and decorated "fighting" spears are now reserved for mock battles and feasts.) Until recent years wild-pig drives involved up to a hundred men. A stockade was constructed ("like a garden fence, but not so strong"), then the hunters would unleash their dogs, form a wide circle, and converge on the stockade, rustling bushes, shouting and blowing on conch shells. Pigs driven into the stockade were then speared. Very large-scale and successful drives are said to have netted up to thirty pigs. If old tuskers were cornered they would usually attack their tormentors, and now and then a hunter or a dog would be maimed or even killed.

Opossum hunting is an adventurous outing. Two or more boys or men equip themselves with "camping" provisions—packets of sago and large quantities of betel-chewing supplies—and remain for two or three days in the forest capturing the little marsupials. After one is treed, sometimes with the help of dogs, a younger native will climb the tree and shake down the opossum while his companions wait on the ground to pounce on the stunned animal. Occasionally a live animal is brought home for a ceremony but more usually the animals are killed, eviscerated, cleaned, and smoked soon after capture. Liver, heart, and blood are promptly eaten, while the smoked carcass is usually put aside for some feast. Opossum hunters appear not to mind the short rations and rough living of the chase, but the Siuais' characteristic uneasiness about tree-climbing is apparent despite the climbers' bravado. The Siuai also set ingenious but rarely successful traps for opossum by rigging a trip-noose over an "opossum trail," a thick vine stretched between two likely trees.

Tree-rats are occasionally captured for food but I discovered few natives who had actually done so or eaten any caught by others. Soups made from flying foxes and flying mice are favorite though infrequent fare, and natives spend hours manufacturing the special four-pronged barbed arrows used in hunting these creatures. They also value their wing bones for making spear and arrow barbs.

Fishing is also an occasional pastime with many Siuai but does not add significantly to their diets. One often sees a solitary male searching for fish and eels with his bow and arrow up and down a stream, hopeful but rarely successful. Or, once a fortnight or so, women and girls will spend a few hours wading in a stream searching by hand for prawns that may hide under ledges and roots. Almost everywhere large and small basket-traps are manufactured and left in likely spots—nearly every two or three hundred feet of a stream's course will harbor one; but these remain empty for weeks at a time, and word of a catch becomes a lively conversation topic in the neighborhood. In addition to these individual and spasmodic attempts to catch fish, natives sometimes—as often as two or three times a year in communities bordering large creeks—engage in coöperative fish drives. One technique is to select a spot where the creek divides around an island, divert the water from one stream by damming, and then proceed to shoot or capture the fish and prawns left floundering in pools in the dry stream bed. In one such fish drive I witnessed, about eighty natives took part and about two hundred pounds of fish plus several hundred prawns were caught. A second large-scale fishing technique involves the use of a long seine-net carried through the wider river pools by a score or more men. Seines are made from dried and shredded bark, and are usually manufactured by several specialists working together. There were only three of these large seine-nets in all northeast Siuai during my stay, and not a single seine-drive took place.

ANIMAL HUSBANDRY

Pig-raising is vastly more important than hunting and fishing in Siuai economy. Nearly every household owns at least one pig, and most average three or four.

Domesticated pigs are fed once a day, during the late afternoon, and the rest of the time they are allowed to run free and forage. According to natives' belief, based apparently on experience, a full-grown pig must be given five to six pounds of food daily in order for it to remain properly domesticated. If fed less it will break through the strongest of fences and devour garden produce, or wander farther from home and invade the less protected potato gardens, or, worse still, it will run wild altogether in the forest. A proper diet for pigs, the Siuai consider, must be balanced and cooked like their own: a boiled taro or potato base, a portion of cooked greens, and some coconut meat. When preparing their own meals natives usually remove thick slices of peeling from taro or potatoes and cook the peel along with some taro tips for their pigs, but sometimes they feed them whole corms or tubers. This feeding is carried out with painstaking care, every animal receiving its portion on a separate basket-tray. Fully domesticated pigs do not have to be called for their daily meal; they return to the dwelling in midafternoon and clamor for it, and often remain nearby all night.

No attempt is made to pen grown pigs until they are held awaiting slaughter. At home, although the larger animals are kept outside the house, they are encouraged to stay nearby, this of course being possible only in the scattered hamlet residences, the "pig-food" houses, and not in the palisaded line villages prescribed by the Administration.

Some care is given to breeding, and a good boar is considered a very valuable resource. Sows usually farrow in thickets near their owners' dwellings; when that happens the owners close all paths to the spot and take the precaution of barring dogs. Young pigs are kept in pens alongside the dwellings; until the animals are domesticated enough to remain near home and large enough to fend for themselves, their owners believe it necessary to stay nearby at least part of each day; otherwise young animals become "lonely," natives say. During the first few months of their lives young pigs are cared for like the pets they are; their food is cooked in the pot along with their owners', and one often sees women premasticate a lump of taro or potato for sickly young animals.

It will be described later on how pigs are ritually named, "baptized," and magically treated for ailments. Here it should merely be noted that young male shoats are gelded without ceremony, as a purely practical measure—"to make them grow." Gelding is carried out with a knife (formerly with a splinter of bamboo) by splitting open the scrotum and removing the testicles. Natives take great interest in this operation and even children are allowed to try it. Pigs are also "branded" by cutting chips out of their ears; this is not an ownership mark but does serve to distinguish domestic from wild pigs. Additional ways of distinguishing between wild and domestic pigs are known to nearly all natives. Wild pigs are smaller, thinner, quicker, more malodorous, pure "razorback"; domesticated pigs are the result of mixing native with European breeds, the latter having been introduced within recent decades by laborers returning home from white colonists' coconut plantations. Before the introduction of European strains, wild pigs were probably not very different from domestic ones—thinner and tougher, perhaps, but probably the same breed. Later on, when Siuai youths finished their terms of indenture on whites' plantations, many of them invested their earnings in European pigs and proudly carried them back home. Older natives recall those times with feeling: how great was the excitement that prevailed upon first sight of the superior animals and how longingly every adult tried to obtain one of its offspring. Disdain for the native breed, including the wild pigs, became so marked that hunting was thereby discouraged. It is certainly obvious that the new mix-breed animal is a great improvement in size and succulence over the old; but it is not all gain, for natives also state that the domesticated native pig stayed nearer home, hence did not menace gardens located farther away than a few hundred yards. It is even claimed by some older informants that during their fathers' childhoods gardens did not require fencing. Whether that be true or not, and I suspect not, the new mixed breeds possibly do rove farther afield and, being larger, probably do require sturdier garden fencing.

Killing and butchering a pig is man's work and most men can butcher quite skillfully. Some men prefer to kill an animal by strangling it—by bending its head to one side to cut off respiration. This is the tidier and more economical method because there is less loss of blood; it is used in killing a pig while a ceremony is going on. At other times the animal is killed by having its lungs caved in and heart crushed with a few hard blows of an ax-butt; this is the quicker method. When the animal is dead —or thought to be near enough dead—it is fastened to a pole and hung over a fire for singeing. After this, soot and burnt hair are scraped away with a knife and the butcher sets to work cutting the animal into twelve longitudinal strips. During the butchering the gullet is knotted near the head in order to prevent the contents of the stomach from spilling over the animal. Blood is highly valued, and is scooped up from the body cavity and placed in containers—either to be drunk at once or made into a pudding. The heart is roasted and is regarded as a great delicacy. Belly fat is also carefully saved, mixed with blood, and cooked in a pot. No attempt however is made to retain stomach or intestines.

Every settlement contains a few fowl, which fend for themselves by stealing food leavings and catching insects. They hide their eggs in the scrub, but most natives do not care for eggs anyway. Only on rare occasions do the Siuai kill and eat one of these athletic birds.

Dogs are also to be found in every settlement—almost in every house. A few of these wretched rail-thin creatures are used in hunting but the rest serve only as pets, if that is the proper word to describe the lot of these half-starved, continually kicked animals. Some households also keep a cat or two for rat-catching and for the amusement of children, and now and then natives capture and keep a cockatoo.

COOKING AND EATING

The Siuai domestic meal, the one full meal of the day, seldom varies in its main outlines: for each individual past early childhood a basic portion of three or four pounds of taro or sweet potato, along with a helping of cooked greens flavored with salt or coconut oil and, now and then, some small taste of relish—meat, fish, grubs, or other delicacy. Sometimes plantains or yams are substituted as staples for taro and sweet potato, but as already indicated they are regarded as second best, most adults insisting that taro alone gives them the feeling of stuffed satiation which should accompany every satisfactory meal. Sago is another substitute, usually eaten with the domestic meal only when some other staple is not available. Invalids are usually given vegetable or meat soups.

The Siuai vary their cooking methods with the occasion. Working in the gardens, hunting in the forests, or traveling far from home, they assuage hunger by simply roasting a plantain, a yam, or a leaf packet of sago on an open hearth. On special occasions they wrap their vegetables and relishes in leaves and bake them by covering them with hot coals. Or more elaborately, they dig a pit and place in it packets of leaf-wrapped food surrounded by hot stones; this is the favorite manner of cooking but it is laborious and hence used only for feasts. The daily meal of the household is cooked by steaming and boiling. A clay pot is wedged upright between stones on the hearth and into the pot are poured a few inches of water. Then it is filled to the brim with chunks of taro and potatoes, unpeeled plantains, small packets of greens, and any other supplement available; a covering of large leaves is fixed tightly over the top; and the pot is allowed to boil and steam until the starchy staples have reached a consistency which most Americans would find slightly underdone. This means that any meat cooked in the same pot is far tougher than stone-baked meat, and the Siuai recognize its inferiority, but the morsels of home-cooked meat are usually so minute that, natives reason, they are hardly worth while baking. Cooks sometimes use pointed sticks to test whether food is properly cooked, but usually they gauge—or more frequently misgauge—the time by some measure I was unable to fathom and proceed to spear out the food into basket-trays. Onto each tray are placed several chunks of starchy staple, a plantain or two, a helping of greens mixed with oil, a few slivers of coconut meat, and a tidbit of the day's special relish. The solid food is then eaten by hand and washed down by drinks of broth or coconut milk. Then, after eating, comes the betel-chewing and the pipe of tobacco.

Siuai natives chew the betel mixture frequently and smoke almost continually. The betel mixture consists of areca nuts, collected from purposefully planted palms, along with catkins taken from a pepper tree, and lime obtained by burning shells collected on the southern beaches. One variety of areca nut is said to be strongly narcotic but I never noticed any native visibly affected. The Siuai say that betel-chewing staves off hunger, but they also chew it immediately after meals just for its pleasant taste. Native tobacco is smoked in trade-store pipes. It is grown in their gardens along the fences, and although some of it is sun- and smoke-dried before use, these inveterate and hardy smokers often pick a green leaf, "cure" it over a smoky fire for a minute or two, and smoke it forthwith.

9. THE ENERGY THEORY OF CULTURAL DEVELOPMENT *

Changes in technology are much more easy to describe and quantify than changes in polity or religious belief or ideas of beauty. Technological changes also have the advantage of leaving relatively clear evidence of their occurrence—to a considerable extent the archeological record deals with technology. For these reasons, if no other, technological change has often been used as the prime criterion of progress and cultural evolution. It is fatal to confuse these two things, however, since progress demands a kind of evaluation that inevitably compromises objectivity while cultural evolution is theoretically non-evaluative and therefore thoroughly objective. There are many anthropologists who feel that there is no suitable way of applying evolutionary theory to culture. As cultural relativists they ask for the analysis of individual cultures in terms of the culture itself; comparisons illustrate differences, they say, and do not furnish a basis for any hierarchical arrangement. Fundamentally, the relativists deny that any particular aspect of culture, such as technology, has any greater coercive effect on the rest of culture than any other aspect. For this reason, they argue, a developmental sequence of technological changes need not be accompanied by a comparable sequence of changes in other facets of culture.

To the extent that archeology illuminates this problem, it indicates that there has indeed been an evolution of technology. More than that, it indicates an evolution of such aspects of social organization as settlement pattern and population density. Extrapolation to other aspects of society offers a further degree of confirmation. A similar position may be developed with regard to ethnology.

* Leslie A. White, "The Energy Theory of Cultural Development," in K. M. Kapadia (Ed.), *The Ghurye Felicitation Volume* (Bombay: Popular Book Depot, 1954), pp. 1–10. Reprinted by permission of the author.

One of the most forthright of evolutionists, Leslie White has stated in
several ways his hypothesis of the role of energy utilization in cultural
evolution. Here is an example of his approach from a volume
published in India.

$\mathbf{B}$Y *culture* we mean the organization of tools, utensils, language,
customs, institutions, rituals, paraphernalia, beliefs, sentiments, attitudes,
etc., that every people possesses. *Culture* is the name of a distinct class
of phenomena: things and events dependent upon man's unique ability
to symbol.

The function of culture is to serve the needs of man: to provide him
with food and other materials from his habitat, to provide shelter from
the elements and defense from his enemies, to divert him with art, to
give him courage and consolation in the crises of life, and so on. In
short, the function of culture is to make life secure and continuous for
the human species, and, if possible, to make it seem significant and worth
while.

Everything that a cultural system does requires energy, whether it
be catching or cooking a fish, weaving a basket, performing a ritual, observing a custom, entertaining a belief, or uttering a silent prayer. Every
event that takes place in the universe, whether it be physical, biological,
or cultural, is an expression of energy, an instance of energy transformation. All cultural systems, therefore, like all physical and biological systems, can be reduced to a common denominator: energy. Energy is a
universal dimension of culture.

An appreciation of the energy character of culture can be enhanced
by a consideration of biological organisms. According to the Second
Law of Thermodynamics, the universe is breaking down structurally,
running down dynamically. Every event that takes place means an increase in entropy, i.e., an increase of disorder, a more random distribution of material particles, a more diffuse distribution of energy. But living organisms are able successfully to oppose this drift toward increasing entropy. More than this, they have been able to move in a direction
opposite to that specified for the cosmos as a whole by the Second Law.
That is, they have been able to develop more complex structures and
greater concentrations of energy. We call this process biological evolution. How, then, have individual organisms been able to maintain themselves as living systems against the constant attrition of increasing entropy, and how have phyla, genera, and species succeeded in developing
higher forms? How has it been possible for them to swim upstream
against the cosmic flow toward increasing entropy? The answer is, by

capturing free energy. The living organism balances the increases of entropy—positive entropy—that accrue from the process of living, with negative entropy drawn from its environment. The organism is a system through which energy flows, entering the system at higher potentials, leaving it at lower potentials. Thus the organism is able to maintain itself by taking advantage of the cosmic flow of energy downward. And certain species have been able not merely to offset entropy increase of day to day living with "orderliness sucked from their environment" (Schrödinger), but actually to develop more complex structures and higher energy potentials.

We may now understand culture in relation to life: it is an extra-somatic mechanism for capturing free energy, harnessing it, and putting it to work in the service of the human species.

A cultural system does something: it serves human needs. The functions of a cultural system require energy. The amount of energy harnessed by a cultural system within a given period of time is always finite and measurable. The things accomplished by a cultural system, the degree of development of a culture, is proportional to the amount of energy harnessed and put to work, other factors being constant. Culture develops, therefore, as the amount of energy harnessed and put to work per capita per year is increased.

Energy is harnessed culturally with technological means. Social systems and idea systems are functions of technological systems; the latter is the independent variable, the former the dependent variables. Culture evolves in its sociological and ideological aspects, therefore, as it develops technologically.

The first cultural systems were activated by energy derived from the human organism, and for some 990,000 of the million years that have elapsed since man and culture began the human body was virtually their sole source of energy, since fire, wind, and water were extremely insignificant in this respect. The accomplishments of such cultural systems—which is also to say their degree of development—were extremely meager because the amount of energy harnessed and put to work per capita per year was very small—about one-twentieth of one horsepower per capita. All cultures activated exclusively (or virtually exclusively) by human energy have been, as they must be, crude, meager, and of a low degree of development. For culture to evolve, to develop higher and better forms, judged from the standpoint of serving human needs, the amount of energy harnessed and put to work per capita per year must be increased, other factors remaining constant.

After hundreds of thousands of years some cultural systems devised ways of harnessing solar energy—and all life and culture are dependent upon energy from the sun—in new forms and in larger amounts. These new techniques were agriculture and animal husbandry. These arts are, literally, ways of laying hold of forms and magnitudes of solar energy, and of utilizing them as such, just as hydroelectric plants are ways of harnessing solar energy in the form of flowing water. A great and rapid increase of cultural development followed quickly upon the heels of the cultivation of plants and the domestication of animals. The great civilizations of ancient Egypt, Mesopotamia, India, and China, of aboriginal Mexico, Mesoamerica, and Peru were brought quickly into being by these new ways of harnessing solar energy.

Animals were put to operating machinery—in addition to drawing plows and vehicles—shortly before the beginning of the Christian era. And the water wheel came into use at about the same time. The windmill appears in western Europe about the twelfth century A.D., although it may have been used earlier in the near Orient. Solar energy stored up in coal was harnessed practically in the eighteenth century with the development of the steam engine, and oil-energy resources were tapped in the nineteenth century with the development of internal combustion engines. The energy of the nucleus of the atom has been harnessed in our own day. Thus, culture has developed, has advanced from the most primitive levels to the highest cultures of today, as a consequence of harnessing and putting to work energy in larger amounts. The Agricultural Revolution and the Fuel Revolution have been the two great advances of culture that have elevated mankind from savagery to civilization. And we may be sure that the course of culture in the future, as in the past, will be determined by the ways and the magnitudes in which energy is harnessed and expended, whether destruction and chaos or world peace and plenty be the outcome.

As early as 1833, in the first edition of his *Outlines of Astronomy*, Sir John Herschel noted that "the sun's rays are the ultimate source of almost every motion which takes place on the surface of the earth." Their "vivifying action," he observes, brings forth and sustains all life. He included coal and the consequences of its use among the products of solar radiation. George Stephenson (1781–1848), the great pioneer in the development of the steam locomotive, was "one of the first," according to Herbert Spencer, "to recognize the fact that the force impelling his locomotive originally came from the sun." And Spencer himself clearly recognized in *First Principles* the solar source of all socio-cultural, as well as vital, forces. In 1886, the Austrian physicist, Ludwig Botlzmann (1844–1906), applied the Second Law of Thermodynamics to the life process: the struggle for existence is a struggle for free energy.

An American physicist, Joseph Henry (1797–1878), the first secretary of the Smithsonian Institution, presented an energy theory of cultural development in 1873, outlining stages of evolution in terms of harnessing energy in increasing magnitudes and in various forms.

The great German chemist, Wilhelm Ostwald (1853-1932), winner of a Nobel prize, developed an elaborate and comprehensive theory of "energetics" which included an energy theory of cultural development. The "history of civilization," he says, "becomes the history of man's advancing control over energy . . . the objective characteristic of [cultural] progress consists in improved methods for seizing and utilizing the raw energies of nature for human purposes."

A distinguished British physicist, Frederick Soddy (1877—), also a Nobel prize winner, asserted that "the laws expressing the relations between energy and matter are not solely of importance in pure science [i.e., physics]. They necessarily come *first in order . . . in the whole record of human experience,* and *they control, in the last resort, the rise or fall of political systems, the freedom or bondage of nations, the movements of commerce and industry, the origin of wealth and poverty, and the general physical welfare of the race*" (emphasis ours).

Robert A. Millikan (1868—), an American physicist and Nobel prize winner, has expressed an energy theory of cultural development, in brief and partial form at least. Erwin Schrödinger (1887—), also a Nobel prize winning physicist, is "convinced that this Law [i.e., the Second Law of Thermodynamics] governs all physical and chemical processes, even if they result in the most intricate and tangled phenomena, such as organic life, the genesis of a complicated world of organisms from primitive beginnings, [and] *the rise and growth of human cultures* (emphasis ours)."

We find an interesting and sound statement of the energy theory of cultural development in a *Catalog of the Mechanical Collections of the Division of Engineering, U. S. National Museum,* by Frank A. Taylor, an engineer. "Throughout history," he says, "the changing pattern of society has been determined to a large degree by the progress made in exploiting the natural energy resources of the world. . . ." UNESCO has recently issued a brochure, "Energy as the Key to Social Evolution," by W. Tiraspolsky, a mining engineer. Martin Ruhemann, a British physicist, presents a graphic statement of the energy theory of cultural development in his chapter, "Power and Civilization," in his compact and excellent little book, *Power.* Two papers presented recently before the British Association for the Advancement of Science deal with the development of civilization in terms of utilization of energy: (1) "Man's Use of Energy," a presidential address by Sir Harold Hartley, a physical chemist, and (2) "Civilization and the Use of Energy," by Sir Alfred Egerton, also a chemist.

Thus we see that the energy theory of cultural development is not new by any means; it has received explicit expression repeatedly for decades. It is significant to note, however, that most of the statements of this theory have come from men in the physical and chemical sciences rather than from workers in the social sciences.

Some of the early anthropologists held an energy theory of cultural evolution even though this theory may not have been systematically formulated nor very explicitly set forth. Cultivated cereals were the "great moving power of civilization," according to E. B. Tylor. He speaks of "that immense change which is remodelling modern life, by inventions which set the forces of nature to do man's heavy work for him." It was "a great movement in civilization," he observes, "for the water-mill and its companion contrivance the wind-mill to come into use as force-providers . . . [And] within the last century the civilized world has been drawing an immense supply of power from a new source, the coal burnt in the furnace of the steam-engine. . . ."

The energy theory of cultural development was at least implicit in the work of Lewis H. Morgan (1818–1881). Cultural systems rested upon control over the means of subsistence, and their development was brought about by an "enlargement of the means of subsistence" as a consequence of inventions and discoveries.

Léon Winiarski, a European sociologist, treated human societies in terms of energy. He discusses social systems in terms of the First and Second Laws of Thermodynamics, and uses differential equations to describe certain social processes. But for all this he seems merely to present social system as analogous to physical systems, to describe them in the language of physics, rather than to apply physical concepts to gain new insights and understandings of socio-cultural systems.

Two American economists, T. N. Carver and Simon N. Patten, treat the economic process in society—the production and consumption of goods—in terms of energy: there is a transformation "from goods to energy and from energy back to goods." But they appear not to be concerned with the development of culture in general.

The Adams brothers, Brooks and Henry, American historians, have much to say about energy in their discussions of society and culture. The latter discourses easily about electrons, "astronomical or electric mass," the second law of thermodynamics, etc. But both men merely use the vocabulary of physics; it would be a mistake to confuse their pseudo-scientific musings with a genuine thermodynamic conception of culture.

[In August, 1955, the McGraw-Hill Book Company published *Energy and Society*, The Relation between Energy, Social Change and Economic Development, by W. Frederick Cottrell, Professor of Government and Sociology at Miami University, Oxford, Ohio.]

The concept of energy is probably the most fundamental concept in all science. It is as applicable to cultural and to biological systems as it is to physical phenomena. Reality is one and science is one though many-sided. It is the concept of energy that relates the science of culture to the biological and physical sciences. The basic function of cultural and biological systems is revealed in the concept of energy: capturing, harnessing, and utilizing energy. It is the concept of energy that illuminates the structure and behavior of cultural systems, and shows us how and why they evolve.

In view of the fundamental character of the concept of energy and of the possibilities of its fruitful application in the science of culture, it is rather remarkable to note how little attention it has received in contemporary anthropology. To be sure, there has been much work in ethnology during the past few decades that is not incompatible with a thermodynamic conception of culture, and some that is quite in harmony with it. Clark Wissler characterized the present stage of cultural development as "the age of coal." And the late George Grant MacCurdy expressed the energy conception of culture very clearly: "The degree of civilization of any epoch . . . is measured by ability to utilize energy for human advancement. . . ." Grahame Clark, a British archeologist, uses amount of energy harnessed as a criterion of cultural development in *From Savagery to Civilization:* "The low cultural status of savage societies can best be illustrated by considering the amount of energy at their disposal . . . In modern terms the total output of energy in savage Europe at any one time probably never exceeded that of a single four-engined bomber." The energy conception of culture is both explicit and implicit in much of the work of V. Gordon Childe.

But one has only to browse through the literature of anthropology during the last few decades to see how little attention this basic conception has received. There has been much concern with the psyches of primitive peoples; they have been probed with Rorschach and other psychological tests. "Basic personality structure" has become, for some, the basis and motive force of cultural systems. The behavior of nations and even empires has been interpreted in terms of experiences of individual citizens in infancy, particularly those of nursing, weaning, swaddling, and toilet training. Inventions have grown out of personal conflicts of frustrated or maladjusted persons. "Religion and to a lesser extent magic" have been termed "the very foundation of culture." Divine creation, revelation, and original sin find a place in the work of Father Wilhelm Schmidt, the leader of a prominent school of ethnology. And the official organ of the American Anthropological Association recently carried an article assuring us that "man, under God, controls his own cultural destiny."

But we have more than mere indifference to or neglect of an energy theory of cultural development. There has been no little hostility to it. Many years ago Wilhelm Ostwald remarked upon the extent and vigor of attacks upon his theory of energetics. Recently a leading French anthropologist, Claude Lévi-Strauss, commented upon the present writer's criterion of cultural development in terms of amount of energy harnessed as follows: "on voit mal comment procéder a cette détermination pour l'immense majorité des sociétés humaines, où la catégorie proposée parait, au surplus, totalement dénuée de signification." Bernard Mishkin regards "phrasing the laws of culture in terms of the science of thermodynamics" as an "old fallacy." And there is opposition elsewhere, also. We are confident, however, that basic and fruitful concepts will eventually be accepted and exploited. After all, the science of culture is still very young.

10. BEFORE THE MACHINE *

Melville Herskovits is among those who contest evolutionism
as applied to culture because of its deterministic implications. Concluding
that such concepts as "primitive" or "preliterate" reflect invidious
distinctions based on ethnocentric attitudes, he prefers to restrict cultural
contrasts to specific features rather than making blanket statements about
levels of development or complexity.
In line with this attitude, the author of this selection recognizes
differences in economic organization between, he says, machine and
non-machine cultures. But the differences are invariably quantitative
rather than qualitative; in other words, the fundamental institutions of
modern economy are perceptible, if embryonic, in non-literate cultures.

1

Though man has inhabited the earth for more than half a million
years, the invention of the steam engine, which introduced the machine
age, occurred less than two hundred years ago. In this mere instant, as
the life of the human race is counted, the machine has come to hold a
place of such importance in present-day America and Europe that it is
not easy for us to imagine a machineless existence.

* Melville J. Herskovits, *Economic Anthropology* (New York: Alfred A. Knopf,
1952), Chapter 2, "Before the Machine," pp. 25–41. Reprinted by permission of the
author and publisher.
Professor of Anthropology at Northwestern University, Melville J. Herskovits (b.
1895), a pioneer in introducing studies of African culture in the United States, has
made his department a center of African research. He and his wife have done fieldwork in Africa, South America and the Caribbean. Herskovits has also taken and
maintains an active role in theoretical controversy. Among his books are: *The Myth
of the Negro Past* (1941); *Man and His Works* (1948), *Cultural Anthropology* (1955),
Dahomey (1938) and volumes written in collaboration with (Mrs.) Frances Herskovits,
including *Rebel Destiny* (1934) and *Trinidad Village* (1947).

Yet for much of mankind the machine holds little significance. Even in America and in Europe, where the influence of a mechanized technology invades all phases of life, quiet backwaters still exist where farming folk or village communities live lives relatively little touched by the machine. More important are the untold millions who today follow patterns of life almost entirely different from those by which we order our lives and who, in the Americas, the South Seas, Australia, Asia, and Africa meet their needs without the use of any of those complex mechanical aids we hold essential.

The term "primitive" has been applied to most of these folk. Because with but few exceptions, they have developed no written language, the word thus became synonymous with "nonhistoric" or "nonliterate." These terms, however, are actually to be preferred because they do not carry the connotations of inferiority, simplicity, and lack of sophistication that have come to cluster about the word "primitive," and thus to obscure its meaning. Such large differences are, indeed, to be found among nonliterate societies that to characterize them in any general manner is exceedingly difficult. Every institution shows a tremendously wide range of variation in its "primitive" manifestations. It has therefore become a truism that there is no generic difference between "primitive" societies and literate ones, but that, the world over, all cultures represent specialized local developments which have come into being as a result of the unique historical developments that, as was pointed out in the preceding chapter, mark the past of each of them.

This being the case, we may find it worth while to sketch the characteristics of the nonliterate societies that justify us in marking them off for special study. We will, in particular, consider those traits that will occupy us in contrasting and comparing their economics with those of the literate, machine cultures.

At the outset, we are struck by the differences in population size between "primitive" and literate groups. This is true not only where density is concerned, but in the numbers of those who make up the self-conscious social entities which we variously designate as "band" or "tribe" or "kingdom." Another difference between nonliterate and literate folk lies in the respective degree of contact they have with the outside world. In supplying their wants, what the nonliterate tribesman could obtain "was usually near at hand," as it has been put. On the other hand, "the whole world . . . contributes to our needs. A complicated business organization makes this possible, one that stands out in marked contrast to the simple system" of these folk. Even in pre-machine days in Europe, or in the non-machine but literate cultures of Asia, the range of communication and the consequent breadth of horizon of these peoples were and are in general greater than those of an African or a North American Indian tribe, or even, for all their voyaging, of the inhabitants of the Polynesian islands. Literate societies, as we have seen, also manifest a greater degree of specialization of labor, a greater emphasis on the market and on a standard medium of exchange—money—as an expression of value to facilitate market operations, and a resultant greater economic complexity than do nonliterate communities.

The machine, however, most highly developed in the cultures of North America and Europe, has been the outstanding factor in accentuating all those characteristics of an economic order that have been mentioned as distinguishing the lives of literate from nonliterate peoples. The implications of the machine for human society are therefore greatest in these cultures, and it is between these machine cultures and all others, especially the nonliterate ones, that the differences are widest. That is why, at the outset, the role of the machine must be emphasized as a factor in differentiating their life from ours.

2

In considering the influence of the machine in our lives, we must constantly bear in mind the effect the technological perfections that have gone with its development, the greater degree of productivity these have permitted, and the changes they have wrought in the economic sphere have had on some of the more important currents of thought of our day. Especially important is the fact that the achievements of the machine are objectively demonstrable, from which it follows that technological and economic gains can most readily be used when evaluating different cultures. The mechanistic philosophy of our day, when raised in the field of method to a tradition of objective observation, is readily contrasted with the mystical elements in the technology and economic order of nonliterate societies.

This is one of the principal reasons why the identification of the word "primitive" with the concept "lower" as regards social development—or its converse, the use of "civilized" in the sense of something "higher"—has been so convincing and, as expressed in the term "progress," has come to lodge so deeply in our everyday manner of thought. Here is the apparent documentation of the ethnocentrism that makes the appreciation of the values of other cultures than our own so difficult. Descriptions of our technological achievement and the multiple interrelations of our economic organization can seemingly be employed to demonstrate the more complex nature of our culture as compared with the cultures of all other peoples, especially of nonliterate folk. That such a demonstration has had so great an appeal and has been so difficult to dislodge from the popular mind is not strange. It was such an assumption that gave the attempts to establish an evolutionary sequence for human civilizations their greatest psychological force. For from this point of view—but this point of view only—the Australians could be regarded beyond question as a simpler people than the Africans; or the Africans could be demonstrably shown to be on a lower level of culture than the great aggregates that peopled Central America, Mexico, and Peru at the time of the discovery of America; or these latter, in turn, could without fear of contradiction be held less highly developed than ourselves.

In the same way, the concept of progress, so deeply rooted in our habits of thought, has derived its most important sanctions from demonstrations in the field of technology and economics. That a man, working with a machine, can produce more in given units of time with a given expenditure of energy than when working by hand, is not difficult to prove. It is not so easy, however, to show that one set of religious beliefs is more adequate than another, or one type of family organization more effective than the next. Here the validation of judgment must derive from assumptions that lie quite outside objective proof. Even in the economic and technological spheres the argument couched in terms of relative powers of productivity is by no means self-evident when the ultimate ends toward which such activities are directed—as against the values that guide day-to-day living—come to be analyzed. In all societies, that is, the technological and economic order must at least be efficient enough to permit survival. Granting this, we know enough about the psychology of culture to understand that the satisfaction of human wants is by no means dependent upon an abundance of goods. Increased efficiency in production is likewise not necessarily accompanied by a corresponding efficiency in achieving an effective distribution of what the technological system is capable of producing.

It is not alone in evaluating societies as a whole that the machine has shaped our thought. Certain concepts respecting the psychology of nonliterate peoples have been influenced by that phase of our culture which is to be broadly included under the term "science." The scientific tradition, and the nature of the problems with which scientists deal, require that every effort be made to reason from cause to effect, to work under conditions of rigid control, eliminating extraneous factors that might influence the result of any given experiment. It is not generally understood, however, that this technique, which marks scientific thinking, is by no means characteristic of the reasoning of most persons in our society, nor even of scientists in their everyday life. Yet despite this, these particular modes of thought have given rise to a concept which maintains that our ways of thinking differ from those of "primitive" peoples, who are held to be prelogical. Without a tradition of reasoning from cause to effect, they are held to be enmeshed in a body of "collective representations," in which the mechanical relationship between effectuating forces and their objective results is lost in a maze of mystic associations. Life is thus lived in a world where reality, as we know it, constitutes but a portion of valid experience.

We need here do no more than enter a demurrer to this position, for many refutations of it have been written out of the first-hand experience of those who have studied nonliterate societies. The significant thing for us is to realize how a mode of thought, closely associated with the basic technological process of our culture, can be rationalized as a habit of thinking presumably followed by all those who live in this machine society, as against the habits of all who do not.

Another instance of how pervasive the indirect influence of the machine has been may be introduced here, though some of its implications for our subject will be treated at length in later pages. This concerns the theory of economic determinism. The increased productivity of our technology and the accompanying complexity of economic organization has resulted in a corresponding increase in the interdependence of individuals and communities. But it was just when the industrial revolution was at its height, and the economic problems presented by it had attained an order of difficulty perhaps never before experienced, that this theory in its present form, was developed. It seems, therefore, that there might well be a discernible relationship between a point of view that holds economic phenomena to be basic in shaping other aspects of life and the historical setting of the period during which this concept was developed.

There can be little doubt that economic factors do play an important role in influencing non-economic aspects of culture; but this merely recognizes the fact that all phases of life are closely interrelated and, because of this, tend to modify each other. In these terms, ours is by no means the only culture where economic factors are preponderant in influencing the other facets of culture. Yet it does remain an historic fact that it was only among a people—ourselves—whose economy had become more complex than any before experienced by man, and at a time when the problems presented by the economic order were becoming most serious, that this theory made its appearance.

We must, then, be on our guard against a position that fails to take due account of modes of life other than our own, or which disregards directive forces other than those that to us appear to be of the first magnitude. Above all, we must guard against thinking of all the cultures of nonliterate peoples as one undifferentiated mass, to be contrasted with our own particular body of traditions. These reservations must be kept in mind in recognizing that the machine has made it possible for us to live in an order of society which, in its economic aspects, is to be set apart from all others because of its complexity. Only with these reservations can we achieve a workable basis for the analysis of the problems to be considered in this book. We may, therefore, in these terms, proceed to sketch the more outstanding of these distinctions. For though, in most instances, they will be found to comprise differences of degree rather than of kind, we must analyze them so that we will not lose sight of them as we later describe and seek to understand the economic processes employed by nonliterate communities.

3

The relationship between the machine technology and the pecuniary organization of our economy has by no means been made clear. Yet it is apparent that this relationship has given rise to certain special kinds of economic phenomena, such as the business cycle, and the periodic unemployment that has followed on technological advances. These phenomena are the direct result of the increased productivity of the machine, coupled with a system whereby the sale of goods for profit as a technique for amassing wealth has become an end rather than a means in life. This entire complex operates so as to deprive many persons of an opportunity to obtain the basic necessities of living, no matter how willing they may be to work or how able.

Such conditions are unknown to nonliterate man. These smaller groups may live on a level but little removed from subsistence needs, where the margin between starvation and survival is slight. Yet even in such societies, the individual who, as an individual, is reduced to such straits that he must either depend on some agency set up for the purpose of preventing his giving way before the harsh dicta of the economic system, or starve, is rarely, if ever, encountered. In societies existing on the subsistence margin, rather, it is generally the rule that when there is not enough, all hunger alike; when there is plenty, all participate.

This does not mean that in cultures where the margin of available goods is greater than in those existing on such a low economic plane, an equal distribution of available resources exists. Practically all societies where life is lived on more than a subsistence level know the concepts of rich and poor, of leader and follower. But even in societies with relatively complex economies, such as those of West Africa and Melanesia, where buying to sell at a profit is of some importance and the hiring of labor is not unknown, the phenomena of the business cycle, of technological unemployment, and of malnutrition resulting from an inability to obtain the necessities of life are not found. Thus, for example, clan solidarity among the East African Baganda assured that "real poverty did not exist";

furthermore, "no one ever went hungry . . . because everyone was welcome to go and sit down and share a meal with his equals." Again, the labor market, though by no means entirely absent among nonliterate groups, never attains a place comparable to that which it holds in our own economic order.

Among nonliterate folk we encounter conditions in many respects analogous to the economic system of the Middle Ages and before. As in pre-machine-age Europe, the laborer is almost invariably the owner of the means of production and to that extent is the master of his own economic destiny. That is, capitalism, as we have come to know it since the advent of power machinery, is foreign to non-machine economies. Capital goods may be concentrated in the hands of individual members of certain communities of this type, but this merely signifies that the difference between these systems and our machine economy is one of degree rather than of kind. In nonliterate societies, we do find men who control the labor of others, whether completely, as under the institution of slavery, or for limited periods of time, under forms of employment for wages. We can even encounter, in Samoa, something akin to an organized body of workers who do not hesitate to interrupt their labor where this is necessary to enforce their demands, or even to indulge in sabotage. But the demands to be enforced are demands of prestige and not of livelihood, for among these workers there is no one to whom the return for his labor is essential to his existence.

Another outstanding difference between machine and nonmachine cultures is found in their degree of specialization. In the latter, as has been noted, almost every person controls all the techniques essential for his own support and for the support of those dependent upon him. Even the man who excels in building a canoe, or hunting game, or weaving, or iron-working will, with the aid of members of his family, also carry on agriculture or tend the herds, and he can, when necessary, build a house and fashion household utensils, or make the clothing that habitat and tradition dictate as necessities. Similarly, though some women may be better potters than others, or may excel in basketry or in some other occupation, yet all women will know how to do the household tasks and other kinds of work that are allotted to women under the prevalent patterns of labor. Conversely, it is rare, even where individuals surpass in certain skills, that these skills are restricted to them alone.

Thus, among the Ifugao of the Philippines,

Division of labor is not carried further than a mere beginning. Some men are highly skilled blacksmiths. Nearly all know something about blacksmithing. Some are highly skilled wood carvers, but nearly all are wood carvers for all that. Almost the only division of labor is between men and women.

In Samoa,

The division of labor which is of importance to the mere physical well being of the people is the division of labor along sex lines. Every man knows how to build a small house, how to hew out a rough canoe, how to make a coconut cup, or carve a rough food bowl. The carpenters and makers of sennit lashings are essentially specialists, called in for important occasions. But upon the balance of men and women workers within the household, and upon their skill in the usual tasks in which every adult is supposed to be proficient, depends the prosperity of the household.

Among the Hopi of Arizona,

Common wants and desires, fairly standardized, simple and easily satisfied, require no diverse specialization to satisfy them. . . . It is evident that division of labor is primarily conventional, based on sex secondarily and more indefinitely on age.

In Haiti,

The life of the Haitian farmer, though hard, is simple and self-contained. With but few exceptions, he supplies all his necessities, for he commands almost the entire range of techniques known to his culture; hence Haitian economy shows a lack of specialization that in the main is only relieved by the sex division of labor.

The Maori, we learn, employed

. . . no very intricate division of labour, such as occurs in the highly complex social structure of the 'civilized' community. The fairly simple character of economic wants did not necessitate any great diversity of occupations to satisfy them, and every man was able to master something more than the rudiments of the principal crafts. Entire absorption of the working powers of the individual in one industry, or in a single process of an industry, was rare, if not unknown. At the same time division of labour on a limited scale, both as regards separation of employments and of processes, was not absent.

Or, in Dahomey, a non-machine economy outstanding for its complexity, and where craft specialization is marked, "no matter what the rank of a Dahomean or what his trade, he must know how to cultivate the soil, and he will have his fields."

We must recognize that all men and women in non-machine societies can control the techniques essential for obtaining a living, and, where there are specialized crafts, that the craftsmen are never dependent for their livelihood solely upon what they produce. These are sufficiently striking differences between nonliterate economies and our own. Even more striking, however, are the implications of the fact that among nonliterate peoples the extreme forms of specialization known to us, where the worker must restrict his activities to minor operations in the entire production process, is but rarely encountered. Specialization within one industry does occur in non-machine societies, as where an individual will be expert at making one special part of a canoe. But, again, almost without exception, such a worker is found to be a full-fledged member of a larger co-operative work group, and psychologically has no difficulty in identifying himself with the finished product.

The subject of industrial psychology is important in making effective the human resources needed for the kind of mass production that has been developed in our society, since the degree of specialization characteristic of the organization of our larger industries has given rise to serious problems of individual adjustment. A man who for hours on end tightens a bolt on the engine of an automobile which he will probably never see, and with which he can in no way identify himself, or who, in a packing house, makes the same cut on each of an endless procession of carcasses as they pass before him, is deprived of something that is deeply rooted in the human psyche.

It is not necessary to do more than indicate this to cause us to see why questions of this sort have been found so urgent a subject for study. Veblen put it as follows:

The share of the operative workman in the machine industry is (typically) that of an attendant, an assistant, whose duty is to keep pace with the machine process and to help out with workmanlike manipulation at points where the machine engaged is incomplete. His work supplements the machine process, rather than makes use of it. On the contrary the machine process makes use of the workman.

In the unconscious processes of identification an infinite satisfaction is achieved if, at the end of a day or a week or a year, a worker can point to something of which he may be proud, of which he is the maker or in the making of which he has participated, and in which he retains a sense of creativeness. But this is precisely what cannot be achieved by the majority of those employed in the specialized occupations of an industrial society.

Sapir, in developing his idea of "what kind of a good thing culture is," felt that this factor of specialization was so important that it could be used as a criterion to divide cultures into those which are "genuine" and those which are "spurious":

The great cultural fallacy of industrialism, as developed up to the present time, is that in harnessing machines to our uses it has not known how to avoid the harnessing of the majority of mankind to its machines. The telephone girl who lends her capacities, during the greater part of the living day, to the manipulation of a technical routine that has an eventually high efficiency value but that answers to no spiritual needs of her own is an appalling sacrifice to civilization.

. . . The American Indian who solves the economic problem with salmon-spear and rabbit-snare operates on a relatively low level . . . , but he represents an incomparably higher solution than our telephone girl of the questions that culture has to ask of economics.

We need not set up a system of comparative values in modes of living, however, to recognize that in terms of achieving a rounded life, the patterns of production in non-machine societies afford far more satisfactions to one engaged in the industrial process than in a machine society. No more apt illustration of this point could be had than in the following description of the manner of work of the Andamanese and of the drives that underlie their efforts:

In the manufacture of their weapons, utensils, and other articles, they . . . spend . . . hour after hour in laboriously striking pieces of iron with a stone hammer for the purpose of forming spear or arrowheads, or in improving the shape of a bow, etc., even though there be no necessity, immediate or prospective, to stimulate them to such efforts. The incentive is evidently a spirit of emulation, each one priding himself on being able to produce work which will excel, or at least compare not unfavourably with, that of his neighbors.

This may likewise be seen in the choices of occupation made by certain native peoples who are in contact with the world economic system. Thus, of the Malay fishermen of Kelantan, it is stated:

Popular opinion is apt to regard the Malay, in contrast to the Indian and Chinese who share his native land, as lazy, improvident, and lacking in foresight or ability to work hard and to save. . . . Because a Malay refuses to do long and monotonous work on rubber plantations away from his family, under conditions which Chinese and Indians willingly accept for the sake of the wages, it is assumed that he is lazy. No one who has seen the long, often cold, exhausting and disappointing labour of fishermen on the east coast would doubt that the Malay is capable of sustained, skilful and energetic labour. But he needs to have interest in his work, a factor which modern industrial organization has subjugated to the desire for a higher standard of living.

Certainly the resources an individual in a non-machine society brings to his task must be greater and more varied, in terms of productive activity, than when he carries on the intense specialization demanded of him in a machine technology. What in the field of art has been termed the drive toward virtuosity can be given full play where every step in a process is in the hands of the producer, from the gathering of the raw materials to the finished product that may be admired by the worker's fellows.

Yet another distinction between machine and non-machine societies lies in the development of the tradition of business enterprise, as we know it. As will be shown in later pages, practically no present-day human group is entirely self-supporting, and there is good reason to believe that trade existed in quite early prehistoric times. Where tribal specialization has followed on the localization of natural resources, the needs of a people for those goods they cannot produce because of a lack of essential raw materials cause them to trade for what they desire, and much of their own productive activity is devoted to the making of their own specialty for this same market. A comparable phenomenon is found within certain tribal economies, as where the makers of iron objects, to the degree that they devote their time to this work, must exchange their products for such food, utensils, or non-utilitarian objects as they need or desire if they are to have them. In a number of nonliterate societies where trading is a recognized occupation, and where, as in West Africa, trade is carried on by the use of money rather than by barter, buying in order to sell at a profit, or manufacture of goods primarily for disposal in the market, is well known. We shall also encounter cultures in Melanesia, in East Africa, and in North and South America where the trader as middleman plays an important part in the circulation of commodities from tribe to tribe. But the role which these aspects of trade play in the economic life of such peoples does not have an importance comparable in any way to that held by business in our own economy.

Though in non-industrial societies sparring between traders for advantage does, of course, mark their operations, sometimes even this seems to be absent where values in terms of goods exchanged by direct barter are fixed by traditional usage. Nonetheless, among nonliterate groups the conduct of business transactions has nothing of the impersonal quality that has come to be an outstanding characteristic of our economic system. It is well known that where a non-European has to deal with a European in a matter involving trade, both parties to the transaction are often subject to no little irritation because of differing traditions of trading. Among many who live in non-machine societies, sparring for advantage in the exchange of goods is something of a pleasurable contest of wits.

Nonliterate societies also differ from our own in the relative stress they lay on pecuniary standards of evaluation. Among ourselves, these standards assume such importance that values in terms of money not only dictate our economic judgments, but tend to invade evaluations of all other phases of our culture as well. This has brought it about that money, by and of itself, has come to have a place quite aside from its function as the least common denominator of the market-place. As a matter of fact, it is not easy for us to think of ends that are not expressed as monetary values, even though they concern art or religion or family relations. That we use phrases such as "to have a heart of gold," or to "give a gilt-edged promise," means only that our linguistic usage, like that of all peoples, reflects our standard of values—not as this standard may operate in an

economic sense, but as the phrase is applied to moral and personal judgments of the broadest sort.

Now this kind of evaluation is a rarity in nonliterate societies. It is
found, notably in Melanesia and in northwestern North America, where
outward emblems of wealth are psychologically as important as among
ourselves. Yet, in general, there are many more of these groupings where
goods, to say nothing of people, are not to be bought at a price, than
where the opposite is true. Many instances have been recorded where
objects desired by a purchaser have been refused him in the face of
fabulous offers—fabulous, that is, in terms of the values set by the people
among whom the owner of the desired object lived. It is more revealing
of our own psychology than that of those against whom the charge of
economic irresponsibility has been laid that the basis of this charge, so
often repeated in the accounts of contacts between natives and Europeans,
is that these peoples are prone to accept trifles, such as beads, in recom-
pense for objects which we hold to have the highest value, such as golden
ornaments or precious stones. In reality, this merely means that in such
cases the standards of value brought into play differ from our own.

One of the most widely spread traits of human beings, manifest under
the most diverse types of social order, is the desire for prestige. As we
shall see, there is an intimate relationship between prestige and the
control of economic resources in most societies living above a subsistence
level. The degree to which those who live under the regime of the machine are dependent upon others for almost every necessity of life,
whether material or psychological, and the extent to which it has become
necessary to translate experience into terms of those monetary units on
which we are so dependent for the goods and services we find essential or
desirable, demonstrate the economic consequence of extreme specialization. Here we see money assuming an importance out of all proportion to
its manifestation in other cultures or at other times.

It is a commonplace that Europe of the Middle Ages stressed other-
worldliness in evaluating its satisfactions and directives. This, however,
is merely one way of recalling to ourselves that prestige and the resultant
power associated with it can and, in most societies, is to be gained
through excellence in other fields than the accumulation of wealth, that
the rewards for outstanding accomplishment can be conceived in terms
other than those of money.

All caution must understandably be exercised in making statements
such as these. In some nonliterate groups, especially where a money
economy prevails, motivations quite similar to those found in any community living under a machine technology are not lacking. On the other
hand, we must not forget that many persons in our culture are not dominated by the pecuniary ideal to anything like the extent of the majority.

However, granting the existence of exceptions both in nonliterate societies and our own, the broad differences in the patterned attitudes toward money in machine and non-machine cultures must be recognized.

4

A final distinction between machine and non-machine societies has to do with the utilization of economic resources for the support of non-subsistence activities. Because of greater powers of production, the goods available under a machine technology to release man-power from direct concern with the tasks of producing the necessities of life are more numerous among ourselves than in any other society. The conversion of these resources into what is to be termed social leisure is of the highest importance for the understanding of many aspects of the organization of human societies, wherever they are found and whatever their complexity. As such, this point will be given extended treatment in a later chapter. Here we will consider only that phase of the development of a mechanistic approach to life that accompanied the advent and growth of a machine technology, which finds its most characteristic expression in the scientific tradition.

From the beginning of the industrial revolution, the amount of economic resources devoted to the support of the scientific investigation of the world in which we live has become ever larger. This in turn has so helped to increase the efficiency of the processes of production that much more consumption and capital goods have been available than ever before. But the relationship is a reciprocal one, which has released an ever increasing measure of social leisure; and this, in turn, has permitted the investigation of a constantly wider range of problems.

Science, of course, did not begin with the machine age, as is apparent when we consider the history of physics and mathematics. Medicine, one of the scientific disciplines that has most flowered in our culture, also has a history that long antedates the coming of the machine. Those whose task it is to care for human life and assuage human suffering, whether as practitioners of scientific medicine or as magic healers, are in all societies held to be worthy of support out of the subsistence goods produced by those who are always potentially, at least, in need of them. As regards science in general, however, since there was more to consume, more social leisure has been available since the advent of the machine age to release scientists for the pursuit of their investigations. The increased efficiency of the productive processes that have resulted from the application of discoveries in the fields of the exact and mechanical sciences to industry is striking. In such matters as housing and all its related conveniences, or quantity and variety of foods, or aids to health and the prolongation of the life-span, or the wider recreational facilities and opportunities for a broader outlook on the world, the resources of machine societies are not to be compared with those where the technology does not permit an equivalent production of material goods.

There is no intention to suggest in what has just been set forth that the machine technology, by and of itself, causes the societies in which it develops to live under optimum conditions, any more than there is of indicating that the societies in which man lived or lives in what is sometimes termed a state of nature—in non-machine cultures, that is—represent a golden age.

What is meant is that the more admirable developments of science and the multiplication of resources, like those less desirable aspects of life under this same order of society, are concomitants of the machine as against other technologies. In non-machine cultures, life, though lived at a slower pace, must be lived with far more constant regard for the demands of the natural environment, and often in actual fear of not surviving. That is perhaps why the most convincing exposition of the values of our culture to native peoples is on the technological and scientific level; and this is also why we are so prone to insist that our way of life is the best.

One further point must be clarified before we proceed to an exposition of the data descriptive of the economic aspects of nonliterate societies with which we shall deal in succeeding chapters. The division of labor in the intellectual field has brought it about that students who investigate nonliterate cultures have had but little contact with those whose special concern is with the economic aspects of life; while those who study our economic organization have been so occupied with the problems of our complex industrial order that they do not customarily turn to other cultures for relevant materials against which to project their generalizations. For the problems with which we are concerned in this book, the implications of the fact that there is no established discipline of the kind envisaged by Gras under the term "economic anthropology" is crucial. Hence, in probing these implications, we shall profit by a clearer view of the usefulness of the materials with which we shall be dealing.

11. ANTHROPOLOGY AND ECONOMIC THEORY *

The kinds of assumptions made in the previous selection lead inevitably to attempts to apply modern economic theory to all cultures. Basically, it is assumed that value is determined by scarcity, and with various degrees of sophistication, use is made of the concepts of supply and demand, price, capital, and all of the other words which represent tools of economic inquiry.

Among economists, there is one whose denunciations of the application of modern economic theory to all economies in general has attracted considerable attention among anthropologists. Arguing that modern economic theory is designed for the analysis of systems in which values are determined through market transactions, this economist contends that neither primitive cultures nor the societies of classical antiquity operated according to such a system. He suggests, instead, that there are three fundamental kinds of economic system, two in addition to the market type. Simplest of these is the reciprocal economy in which goods move from one person or group to another and back, each pair of participants constituting a complete and independent unit. The other is the redistributive economy which sees goods and services flow into a central store, then redistributed (though not necessarily in equivalent repayments to contributors so as to exhaust the central store). The content of this approach and its implications are given in the article below.

* Karl Polanyi, *Semantics of General Economic History* (*Revised*) (New York: Columbia University Research Project on "Origins of Economic Institutions," 1953). Reprinted by permission of the author.

Adjunct Professor of Economics at Columbia University, the author (b. 1886) is the senior organizer of the University Seminar on Origins of Economic Institutions which took its character from the paper reproduced here and ultimately published its findings under the combined editorship of Karl Polanyi, Conrad M. Arensberg and Harry K. Pearson, *Trade and Market in the Early Empires* (1957). Professor Polanyi is also the author of *The Great Transformation* (1944).

1. THE TWO MEANINGS OF ECONOMIC

The PURPOSE of this paper is to determine the meaning that can be attached with consistency to the term 'economic' in the social sciences.

The need for an inquiry of this kind can hardly be in doubt. Naturally, the sphere of man's livelihood is not the concern of the discipline of economics alone. Embedded and enmeshed, as it is, in a variety of institutions, man's livelihood is the subject matter of the other social sciences as well, such as sociology, anthropology and, of course, economic history. None the less, up till recently it was taken for granted that the definition of that concept fell in the sole competency of the economist. True, the degree to which his analytical terms were relevant to other than market dominated economies—such as primitive economies, feudal economies or advanced socialist economies—was always held to be somewhat problematical. But only with the present recession of market institutions from their nineteenth century predominance has the limited character of economic analysis become apparent. The social sciences, as such, are now faced with the overdue task of constructing a frame of reference in regard to matters economic, which would no longer suffer from the limitations imposed by the traditional setting of economic science.

The simple recognition from which all such attempts must start is the fact that in referring to human activities the term economic is a compound of two meanings that have independent roots. We will call them the substantive and the formal meaning.

The substantive meaning of economic derives from man's dependence for his livelihood upon nature and his fellows. It refers to the interaction with his natural and social environment, insofar as this results in supplying him with the means of material want satisfaction.

The formal meaning of economic derives from the logical character of the means-ends relationship, as apparent in such words as 'economical' or 'economizing'. It refers to a definite situation of choice, namely, that between the different uses of means induced by an insufficiency of the means. If we call the rules governing choice of means the logic of rational action, then we may denote this variant of logic, with an improvised term, as formal economics.

The two root meanings of economic, the substantive and the formal, have nothing in common. The latter derives from logic, the former from fact. The formal meaning implies a set of rules referring to choice between the alternative uses of insufficient means. The substantive meaning implies neither choice nor insufficiency of means; man's livelihood may or may not involve the necessity of choice and, if choice there be, it need not be induced by the limiting effect of a 'scarcity' of the means;

indeed, some of the most important physical and social conditions of livelihood such as the availability of air and water or a loving mother's devotion to her infant are not, as a rule, so limiting. The cogency that is in play in the one case and in the other differs as the power of syllogism differs from the force of gravitation. The laws of the one are those of the mind; the laws of the other are those of nature. The two meanings could not be further apart; semantically they lie in opposite directions of the compass.

It is our proposition that only the substantive meaning of economic can yield the basic concepts that are required by the social sciences for an investigation of the empirical economies of the past and present. The frame of reference that we are endeavoring to construct requires, therefore, treatment of the subject matter in substantive terms.

The immediate obstacle in our path lies, as indicated, in that concept of economic in which the two meanings, the substantive and the formal, are compounded. In popular terms, this current concept fuses the 'material' and the 'scarcity' meanings of economic. Such a merger of meanings is, of course, unexceptionable as long as we remain conscious of its restrictive effects. Actually, it excludes from the concept of economic (with the exception of some services) all scarce means other than material ones, as well as all material means and all services, other than scarce ones. This combination of terms sprang from logically adventitious circumstances. The last two centuries produced in Western Europe and North America an organization of man's livelihood to which the rules of choice happened to be singularly applicable. This form of the economy consisted in a system of price-making markets. Since the acts of exchange, as practiced under such a system, of necessity involve the participants in choices induced by an insufficiency of their means, the system could be reduced to a pattern that lent itself to the application of methods based on the formal meaning of economic. As long as the economy was controlled by such a system, the formal and the substantive meanings would run parallel. Laymen accepted this compound concept as a matter of course; but Marshall, Pareto and Durkheim equally adhered to it. Menger alone in his posthumous work criticized the term but neither he nor Max Weber, nor Talcott Parsons after him apprehended the significance of the distinction for sociological analysis. Indeed, there seemed to be no valid reason for distinguishing between the two root meanings of a term which were bound to coincide in practice.

While in common parlance it would have been sheer pedantry to distinguish between the two meanings of economic, their merging in one compound concept nevertheless was a bane to the social sciences. Economics naturally formed an exception since under the market system its terms were bound to be fairly realistic. But the anthropologist, the sociologist or the historian in his study of the place occupied by the economy in human society was faced with a great variety of institutions other than markets, in which the sphere of man's livelihood was embedded. [Such problems could not be attacked with the help of concepts devised for a special form of the economy, which was dependent upon the presence of definite market elements. The employment of the compound concept fostered what may well be called the "economistic fallacy." It consisted in an artificial identification of the economy with its market form. From Hume and Spencer to Frank H. Knight and Northrop, social thought suffered from this limitation wherever it touched on the economy. Lionel Robbins' essay (1932), though useful to economists, fatefully distorted the problem. In the field of anthropology Melville Herskovits' recent work (1952) represents a relapse after his pioneering effort of 1942. That fallacy had consequences for our general outlook that transcended the sphere of the human economy. However, we can not here treat of this important philosophical aspect of the subject.]

This lays down the rough sequence of our argument. After a closer examination of the concepts derived from the two meanings of economic, starting with the formal and proceeding to the substantive, it should prove possible to apply the substantive approach first to a classification of empirical economies and eventually to trade, money and market institutions. These provide a test case. They have previously been defined in formal terms only; thus any other than a narrow marketing view of these important economic institutions was barred. The treatment of forms of trade, money uses and market elements in substantive terms should, then, bring us considerably nearer the desired frame of reference.

Let us then first examine the manner in which the logic of rational action produces formal economics, and the latter, in turn, gives rise to economic analysis.

Rational action is here defined as choice of means in relation to ends. Means are anything appropriate to serve the end, whether by virtue of the laws of nature or by virtue of the laws of the game. Thus 'rational' does not refer either to ends or to means, but rather to the relating of means to ends. It is not assumed, for instance, that it is more rational to wish to live than to wish to die, or that, in the first case, it is more rational to seek a long life through the means of science than through those of superstition. For whatever the end, it is rational to choose one's means accordingly; and as to the means, it would not be rational to act upon any other test than that which one happens to believe in. Thus it is rational for the suicide to select means that will accomplish his death; and if he be an adept of black magic, to pay a witch doctor to contrive that end.

The logic of rational action applies, then, to all conceivable means and ends covering an almost infinite variety of human interests. In chess or technology, in religious life or philosophy ends may range from commonplace issues to the most recondite and complex ones. Similarly, in the field of the economy, where ends may range from the momentary assuaging of thirst to the attaining of a sturdy old age, while the corresponding means comprise a glass of water and a combined reliance on filial solicitude and open air life, respectively.

Let us now assume that the choice is induced by insufficiency of means and the logic of rational action produces the variant of the theory of choice that we have called formal economics. It is still logically unrelated to the economy, but it is closer to it by one step. Formal economics refers, as we said, to a situation of choice that arises out of an insufficiency of means. This is the so-called scarcity postulate. It requires, first, insufficiency of means; second, that choice be induced by it. Both conditions are factual. Insufficiency of means in relation to ends is simply determined with the help of the operation of 'earmarking', which demonstrates whether there is or is not enough to go round. For insufficiency to induce choice there must be given more than one use to the means, as well as graded ends, i.e., at least two ends ordered in sequence of preference. It is irrelevant whether the reason for which means can be used in one way only happens to be conventional or technological; the same is true of the grading of ends. Having thus defined choice, insufficiency and scarcity in operational terms, it is easy to see that as there is choice of means without insufficiency, so there is insufficiency of means without choice. In effect, scarcity may or may not be present in almost all fields of rational action. Not all philosophy is sheer imaginative creativity, it may also be a matter of economizing with assumptions. Or, to get back to the sphere of man's livelihood, in some civilizations scarcity situations seem to be almost exceptional, in others they appear to be painfully general. However, in either case the presence or absence of scarcity is invariably a question of fact, natural or conventional.

Last but not least is economic analysis. This discipline results from the application of formal economics to an economy of a definite type, namely, a market system. The economy is here embodied in institutions that cause individual choices to give rise to interdependent movements of objects and activities. This is achieved by generalizing the use of price making markets. All goods and services, including the use of labor, land and capital are available for purchase in markets and have, therefore, a price; all forms of income derive from the sale of goods and services— wages, rent and interest, respectively, appearing only as different instances of price according to the items sold. Since money is useless unless it is scarce, the general introduction of purchasing power as the means of acquisition converts the process of meeting requirements into an allocation of scarce means, namely, money. It follows that both the conditions of choice and its results are quantifiable in the form of prices. It can, therefore, be asserted that by concentrating on price as the economic fact *par excellence,* the formal method of approach offers a total description of the economy as determined by choices induced by an insufficiency of means. The conceptual tools by which this is performed constitute the discipline of economic analysis.

From this follow the limiting conditions under which economic analysis can prove effective as a method. The use of the formal meaning denotes the economy as a sequence of acts of economizing, i.e., of choices induced by scarcity situations. While the rules governing such acts are universal, the extent to which they are applicable to a definite economy depends upon whether or not that economy is, in fact, a sequence of such acts. And for application to be effective, i.e., to produce relevant quantitative results, movements must moreover present themselves as functions of the allocation of insufficient means oriented on resulting prices.

We find, then, that the relation between formal economics and the human economy is, in effect, contingent. Outside of the institutional system of price making markets economic analysis loses most of its relevance as a method of inquiry into the working of a definite economy.

The fount of the substantive concepts is the empirical economy itself. It can be briefly (if not engagingly) defined as an institutionalized process of interaction between man and his environment, which secures him material want satisfaction. Want satisfaction is 'material' if it directly or indirectly involves the use of material means to satisfy ends; also in the case of a definite type of physiological wants, such as food or shelter, that of services only.

Two terms stand out in our definition of the economy: the 'process' and its institutionalizing, or as we will more briefly say, its 'instituting'. Let us see what they contribute to our frame of reference:

The process aspect of the economy suggests analysis in terms of motion. The movements of the useful objects and activities are either changes in location, or appropriation, or both. In other words, the objects and activities may alter their position either by changing places or by changing hands; again, these otherwise very different shifts of position may go together or not.

Between them, these two kinds of movements may be said to exhaust the possibilities comprised in the economic process as a natural and social phenomenon. The locational movement includes production— alongside of transportation—to which the spatial shifting of objects is equally essential. The appropriative movement governs both what is usually referred to as the circulation of goods and their administration. Roughly, in the first case, the appropriative movement results from transactions, in the second, from dispositions. Accordingly, a transaction is an appropriative movement as between hands; a disposition is a one-sided act of the hand, to which by custom or law definite appropriative effects are attached. The term 'hand' here serves to denote public bodies and offices, as well as private persons or firms, the difference between them being mainly a matter of organization. However, it should be admitted that private hands are associated with transactions, while public ones are usually credited with dispositions.

In this description a number of further definitions are implied. Activities, insofar as they form part of the process may be called economic; institutions are so called to the extent to which they contain a concentration of such activities; any components of the process may be regarded as economic elements. The elements again can be conveniently grouped as ecological, technological or societal according to whether they belong primarily to the natural environment, the mechanical equipment, or the human setting. In the ecological group, geography and climate, land, cattle and raw materials stand out; in the technological, tools and machines are prominent, together with modes of collecting, growing, manufacturing, transporting, storing and consuming of goods; in the societal category, which would tend to occupy the center of interest in the sciences dealing with the human setting, an even greater diversity of matters is compounded, such as labor itself, man's wants and needs, as well as the appropriational aspects of the economy.

Another grouping of the elements as based on substantive criteria is no less significant. Goods are of lower order or of higher order, according to the manner of their usefulness from the consumer's point of view. This famous 'order of goods' sets consumers' goods against producers' goods, according to whether they satisfy wants directly, or only indirectly, through a combination with other goods. This type of interaction of the elements represents an essential of the economy in the substantive sense of the term, namely, production.

Thus a series of concepts old and new accrues to our frame of reference by virtue of the process aspect of the economy. However, reduced to a physical, physiological and psychological interaction of elements that process would possess no all-round reality. True, from the ecological and technological angle it represents an important subject for study, since it contains the bare bones of the processes of production and transportation, (as well as the items of appropriative changes). Yet in the absence of any indication of societal conditions from which the organized and structured motives of the individuals spring, there would be little, if anything, to sustain the interdependence of the movements or their recurrence on which the unity and the stability of the process depends. The interacting elements of nature and humanity would form no coherent unit, in effect, no structural entity that could be said to have a function in society or to possess a history. That process would lack, therefore, the very qualities which cause common thought as well as scholarship to turn towards matters of human livelihood as a field of eminent practical and theoretical interest.

Hence the transcending importance of that other, the institutional, aspect of the economy. What occurs on the process level between man and soil in hoeing a garden plot or what happens on the conveyor belt in the constructing of an automobile is, *prima facie* a jig-sawing of human and non-human movements. Yet, from the institutional point of view this process of interaction is the referent of the terms labor and capital, craft and union, slacking and speeding, the spreading of risks and all the other semantic units of the social context. The choice between capitalism and socialism, for example, refers to two different ways of instituting modern technology for the purposes of production. Or, to give another instance: the industrialization of underdeveloped countries involves, on the one hand, alternative techniques, on the other, alternative methods of their instituting.

The instituting of the economic process vests that process with unity and stability; it produces a structure with a definite function in society; in shifting its place in society, that entity acquires a history; interest is, as a rule, related to action or policy. Unity and stability, structure and function, history and policy spell out the operational content of the statement that the human economy is an instituted process.

The human economy, then, is embedded and enmeshed in institutions, economic and non-economic. The inclusion of the latter is vital. For religion or government may be as important for the structure and functioning of the economy as are monetary institutions or the improvement of tools that lighten the toil of labor.

The study of the shifting place occupied by the economy in society is the study of the manner in which the economic process is instituted at different times and places.

2. THE CLASSIFICATION OF EMPIRICAL ECONOMIES, PAST AND PRESENT

The classification of empirical economies, then, might best take its start from the manner in which economies are integrated. Integration is one of the effects of the instituting of the economic process—a condition, apart from which such a process, as we saw, can not actually exist. The societal background of the process structures the motives which are responsible for the tendency of the movements towards interdependence and recurrence. The different types of movements through which the effect is achieved we will call forms of integration. Their number being small, they are convenient for classification. Since, however, different forms of integration may occur side by side on different levels and in different sectors of the economy, we shall regard that one as dominant which integrates the factors of production, land and labor, with the rest of the economy.

Empirically, we find the main forms of integration to be reciprocity, redistribution and exchange. Reciprocity denotes movements between correlative points of symmetrical groupings in society; redistribution designates movements toward an allocative center and out of it again; exchange refers to vice-versa movements taking place as between 'hands' under a market system. Reciprocity, then, requires as its background, symmetrically arranged groupings; redistribution is dependent upon some measure of centricity in the group; exchange, in order to produce integration requires the presence of a system of price-making markets. It is apparent that the different forms of integration involve the presence of definite institutional supports.

At this point a terminological clarification may be welcome. The terms reciprocity, redistribution and exchange, by which we refer to our forms of integration are also loosely employed to denote personal relationships. Thus it might seem as if our forms of integration merely reflected aggregates of the respective forms of individual behavior: If reciprocation or mutuality between individuals were frequent, a reciprocative integration would emerge; where sharing or voluntary distribution among individuals were common, redistributive integration would be present; similarly frequent acts of barter or exchange between individuals would result in exchange as a form of integration. If this were so, our forms of integration would be indeed no more than societal aggregates of corresponding forms of behavior on the personal level. To be sure, we insisted, that the integrative effect was conditioned by the presence of definite structure patterns, such as symmetrical arrangements, central points and market systems, respectively. But can these structures be accepted as independent variables? Or rather, do they not represent merely a form of the self-same personal behavior pattern the eventual effects of which they are supposed to condition? The significant fact is that they do *not*.

Mere aggregates of the personal behavior in question do not produce such structure patterns. Reciprocity behavior between individuals, for instance, integrates the economy only if symmetrically organized structures, such as a symmetrical system of kinship groups are given. Yet in the nature of things, a kinship system does not arise as the result of reciprocating individual behavior on the personal level. Similarly, in regard to redistribution. It presupposes the presence of an allocative center in the community, yet the organization and validation of such a center does not come about merely as a consequence of frequent acts of sharing or distribution as between individuals. Finally, the same is true of the market system. Acts of exchange or barter on the personal level produce prices only if they occur under a system of price-making markets, an institutional setup which is nowhere created by mere random acts of exchange. We do not wish to imply, of course, that those supporting patterns are the outcome of some mysterious forces acting outside the range of personal or individual behavior. We merely insist that if, in any given case, the societal effects of individual behavior depend on the presence of definite institutional conditions, these latter conditions do not for that reason result from the personal behavior in question. Superficially, the supporting pattern may sometimes seem to result from a mere cumulation of a corresponding kind of personal behavior, but the vital element of validation is necessarily contributed by a different type of behavior.

The first writer to our knowledge to have hit upon the factual connection between reciprocative behavior on the personal level, on the one hand, and independently given symmetrical groupings on the other, was the anthropologist Richard Thurnwald, in 1915, in an empirical study on the marriage system of the Banaro of New Guinea. Bronislaw Malinowski, some ten years later, referring to Thurnwald, predicted that socially relevant reciprocation would regularly be found to rest on symmetrical forms of basic social organization. His own description of the Trobriand kinship system as well as of the Kula trade bore out the point. This lead was followed up by the author, in regarding reciprocity as merely *one* of several forms of integration, and symmetry as *one* of several supporting patterns. He then added redistribution and exchange to reciprocity, as further forms of integration; similarly, he added centricity and market to symmetry, as other instances of institutional support.

This should help to explain why in the economic sphere personal behavior so often fails to have the expected societal effects in the absence of definite pre-conditions. Only in a symmetrically organized environment will reciprocative behavior result in economic institutions of any importance; only where allocative centers have been set up can individual acts of sharing produce a redistributive economy; and only in the presence of a system of price-making markets will exchange acts of individuals result in fluctuating prices that integrate the economy. Otherwise such acts of barter will remain ineffective and therefore tend not to occur. Should they nevertheless happen, in a random fashion, a violent emotional reaction would set in, as against acts of indecency or acts of treason, since trading behavior is never indifferent behavior and is not, therefore, tolerated by opinion outside of the approved channels.

Let us now return to our forms of integration.

A group which deliberately undertook to organize its economic relationships on a reciprocative footing would, to effect its purpose, have to split up into sub-groups, the corresponding members of which could identify one another as such. Members of Group A would then be able to establish relationships of reciprocity with their counterparts in Group B and vice versa. But symmetry is not restricted to duality. Three, four, or more groups may be symmetrical in regard to two or more axes; also members of the groups need not reciprocate with one another but may do so with the corresponding members of third groups towards which they stand in analogous relations. A Trobriand man's responsibility is towards his sister's family. But he himself is not on that account assisted by his sister's husband, but, if he is married, by his own wife's brother—a member of a third, correspondingly placed family.

Aristotle taught that to every kind of community (koinōnia) there belonged amongst its members a corresponding kind of good will (philia) which expressed itself in reciprocity (antipeponthos). Assuming this to be true, human communities are endowed with a tendency towards multiple symmetry in regard to which reciprocative behavior may develop. Of communities in this broad sense there exist a large number, for a permanent community, i.e., a tribe or village would include many other subordinate ones. It may be said that the closer the members of the encompassing community feel drawn to one another, the more general will be the tendency among them to develop reciprocative attitudes in regard to specific relationships limited in space, time or otherwise. Kinship, neighborhood, or totem belong to the more permanent and comprehensive groupings; within their compass voluntary and semi-voluntary associations of a military, vocational, religious or social character would create situations in which at least transitorily or in regard to a given locality, or a typical situation there would form symmetrical groupings the members of which practice some sort of mutuality.

Reciprocity as a form of integration gains greatly in power by its capacity of employing both redistribution and exchange as subordinate methods. Sharing of the burdens of labor may be subject to reciprocity, if the sharing is done according to definite redistributive rules, as e.g. taking things 'in turn.' Similarly, exchange at set equivalencies may be practiced reciprocally for the benefit of the partner who happens to be short of some kind of necessities—a fundamental institution in ancient Oriental societies.

Redistribution obtains within a group to the extent to which the allocation of goods is collected in one hand and takes place by virtue of custom, law or *ad hoc* central decision. Sometimes it amounts to physical collecting accompanied by storage-cum-redistribution, at other times the 'collecting' is not physical, but merely appropriational, rights of disposal being collected in one hand, without any accompanying change in the physical location of the goods. Redistribution occurs for many reasons, on all civilizational levels, from the primitive hunting tribe to the vast storage systems of ancient Egypt, Sumeria, Babylonia, or Peru. In large countries differences of soil and climate may make the reuniting of labor necessary; in other cases it is caused by discrepancy in point of time, as between harvest and consumption. With a hunt, any other method of distribution would lead to disintegration of the horde or band, since only 'division of labor' can here ensure results; a redistribution of purchasing power may be valued for its own sake, i.e. for purposes demanded by social ideals as in the modern welfare state. The principle remains always the same—collecting into, and redistributing from, a center. Redistribution may also apply to a group smaller than society, such as the household or manor irrespective of the way in which the economy as a whole is integrated. The best known instances are the Central African *kraal*, the Hebrew patriarchal household, the Greek estate of Aristotle's time, the Roman *familia*, the medieval manor, or the typical large peasant household before the general marketing of grain. However, only under a comparatively advanced form of agricultural society is householding practicable, and then, fairly general. Before that the widely spread institution of the 'small family' is not economically instituted, except for some cooking of food; the use of pasture, land or cattle is still dominated by redistributive or reciprocative methods on a broader than family scale.

Redistribution, too, is apt to integrate groups at all levels and of all degrees of permanence from the state itself to units of a transitory character. Here, again, as with reciprocity, the more closely knit the encompassing unit, the more varied will be the subdivisions in which redistribution can effectively operate. Plato taught that the number of citizens in the state should be 5040. This figure is divisible in 59 different ways, including division by the first ten numerals. For the assessment of taxes, the carrying of military and other burdens 'in turn,' etc., it would allow the widest scope, he explained.

Exchange as a form of integration requires the institutional support of a system of price-making markets. Insofar as exchange at set prices is in question, the economy is integrated by the factors which fix the price, not by the market mechanism. Even price-making markets are integrative only if they are linked up in a system which tends to spread the effect of the prices to other markets than those directly affected.

Higgling-haggling has been rightly recognized as being of the essence of bargaining behavior. In order for exchange to be integrative it must be oriented on producing a price that is as favorable to either partner as he can make it. Such a behavior contrasts sharply with that of exchange at a set price. The ambiguity of the term 'gain' tends to cover up the difference: Exchange at set prices involves no more than the gain to either party implied in the decision of exchanging; exchange at fluctuating prices aims at a gain that can be attained only by an attitude involving a distinctive relationship between the partners. The element of antagonism, however diluted, that accompanies the latter variant of exchange is ineradicable. No community intent on protecting the fount of solidarity between its members can allow such a latent hostility to develop around a matter as vital to animal existence and, therefore, capable of arousing as tense anxieties as food. Hence the universal banning of transactions of a gainful nature in regard to food and foodstuffs in primitive and archaic society. The very widely spread ban on higgling-haggling over victuals automatically removes price-making markets from the realm of early institutions.

A classification of economies according to the dominant form of integration is illuminating. What historians are traditionally wont to call 'economic systems' falls fairly into this pattern. The dominance of a form of integration depends, as stated, on the degree to which it comprises land and labor in society. A tribal community or, in even looser terms, a savage society, is characterized by the integration of land and labor into the economy by way of the ties of kinship. In feudal society the ties of fealty determine the fate of land and the labor that goes with it. In the floodwater empires land was largely distributed and sometimes redistributed by temple or palace, and so was labor, at least in its dependent form. The rise of the market to a ruling force in the economy can be traced by noting the extent to which land and food were mobilized through exchange, and labor was turned into a commodity free to be purchased in the market. This may help to explain the relevancy of the historically untenable stages theory of slavery, serfdom and wage labor that is traditional with Marxism—a classification which flowed from the conviction that the character of the economy was set by the status of labor. However, the integration of the soil into the economy should be regarded as hardly less vital.

In any case, forms of integration do not represent 'stages' of development. No sequence in time is implied. Several subordinate forms may be present alongside of the dominant one, which may itself recur after a temporary eclipse. Tribal societies practice reciprocity and redistribution, while archaic societies are predominantly redistributive, though to some extent they may allow room for exchange. Reciprocity, which plays a dominant part in some Melanesian communities, survives as a not unimportant although subordinate trait in the redistributive archaic empires, where foreign trade is still largely organized on the principle of reciprocity. Indeed, during an emergency it was reintroduced on a large scale in the twentieth century, under the name of lend-lease, with societies where otherwise marketing and exchange were dominant. Redistribution, the ruling method in tribal and archaic society beside which exchange plays only a minor part, grew to great importance in the later Roman Empire and is actually gaining ground today in modern industrial states. The Soviet Union is an extreme instance. Conversely, more than once in the course of human history markets have played a part in the economy, although never on a territorial scale, or with an institutional comprehensiveness comparable to that of the nineteenth century. However, here again a change is noticeable. In our century, a recession of markets from their nineteenth century peak set in—a turn of the trend which, incidentally, takes us back to our starting point, namely, the increasing inadequacy of marketing definitions for the purposes of the social scientist.

3. TRADE, MONEY AND MARKET INSTITUTIONS

Once economic phenomena are equated with market phenomena, logically no room is left for the problems of trade and money as apart from markets. Catallactically, trade and money are functions of the market; the three form one conceptual whole. Trade appears as a two-way movement of goods through the market, and money as a means of exchange designed to facilitate that movement. Since trade is directed by prices, and prices are a function of markets, all trade is market trade just as all money is exchange money.

Consider the effects of such concepts on empirical research. Eventually, they must induce an acceptance of the heuristic principle, according to which where trade is in evidence, markets should be assumed, and where money is in evidence, trade and markets should be assumed. Again, this must result in a tendency of seeing markets where there are none, and ignoring trade and money where they are present, if markets happen to be absent.

As against this web of preconceptions stands the fact that trade is as old as mankind, and so are some money uses. Markets, on the other hand, although meetings of a broadly similar character may have existed as early as the neolithic age, emerge as integrative institutions at a comparatively very late state in history. However, not even these massive facts could be uncovered as long as the concepts of trade and money were derived, as in the Ricardian system, from exchange as a form of integration. The study of trade and money institutions during those early periods of history when reciprocity and redistribution integrated the economy were, in effect, put out of bounds by a restrictive terminology. Our task, then, is to develop substantive terms of trade, money and market that are suitable for the study of these institutions under all forms of integration.

Trade from the catallactic view point is, as we saw, the movement of goods on their way through the market. All commodities—goods produced for sale in the market—are here potential objects of trade; one commodity is moving in one direction, the other in the opposite direction; the movement is controlled by prices; trade and markets are coterminous.

The substantive meaning of trade is independent of markets. Essentially, it is a method of procuring goods that are not available on the spot. Emphasis upon this aspect brings out the dominance of the import interest in the history of trade. The export interest—a typically catallactic phenomenon—loomed large only since the Nineteenth Century.

Trade therefore resembles activities which we are used to associating with hunts, slave expeditions, or piratic raids, the point of similarity being the acquisition and carrying of goods from a distance.

Like hunt, expedition or raid, trade is under undisturbed native conditions not so much an individual as a group activity. In this regard it is akin to tribal forms of wooing and mating, which are often concerned with the acquisition of wives from a distance by more or less peaceful means (and are undertaken as a public venture). In the same way, trade centers in an external contact: the meeting of communities. Whether a chief collects the 'export' goods from the members of the group and then acts for the community, or whether the members in the flesh meet their counterparts on the beach—in either case the proceedings are collective.

What distinguishes trade from questing for game, booty and plunder is the two-sidedness of the movement, which also ensures its broadly peaceful and fairly regular character. According to the manner in which the two-sidedness of the movement is instituted, three main types of trade can be distinguished: gift trade, administered trade, and market trade.

Gift trade links partners who stand in relationship of reciprocity, such as guest-friends; Kula partners; visiting villages; military allies practicing lend-lease. Over millennia trade between empires was largely carried on as gift trade—no other *rationale* of two-sidedness would meet quite as well the needs of the situation. The organization of trading is ceremonial, involving mutual presentations; embassies; political deals between chiefs, kings, or governments. The goods are often treasure goods, and as such objects of elite circulation; in the border case of 'visiting parties' the goods may be of a more 'democratic' character. However, contacts are always tenuous and exchanges mostly far-between.

Administered trade has its foundations in governmental agreements of a more or less formal nature. At least one of the parties favors redistributive methods in its foreign trade set-up. The understanding between the parties may be tacit, as in the case of traditional or customary relationships. Between sovereign bodies such trade, if carried on on a large scale, assumes, as a rule, the existence of regular treaties. Even in the relatively early days of the second millennium B. C. with its occasional gift trade between sovereigns, administered trade is regularly carried on through governmental or guild channels or other relatively permanent trading bodies such as we meet later in the chartered companies of the mercantilist period in Europe.

The specialized organ of administered trade is the Port of Trade, usually situated on the borders of at least one of the trading territories. It may be coastal, riverain or inland. Its main function is to offer military security for access to trade as well as civil protection to the foreign trader, besides a number of vital facilities to both parties.

Many matters have to be coped with, such as arrangements concerning 'rates' or 'proportions' of the units that form an assortment; the weighing and checking of the quality of the goods; their physical exchange; storage, safekeeping; the control of the trading personnel; regulation of 'payments'; credits; and price-differentials. Much of this falls under the heading of the actual collection of the export goods and the repartition of the imported ones—procedures which both belong to the redistributive sphere of the domestic economy. The goods which are mutually imported are standardized in regard to quality and package, weight, or other easily ascertainable criteria. Only such 'trade goods' can be traded. Their equivalencies are set out in simple unit relations; in principle the ratio is 1:1.

Once a treaty has been negotiated, higgling-haggling is no longer part of the proceedings; rather, the purpose is to exclude it. But since in order to meet changing circumstances bargaining often cannot be avoided, it is preferably practised on other items than 'price', such as measures, quality, means of payment, and even profits. The rationale of this astonishing procedure is, of course, to keep equivalencies unchanged; if adjustment to supply situations is unavoidable, as in an emergency, this is phrased as trading 2:1 or $2\frac{1}{2}$:1, or as the European traveler would put it, at 100% or 150% profit. This method of negotiating on profits in terms of stable prices, a practice which must have been fairly general in archaic society, is well authenticated for the Central Sudan at as late a period as the first quarter of the nineteenth century.

Market trade is the third typical form of trading. This comparatively recent form of trade released a torrent of material wealth over Western Europe and North America. Though no longer the only form of modern trading, it is still by far the most important. The organization of trade is here embedded in the market. The range of tradable goods—the commodities—is practically unlimited. And the supply-demand-price mechanism is adaptable to the handling not only of goods proper but of every feature or element of trade itself—storage, transportation, risk, credit, payments, etc.—by forming special markets for freight, insurance, short-term credit, capital, warehouse space, banking facilities, and so on. The preponderance of that mechanism is in our days so great that the very distinction between trade and market may appear artificial; while the sharp contrast that characterized them in their beginnings seems to us almost paradoxical.

Take the role played by the specificity of goods in trade and market, respectively. While neither of them can escape the influence of specificity, the market is a leveller—it renders homogeneous what nature and history made different. Trade, on the other hand, tends to be specific. Unless full weight is accorded to this fact, no understanding of the early development of trade is possible.

There is originally no such thing as trading 'in general.' A brief list of the early goods will show why trading had several separate and independent origins. Note the characteristics of the various goods. Cattle and captives can be driven away by raiders; slabs of stone and trunks of trees employed in the construction of imposing temples must be hauled by expeditionary forces; gold and silver objects are treasure that circulates only among the elite of gods, kings and chiefs; copper, tin, and, later, iron go to equip armies; timber, hemp and tar to build navies. Exports are collected in the archaic state by administrative methods as was grain in Sumeria; wool and dried fish under the Third Dynasty of Ur; fur and wax under the Varaengian princes of Kiev. Imports are a different matter again. The great empires of antiquity largely secured them in kind, as tribute. Even classical Attica mostly procured its corn or at least a reduction of its price by political means. It would be easy to show how all these 'branches of trade', even after two-sidedness had become a prominent feature of trade, were still found to be organized along the lines of their sociologically and technologically variegated origins.

The specificity of early trade would therefore be enhanced rather than diminished by the two-sidedness of the act. Under non-market conditions, imports and exports may fall under separate and different administrative regimes. The process through which goods are made available for export is frequently distinct from, and independent of, that by which the imported goods are distributed domestically. Exports may be extracted from a subject population, while the repartitioned imports cascade along more exalted lines.

This specificity of non-market trade is chiefly responsible for the absence of continuous enterprise under archaic conditions. Trade is here restricted to single undertakings, a circumstance, which limits the development of trade partnerships. As a rule, a business deal comprises only one venture that is liquidated before another one is started. The Roman *societas*, and the medieval *commenda* formed such *ad hoc* partnerships. The *societas publicanorum* of all trade associations alone was incorporated—it was the one great exception. Not before modern times was continuous business partnership in trade known.

Trade routes as well as means of carriage are of no less incisive importance for the forms of trade than the types of goods carried. In either case geographical and technological facts interpenetrate with the social structure to create institutional diversity.

The market does away with all these distinctions. Matters as different as goods and their transportation are equated since both can be bought and sold in the market, the one in the commodity market, the other in the freight and insurance market. In either case there is supply, demand and price formed in a like fashion; also in each case there is cost, that uniform residue of market alchemy.

The main interest of the economic historian lies in the elucidation of the process by which trade becomes linked with markets. At what time and place do we meet the general result, market-trade? Conversely, why does this form of trade give way once more, as in our days, to administered trade, or still other forms of trading? Strictly speaking, all such questions are precluded under the sway of catallactic logic.

The catallactic definition of money is that of means of indirect exchange. Modern money is used for payment and as a 'standard' precisely because it is a means of exchange. Thus money is 'all-purpose' money. Other uses of money are merely unimportant variants of its exchange use, and all money uses are dependent upon the existence of markets.

The substantive definition of money like that of trade is independent of markets. It is derived from definite uses to which quantifiable objects are put. These uses are payment, standard and exchange. Money therefore is defined here as quantifiable objects employed in any one or several of these uses. The question is whether independent definitions of those uses are possible.

The definitions of the various money uses contain two criteria: the sociologically defined situation in which the use arises, and the operation performed with the money objects in that situation.

Payment is the discharge of obligations through a changing of hands of quantifiable objects. The situation of obligation refers here not to one kind of obligation only, but to several of them, since only if an object is used to discharge various obligations can we speak of it as 'means of payment' in the distinctive sense of the term (otherwise merely an obligation to be discharged in kind is so discharged).

The payment use of money belongs to its most common uses in early times. Obligations do not here commonly spring from transactions. In unstratified primitive society payments are regularly made in connection with the institutions of bride price, blood money, and fines. In archaic society such payments continue, but they are over-shadowed by customary dues, taxes, rent and tribute that give rise to payments on the largest scale.

The standard, or accounting use of money is the equating of amounts of different kinds of goods for definite purposes. The 'situation' is either barter or the management of staples; the 'operation' consists in attaching numerical tags to the various objects to facilitate the manipulation of those objects. Thus in the case of barter, the summation of objects on either side can be eventually equated; in the case of the management of staples the possibility of planning, balancing, budgeting, as well as general accounting is attained.

The standard use of money is essential to the elasticity of the system in redistributive economies. The equating of such staples as barley, oil and wool, i.e. the staples in which the taxes or rents are paid as well as in which rations or wages are claimed is vital, since it ensures the possibility of choice between the different staples for either payer or claimant. At the same time the preconditions of large scale finance 'in kind' are created.

The exchange use of money is the use of quantifiable objects for indirect exchange. The 'operation' consists in acquiring units of quantifiable objects through direct exchange, in order to acquire the desired objects through a further act of exchange. Sometimes the money objects are available from the start, and their indirect exchange is merely designed to net an increased amount of the same objects. Such a use of quantifiable objects develops not from random acts of barter—a favored fancy of eighteenth century rationalism—but only in connection with organized trade, especially through markets. In the absence of markets the exchange use of money is no more than a subordinate culture trait. The reluctance of the great trading peoples of antiquity such as Tyre and Carthage to adopt coins, that new form of money eminently suited for exchange, was due to the fact that the ports of trade of these commercial empires were not organized as markets.

Two exceptions should be noted. The one extends the definition of money to other than physical objects, namely to ideal units; the other extends it to other than the three conventional money uses, namely to the use of money objects as an operational device.

Ideal units are mere verbalizations or written symbols employed as quantifiable units, mainly for payment or as a standard. The 'operation' consists in the manipulation of debt accounts according to the rules of the game. Such accounts are facts of primitive life and not, as was often believed, peculiar to monetarized economies.

The use of quantifiable objects for operational devices is designed as a means by which simple manual operations resolve complex problems by a short cut. It seemed advisable to include under money uses the employment of quantifiable objects to such manipulative ends, since money objects are frequently used in archaic society for arithmetical, statistical, taxational, administrative or other purposes connected with economic life.

Early money is, as we saw, special-purpose money. Different kinds of objects are employed in the different money uses, moreover, these uses are instituted independently of one another. The implications of this fact are of the most far-reaching nature. There is, therefore, no contradiction involved in 'paying' with a means with which one cannot buy, nor in employing objects as a 'standard' which are not used as a means of exchange. In Hammurapi's Babylonia barley was the means of payment; silver was the universal standard; in exchange, of which there was very little, both were used alongside of oil, wool, and many other staples. It becomes apparent why money uses—similarly to trade activities—can reach an almost unlimited level of development, not only outside of market-dominated economies, but in the very absence of markets.

Now, the market itself. Catallactically, the market is the *locus* of exchange; market and exchange are co-extensive. For under the catallactic postulate economic life is both reducible to acts of exchange effected through higgling-haggling and it is embodied in markets. Exchange then can be described as *the* economic relationship, with the market as *the* economic institution. The definition of the market derives logically from the catallactic premises.

Under the substantive range of terms, market and exchange have independent empirical characteristics. What then is here the meaning of exchange and market? And to what extent are they overlapping?

Exchange, substantively defined, is the mutual appropriative movement of goods between hands. Such a vice-versa movement may occur on different levels: Firstly, at indeterminate rates; secondly, at set rates; thirdly, at bargained rates. The third and last is the result of higgling-haggling between the partners. Set rates are either customary, statutory or pro-claimed. Finally, what we referred to as 'indeterminate rates' are neither bargained nor set, they are the outcome of various other operations con-nected with the vice-versa movement of goods, such as Christmas gifts, auctions, lotteries or taxation.

Indeterminate rates are characteristic of reciprocative practices such as are connected with dowry and bride price or international lend-lease, as well as of redistributive arrangements such as picnics or national taxation systems, the actual rate of exchange emerging, as a rule, only subsequent to the movement of the goods. Uncertainty of the rate is some-times of the essence of the matter, though it need not be. In some cases the determining of the rate is deliberately left over, as between friends who regard it as a subordinate matter; also the rate may, in the nature of things, not be capable of determination at the time of the transaction, though afterwards it emerges from a calculus of probability or from the actual course of events.

However, where there is exchange, there is a rate. This principle re-mains unaffected whether the rate be bargained, set, or indeterminate as to the limits within which it is designed to move; the point of time at which it becomes known; or the degree of probability which attaches to it.

We can, then, speak of exchange at the first, second, and third level. It will be noted that the third variant of exchange is identical both with catallactic exchange and with our 'exchange as a form of integration'. This level of exchange alone is limited to market institutions, namely to price making markets.

Market institutions shall be defined as institutions comprising a supply crowd or a demand crowd or both. Supply crowds and demand crowds again, shall be defined as a multiplicity of hands desirous to acquire, or alternatively, to dispose of, goods in exchange. Although market institu-tions, therefore, are exchange institutions, market and exchange are *not* coterminous. Exchange at set rates and, similarly, exchange at indetermi-nate rates occurs under reciprocative or redistributive forms of integra-tion; exchange at bargained rates is limited to price-making markets. It may seem paradoxical that first and second level exchange should be compatible with any form of integration except that of exchange: yet this follows logically since only third level exchange represents exchange in the catallactic sense of the term, in which it is a form of integration.

The best way of approaching the world of market institutions appears to be in terms of 'market elements'. Eventually, this will not only serve as a guide through the variety of configurations subsumed under the name of markets and market type institutions, but also as a tool with which to dissect some of the conventional concepts that obstruct our understanding of those institutions.

Two of the market elements should be regarded as specific, namely, supply crowds and demand crowds; if either or both are present, we shall speak of a market institution (if both are present, we call it a market; if one of them only, a market type institution). Next in importance is the element of equivalency, i.e., the rate of exchange; according to the character of the equivalency, markets are set-price markets or price making markets. Competition is another characteristic of some market institutions, such as price making markets and auctions, but in contrast to equivalencies, economic competition is restricted to markets. Finally, there are elements that can be designated as functional. Regularly they occur apart from market institutions, but if they make their appearance alongside of supply crowds or demand crowds, they pattern out those institutions in a manner that may be of great practical relevance. Amongst these functional elements are physical site, goods present, custom and law. According to the configuration of the elements, markets may be 'visible', insofar as they possess a definite site, or 'invisible', if, as in the modern market, such is not the case; they may have one rate of exchange only for the same kind of goods, or a whole range of rates for practically identical specimens as in the bazaar; they may require 'goods present' as in the medieval 'open market', or goods need not be present as in the invisible market of our day. And so on, with many variants.

This diversity was in recent times obscured in the name of the formal concept of a supply-demand-price mechanism. No wonder that it is in regard to the pivotal terms of supply, demand and price that the substantive approach leads to a significant widening of our outlook.

Supply crowds and demand crowds were referred to above as separate and distinct market elements. In regard to the modern market this would be, of course, inadmissible; here there is a price level at which bears turn bulls, and another price level at which the miracle is reversed. This has induced many to overlook the fact that buyers and sellers are separate in any other than the modern type of market. This again gave support to a twofold misconception. Firstly, 'supply and demand' appeared as combined elemental forces while actually each consisted of two very different components, namely, of *goods,* on the one hand, and *persons,* related to those goods, on the other. Secondly, 'supply and demand' seemed inseparable, while forming, in effect, distinct groups of persons, according to whether they disposed of the goods as of resources, or sought them as requirements. Supply crowds and demand crowds need not therefore be present together. When, for instance, booty is auctioned by the victorious general to the highest bidder only a demand crowd is in evidence;

similarly, only a supply crowd is met with when contracts are assigned to the lowest submission. Yet auctions and submissions were wide-spread in archaic society, and in ancient Greece auctions ranked amongst the precursors of markets proper. This distinctness of 'supply' and 'demand' crowds shaped the organization of all pre-modern market institutions. So much for the Siamese twins 'supply' and 'demand'.

As to the market element commonly called 'price', we generalized it as equivalency. The use of this term should help to avoid misunderstandings. Price suggests fluctuation, while equivalency lack this association. The very phrase 'set' or 'fixed' implies that the price, before being fixed or set was apt to change. Thus language itself makes it difficult to convey the true state of affairs, namely that originally the 'price' is a rigidly fixed quantity, in the absence of which trading can not start. Changing or fluctuating prices of a competitive character are a comparatively recent development and one of the main interests of economic history. Traditionally, the sequence was supposed to be the reverse.

Equivalencies, then, up to a point correspond to forms of integration. 'Price' is the designation of quantitative ratios between goods of different kinds, effected through barter or higgling-haggling. It is that form of equivalency which is characteristic of economies that are integrated through bargaining exchange. But equivalencies are by no means restricted to such relations. Under a redistributive form of integration equivalencies are also common. They designate here the quantitative relationship between goods of different kinds that are acceptable in payment of taxes, rents, dues, fines, or that denote qualifications for a civic status dependent on a property census. At the same time the equivalency sets the ratio at which wages or rations in kind can be claimed, at the beneficiary's choosing. The necessary elasticity of a system of staple finance—the planning, balancing and accounting—hinges on this. It is not what should be given *for* another good, but what can be claimed *instead* of it. Under reciprocative forms of integration, again, equivalencies determine the amount that is 'adequate' in relation to the symmetrically placed party. Clearly, this behavioral context is different from either exchange or redistribution.

Price systems, incidentally, may contain layers of equivalencies that historically originated under different forms of integration. Hellenistic market prices show ample evidence of having derived from redistributive equivalencies of the cuneiform civilizations that preceded them. The 30 pieces of silver received as the price of a man by Judas for betraying Jesus was a close variant of the equivalency of a slave as set out in Hammurapi's Code some 1700 years earlier. Soviet redistributive equivalencies, on the other hand, for a long time echoed nineteenth century world market prices. These, too, in their turn, had their predecessors.

Max Weber remarked that Western capitalism would not have been possible for lack of a costing basis but for the medieval network of statuated and regulated prices, customary rents etc., the legacy of gild and manor. Thus price systems may have an institutional history of their own in terms of the types of equivalencies that entered into their making.

It is with the help of non-catallactic concepts of this kind that such fundamental problems of economic and social history as the origin of fluctuating prices and the development of market trading can be tackled and will be eventually resolved.

To conclude: A critical survey of the catallactic definitions of trade, money and market should make available a number of concepts which form the raw material of the social sciences in their economic aspect. The scarcity definition of economic has its special use in the sphere of market institutions; outside of that restricted field substantive definitions alone are appropriate.

The bearing of this recognition on questions of theory, policy and outlook should be viewed in the light of the institutional transformation that has been in progress since the first World War. Even in regard to the market-system itself, the market as the sole frame of reference is out of date. Yet, as should be clearly realized, the market can not be superseded in that function unless the social sciences succeed in developing a wider frame of reference to which the market itself is referable. Such a conceptual structure, as we have attempted to show, will have to be grounded on the substantive meaning of economic.

D. Social and Political Organization

If the study of societal structure is the focus and core of social anthropology, it is really no less important to a good number of scholars who identify themselves as cultural anthropologists. To some extent the anthropological study of social organization, particularly the systems of kinship, is an American invention associated with Lewis Henry Morgan (No. II:15); the study of political organization is a traditional European malady the roots of which go back into classical antiquity. Actually, while interest in political theory has always been a feature of anthropological work, problems of sanction and law, social control and government, have only recently attracted extensive anthropological specialization.

Political organization is really a subdivision of the more comprehensive category of structured human relationships known as social organization. The readings which follow give only a sample of the field and many kinds of inquiry and certain types of problem are entirely omitted. We have not even included a specimen of the monographic treatment of social organization accorded a particular society. So varied is the subject matter and its approaches that a single example representative of all does not exist.

Instead, the selections deal generally and comparatively with some of the major institutions of human society. Beginning with the family we move into larger and larger social realms until we reach the state. The selections do not stress controversy (as is the case elsewhere in this book), but this is not to be taken as a sign of agreement.

12. THE SOCIAL LIFE OF MONKEYS, APES AND PRIMITIVE MEN *

The very title of this essay is anathema to many anthropologists, yet its formulation was quite deliberate. To juxtapose primitive society and the groupings formed by various non-human primates seems, on the one hand, the worst kind of pejorative classification (though the reader will discover that, in fact, Sahlins concludes that human society is qualitatively different from all others). On the other hand, the attempt to understand the relationship between primate and human social grouping seems to violate the autonomy of culture as a realm of phenomena (see Nos. I:3 and I:15).

Yet the problem tackled below is an old one. During the nineteenth and early twentieth century, many statements were made about the nature of "original" human society, particularly about mating and the family. Without exception, these hypotheses were found untenable in the light of research but the void created by the annihilation of old speculations was not filled by the presentation of new theories.

The article which follows surveys the results of research on primates and among primitives. It furnishes a modest but substantial basis for understanding contemporary ecological approaches to problems of analysis of the simpler human societies.

* Marshall D. Sahlins, "The Social Life of Monkeys, Apes and Primitive Men." Originally presented at a joint session of the meeting of the American Anthropological Association in 1957. The paper is appearing simultaneously in *Human Biology*, Vol. 31:1 (1959).

The author (b. 1930) is Assistant Professor of Anthropology at the University of Michigan. He has done fieldwork in Turkey and Fiji and is preparing a book on the latter. In addition to articles he has written *Social Stratification in Polynesia* (1958).

1. INTRODUCTION

T HIS STUDY compares societies of infrahuman primates with the most rudimentary of documented human social systems. The objectives are to describe general trends in primate social organization leading to human society, and to delineate the major advances of the latter, cultural society, over precultural society.

For comparative materials, we rely on field studies of monkey and ape social behavior, supplementary observations of these animals in captivity, and ethnographic accounts of simple hunters and gatherers. The quality and quantity of published studies of free ranging subhuman primate societies do not provide comfortable support for weighty generalizations. Aside from the anecdotal literature, we have only Carpenter's accounts of spider monkeys, rhesus, howling monkeys, and gibbons; Nissen's chimpanzee material; Zuckerman's observations of baboons (perhaps biased by his captivity studies); the as yet incomplete reports on the Japanese monkey and some peripheral notes on the African red-tailed monkey by Haddow, and on the gorilla by Schwab. *Considering this, our interpretations of subhuman primate social behavior are entirely provisional.* The data on primitive food gatherers are more abundant. We include in our comparison the following primitive societies: Australian Aborigines, Tasmanians, Semang, Andamanese, Philippine and Congo pygmies, Bushmen, Eskimo, Great Basin Shoshoni, Naskapi, Ona and Yahgan. It is assumed that these societies parallel early cultural society in general features. This is simply an assumption of order and regularity. The technologies and low productivity of modern hunters and gatherers resemble the archaeologically revealed productive systems of early cultures. Granting that a cultural social system is functionally related to its productive system, it follows that early human society resembles rudimentary, modern human society. This reasoning is supported by the large degree of social similarity among the present hunters and gatherers themselves, despite the fact that some of them are as historically distant from each other, as separated in contact and connection, as the paleolithic is separated from modern times. Further, simply because many food gatherers have been driven into marginal areas, they are not thereby disqualified from consideration. There still remain strong social resemblances between marginal peoples, such as Bushmen, Ona, and Eskimo, and those found in isolated, but otherwise not ecologically marginal areas, such as many Australian groups and the Andaman Islanders.

A comparison of subhuman primate and primitive society must recognize the qualitative difference between the two. Human society is cultural society; the organization of organisms is governed by culture traits.

The social life of subhuman primates is governed by anatomy and physiology. Variations in human society are independent of, and are not expressions of biological variations of the organism. Variations in primate society are direct expressions and concomitants of biological variation. Nissen writes: ". . . with one notable exception the phylogenetic course of behavioral development has been gradual . . . it has been a continuous affair, proceeding by quantitative rather than qualitative changes. The one exception is that which marks the transition from the highest non-human primates to man . . . At this point a new 'dimension' or mode of development emerges: culture."

It follows that assertions of specific phylogenetic continuities from anthropoid to primitive society must be summarily rejected, such as Yerkes' suggestion that delousing among primitives is a genetic survival of primate grooming, an activity which, Yerkes writes, also led to: "tonsorial artistry, nursing, surgery, and other social services of man." In the same vein is Kempf's identification of the presenting behavior of a subordinate rhesus monkey with human prostitution. Furthermore, the terminology of cultural social and political organization should be disavowed when describing infrahuman primate society. The cultural anthropologist justifiably shudders when he reads of "clans," "communism," and "socialism," among howler monkeys, or of "harems," "overlords," "despots," "tyrants," "absolutism," and "slavery," among baboons.

The determinants of sociability are different in cultural and precultural society. We find useful Zuckerman's contention that social organization in general is based upon, "three main lines of behavior—search for food, search for mates, avoidance of enemies." Of these factors, the sexual one appears to be primary in the genesis of subhuman primate society: "The main factor that determines social groupings in subhuman primates is sexual attraction." Speaking of sexual attraction, Chance and Mead write, "The emergence of this feature into prominence in their behavior has created primate society." It was the development of the physiological capacity to mate during much of, if not throughout the menstrual cycle, and at all seasons that impelled the formation of year round heterosexual groups among monkeys and apes. Within the primate order, a new level of social integration emerges, one that surpasses that of other mammals whose mating periods, and hence heterosexual groupings, are very limited in duration and by season. Certainly, defense against predation is also a determinant of subhuman primate sociability, but it, and the search for food, appear to be secondary to sex. The influence of sexual attraction in promoting solidarity among subhuman primates has been noted in the field. Carpenter has observed of the howlers: "With repetition of the reproductive cycle in the female and with interrupted breeding throughout the year, the process of group integration through sexual behavior is repeatedly operative, establishing and reinforcing intersexual social bonds."

Sexual attraction remains a determinant of human sociability. But it has become subordinated to the search for food, to economics. A most significant advance of early cultural society was the strict repression and canalization of sex, through the incest tabu, in favor of the expansion of kinship, and thus mutual aid relations. Primate sexuality is utilized in human society to *reinforce* bonds of economic and to a lesser extent, defensive alliance. As Miller says, "All marriage schemes are largely devices to check and regulate promiscuous behavior in the interest of human economic schemes." This is not to underplay the importance of primate sexuality in determining certain general characteristics of human society. If culture had not developed in the primate line, but instead among sexless creatures, marriage and rules of exogamy and endogamy would not be means of establishing cohesive groups in cultural society. But, in the transition from subhuman to human society, cooperation in subsistence activities became the dominant cause of solidarity, avoidance of enemies a secondary cause, while sex became simply a facilitating mechanism.

These propositions are best documented by detailed consideration of primate and primitive society, wherein the differences in causes of sociability will be seen to pervade the comparison, and to turn generic continuity into specific discontinuity.

2. PRIMATE AND PRIMITIVE SOCIETIES

Territoriality is one of a number of common features of primate and primitive social behavior. It is also general among lower vertebrates— perhaps it is a universal characteristic of society. Territoriality arises from competition over living conditions, and has the selective advantage of distributing the species in its habitat so as to maintain population density at or below its optimum.

Territorial relations among groups of subhuman primates of the same species are generally exclusive. Except for the few animals that are driven out of one group and may attach themselves to another, primate societies are usually semi-closed societies. Each horde has a focus of favorite feeding and resting places to which it is often deflected by contact with other groups. Contact between groups of the same species at territorial borders is generally competitive and antagonistic, sometimes violently so. Subhuman primate groups apparently have little tendency to federation. They, "*do not have supergroup social mechanisms* . . . Kinship relations are not operative and inbreeding is the rule rather than the exception. . . ." Carpenter finds the origin of intergroup cooperation characteristic of primitive tribalism, "difficult to trace in subhuman primates which I have studied."

Primate territorial relations are altered by the development of culture in the human species. Territoriality among hunters and gatherers is never exclusive, and group membership is apt to shift and change according to the variability of food resources in space and time. Savage society is open, and corresponding to ecological variations, there are degrees of openness: 1) Where food resources are evenly distributed and tend to be constant year to year, territory is clearly demarcated and stable, and, considering the nucleus of males, the same for group membership. The Ona and most Australian groups are representative of this condition. Stability of membership is effected through customary rules of patrilocal residence, which is usually coupled with local exogamy. Patrilocal residence confers the advantage of continuity of occupation for hunters in areas with which they are familiar. 2) Where food resources are evenly distributed during some seasons, and variably abundant during others, exclusiveness of territory and membership are only seasonal. Local groups of Central Kalahari Bushmen, for example, remain fixed in territories focused around water holes during the dry season; whereas, in the rainy season, such groups mingle and hunt together. Similarly the Semang have seasonal territories fixed by the distribution of the durian tree; after the harvest, territories and exclusive groups dissolve, to be reconstituted at the next durian season. Under these conditions, patrilocal residence and local exogamy are preferred but not strict rules, and local endogamy and matrilocality occur. The Andaman Islanders, with relatively fixed territories, a tendency toward local exogamy, and no residence rule, and the Yahgan, who tend to be locally exogamous, patrilocal, and territorially exclusive, may also fall into this ecological type. However, data available for classification of these groups are inadequate. 3) Finally, there are food gatherers among whom territoriality is *de facto* nonexistent, and local group composition highly variable. These occupy areas where food resources vary in local abundance seasonally and annually. Families coalesce and separate *ad hoc* corresponding to accessibility of supplies. Postmarital residence may be in the group of either spouse, and band aggregates are agamous—there are no rules. The Great Basin Shoshoni, the Eskimo, and the pre-fur trade Naskapi fall into this category.

[Philippine and Congo pygmies are presently of the first type: rigid territory, patrilocal, exogamous. However, both live in symbiotic, subservient relation to agricultural peoples; and at least for the Congo Twides, territorial exclusiveness is clearly a function of boundaries between patron Bantu villages (though Gusinde would disagree). The Heikum Bushmen, also in symbiotic, subservient status to patrilineal Hottentot and Bantu groups, are another instance of the same thing. Unlike other Bushmen, the Heikum live in well defined territories and practice strict patrilocality and local exogamy. Leacock's Naskapi studies suggest that bilocal, nonterritorial, unstable bands commonly become so formalized under outside influences of this general sort.]

Territorality among hunters and gatherers is sometimes maintained by conflict. There appears to be a direct relationship between intensity of intergroup feud and exclusiveness of territory and membership. Thus trespass is strongly resented and interband feuds are relatively frequent among Australians and the Ona; whereas, where territoriality is weak, the concept of trespass is naturally poorly developed, and fighting consists of squabbles between particular families. However, in all cases the outcome of trespass depends on the previous relations between neighbors, and these are usually *friendly*. Even among the Australians, adjacent groups would be allowed to hunt in a band's territory if in need; there is, in Spencer and Gillen's phrase, "no constant state of enmity" between neighbors. Everywhere, no matter how strict the rules of territory, constant visiting between bands prevents the development of closed groups. And everywhere exclusiveness is easily broken down if there is some food windfall, or if food is differentially abundant in adjacent locales.

Hunters and gatherers live in relatively open groups between which relations are usually friendly; infrahuman primates of the same species live in relatively closed groups, between which relations are usually competitive. The invention of kinship and the incest tabu of cultural society are responsible for this difference. Through marrying out, friendly, cooperative relations are established between families. When exogamy can be extended to the local group, cooperation between bands is effected. Intermarrying Australian bands are described by A. P. Elkin as, "a family of countries bound together by those sentiments which function between members of a family and its near relations." It is the kinship ethic of mutual aid that permits populations of hunters and gatherers to shift about according to the distribution of resources. Kinship is thus selectively advantageous in a zoological sense; it permits primitives to adjust to more variable habitats than subhuman primates. Moreover, the kinship relations between groups, and the ceremonies and exchanges of goods that frequently accompany interband meetings, give rise to a further social development: tribalism. Common custom, common dialect, a name and a feeling of unity are created among otherwise independent groups. The stage for further political evolution is thereby set.

We turn now to the internal organization of primate and primitive societies.

The subhuman primate horde varies in size from an average of four animals among the gibbon to several hundred baboons. Group size is not correlated with suborder differences, except that great ape hordes are generally at the lower end of the primate range; orang groups are apparently as small as gibbons, and chimpanzee average 8.5 per group.

The horde may remain together at all times, or may disperse into segments of various constitution—mating groups, female packs, male packs —during daytime feeding, concentrating at night resting places. Howling monkeys typically travel together; spider and baboon groups are instances of segmented hordes.

With the exception of the gibbon, the primate horde characteristically contains more adult females than adult males. In observed wild groups the ratio ranges from nearly 3:1 for howlers, to 1:1 for gibbons. The ratio for spider monkeys, 1.6 females per male, is probably near the average for the primates. The usual inequality apparently reflects the degree of dominance and competition among males for female sexual partners. There are almost always unmated males, either peripherally attached to heterosexual groups, or existing outside the horde.

We have argued that sexual attraction is the primary cause of subhuman primate sociability. Indeed, in many cases the entire horde is a single reproduction unit or mate group. But there are significant species variations in the constitution of hordes and mate groups. There appears to be a progressive development in the primate order from promiscuous relations within the group to the establishment of exclusive sex partnerships, one of which comprises the nucleus of a horde. Since the young remain attached to adult females throughout, the highest forms of primate mate groups resemble the elementary human family in composition. The emergence of exclusive, independent mate groups includes the following steps: 1) Among New World monkeys observed in freeranging conditions, howlers and spiders, the only stable relations within a horde are between females and their young. Only when females are in the oestrus period of the menstrual cycle do they leave the female-offspring pack and become attached to specific males, and then not exclusively, but to several in succession. The mated pair is a temporary, non-exclusive unit. 2) Old World monkeys develop more permanent sex partnerships. Rhesus shows the trend toward exclusiveness. Again in rhesus, the female-young pack is a separate unit, and sex partnerships are only temporarily established while a female is in heat. However, for every female the succession order among her male partners corresponds to their dominance position. Therefore, dominant males have all females in oestrus, while subordinate males are excluded from some when there are not enough to go around. The mate group of the Japanese monkey, in the same genus as rhesus, is very similar. 3) The baboon mate group is a simple extrapolation from rhesus. The steps involved are: the exclusion of subordinate males from sexual relations with females, and the development of constant association between a dominant male, females and young. The baboon mate group is a permanent, exclusive relationship between a dominant male and his several females, the young following their mothers. Subordinate males may remain attached to the group on its fringes, or form unisexual bands. The baboon horde consists of several such mate groups and male bands, each relatively independent. 4) The ape horde tends to be composed of a single, independent mate group of the baboon type. In the gibbon, this consists of one male, one female plus young. The evidence from the other anthropoid apes is not conclusive; however, gorilla, orang and chimpanzee hordes apparently consist of mate groups of one male, two or more females and their young, and perhaps subordinate males.

The emergence of exclusive, permanent mate groups among higher primates is explained by the progressive emancipation of sexual behavior from hormonal control running through the order. In monkeys, copulation outside the female's fertile period is relatively rare. In apes—more so, in man—sex is freed from hormonal regulation, being subject instead to cortical and social control. The oftmade alternative assertion that the development of the family is due to increasing duration of infant dependency is not supportable. With one minor exception, subhuman primate males are never significantly involved in rearing the young, save in retrieving the fallen, and indirectly as group defenders. The exceptional case of the male Japanese monkey that rears the older infant if a female has two in succession is not significant here, since there is no family-type group involved. This behavior was observed only in one of a number of hordes of Japanese monkeys, and is entirely unique among subhuman primates. Baboon and rhesus males are known to have killed young in the course of sexual attacks upon their mothers. A long dependency period cements mother-offspring bonds but not necessarily father-mother-offspring relations. Only when there is an economic division of labor by sex can infant dependency produce this effect. In subhuman primates there is no sexual division of economic labor.

Social relations within the subhuman primate horde vary according to the age, sex and dominance statuses of interacting animals. Leaving aside dominance for a moment, most social interaction can be adequately described by utilizing three elemental status categories: adult male, adult female, and young. Interaction of animals of these categories produce six "qualitatively distinct" social relations: male-male; female-female; male-female; male-young; female-young; young-young. The content of most of these relations can be inferred from the preceeding and succeeding discussion. It will be seen that age and sex differences remain important social distinctions among primitive hunters and gatherers.

Dominance statuses are found among all known monkeys and apes, as well as many lower vertebrates. Dominance is established by competition for mates, for food, for position in progression, and the like—Carpenter has remarked that, ". . . in every known typical grouping of monkeys and

apes there is persisting competition for priority rights to incentives." Conflict is often particularly prominent among males over females in oestrus.
Males are usually dominant over females. [This last is subject to exception
when females are in heat. Dominance has been experimentally raised in
primates and other vertebrates by injections of male sex hormones.] Dominance status affects behavior in every aspect of social life: play, feeding,
sex, grooming, competition between groups, and it even determines the
spatial relations of animals within the horde. Dominance among paired
animals is easily determined experimentally by introducing a series of food
pellets to which there is limited access, and noting which animal consistently appropriates them. Nowlis' food appropriation experiments, performed with differentially satiated animals, show that dominance is a social
behavior arising from conflict—not a simple, independent drive for "prestige," as is sometimes claimed.

Maslow contends that the quality of dominance varies among New and
Old World monkeys and the apes, and that variation in dominance
quality is correlated with differences in social organization. Platyrrhines,
according to Maslow, show the greatest indifference in social relations.
Dominance is "tenuous," "non-contactual," frequently not expressed, and
often ascertained in the laboratory only with difficulty. In contrast,
"Catarrhine dominance is rough, brutal and aggressive; it is of the nature
of a powerful, persistent, selfish urge that expresses itself in ferocious
bullying, fighting and sexual aggression." Weak and sick animals are attacked; in competition over food, a subordinate animal would starve.
Chimpanzees however, show "friendly dominance." Dominant animals
protect subordinates, never attack them except in the form of rough play.
Crawford in one laboratory experiment noted that only 0.4 per cent of
chimpanzee social behavior could be described as aggressive, and other
field and captivity data generally bear out Maslow's hypothesis of suborder differences in dominance quality.

There appear to be correlated differences in the grooming behavior of
the suborders. Yerkes advances the notion that social, as opposed to self
grooming, increases in frequency from prosimian through anthropoid ape.
Grooming serves a biological function in removing parasites and the like,
but this is nearly equally accomplished by self or social grooming. Therefore, social grooming takes on added significance as a "social service" in
the higher primates. Moreover, grooming in higher primates is not only
social, but reciprocal. Social grooming among wild gibbons has been
noted to be frequent and reciprocal. By contrast, evidence from field and
laboratory indicates that social grooming is comparatively infrequent
among New World monkeys. It is difficult to say from present evidence
that social and reciprocal grooming increase from Old World monkeys to
anthropoids, but on the whole, Yerkes' assertions are supportable.

The emergence of reciprocal social behavior and the progressive tempering of dominance relations are significant trends in the primate line —trends which, we shall note, are continued in primitive society. On the other hand, economic teamwork and mutual aid are nearly zero among subhuman primates, including anthropoids. Spontaneous cooperation— as opposed to one animal helping another—has not been observed among them. Chimpanzees have been trained to solve problems cooperatively, but fail to do so without tuition. Monkeys apparently cannot even be taught to cooperate. Spontaneous teamwork supposes symbolling: "Teamwork makes intellectual demands of the same order as those made by language. Psychologically, it may, in fact, be difficult to distinguish between the two." Much has been made of food solicitation and sharing among chimpanzees—one case was noted in the field. Nissen and Crawford's elaborate experiment showed that chimpanzees share food pellets and tokens, although sharing was much less frequent than not, and was evidently non-reciprocal. However, in a similar experiment using animals tested for dominance, Nowlis observed that every case of sharing—1/10 of the food shared in 80 of 480 trials—was from subordinate to dominant; dominants never gave food to subordinates. Therefore, "food sharing" here is a function of previous dominance competition and actually indicates monopolization, not pooling, of a limited supply.

We now consider the social system of hunters and gatherers among whom the usual band contains twenty to fifty people. During poor seasons, however, it may fragment into small family groups. We have already looked at band structure. Corresponding to ecological conditions, bands range in composition from an enlarged patrilocal family to a congeries of variably related nuclear families. Almost all members will be kinsmen, and the etiquette of kinship behavior regulates social life. Radcliffe-Brown noted that in Australia, for example, kinship: ". . . regulates more or less definitely the behavior of an individual to every person with whom he has any social dealings whatsoever."

The family is the only social unit inside the band; where bands are unstable, it is the major form of social organization. Among primitives, the division of economic labor by sex is fundamental to the family and makes marriage an economic alliance—or, in Westermarck's terms, ". . . marriage is something more than a regulated sexual relation. It is an economic institution." The complementary economic roles of the sexes determine certain qualities of primitive marriage. First, it is a necessity for all adults; the unmated adult male of the primate horde rarely has a counterpart in primitive bands. Secondly, polygamy is usually economically impractical; monogamy is prevalent. Finally, as indicated, stable heterosexual relations are not simply determined by sexual attraction, but by economics. Sex is easily had in many hunting and gathering groups, both before and beside marriage, but such neither necessarily establishes the family nor destroys it. Legal rights to sexual privileges of spouses are often waived in favor of socio-economic advantages, as in wife lending. The very rules of exogamy and incest prevent the formation of the family on a basis of simple sexual attraction. Steward's statement of the economic basis of the Shoshoni marriage can be duplicated from accounts of other simple societies: "Marriage was an economic alliance in a very real sense . . . a union which brought into co-operation the complementary economic activities of the sexes—a person could not, in the interest of self-preservation, afford to remain long single . . . the role of exclusive sex privileges in matrimony seems to have been secondary." Compare Radcliffe-Brown on the Australians: "The family is based on the co-operation of man and wife, the former providing the flesh food and the latter the vegetable food . . . this economic aspect of the family is a most important one . . . I believe that in the minds of the natives themselves this aspect of marriage, i.e., its relation to subsistence, is of greatly more importance than the fact that man and wife are sexual partners."

In man, therefore, primate sexuality has been brought under cultural control; it has become a means to other ends. Another aspect of primitive marriage teaches the same lesson. Unlike primate unions, created and maintained in conflict, primitive marriage is a powerful factor in inter-familial and interband alliance. Again, as Steward writes of the Shoshoni, and one can find countless ethnographic paraphrases of this truism: "Marriage was more a contract between families than between individuals." Among hunters and gatherers, marriages are frequently arranged (or at least approved) by the families rather than the spouses. Considerations often pass between the groups, thus setting the pattern for future cooperation. Women may be exchanged between groups, or intermarriage between certain parties preferred and repeated, solidifying both the marriages and group relations. The alliance between families may be paramount to the extent that a marriage can survive the death of one of the partners, he or she being replaced through the levirate or sororate.

There is an outstanding implication of these characteristics of primitive marriage and the family. Given the division of labor by sex and the formation of domestic units through marriage, it follows that sharing of food and other items, rather than being non-existent, as among monkeys and apes, is a *sine qua non* of the human condition. Food sharing is an outstanding functional criterion of man. In the domestic economy of the family there is constant reciprocity and pooling of resources. And, at the same time that kinship is extended throughout the band of families, so are the principles of the domestic economy. Among all hunters and gatherers there is a constant give and take of vital goods through hospitality and gift exchange. Everywhere, generosity is a great social virtue. Also general is the custom of pooling large game among the entire band, either as a matter of course, or in times of scarcity. Where kinship is extended beyond the local group by interband marriage, so are reciprocity and mutual aid. Goods may pass over great distances through a series of kinship transactions. "Trade" is thus established. Hunters and gatherers are able to take mutual advantage of the exploitation of distant environments, a phenomenon without parallel in the primate order. This emphasis on generosity, on mutual aid, and the attribution of social prestige for generosity, stand in direct opposition to the tendency among primates to monopolize vital goods. Perhaps the elaborated emphasis on sharing among primitives is to be partially understood as a cultural means for overcoming primate tendencies in the opposite direction.

In the system of social status, there is a generic continuity between primate and primitive society. Qualitative social differences of sex and age that are marked in subhuman primate groups are major principles of status and role allocation among hunters and gatherers. The division of labor by sex is an example. So is the pervasive recognition of sex, seniority and generation in kinship behavior and terminology.

There is also some continuity in dominance status. Leadership falls to men among hunters and gatherers, although, what is possibly different from subhuman primates, it is especially the elders that are respected. There are, however, important qualitative differences in dominance relations among hunters and gatherers and subhuman primates. Each primitive band usually has an elderly headman. The respect accorded him and other elders is not due to their physical ability to appropriate a limited supply of desired objects. (They may be preferentially treated in communal food distribution, but this is another thing.) Quite the opposite from subhuman primates, a man must be generous to be respected. Prestige among hunters and gatherers can be estimated by noting who gives away the most—precisely the reverse of the test for dominance status among subhuman primates. The position of the headman rests primarily on superior knowledge of game movements, water and other resources, ritual and other things which govern social life. Thus Boas pointed out that there is a direct relation between the authority of Eskimo headmen of various groups and the distance and difficulties involved in traveling between winter and summer huntings grounds. But such knowledge alone cannot breed power. The leader of the band has no means to compel obedience. He is commonly described as ruling through "moral influence." A Congo pygmy leader bluntly told Schebesta, "There would be no point in his giving orders, as nobody would heed them." Steward comments that the title, "talker", given to a Shoshoni

leader, "truly designates his most important function." The leader of the
Central Eskimo camp is picturesquely referred to as *isumataq*, 'he who
thinks' (for the others). In all hunters and gatherers, the heads of the
separate families exercise more control than the informal headmen over
the whole. Compared to infrahuman primates, ranking hierarchies and
dominance approach zero among hunters and gatherers. Yet, where all
interact as kinsmen, and sharing a scanty food supply replaces conflict
over it, this is expectable.

3. SUMMARY AND CONCLUSIONS

The transition from subhuman primate society to rudimentary cultural
society was at the same time a process of generic continuity and of
specific discontinuity. If culture had not developed among a species of
primates, but among animals of different behavioral characteristics, then
the forms and development of culture would be basically different. The
social behavior of primates is the foundation of some general features
of human society. On the other hand, no specific trait of cultural society,
even in its most rudimentary state, is, in both form and functioning, a
direct survival of some specific trait of primate social behavior. This
discontinuity is due to the fact that subhuman primate society is a direct
expression of the physiology of the species operating in a given environment; whereas cultural traits govern the social adaptation of the human
primate. The development of culture did not simply give expression to
man's primate nature, it replaced that nature as the direct determinant
of social behavior, and in so doing, channeled it—at times repressed it
completely. The most significant transformation effected by cultural
society was the subordination of the search for mates—the primary
determinant of subhuman primate sociability—to the search for food. In
the process also, economic cooperation replaced competition, and kinship
replaced conflict as the principal mechanism of organization.

What are the generic continuities? Territoriality is one. But similarities
such as these are common to a wide variety of societies, including those
of lower vertebrates. A more restricted continuity is the utilization of
the powerful social functions of primate sexuality in human social organizations. To repeat an earlier observation, it is only against the unique
background of primate sexual behavior that one fully understands why
marriage and marriage rules are general mechanisms for integrating co-
operative human groups. Another generic survival of simian society is
the allocation of social functions on the lines of sex and age among
hunters and gatherers.

Of particular interest are social advances within the primate order
upon which cultural society directly elaborated. Here the cultural de-

velopments appear capstones to trends which had begun to unfold in precultural conditions. In the primate line the exclusive mate group appears to have developed out of the promiscuous horde. In the transformation to the human family, the anthropoid mate group was altered more in function than in form. A second primate advance is the development of reciprocal social services in grooming. Generalized to food sharing, reciprocity is basic to cultural society. Thirdly, there is the softening of dominance relations among higher primates. In primitive society, dominance or prestige is especially associated with service to the group.

The most significant advances in the early evolution of cultural society can be deduced by comparison of primate and primitive groups. To us these appear to be: 1) the division of labor by sex and the establishment of the family on this basis; 2) the invention of kinship; 3) the incest prohibition and its extension through exogamy, thus extending kinship; 4) the overcoming of primate competition over food in favor of sharing and cooperation; and 5) the abolition of other primate conflicts leading to the establishment of dominance hierarchies.

These five advances are complementary; nothing is said here of their order of appearance or relative significance. It is claimed that they are great triumphs of early culture. These developments are necessary social counterparts of the continuous tool activity which enabled man to become the dominant form of life.

13. THE NATURAL HISTORY
OF THE FAMILY *

Herodotus, who commented on the matrilineal Lykkians, is apparently
the first writer to have noted that the family takes different forms in
different societies. Indeed, if the presence of a married couple is made
essential to the definition of family, there is at least one well documented
case, the Nayar of the Malabar area of India, in which the family did not
occur. Even though the Nayar example is extreme, there are many
societies in which the married couple is completely subordinated to other
small scale kin groups. In such societies the functions we are accustomed
to think of as parental are normally and regularly assumed by other
relatives. The selection which follows outlines the main principles of
family organization and discusses some consequences of the
different groupings which result.

THERE IS every reason to believe that the family is the oldest of
human social institutions and that it will survive, in one form or another,
as long as our species exists. Mark Twain's dictum that nothing is so
continuous as marriage holds true from whatever direction we consider
it. Nevertheless, both the origins of the family and the steps by which it
has developed into its present multiplicity of forms are obscure. Since

* Ralph Linton, "The Natural History of the Family," from Ruth Nanda Anshen
(editor), The Family: Its Function and Destiny (New York: Harper and Brothers,
1947, rev. 1959), pp. 18–38. Reprinted with the permission of the editor and publishers.

The author (1893–1953) was an ethnologist of wide experience though his primary
association was with the cultures of Polynesia and Madagascar. Linton's interests were
most diverse: culture-history, primitive art and relations of anthropology and psychiatry were among his favorite subjects. His last book was The Tree of Culture
(posthumous, 1955). Among his other works are The Study of Man (1936) and The
Cultural Background of Personality (1945).

social institutions are among the most perishable of human artifacts, we have no direct evidence regarding any of the types of family organization which existed prior to the beginning of written records. The great variety of familial institutions found among existing "primitives" serves to show the range of possibilities but provides few clues as to what may have been developmental sequences. At most, we can say that certain forms of family are quite unsuited to particular environmental-cultural configurations. For example, no group which lives by hunting and food gathering could seclude its women in harem fashion. Nor would a group in which there was a persistent surplus of women over men be likely to practice polyandry. Beyond such simple generalizations it is impossible to go. All statements about the origin and evolution of family types must be classed as suppositions. Some of these suppositions appear much more probable than others, but none of them is susceptible of scientific proof.

This caveat is made necessary by the calm assurance with which certain authors have discussed the development of the family and by the way in which certain nineteenth-century speculations on the subject have been incorporated into our folklore. Partly because of the almost psychopathic interest of nineteenth-century Europeans in everything connected with sex, the family was one of the first institutions to be investigated by social scientists. The thinking of these scientists was dominated by the recently promulgated theory of evolution and by a calm ethnocentrism which placed their own social institutions at the apex of all lines of development. It was assumed that the western European, and especially the Victorian English, type of family must be the ultimate flowering of the institution. Given such a datum point, it was possible to arrange all other forms of family in an evolutionary series simply by seeing how far each fell short of this ideal. Sexual promiscuity was put at the most distant point—that is, at the beginning of the series —to be followed by group marriage, then polyandry, then polygyny, and lastly monogamy. It was assumed that, running parallel with this, there had been an evolution of patterns of descent and family control. Children were at first the common property of the promiscuous group. This was followed by a development of matriarchal, matrilineal institutions, which in turn were transformed, after a struggle, into the patriarchal family.

All that we know of the physical and psychological characteristics not only of man but of the primates in general makes these early speculations look like pure fantasy. Apparently the only primates who live in sexually promiscuous hordes are the South American howler monkeys, a species very remote from our own line of ancestry. All other primates appear to be either monogamous or polygynous, with partnership durations which would not be considered a bad record in Hollywood. Although most species show active sexual curiosity and will make advances to strange individuals, such episodes do not disrupt the family pattern.

In the face of this evidence the old theory of primitive promiscuity has been discarded by practically all social scientists. Men may be different from the other primates, but they are not that different. Recent years, however, have witnessed the resuscitation of another early theory of family origins and primordial events. According to certain psychoanalysts the original human family (and in reading their accounts one has the feeling that there was only one) was completely patriarchal. It consisted of a group of females and young, dominated by a single irascible and highly jealous old male. This "old man" preempted all females, including his own daughters, and drove away his sons. Eventually these sons found release for both their sex and their hunger tensions in the murder of their father and his subsequent consumption. We need not go into the catastrophic effects of all this on their super-egos—effects still reflected in some of our social institutions.

Aside from its cannibalistic features this theory is more in keeping with the habits of our closest sub-human relatives, the anthropoids, than is the initial promiscuity theory. Its credibility—for of course it can be neither proved nor disproved—rests in large part on the point in our ancestors' evolution which we take as the beginning of human status. Even at a time when our ancestors looked more like gorillas than like us, they were living in groups larger than single families and hunting in packs. None of the living species of gregarious primates drives young males out of the band or resorts to the murder of old ones. At the human level such practices would weaken the unit to the point where it would be unable to maintain itself. If there ever was the "old man" type of family organization it must have ended long before our ancestors became recognizably human.

In view of what we know of the organization of those human societies which are still at the simplest levels of economic and technological development, it seems safe to assume that even the earliest representatives of our species had fairly permanent matings. Moreover, it is highly probable that the bulk of such unions, as in all societies of which we have record, were monogamous. Presumably there was a certain casualness in sex relations, tempered by a lively jealousy on the part of both sexes, and a lack of formal regulation as to the number of spouses. No female of breeding age would remain unattached for long, and, if there were more females than males in the band, the better hunters would absorb the surplus into their family groups. The less common surplus male would attach himself to some family group and might even be permitted to share the wife's favors if he showed proper submission and gratitude to the real husband.

Simple family organization of this sort could serve as a starting point for the development of all later familial forms, but it seems highly improbable that there was any regular order for the emergence of these forms. In other words, there has been not a single universal evolution of the family but a series of local evolutions moving by different paths to different ends. We cannot trace these paths in detail, but by the study and comparison of existing family forms we can get a fairly good idea of the forces which have been at work to produce them.

The first difficulty in making such a comparative study is that of delimiting the field. The English term "family" is applied indiscriminately to two social units which are basically different in their composition and functional potentialities. The word may be taken to mean either an intimate, closely organized group consisting of spouses and offspring or a diffuse and in our case almost unorganized group of blood relatives. To avoid confusion, these two types of grouping will be referred to respectively as the *conjugal family* and the *consanguine family*. Both types of grouping are recognized by practically all societies and are terminologically distinguished in many languages.

There can be no question that the conjugal type of family, as a functional unit, is the earlier in human history and was the first to be integrated into social structures. Blood relationship, of course, is as old as mating and reproduction, but its recognition and especially its employment as a criterion for delimiting the membership of organized, functional social groupings must have required a considerable degree of sophistication. Even in the current social systems which place most stress on the consanguine family, this unit has a certain artificial quality. It is never delimited on a completely biological basis, that is, on blood relationship alone. Such relationship is always stressed with relation to a particular line of descent or certain degrees of consanguinity or both. In other words, the consanguine family is a social artifact whereas the conjugal family is a biological unit differing little, in its essential qualities, from similar units to be observed in a great variety of mammalian species. Even as a formal institution the conjugal family everywhere incorporates a series of behavior patterns which are so closely interrelated with the physiological and psychological characteristics of our species that it is difficult to see how that species could have survived without it.

At the foundation of every variant of the conjugal family lies an assumption of continuity in the mated relationship. Even in those societies which impose no formal strictures on the separation of mates, the role of the conjugal group is based on an anticipation of permanence, and the average individual establishes an enduring partnership with someone of the opposite sex at least by middle age. This continuity of mating has a physiological basis in certain characteristics which man shares with most of the sub-human primates. The primate order is characterized by the absence of any clearly defined rutting season and by constant sexual activity and interest on the part of the male. It is also characterized by marked differences in the size and vigor of males and females, with consequent patterns of male dominance. There are a few exceptions to the second generalization, but it holds for most primate species, including our own. The combination of male dominance and of constant male interest in females as sexual objects operates to give matings stability and presumably did so even before our ancestors had achieved full human status. Even the earliest men were able to keep particular women to themselves and to prevent these women from bestowing their favors on other men, at least as long as their husbands were present.

Very early in human history these physiological factors must have been reinforced by psychological ones. Although man is the most flexible and the most easily conditioned of all the primates, he has an acute need for security in his personal relationships and a desire for congenial companionship and perfected response. These needs, although less immediately compulsive than the physiological tensions of sex, are far more continuous in their operations. Relationships which will satisfy them cannot be established between any and all individuals and can only be established through long-continued association. When one had found a partner who could satisfy both these needs and the sexual ones, such a partner was to be valued and retained even though sexual curiosity might lead to occasional unfaithfulness.

Presumably the factors just discussed had given considerable permanence to human matings before any cultural factors came into play. At least the development of the most important cultural feature making for permanence in modern unmechanized societies could scarcely have taken place without some pre-existing pattern of continuous partnerships. This feature is the universal differentiation of economic activities along sex lines. In all known societies men are trained in certain skills and women in other skills, and the division is so adjusted that a man and a woman together form a largely self-sufficient unit for production and consumption. Typically, the man is the provider and the woman the preparer of raw materials. They are able to satisfy their basic needs for food, shelter, and comfort while together but not if separated. It is only in recent times that this basic pattern of economic interdependence of the sexes has begun to break down, with consequences to the family as an institution which we still perceive only dimly. In the unmechanized society such interdependence does as much to give stability to marriage as all other factors combined. Even uncongenial partners are held together by their need for each other's contribution to their individual physical comfort.

Although the continued partnership of a man and a woman provides the basis for every conjugal family unit, such units also involve other relationships—those of parents to offspring and of offspring to each other. With regard to the parent-child relationship, the mother may be taken as the central point. There are no indications of the existence of anything like a paternal instinct in our species. The group of father, mother, and offspring is held together by the father's attachment to the mother and the child's physical dependency upon her, reinforced at a later period by ties of affection and emotional dependency developed during its infantile period. The association of father and child is a secondary one, deriving from their common interest in the mother and their common residence with her. In this respect it parallels the association between siblings—that is, brothers and sisters—which is also established by common dependence upon the mother and by common residence. The fact that these associations are more or less fortuitous does not prevent them from providing an opportunity for the development of mutual adjustments in personality and of strong ties of affection. There is abundant evidence that similar adjustments and ties can be developed between individuals who have no biological relationship to each other. The ease with which adopted children or stepparents can be incorporated into a conjugal family group is a case in point.

That the conjugal family must be exceedingly old in human history is proved by its close adjustment to certain innate characteristics of our species. Thus it is intimately linked with the difference between the human reproductive cycle and the period of dependency of offspring. It seems that under natural conditions women tend to produce offspring at intervals of eighteen months on the average, whereas the period of the child's dependence upon adults for mere physical survival may be conservatively set at ten years. It is hard to see how a species in which such a disharmony existed could have survived in the absence of permanent matings which assured the female of male assistance in the care of the offspring.

The conjugal family pattern is also in close adjustment with what we know of the optimum conditions for personality development in the young individual. Apparently the infant requires a large measure of affection and adult response over and above the satisfaction of its physiological needs. The high infantile death rate in even the most scientifically run orphan asylums bears witness to this fact. In order to provide this response the mother must transfer to other individuals some of the responsibility for the care of older but still immature offspring. In practice, it is usually the husband or elder siblings who assume such responsibility, but such a transfer would be impossible in the absence of a relatively stable, continuing family group.

As the child grows older the presence of siblings plays an important role in its socialization and in the development of a flexible personality. Elder children provide it with conscious goals and models for behavior which are comprehensible and within the range of its developing abilities. Moreover, in many respects, the sibling group is a microcosm of adult society. The presence of both older and younger children gives the developing individual an opportunity for the simultaneous exercise of dominance and submission while keeping both within limits. Older siblings are unable to enforce or reward patterns of complete submission in the way that adults can. Younger children can resist domination to a degree which makes impossible the development of the spurious sense of power which a child may acquire through the good-natured acquiescence of adults in its demands. In constant interaction with individuals whose abilities are nearly the same as its own, the child can develop a realistic evaluation of its adequacies and inadequacies and patterns of social behavior which will be adjusted to both. The importance of this can be judged from the frequent difficulties of an only child in our own society.

The adjustments to each other which siblings develop during their period of common residence and mutual dependence upon the parents always survive into adult life. This fact lies at the foundation of all consanguine family organization, much as the facts of mating and childhood dependence lie at the foundation of the conjugal family. The habits of mutual dependence and the ties of affection developed between siblings continue to operate even after they have mated and assumed nuclear positions in new conjugal families. This inevitably results in some division of loyalties between the consanguine and the conjugal family groups, and the possibilities for conflict are increased by the fact that the consanguine group can perform most of the functions of the conjugal group. Thus, since it normally includes adults of both sexes, it can be self-contained in terms of the complementary skills required for economic production. For the same reason, it can provide successfully for the care and rearing of children, at least after their weaning. Lastly, it can afford its members a large measure of emotional security and of perfected response in intimate personal relations, thus satisfying their psychological needs. In fact, the only personal needs which it cannot satisfy are the sexual ones. It fails in this because of the existence of incest taboos. The reasons for such taboos appear to be complex and are still imperfectly understood. It is unnecessary to discuss them here. Suffice it to say that practically all societies prohibit the marriage of siblings and thus prevent the fusion of the consanguine and conjugal family units to a single familial institution.

So many of the familial functions can be performed by either a consanguine or a conjugal unit that, to avoid conflict, it is necessary for societies to delimit the roles of each with considerable clarity. Almost every possible type of division of function can be found in one society or another. Our own family organization lies near one end of the series of possible variations. All familial functions are concentrated in the conjugal group, which is surrounded by a fringe of loosely attached and intermittently operative relatives. In many non-European societies, on the other hand, practically all functions except those connected with reproduction are concentrated in the consanguine group. The spouses of group members are never really incorporated into the family and look to their own consanguine families for the satisfaction of many of their practical and most of their emotional needs.

Such a heavy emphasis on the consanguine group has important effects on marriage, which tends to become a matter of contractual arrangement between groups rather than of affinity between individuals. Partners are picked for the younger members mainly with an eye to the advantage of the family. The chances for incompatibility are correspondingly increased, while the economic dependence of the spouses on each other is minimal. Either partner can find in his or her own consanguine group satisfaction for all but sexual needs. Under these circumstances, the marital relationship is intrinsically brittle and partnerships have to be stabilized by external pressures.

In matriarchal societies such pressure is rarely exerted. Any of the functions connected with child care can be performed as well by a mother's brother as by a husband. Actually, marriages appear to be least stable in those societies in which the wife continues to live with her own consanguine group and her children are counted as members of it. In patriarchal societies, on the other hand, there tends to be a high development of machinery for insuring the continuity of marriage. This is especially true in those societies in which the wife leaves her own consanguine group and goes to live with that of her husband. The basis for this seems to be the interest of the husband's family in the children. A mother is far more necessary to their well-being than a father and vastly more difficult to replace. One of the commonest mechanisms for ensuring her continued presence is the giving of a bride price. When this has been accepted by the woman's family, its members will not receive her back except in cases of extreme ill treatment, since if they do so they must either provide a substitute or refund the money.

It is a curious fact that in such attempts to stabilize marriages the sanctions employed are almost always economic. Even in those societies which lean most heavily on supernatural sanctions for the enforcement of socially acceptable behavior, separations entail no supernatural punishment. This is in sharp contrast to the frequency of supernatural punishments for evasion of parent-and-child or sibling obligations. The reasons for this are not clear. Perhaps it stems from a subconscious recognition of the desirability of personal compatibility between spouses and from a sympathy for those who have been forced into unsatisfactory relationships.

In the development of various social systems both the conjugal and consanguine family units have undergone numerous amplifications. The various elaborations of the consanguine group are so foreign to our own experience and have so little bearing on current conditions in our own society that it seems unnecessary to discuss them here. Joint family, lineage and clan, and the intricacies of relationship systems can be left to students of primitive society. The elaborations of the conjugal group, on the other hand, possess more than an academic interest for us, since they appear to be responses to situations which may well arise in our own society in the not too distant future.

Plural marriage is a widespread phenomenon; in fact, it is approved by a majority of the world's societies. Of its three possible forms, one, group marriage, is so rare that we need not concern ourselves with it, especially since it seems to have no functions which cannot be performed equally well by monogamous unions. Polyandry—that is plurality of husbands—is also comparatively rare but seems to be directly related to economic conditions. Contrary to popular belief, most uncivilized peoples exercise some control over population. The simplest method is that of female infanticide, and in groups with limited natural resources this is often carried to the point where it results in a marked surplus of adult males over females. This in itself is not enough to produce polyandry, but, when conditions are so hard that the labor of a single male no longer suffices to support a wife and children, this form of marriage is very likely to develop. Under sufficient economic stress it may even develop, as an alternative form of marriage, in societies where the numbers of the two sexes are approximately equal. Thus any social worker knows that it is not infrequent in the economically depressed sections of our own society, although the secondary husband is usually referred to as a boarder.

Polygyny, plurality of wives, is much more common than polyandry and the reasons for its occurrence appear to be more complex. The frequency of this type of mating among sub-human primates suggests that our own species may have a predisposition toward it, based on the physical dominance and the more constant sexual interest of males. Such a predisposition, if it exists, is reinforced by the presence of more adult females than males in most societies. This is due partly to the higher infant mortality of males, partly to the more dangerous occupations in which they usually engage. It is highly desirable, from the point of view of the society, that these surplus females should be given an opportunity to breed, thus maintaining the man power of the group. It is equally desirable that their offspring should be reared under normal familial conditions, with a mother's husband to teach sons the proper male skills and social attitudes. Lastly, the presence of a number of unmated adults in any society is always a disturbing factor and a threat to the stability of marital relationships. This is especially the case in societies which provide women with no respected careers other than marriage. Except in societies where the men are constantly engaged in war or in extra-hazardous activities, the surplus of females is never large and polygynous marriage tends to be limited to males at the higher economic and prestige levels. Even in societies which consider polygyny the ideal form of marriage most families are monogamous through force of circumstances.

It is always a surprise to persons reared in our own society to discover how smoothly patterns of plural marriage operate in groups which are accustomed to them and especially to find that they are usually approved by both sexes. There are numerous patterns, however, which contribute to this in the societies in question. Sexual jealousy is closely linked with the symbolic importance attached to the sexual act. Although there is reason to believe that such jealousy can never be completely eliminated, it can be greatly reduced by a combination of early conditioning and of rewards for its suppression. All jealousy is essentially a reaction to some situation which the individual perceives as a threat to dominance or to security in a personal relationship. When the individual has been taught that extra-marital relations on the part of the spouse do not constitute a threat to either, such relations lose most of their force as jealousy provocations. This is well illustrated by the frequency of wife lending as a recognized social institution. The man who lends his wife publicly and with social approval does not weaken his own relation with her and even establishes himself in a dominant position with respect to the man who accepts the favor. His psychological reactions under these circumstances are entirely different from those which he has when he discovers that his wife has taken a lover on her own initiative. No jealousy in the first case may well be linked with extreme jealousy in the second.

Still another factor which operates to limit jealousy within a polygamous family is the diffuseness of feelings of dependency and of emotional attachments which growing up in such a family tends to produce in the child. It is reared with several mothers or fathers, as the case may be, to any one of whom it can turn for emotional response and for the satisfaction of its physiological needs. Instead of a fierce and exclusive attachment to one individual, it develops a number of attachments, none of which produces a very high emotional effect. This conditioning makes it possible for it, as an adult, to accept the sharing of a spouse with equanimity if not enthusiasm.

Lastly, all polygamous societies provide plural spouses with rewards for the suppression of jealousy and for willing co-operation in such expanded family units. The woman who is an only wife in a polygynous society tends to be badly overworked and to welcome the addition of other wives because they will lighten her labors. She is also subject to the stigma which attaches in any society to the wife of a man who is a social and economic failure. When plural marriage is a symbol of economic success and advanced social status, wives will often put pressure upon their husbands to contract additional marriages even when the husbands are quite satisfied with the *status quo*.

In spite of all these factors, the possibilities for jealousy and for quarrels between plural spouses are still so strong that nearly all the societies which approve plural marriage go to great lengths to define the relative status and marital rights and duties of spouses. In both polygynous and polyandrous families there is normally a head wife or head husband who dominates the spouses of the same sex and organizes their activities. In many cases this individual is the only real spouse, the other partners of the same sex ranking as concubines or *cicisbei*. In polygynous families it is also a frequent pattern for the husband to spend one day and night in succession with each of the wives, infraction of this rule being punishable as adultery. Property rights within the family, especially as between husbands and wives, also tend to be delimited with great clarity. Lastly, wives are often allowed a right of veto over a husband's plural marriages to insure the creation of a congenial group of spouses who will be able to live and work together with a minimum of friction. All in all, polygynous patterns require an elaboration of formal organization which exceeds that needed even for extended consanguine groups and which is quite foreign to our own concepts of the conjugal family.

It may be added that polygynous patterns do not operate to provide males with any great advantage. Although they may allow somewhat more leeway for the satisfaction of the male's roving sexual interests, the man who will bring a new wife into the family in the face of his established wife's opposition must possess reckless courage. No matter what the public patterns of family life may be, the private patterns seem to be much the same in all societies; most wives know how to reduce their husbands to submission. The husband of several wives inevitably finds himself caught on the horns of a dilemma. Either his wives cannot agree or they agree too well. In the first case he is subjected to multiple, conflicting pressures which leave him no peace. In the second, the wives and children tend to form a closed group from which he is largely excluded.

The main reason for devoting so much space to the polygynous family is that suggestions for the legalizations of polygyny in our own society have been made from time to time. They were frequent immediately after the First World War and may be anticipated following the Second. The reason most commonly advanced is the need of maintaining the population level in the face of war losses. Actually, even severe modern wars rarely result in the destruction of a large enough percentage of males to produce a serious imbalance in the numbers of the two sexes. In modern Western societies, with their well-nigh universal practice of birth control, the numerical losses entailed through the failure of certain women of a war generation to find husbands can easily be made up by a voluntary increase in the number of children produced by those who do. Whether such an increase will occur now that the Second World War has ended is bound up with possibilities of economic and social reform which are beyond the scope of this essay. Wars are more significant for reducing the quality than the quantity of potential husbands, but even at that their adverse genetic effects are likely to be overrated. Only a few of the defects which debar men from military service and none of the injuries received in its course are hereditary. The real problem is less that of providing for the sexual and psychological needs of women who cannot find husbands than that of providing for women who will not be satisfied with second- or third-rate husbands. It seems inevitable that the number of the latter group of women will be increased by the development of independence and self-confidence in those whom the war has brought into responsible and well-paid positions ordinarily pre-empted by men.

How far legalized polygyny would meet these needs in our own society is an open question. We have seen that where it functions smoothly in other societies it is able to do so mainly because of the presence of particular patterns of early conditioning and internal familial organization. Neither of these is present in our own society, and both would require some time for their development. Even if we ignore the strong religious sanctions with which monogamy has come to be surrounded, it is so thoroughly integrated into our social and psychological patterns that any formal departure from it would create serious maladjustments. In particular, our present small families, with their high degree of social isolation and of emotional interdependence between the members, tend to create a personality configuration totally unsuited to polygynous institutions. Individuals who have learned to focus all their emotional attachments and feelings of dependency upon a single parent of the opposite sex will tend to do the same with a spouse and to find any sharing of a spouse a direct threat to their whole security system.

Against this must be placed the fact that membership in a polygynous family would provide women with the best method so far devised for combining domesticity with a career. This is not a mere conjecture, since polygynous institutions operate successfully in these terms in many societies which permit women to engage in business. In those societies the plural wives either take turns at housekeeping and child tending or delegate these duties to some one wife who has a flair for domesticity. In either case, the children receive better care than they could get from servants, the households are under responsible supervision, and there is still time and energy available for outside activities. If polygynous institutions do achieve recognition in our society, they are more likely to originate in the reluctance of women to return to the limited sphere of housekeeping and baby tending after they have experienced the more stimulating life outside the home than they are to stem from a lack of potential husbands. Whether such freedom and increased opportunity would compensate psychologically for the sharing of a husband, even a highly desirable one, would depend largely upon the personalities of the women involved.

These speculations regarding the possible role of polygyny in our society are probably idle. There is no pressing need for it in terms of group perpetuation even in the present world situation, and its formal recognition would do violence to many of our most strongly entrenched mores. Even if it should sometime come to be permitted, the probabilities are that the bulk of American and western European populations will continue to be monogamous for many generations to come. Changes in such a basic aspect of social organization as family structure cannot be imposed suddenly or by legislative fiat. They can only come about through a series of small but cumulative modifications in habits and attitudes. The family of the future will be a direct outgrowth of present familial conditions and trends, and in order to predict its possible forms it is necessary to have an understanding of the current situation.

The outstanding feature of this situation is the almost complete breakdown of the consanguine family as a functional unit. Although the western European consanguine grouping has never dominated the conjugal one, its potentialities for function and its claims on the individual were much stronger even a hundred years ago than they are today. This breakdown seems to be directly correlated with the increased opportunities for both spacial and social mobility which have been created by the current technological revolution. A strong consanguine family organization provides its members with a high degree of economic security, but it also imposes many obligations. When the value of this security becomes less than the handicap imposed on the individual by the associated obligations, he is willing to sacrifice the former in order to avoid the latter. Colloquially speaking, when a man can do better without relatives than with them, he will tend to ignore the ties of kinship.

The unparalleled expansion of western European and American economy in the past century, with the wealth of individual opportunity which it has produced, has struck at the very roots of consanguine family organization. Moreover, the increase in spacial mobility which came with the opening of new areas to settlement and the development of modern methods of transportation made it easy for the ambitious individual to sever his kin ties by the simple process of moving away. At present the consanguine family retains its functions only in long-settled rural districts and in the case of a few capitalist dynasties. In both instances the advantages of membership outweigh the disadvantages. The average city dweller recognizes his extended ties of relationship only in the sending of Christmas cards and in the occasional practice of hospitality to visiting kin.

In spite of this extreme degeneration, it is possible that certain factors quite external to family structure may reverse the present trends. If the social crystallization which now appears to be under way continues, the next few generations will see a marked decrease in individual opportunity. Extended family membership may again become economically valuable, although the value is likely to lie less in joint claims on property than in access to jobs. There is already a strong tendency to make membership in many craft unions hereditary, and the same trend can be observed with respect to the more remunerative executive positions in organizations which are shielded from the threat of active competition. It is also conceivable that the growth of bureaucracy will be accompanied by a growth of nepotism, this trend being most probable in the case of one-party rule of the fascist sort. The consanguine type of family organization, therefore, may simply be in abeyance at present and may play a more important role in the not too remote future.

Whatever these future possibilities may be, the current breakdown of consanguine organization has had significant repercussions on the conjugal family. Historically, the presence of the consanguine group has tended to reinforce rather than to weaken marriage ties. European mores have stressed the continuity of matings, and the separation of partners has been felt as a disgrace by their kindred. As long as kin ties were strong and associations close, the consanguine group could bring heavy pressure to bear on its members. With the weakening of these ties the pressure has been correspondingly reduced. Partners can now separate without fear of effective punishment by their kin and without loss of the already almost non-existent advantages of consanguine family membership.

Another factor, closely comparable in its results, is the increasing anonymity of individuals and conjugal family groups in modern urban society. The disapproval with which other members of a small, closely knit community viewed separation was a deterrent almost as strong as the disapproval of kin. Although it might not entail the same economic penalties, the prospect of social ostracism was enough to daunt all but the bravest. In the modern urban community, with its diffuse and casual social relationships, community pressure toward maintenance of the marriage ties has almost ceased to exist. The former friend who disapproves of such conduct can be avoided, and most of the individuals with whom the offender comes in contact will not even know that the offense has been committed.

Breakdowns of kin ties and of the close social integration of individuals and conjugal family groups are no new thing in history. They were an accompaniment of urbanization and suddenly increased spacial mobility in ancient as well as modern civilization. Nevertheless, there is another factor in the present situation which, if it is not altogether new, is at least of unprecedented importance. This is the progressive diminution of the economic dependence of spouses upon each other. Although in the ancient urban civilizations women of the aristocratic group, inheriting and owning property in their own right, could live in comfort without husbands, the ordinary family still depended upon a rigid division of labor. Spouses living in a Roman slum were almost as dependent upon each other for their creature comforts as spouses living on an isolated farm. Extra-familial substitutes for what were ordinarily domestic services were available only to the wealthy, and opportunities for a single woman to support herself by her own labor were so limited and so unremunerative that they would be turned to only as a last resort.

In the modern urban community the delicatessen, the steam laundry, ready-made clothes, and above all the opening to women of attractive and well-paid occupations have done more to undermine the sanctity of marriage than has any conceivable loss of faith in its religious sanctions. Under present conditions, adult men and women are at last in a position to satisfy their basic needs in the absence of any sort of familial association, either conjugal or consanguine. In the anonymity of city life and with the development of effective techniques for contraception even the sexual needs of both can be met without entering into permanent unions or entailing serious penalties. The revolutionary effect of these developments upon the family as an institution can scarcely be overrated.

Since the rise of modern civilization has stripped the family of so many of the functions which once reinforced the bond between spouses, it may well be questioned whether this unit is still necessary in a "brave new world." It is the writer's firm belief that at least the conjugal type of family will be necessary and will survive. This is based upon the presence of still other functions associated with subtler needs of the individual and of society as a whole. In spite of the steady intrusion of extra-familial institutions such as the day nursery and school into the family's basic function of child rearing, it still remains the best agency for the care and especially for the socialization of the young child. There is good evidence that the proper development of the infant requires not only the satisfaction of its physical needs but also personalized attention, love, and response. These cannot be provided in adequate measure by any institution of the asylum sort. Children reared under the mass-production conditions inevitable in such institutions rarely show normal personality development and usually have great difficulty in adapting themselves to the conditions of adult life. In short, the perpetuation of our society would seem to require the perpetuation of the family institution.

How this perpetuation is to be achieved in the absence of most of the external pressures toward continuity of matings is another question. The simplest and most obvious answer is the application of additional social and legal pressures, but the effectiveness of such punitive measures is questionable, to put it mildly. Informal social presure, always the most effective, is largely ruled out by the conditions of modern urban life. Legal pressure, such as the extreme step of prohibiting divorce, could accomplish its purpose only if supported by a unified public opinion. Otherwise, the law would be more honored in the breach than in the observance, as our recent experience with prohibition has shown. Under present conditions the only effect of outlawing divorce would be to destroy what little influence legal and religious sanctions may still exert toward perpetuating marriages. Extra-legal partnerships would simply become the rule rather than the exception, and the attempt to prevent these by further legal measures would result in an intolerable situation. Moreover, insistence on the continued marriage and cohabitation of individuals who are hopelessly incompatible is fatal to the successful performance of even the surviving functions of the family. Not only are the spouses deprived of any opportunity to establish relationships in which they can satisfy their needs for affection and response, but the environment in which any accidental offspring have to be reared is, if anything, worse than a purely institutional one. It can be said with a good deal of certainty that the legalistic approach to this problem is quite inadequate. It is indeed justifiable to tighten divorce laws to the point where momentary pique will be ruled out as a cause for separation, but any restrictions beyond this point are likely to do more harm than good in the long run.

The best approach would seem to lie in the frank recognition that the basic function of the family today is that of satisfying the psychological needs of the individuals who enter the marital relationship. These needs may be summarized as those for affection, for security, and for perfected emotional response. The need for sexual satisfaction, basic as it is, has become less important under modern conditions, and the extreme attention devoted to it by some of the current writers on marriage must be considered as a reflection of one of the peculiar orientations of our culture. Around this physiological function we have erected a superstructure of taboos and have developed an intensity of interest probably unequaled by any other society. Although active sexual incompatibility is fatal to the marital relationship, any psychologist knows how frequently it is a symptom rather than a cause of tension between spouses.

It happens that the conditions of modern society are such as to increase the compulsive quality of the psychological needs which can best be satisfied by marriage. Childhood experience in small families of the modern type conditions the individual to a focusing of emotional attachments and feelings of dependence upon a single person. With this is linked the relative social isolation of most adults in an urban environment. Under such conditions the desire for a partner who can satisfy these needs becomes doubly strong. It is clearly reflected in the present exaggerated development of the concept of romantic love.

It is unnecessary to trace the history of romantic love. Suffice it to say that the idea originated as a justification for extra-marital relationships in a time and place in which arranged marriages were the rule. It was only at a comparatively late date that the romantic lover came to be identified with a real or even potential spouse. In fact the early Courts of Love ruled that romantic attachment was impossible between husband and wife. From its inception the concept embodied the idea that there was one and only one perfect romantic partner for each individual and that this partner could be recognized even on first meeting by a subjective test. Unfortunately such a subjective test is less valid for the choice of spouses than of lovers. Sudden emotional response may stem from nothing more basic than an item of behavior or appearance which causes the new acquaintance to be subconsciously equated with a parent or other source of childhood pleasure or security. Though this equation may produce an immediate release of tensions, it also rouses expectations which can rarely be fulfilled in the marriage relationship and thus lays a foundation for later disappointment and bitterness. That sudden romantic attachment is not the best possible basis for marriage is abundantly proved by the number of romantically engendered marriages that end in the divorce court.

In all societies the most satisfactory and enduring partnerships are those which are entered into after due deliberation and without too high expectations. These are, typically, the attitudes of mature, experienced individuals who have learned certain things the hard way. In spite of the occasional cases of incurable romantics or delayed adolescents, marriages which are contracted in middle age or survive until middle age tend to be exceedingly stable in all societies. The real problem is that of providing young adults with the knowledge and especially with the point of view required for the intelligent selection of permanent partners. It is taken for granted that, at least for some generations to come, they will do the selecting themselves. Efforts of their elders to do this for them have never been very successful and would have little chance of succeeding under modern conditions.

There appear to be two possible solutions to this problem. The first, based on instruction, requires that the needs which marriage may be expected to satisfy be brought into full consciousness. So as long as the enduring needs for congeniality and placid companionship are ignored or deprecated, their importance is likely to be obscured by desires for immediate sexual satisfaction, for independence from the original family group, or for economic security. In view of our current mythology on love and marriage such a change in emphasis will be difficult to bring about. However, the increasing understanding of mental and emotional processes which is being achieved by psychologists and the gradual spread of this knowledge to the general population should make it possible in the long run.

The second solution, and one already adopted by many societies, is to permit adolescents to gain the experience and knowledge which make for the intelligent selection of a spouse through a series of matings which are frankly transitory. Although this system is repugnant to our formal mores, it must be admitted that it seems to work well in those groups where adolescent experimentation in partnerships is institutionalized. Marriages contracted after such experimentation tend to be stable and emotionally satisfying to the participants. That there is a fairly strong trend in this direction in our own society cannot be denied. This fact is highly disturbing to the moralists, but the alternative is hardly less so. If we insist on marriage as a preliminary to all mating, while leaving the selection of partners to romantic chance, we may expect an increasing brittleness of young marriages as the former religious, social, and especially economic sanctions for the relationship progressively lose their force.

With the passing of the conditions which made almost any sort of marriage preferable to its alternatives, the permanence of marriage will inevitably depend more and more on the successful adjustment of spouses to each other. It may be possible, in some remote future, to assure the lifelong permanence of first matings by some system of preliminary training and supervision. Meanwhile, the current increase in divorce need not give us great concern. Divorce statistics are no guide to the number of really successful marriages in a community. No one would conclude that the sharp decline in the divorce rate during the late depression was an indication that more husbands and wives were happy together at that time than before or after. There are probably as many happy marriages today as there ever have been, the only difference being that unhappy partners are now in a better position to do something about it. A marriage which does not satisfy the needs of the partners is non-functional, and in a modern world there is little reason for insisting on its continuation. Easy divorce is no threat to happy marriages; it may even increase their number by giving individuals an opportunity to rectify their mistakes in new partnerships. A congenial marriage can provide more contentment and emotional security than any other human relationship, and in a world in flux these are becoming increasingly important to individual happiness. A union which provides them needs no formal sanctions or external pressures to insure its continuity.

The ancient trinity of father, mother, and child has survived more vicissitudes than any other human relationship. It is the bedrock underlying all other family structures. Although more elaborate family patterns can be broken from without or may even collapse of their own weight, the rock remains. In the Götterdämerung which over-wise science and over-foolish statesmanship are preparing for us, the last man will spend his last hours searching for his wife and child.

14. FAMILY STABILITY IN
NON-EUROPEAN CULTURES *

Two particular reasons may be given for the inclusion of this essay. First, we may note that one of the most frequently heard criticisms of contemporary American society deplores our rate of divorce and implies that it is an unheralded phenomenon indicating a serious moral failure in the community. The evidence presented below will not shake firmly held opinions as to the morality of divorce, but does raise questions about the interpretation of divorce as a symptom of social disorganization. Second, the reader is introduced to the Human Relations Area Files (HRAF) which is simultaneously a method of research and a storage house of anthropological data. Centered at Yale (there is a separate installation under government auspices in Washington, D.C.), the Files contain carefully collated, indexed and cross-referenced data on over 400 cultures, far more than was the case when this article was written. HRAF is particularly useful in tackling such a question as the comparative cross-cultural frequency of divorce but it is not the universal answer to problems of anthropological analysis. The categories under which data are classified are very extensive as compared, for example, with those advanced by Wissler (see No. II:2), but systems which aid current research may inhibit truly novel approaches. Though the Files have deficiencies, their value is evident in such contributions as that which follows.

* George P. Murdock, "Family Stability in Non-European Cultures," *Annals of the American Academy of Political and Social Science,* Vol. 272 (1950), pp. 195–201. Reprinted with the permission of the author and publisher.
Professor of Anthropology at Yale, the author (b. 1897) supplied much of the guiding force that led to the establishment of the Human Relations Area Files. He has done fieldwork among American Indians, in Micronesia and in a small Connecticut community. Noted for his interest in social organization, he has turned in recent years

T HIS PAPER presents the conclusions of a special study of the stability of marriage in forty selected non-European societies undertaken
in an attempt to place the family situation in the contemporary United
States in cross-cultural perspective. Eight societies were chosen from
each of the world's major ethnographic regions—Asia, Africa, Oceania,
and native North and South America. Within each region the samples
were carefully selected from widely scattered geographical locations,
from different culture areas, and from levels of civilization ranging from
the simplest to the most complex. The data were obtained from the
collections in the Human Relations Area Files, formerly the Cross-Cultural Survey. The selection was made in as random a manner as possible
except that it was confined to cultures for which the descriptive literature
is full and reliable. Once chosen, a particular society was rejected and
another substituted only in a few instances where the sources failed
to provide (1) information on the relative rights of the two sexes in
divorce, or (2) evidence permitting a solid judgment as to the degree of
family stability relative to that in our own society.

SOCIETIES IN SAMPLE

The method, it is believed, comes as close to that of purely random
sampling as is feasible today in comparative social science. The results,
it must be admitted, contain a number of surprises—even to the writer,
who has been steeped for years in the literature of world ethnography.
The forty selected societies are listed and located below.

Asia: the Chukchi of northeastern Siberia, the Japanese, the Kazak
of Turkestan, the Kurd of Iraq, the Lakher of Assam, the Mongols of
Outer Mongolia, the Semang Negritos of Malaya, and the Toda of southern India.

Africa: the Dahomeans of coastal West Africa, the Ganda of Uganda,
the Hottentot of South-West Africa, the Jukun of Northern Nigeria, the
Lamba of Northern Rhodesia, the Lango of Kenya, the Siwans of the
oasis of Siwa in Egypt, and the Wolof of Senegal.

Oceania: the Atayal aborigines of interior Formosa, the Balinese of
Indonesia, the Kalinga of the northern Philippines, the Kurtatchi of the
Solomon Islands in Melanesia, the Kwoma of New Guinea, the Murngin
of northern Australia, the Samoans of Polynesia, and the Trukese of
Micronesia.

---

to studies of African culture and is preparing a book on the subject. Among his works
are *Our Primitive Contemporaries* (1934) and *Social Structure* (1949).

North America: the Aztecs of ancient Mexico, the Creek of Alabama, the Crow of the high plains in Montana, the Haida of northern British Columbia and southern Alaska, the Hopi pueblo-dwellers of Arizona, the Iroquois of northern New York, the Klamath of interior Oregon, and the Yurok of coastal California.

South America: the Cuna of southern Panama, the Guaycuru or Mbaya of the Gran Chaco, the Incas of ancient Peru, the Kaingang of southern Brazil, the Macusi of Guiana, the Ona of Tierra del Fuego, the Siriono of lowland Bolivia, and the Witoto of the northwest Amazonian jungle.

From these cases it emerges, as a first conclusion, that practically all societies make some cultural provision for the termination of marriage through divorce. The Incas stand isolated as the solitary exception; among them a marriage, once contracted in the presence of a high official representing the emperor, could not subsequently be dissolved for any reason. None of the other thirty-nine societies in our sample compels a couple to maintain their matrimonial relationship where there are reasons for separation that would impress most contemporary Americans as genuinely cogent.

DIVORCE RIGHTS—BY SEX

Perhaps the most striking conclusion from the study is the extraordinary extent to which human societies accord to both sexes an approximately equal right to initiate divorce. In thirty of the forty cultures surveyed it was impossible to detect any substantial difference in the rights of men and women to terminate an unsatisfactory alliance. The stereotype of the oppressed aboriginal woman proved to be a complete myth.

The author expected, in line with general thought on the subject, that males would be found to enjoy superior, though perhaps not exclusive, rights in a substantial minority of the cultures surveyed, if not in a majority. They were discovered to possess such prerogatives, however, in only six societies—a bare 15 per cent of the total. In two of the Moslem societies, the Kurd and the Siwans, a husband can dismiss his wife with the greatest of ease, even for a momentary whim. He needs only to pick up three stones and drop them, uttering to his spouse a routine formula of divorce. She has no comparable right; she can only run away and hope that her male relatives will support her. Among the Japanese, divorce is very easy for the husband or by mutual consent, but can be obtained by a woman against the will of her spouse only for serious cause and with considerable legal difficulty. A Ganda man, too, is free to dismiss his wife for any cause, whereas she has no right to initiate a permanent separation. If severely mistreated she can only run away to her male relatives, to whom the husband must justify himself and make amends in order to get her back. For the Siriono it is reported that only men, never women, initiate divorce. A Guaycuru man who wants to terminate his marriage for any reason merely removes for a few days to another hut in the same village, until his wife takes the hint and returns to her family. Women rarely seek a divorce directly, but not infrequently they deliberately act in such a manner as to provoke their husbands into leaving them.

In four societies, or 10 per cent of the total sample, women actually possess superior privileges as regards divorce. Among the Kwoma a wife is relatively free to abandon her husband, but he has no right to dismiss her. His only recourse is to make life so miserable for her that she will leave of her own accord. In the stable form of Dahomean marriage, i.e., that characterized by patrilocal residence and the payment of a bride price, a woman can readily desert her husband for cause, but he cannot initiate divorce proceedings directly; he can only neglect his wife, insult her relatives, and subject her to petty annoyances until she takes matters into her own hands and departs. A Yurok marriage can be terminated at the initiative of either partner, but it involves the return of a substantial bride price. A wife is in a much better position to persuade her male relatives of the justice of her cause than is her husband. His claims are scrutinized with great skepticism, and are often rejected. While in theory he could still agree to an uncompensated separation, no male in his right mind in this highly pecuniary culture would think of incurring voluntarily such a financial loss. A Witoto woman can secure a divorce by merely running away. In such a case the husband is always blamed, because people assume that no woman would leave her male protector unless cruelly mistreated. A man can dismiss his wife for cause, but this makes him a target of damaging ridicule and gossip, and unless he is able to justify his action to the complete satisfaction of the local council of adult men, he becomes a virtual social outcast.

FREQUENCY OF DIVORCE—BY SOCIETY

Analysis of the relative frequency of divorce reveals that, in addition to the Incas, the stability of marital unions is noticeably greater than in our society among Atayal, Aztecs, Creek, Dahomeans, Ganda, Hopi, Hottentot, Jukun, Kazak, Lakher, Lango, Murngin, Ona, Siriono, and Witoto. In the remaining twenty-four societies, constituting 60 per cent of the total, the divorce rate manifestly exceeds that among ourselves. Despite the widespread alarm about increasing "family disorganization" in our own society, the comparative evidence makes it clear that we still remain well within the limits which human experience has shown that societies can tolerate with safety.

In most of the societies with relatively infrequent divorce, the stability is achieved through the mores and the pressure of public opinion rather than through legal enactments and judicial obstacles. The Atayal, Aztecs, and Hottentot constitute partial exceptions. In the first of these tribes divorce is freely allowed for childlessness, but petitions on any other grounds must receive a hearing before the chief. He may refuse or grant the divorce, but in the latter case he usually sentences the guilty party to punishment and may even forbid him or her to remarry. Any other separation is likely to precipitate a feud between the families of the estranged spouses. Among the Aztecs, divorce cases were heard before a special court, and the party adjudged guilty forfeited half of his property to the other. Among the Hottentot, adequate grounds for a divorce have to be proved to the satisfaction of a council consisting of all the adult men of the clan, which may order a runaway wife to return to her husband, or award the property of a deserting husband to his wife.

In only two of the societies with frequent divorce is separation effected by the action of constituted authorities—by village officials among the Balinese and by the courts in an action brought by a Japanese woman. Except in these five societies and the Incas, divorce is everywhere exclusively a private matter, and such restraints as are exercised are imposed by informal social pressures rather than by legal restrictions.

STABILIZING DEVICES

The cases reveal clearly some of the devices whereby different peoples have attempted to make marital unions more stable. One of the most common is the payment of a bride price, which comparative studies have shown to be customary among approximately half of the societies of the earth. Contrary to the popular impression, the bride price is almost never conceived as a payment for a purchased chattel. Its primary function nearly everywhere is that of providing an additional economic incentive to reinforce the stability of marriage. In our sample, the sources on Dahomeans, Klamath, Lango, Mongols, Wolof, and Yurok reveal particularly clear evidence of the stabilizing effect of the bride price.

An even more frequent device is to take the choice of a marital partner largely out of the hands of young men and women and vest it in their parents. Most cultures reflect a marked distrust of sexual attraction as a primary motive in marriage, as it is likely to be in the minds of young people, and it seems to be widely recognized that parents, with their greater worldly experience, are more likely to arrange matches on the basis of factors better calculated to produce a durable union. Having been responsible for a marriage, parents tend to feel humiliated when it shows signs of breaking up, and are likely to exert themselves to restore harmony and settle differences. This is attested very specifically for the Haida and the Iroquois, and the evidence shows that the influence of relatives is also a prominent stabilizing factor among Creek, Hopi, Jukun, Kalinga, Murngin, and Ona.

The lengths to which this precaution can be carried in cases of infidelity is well illustrated by the Jukun. A wife first attempts to persuade her husband to give up an adulterous relationship about which she has learned, whereas the husband in a similar situation merely requests a relative or friend to remonstrate with his wife. If the relationship still continues, the innocent spouse reports the matter to the father, uncle, or elder brother of the other, who exerts all the pressure in his power to bring the delinquency to an end. Only after these steps prove fruitless, and the infidelity continues, is a separation effected.

Occasionally, of course, relatives break up a union that is satisfactory to both the parties primarily concerned. Among the Chukchi, for example, the parents of the groom can send the bride home if they become dissatisfied with her at any time within a year or eighteen months after the wedding, and a woman's relatives attempt to break up her marriage if they become estranged from her husband's family at any time, even going to the extreme of carrying off the unwilling wife by force.

In one of the societies of the sample—the Crow Indians—public opinion, instead of exerting its usual stabilizing influence, actually tends to undermine the marital relationship. Divorce is exceedingly frequent, and a man subjects himself to ridicule if he lives too long with one woman. Rivalrous military societies make a sport of stealing wives from one another, and any husband feels ashamed to take back a wife thus abducted from him, however much against her will and his own.

INCIDENCE OF DIVORCE

The sources rarely give precise statistics on the incidence of divorce in societies where it occurs most frequently. All we have is fragmentary statements, for instance, that one-third of all adult Chukchi women have been divorced, or that the ethnographer encountered Cuna of both sexes who had lived through from seven to nine successive marriages, or that it is not uncommon to meet a Siwan women of forty who has been married and divorced more than ten times.

It is nevertheless possible to segregate one group of societies in which the excessive frequency of divorce is confined to recently contracted marriages and dwindles to a rarity after a union has endured for a year or more, especially after children have been born. This is attested, for example, among the Japanese, the Kaingang, the Kalinga, and the

Macusi. Among the Trukese, marriages are very brittle and shifting with people in their twenties, but by the end of this early period of trial and error the majority have found spouses with whom they are content to live in reasonable harmony for the rest of their lives.

In other societies, like the Semang, while the rate of divorce subsides markedly after the birth of children, it still remains high as compared with our own. All in all, the sample reveals nineteen societies, or nearly half of the total, in which permanent separations appear substantially to exceed the present rate in the United States throughout the lifetime of the individual. Among them, either spouse can terminate the union with little difficulty and for slight or even trivial reasons among Balinese, Chukchi, Crow, Cuna, Haida, Iroquois, Klamath, Kurtatchi, Lamba, Mongols, Samoans, Semang, Toda, and Wolof. In matrilocal communities like the Cuna or the Iroquois, the husband simply walks out, or the wife unceremoniously dumps his effects outside her door. It is more surprising to encounter an equal facility in divorce among patrilocal and even patriarchal peoples like the Mongols, who see no reason for moral censure in divorce and say in perfectly matter-of-fact manner that two individuals who cannot get along harmoniously together had better live apart.

GROUNDS FOR DIVORCE

The societies which condone separation for a mere whim are few. The great majority recognize only certain grounds as adequate. The Lamba, for whom the information is particularly full, consider a man justified in seeking a divorce if he has been continually harassed by his parents-in-law, if his wife commits adultery or theft, if she has contracted a loathsome disease, if she is quarrelsome or disrespectful, or if she refuses to remain at his home after he has taken a second wife. For a woman the recognized grounds are impotence or loathsome disease in her spouse, his failure to prepare a garden or provide her with adequate clothing, persistent wife-beating, or mere cessation of her affection for him. If the marriage produces no issue, husband and wife argue as to who is responsible, and usually agree to separate. If the woman then bears a child to her new husband whereas the man fails to produce offspring by his next wife, the former husband is so overcome with shame that he usually either commits suicide or leaves the community.

Particular societies recognize interesting special grounds as adequate. Thus the Aztecs, who strongly disapproved of divorce and required proof of substantial cause before a special court, readily granted separation to a woman if she showed that her husband had done less than his share in attending to the education of their children. In general, however, a few basic reasons recur repeatedly as those considered justifiable in a wide range of societies. These are incompatibility, adultery, barrenness or sterility, impotence or frigidity, economic incapacity or nonsupport, cruelty, and quarrelsomeness or nagging. Desertion rarely appears, because it is, of course, not usually a reason for divorce, but the actual means by which a permanent separation is effected. The degree to which the more widespread grounds are recognized as valid in the forty sample societies is shown in Table 1. In order to provide comparability, an entry is made under each heading for every society. Judgments that

TABLE 1.   REASONS FOR DIVORCE
(Forty Sample Societies)

Reasons	Permitted				Forbidden			
	Definitely		Infer-entially		Definitely		Infer-entially	
	To Man	To Wife	To Man	To Wife	To Man	To Wife	To Man	To Wife
Any grounds, even trivial	9	6	5	6	14	13	12	15
Incompatibility, without more specific grounds	17	17	10	10	6	7	7	6
Common adultery or infidelity	19	11	8	12	8	10	5	7
Repeated or exaggerated infidelity	27	23	8	10	5	5	0	2
Childlessness or sterility	12	4	15	18	7	7	6	11
Sexual impotence or unwillingness	9	12	24	21	3	4	4	3
Laziness, non-support, economic incapacity	23	22	11	9	4	5	2	4
Quarrelsomeness or nagging	20	7	7	12	6	11	7	10
Mistreatment or cruelty	7	25	19	9	3	4	11	2

are merely inferred as probable from the general context, however, are distinguished from evidence specifically reported or unmistakably implied in the sources.

The data in Table 1 reinforce the earlier comment concerning the extraordinary equality of the sexes in rights of divorce revealed by the present study. Where the table shows notable differences, these have relatively obvious explanations. That cruelty is recognized as an adequate ground for women far more often than for men merely reflects their comparative physical strength. The aggression of women toward their spouses is thus perforce directed more often into verbal channels, with the result that quarrelsomeness and nagging become an adequate justification for divorce much more commonly for the male sex.

CONCERN OVER DIVORCE PROBLEM

The demonstration that divorce tends to be easier and more prevalent in other societies than in our own does not warrant the conclusion that most peoples are indifferent to the stability of the marriage relationship and the family institution. In our sample, such a charge might be leveled with some justification at the Crow, the Kaingang, and the Toda, but for most of the rest the data explicitly reveal a genuine concern with the problem. The devices of the bride price and the arrangement of marriages by parents, already alluded to, represent only two of the most common attempts to reach a satisfactory cultural solution. Others, demonstrated by the author in a previous study (*Social Structure*, 1949), may be briefly summarized here.

One such device is the taboo on primary incest, which is absolutely universal. There is not a single society known to history or ethnography which does not prohibit and penalize, among the general run of its members, both sexual intercourse and marriage between father and daughter, mother and son, and brother and sister. These universal prohibitions are understandable only as an adaptive provision, arrived at everywhere by a process of mass trial and error, by which sexual rivalry is inhibited within the nuclear family so that the unity and integrity of this basic institution are preserved for the performance of its crucial societal services—economic co-operation, sexual reproduction, and the rearing and education of children.

Nearly as universal are prohibitions of adultery. A very large majority of all known societies permit relatively free sexual experimentation before marriage in their youth of both sexes, but this license is withdrawn when they enter into matrimony. In a world-wide sample of 250 societies, only five—a mere 2 per cent of the total—were found to condone adulterous extramarital liaisons. In many of the remaining 98 per cent, to be sure, the ideal of marital fidelity is more honored in the breach than in the observance. Its very existence, nevertheless, can only reflect a genuine and widespread concern with the stability of marriage and the family, which are inevitably threatened by the jealousy and discord generated by infidelity.

It is clear that approximately as many peoples disapprove in theory of divorce as of adultery. They have learned through experience, however, that the reasons are commonly much more urgent for the former than for the latter, and they consequently allow it wider latitude. The vital functions of the family are not likely to be well performed where husband and wife have become genuinely incompatible. Children raised by stepparents, grandparents, or adoptive parents may frequently find their new social environment more conducive to healthy personality development than a home torn by bitter internal conflict. Even though less desirable than an ideal parental home, since this is unattainable divorce may represent for them, as for their parents, the lesser of two evils.

No society in our sample, with the possible exception of the Crow, places any positive value on divorce. The general attitude is clearly that it is regrettable, but often necessary. It represents merely a practical concession to the frailty of mankind, caught in a web of social relationships and cultural expectations that often impose intolerable pressure on the individual personality. That most social systems work as well as they do, despite concessions to the individual that appear excessive to us, is a tribute to human ingenuity and resiliency.

AMERICAN FAMILY COMPARATIVELY STABLE

The cross-cultural evidence makes it abundantly clear that the modern American family is unstable in only a relative and not an absolute sense. From an absolute, that is, comparative, point of view, our family institution still leans quite definitely toward the stable end of the ethnographic spectrum. Current trends could continue without reversal for a considerable period before the fear of social disorganization would acquire genuine justification. Long before such a point is reached, however, automatic correctives, some of them already apparent, will have wrought their effect, and a state of relative equilibrium will be attained that will represent a satisfactory social adjustment under the changed conditions of the times.

15. GENERAL OBSERVATIONS UPON SYSTEMS OF RELATIONSHIP *

There are cultures in which the word equivalent to "mother" is applied to all of mother's sisters and father's too. Similar extension of "father" is frequent and in such societies it is usual to call one's cousins "brother" or "sister." The existence of a variety of alternative vocabularies designating relatives (kin terminological systems), built upon principles unknown in our own culture, has long been known but until Lewis Henry Morgan began his work there was no systematic understanding of either the range of variation or its significance. Though the particular evolutionary scheme Morgan built from his kinship research has suffered subsequent reversal at most of its crucial points, some of Morgan's original contribution retains its utility and his establishment of a whole field of inquiry is a remarkable achievement. Though many of the observations and deductions in this selection are antiquated, the basic view of kin terminological systems and their significance makes an excellent introduction to the subject.

I N CONSIDERING the elements of a system of consanguinity the existence of marriage between single pairs must be assumed. Marriage forms the basis of relationships. In the progress of the inquiry it may become necessary to consider a system with this basis fluctuating, and,

* Lewis Henry Morgan, *Systems of Consanguinity and Affinity of the Human Family* (Washington, D.C.: Smithsonian Institution, Smithsonian Contributions to Knowledge No. 218, 1871), pp. 10–15. Reprinted with permission of the publisher.

The author (1818–1881) is famed for his role in establishing ethnology as a science and for the formulation of a detailed theory of cultural evolution that has been a target ever since. A lawyer and politician, he became interested in the Iroquois and, when 29 years old, was adopted into the Hawk clan of the Senecas. He also travelled to the western United States where he made further observations of Indian cultures. Among his works are *League of the Ho-dé-no-sau-nee, or Iroquois* (1851), *Ancient Society* (1877) and *Houses and House-life of the American Aborigines* (1881).

perhaps, altogether wanting. The alternative assumption of each may be essential to include all the elements of the subject in its practical relations. The natural and necessary connection of consanguinei with each other would be the same in both cases; but with this difference, that in the former the lines of descent from parent to child would be known, while in the latter they would, to a greater or less extent, be incapable of ascertainment. These considerations might affect the form of the system of consanguinity.

The family relationships are as ancient as the *family*. They exist in virtue of the law of derivation, which is expressed by the perpetuation of the species through the marriage relation. A system of consanguinity, which is founded upon a community of blood, is but the formal expression and recognition of these relationships. Around every person there is a circle or group of kindred of which such person is the centre, the *Ego*, from whom the degree of the relationship is reckoned, and to whom the relationship itself returns. Above him are his father and his mother and their ascendants, below him are his children and their descendants; while upon either side are his brothers and sisters and their descendants, and the brothers and sisters of his father and of his mother and their descendants, as well as a much greater number of collateral relatives descended from common ancestors still more remote. To him they are nearer in degree than other individuals of the nation at large. A formal arrangement of the more immediate blood kindred into lines of descent, with the adoption of some method to distinguish one relative from another, and to express the value of the relationship, would be one of the earliest acts of human intelligence.

Should the inquiry be made how far nature suggests a uniform method or plan for the discrimination of the several relationships, and for the arrangement of kindred into distinct lines of descent, the answer would be difficult, unless it was first assumed that marriage between single pairs had always existed, thus rendering definite the lines of parentage. With this point established, or assumed, a natural system, numerical in its character, will be found underlying any form which man may contrive; and which, resting upon an ordinance of nature, is both universal and unchangeable. All of the descendants of an original pair, through intermediate pairs, stand to each other in fixed degrees of proximity, the nearness or remoteness of which is a mere matter of computation. If we ascend from ancestor to ancestor in the lineal line, and again descend through the several collateral lines until the widening circle of kindred circumscribes millions of the living and the dead, all of these individuals, in virtue of their descent from common ancestors, are bound to the "*Ego*" by the chain of consanguinity.

The blood relationships, to which specific terms have been assigned, under the system of the Aryan family, are few in number. They are grandfather and grandmother, father and mother, brother and sister, son and daughter, grandson and granddaughter, uncle and aunt, nephew and niece, and cousin. Those more remote in degree are described either by an augmentation or by a combination of these terms. After these are the affineal or marriage relationships, which are husband and wife, father-in-law and mother-in-law, son-in-law and daughter-in-law, brother-in-law and sister-in-law, step-father and step-mother, step-son and step-daughter, and step-brother and step-sister: together with such of the husbands and wives of blood relatives as receive the corresponding designation by courtesy. These terms are barely sufficient to indicate specifically the nearest relationships, leaving much the largest number to be described by a combination of terms.

So familiar are these ancient household words, and the relationships which they indicate, that a classification of kindred by means of them, according to their degrees of nearness, would seem to be not only a simple undertaking, but, when completed, to contain nothing of interest beyond its adaptation to answer a necessary want. But, since these specific terms are entirely inadequate to designate a person's kindred, they contain in themselves only the minor part of the system. An arrangement into lines, with descriptive phrases to designate such relatives as fall without the specific terms, becomes necessary to its completion. In the mode of arrangement and of description diversities may exist. Every system of consanguinity must be able to ascend and descend in the lineal line through several degrees from any given person, and to specify the relationship of each to *Ego;* and also from the lineal, to enter the several collateral lines and follow and describe the collateral relatives through several generations. When spread out in detail and examined, every scheme of consanguinity and affinity will be found to rest upon definite ideas, and to be framed, so far as it contains any plan, with reference to particular ends. In fine, a system of relationship, originating in necessity, is a domestic institution, which serves to organize a family by the bond of consanguinity. As such it possesses a degree of vitality and a power of self-perpetuation commensurate with its nearness to the primary wants of man.

In a general sense, as has elsewhere been stated, there are but two radically distinct forms of consanguinity among the nations represented in the tables. [These tables, a major portion of Morgan's book, do not appear here—Ed.] One of these is descriptive and the other classificatory. The first, which is that of the Aryan, Semitic, and Uralian families, rejecting the classification of kindred, except so far as it is in accordance with the numerical system, describes collateral consanguinei, for the most part, by an augmentation or combination of the primary terms of relationship. These terms, which are those for husband and wife, father and mother, brother and sister, and son and daughter, to which must be added, in such languages as possess them, grandfather and grandmother, and grandson and granddaughter, are thus restricted to the primary sense in which they are here employed. All other terms are secondary. Each relationship is thus made independent and distinct from every other. But the second, which is that of the Turanian, American Indian, and Malayan families, rejecting descriptive phrases in every instance, and reducing consanguinei to great classes by a series of apparently arbitrary generalizations, applies the same terms to all the members of the same class. It thus confounds relationships, which, under the descriptive system, are distinct, and enlarges the signification both of the primary and secondary terms beyond their seemingly appropriate sense.

Although a limited number of generalizations have been developed in the system of the first-named families, which are followed by the introduction of additional special terms to express in the concrete the relationships thus specialized, yet the system is properly characterized as descriptive, and was such originally. It will be seen in the sequel that the partial classification of kindred which it now contains is in harmony with the principles of the descriptive form, and arises from it legitimately to the extent to which it is carried; and that it is founded upon conceptions entirely dissimilar from those which govern in the classificatory form. These generalizations, in some cases, are imperfect when logically considered; but they were designed to realize in the concrete the precise relationships which the descriptive phrases suggest by implication. In the Erse, for example, there are no terms for uncle or aunt, nephew or niece, or cousin; but they were described as *father's brother, mother's brother, brother's son,* and so on. These forms of the Celtic are, therefore, purely descriptive. In most of the Aryan languages terms for these relationships exist. My father's brothers and my mother's brothers, in English, are generalized into one class, and the term *uncle* is employed to express the relationship. The relationships to *Ego* of the two classes of persons are equal in their degree of nearness, but not the same in kind; wherefore, the Roman method is preferable, which employed *patruus* to express the former, and *avunculus* to indicate the latter. The phrase "father's brother" describes a person, but it likewise implies a bond of connection which *patruus* expresses in the concrete. In like manner, my father's brother's son, my father's sister's son, my mother's brother's son, and my mother's sister's son are placed upon an equality by a similar generalization, and the relationship is expressed by the term *cousin.* They stand to me in the same degree of nearness, but they are related to me in four different ways. The use of these terms, however, does not invade the principles of the descriptive system, but attempts to realize the implied relationships in a simpler manner. On the other hand, in the system of the last-named families, while corresponding terms exist, their application to particular persons is founded upon very different generalizations, and they are used in apparently arbitrary manner. In Seneca-Iroquois, for example, my father's brother is my father. Under the system he stands to me in that relationship and no other. I address him by the same term, *Hä-nih'*, which I apply to my own father. My mother's brother, on the contrary, is my uncle, *Hoc-no'-seh*, to whom, of the two, this relationship is restricted. Again, with myself a male, my brother's son is my son, *Ha-ah'-wuk*, the same as my own son; while my sister's son is my nephew, *Ha-yä'-wan-da;* but with myself a female, these relationships are reversed. My brother's son is then my nephew; while my sister's son is my son. Advancing to the second collateral line, my father's brother's son and my mother's sister's son are my brothers, and they severally stand to me in the same relationship as my own brother; but my father's sister's son and my mother's brother's son are my cousins. The same relationships are recognized under the two forms, but the generalizations upon which they rest are different.

In the system of relationship of the Aryan, Semitic, and Uralian families, the collateral lines are maintained distinct and perpetually divergent from the lineal, which results, theoretically as well as practically, in a dispersion of the blood. The value of the relationships of collateral consanguinei is depreciated and finally lost under the burdensomeness of the descriptive method. This divergence is one of the characteristics of the descriptive system. On the contrary, in that of the Turanian, American Indian, and Malayan families, the several collateral lines, near and remote, are finally brought into, and merged in the lineal line, thus theoretically, if not practically, preventing a dispersion of the blood. The relationships of collaterals by this means is both appreciated and preserved. This mergence is, in like manner, one of the characteristics of the classificatory system.

How these two forms of consanguinity, so diverse in their fundamental conceptions and so dissimilar in their structure, came into existence it may be wholly impossible to explain. The first question to be considered relates to the nature of these forms and their ethnic distribution, after the ascertainment of which their probable origin may be made a subject of investigation. While the existence of two radically distinct forms appears to separate the human family, so far as it is represented in the tables, into two great divisions, the Indo-European and the Indo-American, the same testimony seems to draw closer together the several families of which these divisions are composed, without forbidding the supposition that a common point of departure between the two may yet be discovered. If the evidence deposited in these systems of relationship tends, in reality, to consolidate the families named into two great divisions, it is a tendency in the direction of unity of origin of no inconsiderable importance.

After the several forms of consanguinity and affinity, which now prevail in the different families of mankind, have been presented and discussed, the important question will present itself, how far these forms become changed with the progressive changes of society. The uses of systems of relationship to establish the genetic connection of nations will depend, first, upon the structure of the system, and, secondly, upon the stability of its radical forms. In form and feature they must be found able, when once established, to perpetuate themselves through indefinite periods of time. The question of their use must turn upon that of the stability of their radical features. Development and modification, to a very considerable extent, are revealed in the tables in which the comparison of forms is made upon an extended scale, but it will be observed, on further examination, that these changes are further developments of the fundamental conceptions which lie, respectively, at the foundation of the two original systems.

There is one powerful motive which might, under certain circumstances, tends [sic] to the overthrow of the classificatory form and the substitution of the descriptive, but it would arise after the attainment of civilization. This is the inheritance of estates. It may be promised that the bond of kindred, among uncivilized nations, is a strong influence for the mutual protection of related persons. Among nomadic stocks, especially, the respectability of the individual was measured, in no small degree, by the number of his kinsmen. The wider the circle of kindred the greater the assurance of safety, since they were the natural guardians of his rights and the avengers of his wrongs. Whether designedly or otherwise, the Turanian form of consanguinity organized the family upon the largest scale of numbers. On the other hand, a gradual change from a nomadic to a civilized condition would prove the severest test to which a system of consanguinity could be subjected. The protection of the law, or of the State, would become substituted for that of kinsmen; but with more effective power the rights of property might influence the system of relationship. This last consideration, which would not arise until after a people had emerged from barbarism, would be adequate beyond any other known cause to effect a radical change in a pre-existing system, if [it] recognized relationships which would defeat natural justice in the inheritance of property. In Tamilian society, where my brother's son and my cousin's son are both my sons, a useful purpose may have been subserved by drawing closer, in this manner, the kindred bond; but in a civilized sense it would be manifestly unjust to place either of these collateral sons upon an equality with my own son for the inheritance of my estate. Hence the growth of property and the settlement of its distribution might be expected to lead to a more precise discrimination of the several degrees of consanguinity if they were confounded by the previous system.

Where the original system, anterior to civilization, was descriptive, the tendency to modification, under the influence of refinement, would be in the direction of a more rigorous separation of the several lines of descent, and of a more systematic description of the persons or relationships in each. It would not necessarily lead to the abandonment of old terms nor to the invention of new. This latter belongs, usually, to the formative period of a language. When that is passed, compound terms are resorted to if the descriptive phrases are felt to be inconvenient. Wherever these compounds are found it will be known at once that they are modern in the language. The old terms are not necessarily radical, but they have become so worn down by long-continued use as to render the identification of their component parts impossible. While the growth of nomenclatures of relationship tends to show the direction in which existing systems have been modified, it seems to be incapable of throwing any light upon the question whether a classificatory form ever becomes changed into a descriptive, or the reverse. It is more difficult, where the primitive system was classificatory, to ascertain the probable direction of the change. The uncivilized nations have remained substantially stationary in their condition through all the centuries of their existence, a circumstance eminently favorable to the permanency of their domestic institutions. It is not supposable, however, that they have resisted all modifications of their system of consanguinity. The opulence of the nomenclature of relationships, which is characteristic of the greater portion of the nations whose form is classificatory, may tend to show that, if it changed materially, it would be in the direction of a greater complexity of classification. It is extremely difficult to arrive at any general conclusions upon this question with reference to either form. But it may be affirmed that if an original system changes materially, after it has been adopted into use, it is certain to be done in harmony with the ideas and conceptions which it embodies, of which the changes will be further and logical developments.

It should not be inferred that forms of consanguinity and affinity are either adopted, modified, or laid aside at pleasure. The tables entirely dispel such a supposition. When a system has once come into practical use, with its nomenclature adopted, and its method of description or of classification settled, it would, from the nature of the case, be very slow to change. Each person, as has elsewhere been observed, is the centre around whom a group of consanguinei is arranged. It is my father, my mother, my brother, my son, my uncle, my cousin, with each and every human being; and, therefore, each one is compelled to understand, as well as to use, the prevailing system. It is an actual necessity to all alike, since each relationship is personal to *Ego*. A change of any of these relationships, or a subversion of any of the terms invented to express them, would be extremely difficult if not impossible; and it would be scarcely less difficult to enlarge or contract the established use of the terms themselves. The possibility of this permanence is increased by the circumstance that these systems exist by usage rather than legal enactment, and therefore the motive to change must be as universal as the usage. Their use and preservation are intrusted to every person who speaks the common language, and their channel of transmission is the blood. Hence it is that, in addition to the natural stability of domestic institutions, there are special reasons which contribute to their permanance, by means of which it is rendered not improbable that they might survive changes of social condition sufficiently radical to overthrow the primary ideas in which they originated.

These preliminary statements being made, it is now proposed to explain and compare the systems of relationship of the several nations and families represented in the tables. In doing this the order therein adopted will be followed. Invoking the patient attention of the reader, I will endeavor to perform this task with as much brevity and clearness as I may be able to command.

16. CLASSIFICATORY SYSTEMS
OF RELATIONSHIP *

Once begun, the study of kinship systems became a vital part of anthropology. Field workers collected terminologies not only for their obvious comparative value or the insights which the terminology gave into the behavior and relations of the local populace, but also because the technique of collecting kin terms, the genealogical method, provided entré into the society and furnished a topic of inquiry which hardly ever arouses anxiety or resentment.

Among the earliest general contributions to the search for regularities underlying kin terminological systems was Kroeber's induction of eight principles which, in varying combinations, entered into the logical formulation of all known terminologies, and which explicitly contradict certain of the contrasts which Morgan (see No. II:15) drew between 'descriptive' and 'classificatory' terminologies. Going further, Kroeber disputed the arguments of the British anthropologist Rivers, who maintained that kin terms reflected antecedent sociological conditions. The last paragraph of the following selection asserts that kin terms are primarily linguistic and psychological phenomena. In 1952, Kroeber reviewed much of his earlier work, including this article. He concluded by reasserting his conviction that the use of kin terminological analysis for sociological reconstruction was dangerous, but he berated himself for the unfortunate use of the word 'psychological,' which, he now believes, is not what he really intended. He suggests instead that "as part of language, kin term systems reflect unconscious logic and conceptual patterning as well as social institutions." The matter is not yet completely resolved but theories of sociological causation are predominant in contemporary analyses.

* Alfred L. Kroeber, "Classificatory Systems of Relationship," *Journal of the* [*Royal*] *Anthropological Institute,* Vol. 39 (1909), pp. 77–84. Reprinted with the permission of the author and the publisher.

THE DISTINCTION between classificatory and descriptive systems of relationship has been widely accepted, and has found its way into handbooks and general literature. According to the prevalent belief the systems of certain nations or languages group together distinct relationships and call them by one name, and are therefore classifying. Other systems of consanguinity are said to indicate secondary differences of relationship by descriptive epithets added to their primary terms, and to be therefore descriptive.

Nothing can be more fallacious than this common view. A moment's reflection is sufficient to show that every language groups together under single designations many distinct degrees and kinds of relationship. Our word brother includes both the older and the younger brother and the brother of a man and of a woman. It therefore embraces or classifies four relationships. The English word cousin denotes both men and women cousins; cousins on the father's or on the mother's side; cousins descended from the parent's brother or the parent's sister; cousins respectively older or younger than one's self, or whose parents are respectively older or younger than the speaker's parents; and cousins of men or women. Thirty-two different relationships are therefore denoted by this one English word. If the term is not strictly limited to the significance of first cousin, the number of distinct ideas that it is capable of expressing is many times thirty-two. Since then it is not only primitive people that classify or fail to distinguish relationships, the suspicion is justified that the current distinction between the two classes or systems of indicating relationship is subjective, and has its origin in the point of view of investigators, who, on approaching foreign languages, have been impressed with their failure to discriminate certain relationships between which the languages of civilized Europe distinguish, and who, in the enthusiasm of formulating general theories from such facts, have forgotten that their own languages are filled with entirely analogous groupings or classifications which custom has made so familiar and natural that they are not felt as such.

The total number of different relationships which can be distinguished is very large, and reaches at least many hundred. No language possesses different terms for all of these or even for any considerable proportion of them. In one sense it is obvious that a language must be more classificatory as the number of its terms of relationship is smaller. The number of theoretically possible relationships remaining constant, there must be more ideas grouped under one term in proportion as the number of terms is less. Following the accepted understanding of what constitutes classificatory consanguinity, English, with its twenty terms of relationship, must be not less but more classificatory than the languages of all primitive people who happen to possess twenty-five, thirty, or more terms.

It is clear that if the phrase classificatory consanguinity is to have any meaning it must be sought in some more discriminating way. The single fact that another people group together various relationships which our language distinguishes does not make their system classificatory. If there is a general and fundamental difference between the systems of relationship of civilized and uncivilized people, its basis must be looked for in something more exact than the rough and ready expressions of subjective point of view that have been customary.

It is apparent that what we should try to deal with is not the hundreds or thousands of slightly varying relationships that are expressed or can be expressed by the various languages of man, but the principles or categories of relationship which underlie these. Eight such categories are discernible.

1. *The difference between persons of the same and of separate generations.* The distinctions between father and grandfather, between uncle and cousin, and between a person and his father, involve the recognition of this category.

2. *The difference between lineal and collateral relationship.* When the father and the father's brother are distinguished, this category is operative. When only one term is employed for brother and cousin, it is inoperative.

3. *Difference of age within one generation.* The frequent distinction between the older and the younger brother is an instance. In English this category is not operative.

4. *The sex of the relative.* This distinction is carried out so consistently by English, the one exception being the foreign word cousin, that the discrimination is likely to appear self-evident. By many people, however, many relationships are not distinguished for sex. Grandfather and grandmother, brother-in-law and sister-in-law, father-in-law and mother-in-law, and even such close relationships as son and daughter, are expressed respectively by single words.

5. *The sex of the speaker.* Unrepresented in English and most European languages, this category is well known to be of importance in many other languages. The father, mother, brother, sister, and more distant relatives may receive one designation from a man and another from his sister.

6. *The sex of the person through whom relationship exists.* English does not express this category. In consequence we frequently find it necessary to explain whether an uncle is a father's or a mother's brother, and whether a grandmother is paternal or maternal.

7. *The distinction of blood relatives from connections by marriage.*

While this distinction is commonly expressed by most languages, there are occasional lapses; just as in familiar English speech the father-in-law is often spoken of as father. Not strictly within the domain of relationship, but analogous to the occasional failure to express this category, is the frequent ignoring on the part of primitive people of the difference between actual relatives and fictitious clan or tribal relatives.

8. *The condition of life of the person through whom relationship exists.* The relationship may be either of blood or by marriage; the person serving as the bond of relationship may be alive or dead, married or no longer married. Many North American Indians refrain from using such terms as father-in-law and mother-in-law after the wife's death or separation. Some go so far as to possess terms restricted to such severed relationship. It is natural that the uncle's relation to his orphaned nephew should tend to be somewhat different from his relation to the same boy while his natural protector, his father, was living. Distinct terms are therefore sometimes found for relatives of the uncle and aunt group after the death of a parent.

The subjoined table indicates the representation of the eight categories, and the degree to which they find expression, respectively in English and in several of the Indian languages of North America.

	English	N.A. INDIAN					CALIFORNIA INDIAN						
		Arapaho	*Dakota*	*Pawnee*	*Skokomish*	*Chinook*	*Yuki*	*Pomo*	*Washo*	*Miwok*	*Yokuts*	*Luiseño*	*Mohave*
Number of terms	21 [1]	20	31	19	18	28	24	27	28	24	28	34	35
Generation	21	20	31	11	13	23	24	21	27	24	22	30	26
Blood or marriage	21	19	31	17	18	26	24	24	28	24	32	34
Lineal or collateral	21	10	20	5	11	25	24	21	28	18	26	34	28
Sex of relative	20	18	29	17	2	12	16	21	20	20	17	18	22
Sex of connecting relative	0	6	6	2	0	20	13	13	14	10	14	19	21
Sex of speaker	0	3	18	4	0	15	3	3	10	2	12	10	14
Age in generation	0	3	7	2	2	2	3	4	4	4	4	12	8
Condition of connecting relative	0	0	0	0	8	1	0	0	0	0	2	0	1

[1] All terms are omitted, such as great grandfather, great-uncle, and second-cousin, which are not generally used in ordinary speech and exist principally as a reserve available for specific discrimination on occasion.

[2] Terms denoting relatives by marriage undergo a vocalic change to indicate the death of the connecting relative.

It appears that English gives expression to only four categories. With the exception, however, of the one and foreign word cousin, every term in English involves the recognition of each of these four categories. All the Indian languages express from six to eight categories. Almost all of them recognize seven. But in all the Indian languages the majority of the categories occurring are expressed in only part of the terms of relationship found in the language. There are even Indian languages, such as Pawnee and Mohave, in which not a single one of the seven or eight categories finds expression in every term. While in English the degree of recognition which is accorded the represented categories is indicable by a percentage of 100 in all cases but one, when it is 95, in Pawnee corresponding percentages range variously from about 10 to 90, and in Mohave from 5 to 95. All the other Indian languages, as compared with English, closely approach the condition of Pawnee and Mohave.

It is clear that this difference is real and fundamental. English is simple, consistent, and, so far as it goes, complete. The Indian systems of relationship all start from a more elaborate basis, but carry out their scheme less completely. This is inevitable from the fact that the total number of terms of relationship employed by them is approximately the same as in English. The addition of only one category to those found in English normally doubles the number of terms required to give full expression to the system; and the presence of three additional categories multiplies the possible total by about eight. As the number of terms occurring in any of the Indian languages under consideration is not much more than half greater than in English, and sometimes is not greater at all, it is clear that at least some of their categories must find only very partial expression.

In short, as far as the expression of possible categories is concerned, English is less complete than any of the Indian languages; but as regards the giving of expression to the categories which it recognizes, English is more complete. In potentiality, the English scheme is poorer and simpler; but from its own point of view it is both more complete and more consistent. As English may evidently be taken as representative of European languages, it is in this point that the real difference is to be found between the systems that have been called classificatory and those that have been called descriptive.

The so-called descriptive systems express a small number of categories of relationship completely; the wrongly-named classificatory systems express a larger number of categories with less regularity. Judged from its own point of view, English is the less classificatory; looked at from the Indian point of view it is the more classificatory, inasmuch as in every one of its terms it fails to recognize certain distinctions often made in other languages; regarded from a general and comparative point of view, neither system is more or less classificatory.

In short, the prevalent idea of the classificatory system breaks down entirely under analysis. And in so far as there is a fundamental difference between the languages of European and of less civilized peoples in the method of denoting relationship, the difference can be determined only on the basis of the categories described and can be best expressed in terms of the categories.

The categories serve also to indicate the leading characteristics of systems of the same general order. It is obvious, for instance, that the most important difference between Dakota and Arapaho is the strong tendency of the former to recognize the sex of the speaker. Chinook is notable for laying more stress on the sex of the speaker and of the connecting relation than on the sex of the relative. General differences such as naturally occur between the languages of one region and of another can also be expressed in terms of the categories. All the California systems, for instance, lay much more stress upon the sex of the connecting relative than do any of the Plains languages examined. The Plains systems are conspicuous for their weak development of the distinction between lineal and collateral relationship, this finding expression in two-thirds of all cases in Dakota, half in Arapaho, one-fourth in Pawnee. In seven California languages the corresponding values lie between three-fourths and complete expression. The method can be applied successfully even in the case of smaller and contiguous geographical areas. Of the seven California languages Luiseño and Mohave are spoken in southern California. Their systems show a unity as compared with the systems of the five languages from northern and central California. Both the southern California languages have a greater number of terms; both are stronger in the expression of the categories of the sex of the connecting relative and of age within the same generation; and both are weaker in the category of sex of the relative, than the others. Again, Chinook and Skokomish, both of the North Pacific Coast, are alike in indicating the condition of the connecting relative and in failing, on account of the possession of grammatical sex gender, to distinguish the sex of relatives themselves in many terms of relationship. There is a very deep-going difference between them, however, in the fact that Skokomish is as free as English from recognizing the sex of the speaker and of connecting relatives, while Chinook generally expresses both categories. In short, the categories present a means of comparing systems of terms of relationship along the basic lines of their structure and of expressing their similarities and differences without reference to individual terms or details.

The reason why the vague and unsatisfactory idea of a classificatory system of consanguinity has found such wide acceptance is not to be sought in any primary interest in designations of relationship as such, but in the fact that terms of relationship have usually been regarded principally as material from which conclusions as to the organization of society and conditions of marriage could be inferred. If it had been more clearly recognized that terms of relationship are determined primarily by linguistic factors and are only occasionally, and then indirectly, affected by social circumstances, it would probably long ago have been generally realized that the difference between descriptive and classificatory systems is subjective and superficial. Nothing is more precarious than the common method of deducing the recent existence of social or marital institutions from a designation of relationship. Even when the social condition agrees perfectly with expressions of relationship, it is unsafe to conclude without corroborative evidence that these expressions are a direct reflection or result of the condition.

In the Dakota language, according to Riggs, there is only one word for grandfather and father-in-law. Following the mode of reasoning sometimes employed, it might be deduced from this that these two relationships were once identical. Worked out to its implications, the absurd conclusion would be that marriage with the mother was once customary among the Sioux.

In the same language the words for woman's male cousin and for woman's brother-in-law have the same radical, differing only in a suffix. Similar reasoning would induce in this case that marriage of cousins was or had been the rule among the Sioux, a social condition utterly opposed to the basic principles of almost all Indian society.

The use of such identical or similar terms for distinct relationships is due to a considerable similarity between the relationships. A woman's male cousin and her brother-in-law are alike in sex, are both of opposite sex from the speaker, are of the same generation as herself, and are both collateral, so that they are similar under four categories. In view of the comparative paucity of terms as compared with possible relationships, it is entirely natural that the same word, or the same stem, should at times be used to denote two relationships having as much in common as these two.

No one would assume that the colloquial habit in modern English of speaking of the brother-in-law as brother implies anything as to form of marriage, for logically the use of the term could only be an indication of sister marriage. It is easily conceivable that in the future development of English the more cumbersome of these two terms might come into complete disuse in daily life and the shorter take its place, without the least change in social or marital conditions.

The causes which determine the formation, choice, and similarities of terms of relationship are primarily linguistic. Whenever it is desired to regard terms of relationship as due to sociological causes and as indicative of social conditions, the burden of proof must be entirely with the propounder of such views.

Even the circumstances that the father's brother is frequently called father is not necessarily due to or connected with the custom of the Levirate; nor can group marriage be inferred from the circumstance that there is frequently no other term for mother's sister than mother. A woman and her sister are more alike than a woman and her brother, but the difference is conceptual, in other words linguistic, as well as sociological. It is true that a woman's sister can take her place in in-numerable functions and relations in which a brother cannot; and yet a woman and her sister, being of the same sex, agree in one more cate-gory of relationship than the same woman and her brother, and are therefore more similar in relationship and more naturally denoted by the same term. There are so many cases where the expression of rela-tionship cannot have been determined by sociological factors and must be purely psychological, as in the instances just discussed, that it is fair to require that the preference be given to the psychological cause, or that this be admitted as of at least equal probability, even in cases where either explanation is theoretically possible and supporting evi-dence is absent.

On the whole it is inherently very unlikely in any particular case that the use of identical terms for similar relationships can ever be con-nected with such special customs as the Levirate or group marriage. It is a much more conservative view to hold that such forms of linguistic expression and such conditions are both the outcome of the unalterable fact that certain relationships are more similar to one another than others. On the one hand this fact has led to certain sociological institutions; on the other hand, to psychological recognitions and their expression in language. To connect the institutions and the terms causally can rarely be anything but hazardous. It has been an unfortunate characteristic of the anthropology of recent years to seek in a great measure specific causes for specific events, connection between which can be established only through evidence that is subjectively selected. On wider knowledge and freedom from motive it is becoming increasingly apparent that causal explanations of detached anthropological phenomena can be but rarely found in other detached phenomena, and that it is even difficult to specify the most general tendencies that actuate the forms taken by culture, as the immediate causes of particular phenomena.

The following conclusions may be drawn:

1. The generally accepted distinction between descriptive and classi-ficatory systems of terms of relationship cannot be supported.
2. Systems of terms of relationship can be properly compared through an examination of the categories of relationship which they involve and of the degree to which they give expression to these categories.

3. The fundamental difference between systems of terms of relationship of Europeans and of American Indians is that the former express a smaller number of categories of relationship than the latter and express them more completely.

4. Terms of relationship reflect psychology, not sociology. They are determined primarily by language and can be utilized for sociological inferences only with extreme caution.

17. THE ORIGINS OF SOCIAL ORGANIZATION *

Social anthropologists are rarely given to discussions of origins and the fact that the title above appeared over the signature of a leading social anthropologist may occasion surprise. Perusal of its contents will show, however, that the question of origins with specific reference to the remote past is treated with some scepticism and a great deal of caution. Emphasis is laid upon the conditions under which certain social institutions may be expected to appear regardless of time or sequence. The selection is valuable, therefore, in reflecting some of the basic assumptions and procedures of "functionalism," a theoretical approach which has pervaded and shaped social anthropology but plays a somewhat lesser though still very important role in cultural anthropology. Note also the close connections which the author develops between economic and social relations.

GENERALLY when we speak of 'The Origins of Social Organization' we think of the ways in which our first manlike ancestors organized their society. On the whole, anthropologists no longer attempt to discover what these were. All that survives to us from those distant times are stone implements, shells, bones, potsherds, a few paintings and carvings. From these archaeologists have worked out forms of dwellings,

* Max Gluckman, "The Origins of Social Organization," *Human Problems in British Central Africa* (*The Rhodes-Livingstone Journal* No. 12, 1951), pp. 1–11. Reprinted with permission of the author and publisher.

The author (b. 1911) is Professor of Anthropology at the University of Manchester. A specialist in the cultures of Southeast Africa, Dr. Gluckman has recently been concentrating on problems of political organization. He is the author of several books, among them: *An Analysis of the Sociological Theories of Bronislaw Malinowski* (1941), *Essays on Lozi Land and Royal Property* (1943) and *Custom and Conflict in Africa* (1955).

size of settlements, and various outlines of social organization based on observations of modern primitive societies. They have shown too that great developments must have followed on the domestication of plants, the first establishment of larger settlements, and other crucial changes in associations and technology. Archaeologists have in fact achieved wonders in creating for us accounts of how early men lived, as can be seen in Gordon Childe's *What Happened in History* and *The Dawn of European Civilization*, or Sir Leonard Woolley's *Digging up the Past* and *Ur of the Chaldees*, all published in the Pelican series. The recital of this work of archaeologists is a whole story in itself, which I am not competent to tell. I am a social anthropologist, which in brief is a sociologist who specializes on the study of what we call the primitive peoples: African tribes, Red Indians, South Sea Islanders, Australian blackfellows, and other peoples of that stage of development.

Nowadays when sociologists and social anthropologists speak of the origins of social organization they mean those conditions of human life in society which produce specific ways of organizing the relationships between members of a community. I shall return to these conditions later. First, I want to discuss the history of our own study, for when it began in the last century anthropologists thought they could, by studying primitive peoples, find out how the first men lived, and trace the paths our ancestors followed until they came into written history. They assumed, and it is reasonable enough, that primitive tribes were nearer to the conditions of original man than we are, and that the tribes could be arranged in order of development to give a picture of a large part of the history of human society. That is, they wished to work out how human society had evolved from savagery to that civilization represented by the Victorian middle class. This was even before Darwin had produced his theory of the evolution of animal species.

I can best show you how these anthropologists argued by a few examples. Travellers in Australia had reported that the Australian aborigines knew nothing of the role of men in begetting babies. These aborigines thought that a woman conceived when the spirit of an ancestor entered her body as she passed one of a number of sacred spots. Then when a woman felt a baby stir in her as she passed one of these spots, she would ascribe it to the entry of a spirit, and her child would be supernaturally linked with that place. The Australians were already cast for a lowly place in the ladder of social development, so this belief fitted in well with another class of facts which anthropologists had thrown into a scheme of evolution. In many tribes a man inherits clan-name or surname, property, office, from his mother's brother, and not from his father. The child belongs to the mother's family, not to the father's. Most primitive tribes also have customs by which they class together large groups of relatives, so that a man has many fathers, many mothers, many children, brothers, sisters, grandchildren and so on. To explain all these facts anthropologists created a number of theories, something on the following model.

At first, men and women were promiscuous, and did not pair in marriage. Therefore no-one knew who the father of a child was; only its mother was definitely known. Then groups of men began to marry groups of women, all of the women caring for their children and being 'mothers' to them, and all of the men being 'fathers' to the children. After that, because a child's mother was known with certainty, descent was traced through the mother's line, and power over the child lay with the mother's brother—for as a mother is known, so is her brother by the same mother. The father was still not known, because women had many husbands; and hence the role of men in begetting children was not known. This rule of mother-right was broken when individual men in one tribe began to steal women from other tribes; the children of these captured wives were their own, and did not belong to the mother's family. These forcible marriages, of which a model is the Roman rape of the Sabine women, became the pattern for marriages within the tribe. The anthropologist argued that the practice of stealing brides survived in symbolic form as the reluctance which the bride in many tribes has to show at coming to her husband. In some tribes, she is ceremonially seized by her husband's friends in a mock fight; in others, she has to weep and be given gifts; among ourselves, she should be carried by the bridegroom over the threshold as if he had abducted her. From this stage of capturing brides, as men and women became paired in marriage or men began to take many wives, the father got increasing control over the children, the father-right steadily ousted mother-right. In all tribes which have father-right, the mother's relatives have some rights over the child, and these were ascribed to customs surviving from an early stage of mother-right. Thus the scheme was supported with finely worked out, learned, logical arguments.

This theory is neatly logical, but it is purely conjecture. It cannot be proved or disproved. And other theories have been advanced, with equally good logic. Some writers have argued that father-right must be more fundamental than mother-right. We know that in many animal societies one old male dominates the herd or troop, and drives away his own sons while he keeps the females, so, it was argued that early human society must have been similar. Yet others said that the higher apes lived in pairs, and that that was the original condition of human beings, from which they fell from grace into group-marriage, or man took several wives, or more rarely one woman several husbands. Logical arguments can be worked out to support all these schemes and there is no means of proving that one is right rather than the other. More than this, the theories are sterile, for they do not pose further problems. When you have worked out your scheme you just fit each tribe as it is described into its place on the ladder, and that is that. If in a society with mother-right you find customs of father-right, they indicate the beginnings of the assertion of father's power; if in a society with father-right, you find customs giving power to the mother's family, these are survivals from the stage of mother-right.

Let us now glance at what modern anthropologists do about these problems. When we examine a whole series of tribes which we call primitive, one dominant set of facts emerges. All these societies have goods which are primary, and no luxuries. That is, their goods must be consumed at once, and since these are simple foods, skin clothes, mud and grass houses, and so on, the rich man cannot use wealth to raise his standard of living markedly above his fellows. Chiefs cannot build palaces, have luxurious feasts, wear jewels and costly robes. A man with a thousand head of cattle cannot himself consume all their milk, meat or skins. He can only use them to attract and support dependents, and thus acquire power over people. This situation gives a limiting framework to the conditions of primitive life. In these tribes too there is no widespread trade by which a man can get other kinds of goods for himself, for the products of neighbouring tribes are of the same general kind. From North America, Oceania, and Africa, in tribes which have chiefs, aristocrats and slaves, reports all speak of the essential equality of living standards between all these classes. Thus Hobgin writes that the

possession of wealth in the Solomon Islands, as amongst ourselves, ensures prestige. But in a Native community the same scale of comforts—or lack of them—is available for all; everyone has to spend several hours of the day at the same kind of work, all eat the same kind of dishes prepared in the same type of utensils from similar raw foods, and all sleep on the same kind of mats for beds. The house of a wealthy man may be larger it is true and better built than that of one who is insignificant, and he may have several wives, but the difference otherwise is negligible. Reputation is accordingly enhanced not by accumulating possessions in order to use them oneself, but by giving them away.

Similarly Goldenweiser says of the Tlingit and Haida of North-West America:

It must not be imagined, however, that this development of proprietary ideas stands for distinction of economic status among individuals. There is but the dimmest foreshadowing of a possible division into rich and poor. All live in about the same way. The noble and the commoner, the slave and his master, share in the same work and enjoy approximately the same comforts and pleasures.

Finally, I illustrate with a missionary's description of how a Central African people remembered a tyrant after his death: they forgot his harsh punishments and rule and remembered his successful raids:

They don't study that aspect of Msidi's life which pictures him as thundering out the death warrant . . . and even tasting from his executioner's hand the warm life-blood of his dying victim; but they recall how he could show himself to be kindness and liberality itself, and how he himself would wear, day in and day out, a miserable two yards of dirty calico and yet would give away, to the last yard, the bales upon bales of cloth brought into the country by the many caravans from the east and west coasts.

Note that this persisted even after European goods entered the land. In primitive tribes which are fortunate enough to live in bountiful environments, people even compete with each other in destroying property, because they cannot do anything else with it. The North-West Coast Red Indians used to burn huge quantities of seal and whale oil, blankets, and other valuables, in feasts at which they challenged others, who then lost face until they had replied with an even greater feast. Melanesian Islanders similarly exposed food to rot in competition. Incidentally, we ourselves have this kind of behaviour in what Veblen has called 'the conspicuous consumption' of the rich. A millionaire cannot use all his income for food, housing, etc., and if he cannot invest it all, he spends a lot unnecessarily—and he puts a lot into public benefactions.

In these competitions of destruction a man relies on his kinsfolk to help him outface his opponents. In meagre environments, he relies on his kin to help him survive. This involves another important condition of primitive economies. On the whole they have simple and undeveloped tools so that a man can produce little beyond his own needs. In these conditions one man cannot live off the labour of others, or if he gets power over others cannot use them to raise his own standards of living.

At the beginning of the nineteenth century a small chief, Shaka created the great Zulu nation. He had tens of thousands of subjects but this made no change in his way of life. A writer on Zulu history says:

It is, perhaps, easier to secure increased means than a corresponding increase of capacity for enjoying them. Thus the great wealth which the spoils of fallen tribes supplied made but little change in Tshaka's personal wants. His fare differed but little from that of a native of ordinary means. He knew of no choicer food than boiled beef, and the beer which was the beverage of any man successful in raising a crop of grain. His eyes were reddened by the smoke which filled the ventless hut in which he lived. He slept on a straw mat, with a wooden pillow to support his head, and a mantle made of the skins of animals to cover his body. His apparel was neither so rare nor so costly as to be beyond the means of a common man.

Shaka had thousands of warriors in constant attendance on him; he could not put them to productive labour. When he built a new village they marched off and each man returned bearing a single sapling.

Similarly, David Livingstone quoted with approval a missionary who had worked among the Matabele, a group of Zulu in the present Southern Rhodesia:

The African slave, brought by a foray to the tribe, enjoys, from the beginning, the privileges and name of a child, and looks upon his master and mistress in every respect as his new parents. He is not only nearly his master's equal, but he may, with impunity, leave his master and go wherever he likes within the boundary of the kingdom: although a bondman or a servant, his position . . . does not convey the true idea of a state of slavery; for, by care and diligence, he may soon become a master himself, and even more rich and powerful than he who led him captive.

Of the working of the slave system this missionary said:

Neither the punctuality, quickness, thoroughness, nor amount of exertion is required by the African as by the European master. In Europe the difficulty is want of time; in Africa, what is to be done with it.

This then is the economic situation in which primitive people live, and in this situation they live together in self-subsistent groups, which on the whole produce everything they want and consume it together. Social relationships are undifferentiated, for there is little scope for specialization. A man does not have specific economic relationships, and economic relationships alone, with other men. He does his economic work with the same people with whom he lives, plays, shares good and ill fortune, celebrates weddings, and mourns at funerals. Even specialists like smiths are peasants. These associates are kinsmen, linked with him by different kinds of ties; hence, the kinship system is widely extended, and many distant relatives are grouped with close relatives. As a man grows up in one of these groups, there is no special work to draw him away from those who gave birth to him and nurtured him. What can he do elsewhere? What labour is there elsewhere for him? More than this, there are pressures to keep him with his kinsfolk, who love him and will support him. Elsewhere he will be alone and friendless; if he is killed or injured, who will care or avenge him? So it is clear why men remain on the land of their ancestors as long as there is land, working with their kin, supporting them in quarrels and so on. In many economic activities, however, there must be co-operation if they are to be successful. It is therefore in this economic situation that we now seek the 'origins' of the widely extended system of kinship relationships which is characteristic of primitive tribes, and which our own ancestors once had. We do not need to conjecture about forms of extraordinary marriage which we cannot observe but can only guess at; we can understand the system on the basis of observations.

Given a widely extended kinship system, we have to explain why some peoples have father-right and other mother-right. Anthropologists have not yet worked out successfully any specific conditions to explain why one line of descent should dominate over the other, save that it is true that almost all dominantly pastoral peoples have father-right. There does seem to be something in the conditions of nomadic pastoral life which gives power to the father. The mother-right pastoral peoples I know are all settled. There are nomadic hunters who have mother-right. Agriculture however allows of both father-right and mother-right. But we have been able to throw light on the way in which father's and mother's families both have duties to and rights over the children, and on the effects of these on behaviour. We do not treat the power of the mother's kin in a father-right society as a survival from the past. We study the balance of the power. For a child is born of a marriage linking not only people of different sexes but linking also two different sets of kin, and this situation is the origin of a struggle between the two groups. I have not time to expand on this problem here.

In our general study of this kind of extended kinship system, we have found that the family is always recognized and identified, that is, it is an institution which originates in the fundamental conditions of human life in society. Detailed studies, based on observation, have been made of how a child grows out of the close intimacy of family life into wider kinship relationships. But the kinship system does not arise out of a simple extension of the ties in the family. It is related to the economic situation. In fact, it seems that the structure of the kinship system affects the nature of the family ties. Thus it is probable that in tribes with strongly developed father-right the family is stable and divorce is rare, while in all other tribes the family is unstable and divorce is frequent. If this hypothesis is supported by further research, it will not be easy to apply the argument to our very complex and differentiated society, but clearly we shall have isolated one factor affecting family stability. And that is an example of how research on primitive peoples throws light on our own social problems.

Analyses have also been made of the structure of these extended kinship systems, and a number of general rules have been established for them all. The most important is that brothers and to some extent their sisters are socially equivalent. That is, whatever their individual differences, their role in society is identical in primitive society—and you can easily see why. This is so among ourselves: our parents call all of us 'child', we all call them 'parent'. In communities where wider kinship ties are more important this principle is extended. A man regards all his father's brothers as a group with his father, and therefore calls them all 'father'. This identification may even embrace those of opposite sex, so that the father's sister (the paternal aunt) is often called 'female father' and the mother's brother (the maternal uncle) is called 'male mother'. These are not just terms of address; the father's sister tends to be treated as a father, and the mother's brother as a mother. An African soldier once overstayed his leave, and said he had been delayed by his mother's funeral. The Army asked the local British administrator to find out if it was true. The administrator made enquiries and found it was the man's mother's brother who had died. He wrote to the army: 'Ask the soldier if his mother was a man or a woman. If he says his mother was a woman, he is lying; if he says his mother was a man he is telling the truth.'

In many tribes there is an identification of alternate generations, so that grandfather and grandson call each other 'brother'. This custom is found in parts of Wales. Professor Radcliffe-Brown has suggested the origin of this custom. When a man attains the age of 20 and begins to come into social life as mature, his father is, say, 40, and still has a dominant position in social life. There is therefore hostility and competition between them, which indeed we record frequently between adjacent age-groups. But the grandfather is 60, and ready to move out of active social life; so that he is replaced by his grandson, and not by his son with whom his relations, though loving, were charged with submerged hostility. This is why alternate generations are identified, and why grandparents are accused of spoiling the children, as also among ourselves. Incidentally, it also explains why the grandson often call the grandfather's wife 'my wife', and there is no need to postulate, as anthropologists have done in the past, a now extinct form of marriage between grandmother and grandson to explain this very reasonable behaviour.

I do not want to spend all my time in the intricacies of kinship analysis, but I give one more example from it. Many thinkers have tried to explain the historical origin of the incest taboos, and how the extension of these taboos to other kin produced what we call exogamy—rules forbidding marriage with distant blood-relatives or in-laws, or members of the same clan. For instance, Westermarck suggested that boys and girls who grow up together did not desire each other, which is not confirmed by observation, and he also drew a picture of primitive man at one stage working out that inbreeding produced less satisfactory children than marrying out, a picture I can hardly accept, especially as it is not yet proved by eugenists. Indeed, some tribes only marry their cross-cousins (the children of their mother's brother or father's sister) and this is similar to brother-sister marriage. Cleopatra was the product of some 37 brother-sister marriages. Freud made up a Just-So story of how the sons, kept from their mother and sisters by their jealous father, killed and ate him, and then horrified by their deed, instituted strong taboos against the desires which had motivated it; and these incest taboos were extended into exogamous bans.

I will not go into the complicated problem of incest, but glance at exogamous rules. Exogamous bans are not the same as incest taboos; in some tribes some of the women you cannot marry are ideal mistresses. These historical explanations have tended to seek their origin within single groups, save for one theory that marriages by capture established the practice of seeking brides elsewhere. But, as we observe the exogamous bans in any primitive tribe, they exist not simply as a ban on marrying certain kinswomen but as rules compelling men to marry women from other groups. That is, the origin of the rules must be sought by observation of how they work in a system of exogamous groups. Then we can see how the marriages they compel interlink these groups, and as children are born give these children rights in different groups. In tribes without chiefs these links are the main means by which members of separate groups can move about the country in safety, and they are frequently the mechanism for peacemaking.

This manner of interpretation epitomizes our basic approach to the problems of origins. I illustrate this approach further with another type of example; how the belief in the immortality of the soul arose, leaving aside the question of whether it is true or not, which we cannot judge scientifically at present. The late Sir Edward Tylor suggested that early man pondered on sleep, fainting, trance, death, in which the body is the same but different, and on the appearance of images in dreams, fantasy and memory. Man then explained these facts to himself by saying that the personality is dual. In addition to the body there are the life and the image which become identified as the ghost-soul, which leaves the body temporarily in trance and sleep and unconsciousness, and leaves it permanently in death. The soul in sleep travels to other places and others' souls can visit one in one's dreams. Tylor supported this reconstruction skilfully, by citing beliefs from all over the world, such as that of the Fijians, who think a man must be wakened gradually, lest he be roused before his soul has time to re-enter his body. Tylor's analysis is very valuable, but while he plausibly explained how the belief in the soul could have originated, we are left with no problem to test in any living society. Nor does the theory explain the nature of funeral rites, nor the varying attributes of the soul in the same society or different societies, nor the fear of death.

Professor Radcliffe-Brown gives us a theory which does enable us to study these problems. He points out that two things do in fact survive a man's death. The first is the body which has to be disposed of in some way. The second is what Radcliffe-Brown calls the social personality, which is the total set of the man's relationships with other members of the community, that is, his position as father to children, as son to father, as husband to wife, as subject to chief, and so on. After a man's death these relationships continue to exist, though he is dead; so his social personality survives. In the funeral rites these relationships are adjusted to accommodate them with the fact of his death. If he is full grown, an heir may be appointed who takes over his place, reconstituting the network of relationships. The widows may be taken in marriage by the heir, or may remain married to the dead man, in the levirate of which you've read in the Bible. They bear sons to him by another kinsman. This formulation of the origin of the soul-belief enables us to study funeral rites as they occur in living societies. We see immediately, for instance, why the rites vary for chiefs and commoners, men and women, adults and children, and so on. Each of them had a different social personality, though each of them had the same soul on Tylor's theory (not his descriptions of the variation). It is clear too why so many peoples believe that the soul undergoes a period when it wanders loose, in the wilds, before it is instituted among the ancestral spirits or makes a safe journey to the other world. This is the period during which the survivors, the community, are adjusting themselves to the alteration in the pattern of their interrelationships which must follow on a death. The theory also explains why death is feared. It is an attack on the society of living men for it wrenches and dislocates their inter-relationships; once it has gained a foothold it may not be content with a single victim.

The theory has another advantage. Correctly it sees that men are born into a society and a culture which impose certain ideas and beliefs on them, such as the idea of survival after death. Men do not believe in immortality because of their individual feelings or efforts of mind, but because they are taught to do so. Other anthropologists have sought the origin of the belief in man's inability to accept his own extinction. As one has put it: 'man's hopes will hurdle death itself'; and another: in 'the conflict and chaos of death' religion 'standardises the comforting, the saving belief. We would say that individuals may in this situation get comfort and hope from the belief, but that the belief transcends any individual. It must originate in the conditions of social life, that is why it is found wherever men live in society, and why all peoples attach such importance to the proper performance of funeral rites. For the social importance of the belief is far greater than the comfort it gives the dying individual; and this is shown by the way in which tribes who worship their ancestors give little heed to the after-life of the spirits, but emphasize always the bonds of the spirits with their surviving descendants, and the effects of those bonds on the relationships of those descendants.

It is important to see all social beliefs as imposed on the individual members of the society, and not as created by their own minds. The behaviour of men has also to be understood not by seeking its origins in conjectural history, any more than in individual psychology alone. Professor Evans-Pritchard has demonstrated this vividly in his analysis of witchcraft beliefs in a Central African tribe. It is commonly believed that primitive men think they have been bewitched and then fall ill. Evans-Pritchard shows that the reverse is true. When a man suffers some misfortune he seeks for the witch who has caused it. The African knows very well that the misfortune has an objective cause, in our sense of the word. That is, for example, he sees that his son has been killed by an elephant. But he wants to know why his son and not another hunter was killed, by one elephant and not another, on that hunt and not another hunt. A witch is the explanation. Thus where we say it is chance that makes, say, my going home from here intersect the path of a motorcar so that I am killed, the African says it is the evil-doing of a witch. He seeks the witch by oracles. The oracles are consulted by putting names to them, and eventually must answer 'yes' to some name. The sufferer puts to the oracles the names of his personal enemies; for though many people may have the power of witchcraft, only a man who wishes another ill will hurt him. So malicious, envious, spiteful, people tend to be detected as witches. The moral code contained in witchcraft beliefs disapprove of the same qualities as anti-social, which our moral code regards as evil. It is believed that the witch may have the power of witchcraft and not be conscious that it is acting. If the misfortune is past and done with, like a death, he will be made to pay compensation should the chief's oracles confirm the accusation. If the misfortune is in the making, like a long illness, he will be asked to withdraw his evil influence. The accused may not believe he is guilty, but to show his clean heart will say, 'If I have witchcraft and it is acting, I do not know and it will stop'.

Note here that beliefs in witchcraft are a philosophy explaining not the physical causes of events, but why misfortunes happen to people. They do so by relating the misfortunes to personal enmities. These enmities arise, or are feared, wherever a man is unduly prosperous— if he has children while others' children die, his crops flourish while his neighbours' fail, and so on. The lucky man fears he will be attacked by envious witches; his neighbours suspect he is using witchcraft to prosper at their expense. Clearly this type of witchcraft belief is associated with the economic system I described earlier—a system with no drive to heavy production by the individual. It is part of an organization which is dominated by intense concentration on close personal relationships. Among ourselves, you can sue another only if he has directly injured you, so that you can prove a tort in court. In these primitive societies in effect every misfortune becomes a tort; it is blamed on a specific person who is charged with wronging you. So that the system of beliefs is related to the form of organization of the society—it originates in them.

These beliefs are imposed on the individual by his birth into a tribe with them. Bring him up elsewhere and he would not have them. The African is reared so that he cannot think outside witchcraft. It is a complete system of ideas. In general, it is so cast that it coincides with reality; witches, reasonably, are personal enemies. Failures are explained inside the system, and do not prove it all wrong. Thus the man accused of witchcraft, feeling himself innocent, will suspect that the real witch has twisted the oracles by his power. If magic fails, the failure is explained by the work of witches, or by the magician's having broken a taboo. Thus, if an African magically treats his village to prevent lightning striking it, and lightning does strike it, he will say that he used bad medicines, or called in an inefficient magician, or the magical power of the lightning was too strong. So if your house is struck despite its having lightning conductors, you will say that the wires were no good, the workman was bad, or the power of a particular flash was too strong. You do not say that all modern science is wrong.

All societies have these systems of beliefs which are imposed on their members, and which are rooted in their forms of social organization. Within the systems, human beings in various communities reason in the same way. It must be so, for the same forms of social organization occur in all societies, though in varying forms; they all have marriages and families, and means of nurturing and educating children; men all have the same bodily needs; they all suffer misfortune and fall ill; they all die. People everywhere settle with their fellows. All societies have to make a livelihood, and cope with quarrels among their members. These forms of organization and belief, however, do not originate only in the biological and mental necessities of human existence. You cannot explain economic organization by the appetite of hunger, or exogamous rules by the appetite of sex. Men live in communities which have cultures transmitted down through the generations, and these conditions are the source of forms of organization. Man is so far transformed by living in cultured society that it has proved impossible to arrive at his basic biological constitution, free of culture, to test intelligence between groups. Such fundamental perceptions as those of shape and colour vary from society to society, and so do cultural ideals and characters.

Nevertheless, in society after society we find the same forms of social organization, originating in the same conditions. As soon as men collect in villages and towns, they develop similar constitutions and conflicts. Every society moves through situations in which it makes its living and confronts dangers, new members are born into it and grow up and die; and as it moves through time the parties to its structure change, quarrel, and settle their differences. We are only at the beginning of our study of the processes by which this happens, and in fact we know very little of what is to be known. I have sketched a little of the little we know. What I have tried to emphasize is that when we speak of the origins of social organization, we do so not in the sense of delving into conjectural history to speculate about how early man lived (though true history is an important branch of sociology), but in the sense of searching for the processes by which men live in community. The origins of social organization have to be sought in social organization itself, both in primitive and in our own society.

18. THE PRINCIPLES OF CLANSHIP IN HUMAN SOCIETY *

The definition of the word "clan" represents a formidable and complex problem and the way an anthropologist uses the word can reveal many of his basic assumptions and the fundamental theoretical framework in which he works. We may begin with a point generally agreed upon: a clan is a social unit composed of persons who trace their descent to a common ancestor, through connecting relatives who are all of the same sex. In a society with matrilineal clans a man belongs to the same group as his mother and his maternal grandmother but not to the group of his father.

While clans are found in some societies but not others, and while we know beyond doubt that societies do not have to go through a stage of clan organization, the number of societies that have had or continue to include clans is remarkable. Furthermore, the functions of the clan are so extensive that this grouping frequently dominates the society in which it is found.

But the essay which follows goes beyond this point. Suggesting the value of clan organization in certain economic contexts, it goes on to distinguish two types of grouping which have been confused. One of these differs from the other in ways which show how a more complex and truly political society can emerge from a kin background.

* Paul Kirchhoff, "The Principles of Clanship in Human Society." Originally written in 1935, this important paper failed to reach publication until 1955 when it appeared in the *Davidson Journal of Anthropology* which is produced by graduate students at the University of Washington. It is printed here with the permission of the author.

The author (b. 1900) is Professor of History at the National School of Sciences in Mexico City. Contributor of several fundamental concepts to the theory of social organization, Kirchhoff has spent most of the recent years in intensive studies of Mexican culture in pre-Hispanic times. An authority on the Toltec calendrical system, he spent an interlude of several years at the University of Washington making an analysis of Tibetan polity in the 6th and 7th centuries A. D. He has published for the most part in German and Spanish.

1

I F ONE WERE ASKED to single out one outstanding social phenomenon which dominates the early evolution of human society the answer
would undoubtedly have to be that this phenomenon is the clan. Proof
for this assertion will hardly be necessary. The decisive role of the clan
in early human history manifests itself in a striking manner in the fact
that its disappearance as the dominating form of social organization
marks the end of a whole historical phase, and the beginning of another
i.e., that dominated by social classes and their struggles.

It would, of course, be incorrect to say that the history of human
society begins only with the emergence of the clan. A very important
chapter precedes this event. But while the beginning of this chapter of
the evolution of human society is still characterised by the comparative
shapelessness of all social forms, in its later part the subsequent emergence of the clan casts its shadow ahead as it were: here the main theme,
and consequently the main problem confronting the student, are the
various facts and forms leading towards the emergence of the clan.

One of the outstanding tasks before the student of early human society
is, therefore, the study of the various forms the clan has taken in the
course of its development, of the factors which brought the clan in its
various forms into existence, and of the factors which led to its replacement, as the dominating form of social organization, by other forms.

The study of this complex of problems has dominated the first decades
of anthropological research. Within the last two decades, however, it
has almost completely receded into the background as a result of the
present anti-evolutionist trend of anthropology.

The early evolutionist school in anthropology, with Morgan as its most
gifted spokesman, fell into an error for which anthropology subsequently
had to pay a heavy fine, i.e., the fine of experiencing the growth of anti-
evolutionist tendencies, the unchecked growth of which today threatens
anthropology with ever-increasing sterility. This error consists in replacing the concept of *multi*lineal evolution, as applied by leading students to both natural history and the *later* phases of the history of
society, by the concept of *uni*lineal evolution, as far as *early* society is
concerned. The application of this mistaken concept led to the distortion
of many facts—and it may be said that anthropology since Morgan has
to a very large extent lived on these distortions. It has become the
fashionable pursuit of many a writer to demonstrate that the unilineal
evolutionism of Morgan and others operated with distorted or misin-
terpreted facts, and that—therefore!—the facts unearthed by anthropology, both before, and even more so since Morgan, prove the inap-

plicability of the concept of evolution to primitive society—and therefore to society generally. All that has to be done, on the contrary, in order to demonstrate its applicability is to replace the unilineal concept of Morgan by the multilineal concept as applied in other sciences.

One of the tasks, therefore, which confronts us in studying the evolution of the clan and its role in the history of society is to inquire which different *forms of the clan* are found to exist, and what *their mutual genetic relation is*. The present paper is in the main confined to this task.

2

The most primitive stage of societal development known shows relatively small communities with a non-productive economy. The communities, several of which are united by bonds of common speech, customs and beliefs into what usually is called a tribe, apparently everywhere consist of a nucleus of near relatives (relatives both by blood and by marriage)—to which nucleus are frequently attached more distant relatives and unrelated individuals who for one reason or other have left their original community. Everywhere, however, the decisive element is the group of relatives, by blood and by marriage. Very frequently the community consists only of this group: a married couple and their unmarried and some of their married children—usually the married sons only, or the married daughters only, together with their husbands and wives and unmarried children.

This group, and the whole community, if larger than the kernel of relatives, is by no means a permanent unit. Ever again it splits up into smaller units of similar composition, be it at the death of the leading member of the community, as the result of the impossibility of the existence of a group above a certain size in one locality at this stage of economy and organization, or be it as the result of friction between members of the group, e.g., between brothers or sisters. Marriage of a member of the community frequently leads to his settling apart. This lays the foundation for a new community which in the course of time will go through the same process as the original one.

No bond beyond that of sentiment ties the members of this community to the one in which they were born. What matters is where people live at a given moment: in other words, *the concept of descent is still completely absent.*

Relatives by blood and relatives by marriage are here, as to their place in the community, on a far more equal footing than at any subsequent stage of societal development.

The ties and obligations of kinship cut, of course, across several such communities, where there is intermarriage between several of them. But these ties and obligations do not themselves constitute communities. They do, therefore, not enter into our problem directly.

It is, on the other hand, only these ties of kinship which apparently everywhere at this stage regulate marriage. If we confine the term exogamy to the rule that marriage must be outside of a group larger than that composed of relatives in the first degree, and if we mean by group a constant body of people whose extent is the same for any of its members, then there is no such thing as exogamy to be found at this stage. Society here can still do without the concept of descent and consequently without the rule of exogamy.

The conditions described here are found mainly amongst mere food-gatherers and hunters, and may be said to be typical for them.

In certain cases, however, as, e.g., in many tribes in the Amazon area of South America, where the tilling of the soil has already replaced the mere hunting and collecting of food, and where the communities are considerably larger than, let us say, those of the Shoshoni or Apache, the concept of descent is nevertheless still unknown. Such cases undoubtedly present exceptions to the rule that mere foodgathering and hunting go together with the absence of groups based on the concept of descent. Lowie has quoted these South American cases as proof for his contention that there is "little evidence of complex laws of sequence." It would, however, seem to be very unsafe to base such a far-reaching contention on what so obviously are exceptional cases. Similarly futile it would be to arrive at general conclusions from the reverse cases of, e.g., many Australians or the tribes of the North American northwest coast where we find more advanced forms of kinship organization combined with lower forms of economy. These cases have to be explained on the individual merits of the case, and clearly understood as exceptions due to exceptional historical circumstances which in most cases we probably shall be able to demonstrate.

3

In the overwhelming majority of cases higher forms of economic activity are found together with higher forms of kinship organization.

The increasingly cooperative character of economic activity requires forms of kinship organization which assure greater stability of the cooperating groups (which in primitive society predominantly means groups of relatives). Greater stability of the cooperating groups of relatives requires some principle which more clearly sets off one such group from the other, and which at the same time, assures their continuity in time.

The principle of clanship, based on the concept of descent, does both.

In other words, the function of the clan is to assure stable and continuous cooperation. It takes a number of different forms, but its essence appears to be the same everywhere: to group together in one permanent unit all those persons, living or dead, who can claim common descent. This group is commonly called a clan or sib. Its invention, if we may call it that, is one of the greatest achievements of early man. It provided the form of social organization under which the forces of production could grow, slowly but steadily, to the comparative height attained, e.g., by the mountain tribes of Luzon, with their magnificent terraced fields and irrigation works, or, higher still, by Homeric society.

In this respect, however, and in the complexity and perfection attained by the developing forms of kinship organization themselves, there are important, even striking differences between some of the main forms which the principle of clanship took concretely. To anticipate one of the main results of our survey: some of these forms seem to lead comparatively early to the stage of stagnation, or into a blind alley if we may say so, while others seem to possess far greater possibilities of development.

At the present stage of the investigation of the problem, I conceive of these various forms of clans not as of consecutive stages, so that one could be explained as developing out of the other, but rather as stemming from the same root, i.e., from the more amorphous type of kinship organization outlined before. Whether they actually grew out of this common root *at the same time* is quite another question. In fact, it would seem that they, or at least some of them, rather represent *successive* branches off the same tree. In other words, while none can be explained out of the others, still some appear to be more archaic, others more recent. This concept is, of course, thus far but a working hypothesis, and may remain so for a good time, until a complete survey has been made of the known forms of kinship organization and the other cultural forms accompanying them in every specific case. The detailed evidence on which these provisional conclusions are based can unfortunately not be given here for reasons of space. I hope to be able to present this evidence, in part at least, soon in a second article dealing with this question.

Out of the several forms of clans which have to be distinguished I shall here omit some, especially that found in most Australian tribes, and single out for discussion two only. It appears that the overwhelming majority of tribes whose social units are known to be based on descent, belong to one or the other of these two types.

4

The first of these two types is that of *unilateral exogamous clans,* either of the patrilineal or matrilineal variety. Since these two varieties are alike in all other points except that one is matrilineal, the other patrilineal, no attention needs to be paid here to this difference, since our main aim is to show what distinguishes *both* of them from the other type of clan which is neither unilateral nor exogamous.

The formative features of the first type of clan, in both of its varieties, are: (1) The clan consists of people who are related to each other either through women only or through men only—according to the customs of the tribe; (2) every member of the clan is, as far as clan membership goes, on an absolutely equal footing with the rest: the nearness of relation to each other or to some ancestor being of no consequence for a person's place in the clan; (3) members of the clan may not marry each other.

In other words, the principles underlying this type of clan are: unilateral, "equalitarian", exogamous. They constitute one indivisible whole. It is no accident that practically everywhere where we find one of them we find the other two. Neither of them would, in fact, by itself, produce the same result.

These principles of clanship, or rather this threefold principle, leads to sharply defined, clearly separate units, comparable to so many blocks out of which society is built. There have to be always at least two such blocks—two clans living in connubium. Usually there are more than two.

The most striking aspect of this threefold principle of clanship is its extreme rigidity. It is hard to imagine in which direction this type of clan could develop further. The classical form in which we know it from hundreds of tribes seems to exhaust all its possibilities, and no forms leading beyond it seem to have been reported from anywhere—unless the Australian systems should fall into this category.

This type of clan makes possible a kind of economic and general cultural cooperation which in its way seems perfect. But, as the term perfect implies, it seems to be the highest type of cooperation which can be achieved along *this* line of development. The growing forces of production at a certain stage demand important readjustments in the form of kinship organization of which this type appears to be incapable. Its absolute equalitarianism, combined with the complete subordination of each of its members to the interests of the clan as a whole, while making possible a certain type of primitive cooperation, obstructs very effectively the evolution of these tight forms of cooperation which are based upon economic and social differentiation. Where, therefore, with this type of clan higher forms of economy have come into existence, as, e.g., those based on animal breeding, the development of which requires higher forms of cooperation, there this new economy has usually not gone beyond rather meagre beginnings. It is, on the other hand, significant that the forms of irrigated agriculture found amongst so-called primitive tribes appear to be in the main confined to tribes with the second type of clan, the characteristics of which we will describe presently.

The first type of clan, the unilateral, equalitarian, exogamous clan, is, in the main, typical of tribes with migratory agriculture or with primitive forms of animal breeding. It is probably no accident that it is found above all in those parts of the world where cultural development seems to have reached a point of stagnation, except where subject to foreign stimuli, i.e., in the Americas, in large parts of Negro Africa, in Melanesia and New Guinea, etc.

The form of kinship organization which the unilateral-exogamous principle of clanship creates appears definitely as a blind alley, and more than that; at a certain stage of economic and general cultural evolution as an obstacle to further development. What constitutes its greatness at the same time constitutes its limits.

5

We are presented with a strikingly different picture the moment we turn to the second type of clan, found amongst the early Indoeuropean and Semitic tribes, amongst the Polynesians and most of the Indonesians, including the inhabitants of the Philippines, and a few tribes in other parts of the world. At whatever stage of development we find these tribes, we discover in their economic and social life, factors making for further development, everywhere in the direction of further economic and social differentiation.

What, then, is the type of clan found among these tribes? The answer to the question is not a simple one, at any rate, not if a simple designation like "unilateral", "exogamous", etc., is expected. In fact, the very names "clan", "Sippe", "gens", etc., while taken from the vocabulary of tribes having the *second* type of clan, have been for such a long time and so exclusively used for clans of the first, i.e., the unilateral-exogamous type, that it is very difficult indeed to break down the confusion which anthropologists themselves have created. This confusion consists in the belief that the unilateral-exogamous clan is *the* clan, and that everything else, including the clan of the Gaels, the Sippe of Germans, and the gens of the Romans, is a deviation, or at any rate a special development, from the type of clan found among the Iroquois or in the Trobriand islands. If there is one question in which there is full continuity from Morgan to our own days, then it is this misconception.

Very few indeed are the anthropologists who have tried to understand the clans, e.g., of the Polynesians as a type in itself, as opposed to that, e.g., of the Melanesians. And there is hardly any modern anthropologist who has tried to re-evaluate the principles underlying the clans and sibs and gentes of the early Indoeuropean tribes. In fact, it has somehow become a habit to shun tribes which have this type of clan, both in library research and in field work. They do not fit into the accustomed pattern. Yet, it is precisely the study of these tribes which will allow us to bridge the still existing gulf between the facts of anthropology and those of early European history. These tribes are closer to our own past than any others, and if anthropology aims at being a "useful" science in the sense that its researches and findings fit into a larger body of scientific knowledge, then we must undoubtedly pay more attention to tribes the study of which promises to give us the key to the earliest written history of the Jews, the Greeks, the Romans, the Germans, etc. Thus far, anthropology has completely failed in this task which Morgan regarded as one of the main tasks of our science. In fact, there are probably very few anthropologists today who would agree that this *is* one of the main tasks of anthropology.

The decisive difference between the first and the second type of clan is that what matters in the one is relationship *through* either men or women (according to the customs of the tribe), irrespective of the nearness of such relationship to the other members of the group or to some ancestor —whereas, on the contrary, in the other type it is precisely the *nearness* of relationship to the common ancestor of the group which matters. The first of the two principles of clanship results in a group the members of which are of absolutely equal standing, as far as this standing is determined by membership in the group (leaving aside the question of age). The second principle results in a group in which every single member, except brothers or sisters, has a different standing: the concept of the *degree of relationship* leads to *different degrees of membership* in the clan. In other words, some are members to a higher degree than others.

The logical consequence of this state of affairs is that at a certain point it becomes doubtful whether a person is still to be regarded a member of a certain clan—a question that could never arise in a unilateral-exogamous clan. Clan membership so-to-speak shades off the farther one is away from the center-line of the clan—the real core of the group. This core, the *aristoi*, consist of those who are the nearest descendants of the common ancestor of the clan.

In most tribes descent is customarily either through men or, more rarely, through women, but very frequently, especially in the case of the *aristoi*, descent may be counted through either of them. That side being chosen which gives a person a higher descent, i.e., a closer relationship with the ancestor of the group. The term "ambilateral" has been coined for this system.

Genealogies, unknown and unnecessary in a unilateral clan, are here the means of establishing the "line" of descent of the nobles—this "line" being another concept unknown in unilateral clans.

A corollary of the second principle of clanship is that there is no exogamy in the sense defined above. In fact, there could be none, since there are no groups with definite and fixed "boundaries". On the contrary, we frequently find close endogamy—however, usually only for the *aristoi*. Marriage between relatives of high descent assures that their offspring will be of still higher descent.

The type of preferential marriage most characteristic for this type of clan is that with parallel relatives:—the brother's daughter and/or the father's brother's daughter. We find this marriage all the way from ancient Prussia, Greece, and Arabia, to the Kwakiutl of the North American northwest coast who together with the Nootka seem to be the only representatives of this type of clan organization on North American soil. Marriage with either the brother's daughter or the father's brother daughter may almost be regarded as a "leitfossil" of this type of clan.

Another type of preferential marriage found frequently with it is marriage with a half-sister, i.e., a sister by the same father, but a different mother. Neither of these two types of preferential marriage seems to be ever found in societies organized into unilateral-exogamous clans.

The distinction between rules of behaviour for the noble core of the clan and for its outer membership runs through all societies organized into clans of the second type. It is the feature which most clearly and sharply sets off this type of clan from the "equalitarian" unilateral-exogamous clan, and it is this feature which lies at the root of the very different role which tribes organized into the one or the other type of clan have played in the history of mankind. In fact, this difference inevitably flows from the opposite principles which determine the structure of these two types of clans. The one divides the tribe into a number of solid blocks with clear cut boundary lines, each homogeneous within. The other results in a type of society which may be likened to a cone, the whole tribe being one such cone, with the legendary ancestor at its top,—but within it are a larger or smaller number of similar cones, the top of each coinciding with or being connected with the top of the whole cone. The bases of these cones, representing the circles of living members of the various clans at a given moment, overlap here and there.

The tribe as a whole has essentially the same structure as each of its component parts: it is, therefore, only a question of a choice of words whether we call both of them "tribe", or both of them "clan", or the larger one "tribe" and the smaller ones "clans". Professor Boas' presentation of Kwakiutl kinship organization illustrates this point.

Any one of these cones, large or small, can exist by itself. With the unilateral-exogamous type of clan, on the other hand, always at least two such clans must exist, and the body comprising two, or more, of them together does not have the structure of a clan.

In other words, the two types of clan differ in every single aspect, except the basic one, namely that they are *both based on the principle of descent* (though a different one).

6

In societies of the "conical" clan type, it is regarded as a matter of course that all leading economic, social, religious functions are reserved to those of highest descent, i.e., those closest to the ancestor of the clan and tribe, who frequently is regarded as a god. With the development of production and of culture as a whole, the role of these *aristoi* within the life of the clan and the tribe becomes ever more important. The nearer in descent to the godlike ancestor a person is, the greater are his chances in the process of ever-growing economic and social differentiation. Social differentiation, at this stage of evolution of society, the *condition sine qua non* of the development of higher forms of cooperation, not only finds no obstacle in this type of clan, but on the contrary an extremely flexible medium, namely a hierarchy of relatives, based on the principle of near-ness of descent.

For a long period to come this principle of clanship is able to adapt itself to the ever-growing complexity of social relations. A survey of the tribes organized into clans of this type shows a whole scale of such adaptations to the increasing degree of social differentiation within the tribes: mainly along the line of a more marked stratification of the members of one and the same group. Thus, some members of the clan may be chiefs and near-gods, while others, at the opposite end of the scale, may be slaves: yet all of them are regarded as relatives, and in many cases, are able to prove it.

The process of differentiation within the clan, while for a long time taking place within this flexible unit, finally reaches the point where the interests of those of equal standing, in *all* the clans of the tribe, come into such sharp conflicts with the interests of the other strata that their struggles, the struggle of by now fully-fledged social classes, overshadows the old principles of clanship and finally leads to the break-up of clan, first as the dominating form of social organization and then to its final disappearance. This point, the end of one phase of human history, and the beginning of another, has just been reached when the Greeks, the Romans and the Germans enter into the light of documented history.

However, none of the tribes with which anthropology usually deals have reached this stage. The highest stage found here is, on the contrary, one where it is still to the advantage of the *aristoi* to keep the clan organization intact because it still serves them as the best instrument in their struggle against the lower orders. The reason for this is not difficult to see. In clans of the unilateral-exogamous type the obligations and privileges of every clan member in the final account equal each other. Whatever benefits the individual benefits the clan as a whole, and reversely; whatever strengthens the clan strengthens every one of its members in an equal measure. In this lies the greatness, but at the same time, the limitation of this type of clan. In the cone-shaped clan, on the contrary, everything that strengthens the clan strengthens, above all, its core and correspondingly: whatever any member contributes to the welfare of the clan as a whole benefits above all, the *aristoi*.

Up to a certain point of economic and general cultural development, this strengthening of the core of the clan means, at the same time, a strengthening of the whole clan. But, in the course of time, this becomes less and less true. The interests of the *aristoi*, and to a lesser degree, those of the middle strata where these have come into existence, become ever more separate from and finally opposed to the interests of the group as a whole. But, the bonds of clanship still exist, and, again up to a certain point, it is to the advantage of the *aristoi* to utilize them against the other strata within the clan.

7

A most instructive example of this state of affairs is offered by the Igorot tribes of the northernmost of the Philippine Islands, Luzon. Amongst these tribes whose economy is based on terraced agriculture and irrigation, we are able to study certain still rather embryonic forms of struggle between the developing classes of landlords and landless. Both sides fight here completely within the confines of the old clan organization which is still fully intact. The struggle has certain outward forms of a religious character which, however, do not conceal from the observer the essentials of the struggle.

Both weddings and funerals necessitate amongst these tribes the sacrificial slaughtering of a pig by the nearest relative. The majority of the population, however, have no pigs. If they still own a piece of land, they have to pawn it to a rich man in order to get the required pig. If they have already, at the previous occasion, lost their land, they have to work off the price of the pig. Thus the concentration of land in the hands of a few proceeds at a rapid pace.

The mechanism through which this process operates is the equality of the obligations, on the surface religious in character, for every member of the clan, be he rich or poor. The continuation of equal obligations unquestionably works to the advantage of some against others, at a moment when the development of the forces of production has already led to far-reaching economic and social differentiation. Now, the important point for our problem in all this lies in the fact that both contending sides are very frequently, possibly in the majority of cases, members of the same clan. In fact, they are under the mutual obligation of blood vengeance. But his obligation, too, under the conditions of economic unequality and of the peculiar ties of this type of clan system, works to the advantage of the *aristoi* who can, more or less, force the lesser members of the clan to come to their assistance, and thus, through composition fines extracted from the offender, are able continuously to increase their resources, which in turn gives them a still greater hold over their poorer clan fellows.

The role which this principle of clanship plays here, at a comparatively advanced stage of the evolution of economy and social relations, shows its extraordinary flexibility and adaptability. Its contrast to the rigid unilateral-exogamous principle of clanship is striking. However, this contrast should not induce us to overlook the fact that both of these principles of clanship and the form of clan to which they lead, belong essentially to the same phase of the evolution of society. If we compare them either with the stage of kinship organization which preceded it, or with the breakdown of kinship organization which followed it, the common features, which by grouping the living and the dead together into stable and permanent units, permit of higher forms of cooperation than those known before.

One of these, however, seems, through its rigidity, to lead into a blind alley, while the other, more flexible, has become the form within which social differentiation in a long course of evolution reached the point where it led to the formation of social classes and its own consequent destruction.

19. BILATERAL KIN GROUPINGS
AS A STRUCTURAL TYPE *

The emphasis on unilineal descent groups like clans has been so
intensive that sight has sometimes been lost (as by Kirchhoff in the
preceding selection) of the fact that societies without unilineal emphasis
seem to exist on every level at which unilineal groups are found. The
selection below represents (despite its recent date) a pioneer attempt to
establish the structural regularities of bilateral organization.

A GOOD DEAL of anthropological theory concerning social organization is derived from investigations of societies based upon unilateral
descent groups. The lineage looms large in our picture of non-Western
societies. It is frequently assumed that societies based upon the bilateral
principle of descent are "amorphous," "unstructured," "loosely organized"
or "infinitely complex." I wish to examine the local group organization
and marriage residence patterns of one bilaterally organized society in
order to suggest that there is structure to this type of society but that
the structure may be obscured by approaching it from a unilateral viewpoint.

My model of bilateral organization derives from research among the
North Lapp reindeer nomads who migrate near Karesuando, Sweden;
Enontekio, Finland, and Kautokeino, Norway. The fundamental bilateral-
ism of Lapp society first becomes apparent in the reindeer nomads' inheritance rules and kinship nomenclature.

Among the Lapps, property is owned individually. Wealth is deter-

* Robert N. Pehrson, "Bilateral Kin Groupings as a Structural Type," *Journal of
East Asiatic Studies*, Vol. 3 (1954), pp. 199–202.

The author (1926–1955) died of illness while doing fieldwork in West Pakistan
where he was investigating a second nomadic culture, having previously lived with
a Lapp band in northern Sweden. Pehrson published several articles and a book, *The
Bilateral Network of Social Relations in Könkämä Lapp District* (1957), appeared
posthumously. Other completed manuscripts are being prepared for publication.

mined by the number of reindeer possessed and these are inherited and transmitted equally through the male and female lines. The reindeer are herded collectively by the migratory local group on pasturelands allocated according to customary rights of usage.

Neither is there any unilateral emphasis in the kinship terminology as shown by the complete bilaterality and symmetry of Lapp consanguineal kinship terms and by the rigid differentiation into generations. A third significant feature is the equivalence of siblings, terminologically expressed by classifying cousins with siblings (in Ego's generation, the term of cousin is derived from the sibling term). This equivalence of siblings also occurs in the affinal terminology; Ego classes together his or her spouse's sister and female cousin and brother and male cousin and brother's wife and male cousin's wife.

These terminological features are paralleled in local group organization which, among the Lapps, takes the form of migratory units or bands. Within the band, each generation has its own sphere of activities, rights and obligations. Band members of the same generational level are unified by the classification of cousins with siblings. The principle of the equivalence of siblings also acts to increase the number of band members available for economic activities. In examining kinship behavioural patterns, I came to the conclusion that sibling solidarity is the fundamental kinship bond of Lapp society.

A cursory glance at Lapp band genealogies does not, at first, reveal any clear organizational pattern. The reason for this, I believe, is that a Lapp migratory unit is not a corporate body as such is generally conceived in social anthropology. That is, it lacks such corporate attributes of unilateral kin groupings as perpetuity through time, collective ownership of property and unified activity as a legal individual. Instead of thinking of the Lapp band as a corporate body, we must think of it as a series of alliances between sibling groups. Since these alliances have varying degrees of permanence, a Lapp may be a member of several bands during his life. Within the band, every person is related by blood or marriage to every other person either directly or through a third person. However, the Lapp band is not an "extended family" but, to repeat, an alliance between sibling groups, one of which is dominant. The dominant sibling group provides a nucleus to the genealogical structure of the band since it is the basic point of reference of that structure. The dominant sibling group also gives continuity to leadership since the leader is one of the dominant siblings and his successor is chosen from his sons or sons-in-law.

One of the problems involved in analyzing local group organization is the problem of marriage residence patterns. (I might add in passing that this is not the only problem involved in local group organization as some social anthropologists have assumed. It is also necessary to account for the presence of such unmarried adults as the hired herders found in many Lapp bands.) In analyzing marriage residence, I found no clear-cut matrilocal or patrilocal rules. I also found that the bands are not exclusively exogamic or endogamic. The concepts of complete exogamy or endogamy in relation to local groups may be useful in dealings with societies based on unilateral descent. However, where the local group is neither exclusively exogamic or endogamic (and this seems to be true of many bilateral societies in addition to the north Lapps), the problem becomes one of determining effective range of relationship covered by incest taboos. This is so because the Lapp band is not a corporate entity. By analyzing Lapp sociological concepts, it becomes apparent that the Lapp conceives of himself as a point in a network of kinship relations and not as a member of any corporate entity greater than the sibling group. In selecting a spouse, the Lapp must determine his position in this network of kinship ties in relation to the position of his prospective mate rather than whether or not she belongs to his local group. Thus, if two people in the same band are not directly related or if they are not too closely related, then they may marry. Ideally, incest taboos extend to third cousins but I found in analyzing genealogical connections between spouses that there is a certain amount of cousin marriage. Here there was a discrepancy between the statements of informants and a statistical analysis of the actual situation.

I noted the same discrepancy in statements as to change of residence upon marriage. The Lapps invariably state that at marriage, the woman should join her husband's band but an analysis of all marriages shows that about equally often, the man joins his wife band and remains there. Occasionally, the spouse who moves brings his or her parents and parental siblings and families into the new band. Thus, it became apparent that the Lapps have no simple rules of residence, that the matrilocal and patrilocal characterizations do not apply to a society where parents change residence upon the marriage of their children and that each case of residence change has to be investigated to determine the sociological factors at work.

Such an investigation reveals the following factors underlying marriage residence patterns (although not necessarily in the following order of importance):

1. *Relative wealth.* The spouse with less reindeer often moves to the band of the richer spouse. Rich Lapps frequently consider it desirable to marry off their children to poor Lapps since, by so doing, they gain an addition to their labour force and do not lose their children's reindeer.

2. *Relative status of the spouses' parents or siblings.* Status is not de-

termined exclusively by the individual's wealth. It may also derive from membership in the dominant sibling group of a particular band.

3. *Relative labour convenience.* A person who has several siblings may join his spouse's band if the latter lacks sufficient manpower to herd efficiently.

4. *Relative age considerations.* These are of two sorts. First, one must consider the age of the partners relative to their respective siblings. The eldest son tends to remain at home upon marriage if he is the son of a band leader or wealthy man. In poor families where the mother is widowed, the youngest son often remains at home while the elder siblings are employed as servants in other bands. One must also consider the age of husband and wife relative to each other. If there is a great age difference, the younger spouse may join the band of the elder spouse since the latter has had more time to accumulate property.

Demographic factors are also important in determining residence after marriage. If a herding leader has only daughters, then most of the adult males in the band are liable to have come from other bands (as Mr. Ian R. Whitaker, University of Edinburgh, has shown).

Finally, ecological factors help to determine marriage residence. For example, the son of a rich man may decide to join his wife's band if his father and his own siblings have too many reindeer in relation to the available pastureland.

Now, throughout this consideration of factors determining residence, you may have noted that people may move in relation to their siblings instead of in relation to their parents. This may be correlated with the tendency for Lapps to marry at a relatively late age or when they have attained enough reindeer to set up their own household. By the time a Lapp is ready to marry, band and family leadership may reside in the person of a sibling or cousin rather than in a member of the parental generation. In other words, a Lapp's relation to his siblings may be as important as his relation to his parents in determining local group membership. Therefore, the terms "matrilocalism" and "patrilocalism" do not correctly characterize the whole situation. The terms "virilocal" and "uxorilocal" are more useful here. Virilocalism means that the married couple lives at the locality of the husband's kinsmen, uxorilocalism that the married couple lives at the locality of the wife's kinsmen. The uxorilocal-virilocal characterization emphasizes relationship within one generation, a relationship which may be diagrammed as follows:

This relationship I believe to be crucial in bilateral society. The matrilocal and patrilocal characterizations emphasize the relationship over several generations, a relationship important in unilateral societies and diagrammed as follows:

Thus, when dealing with a bilaterally organized society which emphasized sibling solidarity it seems apropos to use the terms "virilocal" and "uxorilocal" in place of the terms "matrilocal" and "patrilocal" with their implications of unilaterality.

Leonhard Adam suggests that virilocal and uxorilocal are preferable to matrilocal and patrilocal which he considers etymologically incorrect and logically misleading. I also found the former terms more helpful in analyzing marriage residence patterns in a bilateral society. In using them to characterize all marriages, it became clear the Lappish marriage residence patterns are, in fact, bilocal, that there appears to be equal chances of uxorilocalism and virilocalism with the issue settled in each case by the various factors I have discussed before (as was suggested to me by Mr. Ralph Bulmer, Cambridge University).

The structural features of Lapp bilateral organization which emerge from these considerations of kinship, marriage and local group affiliation may be summarized as follows:

1. The society is horizontally separated into generations.
2. The sibling group is the fundamental structural unit of the society. The sibling group is the basic point of reference of Lapp social structure.
3. When the society must act as a unit, these sibling groups form alliances by bilaterally tracing relationship over a network of kinship ties. The temporary nature of these alliances gives flexibility to the structure.

I have not tried in this paper to trace all of the structural ramifications of bilateral organization. Rather, I have attempted to establish that bilateral organization has more structure than has been allowed and that this structure must be studied in its own terms.

20. AFRICAN POLITICAL SYSTEMS *

Some of the questions about the nature of political organization which are raised in current anthropology are clearly inherited from other times and other disciplines. Others seemed, until recently, peculiarly anthropological but now regularly attract analytical talents from other fields. In any case the anthropological approach to these problems is rather distinctive though not necessarily more correct or rewarding.

In the former group of problems are two which, like the Sibyl, refuse to grow old. One is the problem of law and the other deals with the state; they are twins. To pose one is to invoke the other: is law universal, an aspect of social control in all cultures? Is the state present only in the form of certain definite institutions and therefore a characteristic of some societies but not others? Political philosophers and jurisprudes have made intellectual badminton of these questions. The anthropologist comes late to the game but brings his special equipment in the form of ethnographic data.

The book from which the next selection came was a significant attempt to bring together some of the field materials of social anthropology in order to assist in forming generalizations of value to the preceding questions. Though certain of the statements found below are still debated rather than accepted, the essay is a fine introduction to a complex topic.

* Meyer Fortes and E. E. Evans-Pritchard, *African Political Systems* (London: International African Institute, 1940), "Introduction," pp. 1–23. Reprinted by permission of the authors and the publisher.

Meyer Fortes (b. 1906) is William Wyse Professor of Social Anthropology at Cambridge. Specializing in social and political structure, he has made intensive studies among the Tallensi, a people of northern Ghana. He is the author of *The Dynamics of Clanship among the Tallensi* (1945) and *The Web of Kinship among the Tallensi* (1949).

1. AIMS OF THIS BOOK

O NE object we had in initiating this study was to provide a convenient reference book for anthropologists. We also hope that it will be a contribution to the discipline of comparative politics. We feel sure that the first object has been attained, for the societies described are representative of common types of African political systems and, taken together, they enable a student to appreciate the great variety of such types. The eight systems described are widely distributed in the continent. Most of the forms described are variants of a pattern of political organization found among contiguous or neighbouring societies, so that this book covers, by implication, a very large part of Africa. We are aware that not every type of political system found in Africa is represented, but we believe that all the major principles of African political organization are brought out in these essays.

Several contributors have described the changes in the political systems they investigated which have taken place as a result of European conquest and rule. If we do not emphasize this side of the subject it is because all contributors are more interested in anthropological than in administrative problems. We do not wish to imply, however, that anthropology is indifferent to practical affairs. The policy of Indirect Rule is now generally accepted in British Africa. We would suggest that it can only prove advantageous in the long run if the principles of African political systems, such as this book deals with, are understood.

2. A REPRESENTATIVE SAMPLE OF AFRICAN SOCIETIES

Each essay is a condensation of a detailed study of the political system of a single people undertaken in recent years by the most advanced methods of field-work by students trained in anthropological theory. A degree of brevity that hardly does justice to some important topics has been necessary for reasons of space. Each essay furnishes, nevertheless, a useful standard by which the political systems of other peoples in the same area may be classified. No such classification is attempted in this book, but we recognize that a satisfactory comparative study of African

---

E. E. Evans-Pritchard (b. 1902) is Professor of Social Anthropology at Oxford. Also an Africanist, he has specialized in the Azande and the Nuer, two peoples in the Sudan. While his interests and approach are generally similar to those of Fortes, Evans-Pritchard has also concentrated on religion. He is the author of *Witchcraft, Oracles and Magic among the Azande* (1937), *The Nuer* (1940), *Kinship and Marriage among the Nuer* (1951) and other books.

political institutions can only be undertaken after a classification of the kind has been made. It would then be possible to study a whole range of adjacent societies in the light of the Ngwato system, the Tale system, the Ankole system, the Bemba system, and so on, and, by analysis, to state the chief characters of series of political systems found in large areas. An analysis of the results obtained by these comparative studies in fields where a whole range of societies display many similar characteristics in their political systems would be more likely to lead to valid scientific generalizations than comparison between particular societies belonging to different areas and political types.

We do not mean to suggest that the political systems of societies which have a high degree of general cultural resemblance are necessarily of the same type, though on the whole they tend to be. However, it is well to bear in mind that within a single linguistic or cultural area we often find political systems which are very unlike one another in many important features. Conversely, the same kind of political structures are found in societies of totally different culture. This can be seen even in the eight societies in this book. Also, there may be a totally different cultural content in social processes with identical functions. The function of ritual ideology in political organization in Africa clearly illustrates this. Mystical values are attached to political office among the Bemba, the Banyankole, the Kede, and the Tallensi, but the symbols and institutions in which these values are expressed are very different in all four societies. A comparative study of political systems has to be on an abstract plane where social processes are stripped of their cultural idiom and are reduced to functional terms. The structural similarities which disparity of culture conceals are then laid bare and structural dissimilarities are revealed behind a screen of cultural uniformity. There is evidently an intrinsic connexion between a people's culture and their social organization, but the nature of this connexion is a major problem in sociology and we cannot emphasize too much that these two components of social life must not be confused.

We believe that the eight societies described will not only give the student a bird's-eye view of the basic principles of African political organization, but will also enable him to draw a few, perhaps elementary, conclusions of a general and theoretical kind. It must be emphasized, however, that all the contributors have aimed primarily at giving a concise descriptive account and have subordinated theoretical speculations to this end. In so far as they have allowed themselves to draw theoretical conclusions, these have been largely determined by the view they have taken of what constitutes political structure. They do not all take the same view on this matter. In stating our own views we have found it best to avoid reference to the writings of political philosophers, and in doing so we feel sure that we have the support of our contributors.

3. POLITICAL PHILOSOPHY AND COMPARATIVE POLITICS

We have not found that the theories of political philosophers have helped us to understand the societies we have studied and we consider them of little scientific value; for their conclusions are seldom formulated in terms of observed behaviour or capable of being tested by this criterion. Political philosophy has chiefly concerned itself with how men *ought* to live and what form of government they *ought* to have, rather than with what *are* their political habits and institutions.

In so far as political philosophers have attempted to understand existing institutions instead of trying to justify or undermine them, they have done so in terms of popular psychology or of history. They have generally had recourse to hypotheses about earlier stages of human society presumed to be devoid of political institutions or to display them in a very rudimentary form and have attempted to reconstruct the process by which the political institutions with which they were familiar in their own societies might have arisen out of these elementary forms of organization. Political philosophers in modern times have often sought to substantiate their theories by appeal to the facts of primitive societies. They cannot be blamed if, in doing so, they have been led astray, for little anthropological research has been conducted into primitive political systems compared with research into other primitive institutions, customs, and beliefs, and still less have comparative studies of them been made. We do not consider that the origins of primitive institutions can be discovered and, therefore, we do not think that it is worth while seeking for them. We speak for all social anthropologists when we say that a scientific study of political institutions must be inductive and comparative and aim solely at establishing and explaining the uniformities found among them and their interdependencies with other features of social organization.

4. THE TWO TYPES OF POLITICAL SYSTEM STUDIED

It will be noted that the political systems described in this book fall into two main categories. One group, which we refer to as Group A, consists of those societies which have centralized authority, administrative machinery, and judicial institutions—in short, a government—and in which cleavages of wealth, privilege, and status correspond to the distribution of power and authority. This group comprises the Zulu, the Ngwato, the Bemba, the Banyankole, and the Kede. The other group, which we refer to as Group B, consists of those societies which lack centralized authority, administrative machinery, and constituted judicial institutions—in short which lack government—and in which there are no sharp divisions of rank, status, or wealth. This group comprises the Logoli, the Tallensi, and the Nuer. Those who consider that a state should be defined by the presence of governmental institutions will regard the first group as primitive states and the second group as stateless societies.

The kind of information related and the kind of problems discussed in a description of each society have largely depended on the category to which it belongs. Those who have studied societies of Group A are mainly concerned to describe governmental organization. They therefore give an account of the status of kings and classes, the roles of administrative officials of one kind or another, the privileges of rank, the differences in wealth and power, the regulation of tax and tribute, the territorial divisions of the state and their relation to its central authority, the rights of subjects and the obligations of rulers, and the checks on authority. Those who studied societies of Group B had no such matters to discuss and were therefore forced to consider what, in the absence of explicit forms of government, could be held to constitute the political structure of a people. This problem was simplest among the Nuer, who have very distinct territorial divisions. The difficulty was greater for the Logoli and Tallensi, who have no clear spatially-defined political units.

5. KINSHIP IN POLITICAL ORGANIZATION

One of the outstanding differences between the two groups is the part played by the lineage system in political structure. We must here distinguish between the set of relationships linking the individual to other persons and to particular social units through the transient, bilateral family, which we shall call the kinship system, and the segmentary system of permanent, unilateral descent groups, which we call the lineage system. Only the latter establishes corporate units with political functions. In both groups of societies kinship and domestic ties have an important role in the lives of individuals, but their relation to the political system is of a secondary order. In the societies of Group A it is the administrative organization, in societies of Group B the segmentary lineage system, which primarily regulates political relations between territorial segments.

This is clearest among the Ngwato, whose political system resembles the pattern with which we are familiar in the modern nation-state. The political unit is essentially a territorial grouping wherein the plexus of kinship ties serves merely to cement those already established by membership of the ward, district, and nation. In societies of this type the state is never the kinship system writ large, but is organized on totally different principles. In societies of Group B kinship ties appear to play a more prominent role in political organization, owing to the close association of territorial grouping with lineage grouping, but it is still only a secondary role.

It seems probable to us that three types of political system can be distinguished. Firstly, there are those very small societies, none of which are described in this book, in which even the largest political unit embraces a group of people all of whom are united to one another by ties of kinship, so that political relations are coterminous with kinship relations and the political structure and kinship organization are completely fused. Secondly, there are societies in which a lineage structure is the framework of the political system, there being a precise co-ordination between the two, so that they are consistent with each other, though each remains distinct and autonomous in its own sphere. Thirdly, there are societies in which an administrative organization is the framework of the political structure.

The numerical and territorial range of a political system would vary according to the type to which it belongs. A kinship system would seem to be incapable of uniting such large numbers of persons into a single organization for defence and the settlement of disputes by arbitration as a lineage system and a lineage system incapable of uniting such numbers as an administrative system.

6. THE INFLUENCE OF DEMOGRAPHY

It is noteworthy that the political unit in the societies with a state organization is numerically larger than in those without a state organization. The largest political groups among the Tallensi, Logoli, and Nuer cannot compete in numbers with the quarter to half million of the Zulu state (in about 1870), the 101,000 of the Ngwato state, and the 140,000 of the Bemba state. It is true that the Kede and their subject population are not so populous, but it must be remembered that they form part of the vast Nupe state. It is not suggested that a stateless political unit need be very small—Nuer political units comprise as many as 45,000 souls—nor that a political unit with state organization need be very large, but it is probably true that there is a limit to the size of a population that can hold together without some kind of centralized government.

Size of population should not be confused with density of population. There may be some relation between the degree of political development and the size of population, but it would be incorrect to suppose that governmental institutions are found in those societies with greatest density. The opposite seems to be equally likely, judging by our material. The density of the Zulu is 3.5, of the Ngwato 2.5, of the Bemba 3.75 per square mile, while that of the Nuer is higher and of the Tallensi and Logoli very much higher. It might be supposed that the dense permanent settlements of the Tallensi would necessarily lead to the development of a centralized form of government, whereas the wide dispersion of shifting villages among the Bemba would be incompatible with centralized rule. The reverse is actually the case. In addition to the material collected in this book, evidence from other African societies could be cited to prove that a large population in a political unit and a high degree of political centralization do not necessarily go together with great density.

7. THE INFLUENCE OF MODE OF LIVELIHOOD

The density and distribution of population in an African society are clearly related to ecological conditions which also affect the whole mode of livelihood. It is obvious, however, that mere differences in modes of livelihood do not determine differences in political structure. The Tallensi and the Bemba are both agriculturalists, the Tallensi having fixed and the Bemba shifting cultivation, but they have very different political systems. The Nuer and Logoli of Group B and the Zulu and Ngwato of Group A alike practise mixed agriculture and cattle husbandry. In a general sense, modes of livelihood, together with environmental conditions, which always impose effective limits on modes of livelihood, determine the dominant values of the peoples and strongly influence their social organizations, including their political systems. This is evident in the political divisions of the Nuer, in the distribution of Kede settlements and the administrative organization embracing them, and in the class system of the Banyankole.

Most African societies belong to an economic order very different from ours. Theirs is mainly a subsistence economy with a rudimentary differentiation of productive labour and with no machinery for the accumulation of wealth in the form of commercial or industrial capital. If wealth is accumulated it takes the form of consumption goods and amenities or is used for the support of additional dependants. Hence it tends to be rapidly dissipated again and does not give rise to permanent class divisions. Distinctions of rank, status, or occupation operate independently of differences of wealth.

Economic privileges, such as rights to tax, tribute, and labour, are both the main reward of political power and an essential means of maintaining it in the political systems of Group A. But there are counter-

balancing economic obligations no less strongly backed by institutionalized sanctions. It must not be forgotten, also, that those who derive
maximum economic benefit from political office also have the maximum
administrative, judicial, and religious responsibilities.

Compared with the societies of Group A, distinctions of rank and
status are of minor significance in societies of Group B. Political office
carries no economic privileges, though the possession of greater than
average wealth may be a criterion of the qualities or status required
for political leadership; for in these economically homogeneous, equalitarian, and segmentary societies the attainment of wealth depends either
on exceptional personal qualities or accomplishments, or on superior
status in the lineage system.

8. COMPOSITE POLITICAL SYSTEMS
AND THE CONQUEST THEORY

It might be held that societies like the Logoli, Tallensi, and Nuer,
without central government or administrative machinery, develop into
states like the Ngwato, Zulu, and Banyankole as a result of conquest.
Such a development is suggested for the Zulu and Banyankole. But the
history of all the peoples treated in this book is not well enough known
to enable us to declare with any degree of certainty what course their
political development has taken. The problem must therefore be stated
in a different way. All the societies of Group A appear to be an amalgam
of different peoples, each aware of its unique origin and history, and
all except the Zulu and Bemba are still to-day culturally heterogeneous.
Cultural diversity is most marked among the Banyankole and Kede,
but it is also clear among the Ngwato. We may, therefore, ask to what
extent cultural heterogeneity in a society is correlated with an administrative system and central authority. The evidence at our disposal in
this book suggests that cultural and economic heterogeneity is associated
with a state-like political structure. Centralized authority and an administrative organization seem to be necessary to accommodate culturally diverse groups within a single political system, especially if they
have different modes of livelihood. A class or caste system may result
if there are great cultural and, especially, great economic divergencies.
But centralized forms of government are found also with peoples of
homogeneous culture and little economic differentiation like the Zulu.
It is possible that groups of diverse culture are the more easily welded
into a unitary political system without the emergence of classes the
closer they are to one another in culture. A centralized form of government is not necessary to enable different groups of closely related culture and pursuing the same mode of livelihood to amalgamate, nor does

it necessarily arise out of the amalgamation. The Nuer have absorbed large numbers of conquered Dinka, who are a pastoral people like themselves with a very similar culture. They have incorporated them by adoption and other ways into their lineage system; but this has not resulted in a class or caste structure or in a centralized form of government. Marked divergencies in culture and economic pursuits are probably incompatible with a segmentary political system such as that of the Nuer or the Tallensi. We have not the data to check this. It is clear, however, that a conquest theory of the primitive state—assuming that the necessary historical evidence is available—must take into account not only the mode of conquest and the conditions of contact, but also the similarities or divergencies in culture and mode of livelihood of conquerors and conquered and the political institutions they bring with them into the new combination.

9. THE TERRITORIAL ASPECT

The territorial aspect of early forms of political organization was justly emphasized by Maine in *Ancient Law* and other scholars have given much attention to it. In all the societies described in this book the political system has a territorial framework, but it has a different function in the two types of political organization. The difference is due to the dominance of an administrative and judicial apparatus in one type of system and its absence in the other. In the societies of Group A the administrative unit is a territorial unit; political rights and obligations are territorially delimited. A chief is the administrative and judicial head of a given territorial division, vested often with final economic and legal control over all the land within his boundaries. Everybody living within these boundaries is his subject, and the right to live in this area can be acquired only by accepting the obligations of a subject. The head of the state is a territorial ruler.

In the other group of societies there are no territorial units defined by an administrative system, but the territorial units are local communities the extent of which corresponds to the range of a particular set of lineage ties and the bonds of direct co-operation. Political office does not carry with it juridical rights over a particular, defined stretch of territory and its inhabitants. Membership of the local community, and the rights and duties that go with it, are acquired as a rule through genealogical ties, real or fictional. The lineage principle takes the place of political allegiance, and the interrelations of territorial segments are directly co-ordinated with the interrelations of lineage segments.

Political relations are not simply a reflexion of territorial relations. The political system, in its own right, incorporates territorial relations and invests them with the particular kind of political significance they have.

10. THE BALANCE OF FORCES IN THE POLITICAL SYSTEM

A relatively stable political system in Africa presents a balance between conflicting tendencies and between divergent interests. In Group A it is a balance between different parts of the administrative organization. The forces that maintain the supremacy of the paramount ruler are opposed by the forces that act as a check on his powers. Institutions such as the regimental organization of the Zulu, the genealogical restriction of succession to kingship or chiefship, the appointment by the king of his kinsmen to regional chiefships, and the mystical sanctions of his office all reinforce the power of the central authority. But they are counterbalanced by other institutions, like the king's council, sacerdotal officials who have a decisive voice in the king's investiture, queen mothers' courts, and so forth, which work for the protection of law and custom and the control of centralized power. The regional devolution of powers and privileges, necessary on account of difficulties of communication and transport and of other cultural deficiencies, imposes severe restrictions on a king's authority. The balance between central authority and regional autonomy is a very important element in the political structure. If a king abuses his power, subordinate chiefs are liable to secede or to lead a revolt against him. If a subordinate chief seems to be getting too powerful and independent, the central authority will be supported by other subordinate chiefs in suppressing him. A king may try to buttress his authority by playing off rival subordinate chiefs against one another.

It would be a mistake to regard the scheme of constitutional checks and balances and the delegation of power and authority to regional chiefs as nothing more than an administrative device. A general principle of great importance is contained in these arrangements, which has the effect of giving every section and every major interest of the society direct or indirect representation in the conduct of government. Local chiefs represent the central authority in relation to their districts, but they also represent the people under them in relation to the central authority. Councillors and ritual functionaries represent the community's interest in the preservation of law and custom and in the observance of the ritual measures deemed necessary for its well-being. The voice of such functionaries and delegates is effective in the conduct of government on account of the general principle that power and authority are distributed. The king's power and authority are composite. Their

various components are lodged in different offices. Without the co-operation of those who hold these offices it is extremely difficult, if not impossible, for the king to obtain his revenue, assert his judicial and legislative supremacy, or retain his secular and ritual prestige. Functionaries
vested with essential subsidiary powers and privileges can often sabotage
a ruler's acts if they disapprove them.

Looked at from another angle, the government of an African state
consists in a balance between power and authority on the one side and
obligation and responsibility on the other. Every one who holds political
office has responsibilities for the public weal corresponding to his rights
and privileges. The distribution of political authority provides a machinery by which the various agents of government can be held to their
responsibilities. A chief or a king has the right to exact tax, tribute, and
labour service from his subjects; he has the corresponding obligation
to dispense justice to them, to ensure their protection from enemies and
to safeguard their general welfare by ritual acts and observances. The
structure of an African state implies that kings and chiefs rule by consent. A ruler's subjects are as fully aware of the duties he owes to them
as they are of the duties they owe to him, and are able to exert pressure
to make him discharge these duties.

We should emphasize here, that we are talking of constitutional arrangements, not of how they work in practice. Africans recognize as
clearly as we do that power corrupts and that men are liable to abuse
it. In many ways the kind of constitution we find in societies of Group
A is cumbrous and too loosely jointed to prevent abuse entirely. The
native theory of government is often contradicted by their practice.
Both rulers and subjects, actuated by their private interests, infringe
the rules of the constitution. Though it usually has a form calculated
to hold in check any tendency towards absolute despotism, no African
constitution can prevent a ruler from sometimes becoming a tyrant.
The history of Shaka is an extreme case, but in this and other instances
where the contradiction between theory and practice is too glaring and
the infringement of constitutional rules becomes too grave, popular
disapproval is sure to follow and may even result in a movement of
secession or revolt led by members of the royal family or subordinate
chiefs. This is what happened to Shaka.

It should be remembered that in these states there is only one theory
of government. In the event of rebellion, the aim, and result, is only
to change the personnel of office and never to abolish it or to substitute
for it some new form of government. When subordinate chiefs, who are
often kinsmen of the king, rebel against him they do so in defence of
the values violated by his malpractices. They have an interest greater
than any other section of the people in maintaining the kingship. The

ideal constitutional pattern remains the valid norm, in spite of breaches of its rules.

A different kind of balance is found in societies of Group B. It is an equilibrium between a number of segments, spatially juxtaposed and structurally equivalent, which are defined in local and lineage, and not in administrative terms. Every segment has the same interests as other segments of a like order. The set of intersegmentary relations that constitutes the political structure is a balance of opposed local loyalties and of divergent lineage and ritual ties. Conflict between the interests of administrative divisions is common in societies like those of Group A. Subordinate chiefs and other political functionaries, whose rivalries are often personal, or due to their relationship to the king or the ruling aristocracy, often exploit these divergent local loyalties for their own ends. But the administrative organization canalizes and provides checks on such inter-regional dissensions. In the societies without an administrative organization, divergence of interests between the component segments is intrinsic to the political structure. Conflicts between local segments necessarily mean conflicts between lineage segments, since the two are closely interlocked; and the stabilizing factor is not a superordinate juridical or military organization, but is simply the sum total of inter-segment relations.

11. THE INCIDENCE AND FUNCTION OF ORGANIZED FORCE

In our judgement, the most significant characteristic distinguishing the centralized, pyramidal, state-like forms of government of the Ngwato, Bemba, &c., from the segmentary political systems of the Logoli, the Tallensi, and the Nuer is the incidence and function of organized force in the system. In the former group of societies, the principal sanction of a ruler's rights and prerogatives, and of the authority exercised by his subordinate chiefs, is the command of organized force. This may enable an African king to rule oppressively for a time, if he is inclined to do so, but a good ruler uses the armed forces under his control in the public interest, as an accepted instrument of government—that is, for the defence of the society as a whole or of any section of it, for offence against a common enemy, and as a coercive sanction to enforce the law or respect for the constitution. The king and his delegates and advisers use organized force with the consent of their subjects to keep going a political system which the latter take for granted as the foundation of their social order.

In societies of Group B there is no association, class, or segment which has a dominant place in the political structure through the command of greater organized force than is at the disposal of any of its congeners. If force is resorted to in a dispute between segments it will be met with equal force. If one segment defeats another it does not attempt to establish political dominance over it; in the absence of an administrative machinery there is, in fact, no means by which it could do so. In the language of political philosophy, there is no individual or group in which sovereignty can be said to rest. In such a system, stability is maintained by an equilibrium at every line of cleavage and every point of divergent interests in the social structure. This balance is sustained by a distribution of the command of force corresponding to the distribution of like, but competitive, interests amongst the homologous segments of the society. Whereas a constituted judicial machinery is possible and is always found in societies of Group A, since it has the backing of organized force, the jural institutions of the Logoli, the Tallensi and the Nuer rest on the right of self-help.

12. DIFFERENCES IN RESPONSE TO EUROPEAN RULE

The distinctions we have noted between the two categories into which these eight societies fall, especially in the kind of balance characteristic of each, are very marked in their adjustment to the rule of colonial governments. Most of these societies have been conquered or have submitted to European rule from fear of invasion. They would not acquiesce in it if the threat of force were withdrawn; and this fact determines the part now played in their political life by European administrations.

In the societies of Group A, the paramount ruler is prohibited, by the constraint of the colonial government, from using the organized force at his command on his own responsibility. This has everywhere resulted in diminishing his authority and generally in increasing the power and independence of his subordinates. He no longer rules in his own right, but as the agent of the colonial government. The pyramidal structure of the state is now maintained by the latter's taking his place as paramount. If he capitulates entirely, he may become a mere puppet of the colonial government. He loses the support of his people because the pattern of reciprocal rights and duties which bound him to them is destroyed. Alternatively, he may be able to safeguard his former status, to some extent, by openly or covertly leading the opposition which his people inevitably feel towards alien rule. Very often he is in the equivocal position of having to reconcile his contradictory roles as representative of his people against the colonial government and of the latter against his people. He becomes the pivot on which the new system swings precariously. Indirect Rule may be regarded as a policy designed to stabilize the new political order, with the native paramount ruler in this dual role, but eliminating the friction it is liable to give rise to.

In the societies of Group B, European rule has had the opposite effect. The colonial government cannot administer through aggregates of individuals composing political segments, but has to employ administrative agents. For this purpose it makes use of any persons who can be assimilated to the stereotyped notion of an African chief. These agents for the first time have the backing of force behind their authority, now, moreover, extending into spheres for which there is no precedent. Direct resort to force in the form of self-help in defence of the rights of individuals or of groups is no longer permitted; for there is now, for the first time, a paramount authority exacting obedience in virtue of superior force which enables it to establish courts of justice to replace self-help. This tends to lead to the whole system of mutually balancing segments collapsing and a bureaucratic European system taking its place. An organization more like that of a centralized state comes into being.

13. THE MYSTICAL VALUES ASSOCIATED WITH POLITICAL OFFICE

The sanction of force is not an innovation in African forms of government. We have stressed the fact that it is one of the main pillars of the indigenous type of state. But the sanction of force on which a European administration depends lies outside the native political system. It is not used to maintain the values inherent in that system. In both societies of Group A and those of Group B European governments can impose their authority; in neither are they able to establish moral ties with the subject people. For, as we have seen, in the original native system force is used by a ruler with the consent of his subjects in the interest of the social order.

An African ruler is not to his people merely a person who can enforce his will on them. He is the axis of their political relations, the symbol of their unity and exclusiveness, and the embodiment of their essential values. He is more than a secular ruler; in *that* capacity the European government can to a great extent replace him. His credentials are mystical and are derived from antiquity. Where there are no chiefs, the balanced segments which compose the political structure are vouched for by tradition and myth and their interrelations are guided by values expressed in mystical symbols. Into these sacred precincts the European rulers can never enter. They have no mythical or ritual warranty for their authority.

What is the meaning of this aspect of African political organization?

African societies are not models of continuous internal harmony. Acts of violence, oppression, revolt, civil war, and so forth, chequer the history of every African state. In societies like the Logoli, Tallensi, and Nuer the segmentary nature of the social structure is often most strikingly brought to light by armed conflict between the segments. But if the social system has reached a sufficient degree of stability, these internal convulsions do not necessarily wreck it. In fact, they may be the means of reinforcing it, as we have seen, against the abuses and infringements of rulers actuated by their private interests. In the segmentary societies, war is not a matter of one segment enforcing its will on another, but is the way in which segments protect their particular interests within a field of common interests and values.

There are, in every African society, innumerable ties which counteract the tendencies towards political fission arising out of the tensions and cleavages in the social structure. An administrative organization backed by coercive sanctions, clanship, lineage and age-set ties, the fine-spun web of kinship—all these unite people who have different or even opposed sectional and private interests. Often also there are common material interests such as the need to share pastures or to trade in a common market-place, or complementary economic pursuits binding different sections to one another. Always there are common ritual values, the ideological superstructure of political organization.

Members of an African society feel their unity and perceive their common interests in symbols, and it is their attachment to these symbols which more than anything else gives their society cohesion and persistence. In the form of myths, fictions, dogmas, ritual, sacred places and persons, these symbols represent the unity and exclusiveness of the groups which respect them. They are regarded, however, not as mere symbols, but as final values in themselves.

To explain these symbols sociologically, they have to be translated into terms of social function and of the social structure which they serve to maintain. Africans have no objective knowledge of the forces determining their social organization and actuating their social behaviour. Yet they would be unable to carry on their collective life if they could not think and feel about the interests which actuate them, the institutions by means of which they organize collective action, and the structure of the groups into which they are organized. Myths, dogmas, ritual beliefs and activities make his social system intellectually tangible and coherent to an African and enable him to think and feel about it. Furthermore, these sacred symbols, which reflect the social system, endow it with mystical values which evoke acceptance of the social order that goes far beyond the obedience exacted by the secular sanction of force. The social system is, as it were, removed to a mystical plane, where it figures as a system of sacred values beyond criticism or revision. Hence people will overthrow a bad king, but the kingship is never questioned; hence the wars or feuds between segments of a society like the Nuer or the Tallensi are kept within bounds by mystical sanctions. These values are common to the whole society, to rulers and ruled alike and to all the segments and sections of a society.

The African does not see beyond the symbols; it might well be held that if he understood their objective meaning, they would lose the power they have over him. This power lies in their symbolic content, and in their association with the nodal institutions of the social structure, such as the kingship. Not every kind of ritual or any sort of mystical ideas can express the values that hold a society together and focus the loyalty and devotion of its members on their rulers. If we study the mystical values bound up with the kingship in any of the societies of Group A, we find that they refer to fertility, health, prosperity, peace, justice —to everything, in short, which gives life and happiness to a people. The African sees these ritual observances as the supreme safeguard of the basic needs of his existence and of the basic relations that make up his social order—land, cattle, rain, bodily health, the family, the clan, the state. The mystical values reflect the general import of the basic elements of existence: the land as the source of the whole people's livelihood, physical health as something universally desired, the family as the fundamental procreative unit, and so forth. These are the common interests of the whole society, as the native see them. These are the themes of taboos, observances and ceremonies in which, in societies of Group A, the whole people has a share through its representatives, and in societies of Group B all the segments participate, since they are matters of equal moment to all.

We have stressed the fact that the universal aspect of things like land or fertility are the subjects of common interest in an African society; for these matters also have another side to them, as the private interests of individuals and segments of a society. The productivity of his own land, the welfare and security of his own family or his own clan, such matters are of daily, practical concern to every member of an African society; and over such matters arise the conflicts between sections and factions of the society. Thus the basic needs of existence and the basic social relations are, in their pragmatic and utilitarian aspects, as sources of immediate satisfactions and strivings, the subjects of private interests; as common interests, they are non-utilitarian and non-pragmatic, matters of moral value and ideological significance. The common interests spring from those very private interests to which they stand in opposition.

To explain the ritual aspect of African political organization in terms of magical mentality is not enough; and it does not take us far to say that land, rain, fertility, &c., are 'sacralized' because they are the most vital needs of the community. Such arguments do not explain why the great ceremonies in which ritual for the common good is performed are usually on a public scale. They do not explain why the ritual functions we have been describing should be bound up, always, with pivotal political offices and should be part of the political theory of an organized society.

Again, it is not enough to dismiss these ritual functions of chiefship, kingship, &c., by calling them sanctions of political authority. Why, then, are they regarded as among the most stringent responsibilities of office? Why are they so often distributed amongst a number of independent functionaries who are thus enabled to exercise a balancing constraint on one another? It is clear that they serve, also, as a sanction against the abuse of political power and as a means of constraining political functionaries to perform their administrative obligations as well as their religious duties, lest the common good suffer injury.

When, finally, it is stated as an observable descriptive fact that we are dealing here with institutions that serve to affirm and promote political solidarity we must ask why they do so. Why is an all-embracing administrative machinery or a wide-flung lineage system insufficient by itself to achieve this?

We cannot attempt to deal at length with all these questions. We have already given overmuch space to them because we consider them to be of the utmost importance, both from the theoretical and the practical point of view. The 'supernatural' aspects of African government are always puzzling and often exasperating to the European administrator. But a great deal more of research is needed before we shall be able to understand them fully. The hypothesis we are making use of is, we feel, a stimulating starting-point for further research into these matters. That part of it which has already been stated is, perhaps, least controversial. But it is incomplete.

Any item of social behaviour, and therefore any political relation, has a utilitarian or pragmatic content. It means that material goods change hands, are disbursed or acquired, and that the direct purposes of individuals are achieved. Items of social behaviour and therefore political relations have also a moral aspect; that is, they express rights and duties, privileges and obligations, political sentiments, social ties and cleavages. We see these two aspects clearly in such acts as paying tribute to a ruler or handing over blood-cattle in compensation for murder. In political relations, consequently, we find two types of interests working conjointly, material interests and moral interests, though they are not separated in this abstract way in native thought. Natives stress the material components of a political relation and generally state it in terms of its utilitarian and pragmatic functions.

A particular right or duty or political sentiment occurs as an item of behaviour of an individual or a small section of an African society and is enforceable by secular sanctions brought to bear on these individuals or small sections. But in a politically organized community a particular right, duty, or sentiment exists only as an element in a whole body of common, reciprocal, and mutually balancing rights, duties, and sentiments, the body of moral and legal norms. Upon the regularity and order with which this whole body of interwoven norms is maintained depends the stability and continuity of the structure of an African society. On the average, rights must be respected, duties performed, the sentiments binding the members together upheld or else the social order would be so insecure that the material needs of existence could no longer be satisfied. Productive labour would come to a standstill and the society disintegrate. This is the greatest common interest in any African society, and it is this interest which the political system, viewed in its entirety, subserves. This, too, is the ultimate and, we might say, axiomatic set of premisses of the social order. If they were continually and arbitrarily violated, the social system would cease to work.

We can sum up this analysis by saying that the material interests that actuate individuals or groups in an African society operate in the frame of a body of interconnected moral and legal norms the order and stability of which is maintained by the political organization. Africans, as we have pointed out, do not analyse their social system; they live it. They think and feel about it in terms of values which reflect, in doctrine and symbol, but do not explain, the forces that really control their social behaviour. Outstanding among these values are the mystical values dramatized in the great public ceremonies and bound up with their key political institutions. These, we believe, stand for the greatest common interest of the widest political community to which a member of a particular African society belongs—that is, for the whole body of interconnected rights, duties, and sentiments; for this is what makes the society a single political community. That is why these mystical values are always associated with pivotal political offices and are expressed in both the privileges and the obligations of political office.

Their mystical form is due to the ultimate and axiomatic character of the body of moral and legal norms which could not be kept in being, as a body, by secular sanctions. Periodical ceremonies are necessary to affirm and consolidate these values because, in the ordinary course of events, people are preoccupied with sectional and private interests and are apt to lose sight of the common interest and of their political interdependence. Lastly, their symbolic content reflects the basic needs of existence and the basic social relations because these are the most concrete and tangible elements of all social and political relations. The visible test of how well a given body of rights, duties, and sentiments is being maintained and is working is to be found in the level of security and success with which the basic needs of existence are satisfied and the basic social relations sustained.

It is an interesting fact that under European rule African kings retain their 'ritual functions' long after most of the secular authority which these are said to sanction is lost. Nor are the mystical values of political office entirely obliterated by a change of religion to Christianity or Islam. As long as the kingship endures as the axis of a body of moral and legal norms holding a people together in a political community, it will, most probably, continue to be the focus of mystical values.

It is easy to see a connexion between kingship and the interests and solidarity of the whole community in a state with highly centralized authority. In societies lacking centralized government, social values cannot by symbolized by a single person, but are distributed at cardinal points of the social structure. Here we find myths, dogmas, ritual ceremonies, mystical powers, &c., associated with segments and defining and serving to maintain the relationship between them. Periodic ceremonies emphasizing the solidarity of segments, and between segments, as against sectional interests within these groups, are the rule among the Tallensi and Logoli no less than among the Bemba and Kede. Among the Nuer, the leopard-skin chief, a sacred personage associated with the fertility of the earth, is the medium through whom feuds are settled and, hence, inter-segment relations regulated. The difference between these societies of Group B and those of Group A lies in the fact that there is no person who represents the political unity of the people, such unity being lacking, and there may be no person who represents the unity of segments of the people. Ritual powers and responsibility are distributed in conformity with the highly segmentary structure of the society.

14. THE PROBLEM OF THE LIMITS OF THE POLITICAL GROUP

We conclude by emphasizing two points of very great importance which are often overlooked. However one may define political units or groups, they cannot be treated in isolation, for they always form part of a larger social system. Thus, to take an extreme example, the localized lineages of the Tallensi overlap one another like a series of intersecting circles, so that it is impossible to state clearly where the lines of political cleavage run. These overlapping fields of political relations stretch almost indefinitely, so that there is a kind of interlocking even of neighbouring peoples, and while we can see that this people is distinct from that, it is not easy to say at what point, culturally or politically, one is justified in regarding them as distinct units. Among the Nuer, political demarcation is simpler, but even here there is, between segments of a political unit, the same kind of structural relationship as there is between this unit and another unit of the same order. Hence the designation of autonomous political groups is always to some extent an arbitrary matter. This is more noticeable among the societies of Group B, but among those of Group A also there is an interdependence between the political group described and neighbouring political groups and a certain overlapping between them. The Ngwato have a segmentary relationship to other Tswana tribes which in many respects is of the same order as that between divisions of the Ngwato themselves. The same is true of the other societies with centralized governments.

This overlapping and interlocking of societies is largely due to the fact that the point at which political relations, narrowly defined in terms of military action and legal sanctions, end is not the point at which all social relations cease. The social structure of a people stretches beyond their political system, so defined, for there are always social relations of one kind or another between peoples of different autonomous political groups. Clans, age-sets, ritual associations, relations of affinity and of trade, and social relations of other kinds unite people of different political units. Common language or closely related languages, similar customs and beliefs, and so on, also unite them. Hence a strong feeling of community may exist between groups which do not acknowledge a single ruler or unite for specific political purposes. Community of language and culture, as we have indicated, does not necessarily give rise to political unity, any more than linguistic and cultural dissimilarity prevents political unity.

Herein lies a problem of world importance: what is the relation of political structure to the whole social structure? Everywhere in Africa social ties of one kind or another tend to draw together peoples who are politically separated and political ties appear to be dominant whenever there is conflict between them and other social ties. The solution of this problem would seem to lie in a more detailed investigation of the nature of political values and of the symbols in which they are expressed. Bonds of utilitarian interest between individuals and between groups are not as strong as the bonds implied in common attachment to mystical symbols. It is precisely the greater solidarity, based on these bonds, which generally gives political groups their dominance over social groups of other kinds.

21. LAW AND ANTHROPOLOGY *

Very few American and, until quite recently, relatively few British anthropologists made special efforts to collect legal materials. Monographs written about primitive cultures might mention deviations from normal modes of behavior and methods of correction and punishment but vagueness was the rule and the reporting of actual cases and their specific disposition was virtually lacking.

The author of the next selection is one of the rare American anthropologists whose interest in primitive law is on the specialist level. His approach is reminiscent of Herskovits' position in the field of economic anthropology (see No. II:10) to wit, both see that the difference between modern and primitive societies is essentially one of degree rather than kind. Thus Hoebel finds law and the state foreshadowed on the simplest cultural levels. While this is in sharp contrast to other widely held views (see No. II:20) it is a major opinion that has an important body of adherents.

"It is perfectly proper to regard and study the law simply as a great anthropological document."—Oliver Wendell Holmes

1

I F the integration of law and anthropology is to flourish, it must be on a truly functional basis. Each must contribute to the dynamics of the other; each must add to the operative effectiveness of the other;

* E. Adamson Hoebel, "Law and Anthropology," *Virginia Law Review*, Vol. 32 (1946), pp. 836–854. Reprinted by permission of the author and publisher.
The author (b. 1906) is Professor of Anthropology at the University of Minnesota.

each must nourish the other as a process. Mere static comparison, a paralleling of civilized rules of law with selected examples from sundry primitive tribes, is a sterile accomplishment. It may pique the curiosity and it may amuse; if done with sufficient coverage, it may even make a limited contribution to the understanding of the core and limits of law in human affairs. But jurisprudence as a part of the study of man cannot be content to deal with static juridical tidbits served up for exhibition as ethnological *curiosa*. Both the lawyer and the jurisprude are much too busy with the daily grist of their humming mills to give more than scant attention to what the anthropologist has to say unless anthropology is patently offering something of dynamic and vital significance for their use.

The reason for the "If" with which this discussion has been opened rests in the fact that the integration of law and anthropology on a broad scale is still more a goal to be striven for rather than an accomplished fact. In projecting this symposium it was wisely observed that the day had passed when the social anthropologist and the lawyer could afford to treat each other as foreigners. Each is dealing with different aspects of the same questions, and society can no longer afford to have either ignore the learning and experience of the other if we are to solve the complex problems of modern civilization. The day has indeed passed when anthropologists and lawyers can afford to ignore each other. But why, when distinctive progress has been made between others of the social sciences, have law and anthropology lagged in the union of their forces?

We can place the remissness of anthropologists to two conditions: (1) a misconception (or non-conception) of the nature of law; and (2) a failure to set realistic and genuine problems for their attack in the field of jurisprudence.

The lawyer, on his part, is to a great degree responsible for the anthropologist's failure to understand the nature of law. There has been too much parochialism among the men of law. Their craft is amazingly shielded behind a curtain of technical jabberwocky. It is parochialism which sets up a conception of law in terms of the specialized characteristics of law in western civilization. Craft secrecy and traditional disregard of the purpose of the law have induced among our lawyers a disinclination to reduce the problems, the functions, the nature of the raw materials and their processing to simplicity and clarity with which nonspecialists can cope. Historians of law and analytical jurisprudes have

He has done both archeological and ethnographic fieldwork and is a specialist on the Plains Indians. Among his books are: *The Cheyenne Way* (with K. N. Llewellyn) (1941), *The Law of Primitive Man* (1954), *The Archaeology of Bone Cave, Miller County, Missouri* (1946), *Man in the Primitive World* (1949; 1957).

told us, for instance, that nothing so refined and sophisticated, as authoritarian and well-organized, nothing so purposeful as is the law could exist on the primitive level. Almost all anthropologists have placidly accepted this viewpoint, and the legal life of primitive man has been treated less as unexplored than as non-existent. This, we may say, is a tribute to the prestige and awe with which law and the students of law are held, for anthropologists as a tribe are otherwise a skeptical and inquiring lot.

In order to rationalize their neglect of law in the study of primitive society, a number of anthropologists have turned to an exaltation of custom. "Custom is King," they cry. Custom is everything. Either there is no law, because custom takes care of everything and the savage is its automatic slave, or law is by a strange act of sophistry merged in mere custom. In either event, law as a distinct social phenomenon does not then exist in primitive society. Says the English anthropologist, E. Sidney Hartland, who has written a book on primitive law, "Primitive law is in truth the totality of the customs of the tribe." In concurrence, his compatriot Driberg echoes: ". . . law comprises all those rules of conduct which regulate the behavior of individuals and communities. . . ." A typical American declaration on the same subject is that of J. P. Gillin who said that law broadly considered is simply that body of opinion which regulates the behavior of the members of a group.

Not unsymptomatic of this anthropological attitude are the Lynds' famous Middletown studies of 1929 and 1937, introduced by Professor Clark Wissler as the first application of the methods of social anthropology to a contemporary American community: a study of "the whole round of its activities." And yet, of this social anthropology of the whole round of an American community, Karl Llewellyn observed with wry cogency: "the legal aspects of behavior there did not seem worth canvass —or capable thereof."

Outside of America, notably in Germany, serious attempts have been made to bring anthropology to bear on the problems of law. A German school of ethnological jurisprudence under the leadership of Kohler, Post and Steinmetz flourished during the last decade of the past century and the first quarter of the present. It brought forth a mountain of materials in the *Zeitschrift für Vergleichende Rechtswissenschaft,* laid down its principles in Post's *Grundriss der Ethnologischen Jurisprudenz* and Steinmetz's *Ethnologische Studien zur Ersten Entwicklung der Strafe,* and produced finally a bulky set of monographic reports on the native law of the erstwhile German colonies.

Unfortunately, the chief concern of this prodigious effort was to devise systems of legal "evolution" on the basis of sets of assumed premises that prove untenable in the light of empirical anthropology. The Germanic efforts were devoid of dynamic analysis of the juridical process or the functions of legal interrelations. Consequently, little impress was made on anthropology, outside the involuting circle of German ethnologists, and scarcely any impress on law anywhere.

The enormous contributions of the Dutch to law and anthropology are somewhat different. The Dutch legal and anthropological scholars actually lead the world in the study of primitive law both qualitatively and quantitatively. Their research in the *adat* (custom) law of the Netherlands East Indies runs into hundreds of published volumes. But it is all in Dutch—a marginal language read by no more than a handful of non-Dutch social scientists and lawyers. The Dutch have gone far in the integration of law and anthropology because they have used their first-hand knowledge of native law as an active base for the legal administration of the native village communities. These communities are inhabited by fully ninety-five percent of the population of Indonesia. The interest of the Dutch has been at once practical and scholarly (as legal studies ought to be). There is much we could learn from the Dutch if more of us would learn to read their language or if they would put more of their findings into a less exotic tongue. Nevertheless, their legal anthropology suffers several shortcomings. They have arbitrarily limited their studies by the artificial boundaries of the Netherlands East Indies: a negative consequence of their administrative interest. They are overinterested in systematization, as may well be expected from jurists trained in continental civil law. They are little concerned with process and the social psychology of law or with the theory of law as a social science.

2

To seek a definition of law is like the quest for the Holy Grail. We can readily lend a sympathetic ear to Max Radin, who with well-seasoned wisdom warns us that: "Those of us who have learned humility have given over the attempt to define law." However, for law and anthropology to cross-fertilize, there must be some recognized common denominator in primitive law and modern law to serve as a starting point. Law, viewed from the modern position of social science (not from that of the lawyer in court), is simply a specialized machinery of social control: a complex of certain kinds of human behavior. The question is: *what* kinds of behavior? What kind of machinery of social control in societies differently organized from ours corresponds significantly to that which we call law in our own? It is here that modern jurisprudence makes its basic contribution.

There is a strange notion prevalent among many anthropologists that the field worker going out to study a primitive culture must have no preconceptions about social institutions for fear that he may warp the behavior of the primitives into a mold cast in the image of preconceptions taken from our civilization. He has seen how the early Spanish recorders made a Catalonian monarchy of the Aztec empire when in fact it was something quite different. He knows how easy it is to phrase primitive property concepts in terms of our framework when the property institutions of the primitives may have an entirely different quality. He fears that if he has *any* preconceptions about legal institutions, he may find himself seeing and phrasing primitive law in terms of our modern experience and not in terms of the primitives'. As a canon of method the kernel of this caution is eminently sound. A social science has always to struggle to keep the biases and cultural compulsives of its formulators under strict control. But the flowering of this germ into a rejection of all preconceptions is a rank weed of noxious quality. Without "preconceptions," *i. e.*, hypotheses, properly shaped and properly used, a scientist has no tools with which to work. He cannot "see" for he cannot organize, interpret or test what he does see. Specifically, if he has no idea as to what constitutes law, he will be unable to see law. He should not forget that the very reason anthropologists are able to draw attention to much in primitive society that misses the eye of the ordinary layman is just because they have already learned a good deal of what to expect and look for before they ever visit a primitive society in the field.

If, then, it is imperative that we have a suitable conception of what may constitute law or be significant in relation to law, we may properly put the question: what is it that makes law law?

It is not legislation despite contrary notions of typical code-trained European lawyers. Most primitive law is not legislated, and modern sociological jurisprudence and legal realism from Holmes down have made it perfectly clear that much of modern law is not legislated either. English jurisprudence has long since given assent to this point of view, as witness the remarks by Salmond: "But all law, however made, is recognized and administered by the Courts, and no rules are recognized by the Courts which are not rules of law. It is therefore to the Courts and not to the Legislature that we must go in order to ascertain the true nature of Law." The now classic formulation of this concept of the nature of law is Cardozo's statement that law is "a principle or rule of conduct so established as to justify a prediction with reasonable certainty that it will be enforced by the courts if its authority is challenged."

This behavioristic concept of law gives the anthropologist a handle he can grasp, but it is still not enough. For if we think of courts in our traditional manner, *i.e.*, a formal sitting of professional judges, with bailiffs, clerks and advocates, we must conclude: no courts, no law.

This is what bothered Max Radin who well understands the anthropologist's problem and, perhaps, led him to assert: "But there is an infallible test for recognizing whether an imagined course of conduct is
lawful or unlawful. This infallible test, in our system, is to submit the
question to the judgment of a court. In other systems exactly the same
test will be used, but it is often difficult to recognize the court. None
the less, although difficult, it can be done in almost every system at any
time." Max Radin is right. But what sort of courts does he have in mind?
Some courts are difficult to identify. Anthropologically, they may be
regularly constituted tribal courts such as the tribal council of an American Indian pueblo sitting in judicial capacity, or a court of the West
African Ashanti, constituted of the chief, his council of elders and hench-
men.

That type of primitive court is not hard to recognize. Any member of
the American Bar Association would readily see it for what it is. But
a more obscure type of "court" may be found in the Cheyenne Indian
military society. Consider the case of Wolf Lies Down, whose horse
was "borrowed" by a friend in the absence of the owner. When the
friend did not return from the war path with the horse, Wolf Lies Down
put the matter before his society—the Elk Soldiers. "Now I want to
know what to do," he said. "I want you to tell me the right thing." The
society chiefs sent a messenger to bring the friend in from the camp
of a remote band. The friend gave an adequate and acceptable explanation of his conduct and offered handsome restitution to the com-
plainant in addition to making him his blood brother. Then said the
chiefs: "Now we have settled this thing." But they went on, half as a
legislature: "Now we shall make a new rule. There shall be no more
borrowing of horses without asking. If any man takes another's goods
without asking, we will go over and get them back for him. More than
that, if the taker tries to keep them, we will give him a whipping." Can
any one deny that the Elk Soldiers were in effect sitting as a court for
the entire tribe? The test is first, one of responsibility. That they knew.
It is second, one of effective authority. That they achieved. It is third,
one of method. Unhampered by a system of formal precedent which
"required" them to judge according to the past, they *recognized* that the
rule according to which they were settling this case was *new*, and so
announced it.

Among the Yurok Indians of California, as typical of a less specifically
organized people, the "court" was less definite but it was nevertheless
there. An aggrieved Yurok who felt he had a legitimate claim engaged
the services of two non-relatives from a community other than his own.
The defendant did likewise. These persons were called "crossers" because
they crossed back and forth between the litigants. The litigants did not

face each other in the dispute. After hearing all that each side offered in evidence and argument, the "crossers" rendered a judgment on the facts. If the judgment was for the plaintiff, they rendered a decision for damages according to a well-established scale that was known to all. For their footwork and efforts each received a piece of shell currency called a "moccassin." Here again we have a court.

On an even more primitive level, if an aggrieved party or his kinsmen must institute and carry through the prosecution without the intervention of a third party, there will still be a "court" if the proceedings follow the lines of recognized and established order—there will be then at least the compulsion of recognized "legal" procedure, though the ultimate court may be the "bar of public opinion." When vigorous public opinion recognizes and accepts the procedure of the plaintiff as correct and the settlement or punishment meted out as sound, and the wrongdoer in consequence accedes to the settlement because he feels he must yield, then the plaintiff and his supporting public opinion constitute a rudimentary sort of "court," and the procedure is inescapably "legal."

Consider the Eskimo dealing with recidivist homicide. Killing on a single occasion merely leads to feud, inasmuch as the avenger enjoys no recognized privilege of imposing the death penalty on the murderer or his kinsman with immunity against a counter killing. A feud, of course, is an absence of law, since blood revenge is more a sociological law than a legal one. But to kill someone on a second occasion makes the culprit a public enemy in the Eskimo view. It then becomes incumbent upon some public spirited man of initiative to interview all the adult males of the community to determine whether they agree that he should be executed. If unanimous consent is given, he then undertakes to execute the criminal, and no revenge may be taken on him by the murderer's relatives. Cases show that no revenge is taken. A community "court" has spoken. Such are the kinds of courts Max Radin has in mind.

Although courts in this sense exist in most primitive societies, insistence on the concept of courts is not really necessary for the determination of law. The really fundamental *sine qua non* of law in any society is the legitimate use of physical coercion. The law has teeth, and teeth that can bite, although they need not be bared. For as Justice Holmes put it: "The foundation of jurisdiction is physical power, although in civilized times it is not necessary to maintain that power throughout proceedings properly begun. . . ." We would merely add to that declaration that it was not necessary to limit the latency of power to civilized times; primitive men often found that it was not necessary to display the power behind the law when the defendant acceded to proceedings carried through properly. And Jhering has emphasized the factor of force in law, "Law without force is an empty name." Again more poetically we find, "A legal rule without coercion is a fire that does not burn, a light that does not shine." In this we agree.

But force in law has a special meaning. Force means coercion, which in its absolute form is physical compulsion. There are, of course, as many forms of coercion as there are forms of power, and only certain methods and forms are legal. Coercion by gangsters is not legal. Even physical coercion by a parent is not legal if it is extreme in form. The essentials of legal coercion are general acceptance of the application of physical power, in threat or in fact, by a privileged party, for a legitimate cause, in a legitimate way, and at a legitimate time. This distinguishes the sanction of law from other social rules.

The privilege of applying force constitutes the "official" element in law. He who is generally or specifically recognized as rightly exerting the element of physical coercion is a splinter of social authority. It is not necessary that he be an official with legal office or a constable's badge. In any primitive society the so-called "private prosecutor" of a private injury is implicitly a public official *pro tempore, pro eo solo delicto.* He is not and cannot be acting solely on his own, his family's or his clan's behalf and yet enjoy the approval or tacit support of the disinterested remainder of his society. If the rest of the tribal population support him in opinion, even though not in overt action, it can only mean that the society feels that the behavior of the defendant was wrong in its broadest implications, *i. e., contra* to the standards of the society as a whole. Thus it is in itself an injury to the society, although the group feeling may not be strong enough to generate overt and specific action by the group as a group and on its own initiative. Yet the private prosecutor remains the representative of the general social interest as well as that which is specifically his own. This fundamental fact is ordinarily ignored in discussions of primitive law, and it is in this sense that we may say that the difference between criminal law and private law is a difference in degree rather than in kind, though there can be doubt that some matters touch the general interest in fact and feeling much more vigorously than others in primitive law, as for example, sacrilege, homicidal tendencies, and, frequently, treason.

These observations are not intended to deny the usefulness of our modern concept of criminal as against private law. Those concepts are of the greatest value in reaching an understanding of a difference in emphasis that tends to pervade the law of primitive societies as compared to the more highly organized legal systems of civilizations. Private law predominates on the primitive scene.

A third explicit feature of law is regularity. Regularity is what law in the legal sense has in common with law in the scientific sense. Regularity, it must be warned, does not mean absolute certainty. There can be no true certainty where human beings enter. Yet there is much regularity, for all society is based on it. In law, the doctrine of precedent is not the unique possession of the Anglo-American common law jurist. As we shall see, primitive law also builds on precedents, for there new decisions rest on old rules of law or norms of custom and new decisions which are sound tend to supply the foundation of future action.

Hence we may say that force, official authority, and regularity are the elements that modern jurisprudence teaches us we must seek when we wish to differentiate law from mere custom or morals in whatever society we may consider.

The role of the claimant and the crucial importance of the trouble-case are other factors that modern jurisprudence forces upon the attention of the anthropologist. The role of the claimant is the most important single factor in the development of law in primitive societies. Numerous writers have commented upon the relative absence of legislative enactment by primitive government. Professor Robert Lowie, who is distinguished among American anthropologists for his unique contributions to the study of legal phenomena, has offered a general statement that is fairly typical of the prevailing opinion: ". . . it should be noted that the legislative function in most primitive communities seems strangely curtailed when compared with that exercised in the more complex civilizations." Salmond parallels this with the statement that, "The function of the State in its earlier conception is to *enforce* the law, not to *make* it." Lowie continues: "All the exigencies of normal social intercourse are covered by customary law, and the business of such governmental machinery as exists is rather to exact obedience to traditional usage than to create new precedents." Now this would be true for wholly static societies, but Professor Lowie would be among the first to acknowledge, I believe, that no society is wholly static. New exigencies must always arise. One thing permanent about human society is its impermanence. Especially when strange cultures come into contact do new materials, new ways of behaving and ideas enter into the cultural picture.

These new elements are not usually adopted simultaneously by all members of the society. The inevitable consequence is that when some members get new goods and new ideas, they have new interests for which the old lines of the culture have made no provision. Their use of their new acquisitions almost certainly comes into conflict with the old standards held by others. New custom and new law must then be generated.

Recently anthropologists have given considerable attention to the processes of acculturation, but it is notable how little attention they have paid to the legal devices of cultural adjustment. Parenthetically, we may add, not much recognition has been given to the day by day, person by person process by which such changes occur.

Modern jurisprudence has much to tell the anthropologist about leads for the study of the formation of law through the process of litigation. Sociological jurisprudence points up the fact that breach and disputes in conflicts of claims are the most constant source of the law. "Breach," says Seagle, "is the mother of law as necessity is the mother of invention." On the authority of Holmes we have it that "a law embodies beliefs that have triumphed in the battle of ideas and then translated themselves into action," and in the same vein Roscoe Pound has written: "The law is an attempt to reconcile, to harmonize, to compromise . . . overlapping or conflicting interests." Law exists in order to channel behavior so that conflicts of interest do not come to overt clash. It comes into existence to clear up the muddle when interests do clash, and the new decision, if it sticks, is usually so shaped as to determine which interests best accord with the accepted standards of what is good for the society. Of course, it is unfortunately true that tyrants, usurpers and pettifoggers can and do pervert the ends of law to their own designs without regard to social interests or prevailing standards of what is right.

As a canon of realistic law it may be said, and this is particularly important for anthropologists, that unless a dispute arises to test the principles of law in the crucible of litigation, there can be no certainty as to the precise rule of law for a particular situation, no matter what is said as to what will or should be done. A "law" that is never broken may be nothing more than an omnipotent custom, for one will never know more than this until it is sustained in a legal action with a legal sanction.

The field investigator, while among those primitives who are not given to verbalization of their norms, is virtually forced into a utilization of the case test of law, wherever cases can be found. For example, when I would experimentally ask Comanche Indians what was the tribal law in cases of wife absconding, the answer would usually be something like this: "Well, I can't tell about that. But I can tell you what happened when my uncle, Grey Robe, ran off with the wife of Howling Wolf." And when you find a thread of regularity running surely through a number of similar cases, the law begins to emerge.

When you put your eye on the trouble-case you cannot escape the crucial rôle of the claimant and the defendant in the shaping of the law. We all know from case-law experience that law grows in action, as in a test case, but this knowledge is more often neglected than used in the ethnological field. Experience supports the conclusion of Parker when he says: "Although in logical theory substantive law is prior to procedural law, historically the opposite is the case. Primitive *codes* consist almost entirely of procedural rules; and the classical *dictum* that 'law is secreted in the interstices of procedure' must never be forgotten."

However or by whomsoever the judgment may be rendered in any dispute, it is the claimant and the defendant who will lay the grounds of claim, counterclaim or denial. And if one or the other does it skilfully, soundly and wisely, the *ratio decidendi* is likely to be found in his statement of his claim. No matter how selfish the drive of a disputant may be, unless he be a fool indeed, he poses his claim against the background of "right" social principles, of general rightness and the well-being of the entire social group. How else can he gain enduring social acceptance of his position? Naturally, also, the keener his acuteness, the more skilfully he lays his record and argues his case in terms of the consonance of his claim with the well-established principles of social order, the greater the probability that he will shape the law as he wishes it determined.

There is not the space here to unfold case examples of this process in proof of its action in primitive society, but Karl Llewellyn and I found rich evidence in the law-ways of the Cheyenne Indians, which we have presented in full detail elsewhere. Dr. Jane Richardson's Kiowa materials also reveal the building effect of pleading in primitive jurisprudence, but the Kiowa did not develop the unusual juristic skill that marks the work of the Cheyennes.

Still another instrument created by modern jurisprudence, which is of significance for the understanding of law in primitive society, is the Hohfeldian system of legal analysis. Use of the Hohfeldian fundamental concepts will help the anthropologist in at least four ways.

First. It keeps attention focused on the fact that all legal relations are relations between particular persons, and that this fact is primary in any understanding of law. Courts, constables and jails are secondary instruments, not the fundamentals of a legal system, when set up as a system of imperatives or relations. They are the behavior-data from which a system is constructed.

Second. The Hohfeldian analysis clarifies the exact meaning and content of the basic elements in legal relations through definition and functional demonstration of the operation of the demand-right—duty, privilege-right—no demand-right, power—liability, immunity—no-power relations. Hohfeld, as Cook has said, showed by many examples how our courts are constantly confronted by the necessity of distinguishing between the eight concepts, and are all too often confused by the lack of clear concepts and precise terminology. The same need and the same confusion confront the anthropologist who tries to unravel the legal institutions of primitive man. Yet, as Radin has assured us, by use of Hohfeld's sharp, clear concepts it is possible ". . . to reduce any legal transaction, however complicated, to its actual constituent elements or atoms. . . ." And so, "Thinking this, in nicer terms, with nicer tools of thought, you pull the issue into clarity . . . unambiguously, because your terms are not ambiguous." The proof of the pudding is in the eating. Pudding available for testing can be found in Hallowell's brilliant analysis of the institution of property (modern and primitive) and the application that has been made of Hohfeld to Yurok law and certain other primitive examples.

Third. Hohfeld's analysis conclusively demonstrates that the *components* of primitive legal relations are fundamentally identical with those of civilized law, *i. e.*, there is a least common denominator for primitive law and modern.

Fourth. It can be applied effectively to any social complex of imperative reciprocal relations, even though non-legal, and therefore aids in the understanding of other phases of social organization as well.

In short, Hohfeldian concepts are capable of being used and understood by any social scientist. They are the sharpest and surest tools for cutting through the fog of confusion that besets the anthropologist who would work with law. They are deserving of wide adoption by all who seriously undertake the full analysis of culture.

3

Thus far we have dwelt for the most part on what the integration of law and anthropology means for the science of anthropology. What then does it mean for law?

The essential value of anthropology in the study of human behavior is that it enables us to get outside of our own "cake of custom," providing a series of vantage points from which we can view our own culture and doings. Thus viewed, we can see how different people accomplish similar ends by similar means or by other devices; we can see how they conceive even totally different goals from those we are accustomed to hold dear; and so the findings of anthropology serve to stimulate new ideas and new thought in the solution of the problems that beset us. It also provides us with a test tube situation when we can find social set-ups already in existence that approximate conditions with which we might like to experiment. Anthropology is thus often able to supply the social scientist with a sort of substitute laboratory situation to provide already prepared controls to test his observations made on the data provided in our own social experience.

When Ehrlich claimed that "the history of law and ethnological legal science will not be of value for the understanding of existing law but only for the study of the development of law," and that "the attempt to arrive at an understanding of the present through the study of history or of prehistoric times, *i. e.*, of ethnology, is an error in principle," he was thinking exclusively of the evolutionary kind of German anthropology of law that we have condemned at the outset.

Among the moderns, Bronislaw Malinowski was the first of the anthropologists to make a real impact on legal doctrine through his now famous *Crime and Custom in Savage Society*. He described what he saw as law not in terms of rules and principles but in terms of the behavior of real people whom he had observed, namely, Trobriand Islanders. "It is characteristic of Malinowski's method," wrote Sir James Frazer, "that he takes full account of the complexity of human nature. He sees man, so to say, in the round and not in the flat. He remembers that man is a creature of emotion at least as much as of reason, and he is constantly at pains to discuss the emotional as well as the rational basis of human action." Because of this quality in his work, Malinowski breathed life into the moribund still-birth that was anthropological jurisprudence two decades ago. Because his materials were real and vital, they were a challenge to the jurisprude that could not be ignored. This was so, even though his concepts of law were somewhat inexact; even to the end he refused to recognize the significance of breach and authoritative sanction in the determination of law. He insisted that the key to law is reciprocity and its basic sanction the withdrawal of reciprocal services. His concept of law was over-broad, over-sociological and subject to devastating attack from the lawyer's point of view. Nevertheless, he entered a lustily driven wedge into the shell of orthodox jurisprudence, and he added momentum to the doctrine that law is social behavior and not logical abstraction.

It is in just this last named effect that the study of primitive law makes its most fundamental contribution to jurisprudence. The lawyer who reads and digests the meat of the materials from primitive man will find himself orienting his legal thought in terms of law as a social device, *viz.*, a means to an end, not an end in itself. How far this may intensify his social conscience, I cannot say, but there can be no doubt but that it will stimulate his social science consciousness by building an attitude of the scientist at his work and in laying the base of a "social physiology of law." This is good, for the lawyer is to the body politic as the physician is to the anatomy of man.

Anthropology makes even more specific contributions to legal craft and legal doctrine. Perhaps the deadliest social sin of the law profession is legalism: the gross hypertrophy of the controlling power of substantive rules and procedural decorum. Technicality overwhelms technique. Legalism has fortunately never wholly hardened the arteries of American law, although it has sometimes clogged them in an uncomfortable way. We, too, find that justice and law are not always synonymous, and that sometimes the law leads to outrageous results. The need for regularity, the quest for certainty, and the desire for a socially sound decision for the case at hand set the elements of a persistent dilemma for the jurist. When the urge for regularity rules with a tyrant hand and legalism prevails, the layman curses law and the men of law, and, if we are to believe the poet, causes sympathetic hearse horses to snicker "hauling the bones of a lawyer."

Now contrary to the assertion of legal historians, legalism is not a general characteristic of primitive law. Except for the despotic monarchies of the African Negroes, who show a remarkable penchant for litigation and ritualistic procedure, most primitives have not developed legal techniques to be used as perverse tools by specializing functionaries. Law is largely in the hands of the people. Nor is it nearly so involved in magic as is commonly thought. Each litigant wants what he thinks is his due, and so long as he has a considerable degree of control over the procedure, his interests act as a check on the human tendency to ritualize beyond functional effectiveness.

However, some primitives are more consciously aware of their cultures as devices for getting things done than are others. Malinowski scoffed the benighted notion that the savage is the automatic slave of custom. Like moderns, all of them are more or less aware of the fact that culture is something to be used, or sometime to be avoided when it stands in the way and cannot be wholly manipulated. When this awareness is acute and men have the skill to turn it to the solution of their legal problems they have the essence of what Karl Llewellyn has aptly called "legal method." When that skill is such that they can solve their internal conflicts in such a way that substantive rules are sound and fair, so that procedure channels the course of legal action towards the resolution of conflict in terms of social wisdom, the method that that skill produces is "juristic method." It is what the jurist who has pride in his work strives for as a high art. It is that which the layman senses with satisfaction and the legal craftsman views with joy. It is that towards which the pettifogger or higher legalist has no sensitivity.

The great difficulty in this matter of juristic method is that there seems to be little technique for communicating its ways to others on the part of those who have it. Are the law teachers able to do it? Perhaps a few of the very great ones do it. Can the experienced judge pass it on to the lawyer who is ascending to the bench? Some lawyers sense it in the work of the best judges. But Cardozo is on record with testimony that few judges can verbally communicate even the techniques of the judicial process of finding the decision, to say nothing of the more subtle juristic method. When judges and lawyers find it difficult to transmit knowledge of the techniques of sure juristic method, it is more a matter of chance than purpose when we find men exercising it in our law courts and legislatures.

Where does the ethnology of law enter into this problem? It is often easier to see the working of juristic method when we see it operative in situations in which we are not involved. Then we can recognize the thing, can formulate its ways, and with our own hands wilfully apply it to our own legal doings to the betterment of our lot.

4

In the integration of the new world that must come, anthropology and law have their great opportunity to join hands in the service of mankind. Hundreds of millions of peoples in Africa and Asia are emerging with the consciousness of self that demands self-determination. The majority of the world's nations are met to join mankind in a world organization. Now as never before, does the integration of the world's myriad legal systems become an imperative need in the satisfaction of human aspirations. As the United Nations matures into the real government that the present status of mankind demands, a wide knowledge of the fundamentals of the legal systems of all mankind will become an absolute imperative for those who would legislate for all humanity. There must be more and more study and research in comparative law. Lawyer and anthropologist must work hand in hand to find the facts, the methods and the values that human legal experience on all levels prove best suited to meet the challenges that lie ahead.

E. Anthropology and More Complex Cultures

22. THE FOLK SOCIETY *

The anthropological study of complex societies begins with an understanding of primitive culture. The generalizations, both functional and developmental, that are characteristic goals of anthropological inquiry are possible because of reliance, often unstated, upon the comparison and contrast of models (empirically derived hypothetical types) of primitive and more complex societies. Our knowledge of simple culture is essentially derived from ethnography. Despite various limitations, reliable generalizations about primitive society can be offered in fair number.

One of the very useful formulations of the general character of primitive society is that of Robert Redfield. Modestly acknowledging the prior work of others in deriving his so-called "folk-urban continuum," Redfield contributed ethnographically derived characterizations of primitive and complex society and a theory of the relation each bore to the other. For almost two decades Redfield's ideas have been a reference point in a many-sided discussion and critique of the folk-urban problem. Though some more recent articles by such scholars as Foster, Lewis, Mintz, Sjoberg and Wolf call for revision and amplification of the theory as originally presented, the selection below is a classic view of folk society and needs no apology.

* Robert Redfield, "The Folk Society," *American Journal of Sociology*, Vol. 52 (1947), pp. 293–308. Reprinted by permission of the author and the University of Chicago Press.

Originally trained in the law, Robert Redfield (1897–1958) was Professor of Anthropology at the University of Chicago. He did fieldwork in Mexico and India and

1

U NDERSTANDING of society in general and of our own modern
urbanized society in particular can be gained through consideration of
the societies least like our own: the primitive, or folk, societies. All societies are alike in some respects, and each differs from others in other respects; the further assumption made here is that folk societies have certain features in common which enable us to think of them as a type—a
type which contrasts with the society of the modern city.

This type is ideal, a mental construction. No known society precisely
corresponds with it, but the societies which have been the chief interest
of the anthropologist most closely approximate it. The construction of
the type depends, indeed, upon special knowledge of tribal and peasant
groups. The ideal folk society could be defined through assembling, in
the imagination, the characters which are logically opposite those which
are to be found in the modern city, only if we had first some knowledge
of nonurban peoples to permit us to determine what, indeed, are the
characteristic features of modern city living. The complete procedure
requires us to gain acquaintance with many folk societies in many parts
of the world and to set down in words general enough to describe most
of them those characteristics which they have in common with each
other and which the modern city does not have.

In short, we move from folk society to folk society, asking ourselves
what it is about them that makes them like each other and different from
the modern city. So we assemble the elements of the ideal type. The more
elements we add, the less will any one real society correspond to it. As
the type is constructed, real societies may be arranged in an order of
degree of resemblance to it. The conception develops that any one real
society is more or less "folk." But the more elements we add, the less possible it becomes to arrange real societies in a single order of degree of
resemblance to the type, because one of two societies will be found to
resemble the ideal type strongly in one character and weakly in another,
while in the next society strong resemblance will lie in the latter character and not in the former. This situation, however, is an advantage, for
it enables us to ask and perhaps answer questions, first, as to whether certain characters tend to be found together in most societies, and then, if
certain of them do, why.

---

was noted for his insistence on combining humanism and cultural anthropology. Among
his publications are The Folk Culture of Yucatan (1941); Tepotzlan: A Mexican
Village (1930); A Village that Chose Progress (1950); The Primitive World and
its Transformations (1953) and The Little Community (1955).

Anyone attempting to describe the ideal folk society must take account of and in large degree include certain characterizations which have been made of many students, each of whom has been attentive to some but not to all aspects of the contrast between folk and modern urban society. Certain students have derived the characterization from examination of a number of folk societies and have generalized upon them in the light of contrast provided by modern urban society; the procedure defined above and followed by the writer. This is illustrated by Goldenweiser's characterization of five primitive societies. He says that they are small, isolated, nonliterate; that they exhibit local cultures; that they are relatively homogeneous with regard to the distribution of knowledge, attitudes, and functions among the population; that the individual does not figure as a conspicuous unit; and that knowledge is not explicitly systematized.

In other cases the students have compared the state of certain societies at an early time with the same, or historical descendant of the same society at a later time. In this way Maine arrived at his influential contrasts between society based on kinship and society based on territory, and between a society of status and one of contract. In the case of this procedure, as in the case of the next, broad and illuminating conceptions are offered us to apply to folk societies as we contrast them with modern urban society. We are to find out if one of the contrasting terms is properly applicable to folk society and the other term to modern urban society.

In the work of still other students there is apparent no detailed comparison of folk with urbanized societies or of early society with later; rather, by inspection of our own society or of society in general, contrasting aspects of all society are recognized and named. This procedure is perhaps never followed in the unqualified manner just described, for in the instances about to be mentioned there is evidence that folk or ancient society has been compared with modern urbanized society. Nevertheless, the emphasis placed by men of this group is upon characteristics which, contrasting logically, in real fact coexist in every society and help to make it up. Here belongs Tönnies' contrast between *Gemeinschaft* and *Gesellschaft*, or that aspect of society which appears in the relations that develop without the deliberate intention of anyone out of the mere fact that men live together, as contrasted with that aspect of society which appears in the relations entered into deliberately by independent individuals through agreement to achieve certain recognized ends. Comparable is Durkheim's distinction between that social solidarity which results from the sharing of common attitudes and sentiments and that which results from the complementary functional usefulnesses of the members of the group. In the "social segment"—the form of society existing in terms of "mechanical solidarity"—the law is "repressive"; in the "social organ"—the form of society existing in terms of "organic solidarity"—the law is "restitutive."

It may be asked how closely the constructed type arrived at by any one investigator who follows the procedure sketched above will resemble that reached by another doing the same. It may be supposed that to the extent to which the real societies examined by the one investigator constitute a sample of the range and variety of societies similar to the sample constituted by the societies examined by the other, and to the extent that the general conceptions tentatively held by the one are similar to those held by the other, the results will be (except as modified by other factors) the same. For the purposes of understanding which are served by the method of the constructed type, however, it is not necessary to consider the question. The type is an imagined entity, created only because through it we may hope to understand reality. Its function is to suggest aspects of real societies which deserve study, and especially to suggest hypotheses as to what, under certain defined conditions, may be generally true about society. Any ideal type will do, although it is safe to assert that that ideal construction has most heuristic value which depends on close and considered knowledge of real folk societies and which is guided by an effective scientific imagination—whatever that may be.

2

"The conception of a 'primitive society' which we ought to form," wrote Sumner, "is that of small groups scattered over a territory." The folk society is a small society. There are no more people in it than can come to know each other well, and they remain in long association with each other. Among the Western Shoshone the individual parental family was the group which went about, apart from other families, collecting food; a group of families would assemble and so remain for a few weeks, from time to time, to hunt together; during the winter months such a group of families would form a single camp. Such a temporary village included perhaps a hundred people. The hunting or food-collecting bands considered by Steward, representing many parts of the world, contained, in most cases, only a few score people. A Southwestern Pueblo contained no more than a few thousand persons.

The folk society is an isolated society. Probably there is no real society whose members are in complete ignorance of the existence of people other than themselves; the Andamanese, although their islands were avoided by navigators for centuries, knew of outsiders and occasionally came in contact with Malay or Chinese visitors. Nevertheless, the folk societies we know are made up of people who have little communication with outsiders, and we may conceive of the ideal folk society as composed of persons having communication with no outsider.

This isolation is one half of a whole of which the other half is intimate communication among the members of the society. A group of recent castaways is a small and isolated society, but it is not a folk society; and if the castaways have come from different ships and different societies, there will have been no previous intimate communication among them, and the society will not be composed of people who are much alike.

May the isolation of the folk society be identified with the physical immobility of its members? In building this ideal type, we may conceive of the members of the society as remaining always within the small territory they occupy. There are some primitive peoples who have dwelt from time immemorial in the same small valley, and who rarely leave it. Certain of the pueblos of the American Southwest have been occupied by the same people or their descendants for many generations. On the other hand, some of the food-collecting peoples, such as the Shoshone Indians and certain aborigines of Australia, move about within a territory of very considerable extent; and there are Asiatic folk groups that make regular seasonal migrations hundreds of miles in extent.

It is possible to conceive of the members of such a society as moving about physically without communicating with members of other groups than their own. Each of the Indian villages of the midwest highlands of Guatemala is a folk society distinguishable by its customs and even by the physical type of its members from neighboring villages, yet the people are great travelers, and in the case of one of the most distinct communities, Chichicastenango, most of the men travel far and spend much of their time away from home. This does not result, however, in much intimate communication between those traveling villagers and other peoples. The gipsies have moved about among the various peoples of the earth for generations, and yet they retain many of the characteristics of a folk society.

Through books the civilized people communicate with the minds of other people and other times, and an aspect of the isolation of the folk society is the absence of books. The folk communicate only by word of mouth; therefore the communication upon which understanding is built is only that which takes place among neighbors, within the little society itself. The folk has no access to the thought and experience of the past, whether of other peoples or of their own ancestors, such as books provide. Therefore, oral tradition has no check or competitor. Knowledge of what has gone before reaches no further back than memory and speech between old and young can make it go; behind "the time of our grandfathers" all is legendary and vague. With no form of belief established by written record, there can be no historical sense, such as civilized people have, no theology, and no basis for science in recorded experiment. The only form of accumulation of experience, except the tools and other enduring articles of manufacture, is the increase of wisdom which comes as the individual lives longer; therefore the old, knowing more than the young can know until they too have lived that long, have prestige and authority.

The people who make up a folk society are much alike. Having lived in long intimacy with one another, and with no others, they have come to form a single biological type. The somatic homogeneity of local, inbred populations has been noted and studied. Since the people communicate with one another and with no others, one man's learned ways of doing and thinking are the same as another's. Another way of putting this is to say that in the ideal folk society, what one man knows and believes is the same as what all men know and believe. Habits are the same as customs. In real fact, of course, the differences among individuals in a primitive group and the different chances of experience prevent this ideal state of things from coming about. Nevertheless, it is near enough to the truth for the student of a real folk society to report it fairly well by learning what goes on in the minds of a few of its members, and a primitive group has been presented, although sketchily, as learned about from a single member. The similarity among the members is found also as one generation is compared with its successor. Old people find young people doing, as they grow up, what the old people did at the same age, and what they have come to think right and proper. This is another way of saying that in such a society there is little change.

The members of the folk society have a strong sense of belonging together. The group which an outsider might recognize as composed of similar persons different from members of other groups is also the group of people who see their own resemblances and feel correspondingly united. Communicating intimately with each other, each has a strong claim on the sympathies of the others. Moreover, against such knowledge as they have of societies other than their own, they emphasize their own mutual likeness and value themselves as compared with others. They say of themselves "we" as against all others, who are "they."

Thus we may characterize the folk society as small, isolated, nonliterate, and homogeneous, with a strong sense of group solidarity. Are we not soon to acknowledge the simplicity of the technology of the ideal folk society? Something should certainly be said about the tools and toolmaking of this generalized primitive group, but it is not easy to assign a meaning to "simple," in connection with technology which will do justice to the facts as known from the real folk societies. The preciseness with which each tool, in a large number of such tools, meets its needs in the case of the Eskimo, for example, makes one hesitate to use the word "simple." Some negative statements appear to be safe: secondary and tertiary tools—tools to make tools—are relatively few as compared with primary tools; there is no making of artifacts by multiple, rapid, machine manufacture; there is little or no use of natural power.

There is not much division of labor in the folk society: what one person does is what another does. In the ideal folk society all the tools and ways of production are shared by everybody. The "everybody" must mean "every adult man" or "every adult woman," for the obvious exception to the homogeneity of the folk society lies in the differences between what men do and know and what women do and know. These differences are clear and unexceptional (as compared with our modern urban society where they are less so). "Within the local group there is no such thing as a division of labor save as between the sexes," writes Radcliffe-Brown about the Andaman Islanders. ". . . . Every man is expected to be able to hunt pig, to harpoon turtle and to catch fish, and also to cut a canoe, to make bows and arrows and all the other objects that are made by men." So all men share the same interests and have, in general, the same experience of life.

We may conceive, also, of the ideal folk society as a group economically independent of all others: the people produce what they consume and consume what they produce. Few, if any, real societies are completely in this situation; some Eskimo groups perhaps most closely approach it. Although each little Andamanese band could get along without getting anything from any other, exchange of goods occurred between bands by a sort of periodic gift-giving.

The foregoing characterizations amount, roughly, to saying that the folk society is a little world off by itself, a world in which the recurrent problems of life are met by all its members in much the same way. This statement, while correct enough, fails to emphasize an important, perhaps the important, aspect of the folk society. The ways in which the members of the society meet the recurrent problems of life are conventionalized ways; they are the results of long intercommunication within the group in the face of these problems; and these conventionalized ways have become interrelated within one another so that they constitute a coherent and self-consistent system. Such a system is what we mean in saying that the folk society is characterized by "a culture." A culture is an organization or integration of conventional understandings. It is, as well, the acts and the objects, in so far as they represent the type characteristic of that society, which express and maintain these understandings. In the folk society this integrated whole, this system, provides for all the recurrent needs of the individual from birth to death and of the society through the seasons and the years. The society is to be described, and distinguished from others, largely by presenting this system.

This is not the same as saying, as was said early in this paper, that in the folk society what one man does is the same as what another man does. What one man does in a mob is the same as what another man does, but a mob is not a folk society. It is, so far as culture is concerned, its very antithesis. The members of a mob (which is a kind of "mass") each do the same thing, it is true, but it is a very immediate and particular thing, and it is done without much reference to tradition. It does not depend upon and express a great many conventional understandings related to one another. A mob has no culture. The folk society exhibits culture to the greatest conceivable degree. A mob is an aggregation of people doing the same simple thing simultaneously. A folk society is an organization of people doing many different things successively as well as simultaneously. The members of a mob act with reference to the same object of attention. The members of a folk society are guided in acting by previously established comprehensive and interdependent conventional understandings; at any one time they do many different things, which are complexly related to one another to express collective sentiments and conceptions. When the turn comes for the boy to do what a man does, he does what a man does; thus, though in the end the experiences of all individuals of the same sex are alike, the activities of the society, seen at a moment of time, are diverse, while interdependent and consistent.

The Papago Indians, a few hundred of them, constituted a folk society in southern Arizona. Among these Indians a war party was not so simple a thing as a number of men going out together to kill the enemy. It was a complex activity involving everybody in the society both before, during, and after the expedition and dramatizing the religious and moral ideas fundamental to Papago life. Preparation for the expedition involved many practical or ritual acts on the part of the immediate participants, their wives and children, previously successful warriors, and many others. While the party was away, the various relatives of the warriors had many things to do or not to do—prayer, fasting, preparation of ritual paraphernalia, etc. These were specialized activities, each appropriate to just that kind of relative or other category of person. So the war was waged by everybody. These activities, different and special as they were, interlocked, so to speak, with each other to make a large whole, the society-during-a-war-expedition. And all these specialized activities obeyed fundamental principles, understood by all and expressed and reaffirmed in the very forms of the acts—the gestures of the rituals, the words of songs, the implied or expressed explanations and admonitions of the elders to the younger people. All understood that the end in view was the acquisition by the group of the supernatural power of the slain enemy. This power, potentially of great positive value, was dangerous, and the practices and rituals had as their purposes first the success of the war party and then the draining-off of the supernatural power acquired by the slaying into a safe and "usable" form.

We may say, then, that in the folk society conventional behavior is strongly patterned: it tends to conform to a type or a norm. These patterns are interrelated in thought and in action with one another, so that one tends to evoke others and to be consistent with the others. Every customary act among the Papago when the successful warriors return is consistent with and is a special form of the general conceptions held as to supernatural power. We may still further say that the patterns of what people think should be done are closely consistent with what they believe is done, and that there is one way, or a very few conventional ways, in which everybody has some understanding and some share, of meeting each need that arises. The culture of a folk society is, therefore, one of those wholes which is greater than its parts. Gaining a livelihood takes support from religion, and the relations of men to men are justified in the conceptions held of the supernatural world or in some other aspect of the culture. Life, for the member of the folk society, is not one activity and then another and different one; it is one large activity out of which one part may not be separated without affecting the rest.

A related characteristic of the folk society was implied when it was declared that the specialized activities incident to the Papago war party obeyed fundamental principles understood by all. These "principles" had to do with the ends of living, as conceived by the Papago. A near-ultimate good for the Papago was the acquisition of supernatural power. This end was not questioned; it was a sort of axiom in terms of which many lesser activities were understood. This suggests that we may say of the folk society that its ends are taken as given. The activities incident to the war party may be regarded as merely complementarily useful acts, aspects of the division of labor. They may also, and more significantly, be seen as expressions of unquestioned common ends. The folk society exists not so much in the exchange of useful functions as in common understandings as to the ends given. The ends are not stated as matters of doctrine, but are implied by the many acts which make up the living that goes on in the society. Therefore, the morale of a folk society—its power to act consistently over periods of time and to meet crises effectively is not dependent upon discipline exerted by force or upon devotion to some single principle of action but to the concurrence and consistency of many or all of the actions and conceptions which make up the whole round of life. In the trite phrase, the folk society is a "design for living."

What is done in the ideal folk society is done not because somebody or some people decided, at once, that it should be done, but because it seems "necessarily" to flow from the very nature of things. There is, moreover, no disposition to reflect upon traditional acts and consider them objectively and critically. In short, behavior in the folk society is traditional, spontaneous, and uncritical. In any real folk society, of course, many things are done as a result of decision as to that particular action, but as to that class of actions tradition is the sufficient authority. The Indians decide now to go on a hunt; but it is not a matter of debate whether or not one should, from time to time, hunt.

The folkways are the ways that grow up out of long and intimate association of men with each other; in the society of our conception all the ways are folkways. Men act with reference to each other by understandings which are tacit and traditional. There are no formal contracts or other agreements. The rights and obligations of the individual come about not by special arrangement; they are, chiefly, aspects of the position of the individual as a person of one sex or the other, one age-group or another, one occupational group or another, and as one occupying just that position in a system of relationships which are traditional in the society. The individual's status is thus in large part fixed at birth; it changes as he lives, but it changes in ways which were "foreordained" by the nature of his particular society. The institutions of the folk society are of the sort which has been called "crescive"; they are not of the sort that is created deliberately for special purposes, as was the juvenile court. So, too, law is made up of the traditional conceptions of rights and obligations and the customary procedures whereby these rights and obligations are assured; legislation has no part in it.

If legislation has no part in the law of the ideal folk society, neither has codification, still less jurisprudence. Radin has collected material suggesting the limited extent to which real primitive people do question custom and do systematize their knowledge. In the known folk societies they do these things only to a limited extent. In the ideal folk society there is no objectivity and no systematization of knowledge as guided by what seems to be its "internal" order. The member of this mentally constructed society does not stand off from his customary conduct and subject it to scrutiny apart from its meaning for him as that meaning is defined in culture. Nor is there any habitual exercise of classification, experiment, and abstraction for its own sake, least of all for the sake of intellectual ends. There is common practical knowledge, but there is no science.

Behavior in the folk society is highly conventional, custom fixes the rights and duties of individuals, and knowledge is not critically examined or objectively and systematically formulated; but it must not be supposed that primitive man is a sort of automaton in which custom is the mainspring. It would be as mistaken to think of primitive man as strongly aware that he is constrained by custom. Within the limits set by custom there is invitation to excel in performance. There is lively competition, a sense of opportunity, and a feeling that what the culture moves one to do is well worth doing. "There is no drabness in such a life. It has about it all the allurements of personal experience, very much one's own, of competitive skill, of things well done." The interrelations and high degree of consistency among the elements of custom which are presented to the individual declare to him the importance of making his endeavors in the directions indicated by tradition. The culture sets goals which stimulate action by giving great meaning to it.

It has been said that the folk society is small and that its members have lived in long and intimate association with one another. It has also been said that in such societies there is little critical or abstract thinking. These characteristics are related to yet another characteristic of the folk society: behavior is personal, not impersonal. A "person" may be defined as that social object which I feel to respond to situations as I do, with all the sentiments and interests which I feel to be my own; a person is myself in another form, his qualities and values are inherent within him, and his significance for me is not merely one of utility. A "thing," on the other hand, is a social object which has no claim upon my sympathies, which responds to me, as I conceive it, mechanically; its value for me exists in so far as it serves my end. In the folk society all human beings admitted to the society are treated as persons; one does not deal impersonally ("thing-fashion") with any other participant in the little world of that society. Moreover, in the folk society much besides human beings is treated personally. The pattern of behavior which is first suggested by the inner experience of the individual—his wishes, fears, sensitivenesses, and interests of all sorts—is projected into all objects with which he comes into contact. Thus nature, too, is treated personally: the elements, the features of the landscape, the animals, and especially anything in the environment which by its appearance or behavior suggests that it has the attributes of mankind—to all these are attributed qualities of the human person.

In short, the personal and intimate life of the child in the family is extended, in the folk society, into the social world of the adult and even into inanimate objects. It is not merely that relations in such a society are personal; it is also that they are familial. The first contacts made as the infant becomes a person are with other persons; moreover, each of these first persons, he comes to learn, has a particular kind of relation to him which is associated with that one's genealogical position. The individual finds himself fixed within a constellation of familial relationships. The kinship connections provide a pattern in terms of which, in the ideal folk society, all personal relations are conventionalized and categorized. All relations are personal. But relations are not, in content of specific behavior, the same for everyone. As a mother is different from a father, and a grandson from a nephew, so are these classes of personal relationship, originating in genealogical connection, extended outward into all relationships whatever. In this sense, the folk society is a familial society. Lowie has demonstrated the qualification that is to be introduced into the statement of Maine that the primitive society is organized in terms of kinship rather than territory. It is true that the fact that men are neighbors contributes to their sense of belonging together. But the point to be emphasized in understanding the folk society is that whether mere contiguity or relationship as brother or as son is the circumstance uniting men into the society, the result is a group of people among whom prevail the personal and categorized relationships that characterize families as we know them, and in which the patterns of kinship tend to be extended outward from the group of genealogically connected individuals into the whole society. The kin are the type persons for all experience.

This general conception may be resolved into component or related conceptions. In the folk society family relationships are clearly distinguished from one another. Very special sorts of behavior may be expected by a mother's brother of his sister's son, and this behavior will be different from that expected by a father's brother of his brother's son. Among certain Australian tribes animals killed by a hunter must be divided so that nine or ten certain parts must be given to nine or ten corresponding relatives of the successful hunter—the right ribs to the father's brother, a piece of the flank to the mother's brother, and so on. The tendency to extend kinship outward takes many special forms. In many primitive societies kinship terms and kinship behavior (in reduced degree) are extended to persons not known to be genealogically related at all, but who are nevertheless regarded as kin. Among the central Australians, terms of relationship are extended "so as to embrace all persons who come into social contact with one another. . . . . In this way the whole society forms a body of relatives." In the folk society groupings which do not arise out of genealogical connection are few, and those that do exist tend to take on the attributes of kinship. Ritual kinship is common in primitive and peasant societies in the forms of blood brotherhood, godparental relationships, and other ceremonial sponsorships. These multiply kinship connections; in these cases the particular individuals to be united depend upon choice. Furthermore, there is frequently a recognizedly fictitious or metaphorical use of kinship terms to designate more casual relationships, as between host and guest or between worshipper and deity.

The real primitive and peasant societies differ very greatly as to the forms assumed by kinship. Nevertheless, it is possible to recognize two main types. In one of these the connection between husband and wife is emphasized, while neither one of the lineages, matrilineal or patrilineal, is singled out as contrasted with the other. In such a folk society the individual parental family is the social unit, and connections with relatives outside this family are of secondary importance. Such family organization is common where the population is small, the means of livelihood are by precarious collection of wild food, and larger units cannot permanently remain together because the natural resources will not allow it. But where a somewhat larger population remains together, either in a village or in a migratory band, there often, although by no means always, is found an emphasis upon one line of consanguine connection rather than the other with subordination of the conjugal connection. There results a segmentation of the society into equivalent kinship units. These may take the form of extended domestic groups or joint families (as in China) or may include many households of persons related in part through recognized genealogical connection and in part through the sharing of the same name or other symbolic designation, in the latter case we speak of the groups as clans. Even in societies where the individual parental family is an independent economic unit, as in the case of the eastern Eskimo, husband and wife never become a new social and economic unit with the completeness that is characteristic of our own society. When a marriage in primitive society comes to an end, the kinsmen of the dead spouse assert upon his property a claim they have never given up. On the whole, we may think of the family among folk peoples as made up of persons consanguinely connected. Marriage is, in comparison with what we in our society directly experience, an incident in the life of the individual who is born, brought up, and dies with his blood kinsmen. In such a society romantic love can hardly be elevated to a major principle.

In so far as the consanguine lines are well defined (and in some cases both lines may be of importance to the individual) the folk society may be thought of as composed of families rather than of individuals. It is the familial groups that act and are acted upon. There is strong solidarity within the kinship group, and the individual is responsible to all his kin as they are responsible to him. "The clan is a natural mutual aid society. . . . . A member belongs to the clan, he is not his own; if he is wrong, they will right him; if he does wrong, the responsibility is shared by them." Thus, in folk societies wherein the tendency to maintain consanguine connection has resulted in joint families or clans, it is usual to find that injuries done by an individual are regarded as injuries against his kinship group, and the group takes the steps to right the wrong. The step may be revenge regulated by custom or a property settlement. A considerable part of primitive law exists in the regulation of claims by one

body of kin against another. The fact that the folk society is an organization of families rather than an aggregation of individuals is further expressed in many of those forms of marriage in which a certain kind of
relative is the approved spouse. The customs by which in many primitive
societies a man is expected to marry his deceased brother's widow or a
woman to marry her deceased sister's husband express the view of
marriage as an undertaking between kinship groups. One of the spouses
having failed by death, the undertaking is to be carried on by some other
representative of the family group. Indeed, in the arrangements for marriage—the selection of spouses by their relatives, in brideprice, dowry,
and in many forms of familial negotiations leading to a marriage—the
nature of marriage as a connubial form of social relations between
kindreds finds expression.

It has been said in foregoing paragraphs that behavior in the folk
society is traditional, spontaneous, and uncritical, that what one man does
is much the same as what another man does, and that the patterns of
conduct are clear and remain constant throughout the generations. It has
also been suggested that the congruence of all parts of conventional behavior and social institutions with each other contributes to the sense of
rightness which the member of the folk society feels to inhere in his traditional ways of action. In the well-known language of Sumner, the ways of
life are folkways; furthermore, the folkways tend to be also mores—ways
of doing or thinking to which attach notions of moral worth. The value
of every traditional act or object or institution is, thus, something which
the members of the society are not disposed to call into question; and
should the value be called into question, the doing so is resented. This
characteristic of the folk society may be briefly referred to by saying that
it is a sacred society. In the folk society one may not, without calling into
effect negative social sanctions, challenge as valueless what has come to
be traditional in that society.

Presumably, the sacredness of social objects has its source, in part, at
least, in the mere fact of habituation; probably the individual organism
becomes early adjusted to certain habits, motor and mental, and to certain
associations between one activity and another or between certain sense
experiences and certain activities, and it is almost physiologically uncomfortable to change or even to entertain the idea of change. There
arises "a feeling of impropriety of certain forms, of a particular social or
religious value, or a superstitious fear of change." Probably the sacredness
of social objects in the folk society is related also to the fact that in such
well-organized cultures acts and objects suggest the traditions, beliefs,
and conceptions which all share. There is reason to suppose that when
what is traditionally done becomes less meaningful because people no
longer know what the acts stand for, life becomes more secular. In the

repetitious character of conventional action (aside from technical action) we have ritual; in its expressive character we have ceremony; in the folk society ritual tends also to be ceremonious, and ritual-ceremony tends to be sacred, not secular.

The sacredness of social objects is apparent in the ways in which, in the folk society, such an object is hedged around with restraints and protections that keep it away from the commonplace and the matter-of-fact. In the sacred there is alternatively, or in combination, holiness and dangerousness. When the Papago Indian returned from a successful war expedition, bringing the scalp of a slain Apache, the head-hairs of the enemy were treated as loaded with a tremendous "charge" of supernatural power; only old men, already successful warriors and purified through religious ritual, could touch the object and make it safe for incorporation into the home of the slayer. Made into the doll-like form of an Apache Indian, it was, at last, after much ceremonial preparation, held for an instant by the members of the slayer's family, addressed in respect and awe by kinship terms, and placed in the house, there to give off protective power. The Indians of San Pedro de la Laguna, Guatemala, recognize an officer, serving for life, whose function it is to keep custody of ten or a dozen Latin breviaries printed in the eighteenth century and to read prayers from one or another of these books on certain occasions. No one but this custodian may handle the books, save his assistants on ceremonial occasions, with his permission. Should anyone else touch a book he would go mad or be stricken with blindness. Incense and candles are burnt before the chest containing the books, yet the books are not gods—they are objects of sacredness.

In the folk society this disposition to regard objects as sacred extends, characteristically, even into the subsistence activities and into the foodstuffs of the people. Often the foodstuffs are personified as well as sacred. " 'My granduncle used to say to me,' explained a Navajo Indian, ' "if you are walking along a trail and see a kernel of corn, pick it up. It is like a child lost and starving." According to the legends corn is just the same as a human being, only it is holier. . . . . When a man goes into a cornfield he feels that he is in a holy place, that he is walking among Holy People. . . . . Agriculture is a holy occupation. Even before you plant you sing songs. You continue this during the whole time your crops are growing. You cannot help but feel that you are in a holy place when you go through your fields and they are doing well.' " In the folk society, ideally conceived, nothing is solely a means to an immediate practical end. All activities, even the means of production, are ends in themselves, activities expressive of the ultimate values of the society.

3

This characterization of the ideal folk society could be greatly extended. Various of the elements that make up the conception could be differently combined with one another, and this point or that could be developed or further emphasized and its relations shown to other aspects of the conception. For example, it might be pointed out that where there is little or no systematic and reflective thinking the customary solutions to problems of practical action only imperfectly take the form of really effective and understood control of the means appropriate to accomplish the desired end, and that, instead, they tend to express the states of mind of the individuals who want the end brought about and fear that it may not be. We say this briefly in declaring that the folk society is characterized by much magic, for we may understand "magic" to refer to action with regard to an end—to instrumental action—but only to such instrumental action as does not effectively bring about that end, or is not really understood in so far as it does, and which is expressive of the way the doer thinks and feels rather than adapted to accomplishing the end. "Magic is based on specific experience of emotional states . . . . in which the truth is revealed not by reason but by the play of emotions upon the human organism . . . . magic is founded on the belief that hope cannot fail nor desire deceive." In the folk society effective technical action is much mixed with magical activity. What is done tends to take the form of a little drama; it is a picture of what is desired.

The nature of the folk society could, indeed, be restated in the form of a description of the folk mind. This description would be largely a repetition of what has been written in foregoing pages, except that now the emphasis would be upon the characteristic mental activity of members of the folk society, rather than upon customs and institutions. The man of the folk society tends to make mental associations which are personal and emotional, rather than abstractly categoric or defined in terms of cause and effect. ". . . . Primitive man views every action not only as adapted to its main object, every thought related to its main end, as we should perceive them, but . . . . he associates them with other ideas, often of a religious or at least a symbolic nature. Thus he gives to them a higher significance than they seem to us to deserve." A very similar statement of this kind of thinking has been expressed in connection with the thinking of medieval man; the description would apply as well to man in the folk society:

From the causal point of view, symbolism appears as a sort of short-cut of thought. Instead of looking for the relation between two things by following the hidden detours of their causal connections, thought makes a leap and discovers their relation, not in a connection of cause or effects, but in a connection of signification or finality. Such a connection will at once appear convincing, provided only that the two things have an essential quality in common which can be referred to a general value. . . . Symbolic assimilation founded on common properties presupposes the idea that these properties are essential to things. The vision of white and red roses blooming among thorns at once calls up a symbolic association in the medieval mind: for example, that of virgins and martyrs, shining with glory, in the midst of their persecutors. The assimilation is produced because the attributes are the same: the beauty, the tenderness, the purity, the colours of the roses are also those of the virgins, their red colour that of the blood of the martyrs. But this similarity will only have a mystic meaning if the middle-term connecting the two terms of the symbolic concept expresses an essentiality common to both; in other words, if redness and whiteness are something more than names for physical differences based on quantity, if they are conceived of as essences, as realities. The mind of the savage, of the child, and of the poet never sees them otherwise.

The tendency to treat nature personally has recognition in the literature as the "animistic" or "anthropomorphic" quality of primitive thinking, and the contrast between the means-ends pattern of thought more characteristic of modern urban man and the personal thought of primitive man has been specially investigated.

In the foregoing account no mention has been made of the absence of economic behavior characteristic of the market in the folk society. Within the ideal folk society members are bound by religious and kinship ties, and there is no place for the motive of commercial gain. There is no money and nothing is measured by any such common denominator of value. The distribution of goods and services tends to be an aspect of the conventional and personal relationships of status which make up the structure of the society: goods are exchanged as expressions of good will and, in large part, as incidents of ceremonial and ritual activities. "On the whole, then, the compulsion to work, to save, and to expend is given not so much by a rational appreciation of the [material] benefits to be received as by the desire for social recognition, through such behavior."

The conception sketched here takes on meaning if the folk society is seen in contrast to the modern city. The vast, complicated, and rapidly changing world in which the urbanite and even the urbanized country-dweller live today is enormously different from the small, inward-facing folk society, with its well-integrated and little-changing moral and religious conceptions. At one time all men lived in these little folk societies. For many thousands of years men must have lived so; urbanized life began only very recently, as the long history of man on earth is considered, and the extreme development of a secularized and swift-changing world society is only a few generations old.

The tribal groups that still remain around the edges of expanding civilization are the small remainders of this primary state of living.

Considering them one by one, and in comparison with the literate or semiliterate societies, the industrialized and the semi-industrialized societies, we may discover how each has developed forms of social life in accordance with its own special circumstances. Among the polar Eskimos, where each small family had to shift for itself in the rigors of the arctic environment, although the ties of kinship were of great importance, no clans or other large unilateral kinship groups came into existence. The sedentary Haida of the Queen Charlotte Islands were divided into two exogamous kinship groups, each composed of clans, with intense pride of descent and healthy rivalry between them. Among the warring and nomadic Comanche initiative and resourcefulness of the individual were looked on more favorably than among the sedentary and closely interdependent Zuni. In West Africa great native states arose, with chiefs and courts and markets, yet the kinship organization remained strong; and in China we have an example of slow growth of a great society, with a literate élite, inclosing within it a multitude of village communities of the folk type. Where cities have arisen, the country people dependent on those cities have developed economic and political relationships, as well as relationships of status, with the city people, and so have become that special kind of rural folk we call peasantry. And even in the newer parts of the world, as in the United States, many a village or small town has, perhaps, as many points of resemblance with the folk society as with urban life.

Thus the societies of the world do not range themselves in the same order with regard to the degree to which they realize all of the characteristics of the ideal folk society. On the other hand, there is so marked a tendency for some of these characteristics to occur together with others that the interrelations among them must be in no small part that of interdependent variables. Indeed, some of the interrelations are so obvious that we feel no sense of problem. The smallness of the folk society and the long association together of the same individuals certainly is related to the prevailingly personal character of relationships. The fewness of secondary and tertiary tools and the absence of machine manufacture are circumstances obviously unfavorable to a very complex division of labor. Many problems present themselves, however, as to the conditions in which certain of these characteristics do not occur in association, and as to the circumstances under which certain of them may be expected to change in the direction of their opposites, with or without influencing others to change also.

A study of the local differences in the festival of the patron village saint in certain communities of Yucatan indicates that some interrelationship exists in that case. In all four communities, differing as to their degrees of isolation from urban centers of modifying influence, the festival expresses a relationship between the village and its patron saint (or cross) which is annually renewed. In it a ritual and worship are combined with a considerable amount of play. The chief activities of the festival are a novena, a folk dance, and a rustic bullfight. In all four communities there is an organization of men and women who for that year undertake the leadership of the festival, handing over the responsibility to a corresponding group of successors at its culmination. So far the institution is the same in all the communities studied. The differences appear when the details of the ritual and play and of the festal organization are compared, and when the essential meanings of these acts and organizations are inquired into. Then it appears that from being an intensely sacred act, made by the village as a collectivity composed of familially defined component groups, with close relationship to the system of religious and moral understandings of the people, the festival becomes, in the more urbanized communities, chiefly an opportunity for recreation for some and of financial profit for others, with little reference to moral and religious conceptions.

In the most isolated and otherwise most folklike of the communities studied the organization of the festival is closely integrated with the whole social structure of the community. The hierarchy of leaders of the community, whose duties are both civil and religious, carry on the festival: It is the chiefs, the men who decide disputes and lead in warfare, who also take principal places in the religious processions and in the conduct of the ceremonies. The community, including several neighboring settlements, is divided into five groups, membership in which descends in the male line. The responsibility for leading the prayers and preparing the festal foods rests in turn on four men chosen from each of the five groups. The festival is held at the head village, at the shrine housing the cross patron of the entire community. The festival consists chiefly of solemnly religious acts: masses, rosaries, procession of images, kneeling of worshipers. The ritual offerings are presented by a special officer, in all solemnity, to the patron cross; certain symbols of divinity are brought from the temple and exposed to the kneeling people as the offerings are made. The transfer of the responsibility to lead the festival is attended by ceremony in an atmosphere of sanctity: certain ritual paraphernalia are first placed on the altar and then, after recitation of prayers and performance of a religious dance, are handed over, in view of all, from the custodians of the sacred charge for that year to their successors.

In the villages that are less isolated the festival is similar in form, but it is less well integrated with the social organization of the community, is less sacred, and allows for more individual enterprise and responsibility. These changes continue in the other communities studied, as one gets nearer to the city of Merida. In certain seacoast villages the festival of the patron saint is a money-getting enterprise of a few secular-minded townspeople. The novena is in the hands of a few women who receive no help from the municipal authorities; the bullfight is a commercial entertainment, professional bullfighters being hired for the occasion and admission charged; the folk dance is little attended. The festival is enjoyed by young people who come to dance modern dances and to witness the bullfight, and it is an opportunity to the merchants to make a profit. What was an institution of folk culture has become a business enterprise in which individuals, as such, take part for secular ends.

The principal conclusion is that the less isolated and more heterogeneous communities of the peninsula of Yucatan are the more secular and individualistic and the more characterized by disorganization of culture. It further appeared probable that there was, in the changes taking place in Yucatan, a relation of interdependence among these changing characteristics, especially between the disorganization of culture and secularization. "People cease to believe because they cease to understand, and they cease to understand because they cease to do the things that express the understandings." New jobs and other changes in the division of labor bring it about that people cannot participate in the old rituals; and, ceasing to participate, they cease to share the values for which the rituals stood. This is, admittedly, however, only a part of the explanation.

The conception of the folk society has stimulated one small group of field workers to consider the interdependence or independence of these characteristics of society. In Yucatan isolation, homogeneity, a personal and "symbolic" view of nature, importance of familial relationships, a high degree of organization of culture, and sacredness of sanctions and institutions were all found in regular association with each other. It was then reported that in certain Indian communities on or near Lake Atitlan in Guatamala this association of characteristics is not repeated. As it appeared that these Guatemalan communities were not in rapid change, but were persisting in their essential nature, the conclusion was reached that "a stable society can be small, unsophisticated, homogenous in beliefs and practices," have a local, well-organized culture, and still be one "with relationships impersonal, with formal institutions dictating the acts of individuals, and with family organization weak, with life secularized, and with individuals acting more from economic or other personal advantage than from any deep conviction or thought of the social good." It was further pointed out that in these Guatemalan societies a "primitive world view," that is, a disposition to treat nature personally, to regard attributes as entities, and to make "symbolic" rather than causal connections, co-exists with a tendency for relations between man and man to be impersonal, commercial, and secular, as they tend to be in the urban society.

These observations lead, in turn, to reconsideration of the circumstances tending to bring about one kind of society or one aspect of society rather than another. The breakdown of familial institutions in recent times in Western society is often ascribed to the development of the city and of modern industry. If, as has been reported, familial institutions are also weak in these Guatemalan villages, there must be alternative causes for the breakdown of the family to the rise of industry and the growth of the city, for these Guatemalan Indians live on or near their farms, practice a domestic handicraft manufacture, and have little or nothing to do with cities. It has been suggested that in the case of the Guatemalan societies the development, partly before the Conquest and partly afterward, of a pecuniary economy with a peddler's commerce, based on great regional division of labor, together with a system of regulations imposed by an élite with the use of force, may be the circumstances that have brought about reduction in the importance of familial institutions and individual independence, especially in matters of livelihood.

The secular character of life in these highland villages of the Lake Atitlan region is not so well established as in the individuated character of life, but if life is indeed secular there, it is a secularity that has developed without the influence of high personal mobility, of the machine, and of science. In a well-known essay Max Weber showed how capitalistic commercialism could and did get along with piety in the case of the Puritans. So it may appear that under certain conditions a literate and, indeed, at least partly urbanized society may be both highly commercial and sacred—as witness, also, the Jews—while under certain other conditions an otherwise folklike people may become individualistic, commercial, and perhaps secular. It is, of course, the determination of the limiting conditions that is important.

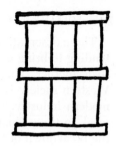

23. LEVELS OF SOCIO-CULTURAL INTEGRATION *

Culture is an emergent: with the advent of massive symboling a new order of phenomena appeared. This order rests upon pre-existing conditions —a physical universe and the fact of life—but the laws of physics and chemistry and the principles of biology and psychology do not explain cultural events. (No combination of these laws and principles can explain why a Chinese eats with chopsticks or a European with a fork.) Observations of the differences between these orders has led to the formulation of a theory of their relationships and sequence, the theory of levels of integration. There are many facets to this theory; one of them deals with the distinctions between the three major kinds of phenomena which are physical (space, time and energy), biological (life) and symbolic (culture). Each of these, however, is internally further subdivided into levels. We cannot here dwell on internal distinctions in either the physical or biological orders but we must note the theory of socio-cultural levels. This is of particular relevance because it gives a framework for the anthropological approach to the study of complex societies. The major social units in this approach are states. Their populations can run into hundreds of millions; they are often divided into regions, and further complicated by class, ethnic, religious and other categories. On another plane, the complex society is composed of families and communities. The following selection is an attempt to set up theoretical coordinates for the studies of complex societies in the face of these difficulties.

* Julian H. Steward, "Levels of Socio-Cultural Integration: An Operational Concept," Chapter 4 of Julian H. Steward, *Theory of Culture Change* (Urbana, Illinois: University of Illinois Press, 1955), pp. 43–63. Reprinted with permission of the author

THE THEORY OF LEVELS OF INTEGRATION

MANY ANTHROPOLOGISTS who began their careers in research on tribal societies now find themselves involved in the analysis of such complicated contemporary sociocultural systems as China, Russia, India, or the United States. It is not surprising that they bring to these newer tasks methodological tools that were devised primarily for the study of tribal society. Valuable as these tools are for many purposes, they are not adequate to deal with all the phenomena encountered either in the study of modern nations or in the analysis of the acculturation of native populations under the influence of these nations. There is some tendency to meet the difficulty by borrowing concepts and methods from the other social sciences which have had long experience in dealing with contemporary societies. Where this leads to new interdisciplinary approaches it is healthy scientific development, but often it appears that anthropologists are ready to abandon the unique methods of their own science and to imitate the other social sciences. While there is no objection to cross-disciplinary fertilization, it should be possible to revise basic anthropological concepts and methods to meet the needs of the new and enlarged subject matter so long as the problem is cultural.

The greatest need is an adequate conceptualization of the phenomena of sociocultural systems above the tribal level. Because anthropology is distinctive in its primary concern with culture—a concept which perhaps represents its greatest contribution to the social sciences—it seems to be widely held that a general definition of culture is sufficient to dictate problem and method in the study of *any* culture. There would probably be no great disagreement with the bare statement that culture consists of learned modes of behavior that are socially transmitted from one generation to the next and from one society or individual to another. To have operational utility, however, this definition would have to be modified in the case of each particular kind of culture. Anthropology's present working definition of culture was devised largely for the study of preliterate, primitive societies, and it does not at all meet certain needs in the analysis of more complicated contemporary cultures.

The concept of primitive or "tribal" culture is based on three fundamental aspects of the behavior of members of tribal societies. First, it is a construct that represents the ideal, norm, average, or expectable behavior of all members of a fairly small, simple, independent, self-contained, and homogeneous society. It is a norm derived from the some-

and publisher. This is a revision of an article of the same title which appeared in the *Southwestern Journal of Anthropology*, Vol. 7 (1951), pp. 374–390.

what varied or deviant modes of individual behavior. It represents essential uniformities which are shared by all persons, despite some special modes of behavior associated with age, sex, occupation, and other roles; for there are definite and fairly narrow limits to deviant behavior in most tribal cultural activities. Tribal society is not divisible into genuine subcultural groups which have a quasi-independent existence and distinctive way of life. The concept of tribal culture emphasizes shared behavior.

Second, tribal culture is usually said to have a pattern or configuration. Pattern has a considerable variety of meanings but it seems generally intended to express some underlying consistency and unity, some over-all integration. Pattern should perhaps connote structuring; but it is difficult to express structure concretely except in terms of some special component of culture, such as social organization. Benedict met this difficulty by conceiving pattern as synonymous with basic attitudes, life view, or value system shared by all tribal members and thereby giving uniformity to behavior. It is a natural step from this definition of pattern to the concept of cultural personality; for attitudes are an expression of a personality type which has been produced by cultural uniformities. Emphasis is again upon shared characteristics, although the auxiliary concept of status- and role-personality is introduced to explain certain special deviants.

Third, the concept of tribal culture is essentially relativistic. The culture of any particular tradition—the norm and the pattern manifest in the tradition—is seen in contrast to cultures of other traditions. It is viewed as unique. The tendency to emphasize the persistence of patterns —and usually also of content—within a tradition plays down the qualitative differences between developmental levels or stages.

Conceptualization of tribal culture in terms of its normative, patterned, and relativistic aspects has been a useful tool for analysis and comparison, especially when contrasts are sought. But as a tool for dealing with culture change it has found little utility, even on the primitive level. Archaeology has continued to deal primarily with element lists, and even ethnology has relied extensively upon element distributions in attempting to reconstruct cultural history by means of the age-area hypothesis. It is significant that the more functional and genuinely holistic ethnological approaches have either stressed the normative and persistent quality of primitive cultures—and in many cases been forthrightly antihistorical or unhistorical—or, if dealing with a culture that has been greatly altered under the influence of modern nations, have paid primary attention to the disruption, imbalance, and internal conflicts of the culture. In cases where the native culture has been substantially changed but has not broken down, the concept of pattern is usually abandoned and acculturation is treated in terms of categories of elements, that is, subpatterns, such as religion, economics, social organization, and the like.

In the analysis of cultural change and acculturation of more complicated sociocultural systems, there are phenomena which cannot be handled by the normative and relativistic concept of culture. The culture of a modern nation is not simply a behavioral norm, which may be ascertained by the observation of all or of a significant sample of individuals. Different groups of individuals are substantially dissimilar in many respects. They have subcultures, which is a concept that has long been understood but surprisingly disregarded in social science. Moreover, certain aspects of a modern culture can best be studied quite apart from individual behavior. The structure and function of a system of money, banking, and credit, for example, represents supra-individual aspects of culture. To say that in the final analysis a banking system, like all culture, exists in the minds of men is not to say that its operation can best be ascertained by using an ethnographic or psychological method to study the behavior of bankers. The system not only has complicated rules, regulations, and principles of its own, but it cannot be understood without reference to world trade, industrial development, marketing, legal systems, and many other factors. The national aspects of banking can be ascertained from economists who have made them their specialty. It would certainly be approaching the problem in the most difficult way to use the ethnographic method.

Not only is the concept that culture consists only of the common denominator of traits shared by all individuals an inadequate characterization of contemporary sociocultural systems, but the nature of culture patterns found among primitive peoples is by no means applicable to contemporary societies. Nations are not patterned in terms of uniformities of individual behavior. They are extremely heterogeneous entities whose total "pattern" consists of intricately interrelated parts of different kinds. It is only subcultural groups—these might be called subsocieties—whose individual members share a substantial core of behavior.

When tribal acculturation under the influence of a modern nation is being examined, it is wholly inappropriate to view the process simply as replacement of individual tribal behavior (the tribal pattern) by a national core of traits of individual behavior (the so-called national pattern). No individuals or groups of individuals carry an entire national pattern. They participate only in very special portions of the entire culture. They are members of a subculture which has a special relation to the national whole. The "assimilation" of any ethnic minority, therefore, means first that certain traits have been adopted from the particular subcultural group with which the minority had contact and second that certain aspects of the national culture have affected the minority culture to the extent of integrating it as a new subculture, that is, a specialized dependent part of the whole. The process of assimilation is by no means a simple replacement of native features by an entire national pattern. Just what traits are adopted to constitute the new subculture and how this is integrated into the larger sociocultural whole differ in individual cases.

The following pages will examine some of the different characteristics or aspects of sociocultural systems that are important both in structural-functional analysis of modern societies and in the historical analysis of the developmental succession of qualitatively different kinds of societies.

In order to delineate some of the significant components of contemporary sociocultural systems and thereby to indicate the features that are susceptible to analysis by the ethnographic method, I have previously suggested that these systems can be viewed in terms of levels of sociocultural integration. According to this concept a total national culture is divisible into two general kinds of features: first, those that function and must be studied on a national level; second, those that pertain to sociocultural segments or subgroups of the population. The former include the suprapersonal and more or less structured—and often formally institutionalized—features, such as the form of government, legal system, economic institutions, religious organizations, educational system, law enforcement, military organization, and others. These institutions have aspects which are national and sometimes international in scope and which must be understood apart from the behavior of the individuals connected with them.

The sociocultural segments or subcultural groups of individuals are amenable to the methods of direct observation used by ethnology. There are several categories of such groups in modern states and nations. First there are localized groups, which may result from differentiation that has occurred during national development—for example, subcultures arising from local specialization in production or cultural ecological adaptations —or which may consist of ethnic minorities. The latter may be native inhabitants who have survived from a prenational period or immigrants who brought a distinctive culture into the nation. Second, there are "horizontal" groups, such as castes, classes, occupational divisions, and other segments, which hold status positions in an hierarchical arrangement and usually crosscut localities to some extent. These, too, may represent segments which either have been differentiated during national development or have been incorporated from the outside.

The ethnographic method is applicable to sociocultural segments but not to national institutions. Much recent anthropology has dealt with "nations," "national culture," and "national characteristics." "National" cannot have the same meaning as "tribal," for many aspects of modern cultures do not represent shared behavior which lends itself to the direct observation of individuals. "National culture" has in fact several special meanings apart from the totality of culture, and it is necessary to distinguish these.

First, "national culture" may signify "cultural products" or national achievements in the fields of science, literature, philosophy, religion, and the like, which presuppose a national level of sociocultural integration. In some societies, these may be limited largely to the upper classes. Thus, national religion, art, writing, and learning in the early irrigation states was produced for and consumed by the upper class far more than for the basic population.

In Latin America, the cultural stereotype is one which emphasizes gracious living, spiritual over material values, political acumen, and other features which of necessity can only be held by an upper class. The subculture of this comparatively small and privileged group has in the past been conditional upon their ownership of wealth, control of most state institutions, and generally superordinate position. While conditions have changed radically in recent decades under industrial influence which has brought business and professional middle and upper class persons into prominence, the national cultural products—philosophy, art, literature, etc.—were largely produced for and consumed by the upper class.

Second, "national culture" may be understood to mean governmental, economic, religious, and other institutions which function on a national scale. Although all members of the society will be affected by these institutions, the effect may be quite different among the various sociocultural segments.

Third, "national culture" may mean the common denominator of behavior that is shared by all members of the nation and that can be ascertained by direct observation of individuals. The method of study requires techniques for sampling large populations, although some use has been made of indirect evidence, such as "cultural content analysis" of novels, motion pictures, and the like. It is not my purpose at present to review the methods for ascertaining the common denominator of national characteristics. I would stress, however, that current research seems to be more concerned with how to ascertain these characteristics than with what they signify. So far as significance is concerned, they are widely supposed, especially by the more psychoanalytically-minded social scientists, to evidence a basic personality or national character which constitutes the mainspring of all national behavior. The national common denominator of shared behavior, however, actually consists of behavior traits of different kinds and origins. For this reason some traits change fairly readily while others, more deeply rooted, are extremely persistent.

If national character is analyzed from the point of view of levels of sociocultural integration, the common denominator will be seen to be affected by the following factors. First, certain behavior and personality traits result from practices of child-rearing. They are acquired by the individual as a member of the family under influences that continue from infancy for many years. In a large heterogeneous society, however, the families of all sociocultural subgroups will not be essentially similar in child-rearing. The nature of differences is a purely empirical question. Morever, socialization with respect to the local in-group or community—at least the social community—starts in early childhood, and, unless the individual shifts residence, it continues throughout life. Community patterns of behavior, however, do not affect so deep a level of the personality because they do not involve food, physical comfort and well-being, and security to the extent involved in family behavior. At the same time, these community patterns will be distinctive of the subcultures. It is extremely important, therefore, that nationally shared features of socialization be distinguished from subcultural features which may differ on both the local and family levels.

Second, there is common behavior of all persons within a nation to the extent that they participate in the same national institutions. All individuals presumably obey the same laws, and they may share in some measure national religious, military, social, and other institutions. Nonetheless, these national institutions may have very unlike effects upon members of subcultural groups.

Third, there may be a common denominator that derives from the influence of mass means of communication. In industrialized nations which have state education, general literacy, newspapers, magazines, radio and television which reach nearly everyone, and nationally standardized and syndicated ideals of behavior, certain uniformities of behavior are introduced to all individuals to an extent unimaginable in pre-industrial societies. As yet, however, there is no way to measure the cultural effects of mass communications on a national scale. Indices of use of mass media are suggestive of the extent of their effects—a qualitative estimate—but since the quality or nature of the effects may well depend upon the subcultural context of their consumption, it must be ascertained through detailed ethnographic analysis of the subcultures. While mass media are therefore undoubtedly potent in helping to level subcultural differences, empirical research must also be alert to the probability that their meaning is somewhat repatterned according to the total point of view of the consumer.

These three kinds of traits are not wholly comparable, and each may change somewhat independently of the others. International relations, we know, have changed recently at a vertiginous rate, and the attitudes of individuals toward other nations have changed correspondingly. Attitudes toward internal political ideologies, however, have not undergone similar abrupt transformations. Nevertheless, the latter may change significantly under the pressure of economic factors and the influence of mass communications. Commensurate alteration of family types and ideals does not occur.

The effects of nationally shared practices of child-training and family patterns, of common participation in national institutions, and of mass communications all serve to develop national uniformities of individual behavior. But, since there remain important regional occupational, ethnic, class, and other differences it cannot be assumed a priori that the national common denominator so outweighs the subcultural differences in importance that individual behavior can be adequately understood with reference solely to the former. A modern society is extremely heterogeneous, and even the common denominator of shared behavior is a composite, a machine of wheels within wheels, some turning faster than others and each geared to some different aspect of national institutions. A broad definition of national culture, therefore, must include many different kinds of features.

The distinctions between the different aspects of national culture clearly imply that a great many different methods must be used to study any national culture in its totality. The problem of how to study a national culture does not ordinarily arise in most of the social sciences. Except anthropology and sociology, the social science disciplines and humanities usually deal with special categories of data representing state or national-level aspects of culture, e.g., economics, political science, philosophy, science, and others. While these disciplines at times relate their state- or national-level institutions to local behavior or the "grass roots," their emphasis is upon the former, and local differences are of interest as they affect specific institutions and not as they manifest total subcultures. These categories of data represent only portions of a national culture. Each category has manifestations on the national level and on the level of the subcultural groups. Religion, for example, may have a state or even international organization and a formal doctrine—viz. Catholicism —but it also has a great variety of local meanings and manifestations. The utility of distinguishing levels of sociocultural integration as well as categories of phenomena can be strikingly illustrated in studies of culture change and acculturation.

In the growth continuum of any culture, there is a succession of organizational types which are not only increasingly complex but which represent new emergent forms. The concept is fairly similar to that of organizational levels in biology. In culture, simple forms, such as those represented by the family or band, do not wholly disappear when a more complex stage of development is reached, nor do they merely survive fossil-like, as the concepts of folkways and mores formerly assumed.

They gradually become modified as specialized, dependent parts of new kinds of total configurations. The many-faceted national culture previously delineated represents a very high developmental level.

The application of the concept of developmental levels, or emergent evolution, to cultural phenomena is not new. The idea that "advanced" cultures are differently integrated than "simple" cultures is implicit in most studies; but its methodological utility has been pretty much ignored. A reason for this may be that it suggests the now widely discredited schemes of cultural evolution. The concept of levels of integration does not presuppose any particular evolutionary sequence. In biology, the concept that higher levels of life have different organizing principles than lower ones is in no way concerned with the evolution of particular life forms, such as birds, mammals, or reptiles. Similarly, this concept applied to culture is essentially heuristic and does not purport to explain the developmental sequences of particular cultural types. The cultural evolution of Morgan, Tylor, and others is a developmental taxonomy based on concrete characteristics of cultures. The concept of levels of sociocultural integration, on the other hand, is simply a methodological tool for dealing with cultures of different degrees of complexity. It is not a conclusion about evolution.

Another obstacle to acceptance of the concept of levels of sociocultural integration is the very strong hold of the concept of relativity. So long as the differences between cultural traditions are regarded as the most important qualitative differences, that is, so long as each culture area is seen primarily in terms of a fixed pattern which endures throughout its history, developmental stages will be thought of in terms only of quantitative differences, as matters of mere complexity. The concept of levels of sociocultural integration provides a new frame of reference and a new meaning to pattern; and it facilitates cross-cultural comparison.

THE FOLK SOCIETY AS
A LEVEL OF INTEGRATION

The research value of the concept of levels of sociocultural integration is largely unexplored. The historical approach to cultural studies has been divided mainly between a relativistic emphasis upon the continuity of traditional patterns of local areas without regard to succession of qualitatively different levels and upon postulation of universal evolutionary stages without regard to local differences.

An outstanding contribution which bears directly upon the problem of integrational levels, even though it approaches it somewhat tangentially, is Redfield's concept of the folk society and the folk culture. The characteristics which Redfield ascribes to folk society and culture and which are presumably attributes of a large number of tribal societies and cultures are more descriptive of a level of integration than of any particular culture type. I judge that Redfield's characterization of the folk society is intended to be applicable to the culture of societies at a certain level of sociocultural integration in wholly different cultural traditions. Further comparative analysis will no doubt require redefinition of the concept, but for the present purposes we can assume that most of the diagnostic features are significant. Folk societies are small, isolated, close-knit, homogeneous, patterned around kinship relations, oriented toward implicit goals and values, and pervaded by general supernaturalism.

Redfield did not attempt to conceptualize suprafolk levels of sociocultural integration, but in his studies of Yucatan, he uses the urban society as a contrasting type. Subjected to urbanization, the folk society is secularized, individualized, and disorganized. Urbanization, however, is but one of the processes through which a folk society may be integrated into a larger sociocultural system; for cities are but specialized parts of such systems. Some folk societies are incorporated into states and nations as regionally specialized subcultures which do not undergo urbanization at all and which are readapted rather than transformed. Even when the folk society is transformed, the individual is not only secularized, individualized, and disorganized but he adopts scientific or naturalistic explanations in place of supernatural ones, he participates in occupational, class, ethnic, or other sociocultural segments of the city, and in general he is reintegrated in a new kind of system.

Redfield's concepts of the folk society and the folk culture are based largely on his studies of the Maya Indians of Yucatan. Historically, the Maya villages were once parts of city states and federations, sometimes called "empires," and they became relatively independent after the Spaniards destroyed the state or national superstructure. The evident stability of their society and culture through the upheavals of the Spanish conquest and later events suggest a fairly high degree of integration. Whether the nature of this integration is essentially similar to that of tribal societies and to what is broadly called "folk societies" in other cultural traditions is a question to be answered by comparative, cross-cultural analysis. It is significant that the term "tribal society" remains an exceedingly ill-defined catchall. Once a typology of integrational levels is established empirically, it will be possible to examine the reintegration of simpler societies into larger sociocultural systems and to make generalizations about processes which go beyond what Redfield derived from the process of urbanization.

It is certain that further discriminations will require recognition of integrational levels that are lower than the folk level. The biological or nuclear family represents a level that is lower in a structural sense, and in some cases it appears to have been historically antecedent to higher forms. Among the aboriginal Western Shoshoni and probably most of the Great Basin Shoshoneans, practically all features of the relatively simple culture were integrated and functioned on a family level. The family was the reproductive, economic, educational, political, and religious unit. It reared its children in comparative isolation, obtained its own food, and cared for its members at birth, sickness, death, and other crises. It made its own decisions on virtually all matters. Family dependence upon outsiders was rare and its patterns restricted. The family sometimes called a shaman to treat the sick, co-operated with other families in communal hunts and dances, and visited relatives and friends when the opportunity permitted. But it could and did exist during most of the year without these extrafamilial relations. Extrafamilial dependency represented only a slight tendency toward a higher level of organization; patterns of multifamily unity had not become fixed.

The nuclear family, despite its many varieties, is basic in every modern society, and it seems safe to suppose that it has always been basic. In many cases, it was probably antecedent to the extended family, band, community, and other multifamily forms. In any event, there are probably several levels of sociocultural integration between the family and the folk society which should be distinguished. And above the folk society there are many significantly different levels of integration. For the purpose of the present exposition, however, it is sufficient to discuss only three levels—the nuclear family, the folk society, and the state. These are qualitatively distinctive organizational systems, which represent successive stages in any developmental continuum and constitute special kinds of cultural components within higher sociocultural systems.

Folk societies or multifamily sociocultural systems develop when activities requiring a suprafamily organization appear. Productive processes may become patterned around collective hunting, fishing, herding, or farming. Property rights requiring interfamilial understandings are established. Unity achieved in economic behavior may be reinforced through group ceremonialism, through patterned forms of extended kinship and friendship, and through recreational activities. Society acquires a structure appropriate to the particular kinds of interfamilial relations that develop in the cultural tradition, and patterns of social control and leadership emerge.

One of the most common forms of multifamily integration is an extended kin group of some kind. Not all peoples, however, have a suprafamily organization based on extended kinship. The nuclear family may be integrated directly into a larger, multikin structure.

What may be called roughly a state level of integration is marked by the appearance of new patterns that bring several multifamily aggregates, or folk societies, into functional dependence upon one another within a still larger system. Communities or other sociocultural segments of a folk type may participate in state projects, such as the construction of irrigation works, roads, religious edifices, and so on; they may produce special foods or manufactured objects for exchange with other communities and for state purposes; they may join other communities in offensive and defensive warfare; they may accept state rules, regulations, and standards concerning property, credit, commerce, and other matters of mutual concern. They frequently accept a state religion. The system of controls arising from economic, military, and religious needs creates a political hierarchy and a social system of classes and statuses. Qualitatively new institutions appear on the state or national level: governmental structure and control of those aspects of life which are of state concern; social stratification; and national cultural achievements. All of these have national aspects that are distinguishable from their varied folk manifestations.

There are many kinds of state sociocultural systems, each having characteristics determined by factors which are peculiar to the area and to the cultural tradition. But all states can be said to represent a broad level of sociocultural organization which is more than the sum total of the families and communities of which it consists.

There is nothing new in the idea that each stage of sociocultural development entails new forms of co-operation and interaction, and that societies may be arranged in general developmental series, such as family, village, and state, *Gemeinschaft* and *Gesellschaft*, and others. But these are primarily taxonomic concepts. The point I wish to stress is that the concept of levels may be used as an analytic tool in the study of changes within any particular sociocultural system, for each system consists of parts which developed at different stages and through different processes and which, though functionally specialized in their dependency upon the whole, continue to integrate certain portions of the culture. The problem of acculturation may be rephrased so that the phenomena can be handled not merely in terms of categories of elements and total patterns but also of functional levels. This is necessary in any acculturational situation involving a modern state or nation, for the different categories of cultural features—religion, economics, government, and the like—cut across the nation, community, class, and family levels and function differently at each. National religions, for example, involve a formal organization and dogma, but their community or class manifestations may be quite varied, while a considerable amount of supernaturalism functions on the individual or family level.

SOCIOCULTURAL LEVELS IN
ACCULTURATION STUDIES

Three brief examples will suffice in the present chapter to illustrate the utility of the concept of sociocultural levels in acculturational studies, although application of the concept will be evident in all the remaining chapters of this volume. The present examples are offered to show how the concept can be used as a research tool and not to present definitive, substantive results, for little detailed research has been done. Western Shoshoni acculturation exemplifies the influence of a modern nation upon a family level of sociocultural integration. Changes in the Inca Empire under the Spanish conquest illustrate how the culture of a native state may be more radically affected at the national level than at lower levels. Post-conquest changes in the Circum-Caribbean culture show loss of state functions and deculturation to a folk level.

Western Shoshoni acculturation. The distinctive features of Western Shoshoni acculturation are best understood if contrasted to the acculturation of other Indians who had a tribal culture. American Indians since post-white times have been potentially subject to influences from both the national and folk levels of European culture. National institutions affecting the Indian include trade relations, such as markets for furs, farm produce, and craft objects and a source of manufactured goods; governmental services, such as schools, hospitals, work projects, grants of money and goods, and farm extension aid; laws; reservations; and many restrictive measures. In some cases there was armed intervention in tribal affairs. National influences likewise have been introduced through special groups, such as churches. All of these influences were mediated through agents of one kind or another. But the contacts with the agents of the national institutions were rarely so continuous and powerful that the personal behavior patterns of the individual agents were adopted to any appreciable degree by the Indians.

In many cases, however, the Indians came into daily contact with white settlers—miners, farmers, and ranchers—which presented the opportunity for acculturation of each group toward the folk culture of the other. In early times, the white trappers were often strongly acculturated toward the Indian way of life. Later, the white farmers introduced rural American patterns which began to influence the Indians.

The reaction of the Indians to these national and folk or community patterns depended upon their own native level of cultural development. Most Indians had some kind of multifamily organization, some fairly cohesive in-group, from which an individual detached himself to enter the context of the neighboring rural white culture only with difficulty.

The reservation is therefore a result as well as a cause of group cohesion. Only the extremely acculturated individuals have been able to break from tribal life and, race prejudice permitting, behave like rural whites.

But native patterns do not necessarily remain intact because individual Indians do not participate in white society. All "tribes" have been brought into a relationship of dependency upon American national culture through economic, governmental, and often religious institutions. In most cases, the influence of the institutions of the larger sociocultural system has been sufficient to destroy the native pattern, often with traumatic effects. It was the most serious weakness of the New Deal policy for the Indians to suppose that an uncontaminated native core of attitudes and values could be preserved while the tribe became increasingly dependent upon national institutions. One of the most tragic cases of present cultural conflict is the Navaho. Their very dependence upon livestock as cash produce for a national market puts them into competition with one another and threatens to destroy the native culture. The situation is aggravated by the limited grazing resources.

The Western Shoshoni were spared the more crucial difficulties experienced by Indians who had a fairly tightly-woven fabric of community culture. When white miners and ranchers entered their country a century ago, individual families readily attached themselves to white communities. When their native hunting and gathering resources were depleted, they worked for wages sufficient to maintain their very low standard of living. Later, they were given reservations, but these consisted of little more than small residence sites. A few who obtained arable land undertook farming in a small way, very like their white neighbors. Most Western Shoshoni, however, were only loosely tied to any definable locality or cohesive social group, for there were no community bonds beyond kinship and friendship. Persons commonly wandered from place to place, covering distances of several hundred miles if they could manage transportation.

On the whole, Western Shoshoni acculturation has come about more through face-to-face association with whites than through governmental services. The influence of schools, health services, work projects, and other federal benefits has been sporadic. Facilities have been poor, and the Indians have been too mobile. Association with rural whites has not been very sustained, but it has been sufficient to acculturate the Shoshoni toward the Great Basin American ranching and mining subculture, especially where economic needs have forced them into the role of nomadic wage laborers. But it has not wiped out all Indian practices. Acculturation has consisted primarily of modification of those patterns necessary to adjust to the rural white culture. It has brought wage labor, white styles of dress, housing, transportation, food, and other material items, use of English and some literacy, and considerable adaptability in dealing with whites, though race prejudice has prevented full participation in white social relations. The Shoshoni retain, however, many practices and beliefs pertaining to kinship relations, child-rearing, shamanism, supernatural powers and magic, and recreation, especially gambling games.

Many other American Indian groups retain features of this kind after other portions of their native culture have been lost. These features, however, are those that functioned on a family level and may survive apart from group patterns. The difference between the Western Shoshoni and most other Indians is that the former did not have to experience the break-up of suprafamily-level institutions. The individual families were quite free to adjust to changed circumstances in the most expedient way without facing conflict. Perhaps this is why they are generally quite amiable toward the whites, exhibiting no deep-seated hostility.

Changes in the Inca Empire. At the time of the Spanish conquest, the Inca of the South American Andes had a fairly elaborate empire. The conquest produced radical changes in the national institutions, but the lower levels of the native sociocultural system were affected far less.

The native Inca Empire was controlled through highly centralized political, military, economic, and religious institutions. These had developed in the course of empire growth, national or imperial institutions being imposed upon the local states just as local state institutions had evidently been imposed upon the earlier communities. The Inca institutions affected the states and communities to the extent that it was necessary to make the empire function, but this did not mean that everything at the lower levels had to be changed. Much was left alone. The imperial political structure consisted of a hierarchy of positions, the more important being held by members of the royal family while the lesser were left to native rulers. Community affairs that did not conflict with the state were evidently handled much as in pre-Inca times. Economic production was reorganized under the empire in order to channel a portion of goods and services to the ruling bureaucracy and to the Inca Sun Temple, but the kinds and quantities of goods produced and consumed in the home and village were not greatly changed, except perhaps through the introduction of methods of quantity production. The Inca Sun God was forced upon all communities as the supreme deity, but local gods, cults, and rites and household fetishes, shrines and beliefs were not disturbed.

Under the conquest, Spanish national institutions replaced those of the Inca, but the lower levels of native culture were not so drastically altered. Spaniards took over the key positions in the political hierarchy and Spanish law was imposed to the extent necessary to maintain the

Spanish institutions. But many native rulers were retained in lower positions and a large portion of village activities went on as in native times. Spanish economic patterns introduced a system of cash produce, money, credit, and commerce, but Spanish policy was designed at first primarily to drain off wealth, especially gold, for the Spanish Crown and the upper classes. Instead of contributing goods and services to the Inca ruling classes, the common people were drafted into the mines to produce gold for export and were forced to pay tribute in various forms to their conquerors. Once these obligations were discharged, however, village and family affairs seem to have been carried on in traditional ways.

Spanish religion likewise affected the Inca culture differently at different levels. The Catholic Church, which in feudal Spain had sanctioned and implemented state policies, completely replaced the Inca sun cult, for it could not tolerate a rival national religion. All Peruvians became nominal Catholics, accepting the Christian God and saints and contributing to Church support, but they did not abandon local shrines, ancestor worship, household gods, shamanism, and other lower level forms of religion. And the Catholic fathers were content to regard these community and family practices as mere "paganism," which was innocuous provided it did not threaten the state religion.

Modern, republican Peru is very different from sixteenth-century colonial Peru, but a great deal of native community and family culture has survived in the areas least touched by commercialism. Over the centuries, however, national economic patterns have struck deeply at the heart of community culture. The production of cash crops, both by independent small farmers and by plantation wage laborers, has linked the people to the national society. Wage labor in pottery, textile, and other factories, service in the army, work on roads and other government projects, and adoption of many cash-oriented occupations, together with loss of lands, is destroying the basis of the native communities and converting the mass of the Indians into a national laboring class. The local sociocultural segments are being replaced by class subcultural groups which extend horizontally across communities. This trend is occurring in all parts of the world as native populations are drawn into the orbit of an industrial world through specialized production of cash commodities.

Post-conquest changes in the Circum-Caribbean Culture. Among certain of the Circum-Caribbean Indians, the Spanish conquest destroyed native state institutions without effectively substituting Hispanic national patterns. These people were consequently deculturated to a community level of sociocultural organization.

This deculturative process may be illustrated by the Cuna-Cueva Indians of the Isthmus of Panama. Archaeological evidence and historical documents show that at the time of the conquest these Indians had a rather elaborate state organization. There was a ruling class consisting of chiefs and nobles whose status is evidenced by rich burials. These rulers were interred with several wives or retainers and a wealth of luxury goods, including gold objects, carved stone, pearls, precious stones, and ceramics. The priests were also members of the upper class, and they presided over a cult which depended in part upon human sacrifice. Since prisoners of war were used as sacrificial victims, warriors could achieve some upward mobility of status through taking captives. The common people were the farmers and the artisans who produced luxury goods for the state. At the bottom of the scale were some kind of so-called slaves, apparently female captives and perhaps those males who were not sacrificed.

The Spanish conquest struck the Cuna with sufficient force to wipe out the national or state institutions. Military expeditions eliminated the upper classes and confiscated their wealth. Human sacrifice and the state religion based on it were suppressed. But Spanish rule and the Catholic Church were not very effectively substituted for the native institutions, for the people moved into regions where the Spaniards did not care to follow. Left comparatively unmolested and yet unable to maintain state functions, the Cuna resumed life on a community basis. The content and organization of the Cuna community in recent times is strikingly like that of the Tropical Forest Indians of South America, and it must be assumed that this type of culture was always part of the more elaborate Circum-Caribbean state organization. Today, the Cuna farm for home consumption and make their own fairly simple household goods and utensils. The luxury objects were no longer made after the upper classes for which they were intended were wiped out. The manufactures now include pole-and-thatched houses, dugout canoes, baskets, simple pottery, and bark cloth. The village is the largest political unit, and it is controlled by a headman assisted by one or more shamans. These shamans do not have the priestly functions of the native Cuna, for loss of state religion has left little more than a simple village religion which centers around girls' puberty ceremonies and death rites.

CONCLUSIONS

In the three cases just described, much of the significance of the acculturation would have been lost if changes in the native society had been viewed solely in terms of a monolithic concept of total cultural pattern or configuration. Whether the substantive conclusions suggested are correct or not, it is clear that cultural and social interaction take place on different levels. National, community, and family levels were selected for illustration, but there are no doubt other levels which will have greater significance for certain problems.

The concept of levels of sociocultural integration is a conclusion about culture change only in the sense that there do appear to be phenomena which cannot be explained by any other frame of reference. Any aspect of culture—economic, social, political, or religious—has different meanings when viewed in terms of its national functions and its special manifestations in different subcultures. Stated differently, the individual's participation in culture is of a somewhat different order at the family, community, and national levels. As a member of the family, he is concerned with the most basic human needs—procreation, subsistence, child-rearing, sickness, and death. Even where community or state institutions intervene to assist the family, these functions still remain the primary reason for the existence of the family. Because they are directly concerned with biological survival, they are charged with emotions—emotions involving sex, hunger, fear of sickness and death, and social anxieties. In the development of the individual, they are among the earliest learned and the most deeply ingrained attitudes. This presumably is why behavior which functions on a family level is the most difficult to change in a changing culture.

The individual, of course, reacts as a total person in his functions as a member of the family, community, and nation. Nevertheless, community functions may develop without completely altering the family. New patterns of co-operation and social interaction lift certain responsibilities from the family and make it a specialized dependency of a larger sociocultural unit. But they by no means supersede all of its functions.

State functions, too, may be mediated to the individual through the community or they may reach him directly. But he does not surrender his role in the family and community by virtue of becoming a member of a nation. His relationship to the nation is specialized according to the subculture of his local group or class.

The inference of these observations for studies of national characteristics and national character is clear. Personal behavior is not something that can be understood simply by studying random samples of the total national population. The several aspects of national culture previously defined—national institutions, national cultural achievements, subcultural patters, family patterns, behavior in situations involving different subcultural groups, and the common denominator—should be distinguished and the role of each appraised. The significance of each of these aspects will depend upon the particular culture, and for this reason proper conceptualization of the culture studied is essential.

These comments on the usefulness of the concept of levels of sociocultural organization to studies of national characteristics and national character are offered because such studies have wide current interest. The concept, however, will have value to another problem or objective of anthropology which will surely become of major importance in the future. The search for cross-culturally valid laws or regularities has suffered as much for want of adequate methodological tools as for lack of interest. So long as developmental stages within any cultural tradition are regarded primarily as quantitative differences and the traditions are assumed to be qualitatively unique, formulation of cross-culturally significant regularities is foredoomed. If, however, stages are recognized as qualitatively distinctive, the way is clear to establish developmental typologies that are valid for more than one cultural tradition. Even if this typology were based solely on general forms of the kind I have discussed, it would facilitate the analysis of the processes of change from one form to another. Distinction of levels of internal organization within sociocultural systems would also facilitate the discovery of regularities. Instead of dealing with total configurations, which are made virtually unique by definition, it would be possible to isolate special components, which, having been analyzed in their relation to the whole, could safely be compared with similar components in other cultural traditions.

24. AMERICAN COMMUNITIES *

One day in 1947, when the editor of this book was just beginning to settle into a community in east-central China, he was summoned to appear at once at the office of the county magistrate. The magistrate was polite but cold: an anthropological study of his country was an affront; anthropologists, said the magistrate, studied only savages and barbarians. For several decades now, anthropologists have made field studies in almost every complex society that would permit such work to be undertaken. For the most part these researches have been community studies—a blending of ethnographic and older sociological interests with methods derived from both. The United States has been the subject of a good many studies and some of the results of this work are given in this selection.

THE COMMUNITY-STUDY METHOD has been fairly widely used in studies of American culture. In that method it has become traditional to use local communities as local samples or microcosms of culture. A good deal of theoretical statement of the justification of the tradition is now accumulating. Nevertheless, no independent treatment of specifically American communities looking toward classifying them in correspondences with a typology of American cultures or subcultures has yet been attempted. It is useful, then, if communities do reflect their cul-

* Conrad M. Arensberg, "American Communities," *American Anthropologist*, Vol. 57 (1955), pp. 1143–1162. Reprinted with permission of the author and publisher.

Professor of Anthropology at Columbia University, the author (b. 1910) is known as a sociologist as well as an anthropologist. A participant in the elaborate study of Newburyport, Massachusetts (*Yankee City*), he also made a detailed study of Irish rural society. Arensberg was associated with the economist Karl Polanyi in a research project on economic institutions (see No. II:11) and is deeply concerned with problems of applied anthropology. Among his works are *The Irish Countryman* (1936); *Family and Community in Ireland* (with Solon T. Kimball) (1940); *Measuring Human Relations* (with Eliot D. Chapple) (1942); and *Trade and Market in the Early Empires* (with Polanyi and Pearson) (1957).

tures, to ask what sorts of communities are distinguishable in the United States and how these sorts reflect one by one American culture or cultures.

CULTURES AND COMMUNITIES

In undertaking to answer such questions, some preliminary decisions must be made. We must take it for granted that communities properly sampled do reflect their cultures. The full proof is not cogent here; I have taken pains to spell out elsewhere how they do so. Communities seem to be basic units of organization and transmission within a culture. They provide for human beings and their cultural adaptation to nature the basic minimum personnel and the basic minimum of social relations through which survival is assured and the content of culture can be passed on to the next generation. Already pan-animal as ecological units, communities are pan-human as transmission units for human culture. It is their function in keeping alive the basic inventory of traits and institutions of the minimal personnel of each kind for which culture provides a role and upon which high-culture specialization and acceptance can be built that makes human communities into cell-like repeated units of organization within human societies and cultures.

We can rely, then, on this hypothesis for ordering the experience of American communities we will cite. Without defending it further, we must notice at once that it implies that each culture has its characteristic community which serves as such unit and that each isolable type of community, as such a unit of cultural organization and transmission, stands for an isolable culture. We can hypothesize a one-to-one correspondence of some kind between culture and community.

Naturally the correspondence will hold for the two only as we take them as cultural data. We must treat them with the same operations of observation and generalization, working on both of them within cultural or social anthropology rather than at random. Cultural data are patterns and wholes and processes among patterns, not matters of size, population, location, economics, etc. Such patterns reach us from comparative ethnographic analysis. They are constructs modeling and explaining the successions and variations in human adaptation and invention, and their first field is the field of *forms*.

That means that our treatment of culture and community need not resemble the results of economic or sociological analysis. Our treatment of communities in America or anywhere, from hamlets and market centers to metropolises, need not coincide with that of modern urban study or with human or economic geography. We must share facts with other disciplines. But we must put them together and add to them new ones of our own quite differently. Anthropology's point of reference is the comparative human record of cultures and communities everywhere. Laws and processes among other phenomena, however sharply they too are reflected in the story of cultures and communities, are to us, at most, ancillary.

Rather our view of communities will rest upon the pioneer cultural analysis in Mumford's *The Culture of Cities* (1937). There the correspondence of community and culture got its first great statement. Mumford demonstrated that for each cultural advance in European life a new form of the city emerged. The medieval borough around market and cathedral, urban counterpart of the manorial village, expressed the high Middle Ages; the baroque capital of parade avenues, palaces, and *places d'armes* mirrored the absolutist national states; the sooty tangle of factory and slum and the residential segregations of the withdrawn squires on the hill in mill towns and mill cities matched the industrial and railroad age. Each community form (here "city") was unique, just as the age, which the anthropologist calls "culture," was unique. Accidental functional, social, economic, and geographical differences, whereby one city was a port and another a fortress, or one climbed a mountainside and another sprawled over rivers, plains, and canals, fell away as Mumford showed us the grand similarity of city form.

We can thus expect American culture, in its many subcultures of region and age, to show similar correspondence in forms. There will be an American community, at least in pattern discernible above accidents of function, size, location, etc., for every American culture. Indeed, conversely, for as many types of communities as we can distinguish from the record there will be *so* many cultures upon the American scene.

CULTURAL ANALYSIS

The trick, as we said, is to treat communities and their cultures with the same analytic devices. Such devices must be empirically descriptive of the real world and use the common data we share with other sciences. But they must also be comparative in the fullest ethnographic sense. They must yield us defensible and recognizable patterns at once generalizing and specific to time and place.

At the present stage of the science of culture such devices do exist. They are ready for use in our abstracting from the many accounts of real American communities, both large and small, the significant patterns of form which we seek. We do not yet, however, have sufficient theory of culture upon which to build comparative patterns for whole cultures. I shall treat only the communities here, and I shall have to leave to other authors any patterns for the wholes of the corresponding American cultures. Nevertheless, it may be that what I think we can discern of patterns in American communities will give us interesting distinguishing features which may help us with recognition and prediction of the wholes.

Hundreds of accounts of American communities already exist. They appear in every stage of completeness of description. They come to us from the prolific pages of American censuses, American rural sociology, agricultural and land economics, urban sociology, social-problems literature, architecture and city or community planning, human and urban geography, regional history, local novels, muckraking investigations, as well as from formal "community studies." Our job is less to cite such abundance of data than to order it into sense. We shall content ourselves with drawing upon fairly common knowledge of American life and its local manifestations. Nothing can be more obvious than most of the facts we shall have to use; anthropology can hope to find few esoterica in our own back yards. Nevertheless, if our comparisons order even obvious facts in genuinely universal and cross-cultural ways, then the patterns we discover in American communities will not only be new but they will be important to the perspective of science and to the record of anthropology.

What are the comparative analytic devices of cultural analysis we can put to work on all human communities in general and on American ones in particular? Clearly they must be such as describe all cases in common, yet still combine for useful comparisons. They must be such as go into the building of structural models. Nowadays it is clear that a model rather than a definition serves to represent the complex variables of a complex situation, thing, or process. A model serves better to put together empirical descriptions economically and surely and to handle summarily things of many dimensions, little-known organization, diverse functions and processes, intricate connections with other things. Definitions are too shallow and too full of verbal traps; summaries of propositions are too slow, piecemeal, and cumbersome. And certainly communities are such complex things.

We shall seek here for a family of models comparing all communities to our known American ones. Our models will not be simple ones. Spare as possible, with one term for each attribute and one relation in the model for each relation in the thing, they must still cover the many attributes which communities can be described for. They must cover size, spread, density, land use, traffic flow, population replacement, and so on. They must treat the many functions for individual lives or for society that communities may have: subsistence, defense, sociability, mate choice, trade, social or political control. They must try to cast these attributes and functions into the connections they have in real life. They must go on to trials of forecasting form, structure, and process, since attributes and functions connect in definite ways that have definite products and lawful properties of change. In the last analysis, a model is predictive, as these must be. It is testable in each new prediction. If a new fact can be predicted to fit in just so, with a result upon the model which foretells the outcome in the thing, then the model is correct and the theory upon which it is built is true.

Thus the models we shall need for American communities must rest on the common terms of description which serve for all others. The terms that we must vary as each successive model of the family represents the changed realities of a common experience of all communities in a new particular one must be terms of universal application. The following are the variable comparative terms which apply to all human and animal communities, out of which our models can be built:

1. Individuals (persons or animals)
2. Spaces (territory, position, movement)
3. Times (schedules, calendars, time-series)
4. Functions (for individual and group life)
5. Structure and Process

1. *Individuals.* Our first operation of description and model building for all communities specifies individuals (persons, animals). It answers: Who? With it we treat populations, memberships, exclusions and inclusions. Communities are, of course, collectivities or "social systems" of specific individuals. These have identities, and in description we select some and not others, and specify who is member, to be observed, and who is not. Once identified they can be counted, located, followed. Further, they can be described for the attributes we, observers, select or they, the observed, distinguish: age, sex, color, size, occupation, class, ethnicity, sect, etc. In dealing with human beings and their cultures we learned long ago to treat as significant those categoric attributes which the members of the community and culture inform us they discriminate and to connect these with behavior and organization. In dealing with animals, it is also a truism that behavior varies with category: age, sex, function. Communities, indeed, are unit minima organizing the individuals realizing such categories.

2. *Spaces.* Communities occupy and use space and its contents, have territories the individuals exploit, create boundaries. They use such space and "environment" differentially. Upon space they produce what the geographer calls culture and the ecologist calls modification of the environment: dumps, blights, houses, canals, roads, harvests, etc. All these are such that maps can record. They assign space differentially to their members, to individuals, to categories of individuals, to functional of-

fices. Thereby they produce settlement patterns, land use and property distributions, assembly points and dispersal zones with tracks between, segregations of sex, age, class, occupation, rank, etc., and the things of each of these. Maps and charts can describe these, and every community and every culture patterns these but patterns them differently, as does every animal species, too. Obviously intricate connections interlace population and space use, (1) and (2) here.

3. *Times.* Communities occupy their spaces in time. They alternately show dispersal of their persons (to the fields, to the hills, by the season, by day, etc.) with assemblage of them (in sleeping quarters, in ceremonies, in communal efforts, in war). There are climatic and economic rounds, calendars, shorter cycles of euphoria and dysphoria, longer rhythms of generational expansion or colonial budding, monthly, weekly, daily periodicities. There are periodic yields of the community's space and things in crops, in production, in volume of transactions or of traffic. All these are such that time rates can record. They engage the members differentially, and the description that tells us which members engage when and which do not in this action or that is a necessary complement to our knowing who they are and where the community places them. We cannot compare communities without confronting these periodicities from one community to the next. It is not enough merely to know that we already make imprecise temporal comparisons implicitly: sedentary versus transhumant communities, tight Apollonian sabbatarian ones versus loose Dionysian ones of occasional and irregular celebrations. We must discover in each case explicitly how the community specifically acts out its own sense of time.

4. *Functions.* Furthermore, communities collectivize in their space, among their members, through their lives (which are generations long and thus longer than those of their members), many gains for individual and for social survival or advantage. We have named some of them already. These too must appear in our models and the gains must be spelled out. But the functions do not define the communities. Any culture has other ways of defense, of mate finding, of socializing, that extend beyond the community or that may supplant the community's. Likewise, communities, like other things, can develop dysfunctions, pain and thwart members, gain or lose functions, without losing identity. Yet some functional reason for any phenomenon's identity certainly exists. In this case the reason seems clear; we will risk repetition to point it out again. The record indicates that some local, continuing grouping of men or animals nearly always comes to exist. Bigger than the family or the mating pair, it insures continuity of the species. Where the species is human—to wit, a culture (for it is only in man that differentiation of kind takes not a genetic but a cultural form)—a characteristic minimal

unit of personnel arises, as surely as in its animal counterpart, to subsist in space and endure over lives, sufficient to insure cultural transmission. Thus a human community, specifically, contains within it—and the content gives us both our definition and our problem—roles for every kind and office of mankind that the culture knows: husband, farmer, old man, mother, child, proletarian, priest, etc. A human community does this as surely as does one of ants, which, too, provides a role for every kind of ant the species has evolved: queen, worker, egg, soldier, larva. But the mechanisms, of course, are now known to be quite different.

Tables of functions performed for persons and for groups, then, are quite necessary tools for analysts of this unit of organization and continuity in cultural transmission in man, just as they are for physiologists of cells, organs, and organisms. But they are no more so than the maps and time charts we have already cited.

5. *Structure and Process.* A model for a community, then, and any models we make for American ones, must put all these things together. It will represent, and help us explore, the characteristic minimal organization of the bearers of a culture in time and space. How will we put these things together; what devices will best represent them and the whole they make? Trial will tell. We cannot predict in advance, in the abstract. Devices for representing empirical structure and process must be invented, searched out of many prior human experiences, tried and fitted to reality again and again.

Once found, invented, tested, they will fit each community's use of time and space and function and follow each community's organization of roles, institutions, and personnel. The models will have form, carry out functions, show structure, unfold process, like the communities. They will both show the properties we know already and ready us to predict effects and also follow laws we do not yet know are theirs. The double promise of such models is the double promise of science: ordering of the commonplace and unexpected discovery of the unknown.

**COMMUNITY PATTERNS IN
THE UNITED STATES**

Let us now take the known historical communities of the United States and submit them to analysis. We can begin with the New England town.

The New England town. There is much distinctive about the New England town. First, there is its historical (cultural) descent. I think it unnecessary to go into the long and difficult controversy within American history about the importation or the invention *in situ* of the New England town. Suffice it to say that the eminent colonial historian Wertenbaker accepts the derivation of the New England town from the

manorial village of the champion country of the English Midlands,
whence most of the Puritans came, a derivation established by Homans
(1942). In the Midlands that village in turn was a local specialization
of the open-field village of the North European plain. It was brought in
to newly opened fenlands by Angles and Saxons from the Elbe mouth
and was of a settlement pattern, village type, and agriculture quite different from that of once-Celtic western Britain and even from that of
nearby once-Belgian and Jutish Kent. Nothing prevents inventors in a
New World from elaborating, adapting, formalizing already familiar,
even unconscious, heritages. In fact, that is the way anthropology tells us
most cultural evolution (*anglice* "invention") proceeds. The urbanizing
Puritans rationally planning new settlements in the wilderness were
elaborating ancestral cultural materials and, as we shall see, every other
American pioneer community did likewise.

Even the distribution of the New England town, its second distinctive
trait, confirms its character as culture trait. The town about the green or
common, with its centered church and town hall, seats of a single village-
wide congregation and town meeting, with its town territory stretching
out over fields and woods used by farmers and artisans clustered at the
square rather than spread through the open countryside, went only
where the New England Yankees went, mixed only where they mixed,
survived or died only where they survived or died as a majority. Outside
New England, as we know, that is only upstate New York and Long Island; in mixture, the Great Lakes country and the upper Middle West;
in descent, Mormon Utah.

Distinctive measures of community use of personnel, space, and time
require we create a very special model for the New England town, either
for its heyday till the coming of the industrial revolution or for its crippled and dying modern isolated back-country remnant. Take membership first, and let us see who belonged. The nucleated settlement pattern
made for close living; the neighbors were fellow-townsmen, visible and
ever-present but not necessarily kinsmen. Endogamy, however, was
fairly usual and exogamy not obligatory. In this the cultural tradition
of the European and Near Eastern but not that of the Indian, Chinese,
or African village was preserved, a community pattern which Murdock
has mistaken for a kinship form he calls the "deme." Hence, fellows of
the town were nearer than kinfolk, and kin moving off to another town
soon fell away. The brittle, easily split "nuclear" or "democratic" ("Eski-
moan") family, the *famille particulariste* of Le Play, native to North
Europe, came with these Yankees from England and fitted well their
egalitarian, unstratified farmer-artisan towns.

These Yankee towns were originally single congregations and autonomous villages. They were under the rule of their own householders, as

heads of families ("town fathers"), and of their own elders, who hired and fired their own clergy, determined their own orthodoxy, enforced conformity and morality, easily mistaking their own common one-class customs, under a Calvinist Protestantism freed of hierarchical and external control, for exclusive religious truth, through the whole gamut of custom from belief to sumptuary law and sabbath meeting. The same direct democracy among fathers and householders prevailed politically, under the larger framework of inherited English law, at least till the crown reasserted control, and the body of the congregants were also the town meeting, an assemblage of the whole. Church and town hall were one building or, if two, stood side by side on the village common, and only the drop of a gavel might separate religious from secular deliberations.

Only later were there any class distinctions, and these grew up *in situ* among kindred, on a functional basis. Later, on the eve of industrializing, classes and sections were to break away from Yankee equality. Poor pioneers were to break away on the outer western fringe, in the "burnt-over country" of York State, into Mormonism and the evangelical sects of the frontier; merchant patricians on the eastern edge were to give Boston and Unitarianism its distinctive character, in a move which left the Puritans' Congregationalism a core church and subculture, still confined to Puritan middle (and middle-class) territory. But, before all that, Yankees were farmers, artisans, shop-keeper-merchants, seamen and fishermen, without distinction or segregation either in community membership, political right, or use of living space. They were all townsmen together.

It may well be this culturally distinctive use of community space, not any agricultural poverty of New England, which made the Yankee an egalitarian jack-of-all-trades, both individualist in motive and deeply trained in civic co-operation and association. The nucleated village of the open-field agriculture of the North European plain shows many parallels to Yankee tradition, even as far out east as the Russian and Ukrainian *mir*. "National character" studies have still to work out what parallels in social organization and psychological traits in culture respond to substrata of common folk tradition and what to superstructures of state and national institutions of special political and historical development.

Thus, like some other *North* Europeans, these one-congregation, egalitarian villages lived by nuclear families, without much functional extended kinship, with equal division of inheritance, some freedom of divorce, and some ancestral near-equality of the sexes (later to flower in special American feminism). They had the habit of setting up children on their own quite young and of supporting the old and indigent "on the town." They had town officers, such as fenceviewers, weighmasters, etc., remote descendants of the village servants, the gooseherds, cowherds, haywards, and swineherds of the medieval Old World. They displayed, too, the republican tradition of a Roman Cincinnatus, best described as a tendency to assign public office in rotation among "pillars of the community" (and of the church, the same thing) but otherwise to show extreme suspicion of one man's getting ahead of his neighbors, to the point of concealing wealth and understating ability.

Just as the consequences of the New England townsmen's use of space were marked, so were those of their use of time. Frequent daily intercourse of neighbours and townsfolk, continuous contact of the young people among themselves at each age of growing up, as well as enforced frequent sabbatarian communion, meant a dense collective experience, a chance for internalization of these rigidities of repetitive role and habit, a readiness to seek consensus coupled with a stubbornness of egalitarian judgment about which much has long been written. Yet little thought is given, outside the New England heritage, to the rarity of such "town meeting democracy" and "Puritan conscience" in the rest of the American scene. Even the generational rhythm of the New England town, which peopled much of the northern frontier (but far less than is usually assumed), was a use of long-wave time both distinctive and congruent with the nucleated, egalitarian "open-field village" of the cultural past. For it was in New England, and in New England alone, that towns, like Greek cities, sent out whole colonies of surplus young people, newly married church "elders" in their late teens, complete with church, town plan, minister, treasury, etc., in short, a full apparatus for nucleated community living. Only the Mormon community and culture, later-day offshoots of New England, still expands so, in our own present, as they spread up into the Bitterroot Mountains of Idaho, town by town up the mountain valleys.

If this Yankee community, the New England town, is a faithful microcosm in its distinctive pattern of the New England culture in its region and in its epochs of rise and flower, are there other American communities equally distinct? Yes, there are many, as we shall see, and we can find others at once in two other well-known original colonial regions where the first American cultures were established.

The Southern county. For ease of recognition, it is best to turn next to the American Old South, tracing it from its Tidewater beginnings through its Deep South extensions south and west over three centuries of movement toward Texas and California. As we shall see, the original sectionalism, North and South, was a too easy division of the complex country, even in colonial times, but it is so familiar that we can begin with it. We know a great deal about this Old South, counterpoise to the Yankee North, but have we analyzed its historical form of community? Plantations, poor whites, Negro slavery, Anglicanism and Methodism, "Bourbonism" and Fundamentalism, are culture traits we did not need to mention for New England. However, it is not the new traits but their organization into a community of new personnel, space, time, functions, and form that we must specify.

The distinctive community form of the South was and is the county. Dispersed a day's ride in and out around the county seat, that community assembled planter and field- or house-hand from the fat plantations, free poor white or Negro from the lean hills and swamps, for the pageantry and the drama of Saturdays around the courthouse, when the courthouse, the jail, the registry of deeds, and the courthouse square of shops and lawyers' row made a physical center of the far-flung community. This is the American counterpart of the Spanish and Portuguese *municipio*, the French and German *commune* and *Gemeinde*, the rural counterpart of the baroque capital which Mumford called the city of the palace and the parade. It is a product of the same age, the age of the rise of the national state, whose community form it represents.

It is a mistake to treat this county and county seat for its separate parts and to try to find the community in the Old South at any other level. The poor white or Negro hamlets about a country church, set in hill or swamp retreat, the plantation, however large and proud and populous, the county seat as town (older ones seldom had distinctive organs apart from their function as county seat), were and are none of them complete communities. The country itself was the unit of dispersal and assemblage, and it was a two-class community from its inception in the gathering-in of nobles into the king's palace and capital along with *noblesse de robe* and rich *bourgeois*. Formed from the coming together of landowner and *peón*, its pattern of dispersal was a double one, with estates covering the good land, and little men, now clients, now runaways, taking up the leavings in the bad. Nowhere is the church, even the baroque cathedral, the center of this community, either physically or spiritually. There are many churches, and these split along the lines of class or ethnicity: rural chapels in the hamlets and the *barrios*, fundamentalist sectarian or Indianly "superstitious," and city ones, seats of fashion and elegance. The church, both as building and as institution, is overshadowed by another, cynosure of all eyes, seat of power and decision, repository of land grants and commercial debt-bonds: the courthouse, the "palacio."

The county of the Old South, spread across the land to California but purest in the Tidewater and the Black Belt, is the American community form of the Baroque Age. Its distinctly American accents— Methodism, Baptism, and White Supremacy—like the distinct American pattern of race relations to which it gave rise, do not separate it generically from its Latin and Old World counterparts. It received, like the New England town, much of English law and of North European and British Protestantism, two culture elements that never penetrated Latin America, but it reworked these into forms which have no semblance of the forms New England gave these things. In no particular of community form can we find the Southern county like the New England town. Neither in land use, nor in dispersal and assemblage, nor in use of time, nor in deploy of functions, is there anything in which the one community resembles the other, despite their common institutional elements and borrowings. And the cultures were and are just as different as the two communities which miniature them.

These two American communities, then, are easily recognizable and as easily contrasted, and it is not hard to see their reflection of their regional American cultures. It is not hard, either, to make similar recognition of well-documented ethnic-minority communities and their reflected cultures in some other instances. The Spanish–New Mexican culture of the Southwest is mirrored faithfully in such a village as the El Cerrito of Leonard and Loomis, lineal descendant of the Castillian *pueblo*, the centered wheat-village of Spain; the Mormon village of Nelson, descendant of the New England town out of upstate Yankee New York, has already been cited, if its palpable miniaturizing of the Mormon culture is not yet fully spelled out. The Cajun line-village, blood descendant of northern French line-villages of France and Canada, is less well known, beyond Smith's references. This is because the Cajun culture itself is as yet unstudied, though the very form of the line-village would suggest that the *famille souche* way of life that Miner found in St. Denis would hardly fall out of an association with this community which marks the French and their children from Normandy to the bayou country. These minority ethnic communities and cultures of the United States are not unpredictable. It is rather to other cultures or subcultures of the "majority" population of the country that we should turn. With them we enter upon scenes less well stereotyped, where our thesis that communities microcosm cultures gets a stiffer test.

Crossroads hamlets and Main Street towns. Very much less known are the cultural derivation and continuation, and the communities, of the great American middle country. The American historian Wertenbaker, referred to earlier, reminds us that the Middle Colonies were just that. They were ethnically neither New England Yankee (English Puritan) nor Southern Cavalier. They were Swedish, Dutch, Quaker English, Welsh, Pennsylvania German, Scots-Irish, and many mixtures of these elements. From the Middle Colonies, too, came two new regions: the Middle West, recipient of streams from all three distinctive seaboard colonial sections but by-and-large continuant of the adjacent Middle Colonies rather than of off-center New England and the South, and the Middle or Appalachian Frontier.

These two new regions, in a historical order the reverse of our naming them here, were the first American regions to stand clear, to rise out of mixture and to shape new and free conditions. They remain distinct today. Any list of American regions must count them in, though the names are various. The best recent treatment of regional cultures still lists them as the Appalachian-Ozark region (i.e., the better-known Hill South) and the Cornbelt. But under any name they must be treated as the full-fledged and distinctive regional cultures that they are. Again, like the original Middle Colonies, that seedbed of mixture that parented them, they still call their majority members by the only possible name: "Americans." Other older regions, where mixture was less, have their own names for such majority members, reminiscent of some degree of common ethnic origin: "Yankees" and "Southerners" of "English ancestry." The majority members of the regions Frontier and Midwest have no such ease in naming themselves. They are only "Americans," not "English stock," except in mix, but as often children of Scots, Welsh, Irish, Germans, Scandinavians, Slavs, Latins, and the endless other inwanderers since. Only the common name will do. The culture that united and unites under that name the diverse minorities of the great Atlantic migration was a local emergent from such mix, and it still must be recognized in three versions: Middle Colonial (now called Middle Atlantic), Frontier (now Appalachian), and Middlewestern.

Are there, then, three American communities to match these three American cultures of the preindustrial past? Are there three, or more, community forms common to our joint national experience of the United States palpably different from the New England town and the Southern county? Indeed there are. They are dealt with often enough in the literature, both scientific and popular, but they have not been recognized for what they are. Only when we put our comparative tests to work and ask about comparative uses of persons, space, time, function, and form do we see that the differences from New England and Southern experience which we all know mark Middle Atlantic, Appalachian, and Middlewestern life are systematic and thus cultural. Only then do we see that our common experience reflects identifiable community forms, not yet recognized comparatively, and that these forms, like those of the town and the county cited so far, faithfully give body to units of their regional cultures.

First of all, there is the matter of the community's use of space. These three regions, a parent and two offspring, share in common their patterns of dispersal and assemblage, facts better known under the rubric "settlement pattern." The distinctively American settlement pattern, an "open-country neighborhood" (*Einzelhofsiedlung*), marks all three of these regions as it does *not* the Plantation South and New England. Whence came this new, now all-American pattern? Before cultural anthropology flourished, it was all too easy to derive such patterns of land use from the necessities of the frontier, or the rational plans of colonizers and land speculators, or the workings of individual ownership and republican ideals. Cultural anthropology, however, teaches us that we must look for the native covert custom and value that underlie such necessities and rationalities. The human mind (perhaps always) works with some prior experience in adapting to new conditions, not in a vacuum, and it needs some experience other than pure logic to rationalize. Just as it was all too easy to assume, till we learned its Swedish derivation, that the log cabin was a "natural" adaptation to the frontier, so is it all too easy to think this settlement pattern, and the communities which came of it, was "naturally" and not culturally given.

The truth of the matter, however, is cultural. The Middle Atlantic region received as its pioneer settlers, of all those who came to the colonies, the very immigrants who already practiced not village or plantation life but *Einzelhof* dispersal of individual farms. The Dutch, especially the Frisians, already put individual farms on polder plots at home. The Pennsylvania "Dutch" (Palatinate, Swiss, Rhenish, and Westfalian) brought individual *Grossbauer* family farms of mixed, intensive agriculture with them from their homelands to fill up the Appalachian valley floors from the Delaware seaboard to the Susquehanna and thence south up the Shenandoah. And the Scots-Irish, that new English-speaking mix of Celts arising in Ulster and the English frontier in Ireland, a group without a name (except "Orangemen" or "Presbyterian") till William Cullen Bryant invented one here for them in 1870, filled up the mountainsides and the forest coves and clearings beyond the English and Quaker towns, farm by farm, with a few cows and a saddle bag of corn seed, from New Hampshire to the Great Smokies, in a New World repetition of the same Celtic dispersed-farm cattle-and-kitchen-garden agriculture that marks Irish small farms and Scots crofts to this day.

Certainly the Revolutionary Land Grants to soldiers and the later Homestead Acts rationalized and generalized open-country individual farm settlement on the Frontier and in the Old Northwest that soon became a mere "Middle," but the pattern was already laid down in the Middle Colonies. Yankees went to the frontier in wagon trains, to planned villages, and Southerners, some of them, to plantations and county seats cut from the virgin woods, but the Midlanders did neither.

They went singly, family by family, into the lands they cleared simply by accretion of farms into "neighborhoods." Their first communities were mere crossroads where scattered neighbors met. Their schools and churches and stores, like their camp meetings and their fairs, were set haphazardly in the open country or where roads met, with no ordered clustering and no fixed membership. But this "pioneer community" is no accident, no "natural" growth of the American frontiers, not even of "isolation" and sparse population. For those who know comparative cultures its Old World origin is plain, and this supposedly "natural," "primitive" pattern is as culturally distinctive and complete as any other.

In such communities the settlers' unit of government, like their point of assemblage, was no town nor *any* fixed place. It was instead a rural "township" or several such diffuse authorities. It was not a single centering but instead a fluid crisscrossing net of emergent countrysides and cantons, variously linking farms in overlapping paths among spreading neighbors, kindred, and fellow-sectarians, about crossroad hamlets or open grounds of infrequent gathering. Even today in the Middle country, from New Jersey to the Rockies, this is the older community form in the countryside, and it persists among the farms despite the growth of towns, burgs, counties, and service centers, marks of later urban consolidation. Even today, in the middle country, the townsman is a separate creature, with no place or vote in the countryside, just as the farmer, chief support of Main Street though he be, is not a citizen of the burg he patronizes but lives and votes beyond the corporate boundaries of the town. Here, in all the middle country, the centered town, either as county seat or as residence of farmers, New England style, is an afterthought. The older communities were the open-country neighborhoods.

Now this sort of community, a rural network of relationships running across countrysides and cantons, round occasional and ephemeral centers of assemblage at shrine or fair or crossroads hamlet, this origin of open-country neighborhoods and townships without urban centering, is honestly come by. As a heritage of culture form it is not unique in the world. To the cultural anthropologist who brings Atlantic Europe into his ken it is very familiar. This is the settlement pattern, community form and cantonal rural republican social organization that marks the fringe of the Atlantic from the Berber country north through "wet Spain" and the Basque and Celtic lands to West Britain, Scotland, and Scandinavia. It is the very community which marked the lands whence the Middle Colonists, so many if not all of them, came. Far older in Europe than the open-field village, or the pueblo, the *latifundium,* and the *municipio,* it is no wonder that its recrudescence and generalization in the English-language cultures' spread across the continent should seem to gentle-folk or pious townsmen a reversion to the primitive. But a submerged culture pattern is not lost, nor is it by reason of submergence any the less capable of further growth. On the Frontier, in the Appalachian region, this community reflected well till just the other day the mostly Scots-Irish-derived culture. Loose, open, Dionysian, kin-based, *famille-souche,* and subsistence farming-rather than commercial- or urban-minded, egalitarian through isolation and personal honor rather than through conscience and congregational control, this culture and this community were and are a match. Both are age-long Atlantic European heritages which Americans have not lost and are not likely to lose in the future. This community, like this culture, is as different from either the town or the county we have already named as is sober Saxon different from wild Scot in the British homeland or Andalusian and Gallego in Spain.

When the settled towns did come to the American frontier, as they had come not so long before to the Atlantic European frontiers, they did not change the community forms of the three Middle cultures of the United States out of hand. The new communities that still exist in the Middle Colonies and the Hill South and the Middle West built around urban centers are neither free of the ethnic traditions of those colonies nor deeply planted in older urbanism like the cities that grew up in New England and the Deep South. There has been no final supplanting of this Atlantic-European dispersed-settlement cultural tradition but rather a mingling and borrowing of traits, in which the older traditions have been deepened and transformed. The Hillman and the Midwesterner are not gone, nor are they likely to disappear, and the different continuities they represent back to pre-Roman, pre-German, pre-Christian Atlantic Europe are nonetheless great because anthropology has just barely come to search for them. When today Zimmerman and Du Wors report Middlewestern Cornbelt and Great Plains towns seeking newer industrial and civic forms, commercializing and abandoning the open countryside for in-town residence, the anthropological reader stands before a further cultural succession and adaptation not yet known in any form, transforming an older "Middle America" still little understood.

In all this, however, we must not neglect the great transformations of internal and continuing cultural evolution. New cultures have overtaken the United States, and new cultures, like old ones, must be expected to show in new communities new organization. The cultures and communities of the social organism called the U.S.A. are no longer confined by any means to those brought by the original settlers of either seacoast or frontier.

The great transformations of the industrial revolution, which ushered in our first great new cultural age, brought also a new community. Naturally, if a community microcosms a culture, then so does a cultural revolution bring along as well a revolution in community form, if the correspondence of the two is to keep pace. That such a new community form struck the United States, beginning in New England and spreading slowly west and south, we already know. It remains only to show how the mill town and factory city, which long ago first supplanted and still continue to supplant the New England town, the Southern county seat, and the open-country neighborhoods and crossroads hamlets of older America, are in fact small and big exemplars of a new community form.

Here, of course, I follow the trail that Mumford (1937) blazed. He showed graphically the huge revolution in living, in cultural and social organization, that the cities of factory and slum brought in. Park and Burgess went on to show us the form within the outward formlessness of Chicago, the railroad city of concentric zones and dynamic succession and decay, the American industrial city in its heyday of 1905. Later in the early thirties when Lynd went to an American "Middletown" it was to such an industrial town, and when Warner and his students gave us Yankee City and Natchez and Jonesville, in New England, South, and Middle West, it was still to mill towns that they went. For mill towns had invaded and transformed all the older communities, just as the Coal and Iron Age sooted up the older rural culture-horizons.

What, then, is a mill town, a factory city, as community form? First, it is a new and distinctive use of space. The new slum-building ("industrial blight"), and the other dynamic succession-and-withdrawal patterns of land and building use in industrial cities, are perfectly lawful and formal patterns, congruent and coincident with the monetarization and the commercialization of the cultural age of the free market and the laissez-faire capitalism they represent. The mill town, born in Britain, has spread, in greater or lesser conjunction with these other patterns of its age, like any other culture wave. It has spread out and around the world for a century and a half, and it is only now in recession and change. In U.S.A. the same mill towns (standard Midwestern American calls them "factory town") web from New England, whence the New England flavor of their name. Mill towns are dying as captured satellites of a still newer metropolitan community form in the homeland, while they win new territory in continuous diffusion into the Southern and Southwestern and Appalachian regions. In all these spreads and migrations the mill-town forms are constant despite accidents of local circumstance and graft to former patterns.

This use of space is telltale. Far from being merely chaotic and lawless, the "unplanned" form the early industrial cities of America took was a new and distinctive (if unlovely) community form. The new use of space gives us the typical banded and stratified zonal ordering of better and better houses from the slums in the industrial valley, on Water Street and River Street, down by the docks or behind the railroad yards, up to the massed squires' houses on the Hill.

This use of space bands and zones the middle-class dwellings and the middle-class shops in the middle and crams the mills and the warehouses and the industrial warrens of factory workers and immigrant hands in the narrow blighted bottoms which once were the marketplaces and the crossroads of the older towns. It creates a new assemblage center in the railroad station and the "downtown center" about it and a new pattern of withdrawal whereby the same railroad or the avenues —pushing out the "Main Line"—put the better-off and higher occupations of the common factories on which all depend in progressively farther removed residential blocks. It makes visible in external display these graded and successive zones of better or worse neighborhoods and mirrors perfectly an open-class system's scalar stratification of incomes, of power, and of prestige in the zonal successions one sees moving inward from withdrawn garden suburb to blighted tenement district.

The once-new mill town's use of time is of a pattern with this use of space. The commutation lines of streetcar and train and the staggered hours of arrival at work, like the loss of play space and park space to mills, yards, and streets, and the sharp separation of work and leisure, spell out in space and time a community tuned to the factory whistle, stratified according to him who obeys it and him who orders it blown, and united about the mill and its livelihood for worker and owner alike. The mill town is the community of the Victorian industrial age, and it is so much with us, especially in memory and survival, that we need hardly spell it out further. But it is also a community form in perfect harmony with the layered, visible, and pecuniary stratification of its age, with the fluid dynamism of its progressive exhaustion and befouling of an environment which in its heyday, as we now know from a hundred commentators, its people treated first and foremost as a workshop for their machines. It is no wonder, then, that the "open-class system" (or the six-class system, if you prefer Warner) and the "pecuniary civilization" should have a distinctive community form in the mill town and its succession, its blight, and its mechanical massing of visible likes and unlikes.

But the once-new mill town and the sooty, cluttered Pittsburghs and Birminghams of a proud Victorian industrial age are no longer young. They are things in transformation, and a new age, with a new community, has fast supplanted them in its turn. On a hundred fronts the

new age of the automobile, of the branch factory with the career manager, of the metropolitan mass-communication city and suburb, of the
leveling of incomes and proliferating of "peer groups" and equalized
consumptive standards, of the "building back" and clearance of slums
and huge desertion of the downtown cities for the Levittowns and highway shopping centers and "rurban fringes" of midcentury, comes relentlessly on. The new age is perhaps easiest to see in the new cities and
suburbs built since the automobile, like Los Angeles, and hardest to
accept in the blighted and abandoned industrial cities of yesteryear.
But all the voices agree that it has come.

The new community that corresponds to the newest age is much less
understood or even perceived. Yet there is a good deal of writing about
it that gives us some evidence of the new form the new metropolitan
community has taken or will take. The difficulty is to see the new form
whole, rather than in disconnected pieces, and for that, as before, a
model must serve.

What are the pieces, then, that we must fit into such a comprehensive
model? First, as always, there is the matter of use of space. The new
metropolitan community, first charted by McKenzie, is the circle of
one and a half to two hours commuting by car from the old downtown
railroad center of the city, from which the new mass communications
of newspapers, radio, and television now radiate. The various metropolitan district devices and authorities in evolution today, for water,
parks, belt highway, and port controls, seem to be political attempts
to cope with the metropolis of this huge area and population. With
numbers divided in many cases nearly half and half between the outer
ring of once independent suburban and satellite settlements and the
inner city, neither suburb nor core city will give up the jealous independence of the last century. (New York has not expanded its city's
official boundaries since 1895, three generations ago.) Only some new
over-arching authority can match the new city form.

Within this huge metropolitan space, the new supercity is struggling
to take the form of a great wheel of internal traffic arteries and peripheral
belts. New factories appear in the empty fields on the outer fringe,
where highways and belt roads serve them better than any railroads,
and new dormitory suburbs mushroom to bring workers to them or to
move workers and white-collars, now less distinguishable, into greener
quarters and automotive mobility. At the nodes between artery and belts,
between spokes and rims of the great new urban wheel-form, huge
new shopping centers arise which duplicate in all particulars, except
the centering of mass communications for the whole itself, the erstwhile
downtown congestions of traffic, shopping, business, and entertainment.
This is the great decentralized city of the automotive age, and no

planning can reverse its evolution, just as no plans which belie its form, from traffic roads to slum clearance, can do more than delay or impede its taking its characteristic shape.

In the great and small segments of the huge circle that artery and belt highways cut out, a new urban life—better, a new suburban one —is already well emerged. This is the life of the "peer groups" of the "lonely crowd" which Riesman rightly sees. It is a huge mosaic of massed segregations of age, class, and ethnic group. Because older with-drawn suburbs, new real-estate developments of massed conformity, enclaved factory satellite towns, old slums and factories, and built-back reclaimed areas are all grown together now and stand contiguous in the unbroken urban-suburban expanse, little remains of the old grada-tions and transitions between house type and house type and class and class. The old graduated concentric zones of the industrial city are fast disappearing. The mosaic that takes their place is a crazy-quilt of discontinuities, where the fault-line between toney garden suburb and Levittown or rich Sutton Place and squalid Dead End is abrupt, sud-den, and hostile, sometimes even policed with a guard or marked by a ten-foot fence. It is no wonder that the persons who grow up in such juxtapositions see nothing of the community pattern as a whole, no longer have intimate connection with and reference toward ordered groups a little "better" or a little "worse" than themselves, but turn inward instead to the welter of their peer-group segregations.

This mosaic of discontinuities of age, class, and ethnicity which is the new metropolitan community is a very different one indeed from the visibly hierarchic and mobile community that preceded it. It is not for us here to explore its new features; the subject is doubly difficult because so few people, in or out of social science, have yet learned to look at the metropolitan city whole. Nevertheless, the new cultural form, with its new social and economic traits and problems, is here be-fore us, in the most violent emergence, and the new age has already found its new unit of transmission and organization.

RECAPITULATION

Enough has been said, in a short paper, to document for the United States a perception that is emerging from comparative ethnological re-search wherever community studies have been carried out. For every American regional (sub-)culture that we can distinguish in American society and civilization, a particular form of the community is to be found. The ones we have spelled out here, each one quite different according to the measures that serve for all communities, are, as they have been often treated by novelists and historians, quite viable microcosms of the cultures whose *florebat* they graced: the New England town, the southern county, the open-country neighborhood and cross-roads hamlet of the Atlantic region, the frontier and the Appalachians, the Main Street "service-center" (so the sociologists call what Mid-westerners know as "a burg"), the Mormon village, the mill town, the metropolitan conglomeration. We have not touched them all; conspicuously absent is the California city of the communities of the factories-in-the-field, with the neat two-class separation of the bungalows of Caucasian overseers and members of the Associated Farmers and the Hoovervilles of the successive migratory laborers, an agricultural factory town well known round the plantation world of commerce overseas. But we have touched the significant majority, and we have answered the question with which we began.

There is in the United States a form of the community for every recognized American culture. Certainly here and perhaps everywhere the correlation of community and culture is one to one.

25. CULTURE CHANGE *

Archeological evidence indicates that, since its obscure origins in the remote past, culture has had the chronic experience of change. Even more, we know that changes in every culture are sometimes local in origin (the result of discoveries and inventions), sometimes introduced from the outside. Whether the change represents the accommodation of one or a few new elements introduced without conspicuous plan or coercion (the whole process known as diffusion) or whether it is the adaptation of one culture to the coercive demands of another (acculturation), the actual situation is likely to follow a complicated course in which the new elements are received, rejected or altered according to the interaction of a large number of variables.
This selection epitomizes some concrete situations of change and the theory which has been developed to handle such phenomena.

As PART of the programme of Section H (Anthropology) at the Dundee Meeting of the British Association in 1947, it was decided to invite a number of papers from social anthropologists dealing with different aspects of culture change among non-European peoples whose ways of life are being profoundly modified by the impact of Western industrial civilisation. It was possible in this way to bring together an exposition and illustration of an important trend in studies in social anthropology which has been developing considerably both before and since the war.

Extended summaries of the four papers, presented at this session of the Section's meetings on September 1, are printed below. Dr. Richards' paper sets out the historical background, practical inducements and theoretical considerations relevant to advances in this field, and Dr. Mair illustrates by an analysis of changes in African land tenure the way in which fundamental generalisations are being reached through com-

* Daryll Forde (editor), "Culture Change: Report of a Colloquium," *The Advancement of Science*, No. 17 (1948), pp. 48–55. Reprinted by permission of the editor, authors, and publisher. The component reports follow without introductory comment.

372

parative studies. Dr. Little and Professor C. von Fürer-Haimendorf illustrate the nature and complexity of the factors involved in cultural change as revealed in studies of West African and Indian peoples among whom they have worked.

CULTURE CHANGE AND THE DEVELOPMENT OF
ANTHROPOGICAL THEORY

By Dr. A. I. Richards *

Most students of human society, whatever their avowed objective, do, in fact, spend much of their time investigating processes of culture change. A people's culture is, by definition, their traditional heritage, but nevertheless their organised activities, their beliefs, their social structure and their artefacts are constantly subject to change. A culture reacts to a physical environment, to contacts with other cultures, and to the working of its own institutions which may be designed expressly to produce or facilitate change. To treat culture as a static phenomenon is a mere heuristic device.

Social scientists, however, differ in their interests and methods. The archæologist, the historian, or the sociologist who wishes to trace the evolution of social forms, may select long periods of time in which to study the sequence of events and, as a result, may be able to frame general laws as to the nature of social change. The economist concentrates on variations in one special sphere of human activities. The anthropologist is reputedly concerned with static societies, small isolated communities in which change takes place so slowly that it is almost invisible and for which there are no written records of the past. Yet, paradoxically enough, the very nature of his material has led him to formulate a number of hypotheses as to culture change which could not easily have been made by any other type of social scientist, and which may prove to be amongst his most important contributions to our knowledge of social laws.

Anthropologists first began to interest themselves in culture change as the result of the methods they were forced to evolve for the reconstruction of the history of peoples for which no written or other records exist. But, as a by-product of this historical work, came a series of generalisations as to the processes of the 'diffusion' of traits from one culture to another. Graebner, Wissler, Dixon, Kroeber and others were in fact

* Audrey I. Richards (b. 1899), teaches anthropology at Cambridge University and was formerly Director, East African Institute of Social Research, Makarere College, Kampala, Uganda. She has done considerable fieldwork, particularly in East Africa. Among her books are *Hunger and Work in a Savage Tribe* (1932), *Land, Labour and Diet in Northern Rhodesia* (1939), and *Chisungu: A Study of Girl's Initiation Ceremonies in Northern Rhodesia* (1956). Dr. Richards is also the editor of *Economic Development and Tribal Change* (1954).

attempting to frame laws of culture contact, as was Rivers when he tried to classify different types of contact situations and the changes likely to be produced by the contact of superior and inferior peoples, or between groups of greater or less size. A large part of the anthropological teaching given in Universities twenty-five years ago was devoted to this type of study of culture change.

A new series of generalisations as to culture contact resulted from a shift in the theoretical interests of anthropologists during the twenties. More detailed field-studies and deeper sociological analysis made the older type of diffusion work seem artificial and mechanical. Malinowski began to publish the results of an intensive study of one particular community. He urged anthropologists to investigate primitive tribes as units actually functioning under present-day conditions and not as reflections of their own past history. Such an approach naturally focussed attention on the observation of changes going on in individual cultures whether through contact with other people or through other forces. Malinowski himself worked in a part of Melanesia in which society was, relatively speaking, stable, but a number of his pupils did their field-work in African communities which were being subjected to particularly powerful European influences. It was inevitable that they should turn their attention to the study of such changes and to describe the disruptive effects of western administration and industrialisation on African political, economic and family life. The practical importance of such investigations became apparent to the administrator in colonial areas and increased the demand for such work.

Malinowski's main theoretical contribution was a functional analysis of culture into a series of interrelated aspects, and this scheme he later adapted to form the basis of a more dynamic type of study of culture contact by which it would be possible to trace the series of related changes which would follow the introduction into a primitive society of, for instance, a new political organisation, a new creed, or a new cash crop. He pointed out that anthropologists working in situations of rapid change could not afford to limit themselves to the study of the native community only. The behaviour of the white administrator or missionary were as much a part of the 'total contact situation' as the native himself. Gluckman used the same concept in an analysis of a modern social situation in Zululand, and Kuper has described the whole of the social structure of the Swazi and their system of rank as part of the whole white-black structure of Swaziland and the Union of South Africa.

Anthropologists began to adopt new techniques suited to the investigation of changing communities. They tried in the first instance to contrast conditions before and after European contact, or to search as Dr.

Mair has described it, for 'a zero point' from which to reckon such changes. They illustrated changing social forms by selecting sample communities which had been more or less in contact with white civilisation. They began to use statistical methods to estimate the variations in behaviour of groups and individuals which are bound to be characteristic of a change situation. They collected village, family and individual case-histories, and made comparisons of the behaviour of different generations.

Anthropologists have been accused of neglecting their scientific work for the sake of doing studies of practical importance to the administrator, such as land-tenure, or urban surveys, but it is a mistake to put 'scientific' and 'practical' work in opposition, as is sometimes done. The application of anthropological knowledge follows the detailed scientific investigation; it does not precede it or do away with it. Moreover, it is as possible to write a scientific article on the position of the urban African as it is to write an unscientific one on totemism among the Australian aboriginees. A number of generalisations as to the processes which result from contact between European and primitive civilisations have been made as well as practical recommendations. Firth suggested, on the basis of Maori material, that there was a rhythm in the acceptance of the new culture, first an eager reception of European goods and ideas, then a rejection with a corresponding idealisation of the past. Chinnery and others have described the appearance of religious cults and revivalist movements as a reaction to the superior culture, Schapera suggests that where Christianity comes in contact with primitive religious and magic systems the religious elements such as ancestor worship go, while the magic remains. The Wilsons have devoted a book to the enunciation of general laws as to the changes produced by contact between small and large-scale societies.

American anthropologists have protested on the other hand that their English colleagues are pre-occupied with culture contact in a very narrow sense; that is to say the reaction between European, and mainly between British, and primitive peoples. Herskovits and Redfield and others have differentiated between the process of 'acculturation' that takes place between two peoples long in contact with each other, and 'culture contact' as used to describe the first stages of such a process. Redfield has studied Mexican communities, where Spanish, Indian and American cultures exist side by side, and Herskovits the mixed cultures of Haiti and Trinidad. Evans-Pritchard has advocated similar widening of the field by the inclusion of Mohammedan-pagan contacts in Africa. Firth has recently argued that the changes produced in primitive society by western industrialisation can be parallelled in Malaya, China, India and other regions where there are peasant societies not usually regarded as

primitive. He suggests in fact that anthropologists should concern themselves with primitive and peasant peoples all over the world and that
they should abandon the term 'culture contact' for the wider concept of
'culture change.'

The new situation is one that needs some examination. Some anthropologists claim to study all peoples and not only those that are reckoned
as 'primitive'; all realise that there are now very few peoples left who
are quite out of touch with our own industrial civilisation. The anthropologist will increasingly need the help of social scientists accustomed
to working in modern communities if he is to complete his picture of a
total contact situation. He is already using many of their statistical and
other techniques. Has the anthropologist then no further contribution
to make to the study of culture change? Having thrown up a number of
subjects for investigation must he now retire from the field and declare
that the situation is too complex for him to handle with his own tools?

I believe that, on the contrary, the anthropologist's contribution to
the study of social change is likely to be greater rather than less during
the next decade. The intensive analysis of particular small scale cultures
gives us the habit of examining the total sequence of changes produced
by the introduction for instance of a cash crop or a new form of education, and to examine them in every aspect of social life. This tradition
and its accompanying techniques will still, I think, produce a number
of hypotheses as to cultural process which no other type of material is
likely to yield. Again, the variety of small cultures we have had to study
has led us to do some, at any rate, of the pioneer work in the field of
culture change, and it still gives us the widest range of contact situations
on which to base general laws. In fact I think it likely that one of our
most fruitful fields of work in the future will be the study of the differential reactions of primitive peoples to contact with the same agents of
change, or to similar processes such as urbanisation. Benedict, Kardiner,
Linton and others have tried to account for these differential reactions
in terms of differing personality structures, but comparisons on the basis
of structural variation and an examination of the basic institutions in
each culture have not yet been systematically developed.

Anthropologists have also the tradition of direct observation of human behaviour in small groups—families, households or villages—and
it is on such observations that finer generalisations as to individual reactions to change must be based, and the very important process of the
education in new values observed. This is a type of data that the historian
has rarely had available in discussing change. Small scale studies of
the institutional background and formalised morals of a people should
prove a basis for psychological investigations of the individual reactions,

and often of the individual maladjustments which are a phenomenon of rapid social change.

CHANGES IN AFRICAN LAND TENURE

By Dr. L. P. Mair *

Customary African land rights were appropriate to a subsistence economy in which land is the basis of existence and therefore cannot be profitably exchanged for any other commodity. With rare exceptions there was ample land available in circumstances where no one wished to cultivate crops other than food crops. Cultivation was shifting; where whole villages were periodically moved, permanent rights could not be established. Otherwise permanent rights of occupation existed over areas large enough to include both cultivated and fallow.

Everyone had a claim for land to cultivate in virtue of his membership of some community. Either he obtained an allocation from the territory of his lineage or it was allotted to him by a chief in return for political allegiance. His rights usually passed to his heirs. Land surplus to the needs of the group could be granted to an outsider, subject to the prior claim in case of need of a member of the group; but this was never a commercial transaction. The principles characteristic of most systems were that every cultivator had recognised rights over a given area of land, which passed to his heirs, but the community, through its representatives, had the right to be consulted if rights were to be created in favour of non-members.

Early European observers thought there could be no security of tenure without full ownership. It is true that there might be political insecurity due to the arbitrary action of chiefs, but there was no economic insecurity in the absence of economic competition. Occasionally the assertion of customary rights has been an obstacle to the planting of permanent crops, but more often custom has adapted itself.

In modern conditions land has acquired an economic value as a scarce commodity. It has also become negotiable for cash. The development of a commercial attitude to land has been stimulated by the general tendency to substitute cash payments for gifts in kind in any situation where custom demands that a gift be made. Such gifts come to be regarded as payment; the harvest gift of the tenant comes to be assimilated to a rent payment.

* Lucy P. Mair (b. 1901) teaches anthropology at the London School of Economics. A specialist in applied anthropology, Dr. Mair has done a great deal of fieldwork in Africa, particularly among the Baganda. Her books include, *An African People in the Twentieth Century* (1934), *Native Marriage in Buganda* (1940), and *Studies in Applied Anthropology* (1957).

A comment which might be made on the process of culture change in general is that the conservative force of tradition is not proof against the attraction of economic advantage, if that advantage is sufficient and is clearly recognised. Of course it does not follow that the resultant changes are necessarily to the general benefit.

Nowadays individuals are prepared to offer money for the exercise of rights in land because they hope to turn those rights to profit in terms of money. They may formally approach the heads of a land-holding group in the traditional manner, but it is recognised on both sides that the group is surrendering its rights. From this it is a short step to open sale.

Complementary to these individuals are those who need money and find in the surrender of land rights a way to meet the need. The method is usually to pledge their land, a transaction recognised by African custom in case of a debt incurred, for example, in order to pay a fine. To-day there are many more opportunities for getting into debt, and the debts incurred are heavier. Gold Coast cocoa farmers established in prosperous times a standard of living that in most years they cannot hope to maintain without borrowing. They do so by pledging their land for money loans at exorbitant interest. Though it is true that progressive farmers need credit, the amount that has been raised to improve the land must be a small proportion of total African indebtedness.

It is now profitable for an individual to cultivate a much larger area of land, and he can do so by ploughing or by employing labour. Those persons who have the authority to allot the land of the group can acquire rights of occupancy over large areas by encroaching on the reserve that should be maintained for future expansion. Another method is for an individual to redeem an area pledged by a group and assert sole rights over it.

Tenants are now really insecure, partly for economic reasons—a man is sometimes evicted just when he has planted up his land with a commercial crop—and partly through the assertion of prior claims by a member of the land-holding group. In the Kikuyu reserves a young man who has grown up in the settled area and decides not to become a labour tenant must return to the reserve and find a holding on the land of the group to which he is related. If a tenant who has succeeded his father and grandfather on his holding is evicted for this reason, he may well feel that he is the long-established occupier who is turned out for a stranger.

Every position of economic privilege is tending to become a private perquisite rather than a position of trust. Many privileges of African chiefs have been curtailed in order to prevent abuses of power. But the ultimate right over land still rests with them, and to remove that would be to remove one of the most important sources of their authority. Yet this right can become a means of abuse in modern conditions.

Changes in African land tenure have been in line with the general response to increased opportunities of economic gain, but those advantages are at first perceived only by the minority and the result is an inadequate adaptation to new conditions.

A STUDY OF MODERN SOCIAL CHANGE IN A WEST AFRICAN COMMUNITY

By Dr. K. L. Little *

In the Sierra Leone Protectorate, as in other parts of West Africa, the prestige of the European and of European civilisation is very great. Its material aspects, in the shape of manufactured goods, housing, etc., offer powerful incentives of a social as well as economic kind to the native people. But there are few ways of satisfying such ambitions except in clerical or some other form of employment for which a European education is required. Farm-work provides a young man with little more than his keep, and even senior posts in the Native Administrations compare unfavourably with a job in Government service or with one of the mercantile firms. The urge towards literacy constitutes, therefore, a fundamental factor in the social changes described below.

In the process of acculturation, two additional sections of Sierra Leone society—the African Creole and the European—have also to be taken into account. The Creoles, who are descended from the original settlers of Freetown and the Colony, have always emulated western habits, and in the present situation they fulfil a special role as cultural media owing to the social distance which separates the ordinary European official from the African community. In the field of inter-personal relations, the Creole missionary, clerk, trader, and teacher supplies a code of etiquettes, and sets a standard of social attainment, which in spending power, educational accomplishments, and mannerisms is approximately intermediate to that of the Europeans and the native people of the Protectorate. It would appear that every native individual undergoes a certain amount of 'creolisation,' i.e. the process of taking on Creole customs, once he begins to disassociate himself from tribal life. The tendency shows itself in a variety of ways, including social selection and adoption of the Creole *patois*, and the general process takes place within a context of group consciousness and resistance from the parties concerned. There is a certain amount of antipathy between the Creoles as a group and natives of the Protectorate who are literate, and between

* Kenneth L. Little (b. 1908) is an anthropologist at the London School of Economics. He has worked in Africa and in his own culture, specializing in the Mende and in race relations. Among his books are *Negroes in Britain* (1947), *The Mende of Sierra Leone* (1951), and *Race and Society* (1952).

literate and illiterate Protectorate people. Attitudes also vary reciprocally between the Europeans and the various sections of the African community.

Indeed, social differences between the groups concerned are sufficient for 'European,' 'Creole,' 'Literate Native,' and 'Illiterate Native' to be regarded as the labels of four fairly distinct classes. These are marked off from each other by various forms and degrees of social distance, the most obvious of which is the residential separation of the 'European' and the deference paid to it by the rest of society. Moreover, the fact that the classes in question are esteemed according to their possession of appropriate educational, occupational, and other traits means that they can be arranged in order of social precedence. For example, the 'European' class, by virtue of its political position and the prestige attached to European customs, is in hierarchical control of the system as a whole. Membership of the classes is to be adjudged on the basis of the individuals composing them, having similarity of occupation, wealth, and education, similar modes of life, a similar stock of ideas, feelings, attitudes, and a feeling of belonging to one group.

Thus, most members of the 'Creole' class have attended a secondary school. Occupationally, they are found in the higher grades of the Government clerical service, or are senior schoolmasters, factors for the European firms, or members of the clergy. Christianity is usually practised. On the whole, relatively few Protectorate-born persons fulfil these criteria. Class consciousness is felt mainly as appreciation of the superior standard of living which the individuals concerned enjoy over the rest of the African community, and in their greater knowledge of the 'correct' way to behave socially. The men wear European clothes on all occasions, and evening dress for dances. The women usually wear a head tie and print frock during the day time and on most week days. On Sundays, a silk dress with hat and stockings are worn; 'long' frocks are *de rigeur* for dances.

The 'Literate Native' class consists in the broadest sense of every other African who has been to school, or can speak English with reasonable proficiency. It is sociologically inclusive not only of the majority of educated Protectorate people, but also of the lesser educated, less wealthy Creole. To a large extent, it is 'Protectorate conscious,' but literate Protectorate-born people and the Creole who moves with them meet, in some respects, on common ground in relation to the illiterate and tribal group. The upper stratum of this class includes junior clerks in Government service, members of the staff of the railway, artisans, motor drivers, and male and female nurses. It includes Moslems as well as Christians, and marriages are polygamic and monogamic. The lower stratum comprises individuals in clerical employment outside the Government, such as assistants to Syrian traders, and tailors, and the permanent but non-clerical staff of Government departments. General behaviour is much more on traditional lines.

Members of this class still retain a close connection with tribal affairs in some cases, and their help and advice are often sought.

Inclusion of the illiterate people as a class within the system is justified on the grounds that it is out of their ranks that the 'Literate Native' class is recruited. In addition, they are clearly characterised as a social class by similarity in occupation, which is farming, in traditional and tribal custom, in a lower standard of living than the rest of society and, to some extent, in consciousness of themselves both as a cultural and social group.

The hierarchical system thus described indicates the dynamic factors at work in a situation which it is conventional to classify as acculturative, and it also exemplifies the main conditions which appear to accompany the process of social change itself. Briefly, these conditions may be summed up as follows:

1. That an increasing number of individuals no longer acknowledge the tribal controls and other sanctions to which they were formerly subject;
2. that the older values and forms of prestige are being replaced by new ones;
3. that there is a growing tendency for an individual's status and role to be socially assessed with reference to society as a whole, rather than to the particular kindred or lineage to which he belongs; and
4. that the kind of relations which individuals whose living is gained by some European form of occupation have with each other is giving rise to a type of social structure which is based on social class rather than kin.

THE ABORIGINAL PROBLEM IN HYDERABAD STATE

By Professor C. von Fürer-Haimendorf *

While the problems of cultural change arising from the impact of western civilisation upon African societies are the subject of a considerable literature, there exist few accounts of the social and economic phenomena resulting from the contact between primitive and advanced communities in the sub-continent of India. Yet cultural change is a cardinal factor in the shaping of the future of twenty-three millions of Indian aboriginals who stand outside the orbit of Hindu and Muslim civilisation. There is, however, one fundamental difference between the

---

* The author (b. 1909) is Professor of Asian Anthropology, School of Oriental and African Studies, University of London. He has done extensive fieldwork in India and adjacent countries. Among his works are *The Naked Nagas* (1939); *The Chenchus* (1943), and *Himalayan Barbary* (1955).

problems of acculturation in India and in Africa. The recent changes in African culture patterns are largely caused by the influence of Europeans on the indigenous societies. In India, on the other hand, most aboriginal tribes have had little direct contact with the exponents of western civilisation and the transformation of their culture and mode of life is largely the result of contact with the more advanced Indian civilisations.

Hyderabad, the premier Indian state, with an aboriginal population of over 250,000, offers a wide range of examples illustrative of the diverse reactions of primitive communities to contacts—both voluntary and enforced—with Hindu and Muslim populations. Here the aboriginals inhabit mainly the hill-tracts and forest-areas situated on the borders of the State along the rivers Kistna and Godavari, regions which until recent years were remote from the centres of civilisation.

The Chenchus of the Amrabad hills on the border of Madras Presidency are a semi-nomadic people of food-gatherers and hunters. In groups of a few families they live in the deciduous forest and subsist on wild jungle produce, such as berries, roots and tubers, and a small amount of game. They dwell in bamboo huts and leaf-shelters, and often camp for weeks under overhanging rocks. For centuries they encountered no other outsiders than the pilgrims journeying to a Hindu temple above the Kistna gorge and the Telugu peasants of nearby plains villages, where they sometimes went to barter jungle produce for iron, salt and cloth. Such contacts were almost entirely voluntary and the Chenchus were free to accept or reject any element of the rustic Hindu civilisation of the plains.

A study of these 'Jungle' Chenchus, who still persist in their old mode of life as food-gathers, reveals that acculturation on a modest scale occurred without a basic readaptation of their economic system or their social organisation. Iron tools, for instance, were introduced to improve established techniques but not to develop new economic activities. Thus digging sticks were furnished with iron spikes and arrows with crude iron heads, iron knives were employed in basket-making and iron axes in the construction of huts and shelters. The borrowed items were fitted into the traditional culture pattern of the Chenchus, but there was no attempt to adopt the plainsmen's method of food production or to imitate their style of housing. The Chenchus seemed content to acquire by barter such products of their neighbours as immediately rewarded existent drives, while through the social interaction involved in this barter they seem to have learnt Telugu, which has completely displaced the older tribal language.

A similar process occurred in the sphere of religion and social custom. Without abandoning essential traditional beliefs, the Chenchus took over certain caste rules such as the taboo on the eating of beef and the attitude towards 'untouchables,' and they adopted the use of cooked rice and turmeric for food offerings. The results of the Chenchus' selectivity in the fields of both economics and ritual were twofold; though using tools produced by more advanced populations they remained on the level of hunters and food-gatherers, but on the other hand, they rose to a fairly high rung in the caste system by conforming to some of the customs of caste Hindus.

Fundamentally different from the voluntary adoption of individual cultural elements in the course of casual trade contacts, was the enforced readaptation of Chenchu culture under the pressure of administrative action. The introduction of forest conservancy and the subsequent commercial exploitation of forests put an end to the Chenchus' freedom to roam the forests and barter their wild produce. In Madras Presidency Chenchus were forcibly concentrated in large settlements and provided with the means of cultivation. But the response was largely negative; very few Chenchus took to plough cultivation, and after nearly half a century of supervision the Chenchus in these settlements continue to depend on the labour and the provisions provided by the Forest Department.

In Hyberabad there was for long little deliberate interference with Chenchu economy. Yet, of themselves, some families began to embark on cattle breeding, keeping a few buffaloes for the sake of their milk and the exchange value of calves. Novel as this occupation was, it did not conflict with their seasonal migrations, and could be added to traditional habits. The scheme for the amelioration of the Chenchus' economic conditions recently introduced by the Hyderabad Government takes into account their unpreparedness for a radical economic readaptation; those still inhabiting the forest have been given a respite through the creation of a Chenchu Reserve, which secures them their hunting and collecting grounds; the collection and sale of forest produce has been organised on co-operative lines and Government has encouraged the breeding of cattle by the free distribution of buffaloes to every family.

Other aboriginal tribes of Hyderabad were faced by the same challenge of contact with advanced populations and have met this challenge in different ways. The Reddis, for instance, a tribe of shifting cultivators in the Eastern Ghats, south of the great Godavari gorge, found their hills surrounded by Telugu peasants almost identical in cultural make-up to the Chenchus' present neighbours. Yet the readjustments in their culture pattern followed a course very different from the acculturation process taking place among the Chenchus. In their old economy the Reddis, too, relied to a certain extent on the gathering of wild jungle produce. But long before they came in touch with Hindu peasants they had learnt to raise food by cultivating millet and pulses on clearings carved from the forest, and by breeding domesticated pigs. Their agricultural methods were primitive—axe, digging-stick, and sickle being their main implements—but the principle of plant raising was firmly established in their culture, and when they encountered the fully developed agricultural civilisation of the Telugu people they realised the advantages of plough and animal-traction and wherever the environment was favourable they effected the transition from shifting cultivation to a settled peasant economy within two or three generations. In this case the innovation of plough-cultivation was readily accepted, because it was aligned with the existent orientation of Reddi culture, and involved an enrichment and not a revolution of the traditional mode of life. Permanent cultivation led in turn to larger and more stable settlements, and these favoured sustained social interaction with neighbouring populations different from the casual trade-contacts of unsettled food-gatherers. But though the Reddis copied certain customs and were anxious to secure specialised goods used by their neighbours, they did not go so far as to learn new crafts or to embrace new occupations; they supplemented their own products by trade and hired specialists from neighbouring groups for activities connected with borrowed rites and ceremonies. A breach in these mutually beneficial relations between the Reddis and the neighbouring peasantry occurred, however, when forest contractors began to employ Reddis as labourers and led them deliberately into economic dependence. This they achieved by fostering the growth of new wants which could be satisfied in no other way than by work for wages. A period of domination by outsiders followed upon the 'benign ethnic relations' of earlier days, but the recent exclusion of forest contractors and the establishment of a cooperative society of aboriginal forest workers under Government control has initiated a new phase, the cultural effects of which are not yet apparent.

In the sphere of religion and ritual the selectivity of Reddi culture could operate without appreciable interference by outsiders with vested interests. The aspects of Hindu ritual adopted by the Reddis are different from those that found acceptance among the Chenchus. The Reddis, familiar with animal sacrifices in honour of the Earth Mother and various hill-deities, readily accepted the bloody sacrifices offered to the mother-goddesses of rustic Telugu civilisation, but the belief in the supreme and benevolent god Bhagavan which the Chenchus share with their Hindu neighbours has as yet found no place in Reddi thought.

Chenchus and Reddis are comparatively small communities which, though persisting until recently in a very primitive economy, succumbed to the linguistic pressure of neighbouring advanced populations and adopted Telugu, at first presumably only for purposes of trade, but ultimately as their only language to the exclusion of their original tribal tongues. The Gonds, on the other hand, who are a branch of the great Gond race and alone in Hyderabad number well over 150,000, have maintained their own language and with it a rich oral literature of myth and legend. Unlike Chenchus and Reddis they have been in touch with Hindu populations for several hundred years, but acculturation occurred only in specific spheres of life. Economically the Gonds have adapted themselves to the system of agriculture prevailing among the other peasant populations of the Deccan and it was only their system of land tenure which retained certain features out of tune with modern conditions. They learnt new skills, such as the blacksmith's art and carpentry, and imitated in style of dress and housing the agricultural castes among their Hindu neighbours. But the influence of Hinduism on religion and social customs remained on the surface. While both Chenchus and Reddis comply with the Hindu taboo on beef-eating, the Gonds sacrifice cows and freely eat beef. They have adopted a number of Hindu feasts, yet their myths refer to Shiva and Parvati in decidedly irreverent terms and in the performance of Hindu rites they show none of the seriousness and religious fervour which characterises the cult of their clan-gods. Social relations within the tribe are ruled by a complicated system of phratries, clans and sub-clans, and there is as yet no sign of Hindu ideas of 'caste' disrupting the fundamental unity of the tribe.

A decline of tribal life set in, however, when outsiders of Hindu and Muslim stock penetrated into Gond country and took possession of part of the cultivable land. Skilfully exploiting the difference between the Gonds' traditional system of land-tenure and the land laws of the State, these settlers were able to oust entire communities from their ancestral lands, and a time of acute conflict between aboriginals and newcomers followed upon the period of peaceful acculturation. Administrative action on the part of H.E.H. the Nizam's Government has succeeded in limiting this conflict and in preventing any further alienation of Gond land. A Gond Education Scheme instituted in 1943, is based on traditional Gond culture and the use of Gondi as medium of instruction in all schools. With the subsequent emergence of Gondi as a written language, and the teaching of Urdu and Marathi in the Gond schools, a new phase in the cultural and social interaction between aboriginals and neighbouring populations has been inaugurated, but it is too early to discern the eventual result of this most recent of acculturation processes.

Cultural changes as observed among the Hyderabad aboriginals exhibit a selectivity of primitive peoples in their borrowing from advanced populations, which accounts for the difference in results when several tribes came in contact with the same dominant civilisation. This selectivity makes it extremely difficult to foretell the outcome of any culture contact and calls for the fullest historical study of individual cases of acculturation.

26. AN ANTHROPOLOGIST LOOKS
AT TECHNICAL ASSISTANCE *

"Underdeveloped nations" is a common journalistic phrase that suggests
countries which, while not primitive by the standards of anthropology,
lack the kinds of technological development and general organization that
characterize the modern industrial state. Without raising the vexing
question of ethnocentrism, it may be agreed that an increase in the food
supply, and a reduction of the death rate are regarded as good in all known
cultures. It will be further agreed that there are various means whereby
such ends can be effected, provided that the required knowledge and
machinery are made available. But there is more to it than this. Even if
offers of technical assistance and medical aid are unencumbered with
economic, military or ideological baggage, there is a problem to be met
in the reaction of the "underdeveloped" society to the innovation and its
mode of introduction. Here is the reaction of an anthropologist to
technical assistance programs.

T HIS PAPER is concerned with conscious attempts to direct or to
accelerate culture change, and is based largely on personal observations
in several Latin American countries. It does not pertain specifically to
the work of any one agency or to technical assistance programs directed

* Charles J. Erasmus, "An Anthropologist Looks at Technical Assistance," *The
Scientific Monthly*, Vol. 78 (1954), pp. 147–158. Reprinted by permission of the
author and publisher. The selection also appears in Lyle Shannon (editor), *Underdeveloped Areas* (New York: Harper & Bros., 1957).

The author (b. 1921) is a Research Associate, University of Illinois Research in
Cross-Cultural Regularities. Presently in the field in Mexico, Dr. Erasmus has also
worked in Chile, Colombia, Ecuador and Haiti. He is the author of *Las Dimensiones
de la Cultura* (1953).

only by agencies and governments foreign to the countries concerned. Many if not most of the examples used are drawn from cases where local governments have attempted to introduce change within their own countries. The purpose of the author is to synthesize these observations into a discussion of the patterns of resistance and acceptance demonstrated by the peoples of "underdeveloped" areas in the face of directed attempts to change their ways and to point out the implications of these patterns for the successful and economical operation of technical assistance programs.

EMPIRICISM

Introduced changes that bear clear and immediate proof of their effectiveness and desirability usually achieve a more rapid and widespread acceptance than changes of long-term benefit or changes in which the relationship between the new technic and its purported results is not easily grasped on the basis of casual observation. In agriculture, for example, the introduction of improved plant varieties (higher yielding or more disease-resistant) which result in a greater profit to the farmer has repeatedly resulted in spectacular success stories in many of the Latin American countries, and with a variety of cash crops. A foreign agency in one country developed an improved hybrid corn through local genetic selection. The first year that samples were distributed to farmers, the yield was so much higher than normal that the agency was deluged with requests for seed at the next planting time. In fact, the demand was so great that private enterprise quickly became interested in taking over the job of seed multiplication. In contrast, attempts to introduce soil conservation practices frequently encounter considerable difficulty. Practices that do not bear clear and demonstrable proof of their efficacy in a short period of time usually do not diffuse well on their own, with the result that their diffusion may often be no greater than the range of the agronomist's personal contacts.

The spectacular nature of certain introduced agricultural practices may vary considerably, however, with local environmental conditions. In arid badlands, as those found in some parts of Arizona, for example, where rainfall is confined to one brief season in the form of intense downpours, soil conservation practices may demonstrate remarkable benefits within a very short period. Dobyns shows us how eagerly such practices may be accepted under these conditions, in his case study of a conservation experiment among Papago Indians.

In the tropical lowlands of one Andean country, improved varieties of mosaic-resistant sugar cane have all but replaced the "criollo" varieties since their introduction some ten years ago. The newer varieties demonstrated their usefulness so successfully in the form of higher yields and greater profits that they diffused from one farm to another with a minimum of extension support and promotion. In only two or three small valleys have the older criollo varieties persisted and in these cases because mosaic disease was never a problem, apparently as a result of certain prevailing dry winds. Here the farmers see no advantage to the newer varieties and prefer their criollo in the belief that it is easier to refine.

In public health programs, spectacular curative measures seem to take precedence over preventive ones in the rapidity with which they are accepted. Yaws campaigns carried on by the Institute of Inter-American Affairs, in collaboration with the governments of Colombia and Ecuador, have quickly and successfully overcome the initial resistance of the coastal Negro groups, among which the disease is endemic, and these campaigns are profoundly altering the folk beliefs and the fatalistic attitude formerly surrounding this disease. Even native curers now admit that modern medicine is more effective in the treatment of yaws than their own herbal and magical treatments. In the case of preventive medicine, however, the story in most countries is quite different. For example, the symptoms of intestinal infection in a young child may be diagnosed as "evil eye" by rural populations. In order for these people to be convinced that boiling their polluted drinking water will prevent the symptoms we attribute to intestinal infection, they must be able to observe some measurable decrease in the incidence of the symptoms as a result of the preventive technic. Owing to the conditions under which they live and their failure to understand the reasons behind the new device, intestinal infection may take place through other media, and consequently no relationship between the two is empirically established.

In the case of crops, naturalistic explanations are usually and understandably given to insect plagues while ailments due to microorganisms are sometimes attributed to supernatural causes for which magical preventive measures may be employed. However, when a commercial fungicide, which effectively protects one man's crop against the supernatural maladies that afflict his neighbor's, is introduced into a rural farming area, an empirically measurable relationship is established between the preventive device and the malady. Even though the farmers may not fully accept and understand the modern explanation nor completely abandon their former beliefs, they quickly adopt the fungicide (if they can afford it).

From these examples we begin to see that the people of the so-called underdeveloped areas do not reason very differently from those of areas considered more advanced. Unaccustomed or unable to read, they lack the one great avenue by which more sophisticated populations avail themselves of a broader range of experience (including laboratory and statistical analyses) than would be possible if they were limited to the range of their own casual observations. The reasoning processes of both groups, however, are largely empirical and rest primarily on a frequency interpretation of events. Thus, in the case of a preventive measure for plant diseases or a remedial campaign for an easily distinguishable endemic disease such as yaws, the great number of individual cases plus conditions involving fewer variables permits a frequency interpretation in their favor within the limits of casual observation, whereas conditions involving a preventive measure for intestinal infections in a family of two or three children may not. Therefore, where a new practice can demonstrate its relationship to the improvements in such a fashion that a frequency interpretation is possible within the limits of casual observation, it has a much greater chance for rapid acceptance among the populations of underdeveloped areas.

Very often the nature of an innovation will depend upon proper follow-through by the innovator. In most of Latin America, new technics must be adapted to conditions on which few reliable data are available. Under such circumstances, an unknown factor, which would have been known and allowed for in the United States, will upset the results in such a way that the new practice fails to make what might have been a spectacular demonstration. In one country, a U.S. technician who was attempting to introduce the practice of broad-base terracing had no data available regarding maximum rainfall and soil conditions to guide him in calculating slope and channel capacity. By diligently checking his first experimental terraces under rainfall conditions, he corrected all errors before any damages might occur. As a result of this careful follow-through and sense of obligation to the farmers, not a single terrace failed when the area was later subjected to a heavy rain of flood proportions. In fact, the erosive action of the storm on adjoining non-terraced fields was such as to make the terracing demonstrations more valuable.

NEED

The needs felt by the people, as distinguished from those felt by the innovators, constitute one of the most important factors pertaining to the acceptability of an innovation in any particular case. If the people fail to feel or to recognize the need for an innovation, it may prove impossible to introduce it on a voluntary basis.

Several of these examples, pertaining to the introduction of new agricultural practices, involved not only the factor of their empirical verification at the level of casual observation but also appealed to a profit motive. An improved crop variety, which results in a higher yield or a greater margin of profit, appeals to the profit motivation and the desire for greater purchasing power when the improved variety is a cash crop. When it is not a cash crop, the story may be different. From a study by Apodaca of the introduction of hybrid corn into a community of Spanish American farmers in New Mexico, we can see how motives other than those of greater profit may affect the outcome when the crop to be improved is not being grown for market. Within two years after the introduction of the hybrid, three-fourths of the community had adopted it. But after four years, all but three farmers had reverted to planting their original variety. The hybrid had doubled production per acre; the farmers had met with no technical difficulties in planting it, and the seed were readily obtainable. However, the corn was raised by the community only for its own consumption. As these people eat their corn largely in the form of tortillas (unleavened corn cakes), an important mainstay in their diet, and since the new hybrid did not yield tortillas of the same color, texture, and taste as their own corn, they reverted to their older variety. These reasons were more important to them than was the quantity produced. Apodaca notes the fact, however, that the hybrid was dropped with considerable reluctance by the farmers because of its much greater yield. They had empirically verified the fact that the hybrid was an improvement over the old in one sense, but not in the prime sense which pertained to their particular needs and values. This illustrates what can happen when an improvement that would normally have high appeal under cash-cropping conditions is introduced into a subsistence-oriented cropping pattern.

Let us now turn to examples where subsistence-oriented agricultural improvements are introduced into a money economy. Several years ago the ministry of agriculture in a South American republic sponsored a program to introduce the planting of soybeans in many rural areas. Today, the only place where this crop is planted on any scale is near a city where it is manufactured into vegetable oil. The object of this program was to induce the rural population to improve their diet. Soybeans, considered more nutritious, were to be produced solely for family consumption. The farmers not only found the new food distasteful but discovered that no one cared to buy it, and the movement quickly collapsed. In this case the appeal was made to a better health rather than a greater profit motive, but for the farmers the improvement was not empirically verifiable. Symptoms of malnutrition are often ascribed by the folk to supernatural and other causes which bear little or no resemblance to the medical explanations of the innovators. Therefore, in such cases no feeling of need for a new practice may arise to offset the disagreeableness of changing long-established food habits.

In numerous countries attempts have been made to induce rural populations to cultivate vegetable gardens for home consumption. In all cases observed this, too, usually fails after the program has terminated, if the farmer has found no market for the new product in the meantime. Vegetable crops generally enter an area close to cities and towns, or along reliable communication routes leading to them, where the market is greater. Once farmers grow vegetable crops for profit, they invariably consume some. In one Latin American mestizo community where a health program had enjoyed some degree of success in introducing family vegetable gardens, several farmers said that the best way to pacify government programs was to go along with them and do as one was told; eventually the program would terminate, and then they would abandon the nuisance of vegetable gardens without creating any disturbance.

In another Latin American republic, a government-sponsored agency, designed to look after the welfare of farmers growing a cash export crop of importance to the national economy, instituted a program of aiding farmers to build new homes and improve farm structures that were necessary for properly processing the crop. The agency found that it received many more requests for the processing structures than for the homes, although the cost of both types of units was being borne largely by the agency. The farmers were required to pay a small percentage of the total construction costs, and a majority of them preferred to invest in the labor-saving devices. Frequently the field men of the program scolded the farmers for thinking only of their own convenience and never of the cramped and unsanitary quarters of their families. Again we find an example where the needs felt by the people were not entirely in accord with those felt by the innovators. Farmers accustomed to living under housing conditions which the innovators considered undesirable did not necessarily share this view. The processing structures, however, were already known to the farmers who were aware of their labor-saving advantages. The theory underlying the housing program was that more sanitary living conditions would result in more able-bodied farmers and in higher production. But a majority of the new houses rapidly returned to the same state as those they had replaced, a further indication that the needs felt by the innovators were not generally perceived by the farmers. New houses built on farms located along main highways or near population centers showed better maintenance than those that had to be reached by mule-back. Apparently, greater contact with external influences and the cultural environment of the innovators created a sense of need similar to that felt by the innovators.

Let us turn next to an instance of rapid change independent of any superimposed direction. Near two large cities along a semitropical coast, dairy farming recently has come into greater prominence because of the increasing market for milk. Large and poorly managed haciendas, formerly devoted to the pasturing of beef cattle, are breaking up into smaller and more efficiently operated dairy farms. The dairy farmers on their own initiative have imported improved dairy strains and have adopted improved feeding practices and silage. Some farmers have learned to keep daily records of the milk production of each cow, and on the basis of these records to practice selective breeding of their best producers. These dairymen are sensitive to new technics and knowledge. The local economy already has created an urgent need for new ideas, with the added promise of a high degree of acceptance. Diffusion of ideas from the most advanced to the least advanced farms is proceeding at a rapid rate.

We can see that when the objective of technical assistance is to increase production in an underdeveloped area, it is easier to realize among people who participate in a money economy. Rural people who are cash-cropping for national or international markets frequently tend to specialize. More attention is usually given to a particular crop, such as coffee, sugar cane, wheat, or potatoes. The local group often forfeits a great deal of its self-sufficiency in the process of specialization and consequently grows more accustomed to purchasing specialized products of other areas. An increasing tendency to purchase products external to the area is in turn usually accompanied by an increase in the number of new products and ideas entering the area, and the number of new needs thereby created. This type of situation seems to be more conducive and sensitive to change. Needs created by the process of specialization and the desire for increased production and profit actually seem the easiest for technicians from another culture or subculture to meet. The solution is often largely technical, fewer cultural barriers to a common understanding are presented, and the perception and feeling of needs are more easily shared by the innovators and the people.

However, when change is being attempted in a field not directly related to increased production in a money economy, in other words not directly in terms of profits, the difficulties increase. In the field of public health, for example, the innovator may consider it highly desirable to introduce basic disease prevention measures into an underdeveloped area. But the folk still subscribed to an age-old system of beliefs about the cause, prevention, and treatment of disease, a system so different that the preventive measures of the innovator were meaningless. Lacking an understanding of the modern concepts of the etiology of disease and consequently the reasons for modern methods of prevention, they may feel no need to adopt the prescribed changes. Thus, despite the fact that they feel a general need for assistance in combatting the ailments common among them, they may fail to perceive the need for the specific measures proposed and may actively resist them.

COOPERATION

Until now this paper has purposely been limited to examples of changes whose acceptance and diffusion are largely an individual matter. As has been seen in the case of spectacular innovations such as improved plant varieties, this type of change frequently spreads with phenomenal rapidity from one individual to another with very little outside stimulus. However, some changes may require group or community adoption, a circumstance that can greatly increase the operational difficulties of introducing them. Not only must the need for the change or changes be perceived by the entire group or a large majority simultaneously, but the members of the group must cooperate for the given end.

Holmberg provides us with an excellent example of an assistance project which depended upon collective acceptance and which failed even though it was concerned with a need already felt by the people. In a community in the Viru Valley of Peru, villagers had petitioned the Peruvian government for aid in obtaining well water to supplement their river supply during periods of shortage in the dry season. A permanent and reliable water supply was important to these people for household and for irrigation and production needs. Although a well was successfully dug, the entire project failed because the technicians did not consult with leaders of local opinion or seek to involve the people. Antagonisms based on local social and political conditions became so great that it was necessary to withdraw the project.

Throughout one Andean country an attempt was made to establish farmer committees, by means of which it was planned to bring about agricultural improvements. In only one small mountain sector did the movement have success, and here only among farmers who until a few years before had been living in indigenous communities. Accustomed to a measure of independent local government in the past, they were organized with very little effort. Obviously, then, the failure of this program must have been due in part to the organizing technics, for the few successful cases were the result of highly favorable local circumstances.

It would seem that in many parts of Latin America there is a tendency to consider rural populations as more cooperative than they really are, or at least to take their cooperation for granted. However, in Latin America today many of the age-old customs promoting cohesion and cooperation in rural society are being or have been replaced by social relationships of a more impersonal and individualistic nature. Such replaced customs would include the mutual aid and assistance patterns involved, for example, in reciprocal farm labor and the ceremonial kinship obligations of godparenthood. Apparently the economic aspects of such mutual assistance customs were functional in a subsistence-oriented rural economy, where the peasants cropped largely for family and local consumption. As roads increased the possibilities of marketing farm surpluses over larger areas, farmers began to specialize and came to be more dependent on other regions and countries for marketing their products and for the food and goods no longer produced on their own farms. Thus, the interdependencies existing between members of the local group in daily contact were gradually superseded by national and international interdependencies between peoples who never met. When the economic interdependencies between members of the local group were superseded by larger and more impersonal ones, the cooperative functions of older customs were unnecessary. The rural peasantry became more individualistic and less dependent on their daily contacts.

Actually, it may be fairly argued that the rural populations of Latin America are becoming more competitive than collective. Perhaps one of the clearest illustrations of this may be found in 4-H club work. Results are usually better when the young people work separate plots in competition than when they work the same land together in such a way that they cannot compare their work. Similarly, when earnings of club members are pooled for the purchase of livestock or tools used in common, the results are usually poorer than when each individual has the right to the fruits of his own labor. In such instances we can see how the profit motive coincides with individualistic and competitive tendencies.

When a technical assistance project in a certain country attempted to contour level rice fields across ownership boundaries in order to facilitate irrigation flooding in a pilot area, it was faced with the problem of obtaining the permission and collaboration of all the small landowners within the area. However, the technicians neglected to unite the various landowners concerned, to explain the project to them, and to seek their cooperative support. The project was carried out as if it were a type of change which could be effected on an individual or family basis. One farmer was induced to permit the contouring, then another, and so on. Because of the severe land fragmentation problem, the owners of neighboring plots were not necessarily neighbors in so far as the residence patterns were concerned. Even when a farmer and several of the friends who lived near him were convinced of the benefits of contouring, their plots within the area were found to be widely separated. As planting time approached, the project officials felt obliged to rush the job through, and so began contouring the individual and widely separated plots as functionally separate units. As the work progressed, other landowners began signing up. Eventually, nearly all gave permission to contour their land and agreed to pay the costs. But the sequence of requests was such that practically all contouring had to be done within, rather than across, ownership boundaries. Inasmuch as nearly all the farmers eventually collaborated, there is reason to believe that with the proper inducement they could have been encouraged to do so before the work began. As a result, one of the major objectives of the project, to contour according to the topography rather than ownership boundaries, was lost.

INDUCEMENT

The problem of inducement, as we shall use the word here, refers to the task of overcoming popular resistance to a proposed change for any of the reasons discussed so far. Even in the case of new technics or traits which demonstrate their effectiveness in a spectacular fashion, there is still the initial problem of bringing them to the attention of the public. If the problem is one of introducing an improved plant variety, some farmer or farmers must be persuaded to try it. If these initial experiments result in a much greater yield, the new variety usually sells itself. Generally, farmers are suspicious of government authorities and prefer to let someone else try the new technic before they adopt it. If a well-known neighbor obtains satisfactory results, others will often rush to follow his example. Demonstration farms are not so readily copied, as the farmers are not sure what additional advantages beyond their own means may have biased the results. When a large brewery in a certain country found that the home production of barley was insufficient to supply its needs, it hired agronomists to stimulate production in new areas. The agronomists circulated through the highland regions, promised farmers a good price for barley, gave instructions for planting, and provided seed. The first year very few farmers in a given area tried the new plant on a very modest scale. However, by the third or fourth year, after all had been convinced that the agronomist would keep his word about the price and that the plant would give profitable yields, barley had become one of the important crops.

Where the advantages of a new technic or trait are long term in nature or difficult to demonstrate empirically, long-term methods of introduction through formal education might be considered. Extension work with adolescents frequently demonstrates that it is easier to instill new habits among individuals who do not have to unlearn old habits. Furthermore, young people usually find it easier to substitute the prestige of the specialist for the prestige of tradition. Even when introducing non-spectacular innovations on a long-term basis through formal educational procedures, it will usually be necessary to take popular beliefs and practices into account so that persons may perceive a relationship between the needs they feel and the remedies proposed. In Quito, Ecuador, tests were given to school children who had been receiving formal lectures in health education, including the use of visual aid technics for some two years. Results showed that the period of instruction had made little or no impression. Whereas modern explanations of the etiology of disease and its prevention were now familiar to the children, they were largely related to modern disease terminologies that had no meaning to them. The symptoms of those diseases were still being classified according to a folk system which included such causes as fright, evil eye, malevolent air, and witchcraft. According to the school children, these folk illnesses could not be caused by modern etiologies, could not be prevented by modern means, and could not be cured by medical doctors. In collaboration with the educators, attempted changes in the methods of instruction were made so as to allow the children to discuss their folk beliefs freely in class. During the discussions the educators attempted to show the children, without deriding their beliefs, that the symptoms they ascribed to fright, evil eye, and the like were the symptoms of the very diseases that the educators had been talking about for the past two years. They also tried to disassociate folk symptoms from folk etiologies and practices and to link them to modern methods of treatment and prevention. Retesting after the lectures gave very different results. Written tests, of course, do not necessarily indicate a change of habits, but these certainly indicated that for the first time the children were cognizant of a relationship between the measures and explanations of the educators and their own maladies. This illustrates the necessity of thoroughly understanding the local culture of a people, in cases where it is difficult for them to perceive the needs felt by the technicians under the ordinary limitations of casual empiricism. Ironically enough, salesmen for patent medicine concerns frequently give very careful consideration to folk beliefs in order to adapt the advertising of their products to the local concepts of disease.

In some cases people can be induced to accept new technics and changes, which they find difficult to accept, by linking them or making them conditional to other changes or services more desirable to them. For example, in anticipation of an irrigation project that they know will materially benefit them, farmers may be more willing to satisfy government wishes concerning secondary improvements which they would ordinarily resist. In the example of the contour leveling of rice fields, it seems very possible that one of the principal mistakes of the program was in failing to obtain commitments by the farmers for the leveling before the irrigation project was completed. As the farmers had already been provided with irrigation water, the inducement value of the irrigation project had been lost.

Similarly, where public health centers give attention to curative as well as preventive measures, their rapport with the public as well as their influence in implementing changes in disease prevention habits is noticeably greater. At a charity maternity hospital in Quito it was found that new practices, in conflict with popular beliefs—but with which mothers had to conform in order to receive treatment at the hospital—were found to be having an important and permanent influence in altering their beliefs. In agriculture, the distribution of seeds and tools at cost may offer a decisive inducement to adopt recommended new cultivation practices. Where farmers can see no need for a program objective, it may be possible to alter the emphasis of the objective so as to enhance its appeal. In one Haitian valley, agronomists were able to effect measures of soil conservation by appealing to a local interest in coffee planting and by helping the farmers to start seed beds of coffee and shade trees for transplanting to hillside plots.

Where joint and cooperative action on the part of a community is necessary for the success of a project, considerable attention must be given to involving the people in the activity at an early stage. Whenever possible, the community should be made to feel that it has participated in the planning of the program. When cooperative programs are simply dropped upon the peoples of underdeveloped areas from some high planning echelon within the government, without any explanation and without any consideration for local opinions, the programs are very likely to fail either partially or totally.

In any technical assistance program one of the most important and most variable aspects of the problem of inducement involves the factor of person to person relationships. Much has been expounded on this subject, but the desideratum usually consists of little more than a consideration for the beliefs and customs of other peoples and a sincere attempt to understand them. Yet understanding can be no greater than allowed by the amount of personal contact and the ability to communicate.

A most effective foreign technician was a U.S. soils scientist attached to an agricultural research station in an Andean country. Good-natured and affable, he set out at once to make a friend of every member of the staff. Within his special field he led the local technicians to adopt several new research procedures, and saw several research projects of considerable importance well under way. Yet he never allowed his name to be attached to any project. He encouraged the local man most interested in the plan to initiate it, carry it through, and take the credit, while he played the part of a counsellor who continued to make suggestions but never gave an order. Three nights a week on his own time he held classes in English because he had discovered that many local technicians wanted to learn the language and that he made friends by helping them.

COMPLEXITY

Frequently a change which seems desirable to the innovator may depend upon so many other secondary accompanying changes that its introduction is difficult. Perishable food products, such as fresh vegetables and fish, are most easily exploited near markets where transportation to markets is reliable, inexpensive, and rapid, or where storage and processing facilities have been developed. Successful adoption of improved livestock may depend upon many correlative changes in husbandry practices. The latter in turn may depend upon the farmer's financial ability to provide better feed and care.

Failure to recognize the factor of complexity is one of the most serious problems in technical assistance work, partly because there are no established principles of diagnosis which can be applied to every case. Oftentimes the standard of living may be so low that the innovator's heart goes out to the evidences of suffering which seems unnecessary to him from his different cultural or subcultural viewpoint. Let us take for example country "X," whose density of population and infant mortality rate are among the highest in the world and whose per capita production is among the lowest. Is the first job of technical assistance to save lives and reduce the immediate evidences of human suffering, or is it to help the country itself to solve its health problems? The answer to this question depends on who provides the funds to build the public health centers, the water purification systems, and the public hospitals, and to educate the doctors and nurses. If the innovators provide these funds, the effort may involve much more than technical assistance; it may involve heavy financial assistance. As a result the population may increase more rapidly than ever, and with it all the existing economic and political stresses may be aggravated. However, if the innovators are concentrating on purely technical assistance, they may endeavor to help country "X" raise per capita production to a point where the country can pay for its own secondary improvements as it feels the need for them. In short, this would mean that technical assistance in country "X" might be aimed first at increasing productivity in agriculture and industry, while assigning the high infant mortality rate to a secondary position on its list of problems.

This extreme case is used simply as an example and does not mean that technical assistance in public health should be relegated to a secondary position in all countries desiring technical aid. In some countries productivity per capita is much higher than in others and public health services for the population are already well established. In such cases, technical assistance for making these services more efficient is readily grasped and utilized and effects of the technical assistance are far more permanent and far reaching. U.S. public health technicians in one small country have played an important role in a malaria campaign to clean up a wide coastal zone that was formerly poorly exploited. Roads are now being cut through the jungles, exploitation of forest products is intensifying, and new settlers are entering the area to establish banana and other plantations. Thus an entire nation has been benefited by these public health workers.

A price-support program for cotton was adopted in one country in order to induce greater home production for local textile industries. Within a period of three years agricultural changes in some areas have been almost revolutionary. On flat coastal plains to the east, land that was formerly yielding a very low rate of income per acre from an extensive type of beef-cattle ranching is rapidly changing into a zone of mechanized agriculture. Cotton has become white gold. Not only have many farmers rushed to exploit the new opportunities with mechanized farm equipment, but they have adopted new farming technics such as the use of fertilizers, insecticides, and crop dusting. This example is not used to justify price-support programs, but it does show how increased profits facilitate the adoption of new practices. They do not make such change automatic, however, for the same factors of need and empiricism still apply. Many farmers started planting cotton without heeding advice to use insecticides. They suffered serious crop damages the first year and saw the difference between their yields and those where insecticides were used, and then they adopted the practice the second year. Nor did cotton planting itself become generally adopted until a few enterprising farmers had made a handsome profit.

In situations of extreme land fragmentation where farmers must supplement their agricultural earnings by means of other endeavors, it is usually extremely difficult to initiate changes in farming practices. A higher yielding plant variety may be readily adopted, but many other innovations are difficult to introduce on uneconomical farm units. However, a desire to help impoverished farmers may lead administrators and technicians to attempt the introduction of improvements of a subsistence nature which require little or no capital expenditure. Programs may thereby develop with the purpose of introducing the household manufacture of family clothes, home gardening of all food necessities, home food-preservation practices, and inexpensive animal varieties such as rabbits as a source of meat for the family. All such devices are aimed at making farm families more self-sufficient and less specialized, a process contrary to the usual economic trends. Social welfare programs of this type seem to require more extension personnel and promotional activity than those designed to bring production-increasing technics to farmers who have the financial means to exploit them.

In one South American country where soil erosion has become extremely severe, U.S. soil conservation experts found that practically no remedial steps were being taken. In some areas, erosion had reached a point where only such drastic measures as complete reforestation would suffice. In others, the erosion problem was complicated by absentee land-ownership patterns or the exploitation of uneconomical farm units. However, by selecting an area of medium-sized mechanized farms personally administered by resident owners, the technicians were very successful in introducing many new soil conservation practices with a minimum of promotional activity. Farmers responded readily, were quick to recognize the benefits of the new measures, and found them easy to carry out at their level of operations. As a result of the impetus given to soil conservation by the successes in this area, the government created a special soil conservation division, within its ministry of agriculture, to attend to the erosion problems of the country as a whole.

In one sense, the areas of worst erosion in a country might be thought of as presenting the greatest need for correction, or the poorest farmers as the ones most in need of improved agricultural practices. Frequently, however, the persons most in need, in the judgment of the innovator, may be those who feel the need the least. For this reason it may often be more expedient and practical to work where the need, from the innovator's standpoint, is less acute but where there is greater willingness on the part of the people to make the change. The interest shown by the people themselves is more often a better index to their ability to successfully adopt a given change than the judgment of the innovator.

ECONOMIC FEASIBILITY

It would be quite logical to suppose that, given unlimited financial and human resources, a technical assistance program could effect any change desired. However, no technical assistance project has such unlimited funds; therefore, in any decision concerning the selection of projects, their feasibility with respect to budgetary limitations must be taken into account.

The kinds of innovations which would seem to be most inexpensive are those which require the least man-hours for strictly promotional purposes. Such innovations include those from which benefits are easily verifiable through casual observation, which are accepted and diffused on an individual basis, which meet a strong need already felt by the people (of particular appeal to a profit motive), and those which are in sequence with local development (not too complex). However, certain circumstances may justify considerable promotional activity. For example, in the case of projects requiring cooperative acceptance and action on the part of the people, the necessary groundwork must be done to involve them in the activities, or the time and money spent in the purely technological aspects may be lost. In such cases the two deciding factors are the amount of money being invested in the technological aspects, and the need which the people feel. In the case of an expensive irrigation project, about which the people are highly enthusiastic and for which their cooperation is requisite, the extension work necessary to iron out local social and operational problems for the maximum success of the project should be considered a functional requirement. However, where considerable money is to be spent on a project in which the cooperation of the people is essential but for which they do not even feel a need, the project should be reexamined to see if it fits into the local sequence of development. If a project is very inexpensive but would require costly promotional work to secure the necessary cooperation from the people, the project should be reexamined to see if the ends really justify the means. It frequently happens, for example, that innovators like to initiate projects which require cooperative action from the people because they consider the encouraging of cooperation and community spirit as good and worthy projects in themselves.

The principal consideration in questions of economic feasibility is that of the needs felt by the people. When the people do not feel a need for the innovations proposed, promotional activity necessarily must be increased. Fortunately, actual situations are usually neither all negative nor all positive; differences exist in degree, and some persons within the same group or area are more receptive than others. In the case of soil conservation, for example, some farmers with better farm equipment, more capital, and a long-term outlook can be shown the benefits of soil conservation with relatively little difficulty, while neighbors with more modest resources continue to take a skeptical view. However, when a nucleus for change can be permanently established, even though the prospects of diffusing the change outside that nucleus in the immediate future are poor, the long-term gains may justify the modest beginning. Eventually others may come to recognize the benefits of an innovation at a time when conditions make it easier for them to adopt it or to appreciate its advantages. Thus, rather than spend time and money to promote the adoption of an innovation among people who cannot perceive its desirability, it may prove more expedient to establish it among strategically located nuclei or groups who can.

Another long-term alternative to costly promotional activity to establish a sense of need for new measures is that, already mentioned, of appealing to the younger members of the society through existing educational institutions. However, few well trained teachers and extension personnel may be available in some underdeveloped countries. Only highly productive nations can afford to maintain large numbers of competent teachers at salaries sufficiently attractive to make the long years of preparation worth the effort or the cost. Many persons overestimate the influence of formal education procedures by underestimating the technological and economic conditions which make them possible. Formal educational procedures become strictly promotional if they require large numbers of foreign personnel on free loan or large numbers of local personnel trained and maintained at the expense of foreign subsidy.

The most unfavorable conditions for introducing innovations are frequently presented by such marginal peoples as Indian groups who more than anything else may simply wish to be left alone. The effort involved in introducing changes among them will be particularly great when their economy is still subsistence-oriented. Their conception of needs may be so different from that of the innovators that the two groups may find it very difficult to establish a common meeting ground for mutual understanding.

In general, the absorption of marginal peoples and cultures into the national sphere seems to follow most rapidly upon their further involvement in the national cash economy. In many cases it may prove more expedient to develop areas bordering on marginal groups in such a way as to draw them more closely into the national economy than to attempt to superimpose an extraneous need system directly upon them. While living in a Mayo Indian *comunidad* in southern Sonora, Mexico, during 1948, the writer had an opportunity to note the effects produced on an indigenous community by the rapid development of bordering areas. The development of irrigation and a more intensive machine agriculture to the north was creating more job opportunities and prosperity. Not only were members of the *comunidad* going north more frequently to work as seasonal agricultural labor, but they were returning with new ideas and wants. In fact, a growing nucleus was advocating division of the communal land as an incentive for wealthy farmers to extend irrigation into the area. Thus it was hoped that a more intensive and profitable type of agriculture would be possible for all.

A similar situation was encountered at the plantation of an American fruit company in a Latin American republic. The labor turnover the first year or two was extremely high, for individuals worked until pay day or worked only until they had earned enough to buy something they had specifically wanted. However, as new laborers kept replacing the old, some inevitably joined the nucleus of steady workers. These valued the permanent income, the clean and comfortable company housing, the superior company school for their children, and the company medical treatment. Within a few years the plantation had a permanent resident labor force. The company showed an interest in the upkeep and attractiveness of the workers' housing and helped them landscape gardens around their homes; thus a model community had been formed that was influencing the entire area. Workers in neighboring locally managed plantations were beginning to demand the same treatment, as they perceived a need for it themselves.

Not everyone can be induced to share the values and needs of the innovators at once but, by working first with those who already share them, the changes may eventually have far-reaching results without the unnecessary expense of promotional methods. In short, action programs among those who already feel a need for an innovation would seem to be more effective and less expensive in the long run than promotional programs for those who must first be inspired to feel the need.

One of the greatest weaknesses in most technical assistance programs is the failure to recognize the indispensable part played by research in increasing their economic feasibility. In this respect, government might conceivably learn from business. One writer on the subject of business management has said that any company that lacks an organized program of research will eventually find itself out of business. Two major forms of business research, market and engineering studies, might be paralleled by technical assistance agencies to their advantage. Market studies could be designed to get all the pertinent facts about the people to be changed, including their needs and wants, their ability to absorb a given innovation, and their previous reactions to similar programs in the past. Engineering studies might include research in any number of technical fields, as well as comparative research in the methods and results of other agencies in other parts of the world, and the continued self-evaluation by the agency of its own programs to perfect the least expensive and most effective means of realizing its objectives. However, in government assistance programs, research can probably be realized best through an organization pattern that recognizes the difference between staff and line functions. Government reporting is prone to be a line function originating with operations personnel, who execute it with a bias toward justifying the further existence of their programs. By avoiding the disclosure of mistakes in specific operations, short-term benefits may accrue which prevent the self-evaluation and self-correction necessary to avoid those seriously damaging setbacks that result from the accumulation of hidden errors.

F. Ideology

MAN deals with his environment by laboring and using tools. In the process, and in preparing his successors for their task, he relies upon symbols and calls culture into being. Within culture lie many things: implements and knowledge of their use, social relations and the understanding of their manipulation, and a further area—more conceptual than these other two—wherein lies a culture's ideas of origin and destiny, the meaning of everyday life, and the relations between man and nature. It is the last area that is denoted as "ideology."

The anthropological approach to ideology obviously enlarges the meaning of the term as commonly used. It includes the popular concept of ideology as attachment to specific political credos and regards patriotism, nationalism, and anarchism as being equally ideological. To the extent that republicanism, socialism, monarchism, fascism, or communism connote intellectual commitments rather than *de facto* political and economic systems they are also ideologies. But there is more than "-isms" to this view of ideology. Religion is included in its various guises, but the comparability of fervor sometimes manifest in the holding of religious and political ideas does not mean that emotional attachment is the fundamental criterion of ideology, though it is often a concomitant.

At the root of ideology is explication: ideologies explain to man why he is, whence he came, what he should be. Ideologies explain how the universe operates, how the environment may be dealt with, and the end to which a culture struggles. Phrased in this way, it will be seen that science, too, is an ideology for, while it constantly revises and refines its techniques and products, it is a way of looking at the universe.

Empiricism and pragmatism have probably played significant roles in every cultural approach to the challenges of life. Nevertheless, most cultures have their greatest ideological investments in supernatural interpretations of cosmic questions. Since this is particularly true of primitive cultures, the following selections consist of two specific treatments of primitive religion and an essay which is critical of the attempts to make general and particularly developmental statements about religion.

404

27. TAPIRAPÉ SHAMANISM *

According to Tylor, the belief in spirits—animism—was the simplest and most common denominator of religious belief. Though Tylor's speculations on the origin of animism have been questioned (cf. II:17) and other religious conceptions have had their priority asserted, the ethnographic evidence reveals that the most widespread religious conception is the belief in spirits. Ghosts, spirits and demons play immediate and crucial roles in human life but may be influenced, placated or controlled through a wide variety of techniques controlled by human intermediaries known as shamans. The selection below describes shamanism in an Indian tribe that lives in the Amazonian jungle of Brazil. More than this, it shows how religious beliefs, rituals and statuses integrate with other aspects of the culture.

INTRODUCTION

THE TAPIRAPÉ INDIANS are a Tupi-speaking tribe living in Central Brazil west of the Araguaya River. Their villages formerly extended some two hundred miles to the north of the Tapirapé River, an affluent of the Araguaya; but today their one remaining village lies west of the Araguaya,

* Charles Wagley, "Tapirapé Shamanism," Boletim do Museu Nacional (Antropologia), No. 3 (1943), pp. 61–92. Reprinted by permission of the author and publisher.

The author (b. 1913) is Professor of Anthropology at Columbia University. He has done fieldwork in various parts of Latin America, particularly in Guatemala and Brazil. In addition to his ethnographic specialization, Wagley has made contributions to problems of cultural typology and racism. Among his works are Economics of a Guatemalan Village (1941); Social and Religious Life of a Guatemalan Village (1949); Race and Class in Rural Brazil (editor) (1952); Amazon Town (1953); and (with Marvin Harris) Minorities in the New World (1958).

about forty miles north of the Tapirapé and 160 miles from the point of union of the two rivers. This settlement contains a total population that does not exceed 150 people, the residue of five villages that probably existed so late as the turn of the century and that are said to have had a population of about two hundred people each. A progressive population decline has followed the acquiring of diseases from contact with the neighboring Carajá Indians of the Araguaya River and from European visitors. Such contacts, however, have left their aboriginal culture little changed.

The Tapirapé are properly a forest people, maintaining an agricultural life on clearings hewed from the great tropical forest. Their cultivated fields are large, producing manioc (both *Manihot manihot* and the sweet species *Manihot palmata aypi*), maize, pumpkins, beans, peppers, yams, kará (*Dioscorea* sp.), cotton, and bananas.

The dry months of June through September of each year are devoted to clearing the garden sites. This work is done by men, frequently working individually, sometimes in communal labor formed by the men's moiety groups. When the clearing is done collectively, the large field is divided into individual plots which become individual property; and planting, which begins after the first light rains of October, is done individually and principally by the men. Cotton and peanuts, however, are women's crops. The women plant these in their husband's garden plots and harvest them themselves. While a new garden plot is cleared each year, a particular garden plot is generally used for two years and then abandoned. A man plants such crops as maize, beans, and peppers on the plot the first year and as they are harvested, he replants the plot with manioc. Maize is harvested from the end of December through February, the season of heaviest rains; while other crops are harvested at the end of the rains in May and June.

Large gardens with many different crops guarantee to the Tapirapé a variety and abundance of garden stuff, but meat and fish are definitely luxuries. People in the village could not remember a time when there had been real hunger among them, but they were frequently hungry for meat and fish. This lack in the diet is supplied by frequent trips to the near-by Tapirapé River and the grass plains that border it where fish and game, principally wild pork (*Tagassu pecari*), deer, peccary (*Tagassu tajacu*), water fowl, and tapir (*Tapirus terrestris*) are found in abundance. During the dry season these plains abound in piqui (*Caryocar villosum*), palm nuts especially andiroba (*Carapa guyanensis*), used for body oil—and other wild fruits.

Among the Tapirapé wealth is not reckoned in terms of basic subsistance, for these goods are so easy to obtain as to be considered with little regard. The possessions that lend real distinction of wealth are such luxury articles as the breast and tail feathers of the red parrot (*Ara chloroptera?*), beads, and pieces of hardware acquired through contact with white men or trading with other Indians. These goods are accordingly the most valued media of exchange in the community. Other goods used for a medium of exchange were urucú (*Bixa orellana*), tobacco, extra hammocks, decorated gourds, string for binding feathers to arrows, and cane arrow shafts.

The houses of a Tapirapé village form a circle around a great central ceremonial men's house. There are nine of these large thatch dwellings with rounded roofs in the modern Tapirapé village; four to eight simple families (father, mother, and children) share a house. Each simple family has a section of the unpartitioned house where they lead a domestic life separate from the others. Residence is matrilocal and the women of such a household are ideally related by kinship; yet each large household has a male leader, a man of prestige, who is usually the husband of one of the older women of the female kinship group. Apart from these residential groupings, the Tapirapé are divided in two other ways.

First, all Tapirapé men belong to one of the two patrilineal non-exogamic ceremonial moieties and each moiety is further divided into three age grades. There are consequently two groups of youths, two groups of adult men of warrior age, and two groups of older men. Each of these groups bears the name of a mythical bird, the word *wirã*—bird—itself being used as the generic name for the groups. These *wirã* function as units in hunting and in clearing garden sites; parallel groups also dance against one another in the ceremonials and offer reciprocal feasts to each other. The warrior-age group of each of these moieties has a "walking leader" for hunting excursions and other communal work and a "singing leader" for ceremonials.

Both men and women of the Tapirapé are also divided into eight "feasting" groups called *tátáupawã*—literally "fire all to eat". Men belong to their father's feasting group and women to their mother's. Feasting groups are not only non-exogamic but people prefer to marry with their own group so that husband and wife may attend feasts together. These groups carry names of the mythological heads of the legendary original eight households of the first Tapirapé village. On occasion during the dry season the feast groups meet at sunset on the dance plaza for a ceremonial feast, each member bringing his or her contribution to the common meal.

The kinship system is perhaps a more important factor in assuring solidarity to the Tapirapé than either the moieties or the household groups. Tapirapé kinship is of the type known as "bifurcate merging"— the chief principle of the system being that all persons of one generation who are related through either mother or father, no matter how distantly, are considered brothers and sisters. Children of persons calling each other siblings are also siblings. The mother's "sisters" are called mother and the father's "brothers", father. The mother's brothers and father's sisters are distinguished by special terms. Similarly, the children of a man's brothers are considered sons and daughters of the man himself, and the children of a woman's sisters are considered her children. Children of a man's sister or a woman's brother are given special terms.

The wide inclusiveness of these kinship affiliations makes it possible for an individual to call the majority of his fellow villagers—and in former days those of other villages—by terms of close relationship. Siblings are under obligation to lend aid to one another when it is needed and, in the case of sorcery, to avenge wrong done to any of them. The kinship system accordingly provides an important bond of solidarity within this society which lacks strong centralized control to hold it together.

SOURCE OF SHAMANISTIC POWER

A multitude of spirits populate the unseen world of the Tapirapé. These spirits, known by the generic term of *ančúnga*, are of two general types: ghosts, *ančúnga iúnwera*, the disembodied souls of the dead; and second, malevolent beings of many classes and descriptions. Ghosts inhabit abandoned village sites where they relive their earthly lives, yet frequently they travel about at night and, especially during the rainy season, they come near the village of the living, for "they are cold" and come near human habitations to get warm. People are accordingly afraid to venture beyond the village plaza at night. Now and again, ghosts appear to living people, frightening them, sometimes throwing a dust-like substance over them and causing them to fall insensible.

Several people fell from fright upon seeing a ghost during my visit. One woman saw a ghost "bathing in the stream" when she went to the small brook to drink water after dark. She said that the ghost approached and struck her. A man walking in his garden after dark saw the ghost of a known person, some years dead. "It was white and his eyes had fallen out. He still had some flesh and he had *urucú* in his hair". Yet another man also met a ghost which was "white with big holes instead of eyes". Ghosts of individuals who have been dead many years "have no flesh; they have only bones". The ghosts that appear to the living follow the pattern of the gradual disintegration of the body.

Ghosts gather around a new grave to carry away the soul at time of burial; so they are especially dangerous to people at the time of funerals. When a Tapirapé dies, men carry machetes and mirrors to the wake for protection against the ghosts. If ghosts see their reflections in mirrors, they are frightened away.

The principal encounters of the Tapirapé with ghosts are in dreams. Dreamers sometimes visit them in their villages and at times learn from them new ceremonial songs which they hear in the traditional Tapirapé ceremonials that the ghosts continue to carry on after they have left the village of the living.

After an indeterminate period the ghosts themselves die and their spirits then become changed into animals. The spirit of the dead ghost of a man of prestige may become a toad (*Pipa pipa*); that of a common man a dove. Among the other animals into which spirits of dead ghosts become changed are frogs, deer, paca (*Cuniculus paca*).

Besides the ghosts there are an infinite number of many different species of *ančúnga* of the demonic class, all generally living at a great distance deep in the forest. It is fortunate that their dwellings are so distant, for these creatures are very dangerous, killing Tapirapé whenever possible. In legendary times these demonic beings were more numerous than at present and killed many Tapirapé, but Waré, a powerful shaman and legendary hero, engaged in a constant warfare of wits with them and succeeded in killing many of them. He destroyed the dangerous *awakú anká* by setting fire to their stringy hair which trailed far behind them as they walked through the forest. He also killed the *munpi anká*, the beings that clubbed men to death and drank their blood.

Some of these demons of the forest are now "pets" of the Tapirapé, and are no longer dangerous to them. The comparatively harmless *ančúnga*, in a sense domesticated by Tapirapé men, come at intervals throughout the year to live in the large central men's house. While an *ančúnga* is inhabiting this ceremonial house, Tapirapé men sing and dance with masks representing the visiting spirit.

Knowledge of the supernatural world is gained chiefly through the dream experiences of shamans or *pančé*, for among the Tapirapé shamanistic power derives from dreams and from powers revealed in them. Dreams are believed to be journeys. The *iungá*, the soul, may free itself from the *eté*, the body, in sleep, and move freely in time and space. Obviously anyone may dream but frequent dreaming is evidence of shamanistic power. Laymen who dream very much are afraid, for they do not belong in this supernatural world, or they believe that they should become shamans.

Campukwi, who was not a shaman, indicated this fear in telling me his dream experience. When he saw dangerous *ančúnga* in his dream, he had no recourse but to run: "I am not a shaman. I was afraid. I ran. They would have killed me". Only shamans have the supernatural power to move freely in this dream-world of ghosts and demons. A shaman is never afraid in his dream travels, for ghosts are his friends and the power of a shaman grows in proportion as he fraternizes with the demonic

spirits of the forest. After a dream-visit from a shaman, breeds of demonic
spirits may become his familiars, obedient to his calls for aid. Turning
himself into a bird or launching himself through the air in his "canoe,"
a half gourd, he travels to the villages of ghosts, to the houses of demonic
spirits, or to such temporal places as the Brazilian settlements or Carajá
villages on the Araguaya River. Then, too, time is no obstacle; in a
sleep of a few minutes he may experience three or four days of dream
adventure.

The dream experience of Ikanancowi, a powerful shaman who died
a few years before my visit, will illustrate these points. In his dream he
walked far to the shores of a large lake deep in the jungle. There he
heard dogs barking and ran in the direction from which the noise came
until he met several forest spirits of the breed called *munpí anká*. They
were tearing a bat out of a tree for food. The spirits talked with Ikanancowi
and invited him to return to their village, which was situated upon the
lake. In the village he saw *periquitos* (Psittacidae) and many *socó*
(*Butorides* sp.), birds which they keep as pets. The *ančúnga* had several
pots of *kauí* and invited Ikanancowi to eat with them. He refused for
he saw that their *kauí* was made from human blood. Ikanancowi watched
one spirit drink of the *kauí* and saw him vomit blood immediately
afterwards; the shaman saw a second spirit drink from another pot and
immediately spurt blood from his anus. He saw the *munpí anká* vomit
up their entrails and throw them upon the ground, but he soon saw
that this was only a trick; they would not die, for they had more intestines.
After this visit the *munpí anká* called Ikanancowi father and he called
them his sons; he visited them in his dreams frequently and he had
munpí anká near him always. When Ikanancowi danced and sang in
the annual shamanistic ceremony against Thunder, he painted his chest
and chin red with *urucu*, representing the *kauí* of blood which drools
from the mouths of the *munpí anká* after they vomit and he called these
spirits to his aid in his songs. Other shamans have had familiar spirits
but none have had such dangerous spirits as the *munpí anká;* "people were
very much afraid of Ikanancowi, for these "*ančúnga* are very dangerous".

In another dream told to me a shaman met the forest spirits called
oréya. These have long hair wound in a mass on top of their heads and
they carry one arrow for the bows with which they kill men. The *oréya*
were about to shoot the shaman, but when he shouted, "No, I am a
shaman", they did not harm him. Instead they gave him food and helped
him return through the deep forest to the village. Another shaman had
ančúnga anú awa as his familiars. These forest demons have protruding
eyes and sharp pointed chins. They kill Tapirapé by grabbing them from
behind as they walk unsuspectingly through the forest, clapping their
hands over the victim's mouth and driving their pointed chins into the

back of his neck. A man caught by one of these *ančúnga* dies gurgling and staring, unable to speak; so, although found alive he may never explain what happened to him. A shaman with such dangerous familiars as these protects the laity by keeping his spirits under control.

One powerful shaman may have several demonic familiars and his responsibility and prestige grow with their numbers and strength. Panteri, perhaps the most powerful shaman living in 1940, had several breeds of familiars garnered from his dreams. He was, of course, accustomed to visiting the villages of ghosts and frequently saw and talked with ghosts in his nightly dreams. He had visited the *anapi ančúnga*, beings with huge penises with which they kill people by sodomy and by copulation. Panteri travelled once in his dreams over a high mountain ridge to the north of the Tapirapé country where he visited with the ghosts of the hostile Gê-speaking Kayapo. These enemy ghosts too became his familiars and he says that they will warn him if and when the living Kayapo plan to attack the Tapirapé. Again, in one of his dreams, Panteri travelled two days through a thick forest through which no paths led. Suddenly he found himself at the mouth of the Tapirapé River where it runs into the Araguaya. Inside a near-by hill he visited *anacówa*, the large red parrot from which supernatural beings and the souls of dead shamans pluck their everlasting supply of red feathers for decoration.

Panteri also visited the forest demons called *peropi awa*, who have the power to send fevers to the Tapirapé. About this visit to their "house" he related the following: "I saw many pets. They have periquitos, parrots, many pets . . . I had not seen them before. I saw there a paca. The paca was cold; it was shivering. The paca had fever [chills], I knew that the Tapirapé would all have fever. I told many people that this would occur but there was nothing I could do about it". During his many dream travels Panteri has also visited Maratawa, the home of heroic ancestors and deceased shamans and he has looked down upon many Brazilian settlements on the Araguaya River.

There are certain of the shamans who are said to make frequent trips to the sky in their "canoes" and to count powerful celestial phenomena among their powers. The Milky Way was spoken of as the "Road of the *Pančě*". Once when comparing his powers with those of another shaman, a shaman told me that he dreamed only on earth level and so was not so powerful as the other who frequently travelled in the sky. The other, he said, "had visited *é éco*, the Pleiades, and *kopia xawana*, the Jaguar of the Skies". When this shaman dies, it is thought that many terrestrial jaguars, sent by the Jaguar of the Skies, will haunt the confines of the village. I was told, too, that when the powerful shaman Wantanam died the "sun was large and red with the blood of the shaman"; it was "hot" and "angry" because a shaman had died.

SORCERY

The Tapirapé tell of great battles between strong shamans, each supported by his own retinue of powers. During my stay with the Tapirapé there were rumors of a possible combat between Urukumu and Panteri, the two strongest shamans. Many people believed that it would be caused by the death of a warm personal friend of Panteri through the suspected sorcery by Urukumu. One man even described how he thought that the combat would take place. "Panteri will smoke much tobaco and then he will go to his hammock to sleep. He will go [in his dream] in his 'canoe' to the top of a high mountain. From there he will look about until he sees [the soul of] Urukumu. From there Panteri will throw his *ankungitána*; will wrap itself around [the soul of] Urukumu, carrying him off into the sky". Now the various familiar powers of both shamans hasten to their aid; it was at this point that the narrator, visualizing the possible battle of powers, listed the powers that would come to the aid of each shaman. A shaman whose soul has thus been captured by another falls prey to chills and fevers and soon dies, with his last breath whispering in song that he leaves the earth and possibly even telling gaspingly the name of the shaman who caused his death. Both shamans involved in the rumored combat denied knowledge or intention to wage it.

As might be expected, the same methods said to be used by shamans against one another may also be used against laymen. Shamans are believed to steal souls that are wandering in dream journeys. The shaman may send his *ankungitána* to strike the soul of his victim over the head or to tie it up and carry it off. The one whose soul is thus either incapacitated or imprisoned soon dies. A shaman may call upon his familiar demonic spirits of the forest to deal with a chosen victim or may in his dreams shoot a victim's spirit with small arrows causing at times death and at times only boils. Still another method of attack is for the shaman to throw a fishbone (*ipirã kunya*) or gnawing worms (*uuáka* or *áwai*) into his victim's body causing illness and death. The treatment of illness consists of removing from the victim's body these malignant arrows, fishbones, and worms that are the cause of illness.

In illness and other misfortune, sorcery is always suspected by the Tapirapé and some shaman is accordingly always believed responsible. Sorcery, however, is believed to be the action of shamans in dreams, and although such a negative statement can obviously not be substantiated, it seems never to be consciously practised. But there is, so far as the writer knows, no use of incantations or mechanical devices for the deliberate inducing of sympathetic magic.

All Tapirapé are thought, however, to die by sorcery and at each death suspicion turns toward a shaman. At the death of a child or woman of low status, suspicion may arise and then soon die down but when the deceased is a man of status, his brothers, sons, or sisters' sons become violent in their grief and may murder the shaman toward whom suspicion points. Sometimes, after a long series of deaths, suspicion is fixed upon one famous and strong shaman and the Tapirapé decide informally that he must be killed. In such cases the revenge-murder occurs within the first few days after a death when the relatives are "sad". If the first depression of mourning wear off without violence to the shaman, the anger toward him passes and he is out of danger. Thus, after a man of rather high status had died both Urukumu and Wantanamu, *pancés* of sufficient power to be suspected of causing his death, both left the village, ostensibly on fishing trips, staying away until the brothers of the deceased had calmed down again.

The eight living men (*marántxunkanera* or "killers") who had killed *pancés* attest to the frequency of revenge killing of shamans because of suspected sorcery. Within the memory of one informant, Kamairá, who was approximately forty years old, ten shamans had been killed. During his youth he had killed a shaman, *Pančewáni,* because he believed him responsible for his younger brother's death. Going to the shaman's house the second night after his brother's death, Kamairá found the shaman asleep and killed him with several arrows through the abdomen. According to various informants, the epidemic of deaths that had been occuring then came to a halt, thus proving *Pančewáni's* guilt. In another case the killer hid in the forest and shot the suspected shaman as he passed on his way to his garden; still another shaman was clubbed to death as he sat with his family in the village plaza. Two living "killers" had murdered women shamans by clubbing them to death. *Kučamančé* (*kučan,* woman; *pančé,* shaman) generally die by violence, according to informants; women shamans "are dangerous". They dream more than men [shamans] and they kill many Tapirapé [in dreams]", said one man. Ironically, all three of the more powerful shamans living today, at least two of whom are currently in danger because they are considered powerful enough to be suspected of "evil dreaming", murdered shamans during their youth.

Informants could not remember any one occasion when a shaman thus murdered was avenged by his relatives; yet informants did say that a shaman with several adult brothers—true siblings—strong enough to avenge him, is generally not murdered. A strong shaman makes an effort to have a strong family group about him for protection. Informants could not remember that murdered shamans had ever been revenged by their familiar spirits, although one man made the point that shamans were murdered only by persons under the influence of great anger or grief, for people normally are afraid of the familiars of shamans. Special rites are observed by anyone who has murdered a shaman, to protect him and the rest of the tribe against possible danger. On the day following the murder the *marántxunkanéra* must retire to his hammock and here eat of a white clay, *iwï činga,* and drink until he vomits of a brew made of boiling a man's leg ornament in water. Vomiting cleanses his body "of the blood of the shaman". The killer must paint his entire body black with *genipa (Genipa americana)* and put red urucu paint in his hair; he should also scratch his chest, arms, thighs, and back with teeth of the dog fish, just as he did in the ceremony he had performed as a young boy to make himself a strong adult. Then, each year at the annual ceremony during the harvests in May and June, all who have killed shamans must drink of *kauió* until they vomit, so cleansing themselves of the shaman's blood for the period until the next harvest.

DUTIES OF THE SHAMAN

Among the Tapirapé tobacco is a sacred plant necessary for curing and for all shamanistic activities; yet, while it is found widely near Tapirapé village and near their gardens, it is not strictly a cultivated plant. People know where a patch of tobacco grows and go there to pick it. Occasionally they transplant tobacco nearer to their houses or to their gardens but for the most part the patches seed themselves. When an individual discovers a new patch of tobacco, he hastily builds a low fence around it to inform others that it belongs to him. This native tobacco is smoked by laymen in short tubular pipes made of wood or clay and by shamans in long clay pipes, sometimes 30 centimeters long.

Tobacco is used for leisure-time smoking for pleasure; but its principal uses among the Tapirapé are as a stimulant and as a medicine. Each night after a long day's work or while travelling or hunting, Tapirapé men blow smoke over their tired legs, arms, and backs and sometimes men can be seen fumigating their tired wives or companions. They accompany the fumigation of their bodies with massage, rubbing their arms and legs toward the extremities. Tiredness and soreness are considered extraneous substances acquired during the day through exercise and it is believed they may be massaged and fumigated from the body.

Treatment of the sick is the shaman's most common duty and the use of tobacco is always a necessary prelude and accompaniment to this. Unless the illness is serious enough to warrant immediate treatment, shamans always cure in the late evening. A shaman comes to his patient, and squats near the patient's hammock, his first act is always to light his pipe. When the patient has a fever or has fallen unconscious from the sight of a ghost, the principal method of treatment is by massage. The shaman blows smoke over the entire body of the patient; then he blows smoke over his own hands, spits into them, and massages the patient slowly and firmly, always toward the extremities of the body. He shows that he is removing a foreign substance by a quick movement of his hands as he reaches the end of an arm or leg.

The more frequent method of curing, however, is by the extraction of a malignant object by sucking. The shaman squats alongside the hammock of his patient and begins to "eat smoke"—swallow large gulps of tobacco smoke from his pipe. He forces the smoke with great intakes of breath deep down into his stomach; soon he becomes intoxicated and nauseated; he vomits violently and smoke spews from his stomach. He groans and clears his throat in the manner of a person gagging with nausea but unable to vomit. By sucking back what he vomits he accumulates saliva in his mouth.

In the midst of this process he stops several times to suck on the body of his patient and finally, with one awful heave, he spews all the accumulated material on the ground. He then searches in this mess for the intrusive object that has been causing the illness. Never once did I see a shaman show the intrusive object to observers. As one treatment a Tapirapé *pančé* usually repeats this process of "eating smoke", sucking, and vomiting several times. Sometimes, when a man of prestige is ill, two or even three shamans will cure side by side in this manner and the noise of violent vomiting resounds throughout the village.

One other method of curing was observed. During an epidemic of fever Panteri made a collective cure to drive fever out of the village and disinfect the people of the village against it. Two men were dispatched to collect wild honey; this was then mixed with water, making a weak honey mixture. Panteri, after first smoking for a time, went from house to house taking the honey mixture in his mouth and spraying it over the houses and its occupants. He carefully sprayed and massaged the patients who had fever and removed the foreign substance from their bodies. For several hours he worked, spraying both the inside and outside of the houses, including the central ceremonial house of the men. It was explained that the honey alone did not have a therapeutic effect against fever but sprayed from the mouth of a *pančé* it drove away fevers.

Shamans also protect the Tapirapé against ghosts. All people who see ghosts faint from fright or from the white substance with which the ghost covers their body. Shamans were called to blow smoke over them and to massage this substance from their bodies. During one funeral dance the shaman Panteri "saw many ghosts" in the environs of the village, recognizing some as long-dead relatives of the deceased. By blowing tobacco smoke about and by going among the ghosts with a large mirror he drove them away before they did any harm.

Shamans are necessary in several life situations other than illness. For instance, shamans are thought among the Tapirapé to control the pregnancy of women. While pregnancy is known to be related to sexual intercourse, conception is thought to take place only when a shaman "brings a child to a woman". Several species of birds, of fish, of insects, and several natural phenomena, especially thunder, have children: that is, they are thought to control "spirits of children". A shaman steals, or more simply, takes spirits of children from these sources and brings them to a woman while she sleeps. Parents who wish children can bring presents to a *pancé* to "make him dream and bring a child to them." Most Tapirapé parents can identify the source of their children and the shaman who brought them. One father explained that he had taken honey to the *pancé* Urukumu, making him dream, and that Urukumu had then travelled to the house of Thunder and brought back a child to his wife. Another gave a present of fish to a shaman who brought back a child from the small fish called piau (*Leporinus* sp.); and yet another gave honey to a *pancé* who brought back a child from the horsefly (Tabanidae).

To the Tapirapé all good and likewise all evil can be laid at the door of the shaman. Consequently a phenomenon such as barrenness is always the fault of the shaman. A barren woman or a man with no children by his wife must have "quarreled much with the *pancé*". For example, it was clear to Kamairaho that his failure to have children by the three wives with whom he had lived during his lifetime was due to the shaman: "They do not want me to have a child", he said. He had no suspicion concerning his own sterility, even though his present and third wife had had a daughter by her first husband; for according to Tapirapé belief, all men who have sexual relations with a woman during her pregnancy are biological fathers of the child, and Kamairaho was in this manner the "father" of several children.

The safety of Tapirapé men depends upon the power of their shaman during the period each October and November when they must swim while they fish and shoot turtles; for in this region of Brazil rivers are infested with alligators, sting rays (*Potamotrygon histrix*), and the carnivorous fish called piranha (Serrasalminae). The Tapirapé also believe that large snakes lurk in deep pools of the rivers ready to wrap themselves around men and pull them beneath the water. During the year men will not swim in deep water unless it is absolutely necessary and they will fish only in shallow clear rapids. When they must swim to catch turtles, a shaman guarantees their safety. A powerful shaman dreams. He travels to the river, ties the jaws of the alligators with wires, strikes the *piranha* across their teeth so they cannot bite, and ties up the large snakes into knots with their own tails.

The abundance of the food supply may also become the responsibility of the shaman. Some powerful shamans have the ability to control the movements and the increase of the bands of pigs. These shamans visit in their dreams the "home of wild pigs" near the Tapirapé River on a hill called by them *Towaíyawá*—Ringed tail of the *coati* (*Nasua* sp.). There the shaman has sexual intercourse with female pigs, causing large increase in the bands. Those pigs that run fastest and are hardest to kill are these "children of the *pančé.*" The shaman's control over the movement of bands of pigs comes through his control over the *ančúnga* called *ampukáya*—"crying spirits". Wild pigs are said to be "pets" of these spirits and follow them about. Shamans who are powerful enough capture these spirits and take them, followed by their pets, to an appointed place where Tapirapé men wait to kill the pigs. None of the living shamans was believed to be capable of these controls over the wild pigs and several of the Indians blamed the recent lack of success of hunting expeditions and the apparent scarcity of pigs on the declining power of the shamans.

The dream journeys of the shamans also give them the power of prophecy, as was indicated by Panteri's vision of the fever in the village of the *peropí áwa*. Such dream experiences are not limited to the demonic world but sometimes occur in other earthly regions. The shaman may visit Carajá villages or Brazilian settlements along the Araguaya, where he sometimes learns facts of great interest or importance to his fellow-tribesmen. When Panteri visited the Brazilian settlements along the Araguaya River for the first time, he said that he recognized faces that he saw, for he had been to these places many times in his dreams. When I returned to the Tapirapé village after three months' absence, one shaman claimed to have prophecied my arrival to the day. He had travelled in his dream, he said, to the Araguaya River and had seen my canoe moving up the Tapirapé River. Another in the same way foresaw the arrival of a young Tapirapé who was returning from several weeks on the Araguaya. Frequently shamans, through their dreams, learn and then tell the Tapirapé where large bands of wild pigs can be found and advise them how to approach the band.

The cleansing of food may be accomplished by the shaman by tasting it or by blowing smoke or his breath over it. Several times each year these rites are performed over the first fruits of harvests to insure their safety before the people taste the crop. In December the first ears of the new maize are picked and presented to a strong shaman who then gives them to his wife to cook. At sundown of the day on which this is done the shaman walks to the central plaza followed by his wife, who carries the cooked maize and places it in a pile before him, ready for the ceremonies that will follow. In 1939, Panteri was the shaman who initiated this ceremony and he was joined by five other proved shamans. The people of the village gathered about this group of shamans who sat in a circle facing the maize. One by one the shamans took deep draughts from their burning pipes and blew the smoke over the maize. Then, one by one again, each pinched off a few grains from an ear and ate them. When the last had tasted the new maize, the ceremony was ended. The youngsters of the village then fell upon the pile of maize; the crop had been tasted by the shamans and found free from danger for the people. The next day maize was eaten in all houses.

A similar ceremony is performed in August or September with the first wild honey of the season, and again about January or February when new corn is ground to make the thick beverage kauí. I did not hear of such "tasting of first fruits" by shamans for other garden crops and informants were unable to remember any one occasion when shamans had found new maize or honey too dangerous for consumption by the people.

Again, each year in the first months of the rainy season when the new crop of maize is threatened by the first heavy rains and electrical storms, Tapirapé shamans must "fight" against Thunder and his minions in order to protect the gardens and even the people themselves from his violence. This four-day ceremony is the culmination of shamanistic activity among the Tapirapé and its most exotic and violent manifestation.

SOCIAL POSITION OF THE SHAMAN

The Tapirapá do not have chieftains with highly centralized authority. Instead one finds among them respected individuals who are described modernly by the Tapirapé with the Portuguese term "capitão". Such men of great prestige have in every instance gained the respect of their fellow tribesmen in one or more—usually at least two—of three ways.

First, an individual may be singled out by his parents, who must themselves be people of some prestige for especial treatment as a čiríkakántu, a favored child. Parents bestow upon such a child a series of important names which in themselves carry respect and he is taught with special care the myths, songs, dances, and manual techniques of the tribe. His parents may wait upon him, bringing him water to drink and to wash himself with and preparing special foods for him. Special care is taken in oiling and painting his body and elaborate decorations are made for him to wear during the annual harvest ceremonies, for the čiríkakántu are the central figures in part of this ceremony. Again, his body decorations are more elaborate than those of an ordinary youth when he dances during the ceremony of reaching maturity.

Secondly, an individual may gain respect through being chosen as a leader of the warrior-age group of his ceremonial moiety. His companions may select him as their "walking leader"—*antá úwa*—or as their "song leader"—*amoniká úwa*—because of his special abilities in hunting, gardening, manual technique, singing, or dancing. It frequently happens that these chosen leaders were *čiríkakántu* when they were children, for the special treatment and educational advantages given such children develop qualities of leadership.

The third and most important road to prestige lies in shamanism. It has been shown that the Tapirapé depend upon their shamans to control the dangerous spirit world, to remove danger from first fruits, to predict the future, to bring spirits of children to their parents, and to cure the ill. In all life situations where chance or the unpredictable figure the Tapirapé depend markedly upon their shamans. Thus the greatest prestige which Tapirapé culture offers accrues to the shaman. This prestige is reflected in the concepts of a separate afterlife for shamans and in the identification of ancestral culture heroes as shamans. Informants telling of Petura, the bringer of such phenomena as fire and daylight to the Tapirapé, and of Ware, who killed so many dangerous *ančúnga*, frequently referred to them as "great shamans". While a Tapirapé layman becomes a disembodied soul at death, the afterlife of a shaman is but a continuation of his present life under ideal circumstances. His soul goes to Maratawa, the home of the culture heroes. This home of the privileged dead lies far to the northwest "where the earth ends and the water begins" and where the sun returns to sleep after its travels across the sky. In Maratawa shamans have an inexhaustible supply of tobacco, many red parrot feathers, much manioc, kauí, bananas, meat, and all the other necessities and luxuries of life. Frequently a shaman is buried with a pipe filled with tobacco in his mouth, so that he may have smoke to drive out fatigue on the trip to Maratawa; and sometimes food is buried with the body so he may eat, for the journey to Maratawa is long.

Aside from these non-material considerations, there is one very real factor which insures social respect to the Tapirapé shaman. Shamans are in general the wealthiest men among the Tapirapé. Although they may at times receive meat or honey for their cures or as presents for bringing the spirits of children to parents, payments to them are usually in those luxury goods that are the marks of wealth. It was readily observed that the beads and hardware which I gave as presents to the Tapirapé soon passed into the hands of shamans as payments for cures.

Payments to the shamans for curing the ill depend upon the seriousness of the illness and upon what the patient or his family has to offer. Frequently a shaman names his fee when his cure has been successful, asking for specific objects, for he knows full well what each family owns. Unsuccessful cures are never paid. For example, for the treatment of his sister's son and of his daughter, who were both sick at once, Kamairaho, a shaman himself, called three shamans and paid each the price that he asked. He paid one, Panteri, a machete and two strings of beads; to another, Urukumu, he gave an axe, a pocket knife, a pair of scissors, and five tail feathers of a red parrot; he gave only four strings of beads to Kamaraí, who was considered a shaman of less power than the other two. Another young man with few possessions gave five arrows to a shaman who successfully treated his wife; still another paid the breast feathers from his parrot and four strings of beads to a shaman. When Txawaniuma killed a *paca*, the meat of which is highly prized by the Tapirapé, he gave some to his companion of the hunt and divided the rest between two shamans who had treated his small daughter successfully. Neither shaman had to ask for any specific gift or payment. People often complain to others about the high price they had to pay to a shaman, but generally they pay what is asked. "Stinginess" is a severe accusation among these people and to complain mildly about a high price is one way of announcing one's liberality.

Liberality is a necessary quality for a man of prestige. At the time of the annual harvest ceremonies, shamans and all other men of prestige must give gifts to all those who drink of *kauió*. Gift giving at this time proves their liberality and validates their prestige. At this time then there is a siphoning off of wealth from the shamans, but throughout the rest of the year fees and gifts channel it back into their hands.

ROAD TO SHAMANISM

Among the Tapirapé, *pančés* are essentially those people who dream much and who, in their dreams, travel widely in the supernatural world, achieving familiarity with the supernatural. At the time of my visit there were six men recognized as fullfledged shamans who were called upon to treat the sick and to perform various ceremonials. Panteri and Urukumu, were the two clearly outstanding; these assumed leadership in shamanistic ceremonies and were the ones most frequently called for cures. Besides these six recognized shamans, there were four young men working to develop shamanistic power to gain recognition as shamans.

Within the memory of persons living in the village there had been three women shamans, but there were none, either practicing as recognized shamans or working as novices, during my visit. The women shamans were remembered as having been especially malevolent. They are supposed to dream more than men and work much harm to the people. People who recalled the women shamans explained that when they had sung in the annual ceremony of calling and fighting Thunder they had sung the part of the music usually sung by the shamans' wives and their husbands had sung the usual men shamans' parts. The women *pančés* had smoked and fallen in trances as the male shamans do. Nothing possible to men shamans appeared to be beyond the power of the women. None of them was described as masculine in behavior; on the contrary, they were described as "good wives", and one of them was remembered as small and particularly attractive.

Certain people regardless of sex are early recognized as future shamans because of their natural inclination to dream. Several informants, for example, told me that a young boy, an orphan, and therefore badly cared for, would certainly be a powerful shaman. He turned and talked in his sleep and had been known to cry during a nightmare. He remembered few of his dreams but did tell of seeing the spirit of his mother, and described an evil spirit which he met during a dream. One of the present powerful shamans is said to have been such a youngster with a predilection for dreaming. Such youngsters are nervous and sensitive; yet no distinctive personality traits were observed among adult shamans. Shamans are frequently emaciated and thin, attributable perhaps to their constant use of tobacco and the resulting nausea, and one shaman, now dead, was described by informants as a nervous ascetic interested only in the supernatural world.

Persons lacking this predilection for dreaming, but with aspirations to shamanism, may solicit dreams. Each year during the days of the dry season all young men who aspire to shamanism, even those who have shown potentialities during boyhood, gather each evening in the central plaza of the village to seek dreams. A novice sits upon the ground near a *pančé*, his mentor, and swallows smoke from his mentor's pipe until violent vomiting occurs. When the novices are too ill to hold the pipe, the shaman holds it for them, forcing them to continue "eating smoke." Generally the neophytes fall backwards unconscious and ill from the smoke; during this state they may dream. In any case, when they regain their senses, the pipe is again placed in their mouth until they fall backwards ill and unconscious once more. The process may be repeated several times over a period of two or three hours. Later, when the novice retires to his hammock for the night, he may expect a dream.

Such sessions occur each night during the few weeks before the Thunder ceremony and a serious novice should attend all sessions. During this period he refrains from sexual intercourse because it will hinder his dreaming; he also refrains from bathing and so becomes grimy. He must not eat of those animals which "walk at night", such as the jaboti tortoise (*Testudo tabulata*) and the monkey, because he must be friendly with all creatures he may meet in his nocturnal dream travels. He should eat manioc flour, yams, pepper, and such bland meats as jacu, coati

(*Nasua* sp.), peccary, mutum (*Crax* sp.), and chicken; of other foods he must eat sparingly or not at all. The novices are "tired" and "thin"; many do not continue after the first few nights because they "are lazy" or because "they are afraid". Campukwi, my informant, did not continue because he did not like the dirt, the nausea from tobacco, the lack of food, and the sexual continence.

Other novices, more successful and more persistent, do dream. At first they see smoky forms of ghosts and sometimes forest demons; they as yet do not know how to talk with such spirits. Usually, the first season or two during which a young man seeks dreams, he may expect mild dreams. After several seasons the novice may see dangerous forest demons in his unconscious states and he may talk with ghosts. Traditionally, young Tapirapé shamans become wild and uncontrollable when they have their first dangerous dreams. They are reported sometimes to stand up suddenly from their induced unconscious state and run wildly through the village, sometimes killing chickens, dogs, and parrots, or breaking pottery. Although no novices "ran" in this way during the 1940 training period, an informant described the state of a young shaman who "ran" several years ago. "He jumped up. He shouted and ran through the village. He carried a club in his hand (usually weapons are placed well out of reach). He killed two chickens and broke through the side of a house. He killed his brother's dog. All the women and children ran from the village, afraid. Finally, Maeumi grabbed him but he was strong and he hit Maeumi with a club and blood ran down Maeumi's face. Many men came and held him and Urukumu (his mentor) blew smoke over him", thus bringing him back to his senses. He had seen dangerous spirits and "was afraid", informants told me. This reaction is common for those who show potentialities toward shamanism.

The mere fact that the young shaman has several dangerous dreams does not make him a proved shaman. He must take part in the "fight" against the beings of Thunder, and by the side of his mentor he may attempt cures. If successful, he may be called now and again by people for cures. With a reputation for several cures and with continual dreaming, during which he has supernatural encounters, he builds up his reputation as a shaman over a period of many years. Panteri and Urukumu were about fifty years old when I visited them; informants gave no indication that their power was expected to decline with old age.

CONCLUSIONS

It is apparent that in studying Tapirapé shamanism we are concerned with patterns which are part of a deep-seated New World shamanistic complex found widespread in both North and South America—from the

Eskimo to the Ona and Yahgan of Tierra del Fuego. Among the Tupi-guaraní peoples, however, shamanism has been an unusual factor in their cultural history. Dr. Alfred Métraux has shown that the numerous and distant migrations of Tupi-Guaraní tribes in post-Columbian times were frequently instigated by powerful shamans. In another study, Dr. Métraux emphasizes the extraordinary powers of the Tupinambá shamans and states that among the coastal Tupi of Brazil shamans at times held great secular powers. Senhor Curt Nimuendaju writes that the basic organization of the Apapocúva-Guaraní, before European contact, was the voluntary subordination to their shaman-chiefs and points out that the failure to recognize their power was the cause of repeated failures to unite the Guaraní in "aldeamentos". My own recent work among the Tupi-speaking Guajajara of the Rio Pindaré of Northeastern Brazil leads me to the opinion that, especially before European administrators gave them secular chiefs, Guajajara shamans exercized such strong religious and social controls over their people. The emphasis upon the role of the shaman in Tapirapé culture shows, therefore, a marked affinity with other Tupi-Guaraní peoples.

28· THE PHILOSOPHY OF
THE NAVAHO INDIANS *

Ideologies comprise matters both sacred and secular. An ideological system is not only the way that a culture regards the surrounding world, but the way in which it regards itself. Various anthropologists have dealt with this aspect of culture: Benedict spoke of it in terms of *patterns* (see No. II:33); Melville Herskovits speaks of *focus;* Morris Opler treats of *themes;* and E. A. Hoebel talks of *postulates.* The author of this article is well known for his analysis of value systems: here he inquires into the basic assumptions of Navaho culture.

T HE PUBLICATION of Paul Radin's *Primitive Man as a Philosopher* did much toward destroying the myth that a cognitive orientation toward experience was a peculiarity of literate societies. Speculation and reflection upon the nature of the universe and of man's place in the total scheme of things have been carried out in every known culture. Every people has its characteristic set of "primitive postulates." As Bateson has said: "The human individual is endlessly simplifying and generalizing his own view of his environment; he constantly imposes on this environment his own constructions and meanings; these constructions and meanings are characteristic of one culture as opposed to another."

* Clyde Kluckhohn, "The Philosophy of the Navaho Indians," *Ideological Differences and World Order,* F. S. C. Northrop (editor) (New Haven: Yale University Press, 1949), pp. 356–383. Reprinted by permission of the author and the publisher.

Professor of Anthropology at Harvard, the author (b. 1905) was trained at Vienna, Oxford and Harvard and has done fieldwork in Greece and among the Hopi. His most extensive (and intensive) work, however, has been with the Ramah Navaho. Kluckhohn is interested in all fields of anthropology but a major focus has long been on the ideological aspects of culture. Among his works are *Navaho Witchcraft* (1944), *The Navaho* (with Dorothea Leighton, 1946), *Mirror for Man* (1949; also in paperback), and *Culture: a Critical Review of Concepts and Definitions* (1952).

It remains true that critical examination of basic premises and fully explicit systematization of philosophical concepts are seldom found at the nonliterate level. The printed word is an almost essential condition for free and extended discussion of fundamental issues. Where dependence on memory exists, there seems to be an inevitable tendency to emphasize the correct perpetuation of the precious oral tradition. Similarly, while it is all too easy to underestimate the extent to which ideas spread without books, it is in general true that tribal or folk societies do not possess competing philosophical systems. The major exception to this statement is, of course, the case where part of the tribe becomes converted to one of the great proselytizing religions such as Christianity or Mohammedanism. But, before contact with rich and powerful civilizations, "primitive" peoples seem to have absorbed new ideas piecemeal, slowly integrating them with the previously existent ideology.

Although there are no organized groups of human beings without their own philosophy, there are, then, some tendencies toward differentiation between literate and nonliterate societies. The abstract thought of the latter is ordinarily less self-critical, less systematic, less elaborated in purely logical dimensions; more concrete, more implicit—perhaps more completely coherent than the philosophy of most individuals in larger societies which have been influenced over long periods by disparate intellectual currents. It must be remembered, however, that these statements are made at a relatively high level of abstraction. There are such wide variations in the philosophies of "primitive" folk that, in empirical detail, any black-and-white contrast between "primitive" and "civilized" philosophy would be altogether fictitious.

This consideration of a single nonliterate philosophy is, therefore, not offered as a representation of "primitive man's thought." It affords merely a single illustration of orientations which are typical of the members of one large (60,000) nonliterate group with a fairly homogeneous culture. In the earlier part of this chapter the presentation will be restricted to "native" (i.e., pre-European) ideas. Later, the effects of ideas from white American culture will be touched upon. By no means every adult, minimally acculturated Navaho would set forth all of the notions that will be described. There are Navaho intellectuals (mainly the singers of their ceremonials), and the more explicit systematic statements have been derived in part from talks with them. Yet it is maintained that "average" Navahos think and act in accord with these premises and concepts, even though they would be hard put to explain them in the fashion carried out here.

IMPLICIT PHILOSOPHY

There is a unifying philosophy behind the way of life of every individual at any given point in his history. Although each personality gives to this philosophy an idiosyncratic coloring, this is primarily in its affective or felt dimensions. The main outlines of the fundamental assumptions and basic abstractions have only exceptionally been created out of the stuff of unique biological heredity and peculiar life experience. They are usually cultural products. From the life-ways that constitute the designs for living of his community or tribe or region or socioeconomic class or nation or civilization the ordinary individual derives most of his "mental outlook."

Cultures or group life-ways do not manifest themselves solely in observable customs and artifacts. There is much more to social and cultural phenomena than immediately meets the ear and eye. If the behavioral facts are to be correctly understood, certain presuppositions constituting what might be termed a philosophy or ideology must also be known. The "strain toward consistency" which Sumner noted in the folkways and mores of all groups cannot be accounted for unless one postulates a more or less systematic pattern of reaction to experience as a characteristic property of all integrated cultures. In a certain deep sense the logic (that is, the *manner* of interpreting relationships between phenomena) of all members of the human species is the same. It is the premises that are different. Moreover, the premises are learned as part of a cultural tradition.

Synthesis within a culture is achieved partly through the overt statement of the dominant conceptions, assumptions, and aspirations of the group in its religious lore, secular thought, and ethical code; partly through unconscious apperceptive habits, ways of looking at the stream of events that are so taken for granted as seldom or never to be verbalized explicitly. These habitual ways of begging certain questions that are distinctive of different cultures may be clearly crystallized in the morphology of the language. For example, the tense system of European languages points to the enormous emphasis upon time in Western culture. To the outsider who is a student of the culture these linguistic forms may constitute invaluable clues to the structure of the implicit culture. But to the naïve participants in the culture these modes of categorizing, of dissecting experience along these planes and not others, are as much "given" as the regular sequence of natural phenomena or the necessity of air, water, and food for life.

Every group's way of life, then, is a structure—not a haphazard collection of all the different physically possible and functionally effective patterns of belief and action but an interdependent system based upon linked premises and categories whose influence is greater rather than less because they are seldom brought out into explicit discussion. Some degree of internal coherence which is apperceived rather than rationally constructed seems to be demanded by most of the participants in any culture. As Whitehead has remarked, "Human life is driven forward by its dim apprehension of notions too general for its existing language."

In sum, the way of life that is handed down as the social heritage of every people does more than supply a set of skills for making a living and a set of blueprints for human relations. Each different way of life makes its own assumptions about the ends and purposes of human existence, about ways by which knowledge may be obtained, about the organization of the pigeonholes in which each sense datum is filed, about what human beings have a right to expect from each other and the gods, about what constitutes fulfillment or frustration. Some of these assumptions are made explicit in the lore of the folk; others are tacit premises which the observer must infer by finding consistent trends in word and deed.

In highly self-conscious Western civilization that has recently made a business of studying itself, the number of assumptions that are literally implicit in the sense of never having been stated or discussed by anyone may be negligible. Yet only a trifling number of Americans could state even those implicit premises of our culture that have been dissected out by social scientists. I remember an astute remark by Lloyd Warner: "If you could bring to the American Scene an Australian aborigine who had been socialized in his own culture and then trained in social science, he would perceive all sorts of patterned regularities of which our sociologists are completely unaware."

In the case of the less sophisticated and less self-conscious societies, the unconscious assumptions characteristically made by individuals brought up under approximately the same social controls will bulk large. The Navaho do talk about their ethical principles and their values. Navaho intellectuals discuss the purposes of life and the principles that govern the universe. But many distinctively Navaho doings and sayings make sense only if they are related to certain implicit convictions about the nature of human life and experience, convictions so deep-going that no Navaho thinks of talking about them in so many words. These unstated assumptions are so completely taken for granted that the Navaho (like all peoples) take these views of life as an ineradicable part of human nature and find it hard to understand that normal persons could possibly conceive life in other terms. Much of what will be said in the two following sections is at this level. This implicit philosophy is an inferential construct based on consistencies in observed thought and action patterns.

UNDERLYING PREMISES

The keystones on which the Navaho view of the world appears to rest may be stated schematically as follows:

1. The universe is orderly: all events are caused and interrelated.
   a. Knowledge is power.
   b. The basic quest is for harmony.
   c. Harmony can be restored by orderly procedures.
   d. One price of disorder, in human terms, is illness.
2. The universe tends to be personalized.
   a. Causation is identifiable in personalized terms.
3. The universe is full of dangers.
4. Evil and good are complementary, and both are ever present.
5. Experience is conceived as a continuum differentiated only by sense data.
6. Morality is conceived in traditionalistic and situational terms rather than in terms of abstract absolutes.
7. Human relations are premised upon familistic individualism.
8. Events, not actors or qualities, are primary.

Each of these presuppositions now needs to be elaborated and, in some instances, qualified. Up to a point the Navaho may be legitimately described as a "primitive mechanist." On the other hand, one does encounter some teleological notions. It is generally agreed that Changing Woman created livestock and other goods for the benefit of the Navaho. Some accounts state that death was created so that "everything would be coming new," that the earth would not get too crowded with people and with livestock. The myth with respect to livestock is obviously post-European, and there are other grounds for suspecting the influence of Christian theology in all versions that attribute an all-embracing purposeful design to the divinities. Recently created myths of flood and of the impending end of the world probably also have an indirect Christian source.

In general, Navaho philosophy makes small provision for teleology and for mysticism. History is not oriented in accord with the master design of all-wise and all-powerful beings; events are the inevitable results of previous events. Visionaries do occasionally appear in Navaho lore and legends. But they did not themselves seek mystical experience; the visions were caused, not willed. The ideas of fasting, self-torture, and pity that were so popular among Plains Indians seem ridiculous to earthy, hedonistic Navahos. Rites of purification occur in the curing ceremonials, but this is not a case of the individual's seeking mystical enlightenment. He is only following a cultural pattern that has nothing to do with his private motives.

It should be noted, however, that the Navaho, although they usually think in terms of mechanical causation, are not thorough-going positivists. They do lay great stress on immediately apprehended sense data. This life is what counts, and experience is not defined mystically but in terms of one's sensations of pain and pleasure and of the existence of persons and objects outside oneself. On the other hand, mountains and other natural phenomena have their "inner forms" as well as the properties obtained from introspection of a succession of sense data. Words, as well as things and processes, are important. Mastery of an exoteric terminology gives one power over supernatural forces, objects, and events to which the terms refer.

The universe is orderly. Everything in the universe is interrelated It is a lawful universe. The notion of causation is essentially mechanical. Although at the beginning of things certain happenings occurred at the will of the divinities, they themselves were henceforth bound by the consequences of their own acts. Once the machine had been started, it ran according to irreversible laws. There is no place in Navaho thought for a god who can capriciously (from the Navaho point of view) grant the petition of humans. The divinities, too, follow the rules. Every event has one or more specifiable causes. If rain does not fall at the expected season it is because "people are too mean" or because "whites are selling liquor to the Navahos." As Dr. Reichard has written: "The balance of all things may break down because of man's own behavior in breaking taboos, because of ghosts and witchcraft, or because of foreign influences, all matters which are considered as being 'out of order.'" However, it should be noted at once that possible causes are multitudinous. Hence, one must not be too disappointed if a ceremonial cure is not successful. There are causes, but identification is not easy. The universe is determinate, but human thought is not determinate. "Perhaps" is one of the words most frequently uttered in Navaho.

There is even in Navaho behavior a touch of the experimental, of the utterly pragmatic. Before committing himself to an expensive nine-day ceremonial the sick individual will try out a brief excerpt. Only if it works will he go on to the full version. Some (though not all) singers will freely admit what certainly goes on in practice: a new herbal medicine or song or bit of equipment will be tried out in a ceremonial; if the results are satisfactory, the new business will be incorporated as a standard procedure and taught to learners of the rite. Whole new ceremonials have been borrowed from neighboring tribes, slightly adapted, kept or discarded on the basis of experience. In secular life the Navaho is prone to try anything once. New foods, clothing, and gadgets are taken over with a freedom that contrasts sharply with the resistance of the Pueblo Indians to innovation.

Knowledge is power. The conception of "good luck" is hard to translate into the Navaho language. In their scheme of things one is not "lucky" or "unlucky." One has the requisite knowledge (sacred or profane) or one hasn't. Even in what European languages call "games of chance" the Navaho depends upon medicines, rites, and verbal formulas. The same is true with hunting. Getting a deer is never a matter of good fortune; it is a matter of ritual knowledge and of one's relations with supernaturals which, again, are controllable.

Complete knowledge, however, is unattainable: "Not even the white people who have been everywhere, go across the ocean, fly in the sky, can see all things and places—even up in the sky—not even they know where the sunrise is nor where the sunset is. Nor will they ever find out." While man can never hope completely to understand and control his destiny, he can, once he learns the right formulas, coerce even supernatural beings, for they too are subject to the lawful processes that control events. If the right mechanical procedures are followed, the divinities *must* restore the patient to health and harmonious living.

The basic quest is for harmony. In so far as Navaho philosophy is goal-oriented, it is directed toward the elimination of friction in human relations and toward the restoration of harmony in that total economy of things in which human affairs constitute only one facet. In the Navaho conception of the relationship between their divinities there is the mechanical notion of a balance of opposing forces. No one divine being has unfettered control over the others. Each is limited by the powers of others as well as by the remorseless working out of processes beyond the control of the whole pantheon. In this equilibrium of forces human effort in the form of observance of taboos and in the performance of compulsive rituals can play its part. Individually acquired knowledge can assist in the restoration of harmony in one person's life, in that of the community, in that of the whole universe.

This dominant conception of balance is reflected in the scrupulous symmetry of ceremonials, formal narratives, and art. Poetry is constructed in the fugue and coda style. In dry paintings, rugs, and silverwork an element rarely appears singly. There is a pair, or more often a group of four. In songs and prayers there are numberless balanced repetitions, four again being the favorite pattern:

That before us there being beauty as we shall walk about, we have told our stories to each other. That behind us there being beauty as we shall walk about, we have told our stories to each other. That below us there being beauty as we shall walk about, we have told our stories to each other. That all about us there being beauty as we shall walk about, we have told our stories to each other.

That our speech will become beautiful, we have told our stories to each other. That out of our mouths there will come beauty, we have told our stories to each other. That we shall walk about in beauty, we have told our stories to each other. That we shall walk about being "that which goes about at the rim of old age," we have told our stories to each other.

That today we are the children of the Earth, we have told our stories to each other. That we are the child of the Black Sky, we have told our stories to each other. That we are the children of the Sun, we have told our stories to each other. That we are the children of the White Shell Woman, we have told our stories to each other. That we are the children of the Changing Woman, we have told our stories to each other. That we are the children of the Talking God, we have told our stories to each other. That we are the grandchildren of the Hogan God, we have told our stories to each other.

Let there be beauty indeed. Let there be beauty indeed.
Let there be beauty indeed. Let there be beauty indeed.

Divinities in all forms of symbolism tend to turn up in pairs or fours (Changing Woman, White Shell Woman, Salt Woman, Turquoise Woman; Monster Slayer and Child of the Water). The final example is a pairing of older and younger—a repeated theme in Navaho culture. Another common form of balance is that between the sexes. Each male divinity has a female counterpart in a dry painting. There are male rains and female rains; male rivers and female rivers; male turquoise and female turquoise; male chants and female chants; male plants and female plants. In part, this is not so much a duality of the sexes as such but rather the complementary nature of stronger and weaker, dominant and submissive, etc.

One price of disorder is illness. In every ceremonial there is a patient ("one sung over"), although all rites, and some in particular, have purposes that go beyond the individual to the group and indeed to the whole world. Illness is not traced to what Europeans would consider "natural" causes. Even a broken limb from an accident may have a deeper etiology. Illness is one possible result of disharmony. The outward and visible form of the disharmony may be a disturbance in human relations, but this, in turn, is the manifestation of malequilibrium in the patient's relations to supernatural forces. The social group, the rest of the animate and inanimate world, and the supernaturals are all part of one scheme. Anything that disturbs the balance of this system as a whole can produce malfunctioning in any part of the system. The symptom may be a physiological disturbance, social friction, lack of rainfall, or a flood.

The universe tends to be personalized. This if you like, is the familiar "animism." As a matter of fact, it is a broadly human tendency, found among peoples not considered "animistic." In contemporary American culture, for example, most persons find it psychologically more satisfying to blame "Wall Street operators" than "the laws of supply and demand," "Stalin's clique" than "Communist ideology." Navaho parallels are: "witches" as opposed to "bad weather," "the spirit of Old Age" as opposed to "physiological process." The Navahos, however, do carry the tendency further. Every feature of nature is animated and has some specific supernatural power. "The spirit of hunger kills me" is preferred to the intransitive "I am hungry." The English language describes the impersonal operation of natural forces, "I am drowning"; Navaho uses the active, personalized "water is killing me." Causes are not only identifiable; they are, up to a point, controllable in the way that people are controllable.

The universe is full of dangers. Every realist is aware that the world is a dangerous place. But the Navaho is distinguished by the variety of threats from the unseen world that he fears and names. Navaho philosophy seems a little like that of the Eskimo who said, "We do not believe; we fear." To be sure, he has also learned from experience in his difficult physical environment that living is hard and dangerous. It should also be understood that this view is interpreted in terms of the first premise. It is part of the nature of things that life is difficult and hazardous. No Navaho ever curses a divinity or a "malign fate." He accepts, though he accepts cheered by the realization that *some* misfortunes can be averted by applying obtainable knowledge and thus influencing the course of events. From old age and death there is no escape, but most mischances result from "error which is either incomplete knowledge or carelessness in the observation of rules which constitute the lubricant to minimize friction in the operation of the universal machine" (Gladys Reichard).

Evil and good are complementary, and both are ever present. Some divinities can be influenced directly by human rituals, some only indirectly, others not at all. Some of the Holy People continually have human interests at heart, but the Sun and Moon each continue to demand a life a day, and First Woman and First Man persist in malevolent activity. But all are necessary to the scheme of things. According to some informants, even the most respected singers must know a little witchcraft—"or they'll go dry." The conception of perfection of personality is not a Navaho abstraction. Some frailties are recorded even of Changing Woman, who, of the divine beings, most nearly approaches the idea of benevolence. The most cherished and respected of family members are thought to have some evil in them, so that when they die their ghosts are feared, though majority Navaho opinion says that the good person who died in a ripe old age is harmless.

Experience is conceived as a continuum differentiated only by sense data. The Navaho find no difficulty in distinguishing one horse from another. The language delights in categorizing the concrete in precise and neat fashion. However, where the senses fail to provide evidence of sharp gradations, the continuum, with one important exception, is undifferentiated. A Navaho cannot conceive of absolute good or of absolute evil, though perhaps it is misleading even to use these two words. The Navaho conceive of what is to be desired and what is to be feared more than of the morally approved and disapproved. That is, to say that a person has evil in him really means in Navaho terms that he has properties that are to be dreaded. At any rate, the two qualities of the sought and of the avoided shade into each other and blend. Categories like "the social," "the economic," "the political" baffle the schooled Navaho. Life is a whole. There is likewise no mind-body problem for the Navaho. Although there is a Navaho word which may be translated "mind" and another which may be tendered "body," the two are conceived as interdependent, with the "mind" (the "in-lying one") as dominant. If a person has bodily aches and pains, his "mind" must be treated. If his mental reactions are aberrant, his body must be put through the same procedures as the man who has a fever. Psychosomatic medicine is no startling discovery to the Navaho! The behavior of the warrior's wife at home is as relevant to his safety and success as are his own actions, for all are part of a continuum of interrelated events. Navaho thought abhors the clear-cut time distinctions that are so necessary to Western thinking. Things have only the isolability evidenced by immediate sense perception. Events seem to be thought of as points in a continuous pattern. When they are separated out from the pattern, all their aspects in vivid specificity are isolated as a whole. The type of abstraction that is the central feature of what Northrop has called the theoretic component is almost entirely lacking in Navaho thinking.

Morality is conceived in traditionalistic and situational terms rather than in terms of abstract absolutes. Conduct that is not defined by custom or by rules involving the supernatural is ordinarily judged in terms of its practicality. But a pattern of conduct that has become invested with symbolic significance has its warrant in tradition rather than in rationality. "That is the old Navaho way." "Women must sit that way because the female Holy People used to sit that way." Any violation of the rules is a disruption of the harmony of things and a sure cause of trouble. There is no rain this year because the young men stamped their feet in the Girl's Dance, and that is not the old way. A woman is sick because she fired pottery in full sight of everyone. Since custom is king, public opinion and not "conscience" is the arbiter. Punishment is predominantly external, not internal. Navahos do not lie awake at night worrying about their secret sins. But the threat of being "shamed" by

being publicly observed in a transgression of customs or the fear of
setting in motion a set of supernatural sanctions is sufficient to induce
proper behavior. The difference between Navaho morality and Christian
morality is not at all that of the presence versus the absence of moral
standards. It is rather a difference in the mechanisms for enforcing those
standards.

Navaho morality is also contextual rather than absolute. This is characteristic of "shame" as opposed to "guilt" culture. Lying is not always
and everywhere wrong. The rules vary with the situation. To deceive
when trading with foreign tribes is a morally accepted practice. Acts
are not in themselves bad or good. Incest is perhaps the only conduct
that is condemned without qualification. It is quite correct to use witchcraft techniques in trading with members of foreign tribes. Behavior
that is disapproved for a Navaho is acceptable for an outsider. There is
an almost complete absence of abstract ideals. Under the circumstances
of aboriginal life Navahos did not need to orient themselves in terms of
abstract morality. They got their orientations from face-to-face contacts
with the same small group of people with whom they have the overwhelming majority of their dealings from birth to death. In a large,
complex society like modern America, where people come and go and
business and other dealings must be carried on by people who never see
each other, it is functionally necessary to have abstract standards that
transcend an immediate concrete situation in which two or more persons
are interacting.

Human relations are premised upon familistic individualism. The
Navaho, particularly as contrasted with the Pueblo and some other com-
munally oriented groups, is surely an individualist. Ceremonial knowledge is acquired—and paid for—by the individual. Certain animals in
the family herd belong to definite persons. Some rites give considerable
scope to individual self-expression. Yet this is equally certainly not the
romantic individualism of American culture. No unacculturated Navaho
feels his independence sufficiently to break from his relatives. There is a
great deal of ordinarily submerged hostility among family members, but
in his cognitive picture of his world the Navaho insists that family life is
the hub of interpersonal relations. He does not consider himself primarily
as a member of a local community, nor of his tribe—let alone of the
United States or of an international brotherhood. His conception of the
ideal society is that of a stable equilibrium between various groups of
related persons. One's first loyalty is neither to oneself nor to society
in the abstract but rather, in attenuating degrees as one moves outward
in the circle of kin, to one's biological and clan relatives.

Events, not actors or qualities, are primary. Navaho is overwhelmingly a verbal language. Most nouns may be thematic, and adjectives are slightly altered verbs. The most fundamental categories distinguish types of activity. Similarly, Navaho thinking is relentlessly concerned with doing, with happenings. This fits with the view of the universe as process, with the belief that effective action influences the process, with the emphasis on the interconnections between events, with the stress on situation as opposed to qualitative absolutes, with the animation attributed even to natural phenomena. It is very difficult in Navaho to make fine precisions as to attributes; it is all too easy to indicate a hundred variations as to how an act of going occurred. Doing—neither being nor becoming—is the keynote of Navaho thought.

NAVAHO LAWS OF THOUGHT

Navaho reasoning proceeds consciously or unconsciously from the above premises. It remains to specify the forms of logical processes recognized as valid. First, negatively, it should be observed that the Aristotelian laws of "identity" and "excluded middle" are only weakly and not consistently observed in Navaho thinking. One never hears a Navaho say "a thing either is or it isn't." "Both-and" is a more familiar form than "either-or"—to the extent that one can point to many examples of the thought process that Lévy-Bruhl designated as *participation mystique*.

The following positive logical canons are by no means distinctly Navaho, but they are so emphasized as to be of indispensable significance for the comprehension of their mental horizon. They need only be listed here, since they have been discussed so frequently in approximately the same form that they are encountered among the Navaho:

(*a*) Like produces like (e.g., the eagle flies swiftly so that the runner can well carry a bit of eagle down).

(*b*) A part can stand for a whole (e.g., witches can work upon hair or nail parings as effectively as upon the victim himself).

(*c*) *Post hoc ergo propter hoc* (e.g., the grass no longer grows as high as in the old days when taboos were strictly kept; therefore, the decrease in vegetation is caused by carelessness in observing the rules).

(*d*) Every subjective experience must have its demonstrable correlate in the sense world. (It is not enough for a Navaho to say "I *know* a witch is after me." Witch tracks must be found or dirt must fall mysteriously from the roof of the hut at night. All interpretations must be documented in terms of actual sensory events. The unacculturated Navaho has difficulty in adjusting to clock time. This is arbitrary and unconvincing because it is not based upon natural phenomena.)

SOME BASIC NAVAHO CATEGORIES

In general the Navaho language is tremendously concrete. Referents of words are unusually delimited and precise. Verbalizations are taken with great literalness. Though some ordinary words have figurative connotations, loose denotations are uncommon, and, since most Navahos have had highly similar experiences associated with the same words, connotations do not spread over nearly as much territory as they do in English.

There are, however, some abstract words, extremely difficult to render adequately in English, which are of the greatest importance for the understanding of Navaho philosopohy. Perhaps the most significant of these is conveyed by the Navaho root hóžǫ́–. This is probably the central idea in Navaho religious thinking. It occurs in the names of two important ceremonials (Blessing Way and Beauty Way) and is frequently repeated in almost all prayers and songs. In various contexts it is best translated as "beautiful," "harmonious," "good," "blessed," "pleasant," and "satisfying." As a matter of fact, the difficulty with translation primarily reflects the poverty of English in terms that simultaneously have moral and esthetic meaning. A number of words in classical Greek come rather close.

Earlier it was remarked that the universe was not only lawful but also an interrelated whole. It is integration with the harmony of all forces, personal and impersonal—a harmony that includes both good and evil —that is sought in Blessing Way. It is sought not only for the individual patient but also for his family and for all present at the rite and indeed for all living beings (animal, human, and divine; Navaho and non-Navaho) and all natural phenomena (rivers, mountains, winds, lightning, and the like). The harmony exists, but no person, human or divine, can hope for complete and permanent participation in it:

> When my spiritual power was strong, I came up with it
> When I was holy, I came up with it
>
> "Second Song of the Flood"

For a limited period a personality can become identified with this harmony, and the integration of all forces in it can be improved by performances of the ceremonial.

It is to be noted that this term is applied to a human being only while he is in a sacred situation (i.e., singer or patient in a ceremonial). This in itself implies that the state is not permanently attainable. It also implies that the word means something different from the actually realizable condition of relative moral goodness. "Holiness" is sharply distinct from "goodness." The descriptive adjectives that designate individuals

who are "good" (in the simply moral nonesthetic sense) have reference
to a number of different qualities. The most general concept seems to
include the notions of industry, responsibility (especially to one's relatives), frugality-generosity, strength-hardihood, pleasant disposition,
avoidance of excess of any kind, tending to one's own affairs.

The conception of evil also has separate profane and sacred dimensions. The root, hóčǫ́–, however, is not a precise antithesis of hóʒǫ́–.
It does not refer explicitly to disorder as hóʒǫ́– refers to harmony. Rather,
its primary reference is to the malevolent activities of ghosts and witches
who are the living embodiments of evil of the sacred variety. Ceremonials
of Evil Way type (intended to free the patients from ghost or witch
attack) are hóčǫ́·ʒí which is sometimes translated "Ghost Way." Various
words applied to persons who are disapproved of in the profane sense
refer to qualities the opposite of those listed for the good person. Individuals who commit incest are abhorred and suspect of witchcraft. To
be sure, some connection between the categories is evidenced. Those
who are violent, lazy, irresponsible, meddlesome are more often accused of witchcraft than is the average Navaho. On the other hand,
singers and the rich and powerful (who are at least industrious and
strong) are still more frequently mentioned as witches.

Another basic concept of the sacred world is that of "immunity." The
patient in a Holy Way ceremonial becomes identified with the Holy
People of that rite, hence holy himself, hence immune to further attack
from these divinities. This conception is, of course, congruent with the
premise that many dangers can be averted through employment of the
proper mechanical means. The word, diγin, which is rendered above as
"immune" may also in certain contexts be translated as "holy" or sacred."
"Charged with positive spiritual electricity" suggests in not too far-
fetched a manner the core of the Navaho concept. One whole group of
Navaho ceremonials is called the Holy (diγin) Way group. One class of
divinities is referred to as the Holy People (diγin diné).

The category "property" is very prominent and has some special
Navaho subdivisions: "hard goods," "soft goods," "flexible goods," etc.
The Navaho concept of "place" is unusual and impossible to convey
briefly and directly. Every thing and every act has spatial position which
must be specified with great precision. Myths are replete with long lists
of place names that are as tiresome to the foreigner as the "Catalogue
of Ships" in the Iliad. Each verb has a special third person form that
grammarians call "place person." Other secular categories tend to follow
the lines set rather obviously by the visible world. Except for certain
plant groups, there is little lumping in accord with use or function as
contrasted with divisions derivable from descriptive physical features.

The absence of various abstract categories that are familiar to whites

should be mentioned. It is not surprising in a "shame" culture that there is no notion of "sin." Nor can the Navaho easily conceive of "laying up treasures in Heaven." Indeed there is no heaven in our sense. The afterworld is a colorless, unattractive place according to Navaho thought. In the native ideology there is no concept analogous to our "personal success." Parents urge their children to be industrious, but this is in order that they may gain "security" or "relative harmony." The attainment of some goal through the correct employment of ritual means is also stressed, of course. Personal ambition—as abstracted from family welfare—is a foreign notion. Prestige for some activities, yes. But the Navaho characteristically shrinks from formal leadership, from being marked out as above his fellows. A hierarchical rating of human beings is avoided as much as is a hierarchy of divinities.

The European concept of personality has little if any counterpart in Navaho thought. There are words that may be translated "in-standing" or "in-lying" beings which express an idea that—in certain respects only—is similar to that of a soul. In Navaho conception a wind is blown into the conceived or born body of a human which is an entirely separate unit from the body. The body is animated and activated by the "in-standing one." This "in-standing one" is responsible for the actions of the individual, though not in a sense that Christians would define as "morally responsible." For instance, a child may become ill as the result of actions of the parents during pregnancy. However, an individual is thought to be mean, gentle, one-eyed, left- or right-handed because of the qualities of the "in-standing one."

There is no notion that a *persona* is a composite of "body and soul" in the sense that the union of the wind with the babe's body creates a person (*"homo hic et nunc"* or *"sic et sic"*). The in-lying one of Blanca Peak does not mean that this being and the respective physical mountain result in a specific personality. In the human case, at death the in-lying being is separated forever from that body. In life, if the in-lying one is sick (i.e., out of harmony) this can affect the body which the in-lying one activates. However, no ceremonial expiates a crime or makes provision for *expiation* of unethical actions. Since there is no total personality that is *morally* responsible, transgressions of taboos, clan code, and the like are not reacted to by the offender in terms of a "guilty conscience."

The concept *bahadzid* ("for it there is fear") is congruent with assumptions of causality, lack of personal *moral* responsibility, and the like. the word may be varyingly translated as "dangerous," "tabooed," "restricted." It is, if you like, "negative *mana*." That is, certain objects, events, and persons are charged with negative power. If they are not approached circumspectly, they backfire with enormous destructive force.

Limitations of space make it impossible to discuss all basic Navaho concepts. The ones considered above seem to be especially important in Navaho thought and also very representative.

NAVAHO ETHICAL CODE AND VALUES

We now come to that portion of Navaho philosophy which even the average Navaho can present explicitly. The very fact that the Navaho find it necessary to talk about their ethical principles suggests that not everybody lives up to them (any more than is the case in white society). But this code is largely the working out in concrete terms of the principles inherent in the absolute logic that have been discussed.

In no human group is indiscriminate lying, cheating, or stealing approved. Cooperation is of course impossible unless individuals can depend upon each other in defined circumstances. Societies differ in how they define the conditions under which lying or stealing is forgivable or tolerable or perhaps even demanded. In their general discussions the Navaho make virtues of telling the truth and of fair dealing much as white people do. In the advice fathers give their children, in the harangues of headmen at large gatherings, these types of action never fail to be extolled.

The difference in presentation by whites and Navahos lies in the reasons advanced. The Navaho never appeals to abstract morality or to adherence to divine principles. He stresses mainly the practical considerations: "If you don't tell the truth, your fellows won't trust you and you'll shame your relatives. You'll never get along in the world that way." Truth is never praised merely on the ground that it is "good" in a purely abstract sense, nor do exhortations ever take the form that the Holy People have forbidden cheating or stealing. Certain other acts are commanded or prohibited on the basis that one or more of the Holy People did or did not behave in a similar fashion, but never in the modes which would seem "natural" to Christians: "Do this to please the Holy People because they love you," or "Don't do this because the Holy People punish wrongdoing." The Navahos do most definitely believe that acts have consequences, but the nature of the consequence is not wrapped up in any intrinsic "rightness" or "wrongness" of the act itself. In the matters of truth and honesty the only appeal to the sentiments (other than those of practicality and getting along with relatives and neighbors) which Navaho "moralists" permit themselves is that of loyalty to tradition. The old Navaho way was not to lie, to cheat, or to steal.

The prevalence of such vices today, they say, is due to white corruption. So much for the theory.

When it comes to practice, it is harder to put the finger on the differences between Navaho and white patterns. One gets the impression that Navahos lie to strangers or indeed to their relatives with fewer qualms than the average well-socialized white adult would feel. (However, the white adult's easy acceptance of "white lies" must not be overlooked.) There are also occasions on which stealing is mostly condoned "if you can get away with it." Again, though, a qualification must be entered; in many parts of the Navaho country one can have an automobile containing valuable articles unlocked for days and return to find not a single item missing. Thefts occur chiefly in the areas under strongest white influence, especially now at "squaw dances" frequented by ne'er-do-well young men who are souls lost between the two cultures. There is undoubted evidence that white contact brings about—at least in the transitional generations—some breakdown in the moralities. This much, however, seems to be a distinctive part of the native attitude: a Navaho does not spend much time worrying over a lie or a theft when he is not found out; he seems to have almost no "guilt" feelings; but if he is caught he does experience a good deal of shame. Ridicule is used to reinforce this sense of shame. The person who gets caught is the butt of many Navaho jokes.

Offenses more strongly condemned are those which threaten peaceful working together. The boaster and the troublemaker are strongly disapproved of. Incest and witchcraft are the worst of crimes. Murder, rape, physical injury, and any sort of violence are disapproved and punished, but some of the penalties seem relatively light to white people. By Navaho custom, murder, for instance, could be compounded for by a payment of slaves or livestock to the kin of the victim. To this day the Navaho way of dealing with violent crimes against the person is not ordinarily retaliation or even punishment of the offender but levying a fine which is turned over not to "the state" but to the sufferer and his family to compensate for the economic loss by injury or death.

The positive behaviors which are advocated center, as has been pointed out, on affectionate duty to relatives, pleasant manners to all, generosity, self-control, minding one's own business. The Navahos say: "Act to everybody as if they were your own relatives." A courteous, non-aggressive approach to others is the essence of decency. Polite phrases to visitors and strangers are highly valued. If an English-speaking Navaho wishes to speak approvingly of another Navaho with whom he has had a chance encounter, he is likely to say, "He talks pretty nice." Quiet strength is highly valued. "Make your mind into something that is hard." Generosity is uniformly praised and stinginess despised. One of the most disparaging things which can be said of anyone is, "He gets mad like a dog." Women will be blamed for "talking rough" to their children. The Navaho word which is most often translated into English as "mean" is sometimes rendered "he gets mad pretty easy." In short, one must keep one's temper; one must warmly and cheerfully do one's part in the system of reciprocal rights and obligations, notably those which prevail between kinfolk.

Health and strength are perhaps the best of the good things of life for the Navaho. If you aren't healthy, you can't work; if you don't work, you'll starve. Industry is enormously valued. A family must arise and be about their tasks early, for if someone goes by and sees no smoke drifting out of the smokehole it will be thought that "there is something wrong there; somebody must be sick." In enumerating the virtues of a respected man or woman the faithful performance of duties is always given a prominent place. "If you are poor or a beggar, people will make fun of you. If you are lazy people will make fun of you."

By Navaho standards one is industrious in order to accumulate possessions—within certain limits—and to care for the possessions he obtains. Uncontrolled gambling or drinking are disapproved primarily because they are wasteful. The "good" man is one who has "hard goods" (turquoise and jewelry mainly), "soft goods" (clothing, etc.), "flexible goods" (textiles, etc.), and songs, stories, and other intangible property, of which ceremonial knowledge is the most important. An old Navaho said to W. W. Hill, "I have always been a poor man. I do not know a single song." The final disrespect is to say of a man, "Why, he hasn't even a dog."

A good appearance is valued; while this is partly a matter of physique, figure, and facial appearance, it means even more the ability to dress well and to appear with a handsome horse and substantial trappings.

Thus possessions are valued both as providing security and as affording opportunities for mild ostentation. But to take the attainment of riches as the chief aim of life is universally condemned. This is a typical pronouncement by a Navaho leader:

The Navaho way is just to want enough to have enough to eat for your family and nice things to wear sometimes. We don't like it when nowadays some of these young men marry rich girls for their money and waste it all right away. The old people say this is wrong. You can't get rich if you look after your relatives right. You can't get rich without cheating some people. Cheating people is the wrong way. That way gets you into trouble. Men should be honest to get along.

Many skills carry prestige: the ability to dance, to sing, to tell stories. Skill at speaking is important and is expected of all leaders. "He talks easy" is high praise. Conversely, "He doesn't talk easy. He just sits there," is a belittling remark. Training in certain occupations is emphasized: a man will spend all the time he can spare from subsistence activities in order to learn a ceremonial; grandmothers and mothers are expected to teach young girls to weave. Knowledge is power to Navahos as to other peoples, but the kinds of knowledge which are significant to the Navaho are naturally limited by his technology and his social organization. The skillful farmer or stockman is admired. So also is he who excels at cowboy sports, but the runner comes in for his meed of praise too, even though this skill is today of minimum social utility.

Personal excellence is thus a value, but personal "success" in the white American sense is not. The Navaho lack of stress upon the success goal has its basis in childhood training but is reinforced by various patterns of adult life. A white man may start out to make a fortune and continue piling it up until he is a millionaire, where a Navaho, though also interested in accumulating possessions, will stop when he is comfortably off, or even sooner, partly for fear of being called a witch if he is too successful. This statement represents tendency rather than literal fact, for a few Navahos have in this century built up fortunes that are sizable even by white standards. The attitudes of the Navaho population generally toward these "ricos" are very mixed. Envy, fear, and distrust of them are undoubtedly mingled with some admiration. But there is almost no disposition for parents to hold these individuals up as models to their children. No elder says, "If you work hard and intelligently you might get to be as rich as Chee Dodge."

Navaho ideas of accumulation are different from those of whites. Riches are not ordinarily identified so much with a single individual as with the whole extended family and "outfit." Indeed the social pressure to support and share with relatives has a strong leveling effect. The members of a well-off family must also spend freely, as in the white pattern of "conspicuous consumption." But all wealth is desired for this purpose and for security rather than as a means of enhancing the power and glory of specific individuals.

That individual success is not a Navaho value is reflected also in the avoidance of the types of leadership which are familiar in white society. To the Navaho it is fundamentally indecent for a single individual to presume to make decisions for a group. Leadership, to them, does not mean "outstandingness." Each individual is controlled not by sanctions from the top of a hierarchy of persons but by lateral sanctions. Decisions at meetings must be unanimous.

Some personal values which bulk large among whites have a place among the Navaho that is measured largely by the degree of white influence. Cleanliness, for instance, is an easy virtue where there is running water, but where every drop must be hauled five miles washing is an expensive luxury. Navaho social and economic life is not geared to fine points of time scheduling. If a Singer says he will arrive "about noon," no one takes it amiss that he appears at sundown, though an arrival a day or more late would call for explanation. Work is not, as it is in our Puritan tradition, a good thing in itself. The Navaho believes in working only as much as he needs to. Industry is praised only as a means to providing decently for one's family and oneself.

In sum, the Navaho concept of "goodness" stresses productiveness, ability to get along with people, dependability and helpfulness, generosity in giving and spending. "Badness" means stinginess, laziness, being "mean" to others, being destructive. The concept of value stresses possessions and their care, health, skills which are practically useful. Concerning all of these topics the Navaho are fully articulate. Such sentiments are enunciated again and again in the oral literature, in formal addresses, and in ordinary conversations. As John Dewey has remarked, "Ideals are goals which, though never completely attained, set the direction of intelligent effort."

THE IMPACT OF AN ALIEN IDEOLOGY

Personal and social disorganization is rampant among the Navaho people today. In part this is the consequence of objective facts. Navaho country is overpopulated, and the range is overgrazed. Few Navahos have the occupational skills to compete with whites in the near-by towns and cities. But that Navaho culture is becoming an ugly patchwork of meaningless and unrelated pieces instead of a patterned mosaic is due at least as much to the power of foreign ideas. The Navaho recognize and respect the strength of white American culture. Many Navahos are saying frankly that their tribe's salvation rests in mastering the language and the way of life of the dominant group. The lack of selective blending and constructive fusion is not due to low intelligence. Navahos are perfectly capable of learning white skills and white customs. But when the traits of another culture are learned externally and one by one without the underlying concepts and premises of that culture, the learners feel uncomfortable. They sense the absence of the fitness of things, of a support which is nonetheless real because difficult to verbalize.

The adoption of our ideas is not, of course, due solely to choice on the part of Navahos. Missionaries, government officials, and traders are consciously and systematically trying to redeem the Navaho from "savagery." Some programs have conscientiously endeavored to take account of individual Navaho customs and even of the more external patterns of Navaho life. But because they have taken no account of underlying

Navaho philosophy they have often produced results regarded as unfortunate by Navahos and whites alike. The rationally desirable innovations have failed to configurate correctly with the unconscious system of meanings characteristic of Navaho implicit culture.

This is no new experience in planned culture change. Many attempts at acculturating on the part of missionary groups have had the (to the planners) unexpected consequences of contributing to the reinvigoration of basically aboriginal religions. Education in white values in government schools has promoted "rugged individualism" without the limiting and integrating controls which the white American absorbs in the home as part of his largely unverbalized philosophy. Such phrases as "compatibility with the pre-existing culture of the borrowers" are frequent in discussions of acculturation, and they are necessitated by the universal experience of students of culture that, over and above the cases of externally observable pattern conflict, there are less tangible forms of compatibility "that you can't quite put your finger on." These relate to lack of congruence between the implicit ideological systems. It is as if there were forces "behind" the explicit culture which made for acceptance of one foreign idea but for rejection of the associated ideas that contribute to discipline and control of behavior. Certainly ideas are retailored with subtle distortion of borrowed patterns of thought and behavior to swing them into line with remarkably tenacious underlying ideas.

There is not space to follow out in detail the ways in which Western conceptions have disturbed or destroyed the relatively smooth fabric of Navaho social life. Let us look merely at some aspects of the effects of white premises and categories with respect to individualism, government, economic institutions, sex, and property. It will be easier to follow out the course of events in these rather concrete realms than to trace, at this time, the effects of ideas from Western culture upon Navaho ideas. The less tangible, more implicit aspects of Navaho philosophy have undoubtedly been altered by the impact of Christianity, for example, but the underlying premises and concepts change more slowly than does behavior. Nevertheless, it is clear that many contemporary deviations make sense only if understood in terms of the influence of Christian notions of individualism, personal responsibility, sex code, and the like.

The category "government," something fixed and powerful to white people, is foreign to Navaho thinking. Authority, to their minds, extends only indefinitely and transitorily beyond the established rules of behavior between sex groups, age groups, and, especially, classes of relatives. There are headmen, but the sphere of their influence widens and narrows with the passage of time, the emergence of a new leader, the rise of a new faction. The prestige of some headmen often spreads beyond their own local region. Through channels excessively informal they can sometimes "swing" most of the population of a number of local groups to a given course of action. By and large, however, control of individual action rests in the group and not in any authoritative individual or body.

The whole mechanism of Navaho social control is too fluid, too informal, too vague to be readily understood by white people who think of authority in terms of courts, police, and legislative assemblies. But Navaho social controls are extremely effective for those who remain within their own group. Never to be lost sight of is the fact that the basis of the system was and still is the family. To live at all in this barren region the individual must have the economic cooperation of others, and such cooperation is hardly likely to come to those who deviate from the "right way of doing things" as the Navaho see it. Thus the major threat which restrains the potential offender is the withdrawal of the support and the good will of his neighbors, most of whom are "family" to the Navaho. Gossip and criticism were and are major means of social control throughout Navaho society. These diffuse sanctions are less effective today than in former times because, by taking up wage work for whites, the offender can escape both the need for economic cooperation by the group and the criticism which the group aims at deviators.

The introduction of the white idea of individualism without the checks and balances that accompany it leads to the failure of collective or cooperative action of every sort. The substitution of paid labor for reciprocal services is not in and of itself a bad thing. But there is not a commensurate growth of the white idea of individual responsibility. There tends to be a distortion of the whole cultural structure which makes it difficult to preserve harmonious personal relationships and satisfying emotional adjustments. Widespread exercise of escape mechanisms, especially alcohol, is the principal symptom of the resultant friction and decay. Human groups that have different cultures and social structures have moral systems that differ in important respects. The linkage is so great that when a social organization goes to pieces morality also disintegrates.

A typical cause for confusion, distrust, and hostility arising out of a difference in the system of categories is the fact that Navahos are today dependent upon a distant and mysterious white institution called "the market." In the days of bartering raw materials, a sheep or a sack of wool maintained a rather constant value. At present, when both are sold to the trader, the Navaho never know in advance whether the lamb will bring ten cents a pound or only five cents, and they see no sense in these variations. They share the common distrust of farmer folk for those who buy and resell the products of their hard labors, but they are at a greater disadvantage than the white farmer because they are unfamiliar with white marketing customs and have no means of understanding the reasons for the apparently senseless fluctuations in price and demand. Moreover, since they feel that they usually are underpaid for their sheep and wool and that the price they will get varies with no rhyme or reason, they feel uncertain about improving their products. Why should they invest money, labor, and time simply to benefit the trader or the more remote livestock dealers? Similar confusion and irritation resulted from the government's program of killing "excess" livestock. From the Navaho point of view only production is ethical. Destruction—except to satisfy immediate hunger—is unethical.

The Navaho have only "object taboos" as regards sex, none of the "aim taboos" which are so marked a development of Western culture. That is, Navahos do feel that sexual activity is improper or dangerous under particular circumstances or with certain persons. But they never regard sexual desires in themselves as "nasty" or evil. In school and elsewhere whites have tended to operate upon the premise that "any decent Navaho" will feel guilty about the sexual act which takes place outside of marriage. This attitude simply bewilders Navahos and predisposes them to withdrawal of cooperation in all spheres. To them sex is natural, necessary, and no more or no less concerned with morals than is eating.

The Navaho and the white administrator may see the same objective facts, and communication may be sufficiently well established so that each is sure the other sees them. Naturally, then there is mutual irritation when the same conclusions are not reached. What neither realizes is that all discourse proceeds from premises and that premises (unfortunately taken for granted by both) are likely, in fact, to be very divergent.

Let us put this in the concrete. A wealthy man dies and leaves considerable property. He has a widow but no children by her. There are, however, two sons by another woman to whom the deceased was never married in either white or Navaho fashion. He left, of course, no written will, and it is agreed that he gave no oral instructions on his deathbed. These are the facts, and there is no dispute about them between the Navaho and the white administrator.

Nevertheless the prediction may safely be made that before the estate is settled the white man will be irritated more than once and some Navahos will be confused and indignant at what seems to them ignorance, indifference, or downright immorality. Each will unconsciously make his judgments and decisions in terms of his own presuppositions. Neither set of premises will be brought out into the open and discussed as such, but the following unstated assumptions will be in the background of thinking:

White	Navaho
1. Marriage is an arrangement, economic and otherwise, between two individuals. The two spouses and the children, if any, are the ones primarily involved in any question of inheritance.	1. Marriage is an arrangement between two families much more than it is between two individuals.
2. A man's recognized children, legitimate or illegitimate, have a claim upon his property.	2. Sexual rights are property rights; therefore if a man has children from a woman without undertaking during his lifetime the economic responsibilities which are normally a part of Navaho marriage, the children—however much he admitted to biological fatherhood—were not really his: "He just stole them."
3. Inheritance is normally from the father or from both sides of the family.	3. Inheritance is normally from the mother, the mother's brother, or other relatives of the mother; from the father's side of the family little or nothing has traditionally been expected. Most of the father's property goes back to his relatives.
4. As long as a wife or children survive, no other relatives are concerned in the inheritance unless there was a will to that effect.	4. While children today, in most areas, expect to inherit something from their father, they do not expect to receive his whole estate or to divide it with their mother only; sons and daughters have different expectations.
5. All types of property are inherited in roughly the same way.	5. Different rules apply to different types of property: range land is hardly heritable property at all; farm land normally stays with the family which has been cultivating it; livestock usually goes back (for the most part) to the father's sisters and sororal nephews; jewelry and other personal property tend to be divided among the children and other relatives; ceremonial equipment may go to a son who is a practitioner or to a clansman of the deceased.

The white administrator would be likely to say that the only heirs to any of the property were the wife, children, and perhaps the illegitimate children. Such a decision would be perplexing or infuriating to the Navaho. To say in the abstract what disposal would be proper at the present complicated point in Navaho history is hardly possible. But it is clear that a verdict which seemed so "right" and natural" to a white person as to require no explanation or justification would probably appear equally "unjust" and "unreasonable" to the Navaho involved.

The pressure of such double standards is highly disruptive. Just as rats that have been trained to associate a circle with food and a rectangle with an electric shock become neurotic when the circle is changed by almost imperceptible gradations into an ellipse, so human beings faced with a conflicting set of rewards and punishments tend to cut loose from all moorings, to float adrift, and become irresponsible. The younger generation of the Navaho are more and more coming to laugh at the old or pay them only lip service. The young escape the control of their elders, not to accept white controls but to revel in newly found patterns of unrestraint.

The Navaho are torn between their own ancient standards and those which are urged upon them by teachers, missionaries, and other whites. An appreciable number of Navahos are so confused by the conflicting precepts of their elders and their white models that they tend, in effect, to reject the whole problem of morality (in the widest sense) as meaningless or insoluble. For longer or shorter periods in their lives their only guide is the expediency of the immediate situation. One cannot play a game according to rule if these are sharp disagreements as to what the rules are. The incipient breakdown of any culture brings a loss of predictability and hence of dependability in personal relations. The absence of generally accepted standards of behavior among individuals constitutes, in fact, a definition of social disorganization.

A stable social structure prevails only so long as the majority of individuals in the society find enough satisfaction both in the goals socially approved and in the institutionalized means of attainment to compensate them for the constraints which ordered social life inevitably imposes upon uninhibited response to impulse. In any way of life there is much that to an outside observer appears haphazard, disorderly, more or less chaotic. But unless most participants feel that the ends and means of their culture make sense, in terms of a unifying philosophy, disorientation and amorality become rampant. Some major Navaho premises are incompatible with some major premises of our culture. A resolution must be sought in terms of wider assumptions.

In this chapter an attempt has been made to describe not only Navaho ethics and values but also some of those highest common factors that are implicit in a variety of the doings and sayings of the Navaho. In the not distant past these recurrent themes, these unstated premises, gave a felt coherence to life in spite of social change, in spite of the diversity of institutions, in spite of differences in the needs and experiences of individuals. These distinctly Navaho values and premises still do much to regulate group life and to reconcile conflicts and discrepancies. But these basic assumptions are now under attack from a competing set of assumptions. The majority of Navahos no longer feel completely at home and at ease in their world of values and significances, and an appreciable minority are thoroughly disoriented. This will continue and increase until new coherent philosophical bases for life are created and widely accepted. As Merton has written, "It is the dominating system of ideas which determines the choice between alternative modes of action which are equally compatible with the underlying sentiments."

29. CONTEMPORARY THINKING
ABOUT PRIMITIVE RELIGION *

Several conflicting schemes have been advanced to account for the development of religious concepts. Among these are Spencer's idea of the priority of ancestor worship, Tylor's view of animism which he believed arose from the attempt to account for such things as dreams and reflections, and Father Wilhelm Schmidt's assertion of original revelation and the belief in a high god. Where lies the truth? The following essay, written by an American sociologist, casts doubt upon our ability to give a meaningful answer. The article bears certain methodological resemblances to a previous selection from the pen of a British social anthropologist (see No. II:17). Such similarity would seem to stem from a common commitment to a functional approach—though the social anthropologist is less energetic in denouncing evolutionism and the quest for origins than is the sociologist. In view of the preponderance of evolutionary views expressed in this volume, the editor urges the thoughtful reader to give special attention to this selection as well as Nos. II:10 and II:17.

W<small>E ARE CROSSING</small> a historic threshold in the scientific study of religion. We move from an era of the unprovable insight, to one of systematic observation. We step from an epoch of individual contemplation, to one of collective onslaught on the problems of religion. The new

* William J. Goode, "Contemporary Thinking about Primitive Religion," *Sociologus*, Vol. 5 (1955), pp. 122–131. Reprinted by permission of the author and the publisher.
The author (b. 1917) is Professor of Sociology at Columbia University. His major interests are in three institutional areas: family, religion and profession. Among his works are *Religion among the Primitives* (1951); *Methods in Social Research* (1952) (with Paul K. Hatt); *After Divorce* (1956); and (with Robert Merton and Mary Jean Huntington) *The Professions in American Society* (forthcoming).

analysis, as opposed to the old, does not look for universal theological truths in other religions, but rather seek sociological generalizations. Our sources of fact become more than the doctrines written by religious leaders, and come to include as well the attitudes, decisions, and actions of ordinary men. Finally, our perspectives become wider. We are no longer confined to a) our own society, to b) the historical tradition of the western world, or even to c) that of the major civilizations of the world, such as Egypt of the New Kingdom, China of the era of Shi Hwang Ti, Assyria of Asshurbanipal, or the final days of the Mayans before the intrusion of the Europeans. We now draw into our focus d) *all* societies whose religious systems and religious behavior we can describe accurately and in adequate detail.

We are required, then, to grant equal *intellectual* and *scientific* importance to the religious systems of the Dahomey and the Augustan Romans, the Zuñi and the Tibetans, the Lacandones and the Unitarians: In short, to the primitive as to the "civilized" religions. Now, it is true that certain religions have had greater impact upon our personal lives, because they form part of our group tradition—the Hebrew, for example. This fact does not make them more fundamental than primitive religions in our research into the major structural facts about religious systems. That is, the *scientific* importance of a religious system is not increased in the slightest by its personal or groupal importance to the researcher. Our generalizations must fit the "primitive" religions as well as the "civilized".

Before accepting this blunt assertion, let us first look briefly at the bases of this distinction, to see whether there are any differences between primitive religions and the religions of civilizations, which would be *obviously* necessary and germinal in the development of scientific theories about religion. An examination of the distinction is particularly worthwhile, for it is too often accepted without question. This distinction had its origins in a commonsense observation. This observation was no more than a self-evident assumption until the Darwinian notions about biological evolution were extrapolated and generalized beyond biological theory, to the social sciences. The observation was made by every explorer, missionary, traveler, hunter, and ethnologist who brought us data about primitive tribes, from the middle 16th Century until the beginnings of the 20th Century. In commonsense terms, the report was this: The natives are "backward." They do not understand what we understand, or according to our ways. Their tools are poor. Their societies seem crude, poor, undeveloped, simple, homogeneous, and in summary—within our habit-bound thoughtways these societies often appear equivalent to those of *primeval* man, perhaps of the early Neolithic period. That theoretical edifice, extrapolated from solid biological theory, swiftly collapsed at the turn of the 20th Century, just as all previous attempts to build social science upon the models of other sciences have collapsed. One sub-field of Darwinian thought, that of *ecology*, did stimulate a minor field of sociology, social ecology, but the latter has had to develop its own techniques and theory. The parent science can stimulate; it rarely furnishes important substantive propositions. The major facts about social structures cannot be classified or organized, much less interpreted, by reference to biological evolution. We came back, perhaps sadly, to the hard work of patient observation of our own facts, small-scale hypothesizing, and tiny bits of theory, won with difficulty from awkward data.

However, the old distinction did not die. A second foundation was used, and once more the old idea lived on as a habit of thinking. In its second transformation, it leads us to take for granted an unproved relationship that is always implicit in it: a correlation or association between 1) *technological* advancement on the one hand, and 2) *sociostructural* patterns on the other. We can of course rank almost all known societies along the continuum of scientific and technological knowledge. The stone cultures of Australia and Tierra del Fuego would fall toward the lower pole, and of course the Western culture complex would be at the other extreme. It is the other variable that is recalcitrant, that of sociostructural patterns. We have no scientifically validated laws which can then predict which institutional and specifically religious patterns will be found for any *given* level of technological development. We have no systematic or reliable body of social theory that represents even the beginnings of unsteady but fruitful steps toward understanding social change. Until we do, this *evolutionary* assumption—i. e., an assumption about *patterns, regularities,* of social change—is useless and even harmful to our thinking. Until we have made such a step, we shall not even know in what ways the distinction *might* be theoretically strategic.

It is a mere literary cliché to refute this frequent distinction by commenting that the *ancestors* of those same Europeans who evolved this observation into systematic social theory would in *their* own epochs have been regarded as "primitives" by the subjects of Iknaton or Alexander, or perhaps by even those of Asoka. We all know that the main locus of advanced learning and technology has shifted from one great civilization to another. This literary answer is irrelevant. The question is, rather, *along what dimensions* the distinction between primitive and civilized religions can be scientifically important. Let us look at some of the dimensions or factors that are often used as a basis for this distinction.

(1) The field anthropologist knows, even if Paul Radin had not made such eloquent polemics about the matter, that the primitive religious

belief is not *homogeneous*. There are atheists and believers, religious traditionalists and creators, in any primitive society. (2) We cannot distinguish these beliefs by their *simplicity*. The complex interweaving of belief, legend, myth, and dogma among the Murngin is as far-ranging and intricate as that of most civilized religions. Doubtless, the rituals of the Dahomey are *more* complex than most. By comparison, most bodies of Protestant ritual and belief seem barren and undeveloped. (3) Although there is considerable *integration between religion and political power* in most primitive societies, as there is in our own, there is also *conflict:* We cannot assume a perfect harmony merely because we have not bothered to collect all the discrepant facts. (4) We cannot even say that Western society is worldly, while primitive cultures are constantly suffused by and oriented toward religion. Many of our own fairly recent historical epochs of the West were deeply concerned with religion, and at least one primitive society has gravely debated whether to change religions (e. g., the Manus) for wordly reasons. (5) We are certainly too sophisticated in our generation to think of primitive religions as somehow "magical", while our own are "truly" religious. All major world religions have a considerable magical content, and the folk beliefs in those religions have strongly developed magical patterns (e. g., the Catholic). (6) Moreover, after the monumental work of Pater Schmidt, we can no longer assume that primitive religions have no *ethical* content, as contrasted with our own. (7) We are also not permitted to think of primitive religions as changing only very *slowly*, in contrast to civilized religions. Aside from the serious problems of *measuring* ideational or ritual change (and if we cannot measure it, we cannot presume to claim that one religious pattern changes more rapidly than another), we simply have no data on indigenous social change among primitives. Primitives *claim* that little change has occurred: "Things have always been so," just as do peasants. But we cannot accept that claim when we have no historical records by which to test that assertion. Moreover, once we move from modern Western civilizations, it is clear that many Eastern societies (even urban ones) have gone long periods without much change. Thus, the variable of *rapidity of change* is not useful as a distinction between primitive and civilized religions. Not even the energetic American exponents of that empty, value-laden concept, "culture lag", with all their research into technical and social change, have ever succeeded in (a) measuring ideational or ritual change; (b) correlating ritual and technological development; or (c) demonstrating how slowly primitive religions change.

In sum, when we seriously compare the behavioral facts of primitive religions in all their richness of emotion, variation, complexity, interrelationships with similar facets and areas of "civilized religions", we understand that (a) the similarities are greater than the differences; (b) the differences *among* the many primitive religions are just as wide as differences among civilized religions; and (c) even if the distinction should later become strategic, we have no *theoretical* or *empirical* *grounds* for using it now. The fact that one occupation (the anthropologists) concentrates on primitives, and another (the sociologists) upon civilized nations is no more than an interesting fact in the history of social science, and this fact does not validate the distinction.

All these facts require us to assent to a still further conclusion: we must not let this (often unconscious) habit lead us to identify *primitive* religion with *primeval* religion. We are absolutely barred from *ever* understanding primeval religion. We shall never have the necessary data. We cannot extrapolate from artifacts, such as presumptively sacred figurines or altars, to the religious *meaning* of these objects. These meanings, the patterns of social interaction in religious behavior, *can* be abstracted and deduced (though poorly) from (a) writings, or from (b) observing and interviewing living human beings. They can*not* be discovered by studying the physical objects alone, and for primeval man we have only these last data. Upon almost any complex of physical objects an almost infinite variety of religious and social patterns can be imagined and developed. It is the *meanings* that are primary. Without these, the objects will forever remain mute. The religions of primeval man will remain forever unknown to all social scientists, though doubtless many poet-scientists will persuade themselves that they have intuited these meanings.

These related propositions do not assert that (a) there is no evolutionary pattern; or that (b) there are no differences between primitive and civilized religions. Rather, we assert that except for technological development we have no worthwhile theory of evolution for social structures and particularly for religious structures; and that (b) the differences that do appear between civilized and primitive religions have not been shown to be theoretically strategic.

If this time-worn distinction be properly viewed with skepticism, then *another* mental bias must be thrown out: the belief that the scientifically most fundamental description of a primitive society must refer to its pre-European phase. This prejudice is a corollary of the above distinction, and contains all its weaknesses. *No* primitive society is, or ever was, "pure". *All* have had many contacts with other societies, and thus may have changed gradually through these contacts. The search for "untouched" primitive societies is a literary, not a scientific, quest. It parallels the old search for "pure" races, and has just as little intellectual significance. If we are looking for social patterns, for social laws, for modes of interaction, for an understanding of social behavior, we must understand these phenomena where we find them. A primitive society undergoing rapid social change because of contact with Western European culture is just as rich a source of social data as the geographically and socially most isolated culture in the world.

From the foregoing argument, a *further* inference is clear: there is no *theoretically* important distinction between anthropology and sociology (or, indeed, between either of these and social psychology) if we are analyzing religious institutions.

Now, in social science we seek pattern, order, laws, generalizations. We know that our sciences are crude. Both our data and our laws do not have the rigor of even, say, 18th Century chemistry. Therefore, we are likely to generalize prematurely. This, however, is no danger so long as we are dedicated to judging the worth of our generalizations by a stubborn analysis of the facts. Our premature generalizations may be destroyed, but if we stick to the facts even our premature theories will be improved *cumulatively*.

Let me, then, attempt these tasks in the remaining paragraphs: (1) Offer some tentative generalizations about religious patterns; (2) Specify one major task that lies immediately before us; and (3) Suggest some of the *operational* consequences that flow from an acceptance of the position outlined here.

Although Durkheim's work was based upon several false premises, it was productive of important hypotheses. In a study published several years ago, I attempted (1) to build upon some of his correct notions, (2) to offer a serious critique of theories of religion, and (3) to take several steps forward in the sociology of primitive religion. In the remaining space, it is possible to do no more than to reproduce some of these generalizations; the careful student can see immediately that they could now be further developed in a more systematic and detailed fashion. They are presented here only to suggest the *beginnings* of generalized hypotheses.

1. Human societies distinguish between secular and sacred things, as defined by the group attitudes in the society.
2. These sacred things include various objects, among which are to be found natural forces and animals; or inanimate objects, deities, acts, areas, words, gestures, etc.; and it is the religious context which defines whether at a given time an *otherwise* secular object is transformed into the sacred.
3. The socialization process, which sometimes includes specific cult training as well (adult socialization), inculcates knowledge of and respect for the sacred.
4. Conformity with religious prescriptions will usually give support

to other institutions and to common (or groupal) goals, due to the integration of the social structure at the common-value level.

5. The religious practitioners gain certain advantages from their relationship to the sacred, such as prestige, power, and goods.

6. The supernatural entities, or gods, are not always held to have bodies like men, but their values, attitudes, perception, and thoughts are "anthroposocial". That is, their "personalities" are like those of members of the society. This is evidenced by these facts:

   (a) The deities take notice of man's actions;

   (b) The deities act broadly to further man's welfare, such welfare conforming closely to the society's desires;

   (c) The deities desire human attention and are pleased by honor paid to them, as well as displeased by neglect;

   (d) The deities usually punish men for not acting in accordance with the rules of the society, such punishment usually occurring in *this* world;

   (e) The deities are not invariably "good", for they may also have "moods", and some are whimsical or destructive at times;

   (f) The relationships between deities and men, and among deities, are also conceived in such social terms, in that there will be communication, promises, reminders, approval, and perhaps even threats.

7. There is a body of religious belief common to the society, which may not always be developed into a "doctrine", but which constitutes the *meaning of ritual*. These beliefs treat the origin and nature of the deities, and their relationships to men, punishment, the nature of human souls and their destiny, etc.; and impute order and sense to the cosmos.

8. Religious rituals make many *actional* demands upon men, and thus form the link between religion and other spheres of action, so that one can observe the *concrete* interrelationships of the religious system with other social action: by diverting, increasing, or decreasing production, distribution, and consumption; and shifting or strengthening the political structure.

9. The sacredness of objects and of rituals is based upon their *symbolic* character, as representative of the will or action of the deities, or as objective embodiments of religious belief.

10. Rituals are not thought of as contractual in character, but they will contain frequent requests for favors.

11. Magic and religion are not dichotomies, but make up a *continuum* along several identifiable dimensions, and are distinguished only ideal-typically. Some of these dimensions are: specificity of goal

desired, manipulative vs. cajoling attitude, type of professional-client relationship, collective vs. private ends, etc.

The fuller hypothetical development and empirical testing of such beginnings require, however, an acceptable *typology* of religious systems: our generalizations will be correct only under specified conditions and for specific institutional complexes. We cannot go far in any generalizing scheme, until we have identified the *variables* which at different values create different *types*. There are in any science only few generalizations that fit nearly all its phenomena; most laws apply to sub-sets of phenomena. We must therefore find out what in *our* area, religious institutions, are the major elements, types, classes—and to do this, we must begin to identify the major characteristics and variables that go to *make up* such types.

This is fundamental, and the answer will not be found in some evolutionary scheme, or in moral evaluations, or in rankings of technological advancement. My own attempt to do no more than *suggest* some of these was certainly *not* satisfactory. It was developed merely to show that certain religious systems varied from one another along theoretically *important* dimensions, and that therefore generalizations applying to all of them would not often occur by accident. Here, we may outline these dimensions without discussing them, only to show in what *direction* such a conceptual development ought to go.

1. Variation in religious personnel
   (a) Extent of formal training;
   (b) Degree of identification between secular leaders, and the sacred leaders and followers.
2. Variation in type of societal matrix
   (a) Degree of emphasis upon affectivity vs. affective neutrality;
   (b) Self-interest vs. collectivity orientation;
   (c) Universalism vs. particularism;
   (d) Functional specificity vs. diffuseness;
   (e) Ascription vs. achievement.
3. Variation in sacred entities: from highly abstract, distant entities not clearly defined; through broad, natural forces; to various degrees of anthropomorphism in gods and spirits; to animals, plants, and other natural objects.
4. Variation in ritual
   (a) Development of symbolism;
   (b) Degree of elaboration of ritual.
5. Variation in religious belief
   (a) Beliefs about the soul;
   (b) Explanations of rituals;

(c) Punishment and expiation;

(d) Origins of gods and men.

Even if these tentative suggestions are rejected, a major typology must be created, using those variables which mainly determine religious patterns, and structure the religious institutions. It is through these institutions that the major social structural forces of the society are implemented, or made active. It is only through the institutional prescriptions, through the institutional definitions of appropriate *role* behavior, that men are made to *want* to do the things that *must* be done if the society is to survive.

As I now view the problem, here are some of the *operational* and *procedural* consequences that seem to flow from the exceedingly condensed theoretical position outlined above:

1. We are thus forced to turn away from the fascinating but unanswerable question as to the "ultimate reality" of religion. We cannot know scientifically what lies behind religion. What we *can* know is in *this* world: the institutional patterns, the social behavior, the human meanings and emotions of religious action.

2. We shall attempt to remain on one major emergent level, the sociological, in our analyses, in order to obtain the maximum generalizing power. When we move from this theoretical level to that of psychodynamics or the economic, we shall at least be aware that we *have* shifted levels. We shall not use the variables of one level as specious solutions of problems at another level.

3. Our studies will be cross-cultural, comparative-historical, so as to obtain as wide a range of data as possible. Only thus shall we be able to develop adequate generalizations. This will require international cooperation between scholars who dedicate themselves to the analysis of religion.

4. We shall try to formulate *specific* hypotheses as deductions from, or inductions to, our general laws. We cannot have a cumulation of knowledge without negating some existing hypotheses. We *cannot negate hypotheses unless they are specific enough to be disproved.* To assert that "religion is somehow integrated with other institutions", for example, is doubtless correct, but it is impossible to disprove its correctness or even its fruitfulness until we deduce detailed hypotheses from it. We are not daring enough in our thinking unless we formulate such specific hypotheses as permit disproof. This means, as a corollary, that we can then begin to specify the conditions of social structure under which given hypotheses are correct. Disproof is not accomplished by merely citing a negative case. The negative case may, rather, give us a

clue to understanding under what definite conditions the previous assertion is correct. *All* scientific laws contain, implicitly or explicitly, a statement of the conditions under which they hold.

5. We shall begin more systematically to formulate research designs,
in as close a logical and concrete approximation to the controlled experiment as is possible. Ample evidence is now available, from the best
of social science research, that this can be done. The fact that *we* as
scientists cannot *ourselves* change the value of the variables in a given
case does not lessen the *logical* rigor of a good research design: the
astronomer, the cosmogonist, the meterologist are even more helpless
than we to "experiment" with the physical world. *With* good research
design, we can at least begin to locate the more important variables and
phenomena.

6. These facts mean that we abandon salon Freudianism, just as we
have already abandoned vulgar Marxism, as being a literary pose rather
than serious attempts to develop a cumulative body of tested generalizations. We are no closer to "the real factors" of religion when we seek
psychodynamic interpretations, than when we look for economic interests. Both these represent potentially important theoretical contributions,
but not refuges (akin to the older refuge of instinctualism) from the
stubborn analysis on a single major theoretical level.

7. We then recognize, when trying to understand any concrete religious system, that religious *behavior, emotion,* and *meaning,* are not a
homogeneous pattern, but must always be described as statistical *distributions:* For any given characteristic, not all people will fall at the
modal point, but some will be distributed between this point and the
extremes. For shorthand purposes, we can say that the Manus are "ascetic, profit-seeking, secular, ghost-ridden" people, but not all of them
are—and this fact is of great importance in interpreting social patterns.
We must, therefore, attempt to analyze these *deviants;* and not in merely
personality terms, since one may be socially deviant and psychologically
quite normal. All major social structures *produce* deviants through pressures on particular social positions. It is the experience of empirical research that the analysis of deviants yields important clues to understanding *major social* patterns.

8. We shall expect to find various areas of *conflict* between (1) religious institutions and (2) other institutions. After all, they lay claim to
time, energy, goods, and people, and all these are limited. In concrete
cases, open conflict will not be actual, but it is always potential. We can
specify it abstractly, when we make *structural* analyses. We are also
required to seek it in the social *roles* that *individuals* play: The same
man is husband, father, brother; acolyte, hierophant, religious appren-

tice, priest; subject, citizen, or subordinate chief. These conflicts are neither accidental nor mysterious. We must know more of them.

9. We must therefore ascertain the *mechanisms* by which actual or potential conflicts are mitigated, avoided—or perhaps intensified. Again, we search on both the grand level of sociostructural analysis, and on the more concrete level of social roles. As we gain more knowledge of such mechanisms within our own societies, we shall know much better which questions we must ask about *any* society, or *any* religious system.

Conclusion. In the brief compass of this paper, I have attempted to accomplish the following four tasks: (1) State the relationship between the social analysis of primitive religion, and that of civilized religion; (2) Suggest the beginnings of some generalizations about primitive religions; (3) Point to the need for an adequate typology of religion, so that we may begin to collect *comparative* data about all known religions; here I have merely noted a few of the variables that might be useful in such a typology; and (4) Outline some of the operational consequences for our research into religion, which appear to be necessary if we accept the prior argument.

The tone of certainty and arrogance in these pages is due to brevity alone. The tasks ahead are difficult, and we shall win our new knowledge no more easily than our predecessors won theirs. Nevertheless, the goals are worthy of our best talents, and the vistas ahead are exciting.

G. Art and Music

$\mathbf{T}$HOUGH some cultures are almost totally lacking in ornamentation and others possess mere rudiments of rhythm, every culture manifests a sufficient degree of each to warrant the generalization that, loosely defined, art and music are universal attributes of culture. Anthropologists have often made studies of art and music as an aspect of their fieldwork. Sometimes this material is used to make a general point as in Franz Boas' study of the ornamentation of Eskimo needle cases which showed that art style could move from abstraction to realism or vice versa. At other times the material is collected by a specialist primarily for its own sake. The selections which follow include an interpretation of paleolithic art which seeks to extrapolate from art to ideology, a general survey of anthropological approaches to art and a sample of the ethnological approach to musicology. The reader who is methodically going through these selections in the order of their appearance will experience something of a shock when he turns the page. He will realize very quickly that Mr. Levine is pursuing a task (in II:30) that Professor Goode (see II:29) said was impossible of fulfillment. If the reader studies carefully the remarks of both scholars—weighing them and testing them against each other and the other available materials—and then comes to a thoughtful conclusion (perhaps even to withhold judgement!), this book will be serving its purpose.

30. PREHISTORIC ART AND IDEOLOGY *

INTRODUCTION

The material remains of past civilizations are like shells beached by the retreating sea. The functioning organisms and the milieu in which they lived have vanished, leaving the dead and empty forms behind . . . understanding . . . of ancient societies must be based upon these static molds which bear only the imprint of life.—GORDON R. WILLEY 1953

THE material remains of past civilizations sometimes include art. Where this is so, as in the spectacular case of Upper Paleolithic art in Western Europe, we may be able to add an ideological dimension to our understanding of the ancient people.

Traditional anthropological interest in art treated the subject as an isolated ethnographic category, focused almost exclusively on the technique of art-making, on the iconography, and on the uses to which art is put. But attention has turned increasingly to questions about the ties between art and other aspects of culture. For example, monographs by Mills and McAllester, produced under the aegis of the Harvard Values Study project, have looked for relationships between esthetic values in Navaho art and music and Navaho value culture as a whole. Malraux's *Voices of Silence* exhibits a convergent trend in art history. These and similar studies are laying the foundation on which efforts to interpret prehistoric art must rest.

Translating into achievement the prospect of reconstituting prehistoric

* Morton H. Levine, "Prehistoric Art and Ideology," *American Anthropologist*, Vol. 59 (1957), pp. 949–962. By permission of the author and publishers. Mr. Levine is a Teaching Fellow at Harvard University. He plans to make a series of related researches on the art of ancient and modern primitive cultures. This is his first published contribution to the field.

"idea culture" through the study of prehistoric art depends upon finding ways and means for archeologists to ask, however indirectly, the same questions which ethnologists increasingly pursue among recent and living art-makers. If relationships between art and other parts of culture can be discerned and described in individual cultures and compared across cultures so as to yield generalizations, if we can make a reasonable case for the idea that a people's art is patterned by the point of view of their culture, if we can suggest the ways in which art exhibits this patterning, we might hope to put the lessons learned to work in behalf of a plausible reconstruction of the attitudes and outlook of a prehistoric people. We might gain a means of narrowing the gap between that span of time for which we know something of man as an economic animal and that much shorter period for which we are acquainted with him as a thinking, believing, feeling creature.

The concern of this paper is two-fold: What kind of controls on interpretation can we derive from the study of ethnographic materials? And, what problems can we approach fruitfully through the analysis of art style? The crucial general issues about the "nature of artistic behavior" and the character of the "relationship between Art and Culture" are not confronted directly.

The present discussion moves beyond ground already taken by anthropological field forces. This has its obvious advantages and disadvantages. The attempt was stimulated by studies in the art of the Upper Paleolithic and in aboriginal Australian art. In pursuing the concerns of this paper, we will have recourse to the former to exemplify problems in reconstruction of ideology, and to the latter for examples of what ethnographic materials can provide by way of suggestions for and limitations on interpretation. Further, we will deal solely with painting and sculpture, the only arts common to the ethnographic and archeological record.

THE ARCHEOLOGICAL RECORD AND
ETHNOGRAPHIC COMPARISON

Drawing on material survivals and on the data of paleo-studies in geology, geography, and zoology, archeology develops a picture of the life of Upper Paleolithic man in broad terms of habitat-economy-society:

He was a cold climate big game hunter. His environment was at once bountiful and threatening. Animal and plant resources abounded; but bringing down game, even with the refined and varied arsenal then at hand, was extremely difficult if not dangerous. The natural setting which enveloped the Ice Age hunter was uncommonly labile and must have seemed brutally capricious: the weather in Würm times was fairly drastic, and the landscape was tortured by tectonic upheavals. But life appears to have been relatively sedentary. Small local societies may have migrated with the change of season; but evidence for a plentiful food supply and the elaborate art in the caves refute any suggestion of incessant wandering. The existence of art of such a high level of achievement points to specialization of some sort within the groups; but we can only wonder whether the artistic function was or was not combined with religious or chiefly roles. Stylized, intentional burials appear in the record to suggest not only some sort of funeral exercise, but an explicit recognition of life and death as opposed and remarkable states.

These people or peoples left for posterity one of the great art collections of all time. It was a refined and varied art, produced over many millennia. Taken as a whole, the artistic universe of the Upper Paleolithic offers large animal "portraits," animal figures bearing geometric designs, other beasts studded with darts, sculptured women in the round and in relief—the famous "Venuses"—anthropomorphs of which the best known is the "Sorcerer" at Les Trois Frères, profusely superposed engravings on the walls of caves and on pebbles, handprints on the cave walls, some of which betray mutilation of the fingers, geometric figures and dots and club-shaped forms, and the vivacious meanders dug into the then soft clay with the fingers or with hafted animal teeth—the so-called "macaroni."

Archeology gives us a sense of the character of existence and the realistic problems which confronted these ancient hunters. We are presented, too, with a rich corpus of art. The "missing link" is what these early men thought and believed—how they perceived reality, what they valued and what they took as problematic. This is precisely what we hope to recover to some extent from a sensitive, systematic study of the art. But we cannot do this by unaided recourse to the art itself. Granting the assumption that values and world view reach expression in art, this general confidence is of no help in the enterprise of specific interpretation. If we want to eschew impressionistic insights and reconstitute the "missing link" in a way which is communicable and subject to restudy and confirmation or revision by others, then we will have to base our work quite explicitly on the clues and limits afforded by researches among living peoples. To illustrate the potential advantages of exploiting ethnographic materials, let us begin with a brief summary of elements in the life situation, thought and belief, and art of the aboriginal Australians. But not without first entering a caveat:

The material here is a compilation, a summary of and selection from diverse researches pursued among various regions and cultures of Australia. The data on art tend to emphasize that which is characteristic of the Oenpelli district of Arnhem Land in particular and north central and northwest Australia in general. The items on ecology and general culture are more widely eclectic. An effort has been made to avoid gross mis-match in coupling material about various aspects of aboriginal life and art; but error or simplistic generalization is built into this kind of summary. This "lumping" is justified, if at all, from the standpoint of our illustrative purpose and does not pretend to be a satisfactory review of the Australian situation as such. Such a summing up must await many more studies like the recent Mountford volume, *Art, Myth and Symbolism,* in which we are provided with a specific account of aboriginal art and belief in Arnhem Land which discriminates three artistic sub-cultures (Groote Eylandt, Oenpelli, and Yirrkalla) and details the corresponding ideology. Pending the availability of such material from many regions of Australia, the generalizations which are offered below must be regarded as at least highly tentative.

The ungenerous character of the Australian ecology, the utter dependence of the aborigine upon the environment, and the intensity and intimacy of his relationship with it form a classical syndrome in the literature. It is vividly and systematically described by Birdsell; and Tindale and other writers going back to Spencer and Gillen have given witness to the picture of a people who live in groups of less than 50, wander constantly within their tribal territory, and sustain themselves on a diet which reads virtually like a biological inventory of their locality.

The life situation of the Australian aborigine is not merely reflected in but rather imprinted on his belief and behavior. Basic is the perception of a profound connection between human life and that of plants and animals—and between all life and the rain. Mythology extends this to the notion of a common origin of men and other natural species. Anxiety, induced by dependence upon the environment and its parsimony, is expressed in various ways: there is a whole complex of belief and action associated with fertility and increase, a theme which pervades mythology and forms one of the main bases for ritual and underlies the exuberant ramification of sexual symbolism. The unpredictability of the evironment echoes in the belief in benign and malevolent spirits, as well as sorcery, as causal agents. And there are rituals of atonement and propitiation which function to redress the feeling of being vulnerable to retribution for the killing of animals. Marrett describes such ritual as a "composition in the matter of blood revenge."

Some of the themes in art and artistic behavior among the Australians are:

1. Art-making as one of the principal forms of ritual and ceremonial action. The Australians hold many designs sacred and, further, believe that a design *is* what it represents. For example, the painted actor in ceremonial *becomes* the mythological personage whose role he enacts by virtue of the ritualistic application ("singing on") of the design.

2. Several other forms of ritual art-making include the palimpsest, or repetitive superposition of engraved and painted forms at certain places; the periodic ritual retouching of the *Wondjina* in the Kimberley caves to "reactivate" their power; ground painting as part of the ceremonial and the remaking or at least repainting of ceremonial objects for each use.

3. The affiliation between men and other living things is a frequent theme in Australian art, especially exemplified in anthropomorphic figures.

4. "X-ray" art is a popular motif, often showing pregnancy or the inner "works" of men and animals, all of this explicitly reflecting an intense concern with life and, more to the point, with fertility and increase. The emphasis on sexual motifs and the outsize portrayal of genitalia in both X-ray and non-X-ray art is another manifestation of this emphasis.

5. The Australian landscape is familiar to the inhabitants on the most intimate level; and features of the landscape are often invested with sacred meaning. The Australians leave their handprints at sacred places as a ritual of personal identification. Elsewhere in this paper we shall have occasion to discuss footprints in the caves and the animal track motif in art as a reflection of elements of the life situation in style.

How much of Australian belief (and its manifestation in art) refers to the particulars of the Australian situation and what may be referred to aspects in which the Australian and Upper Paleolithic situations are comparable? This important stage of analysis requires recourse to material from other living peoples. As an example, let us consider the question of whether the importance of the food quest to the Australian modes of belief is related to the sheer fact of scarcity.

The Chukchee, Gilyak, Lapps, Eskimo, and other hunting peoples of the world live in ecological circumstances which are by no means as adverse as those faced by the Australians; some of the environments may even be described as relatively bountiful. Yet, in one way or another, these people exhibit anxiety in the face of nature, perceive the world in animistic terms, and take various steps to propitiate the spirits and to compensate nature for what has been taken in the hunt.

Sverdrup offers this revealing account of the Chukchee world view:

> The Chukchi concept of nature is fundamentally based on the fear of unexpected and unavoidable events. To them the regularly repeated natural phenomena . . . represent no problem. . . . The hostile nature manifests itself in the unexpected event, in the catastrophes, the storms, the heavy snowfalls . . . disease.
>
> . . . the Chukchi . . . have formed a system of their own which explains nature to their satisfaction, and which they think protects them against the catastrophes. They have populated nature with spirits and consider every unforeseen happening as evidence of the direct action of evil spirits, but . . . they

can approach them and negotiate with them—they can hope that their sacrifices will be accepted by the spirits and that the spirits will show mercy or become reconciled if they have been offended.

The belief in good and evil spirits is also found among the Gilyak, according to Seeland, who notes further that evil spirits predominate and must be propitiated. Hawes reports that the Gilyak have a two-cycle year, marked by the seal and sable hunting seasons respectively. The hunters dedicate their first land-hunting catch to the "lord of the forest" at a special place; and the seal bones are tossed back into the sea. Similar restitution is found among the Lapps, who set aside certain parts of the slain elk for later burial; among the Minnetaree Indians, who believe the skeleton of the bison will again take on flesh if the bones are undestroyed; among the Baffinland and Hudson's Bay Eskimo, where a boy's first seal is stripped of its skin and flesh and the bones are thrown by his mother into a deep hole so that they may rise again as live seals for the boy to catch in later life.

The fertility-increase complex encountered among the Australians is conspicuous by its absence among these people; and this must be regarded as specific to the Australian situation. But it is noteworthy that an animistic view of nature, anxiety about continuity of the food supply, and propitiation and restitution ritual are manifest nevertheless. This persistent syndrome of thought and ritual action, apparently independent of the relative bounty of the environment, seems then to be a function of the dependence upon and intimate relationship with the natural setting. In this case, such characteristics would appear potentially attributable to prehistoric hunters like those of the Upper Paleolithic.

The Gilyak data relating belief and art offer a few details suggesting the extension of certain features in Australia beyond the local situation. We might consider them briefly. The Gilyak make art ritually and impute mana-like power to the art product. Seeland refers to "idols" which are both symbols for and dwelling places of the spirits. Small carved figures are worn as magical charms, recalling the Australian *tjurunga*. Hawes reports crude murals in the village houses: some representations of bears, and a rough design like a chessboard. (Without implying that this has any resemblance of which one could make interpretive use, the reference to a mural chessboard pattern recalls two interesting similiarities: a like design occurs at Lascaux; and Birdsell has shown the writer a map drawn for him by an Australian informant which looks like a multicolored chessboard.) Kreinovich reports this interesting art ritual among the Gilyak: on the sea-going hunt, an indispensable part of the preparation is the making of a carved figure to be placed on the prow or stern of the boat. The ritual is called *tn,aj*, which also means "image" or "picture" or "figure." It affords protection on the hunt.

Now, with respect to connections between art and belief, some extension of the Australian material beyond the specifically local situation may be suggested: The ritual production of art. The equation of a work of art with that which, from our point of view, it merely represents. The investment of pictures or carvings with mana-like power.

Before proceeding to examine similarities and differences in Australian and Upper Paleolithic art, it might be useful to take stock of the procedure thus far. We began with a brief summary of the picture which archeology provides of the life situation of Upper Paleolithic man, and followed this with a very broad inventory of the art. Alongside this account was offered an overview of the conditions of life in Australia, their imprint on belief and behavior, and the expression in art of aspects of Australian world view and values. It then became evident that any extension of the Australian data to Upper Paleolithic man would require further ethnographic comparison to filter out elements specific to the Australians. Examples were offered relevant to two overlapping sets of relationships: (1) the life situation and belief, and (2) belief and the practice of art. Certain very broad positive and negative suggestions were developed in these illustrative comparisons. To narrow the interpretive possibilities further requires that we turn to the art itself, to its content and, above all, to its style. The analysis of style offers two potential contributions. Before exemplifying the more detailed kind of interpretation which can be made when the sort of study outlined above is followed by scrutiny of the art itself, the concept of style and its potential value to our undertaking deserves consideration.

POTENTIAL CONTRIBUTIONS TO THE INTERPRETATION OF PREHISTORIC ART IN STYLISTIC ANALYSIS

A. *Style and Meaning.* "By style is meant the constant form—and sometimes the constant elements, quality and expression—in the art of an individual or a group." In this compact statement by Schapiro are two implications of potential importance for the study of prehistoric art. One is that style, as well as subject matter, yields "meanings." The other is that an art style refers to a specific group. Our discussion of style will be devoted to developing these two implications.

Style is not, as is sometimes assumed, an aspect of art independent of subject matter or "content." This distinction merely refers to different lines of sight on the same phenomena. When we talk about subject matter, the objective is principally to identify the items of experience to which the painter has turned for his models, or to characterize the anecdotal situation which has served him for a metaphor. When we talk about style, we may be said to be concerned with identifying the principle or principles of selection which distinguish the artistic utterance.

Selection occurs on three levels. First, it affects the choice of subject matter. The universe of Upper Paleolithic art is predominantly a carnival of the animals—and the big game animals at that. The art of Australia offers a much more representative sample of the plant and animal life of the region, and humans are frequent subjects. This is a gross contrast, but it will serve to illustrate the point: If we were to approach the matter from a primary interest in "content," our problem would be solved with an inventory of the creatures who inhabit the artistic universe. The stylistic approach, however, aims at detecting the bias which such a census might reveal and then trying to interpret its significance.

Even when the subject matter is merely identified, there is usually some attempt to describe the manner of depiction, the second level on which selection occurs. The suggestion here is that the manner of depiction is properly and usefully regarded as an object of analysis in its own right. The same subject matter is sometimes found in two quite distinct bodies of art—for example, the fish paintings in Arnhem Land and at the Gorge d'Enfer in France. Discriminating the piscine species is hardly sufficient to account for the contrast in point of view expressed by the art. More to the point is the X-ray treatment of the fish in Australia as against the full-fleshed presentation of the Upper Paleolithic fish. The difference in this case is stylistic, a difference in the selection of relevant elements from the model encountered in real life. This is what distinguishes an Altamira bison from the buffalo on a nickel. On this level, selection is defined by such questions as: What aspects of the model are retained? What aspects are stressed, by disproportion or color or other means? What aspects are attenuated or ignored?

Many Australian paintings present a tableau, built either on some situation encountered in daily life or on a fantastic recombination of various individual elements of ordinary experience. In such a work, the artist creates and populates a milieu. This expresses the third level of selection, that which involves patterns of arrangement of the subject matter in the total composition. In the *Mimi* paintings in Arnhem Land, we may see inordinately tall human figures hurling spears at kangaroo. Some of the bark paintings from the same region offer a synthetic situation: A man dominates the center of the picture. He is ringed by fish, two of which are converging on his huge, extended penis. In the former work, the milieu is modeled on a mundane event, whereas the latter presents a microcosmos whose overall arrangement or gestalt is synthetic, a product of fantasy. In both, however, the elements of subject matter have been selected; the depiction of the subjects shows selection; and, in the frame of reference of the total composition, the "environment" is established

through selective principles expressed in juxtaposition, relative size of
the elements, the character of the *lebensraum*, and suggestions about
time through treatment of sequence, and so forth.

In contrast with Australian art, one of the most striking features of
Upper Paleolithic art is the rarity of "scenes." Where they do occur, as in
the famous one at Lascaux, the style is markedly different from the rest
of the art. They are generally very economical delineations, almost stick
figures in some cases, rather than opulent paintings; and their "sketchy"
quality suggests a kind of reportage, perhaps the illustration of a verbal
narrative. Most of the art, however, is "portraiture" of one kind or another, i.e., the presentation of an animal which is not placed in a context
but rather preempts the "milieu" of the painting. Not only does the analysis of compositional selection become much more refined, but we are
faced with interpreting the significance of the absence of any kind of
mise en scène.

Thus far, we have described style as the expression of principles of
selection on three levels and have sought to specify them. In order to suggest the "meanings" which style may yield, we must turn to a more
general canvass of the idea of selection per se.

Boas derives selection from the limitations of the artistic media. The
materials of the painter and sculptor do not permit truly literal imitation,
but constrain them to select. This is self-evident, but it doesn't explain
why the selection should not turn out to be random. The fact is that the
selection is not random, or else we could never talk about "Gothic" art
or "Cubism" and so on; so that we must work toward some idea of the
source of the patterns of selection.

Tylor said that the purpose of art "is not imitation, but what the artist
strives to bring out is the idea that strikes the beholder". In relating
selection to creative intent, rather than to the constraints imposed by the
media, Tylor puts us on the path to a useful conception of meaning in
style. Malraux develops this theme. The artistic enterprise is conceived
by him in the following terms: 1) Selection from an uncharted pro-
fusion of forms and meanings available in the outside world; and, 2) the
composition, by virtue of style, of a coherent universe in which reality is
shaped according to human values.

This will recall the parallel statement by Whorf in quite a different context, worth quoting here because it refers in a more general way to the
source of selection as a function of symbolic behavior in man's organization of reality:

The categories and types that we isolate from the world of phenomena we do
not find there because they stare every observer in the face; on the contrary,
the world is presented to us in a kaleidoscopic flux of impressions which has to

be organized by our minds. . . . We cut nature up, organize it into concepts, ascribe significances as we do, largely because we are parties to an agreement to do it in this way.

A few years earlier, in *Patterns of Culture*, Benedict defined the ethos of a culture as a selection from the great arc of human possibilities. Her analogic reference to the configuration of culture and art style in the same work is not merely heuristic; the conception of art style was as much a model as a metaphor.

An art style is a particular set of selective principles. Taken as a whole, the style of a particular work of art expresses the perceptive bias of the individual artist, as conditioned by (1) his peculiar life history and (2) the context in which his life unfolds, that context being the human group to which he belongs and its culture. But there is also a style attributable to a corpus of art by many artists, as the synoptic collections of any historically organized museum will confirm. Sapir's distinction between individual and social behavior can be projected to reconcile the individual and social dimensions in art style: those aspects of "individual style" which may be referred to shared patterns of selection represent the art style of the group or culture. The "cultural meaning" of an art style, then, is the organization of reality, the conceptual modes, the various levels of value—in short, the collective representations—of the culture which produced it.

B. *Stylistic Units and Cultural Units.* Up to now, we have been concerned with interpreting art—with the use of ethnographic materials and with the meanings which may be derived from the analysis of style. Along with Schapiro, we have assumed that a particular art style is the product of a particular historical sociocultural entity. The concept of style outlined above would seem to warrant this assumption. And, although taxonomic arrangements of non-artistic archeological materials in "industries" and "assemblages" have not been equatable with cultures, archeology has used art styles to achieve culture historical integration. On the premise that art styles refer to historic cultural entities, archeologists have plotted their distribution geographically and chronologically and have been able to order their assemblages in a space-time matrix. Bennett's reconstruction of a Central Andean area co-tradition summed up historical and methodological contributions by Kroeber and Willey, among others, and remains today a prime example of the effective use of art styles in plotting culture history.

But to say that an art style belongs to an historic sociocultural entity doesn't quite do away with the problem of coincidence between an artistic unit and a group unit. We must consider Schapiro's point that a culture may foster two art styles contemporaneously. If this were true, we could not be sure whether our ideological reconstruction referred to part of the outlook of a group, or to the whole of it; and our unit of reference would slip from our grasp.

From the standpoint of the present concern with cultures on the hunting and gathering level, i.e., cultures which are likely to be homogeneous, the problem does not appear formidable. An apparent instance of diverse art styles maintained by a single culture in Arnhem Land disappears upon closer inspection. The Mimi paintings in the caves are, in most stylistic respects, markedly different from the bark paintings and other art produced today and in the recorded past. We cannot assume, because the Mimi paintings figure in contemporary belief and ritual, that they represent another art style of the aborigines of today, who do not make them, do not know or have forgotten who did make them, and regard this art as both representative of and produced by spirits. The fact that present-day aborigines project an explanation on the art does not put them in possession of two art styles.

Turning more directly to Schapiro's point that, "The variation of styles in a culture or group is often considerable within the same period" we are led to inquire into the unit characterized as "a culture or group." Considering the range of examples adduced throughout the article, it is fair to assume that he refers to contemporaneous variety within something like "Western culture." The tremendous diversity within this frame of reference is a plain fact, but are we justified in referring to it as "a culture"? To the extent that we are justified in taking Western culture as a unit, it is vis-à-vis non-Western cultures; and then it is the similarities within our unit, not the differences, that are being stressed. If, however, we are going to focus on variation within this huge geographical, historical, sociocultural framework, then we have to recognize subcultures in space, time, and the organization of society and social thought. And the question becomes one of coincidence between a single art style and a single subculture.

The recent history of modern art gives vivid testimony to the overlapping and side-by-side existence of diverse artistic styles; it is fruitless to seek a common denominator for Expressionism and Cubism or for Norman Rockwell and Picasso. There is parallel diversity in views of reality and values. The artistic subcultures can be characterized by different orientations in belief and behavior. However, in no case can a variety of styles be attributed to one artistic "school." The problem which Schapiro raises is not, in the end, a problem of reconciling cultural homogeneity with stylistic diversity, but one of establishing meaningful coincidences between art styles and sociocultural entities.

This problem is yet to be solved with respect to the Upper Paleolithic. Breuil has organized the art into two great cycles, the Aurignacian-

Périgordian and the Solutréo-Magdalenian, on the basis of archeological evidence, stylistic criteria (which assume a progression toward accomplished naturalistic rendering and increasing elaborateness in technique), and similarities in certain broad features of execution. This grouping of the material, granting its validity, is nevertheless unsuited to the purposes outlined in this paper. The units are chonological and lump obviously disparate art styles. The Altamira polychrome bison are placed in Magdalenian VI. So are the bison at Font-de-Gaume. Yet they are remarkably different in style. The former are thickly outlined, presented in a variety of poses, very detailed, adorned with a stylized, fringe-like treatment of the hair. The latter have more generalized forms, are rather delicately outlined, are mostly standing erect, with emphatic development of the hump and other rounded parts of the body. The refinement of delineation in the French bison contrasts with the Spanish cave paintings as Japanese art might contrast with Rouault or Picasso.

In order to obtain units against which the analysis of style can be projected, it will be necessary to cross-cut Breuil's chronological classification with groupings based on spatial distribution. Despite their apparent contemporaneity, and whatever similarities in outlook they may have shared, there were differences in the principles of selection between the people at Altamira and those at Font-de-Gaume. We have to assume, provisionally at least, that these were variant local cultures. What might, for convenience, be called the "Font-de-Gaume Style" and the "Altamira Style" must be plotted geographically. Once the distribution is known, the archeology of the area which corresponds with the art style must also be treated as a unit distinct from the remainder of the larger region. In short, a stylistic-cultural region must be plotted and dealt with as an entity.

The outcome of such "style-mapping" will be individual units with which we can begin to do interpretive work. It will not result in a sequence of Upper Paleolithic art history, for the present state of our knowledge of art styles and the logic of their progression is totally inadequate to allow us to convert several different art styles into an historical series on internal evidence. For sequences of styles, we will have to continue to depend for a long time on the data of dirt archeology.

SOME TRIAL INTERPRETATIONS OF UPPER PALEOLITHIC ART

Let us proceed now to some attempts at interpretation of some features of Upper Paleolithic art, using the guides developed above. The following suggestions were developed in ethnographic comparisons, taking off from a review of the Australian data:

Dependence upon nature is one of the crucial features of a hunting and gathering subsistence, regardless of the relative bounty of the environment.

The relationship with the natural setting is intimate and intense.

Hunting is difficult with the inadequate arsenal possessed by these peoples; and cornering and killing big game animals is not only problematic but often dangerous.

The unexpected and irregular manifestations of nature produce major crises in the lives of such dependent people.

These situational factors are reflected in several themes in the outlook and behavior:

Nature is perceived as active and purposive and personal, sometimes in animistic terms and sometimes in outright anthropomorphic terms; and there is some tendency to identify to greater or lesser degree with non-human living things.

Even when the food supply is abundant, dependence, unpredictability in the total situation, and the resistance of big game to the hunter's purpose invoke anxiety which is expressed by peopling the universe with spirits or gods which (a) account for the character of the situation, and (b) provide the possibility of appropriate action to control or at least salvage the situation.

Nature, thus regarded, is approached from two directions: It is perceived as accessible to propitiation; and compensation for what man must take from it in order to survive is regarded as possible and necessary.

In turn, these themes are reflected in certain attitudes and patterns of behavior with respect to art:

The main belief in this connection is that a work of art is the same thing as that which it represents.

From this stems the idea that art objects have mana-like power.

In the realm of behavior, we have seen that hunting and gathering people who engage in art-making do so ritually.

This represents the range of possibilities filtered from a description of Australian life, belief, and art by virtue of comparisons with other hunting and gathering peoples designed to distinguish between what is specific to the Australian situation and what might remain for use in interpreting Upper Paleolithic art. In approaching the prehistoric material, the art itself guides us to a still closer range of potential explanation. The selection reflected in the subject matter, depictive treatment, and compositional arrangement of the art is the clue to the selection which characterizes the outlook of the ancient people. In view of what has been said about the need for well articulated art styles for the Upper Paleolithic, it is only possible to deal here with discrete features which cannot be added up and offered as the values and outlook upon reality of a true sociocultural entity.

The handprints in the caves are the remains of a ritual of identification ("Kilroy was here"), the mark of the pilgrim's visit to a sacred place. The very way of life, as we have seen, develops an intimate sense of locality and the imputation of sacred character to features of the landscape. This is elaborately expressed in Australia, where there are also handprints and where the natives are able to identify the owners who have placed them there in a ritual act.

The profusely superposed drawings are the traces of a restitution ritual: whenever an animal was killed, his essence was restored to Nature by ritual rendering of his image at a sacred spot. Basic to this interpretation are the following beliefs: an image is what it represents; restitution can and must be made to the spirits or gods who stand for Nature. These express anxiety over the continuity of the food supply, born of dependence upon nature, and the notion that taking life is dangerous not only vis-à-vis the powerful beast but also the powerful spirits who inspire and protect all life.

The superposed drawings occur at selected places, often surrounded by available areas for drawing. On occasion, as at Les Trois Frères, they are placed in juxtaposition with other art—in this case the "Sorcerer"—in a manner which suggests sacrifice to a spirit or god. Above all, the palimpsests of this kind suggest a compulsive superposition rather than mere overpainting or overdrawing; and this compulsiveness inspires the notion of ritual. Similar artistic phenomena are reported from Australia by Basedow, who cites rock carvings at Yunta in the Flinders mountains where "one design has been carved over the top of another, time after time, until eventually the ground appeared as though it were covered by an elaborate carpet." Speaking of the "impression of profuseness" in the cave galleries of rock painting in Arnhem Land, Elkin says: "The drawings overlay one another. This suggests that satisfaction lies not so much in admiring the finished picture, as in the act of painting it or in some practical desire it expresses and in some result it will effect . . . he believes that this 'ritual' act will bring about the desired result."

The anthropomorphic figures, as a general class of art, express the affiliation between men and other living creatures and, as well, the personification of nature. This is a very vague generalization; but it does suggest the direction of productive analysis. Assuming the significance of anthropomorphic figures suggested here, the most informative path would seem to require a close study of the factors of selection—human and animal elements used—and composition of these elements into a synthetic figure. This is not an easy task for the Upper Paleolithic, where anthropomorphic figures are not a strongly expressed artistic theme and where they tend to occur as one-of-a-kind examples.

The animals which occur with darts or spears sticking in them have been popularly interpreted as imitative magic; and although this kind of interpretation is again very general, it does gain support from other evidence discussed above. This involves the same kind of equation of the artistic depiction with that which is depicted as do the superposed drawings of the palimpsests, although the intent here is clearly not restitution but rather to gain power over the animal. Thus, we have an expression tending to confirm the perception of the game animals as dangerous in a literal sense. In the more specific treatment of *perspective tordue* below, there seems ample justification to impute this sense of problem to Upper Paleolithic man.

Perspective tordue in Upper Paleolithic art is not a manifestation of inept perspective rendering but evidence for the intense concern of the hunter, with his inadequate armament, over the danger he faced from the horned wild beasts. "Twisted perspective" is Breuil's name for an artistic practice encountered in the Upper Paleolithic in which the horns of animals otherwise shown in profile are turned around full face to the viewer. The accepted interpretation of this phenomenon has been that it represents less accomplished naturalism than later art. To put it another way, this style has been designated as earlier and assigned to the Périgordian, largely on the assumption that there is a progression in Upper Paleolithic art as a whole toward the Renaissance ideal of perspective.

This assumes a kind of progressive learning which took place over many thousands of years. It also ignores the possibility that perspective tordue expresses a principle of style, a kind of compositional selection which is designed to stress the significance to the artist of the horns of the animal. However, recourse to the Australian material yields evidence that such twisting of usual appearances is purposeful and refers to aspects of the life experience of the artists.

In Australia there are many pictures in which the figure of a man or an animal is presented in profile, standing or running, but with the soles of the feet turned up to face the viewer. We know why the Australians do this. From early childhood, boys are taught to identify human and animal tracks with extreme subtlety. Their lives depend on the success of the hunt and game is scarce, and no means of detecting the opportunity for a kill can be neglected. Animal tracks themselves are a prominent motif in Australian art; in the pictures described above they merely become an element—albeit an important one—of a larger composition. It should also be noted that footprints of humans, as well as handprints, are found in the caves and are part of the syndrome of identification. Tracks are the mark of men and animals in Australia.

In this light, it is evident that the presentation of the soles of the feet in the Arnhem Land bark paintings and other art represents a selective principle, a violation of literal truth in behalf of a more profound reality, reflecting the intense concern with identifying animals and men and even spirits.

In the Upper Paleolithic, we cannot overlook the possibility of an analogous situation in the art, which takes its shape from the particular situation that obtained then and there. We have referred to the inefficiency of the weapons of Upper Paleolithic man in dealing with large animals; and he doubtless used traps and pitfalls and other means to bring them down. It is also quite likely that one of the perils of wandering around the countryside to hunt or to collect vegetable food was the possibility of attack by these beasts. This was a real problem for him; and the notion that his art features the selective principle which gives prominence to the horns on these grounds seems more plausible than inept rendering—an idea which applies esthetic values limited to a particular period of Western art history. Further, in the famous "wall-scene" at Lascaux, which appears as noted earlier to be illustrating an actual event, we get a depiction of an event in which the disemboweled beast looms over the fallen hunter, horns pointing to the fallen man and to the viewer.

The above are some examples of interpretations of Upper Paleolithic art, offered to illustrate how artistic selection may be projected on a range of possible explanations to narrow that range considerably. This paper has been designed to suggest procedures whereby ethnographic materials, the data about ecology and the life situation and art afforded by archeology, a concept of style as selective perception, can contribute to a systematic, verifiable sequence of analysis and reconstruction. The essence of the procedure is a progressive narrowing down of the variety of explanation for which plausibility can be asserted. The objective is a limitation on plausible explanation; patent demonstration is out of the question. Even so, with much work on a more modest scale than indicated here, on many fronts which demand study, there is some prospect of narrowing the span between that period for which we know something of man as a highly evolved animal and that brief epoch for which his attitudes and outlook are known to us in specific detail.

31. ANTHROPOLOGISTS ON ART *

A TWO-FOLD PROBLEM presents itself in the study of art which is reflected in the methodology of the anthropologists, and others dealing with anthropological materials, whose work we shall consider here. In the first place, information must be gathered regarding forms and styles according to culture or area, and once sufficient material has been gathered, it must be put into some categorical form. Perhaps it is unavoidable that art has been discussed for the most part in the taxonomic and static terms of form and style categories, since categorizing is necessary to the very investigation of the subject. Yet art, like other aspects of culture, is in a constant process of change. This brings us to the second, or *dynamic*, aspect of the problem. It is necessary to study the origins, and changes through time, of forms, designs, and styles; to look for the reasons or causes for these, and to attempt to discover which are most basic. The study of art, thus presented, could well be subjected to scientific methodology. Early anthropological interest in art was decidedly science-oriented.

The men who took up the problem near the end of the last century were from different countries and from somewhat differing backgrounds, but their aims and methods in studying art were remarkably similar. Among them were Ernst Grosse, a German sociologist and anthropologist; Hjalmar Stolpe, a Swedish ethnologist; Henry Balfour, who was Curator of the Pitt-Rivers Collection at Oxford; and Alfred Haddon, an English zoologist who worked in anthropology. These men were vitally interested in the possibility of treating art in a scientific way. They felt

* Donna Taylor, "Anthropologists on Art," *Papers of the 1956 General Studies Anthropology Seminar* (1957), pp. 23–33. Printed with the permission of the author.

Mrs. Taylor is a graduate student of anthropology at Columbia University specializing in Chinese and contiguous cultures. She is also deeply interested in art and material culture. This is her first published work.

that the then recent doctrine of evolution had much to offer in the way of theory, and that ethnology, which, as Grosse says, had already made significant contributions to "other branches of sociological study," had a great deal to offer in the way of materials.

Ethnology could be helpful to a study of art because at that time any general art theory had been based on European art only; but this is not the only art. In constructing any general art theory, and certainly in looking for origins, the art of primitive peoples must come into consideration. Grosse says in *The Beginnings of Art:* "The beginnings of art lie . . . where the beginnings of culture lie. But the light of history illuminates only the last shortest stretch of the long road that mankind has left behind it, and history can give no clew to these beginnings. . . . History knows no primitive peoples. . . . Ethnology, on the other hand, is competent to show us primitive peoples in the light of the present." Or, as Balfour puts it, the true history of the earliest stages "is lost and can never be written, and in forming our opinion of the condition of its early progress we are reduced to reasoning from analogy, and are unable to produce a chain of evidence in the form of events arranged in true chronological order."

Grosse assigns the "science of art" to the field of "sociological science." He points out that there are two approaches to the study of art, the individual and the social. The individual approach, that is, the attempt to illustrate the individual character of an art work from the individual character of the artist, is capable of solution only for a small minority of cases, if at all. The problem in this form would in any case be a psychological one; therefore the problems arising in the science of art are solvable only in the second, or social, form. "We can only undertake to relate the aggregated character of the art groups of a period or a district to a whole people or a whole age."

The science of art would have the goals and methods of science in general. Science looks for regular or fixed relationships of phenomena studied, and for laws that will explain them. In a way, science is superficial, for "it remains on the empirical surface of things" and "has to content itself with demonstrating the normal sequence of phenomena in the general aspects." Thus the science of art is "no metaphysical illumination . . . and does not penetrate into the transcendent depths." Its goals are limited:

If the science of art has taught us one of the laws that reign in the seemingly incalculable and capricious development of art, it has done all that can be asked of it. It has won a new province from the barren sea of vague speculation, on which ground the human mind can secure a firm footing, and sow and reap. A piece of tillable ground is indeed a poor substitute for the mysterious treasures which the old art philosophers promised their adepts.

To some this indeed seems quite dull and uninteresting. As Meyer Schapiro says in his article "Style" in *Anthropology Today* (1953), "scholars will often deny that these 'external' relationships can throw any light on the artistic phenomenon as such. They fear 'materialism' as a reduction of the spiritual or ideal to sordid practical affairs." Grosse says simply that "the science of art has completed its message when it has shown that regular and fixed relations exist between certain forms of culture and art; and when the philosophy of art asks it concerning the inner substance of these forms and relations . . . it is obliged to confess squarely that it not only can not answer these questions, but can not even understand them."

In the search, then, for "laws," Grosse turns our attention to the next best thing to the earliest traces of art, now lost forever—the art of primitive peoples; specifically, the art of hunting peoples. He finds that hunting peoples devote a large part of their time and strength to art. Grosse concludes that a function to which so great a mass of energy is applied by a people whose subsistence requires such effort and hardship must be no idle play, but an indispensable social function. He provides many examples of the art of hunting peoples, wherein he finds great similarities. Looking for some common factor, he finds that the one component which, among all hunting peoples, exercises the strongest influence on the other "departments of cultural life" is the securing of food. This, he says, is "the uniform cause" which produces "the uniform character of primitive art." The function of art in the life of primitive peoples is to strengthen and extend the social bonds so necessary to the securing of food. Grosse says we are "not yet able to follow out clearly the relations between the forms of primitive production and the forms of primitive art in all cases and on all sides"; yet he feels he has made clear "the significance of hunting life in the beginnings of art in general." Primitive art possesses a practical importance to the hunting peoples; thus is art characterized in its earliest recoverable beginnings.

Grosse concedes that throughout history artistic activities were perhaps many times first exercised for the sake of their immediate aesthetic value, but asserts that they have been kept up and developed mainly because of their social value. He states that a consciousness of the importance of art to social welfare has, moreover, existed in man in all ages, and that the art of "civilized" peoples is hardly less practical than that of primitive peoples. Rarely do we find a work which engages and pursues exclusively aesthetic interests. The differences between the two arts are of a quantitative rather than a qualitative nature; primitive art reveals a paucity of materials and technical knowledge and consequent poor and coarse forms, "but in its essential motives, means, and aims the art of the earliest times is at one with the art of all times."

Our other early writers were not only science-oriented but more overtly evolution-oriented. They were convinced that the study of decorative art could use the same methods as biological science, and that designs, like animals, had geographical distribution and histories of evolution governed by laws as fixed as those governing the evolution of animals, following similarly immutable courses in all times and places of the world. Indeed, as has been mentioned, Haddon was a zoologist, and he gives a detailed argument for the application of biological deductions, based on the law of biology "all life from life," to the science of art.

In their assumptions and methodology these men were preceded by, and some overtly followed, the general approach of Pitt-Rivers, who had postulated evolutionary series of development for decorative art, and accumulated material forming a collection of step-by-step series illustrating the origin, growth, and variations of certain patterns. His writings on the subject were, however, fragmentary and scattered among his various papers on other subjects. Balfour was Curator of the Pitt-Rivers Collection when it became a gift to Oxford, and he continued to collect fresh material and information with the intention of developing the subject further. *The Evolution of Art* was the result of this work. His purpose in writing it was to set down certain conclusions he had reached.

He states that aesthetic experience has been observed among animals, and that man, in his pre-human state, must have also experienced some form of aesthetic stimulation. He was perhaps attracted by uncommon or brightly colored objects, and, for instance, perhaps collected small shells and other objects and strung them together for decoration before he thought of the next stage, imitation.

The earliest actual evidence we have of man's attempts at manufacture are flint implements. These are very difficult to work into shape and "utterly unsuited to the application of decoration except in the most expert hands." Thus, the earliest decorations on implements were probably done in soft, now perished materials. The earliest extant art we do have is "cave-art," consisting almost entirely of naturalistic representations. Balfour feels that embellishment of a "purely decorative nature is extremely scarce." The Neolithic shows a decline in realistic representation but an advance in "conventional or fanciful design." This art was "devoted rather to embellishing and beautifying useful objects than to, so to speak, sketching from nature. Its 'school' was a very different one, but by no means necessarily inferior."

Balfour felt that on the basis of the above development an evolutionary series that all art followed could be established. However, the supporting evidence was by no means complete. It was therefore necessary to look to living primitive peoples. Balfour did this, offering considerable evidence for the following "chief stages" in the evolution of decorative art:

I. ADAPTIVE: The appreciation of curious or decorative effects occurring in nature or as accidents in manufacture, and the slight increasing of the same by artificial means in order to augment their peculiar character or enhance their value as ornament.

II. CREATIVE: The artificial production of similar effects where these do not occur; imitation or copying.

III. VARIATIVE: Gradual metamorphosis of designs by—

(a) *Unconscious Variation,* in which the changes are not intentional, but are due to want of skill or careless copying, difficulty of material, or reproducing from memory.

(b) *Conscious Variation,* in which the changes are intentional, and may be made to serve some useful purpose (e.g., marks of ownership), or to increase an ornamental effect; to emphasize some specially important feature in a symbolic design; to adapt the same design to a variety of objects or spaces; by the development of a new idea from the modification of a pre-existing design; etc.

The effects of "successive copying" are paramount in creating variations upon established designs, whether unconsciously or consciously.

Conscious and unconscious variation frequently, usually in fact, act together; the changes being hastened by an association of unskilful copying and a desire to vary.

Haddon presented a very similar series which he called "life-histories of designs," with the difference that he had perhaps a dissimilar value judgment. Where Balfour felt his "variative" stage was not necessarily inferior to the "creative" stage, Haddon calls his three stages: origin, evolution, and *decay.*

Stolpe also presents three stages, those of originating, intermediate, and final forms:

On studying a large collection of ornament we often find that certain details, though at first sight insignificant, yet by means of a series of intermediate forms, become explicable as rudiments of emblems derived from organic nature. The rudiments may be more or less evident, yet they will always resemble and symbolize and suggest the image from which they originated. In their latest stage the primitive signification is, indeed so lost that they pass, degraded, into mere meaningless decoration.

Both Stolpe and Haddon emphasized the importance of realistic representation as an early stage in art which later degenerated into geometric representation. They fell into something of a trap in doing this, for although it was known that "cave-art" was probably not the earliest art in time, since it was the first *evidence* of art, it was used to indicate the first stage in postulated universal and ever-occurring evolutionary series.

Balfour and Haddon were primarily interested in presenting evidence for evolutionary series, and only secondarily interested in the function of art. Balfour mentions that art plays an important part in "beautifying our surroundings, and . . . subduing the monotony of a too matter-of-fact existence," and Haddon briefly discusses aesthetic, communication, wealth, and religious "reasons for which objects are decorated." Stolpe, on the other hand, is as much interested in the function of art as in its evolution. He asserts that all primitive art is primarily symbolic and only secondarily decorative. The earliest renderings, which were mainly of animal and human form, served a purely utilitarian purpose. Magico-religious beliefs established an intimate spiritual and sympathetic relationship between an object and its effigy, so that the possession of an object's effigy could endow the owner with some degree of control over the object represented. Geometric designs were derived originally from realistic representations of animals over which control was desired, or representations of gods whom the people wished to supplicate. This view is of course similar to Grosse's, without, however, his explicit emphasis on the *social function* of primitive art.

All designs have meaning, according to Stolpe. If one asks the reason for some device and gets no satisfactory answer, either the meaning is forgotten or the people don't wish to tell it to the investigator. Yet

our previous investigations suffice of themselves to prove that the forms of development of the old primitive images, highly conventionalized, must have a symbolic significance. They symbolize, they stand in the place of, the primitive image. They are to be considered as a sort of cryptograph. By means of perpetual reiteration of certain ornamental elements, they suggest the divinity to whose service the decorated implement was in some way dedicated.

Stolpe, closely following a terminology which Haddon had taken from Colley March and had modified, classified art decorations according to the forms from which they were originally deliberately copied: anthropomorphic, zoomorphic, phytomorphic (Haddon: phyllomorphic), physiomorphic, ideomorphic; also skeumorphic, unintentional and purely extraneous decorations, the "deliberate retention for ornamental purposes" of such things as clay coils or fingerprint rows on pottery, curved lines becoming of necessity squared designs in weaving, the decoration of handles and rims. Another idea modified by Haddon from March is that of two antagonistic forces at work in the history of the evolution of ornament: a) the disintegrative; "conventionalization," which is gradually produced so that the original motif is no longer recognizable unless one has the intermediate states; b) the conservative, which retains as much of the original as possible, whether the preserved features are essential or not (e.g., rope patterns or binding designs). The latter is widely operative in architecture.

It is to be regretted that in this brief exposition we are unable to do fuller justice to the views and methods of these men. As we shall see, there have been cogent arguments against their methodology and arrangement of materials, and it has been well demonstrated that art can have either geometric or representational origin, and that change can go in either direction. Yet whether we agree with them or not, we cannot help but be impressed by their inquiring spirit and the vitality of their interest in the possibility of treating the subject of art in a new way, of making new contributions to the subject, and their willingness to spare no effort in this attempt, nor refuse to look at or consider anything that might aid it.

Franz Boas (*Primitive Art*, 1927) represents, if indeed he does not originate, an ensuing trend of concern with primitive art. Perhaps its most notable feature is the lack of interest in the determination of possible evolutionary stages or series. Boas asserts that it may be possible to answer the historical questions in art, but that we have not yet sufficient materials to do this. Therefore "the only available method of study is the geographical one, the study of distribution." Within an area, however, Boas does acknowledge the influence of history, but his emphasis is rather different from that of the writers discussed above. He postulates two main sources of art. One is based on the development of control of technique alone, the achievement of a certain standard of excellence in technical treatment so that typical forms are produced. The other source is religious, social, or other emotions and thoughts, as they are embodied in fixed artistic forms—that is, representation. Since Boas asserts both a geometric and a representational source of art, he finds unacceptable the theory that all art is first realistic and expressive and gradually degenerates into geometrization. Rather, interpretations are often later read into originally geometric designs. One proof given of this is the fact that different peoples may have different interpretations of the same design. Further, some designs are made only for the pleasure of making them, for the completed design cannot be seen in the article when it is used. For example, the Thompson Indians hang beads on legging fringe in regular patterned sequence, but the pattern cannot be seen when the fringe hangs down the side of the leggings. Also, parfleche designs are laid out in large over-all patterns which cannot be seen when the decorated skin is folded into its box form, which does not follow the design form of the painting. Boas says further that "it is very seldom only that the steps are found so distributed that they can be proved to follow one another in time. Much oftener all are found at the same time among the same people." Incidentally, neither Boas nor those he criticizes rely heavily on archeology, and the positive chronologies it can contribute to this question.

Rather than art stages or style series, then, it is formal principles that Boas emphasizes. The objects of study in various areas of the world are those that have an aesthetic value, which is a value to be found among all men and recognized by all men everywhere. He finds definite formal principles manifesting themselves universally in all art. It is not his wish to explain their origin, but, finding them in the art of man the world over, he considers them the most ancient and fundamental characteristics of all art. One is symmetry, which is generally right and left and may be due to the symmetry of manual movements as well as the observation of right and left symmetry in animals and in man. Second is rhythm. Rhythmic repetitions of similar units run ordinarily in horizontal bands and may be based on the simple repetitions of the same motifs which are necessitated by technical processes, and on the general observation of natural objects of the same or similar kind arranged in horizontal strata, such as woods, mountains, and clouds; legs, body, and limbs. The third formal element is the emphasis of form, such as the application of lines to the rim of a pot, or decoration around handles where they join the pot.

Other principles underlie art styles. For example, art styles that make use of the spiral show characteristic traits, not only in the form of the spiral, but also in the handling of the decorative field. Similarly, all the tribes in a certain area may use the same kind of triangles and rectangles in their art, and yet there can exist typical differences in the treatment of the decorative field. In decorative art which is highly symbolic "the selection of symbols is of decisive importance in defining the style and . . . the arrangement of the symbols is subject to the same formal treatment of the decorative field which control the arrangement of geometrical motives."

The particular types of geometrical motives that enter into the representative form, as well as the treatment of the decorative field determine the character of the design and . . . the degree of realism depends upon the relative importance of the geometric and representative elements. When the purely decorative tendency prevails we have essentially geometrical, highly conventionalized forms, when the idea of representation prevails, we have, on the contrary, more realistic forms. In every case, however, the formal element that characterizes the style, is older than the particular type of representation. This does not signify that early representations do not occur, it means that the method of representation was always controlled by formal elements of distinctive origin.

Thus it might be said that the "science of art" has been replaced by the "appreciation of primitive art." Probably the main approach today is Boasian. It is the intention of such writers as Covarrubias, Linton, and Wingert—to whose works we can only refer the reader—to illuminate the value of primitive art as equal to Western art, to distinguish the arts by area and culture, and to discuss these arts in terms of those formal elements which will aid our understanding and appreciation. Also necessary is the explanation of special religious ideas, social values, and so forth, which might explain primitive art to the uninitiated. Their methodology reveals the influence of modern Western aesthetics. It leads to a sympathetic and objective approach to all art—ancient, foreign, or primitive. Primitive art is now at one with the art of the rest of the world. As Meyer Schapiro says, "As a result of this new approach, all the arts of the world . . . have become accessible on a common plane of expressive form-creating activity. Art is now one of the strongest evidences of the basic unity of mankind."

There has been, however, some recent interest in historical questions. As is evident from the title of her book, in *The Origins of Art* (1953) Gene Weltfish wishes to return to some of the earlier problems of origin and change. Like Boas, she says that the art of design grew up side by side with naturalistic representation, and that the symbolism of geometric art occurs through a process of secondary association.

It is the geometric art that Weltfish is mainly concerned with in her book. She demonstrates the origin of modern Amazon Indian designs in matwork weaves, the evolution of an elaborate decorative art based on the diagonal-inverted-symmetry textile pattern among the Mimbres Indians of New Mexico, and the development of North American Indian parfleche designs from birchbark decoration. On the basis of elaborate evidence, she demonstrates that certain designs evolved as the techniques needed for the manufacture of some objects gave rise to patterns which were then carried over to other objects in which such technical manipulations are not required; for example, matplaiting and textile-weave patterns to pottery and other painted objects, birchbark designs to parfleche style, and parfleche style to baskets, blankets, and so forth.

Weltfish suggests additional factors from history, religion, mythology, and economics which are later incorporated into art, but does not deal with them systematically. Because of inadequate treatment of various questions raised, the book is not so comprehensive a work as it seems to have been intended to be. The more limited but nonetheless important contribution is a masterly step-by-step demonstration of the adaption of designs arising of necessity in some manufactures to surfaces that do not demand patternings.

In his article "Style," to which we have already referred, Meyer Schapiro indicates a possible direction for inquiry into the general subject of art that might be of some interest to the cultural anthropologist. He points out that common to all the approaches of those concerned with art (archeologist, art historian, synthesizing historian of culture, philosopher of history, art critic) is the assumption that any given culture or epoch of culture has only one style, or a limited range of styles, peculiar to it. Works of a particular style could have been produced only at a certain time, and not at another. The repeated experience of discovering objects later which confirm a connection made between a style and a period, on the basis of a few examples, supports these postulates. Works are related by nonstylistic evidence, whenever this exists, either to the same time and place as do formal traits, or to a culturally associated region. Migration or trade explains the appearance of a style in another region. Style has therefore come to be used with confidence as an independent clue to the time and place of origin of an art work. It has been possible, on the basis of these assumptions, for scholars to construct a systematic, if not entirely complete, picture of the temporal and spatial distribution of styles covering large regions of the globe.

Furthermore, when works of art are grouped according to their original time and space positions, significant relationships will be shown by their styles which can be co-ordinated with the relationships of the works of art to still other cultural features in time and space. Such relationships are reflected in or already suggested by the framework of the history of art, whose main divisions, accepted by all students, are also the boundaries of social units: cultures, empires, dynasties, cities, classes, churches, and periods which mark significant stages in social development. Schapiro says that "the importance of economic, political, and ideological conditions for the creation of a group style (or of a world view that influences a style)" is frequently admitted. Yet with all this experience, there has been no systematic explanation of the connection of art types with social structure types and the general principles underlying the making of this connection; little has been done toward the construction of an adequate comprehensive theory.

Schapiro points out one possible direction that has been indicated for analysis based on the recognition that "between the economic relationships and the styles of art intervenes the process of ideological construction, a complex imaginative transposition of class roles and needs, which affects the special field—religion, mythology, or civil life—that provides the chief themes of art." The great interest of this approach lies in its attempt to interpret the historically changing relation of art and economic life in the light of a general theory of society and also "in the weight given to the differences and conflicts within the social group as motors of development, and to the effects of these on outlook, religion, morality, and philosophical ideas."

In *Social History of Art* (1951) Arnold Hauser, with great competence, deals with just those interrelationships within our own art tradition that Schapiro points up. The anthropologist can extend the investigation to the cultures with which he works. He does not, of course, have the many social referents for these cultures that the art historian has. Yet careful extrapolation may produce meaningful results.

In his article "A Trobriand Medusa?" E. R. Leach argues, cogently and concretely, that a shield design, previously thought to be entirely abstract, is in fact the anthropomorphic representation of a malevolent mythical figure made for magical purposes in war. Leach feels that primitive art is seldom totally abstract, but usually performs some social function. Although in many cases

the evidence that can be adduced is wholly circumstantial, since the objects are no longer made and the memory of them no longer survives in their place of origin; in other cases . . . investigation of "abstract" designs for the contemporary functional significance might prove very rewarding.

CONCLUSION

In anthropology the subject of art has received treatment in terms of various problems, some of which have been indicated in this paper.

A general theory like that of evolution is of course not original with ethnology. Yet when art is conceived of as an aspect of culture—and not merely as the expression of an "aesthetic impulse," thus increasing the complexity of the problem by assigning separate causes to separate phenomena—it becomes possible to apply to it the methodology of the science of culture. Ethnologists, and others working with ethnographic materials, who early struggled with the problem of treating art in the light of ethnology, applied to it the theory of evolution, which was then being applied to ethnology in general. This was done in a rather simplistic fashion and produced some faulty results. Yet these men were perhaps not asking the wrong questions; they did know how to set up a problem on the basis of such materials as they did have. Even Boas did not deny the possibility of investigating the historical questions in art, but only asserted that we had not yet enough materials to deal adequately with such questions. Indeed, evolutionary series which date from quite early stages have now been established by reliable archeological means for some cultures of the world—for example, for Egypt, Crete, Mesopotamia, Greece, China, Nuclear America—and at least some parallelism is evidenced.

Ethnology has had a strong influence on the subject of art in general by the demonstration of the qualitative equality of primitive peoples with all peoples, and of the fact that primitives are not "simple children of nature" but mature members of on-going societies who face daily the problems of existence and who express their experiences and values in their art with depth and feeling. Writers such as Boas and Wingert have done much to establish primitive art on a par with the art of the rest of mankind, although much of their methodology, particularly that having to do with formal principles, is a contribution to aesthetics rather than to ethnology.

When art is viewed as an aspect of culture, the question of what determines style or how we can account for styles and changes of styles is related to questions of the functions that various aspects of culture play in the whole, and which are most basic. Grosse (and of course others) says gaining a livelihood is the most basic activity of primitive man, and that social relations aid this. He feels therefore that primitive art must somehow aid or facilitate social relations and efforts. Stolpe also believes primitive man's main concern is subsistence but he emphasizes the importance religion plays in this concern, and, therefore, in art. Boas emphasizes the aesthetic aspect of art, which he asserts exists among all peoples. It could be said that the aesthetic role of art does not of necessity preclude the other roles we have mentioned; also, social roles, rather than aesthetic, might be more in the province of anthropology.

One contribution to the anthropological study of art is that of the archeologist who can discover and accurately date sequences of styles of prehistoric cultures. Another is the field experience of a modern ethnographer such as Gene Weltfish, who can demonstrate the actual production of designs in primitive industry, and the necessities of technology which preclude the appearance of some designs in advance of others, or the appearance of some designs in certain media in advance of their appearance in other media, and who can thus demonstrate some of the mechanics of design origin and change.

Meyer Schapiro outlines yet another approach which should be of great interest to the modern anthropologist concerned with the special topic of art. Because of the great amount of work that has been done on the subject, we have now available an incomplete but systematic picture of the temporal and spatial distribution of styles throughout large regions of the world. Significant relationships are to be found between works which correspond in time, which can be coordinated with relationships of art works to still other features of cultural life in time and space. These relationships are already suggested by the framework of art history, in which historical art epochs are the same as the epochs of economic history. This is the very problem Grosse was struggling with. Although he felt he could not prove it conclusively, he, and others, have recognized a relationship between economic organization and art. Grosse postulated the relationship only for hunting economies; yet he was aware that the art of more complex cultures did not perform an aesthetic function only. Schapiro points out that the problem has an additional dimension. It is not only a matter of interpreting the relations of art and economic life in the light of a general theory of society; it is also necessary to examine, in particular, how the roles, needs, conflicts within a social group get formed into art objects and expressed through them. The latter analysis has been applied by Arnold Hauser to much of our own art history.

Schapiro says that "a theory of style adequate to the psychological and historical problems has still to be created. It waits for a deeper knowledge of the principles of form construction and expression and for a unified theory of the processes of social life in which the practical means of life as well as emotional behavior are comprised." While there may be valid problems of expression and perception in the field of aesthetics, a unified theory of style can be constructed which is on other levels. The anthropologist can treat of details of technology and of form construction; he can also deal with the subtleties of social and economic relationships and their ideological expression in art. He has special tools for handling problems of such provenience and here can make his best contribution.

32. MUSIC OF THE AMERICAN INDIAN *

THERE ARE two ways in which we may approach the subject of Indian music. One is with the question, "What does Indian music mean to us?" The other is "What does it mean to the Indians?" We must approach it from both standpoints in order to understand it.

You have probably heard Indian music at exhibitions or on the stage and remember the loud drumming and the harsh voices of the singers. Perhaps the Indian would get just such an unfavorable impression from hearing our jazz bands. But the Indian songs you heard at exhibitions were not like our jazz. They were probably songs of social dances or perhaps they were old war songs. Indians sing all sorts of songs in the same way—the manner of rendition has no significance. From our standpoint we might call it abstract, as that word is commonly used at the present time.

The Indians' manner of voice production is their own. I once asked Little Wolf, one of my singers, to hear me sing a song that he had recorded and tell me if it was correct. He listened and said, "The *tune* is right but you haven't an Indian throat."

Indians never "sing with expression," so the style of singing is the same throughout a song, as well as in different songs. We use a syllable for practically every note, but most Indian songs have very few words—2 or 3 are often enough for a song and they occur midway through the melody. The rest of the tones are produced by this strange "Indian throat"—a muscular action that can clearly produce tones as short as sixteenth or even thirty-second notes without any distinct syllables. An Omaha Indian said that we "talk a great deal when we sing."

Indians have no musical system, no rules of composition, few musical composers, no teachers and no concerts. Is it any wonder that their music is a foreign language to the white race?

* Frances Densmore, "Music of the American Indian," *Southern Folklore Quarterly*, Vol. 18 (1954), pp. 153–156. Reprinted by permission of the publisher.

The author (1867–1957) was a devoted student of American Indian music. Among her works are monographs on the music of twenty-one distinct tribes from Acoma to Zuñi. She is also the author of *The American Indians and Their Music* (1936).

My work, as you know, is the recording of Indian songs and transcribing them as nearly as possible in our notation, so that the *eye* can get an impression that the *ear* does not receive when listening to the song. This work has been done almost entirely for the Bureau of American Ethnology of the Smithsonian Institution, a limited amount having been done for the Southwest Museum of Los Angeles, California. Both institutions have published the results in books. A large manuscript on Seminole Music will go to press soon at the Bureau of Ethnology, and two other manuscripts await publication. The field work has included tribes in all the principal areas from Florida to British Columbia and the recordings from the Bureau of Ethnology have been transferred to the Music Division of the Library of Congress. Selected songs are now being issued in a series of long-playing disks.

Early in my work I established a system of analysis for each song and have continued this throughout the whole series. These tabulated analyses make it possible to compare the structure of songs in different areas. At one time I used 22 tables of analysis but later reduced the number when the results were similar in many tribes. This showed the peculiarity to be characteristic of Indian music as a whole, not a peculiarity of a certain tribe.

With these analyses there have been descriptions of the uses of the songs and the personality of the singers, showing the relation of music to the life of the Indian, but the presentation of the subject has been from the standpoint of our own culture.

Now let us consider music from the standpoint of the Indian. He has no written music and his songs are carried in his mind. There is a sort of musical aristocracy among the Indians, and the songs they value most highly are songs that belong to men in that group. Their songs are entirely distinct from the songs of social dances and games, or songs learned from other tribes. Such songs may be sung by anyone, but these special songs belong to individuals who are believed to receive them in "dreams." Such songs are connected with "magic power." They come to the mind of the man who has prepared himself to receive them by fasting and other acts. This might be compared to what we call *inspiration,* and such songs among the Indians have a definite purpose. They are believed to give power for success in war, hunting, the treatment of the sick, or other undertakings. They are songs to *benefit* the Indian by putting him in contact with power above *human* power. The Indian may personalize the source of the song and its power, or he may attribute it to some form of nature. These songs were long ago designated as "dream songs" and in one of these songs the singer says he is "carried by the wind across the sky."

Many "dream songs" are believed to be given by spirit birds or animals, these being birds or animals that live successfully in the environment of the dreamer. Thus a man on the plains might dream of a spirit buffalo that gave him strength or a roving wolf that gave him success in war—the Sioux war songs were called "wolf songs." A man on the Northwest Coast dreamed of a whale. This may seem of little significance, but as we are considering music in the life of the Indian we will recognize in this a friendliness of nature—a desire to help man. Such songs link man with nature in ways that are foreign to us. We talk of conquering nature, but that was not the Indian way. An incident will show this. On the Northwest Coast I was recording songs by a woman from Clayoquot Sound— on the west coast of Vancouver Island, and her husband, who was a Makah, living near Cape Flattery. Neither spoke English. She recorded a song to make the sea calm, with the words "Breakers, roll more gently."

I asked whether the ocean was angry and they seemed surprised, talking together. Then the interpretor said, "They cannot understand why you ask such a question. How could nature be angry with us when we get our food and everything we have from nature?" This communication with nature is a phase of Indian music that extends far into their culture, and is too deep for present consideration.

Among the most important "dream songs" are those used in the treatment of the sick. "Music therapy" was old among the Indians long before it came into use by our own race. The Indian doctors, or medicine men, received the songs with instructions for their use from "spirits" of animals, who continued their aid. Thus a Chippewa doctor had a song with the words, "The big bear, to his lodge I go often." It was considered good for a doctor to dream of a bear, as it is such a healthy animal and has good claws for digging roots, which it eats.

I have recorded about 200 of these healing songs, sung by men and women who were using them at that time in treating the sick. Five such songs were recorded by a Seminole woman known as Susie Tiger. The recording of these and other songs in the Cow Creek group was made possible by the aid of William King, a Creek who was there temporarily and understood their dialect. The rhythm of the songs for the sick is generally peculiar and forms a subject for special consideration.

As Indians have no written language the history of a tribe is preserved by its members, being transmitted from one generation to the next. Songs are often connected with important events in the history of a tribe and the age of the song corresponds with our knowledge of the time of the event. Thus I recorded songs concerning the removal of the Seminole to Oklahoma which took place about 1838. Such songs are still remembered, as, for example, a Chippewa song concerning a certain treaty known as the Salt Treaty which took place in 1847. The tradition of the treaty has come down in the song and our own knowledge supplies the date. In this song the Pillager Band boasts that they will receive salt, which the other bands lack. By the treaty they were to receive 5 barrels of salt annually for 5 years.

The names of successful warriors are preserved in songs, and by an interesting custom the name of one warrior may replace another of more remote accomplishment, the praise of valor remaining the same; thus a song is in praise of Cimauganic, whose name replaced that of a former warrior. The song has only two words, the name Cimauganic and a word meaning "killed," it being understood that he killed a man in war. This is a particularly interesting song.

The poetry of the Indians is another phase of their culture which is preserved in their songs. This can only be procured by the aid of an expert interpretor with a knowledge of the idioms of both languages and a genuine interest in the preservation of the culture of his people. For instance, I once obtained records of songs from Tule Indians from Panama who were temporarily in Washington. One song was interpreted as describing the rapid motion of a boat, saying that the wind in the sails was like the sounds of birds, and the clicking of blocks against the mast was like the sound of a clock. Another interpretor heard the record and said "the words mean the boat is going fast."

Among the Santo Domingo Pueblo Indians the words of the songs were often continuous throughout the melody and described customs in a highly poetic manner. One of these songs was concerning the bringing in of the harvest of corn and spoke of one little ear of corn that stood above the others in the load and sang about what he saw.

Mention has been made of the very few words in some Indian songs. Thus the words of a Chippewa song were translated:

> The bush is sitting under a tree and singing.

On being questioned, the interpreter said that was an exact translation but it meant that the bush, under a tree, was putting forth its magic power. This is beautiful as poetry and also shows the Indian belief in a mysterious power in nature. Another song in that series contained only the words:

> The deer is looking at a flower.

On the Northwest Coast, where the men go far out on the Pacific Ocean to catch whale and seal, an old man recorded a touching song with these words:

> My little son, my little baby boy,
> You will put a sealing spear in your canoe, not
> knowing what use you may make of it when
> you are a man.

The songs of the Chippewa, Sioux, Papago and the Northwest Coast tribes, to which the above references allude, are now available in the Folk Music Series issued by the Recording Laboratory of the Division of Music of the Library of Congress, Washington, D. C.

H. Culture and Personality

MANY DECADES AGO the word "anthropology" conjured up a vision of a bone-measuring scientist. Later this was displaced by the picture of an intrepid fieldworker in a remote and little known land. Today the sophisticate is likely to conceive of anthropology as combining fieldwork and psychoanalysis. None of these images is correct, though each has its justification in genuine anthropological activities. This book is testimony to the breadth of studies which comprise anthropology and obviate any too particularized stereotype of the anthropologist.

Culture and personality studies are an important and specialized branch of cultural anthropology. Actually, these studies are not themselves homogeneous but fall into a number of types associated with different goals and methods. Significantly, the major development of these studies occurred within anthropology itself: though other disciplines have assisted with theoretical and methodological contributions, personality and culture studies are indigenous to anthropology, not importations.

Among the various types of study which are lumped under the culture and personality rubric are two of particular interest: investigations of national character and inquiries into the relation of individual psychological states to the cultures in which they appear. The first of these is not represented below except as Benedict's broad generalizations indicate the approach which brought her fame. The second is illuminated by both Benedict and Mead who display discrete but related interests without exhausting the possibilities of their own work or the field. The third selection is a rigorous criticism of some of the assumptions and methods which have characterized some, but certainly not all, contributions to this field.

33. ANTHROPOLOGY AND THE ABNORMAL *

Ethnographic reports contain numerous examples of various kinds of
behavior which, treated in our culture as symptoms of mental illness, are
regarded as unexceptional, normal or even desirable in other cultures.
Consider the problems this poses. Is mental illness dependent on culturally
defined behavioral norms? Would the mentally ill of one culture be
normal in another? Will the possibility of an objective science of the mind
founder on the rock of cultural relativism?

M ODERN SOCIAL ANTHROPOLOGY has become more and more a
study of the varieties and common elements of cultural environment and
the consequences of these in human behavior. For such a study of diverse
social orders primitive peoples fortunately provide a laboratory not yet
entirely vitiated by the spread of a standardized worldwide civilization.
Dyaks and Hopis, Fijians and Yakuts are significant for psychological and
sociological study because only among these simpler peoples has there
been sufficient isolation to give opportunity for the development of localized social forms. In the higher cultures the standardization of custom
and belief over a couple of continents has given a false sense of the in-
evitability of the particular forms that have gained currency, and we need
to turn to a wider survey in order to check the conclusions we hastily
base upon this near-universality of familiar customs. Most of the simpler

* Ruth Benedict, "Anthropology and the Abnormal," *The Journal of General Psychology,* Vol. 10 (1934), pp. 59–79. Reprinted by permission of the publisher.
Ruth Benedict (1887–1948) was Professor of Anthropology at Columbia University. As the author of *Patterns of Culture* which, in pocket edition, has sold more
widely than any other volume of anthropology, she brought the ideas of cultural
relativism to a vast audience. She did fieldwork among the Indians of the Southwest,
particularly the Pima and Zuni, and pioneered in several areas—personality and
culture, the study of culture at a distance, and cultural integration. Among her works
are *Patterns of Culture* (1934), *Race: Science and Politics* (1940) and *The Chrys-
anthemum and the Sword* (1946).

cultures did not gain the wide currency of the one which, out of our experience, we identify with human nature, but this was for various historical reasons, and certainly not for any that gives us as its carriers a monopoly of social good or of social sanity. Modern civilization, from this point of view, becomes not a necessary pinnacle of human achievement but one entry in a long series of possible adjustments.

These adjustments, whether they are in mannerisms like the ways of showing anger, or joy, or grief in any society, or in major human drives like those of sex, prove to be far more variable than experience in any one culture would suggest. In certain fields, such as that of religion or of formal marriage arrangements, these wide limits of variability are well known and can be fairly described. In others it is not yet possible to give a generalized account, but that does not absolve us of the task of indicating the significance of the work that has been done and of the problems that have arisen.

One of these problems relates to the customary modern normal-abnormal categories and our conclusions regarding them. In how far are such categories culturally determined, or in how far can we with assurance regard them as absolute? In how far can we regard inability to function socially as diagnostic of abnormality, or in how far is it necessary to regard this as a function of the culture?

As a matter of fact, one of the most striking facts that emerge from a study of widely varying cultures is the ease with which our abnormals function in other cultures. It does not matter what kind of "abnormality" we choose for illustration, those which indicate extreme instability, or those which are more in the nature of character traits like sadism or delusions of grandeur or of persecution, there are well-described cultures in which these abnormals function at ease and with honor, and apparently without danger or difficulty to the society.

The most notorious of these is trance and catalepsy. Even a very mild mystic is aberrant in our culture. But most peoples have regarded even extreme psychic manifestations not only as normal and desirable, but even as characteristic of highly valued and gifted individuals. This was true even in our own cultural background in that period when Catholicism made the ecstatic experience the mark of sainthood. It is hard for us, born and brought up in a culture that makes no use of the experience, to realize how important a rôle it may play and how many individuals are capable of it, once it has been given an honorable place in any society.

Some of the Indian tribes of California accorded prestige principally to those who passed through certain trance experiences. Not all of these tribes believed that it was exclusively women who were so blessed, but among the Shasta this was the convention. Their shamans were women, and they were accorded the greatest prestige in the community. They were chosen because of their constitutional liability to trance and allied manifestations. One day the woman who was so destined, while she was about her usual work, would fall suddenly to the ground. She had heard a voice speaking to her in tones of the greatest intensity. Turning, she had seen a man with drawn bow and arrow. He commanded her to sing on pain of being shot through the heart by his arrow, but under the stress of the experience she fell senseless. Her family gathered. She was lying rigid, hardly breathing. They knew that for some time she had had dreams of a special character which indicated a shamanistic calling, dreams of escaping grizzly bears, falling off cliffs or trees, or of being surrounded by swarms of yellow jackets. The community knew therefore what to expect. After a few hours the woman began to moan gently and to roll about upon the ground, trembling violently. She was supposed to be repeating the song which she had been told to sing and which during the trance had been taught her by the spirit. As she revived her moaning became more and more clearly the spirit's song until at last she called out the name of the spirit itself, and immediately blood oozed from her mouth.

When the woman had come to herself after the first encounter with her spirit she danced that night her first initiatory shamanistic dance, holding herself by a rope that was swung from the ceiling. For three nights she danced, and on the third night she had to receive in her body her power from her spirit. She was dancing, and as she felt the approach of the moment she called out, "He will shoot me, he will shoot me." Her friends stood close, for when she reeled in a kind of cataleptic seizure, they had to seize her before she fell or she would die. From this time on she had in her body a visible materialization of her spirit's power, an icicle-like object which in her dances thereafter she would exhibit, producing it from one part of her body and returning it to another part. From this time on she continued to validate her supernatural power by further cataleptic demonstrations, and she was called upon in great emergencies of life and death, for curing and for divination and for counsel. She became in other words by this procedure a woman of great power and importance.

It is clear that, so far from regarding cataleptic seizures as blots upon the family escutcheon and as evidences of dreaded disease, cultural approval had seized upon them and made of them the pathway to authority over one's fellows. They were the outstanding characteristic of the most respected social type, the type which functioned with most honor and reward in the community. It was precisely the cataleptic individuals who in this culture were singled out for authority and leadership.

The availability of "abnormal" types in the social structure, provided they are types that are culturally selected by that group, is illustrated from every part of the world. The shamans of Siberia dominate their communities. According to the ideas of these peoples, they are individuals who by submission to the will of the spirits have been cured of a grievous illness—the onset of the seizures—and have acquired by this means great supernatural power and incomparable vigor and health. Some, during the period of the call, are violently insane for several years, others irresponsible to the point where they have to be watched constantly lest they wander off in the snow and freeze to death, others ill and emaciated to the point of death, sometimes with bloody sweat. It is the shamanistic practice which constitutes their cure, and the extreme physical exertion of a Siberian seance leaves them, they claim, rested and able to enter immediately upon a similar performance. Cateleptic sezures are regarded as an essential part of any shamanistic performance.

A good description of the neurotic condition of the shaman and the attention given him by his society is an old one by Canon Callaway recorded in the words of an old Zulu of South Africa:

The condition of a man who is about to become a diviner is this; at first he is apparently robust, but in the process of time he begins to be delicate, not having any real disease, but being delicate. He habitually avoids certain kinds of food, choosing what he likes, and he does not eat much of that; he is continually complaining of pains in different parts of his body. And he tells them that he has dreamt that he was carried away by a river. He dreams of many things, and his body is muddied (as a river) and he becomes a house of dreams. He dreams constantly of many things, and on awaking tells his friends, 'My body is muddied today; I dreamt many men were killing me, and I escaped I know not how. On waking one part of my body felt different from other parts; it was no longer alike all over.' At last that man is very ill, and they go to the diviners to enquire.

The diviners do not at once see that he is about to have a soft head (that is, the sensitivity associated with shamanism). It is difficult for them to see the truth; they continually talk nonsense and make false statements, until all the man's cattle are devoured at their command, they saying that the spirit of his people demands cattle, that it may eat food. At length all the man's property is expended, he still being ill; and they no longer knew what to do, for he has no more cattle, and his friends help him in such things as he needs.

At length a diviner comes and says that all the others are wrong. He says, 'He is possessed by the spirits. There is nothing else. They move in him, being divided into two parties; some say, "No, we do not wish our child injured. We do not wish it." It is for that reason he does not get well. If you bar the way against the spirits, you will be killing him. For he will not be a diviner; neither will he ever be a man again.'

So the man may be ill two years without getting better; perhaps even longer than that. He is confined to his house. This continues till his hair falls off. And his body is dry and scurfy; he does not like to anoint himself. He shows that he is about to be a diviner by yawning again and again, and by sneezing continually. It is apparent also from his being very fond of snuff; not allowing any long time to pass without taking some. And people begin to see that he has had what is good given to him.

After that he is ill; he has convulsions, and when water has been poured on him they then cease for a time. He habitually sheds tears, at first slight, then at last he weeps aloud and when the people are asleep he is heard making a noise and wakes the people by his singing; he has composed a song, and the men and women awake and go to sing in concert with him. All the people of the village are troubled by want of sleep; for a man who is becoming a diviner causes great trouble, for he does not sleep, but works constantly with his brain; his sleep is merely by snatches, and he wakes up singing many songs; and people who are near quit their villages by night when they hear him singing aloud and go to sing in concert. Perhaps he sings till morning, no one having slept. And then he leaps about the house like a frog; and the house becomes too small for him, and he goes out leaping and singing, and shaking like a reed in the water, and dripping with perspiration.

In this state of things they daily expect his death; he is now but skin and bones, and they think that tomorrow's sun will not leave him alive. At this time many cattle are eaten, for the people encourage his becoming a diviner. At length (in a dream) an ancient ancestral spirit is pointed out to him. This spirit says to him, 'Go to So-and-so and he will churn for you an emetic (the medicine the drinking of which is a part of shamanistic initiation) that you may be a diviner altogether.' Then he is quiet a few days, having gone to the diviner to have the medicine churned for him; and he comes back quite another man, being now cleansed and a diviner indeed."

Thereafter for life when he achieves possession, he fortells events, and finds lost articles.

It is clear that culture may value and make socially available even highly unstable human types. If it chooses to treat their peculiarities as the most valued variants of human behavior, the individuals in question will rise to the occasion and perform their social rôles without reference to our usual ideas of the types who can make social adjustments and those who cannot.

Cataleptic and trance phenomena are, of course, only one illustration of the fact that those whom we regard as abnormals may function adequately in other cultures. Many of our culturally discarded traits are selected for elaboration in different societies. Homosexuality is an excellent example, for in this case our attention is not constantly diverted, as in the consideration of trance, to the interruption of routine activity which it implies. Homosexuality poses the problem very simply. A tendency toward this trait in our culture exposes an individual to all the conflicts to which all aberrants are always exposed, and we tend to identify the consequences of this conflict with homosexuality. But these consequences are obviously local and cultural. Homosexuals in many societies are not incompetent, but they may be such if the culture asks adjustments of them that would strain any man's vitality. Wherever homosexuality has been given an honorable place in any society, those to whom it is congenial have filled adequately the honorable rôles society assigns to them. Plato's *Republic* is, of course, the most convincing statement of such a reading of homosexuality. It is presented as one of the major means to the good life, and it was generally so regarded in Greece at that time.

The cultural attitude toward homosexuals has not always been on such a high ethical plane, but it has been very varied. Among many American Indian tribes there exists the institution of the berdache, as the French called them. These men-women were men who at puberty or thereafter took the dress and the occupations of women. Sometimes they married other men and lived with them. Sometimes they were men with no inversion, persons of weak sexual endowment who chose this rôle to avoid the jeers of the women. The berdaches were never regarded as of first-rate supernatural power, as similar men-women were in Siberia, but rather as leaders in women's occupations, good healers in certain diseases, or, among certain tribes, as the genial organizers of social affairs. In any case, they were socially placed. They were not left exposed to the conflicts that visit the deviant who is excluded from participation in the recognized patterns of his society.

The most spectacular illustrations of the extent to which normality may be culturally defined are those cultures where an abnormality of our culture is the cornerstone of their social structure. It is not possible to do justice to these possibilities in a short discussion. A recent study of an island of northwest Melanesia by Fortune describes a society built upon traits which we regard as beyond the border of paranoia. In this tribe the exogamic groups look upon each other as prime manipulators of black magic, so that one marries always into an enemy group which remains for life one's deadly and unappeasable foes. They look upon a good garden crop as a confession of theft, for everyone is engaged in making magic to induce into his garden the productiveness of his neighbors'; therefore no secrecy in the island is so rigidly insisted upon as the secrecy of a man's harvesting of his yams. Their polite phrase at the acceptance of a gift is, "And if you now poison me, how shall I repay you this present?" Their preoccupation with poisoning is constant; no woman ever leaves her cooking pot for a moment untended. Even the great affinal economic exchanges that are characteristic of this Melanesian culture area are quite altered in Dobu since they are incompatible with this fear and distrust that pervades the culture. They go farther and people the whole world outside their own quarters with such malignant spirits that all-night feasts and ceremonials simply do not occur here. They have even rigorous religiously enforced customs that forbid the sharing of seed even in one family group. Anyone else's food is deadly poison to you, so that communality of stores is out of the question. For some months before harvest the whole society is on the verge of starvation, but if one falls to the temptation and eats up one's seed yams, one is an outcast and a beachcomber for life. There is no coming back. It involves, as a matter of course, divorce and the breaking of all social ties.

Now in this society where no one may work with another and no one may share with another, Fortune describes the individual who was regarded by all his fellows as crazy. He was not one of those who periodically ran amok and, beside himself and frothing at the mouth, fell with a knife upon anyone he could reach. Such behavior they did not regard as putting anyone outside the pale. They did not even put the individuals who were known to be liable to these attacks under any kind of control. They merely fled when they saw the attack coming on and kept out of the way. "He would be all right tomorrow." But there was one man of sunny, kindly disposition who liked work and liked to be helpful. The compulsion was too strong for him to repress it in favor of the opposite tendencies of his culture. Men and women never spoke of him without laughing; he was silly and simple and definitely crazy. Nevertheless, to the ethnologist used to a culture that has, in Christianity, made his type the model of all virtue, he seemed a pleasant fellow.

An even more extreme example, because it is of a culture that has built itself upon a more complex abnormality, is that of the North Pacific Coast of North America. The civilization of the Kwakiutl, at the time when it was first recorded in the last decades of the nineteenth century, was one of the most vigorous in North America. It was built up on an ample economic supply of goods, the fish which furnished their food staple being practically inexhaustible and obtainable with comparatively small labor, and the wood which furnished the material for their houses, their furnishings, and their arts being, with however much labor, always procurable. They lived in coastal villages that compared favorably in size with those of any other American Indians and they kept up constant communication by means of sea-going dug-out canoes.

It was one of the most vigorous and zestful of the aboriginal cultures of North America, with complex crafts and ceremonials, and elaborate and striking arts. It certainly had none of the earmarks of a sick civilization. The tribes of the Northwest Coast had wealth, and exactly in our terms. That is, they had not only a surplus of economic goods, but they made a game of the manipulation of wealth. It was by no means a mere direct transcription of economic needs and the filling of those needs. It involved the idea of capital, of interest, and of conspicuous waste. It was a game with all the binding rules of a game, and a person entered it as a child. His father distributed wealth for him, according to his ability, at a small feast or potlatch, and each gift the receiver was obliged to accept and to return after a short interval with interest that ran to about 100 per cent a year. By the time the child was grown, therefore, he was well launched, a larger potlatch had been given for him on various occasions of exploit or initiation, and he had wealth either out at usury or in his own possession. Nothing in the civilization could be enjoyed without validating it by the distribution of this wealth. Everything that was valued, names and songs as well as material objects, were passed down in family lines, but they were always publicly assumed with accompanying sufficient distributions of property. It was the game of validating and exercising all the privileges one could accumulate from one's various forbears, or by gift, or by marriage, that made the chief interest of the culture. Everyone in his degree took part in it, but many, of course, mainly as spectators. In its highest form it was played out between rival chiefs representing not only themselves and their family lines but their communities, and the object of the contest was to glorify oneself and to humiliate one's opponent. On this level of greatness the property involved was no longer represented by blankets, so many thousand of them to a potlatch, but by higher units of value. These higher units were like our bank notes. They were incised copper tablets, each of them named, and having a value that depended upon their illustrious history. This was as high as ten thousand blankets, and to possess one of them, still more to enhance its value at a great potlatch, was one of the greatest glories within the compass of the chiefs of the Northwest Coast.

The details of this manipulation of wealth are in many ways a parody on our own economic arrangements, but it is with the motivations that were recognized in this contest that we are concerned in this discussion. The drives were those which in our own culture we should call megalomaniac. There was an uncensored self-glorification and ridicule of the opponent that it is hard to equal in other cultures outside of the monologues of the abnormal. Any of the songs and speeches of their chiefs at a potlatch illustrate the usual tenor:

.   .   .   .   .

Wa, out of the way. Wa, out the way. Turn your faces that I may give way to my anger by striking my fellow chiefs.

Wa, great potlatch, greatest potlatch.[1] The little ones [2] only pretend, the little stubborn ones, they only sell one copper again and again and give it away to the little chiefs of the tribe.
Ah, do not ask in vain for mercy. Ah, do not ask in vain for mercy and raise your hands, you with lolling tongues! I shall break,[3] I shall let disappear the great

---

[1] The feast he is now engaged in giving.   [2] His opponents.

[3] To break a copper, showing in this way how far one rose above even the most superlatively valuable things, was the final mark of greatness.

copper that has the name Kentsegum, the property of the great foolish one, the great extravagant one, the great surpassing one, the one farthest ahead, the great Cannibal dancer among the chiefs.[4]

I am the great chief who makes people ashamed.
I am the great chief who makes people ashamed.
Our chief brings shame to the faces.
Our chief brings jealousy to the faces.
Our chief makes people cover their faces by what he is continually doing in this world, from the beginning to the end of the year,
Giving again and again oil feasts to the tribes.

I am the great chief who vanquishes.
I am the great chief who vanquishes.
Only at those who continue running round and round in this world, working hard, losing their tails,[5] I sneer, at the chiefs below the true chief.[6]
Have mercy on them![7] Put oil on their dry heads with brittle hair, those who do not comb their hair!
I sneer at the chiefs below the true, real chief. I am the great chief who makes people ashamed.

.   .   .   .   .

I am the only great tree, I the chief.
I am the only great tree, I the chief.
You are my subordinates, tribes.
You sit in the middle of the rear of the house, tribes.
Bring me your counter of property, tribes, that he may in vain try to count what is going to be given away by the great copper-maker, the chief.
Oh, I laugh at them, I sneer at them who empty boxes[8] in their houses, their potlatch houses, their inviting houses that are full only of hunger. They follow along after me like young sawbill ducks. I am the only great tree, I the chief.

.   .   .   .   .

I have quoted a number of these hymns of self-glorification because by an association which psychiatrists will recognize as fundamental these delusions of grandeur were essential in the paranoid view of life which was so strikingly developed in this culture. All of existence was seen in terms of insult. Not only derogatory acts performed by a neighbor or an enemy, but all untoward events, like a cut when one's axe slipped, or a ducking when one's canoe overturned, were insults. All alike threatened first and foremost one's ego security, and the first thought one was allowed was how to get even, how to wipe out the insult. Grief was little institutionalized, but sulking took its place. Until he had resolved upon a course of action by which to save his face after any misfortune, whether it was the slipping of a wedge in felling a tree, or the death of a favorite

[4] Himself.   [5] As salmon do.   [6] Himself.   [7] Irony, of course.
[8] Of treasure.

child, an Indian of the Northwest Coast retired to his pallet with his face to the wall and neither ate nor spoke. He rose from it to follow out some course which according to the traditional rules should reinstate him in his own eyes and those of the community: to distribute property enough to wipe out the stain, or to go headhunting in order that somebody else should be made to mourn. His activities in neither case were specific responses to the bereavement he had just passed through, but were elaborately directed toward getting even. If he had not the money to distribute and did not succeed in killing someone to humiliate another, he might take his own life. He had staked everything, in his view of life, upon a certain picture of the self, and, when the bubble of his self-esteem was pricked, he had no interest, no occupation to fall back on, and the collapse of his inflated ego left him prostrate.

Every contingency of life was dealt with in these two traditional ways. To them the two were equivalent. Whether one fought with weapons or "fought with property," as they say, the same idea was at the bottom of both. In the olden times, they say, they fought with spears, but now they fight with property. One overcomes one's opponents in equivalent fashion in both, matching forces and seeing that one comes out ahead, and one can thumb one's nose at the vanquished rather more satisfactorily at a potlatch than on a battle field. Every occasion in life was noticed, not in its own terms, as a stage in the sex life of the individual or as a climax of joy or of grief, but as furthering this drama of consolidating one's own prestige and bringing shame to one's guests. Whether it was the occasion of the birth of a child, or a daughter's adolescence, or of the marriage of one's son, they were all equivalent raw material for the culture to use for this one traditionally selected end. They were all to raise one's own personal status and to entrench oneself by the humiliation of one's fellows. A girl's adolescence among the Nootka was an event for which her father gathered property from the time she was first able to run about. When she was adolescent he would demonstrate his greatness by an unheard of distribution of these goods, and put down all his rivals. It was not as a fact of the girl's sex life that it figured in their culture, but as the occasion for a major move in the great game of vindicating one's own greatness and humiliating one's associates.

In their behavior at great bereavements this set of the culture comes out most strongly. Among the Kwakiutl it did not matter whether a relative had died in bed of disease, or by the hand of an enemy, in either case death was an affront to be wiped out by the death of another person. The fact that one had been caused to mourn was proof that one had been put upon. A chief's sister and her daughter had gone up to Victoria, and either because they drank bad whiskey or because their boat capsized they never came back. The chief called together his warriors. "Now I ask you, tribes, who shall wail? Shall I do it or shall another?" The spokesman answered, of course, "Not you, Chief. Let some other of the tribes." Immediately they set up the war pole to announce their intention of wiping out the injury, and gathered a war party. They set out, and found seven men and two children asleep and killed them. "Then they felt good when they arrived at Sebaa in the evening."

The point which is of interest to us is that in our society those who on that occasion would feel good when they arrived at Sebaa that evening would be the definitely abnormal. There would be some, even in our society, but it is not a recognized and approved mood under the circumstances. On the Northwest Coast those are favored and fortunate to whom that mood under those circumstances is congenial, and those to whom it is repugnant are unlucky. This latter minority can register in their own culture only by doing violence to their congenial responses and acquiring others that are difficult for them. The person, for instance, who, like a Plains Indian whose wife has been taken from him, is too proud to fight, can deal with the Northwest Coast civilization only by ignoring its strongest bents. If he cannot achieve it, he is the deviant in that culture, their instance of abnormality.

This head-hunting that takes place on the Northwest Coast after a death is no matter of blood revenge or of organized vengeance. There is no effort to tie up the subsequent killing with any responsibility on the part of the victim for the death of the person who is being mourned. A chief whose son has died goes visiting wherever his fancy dictates, and he says to his host, "My prince has died today, and you go with him." Then he kills him. In this, according to their interpretation, he acts nobly because he has not been downed. He has thrust back in return. The whole procedure is meaningless without the fundamental paranoid reading of bereavement. Death, like all the other untoward accidents of existence, confounds man's pride and can only be handled in the category of insults.

Behavior honored upon the Northwest Coast is one which is recognized as abnormal in our civilization, and yet it is sufficiently close to the attitudes of our own culture to be intelligible to us and to have a definite vocabulary with which we may discuss it. The megalomaniac paranoid trend is a definite danger in our society. It is encouraged by some of our major preoccupations, and it confronts us with a choice of two possible attitudes. One is to brand it as abnormal and reprehensible, and is the attitude we have chosen in our civilization. The other is to make it an essential attribute of ideal man, and this is the solution in the culture of the Northwest Coast.

These illustrations, which it has been possible to indicate only in the briefest manner, force upon us the fact that normality is culturally defined. An adult shaped to the drives and standards of either of these cultures, if he were transported into our civilization, would fall into our categories of abnormality. He would be faced with the psychic dilemmas of the socially unavailable. In his own culture, however, he is the pillar of society, the end result of socially inculcated mores, and the problem of personal instability in his case simply does not arise.

No one civilization can possibly utilize in its mores the whole potential range of human behavior. Just as there are great numbers of possible phonetic articulations, and the possibility of language depends on a selection and standardization of a few of these in order that speech communication may be possible at all, so the possibility of organized behavior of every sort, from the fashions of local dress and houses to the dicta of a people's ethics and religion, depends upon a similar selection among the possible behavior traits. In the field of recognized economic obligations or sex tabus this selection is as nonrational and subconscious a process as it is in the field of phonetics. It is a process which goes on in the group for long periods of time and is historically conditioned by innumerable accidents of isolation or of contact of peoples. In any comprehensive study of psychology, the selection that different cultures have made in the course of history within the great circumference of potential behavior is of great significance.

Every society, beginning with some slight inclination in one direction or another, carries its preference farther and farther, integrating itself more and more completely upon its chosen basis, and discarding those types of behavior that are uncongenial. Most of those organizations of personality that seem to us most incontrovertibly abnormal have been used by different civilizations in the very foundations of their institutional life. Conversely the most valued traits of our normal individuals have been looked on in differently organized cultures as aberrant. Normality, in short, within a very wide range, is culturally defined. It is primarily a term for the socially elaborated segment of human behavior in any culture; and abnormality, a term for the segment that that particular civilization does not use. The very eyes with which we see the problem are conditioned by the long traditional habits of our own society.

It is a point that has been made more often in relation to ethics than in relation to psychiatry. We do not any longer make the mistake of deriving the morality of our own locality and decade directly from the inevitable constitution of human nature. We do not elevate it to the dignity of a first principle. We recognize that morality differs in every society, and is a convenient term for socially approved habits. Mankind has always preferred to say, "It is a morally good," rather than " It is habitual," and the fact of this preference is matter enough for a critical science of ethics. But historically the two phrases are synonymous.

The concept of the normal is properly a variant of the concept of the good. It is that which society has approved. A normal action is one which falls well within the limits of expected behavior for a particular society. Its variability among different peoples is essentially a function of the variability of the behavior patterns that different societies have created for themselves, and can never be wholly divorced from a consideration of culturally institutionalized types of behavior.

Each culture is a more or less elaborate working-out of the potentialities of the segment it has chosen. In so far as a civilization is well integrated and consistent within itself, it will tend to carry farther and farther, according to its nature, its initial impulse toward a particular type of action, and from the point of view of any other culture those elaborations will include more and more extreme and aberrant traits.

Each of these traits, in proportion as it reinforces the chosen behavior patterns of that culture, is for that culture normal. Those individuals to whom it is congenial either congenitally, or as the result of childhood sets, are accorded prestige in that culture, and are not visited with the social contempt or disapproval which their traits would call down upon them in a society that was differently organized. On the other hand, those individuals whose characteristics are not congenial to the selected type of human behavior in that community are the deviants, no matter how valued their personality traits may be in a contrasted civilization.

The Dobuan who is not easily susceptible to fear of treachery, who enjoys work and likes to be helpful, is their neurotic and regarded as silly. On the Northwest Coast the person who finds it difficult to read life in terms of an insult contest will be the person upon whom fall all the difficulties of the culturally unprovided for. The person who does not find it easy to humiliate a neighbor, nor to see humiliation in his own experience, who is genial and loving, may, of course, find some unstandardized way of achieving satisfactions in his society, but not in the major patterned responses that his culture requires of him. If he is born to play an important rôle in a family with many hereditary privileges, he can succeed only by doing violence to his whole personality. If he does not succeed, he has betrayed his culture; that is, he is abnormal.

I have spoken of individuals as having sets toward certain types of behavior, and of these sets as running sometimes counter to the types of behavior which are institutionalized in the culture to which they belong. From all that we know of contrasting cultures it seems clear that differences of temperament occur in every society. The matter has never been made the subject of investigation, but from the available material it would appear that these temperament types are very likely of universal recurrence. That is, there is an ascertainable range of human behavior that is found wherever a sufficiently large series of individuals is observed. But the proportion in which behavior types stand to one another in different societies is not universal. The vast majority of the individuals in any group are shaped to the fashion of that culture. In other words, most individuals are plastic to the moulding force of the society into which they are born. In a society that values trance, as in India, they will have supernormal experience. In a society that institutionalizes homosexuality, they will be homosexual. In a society that sets the gathering of possessions as the chief human objective, they will amass property. The deviants, whatever the type of behavior the culture has institutionalized, will remain few in number, and there seems no more difficulty in moulding the vast malleable majority to the "normality" of what we consider an aberrant trait, such as delusions of reference, than to the normality of such accepted behavior patterns as acquisitiveness. The small proportion of the number of the deviants in any culture is not a function of the sure instinct with which that society has built itself upon the fundamental sanities, but of the universal fact that, happily, the majority of mankind quite readily take any shape that is presented to them.

The relativity of normality is not an academic issue. In the first place, it suggests that the apparent weakness of the aberrant is most often and in great measure illusory. It springs not from the fact that he is lacking in necessary vigor, but that he is an individual upon whom that culture has put more than the usual strain. His inability to adapt himself to society is a reflection of the fact that that adaptation involves a conflict in him that it does not in the so-called normal.

Therapeutically, it suggests that the inculcation of tolerance and appreciation in any society toward its less usual types is fundamentally important in successful mental hygiene. The complement of this tolerance, on the patient's side, is an education in self-reliance and honesty with himself. If he can be brought to realize that what has thrust him into his misery is despair at his lack of social backing he may be able to achieve a more independent and less tortured attitude and lay the foundation for an adequately functioning mode of existence.

There is a further corollary. From the point of view of absolute categories of abnormal psychology, we must expect in any culture to find a large proportion of the most extreme abnormal types among those who from the local point of view are farthest from belonging to this category. The culture, according to its major preoccupations, will increase and intensify hysterical, epileptic, or paranoid symptoms, at the same time relying socially in a greater and greater degree upon these very individuals. Western civilization allows and culturally honors gratifications of the ego which according to any absolute category would be regarded as abnormal. The portrayal of unbridled and arrogant egoists as family men, as officers of the law, and in business has been a favorite topic of novelists, and they are familiar in every community. Such individuals are probably mentally warped to a greater degree than many inmates of our institutions who are nevertheless socially unavailable. They are extreme types of those personality configurations which our civilization fosters.

This consideration throws into great prominence the confusion that follows, on the one hand, the use of social inadequacy as a criterion of abnormality and, on the other, of definite fixed symptoms. The confusion is present in practically all discussions of abnormal psychology, and it can be clarified chiefly by adequate consideration of the character of the culture, not of the constitution of the abnormal individual. Nevertheless, the bearing of social security upon the total situation of the abnormal cannot be exaggerated, and the study of comparative psychiatry will be fundamentally concerned with this aspect of the matter.

It is clear that statistical methods of defining normality, so long as they are based on studies in a selected civilization, only involve us, unless they are checked against the cultural configuration, in deeper and deeper provincialism. The recent tendency in abnormal psychology to take the laboratory mode as normal and to define abnormalities as they depart from this average has value in so far as it indicates that the aberrants in any culture are those individuals who are liable to serious disturbances because their habits are culturally unsupported. On the other hand, it overlooks the fact that every culture besides its abnormals of conflict has presumably its abnormals of extreme fulfillment of the cultural type. From the point of view of a universally valid abnormal psychology the extreme types of abnormality would probably be found in this very group—a group which in every study based upon one culture goes undescribed except in its end institutionalized forms.

The relativity of normality is important in what may some day come to be a true social engineering. Our picture of our own civilization is no longer in this generation in terms of a changeless and divinely derived set of categorical imperatives. We must face the problems our changed perspective has put upon us. In this matter of mental ailments, we must face the fact that even our normality is man-made, and is of our own seeking. Just as we have been handicapped in dealing with ethical problems so long as we held to an absolute definition of morality, so too in dealing with the problems of abnormality we are handicapped so long as we identify our local normalities with the universal sanities. I have taken illustrations from different cultures, because the conclusions are most inescapable from the contrasts as they are presented in unlike social groups. But the major problem is not a consequence of the variability of the normal from culture to culture, but its variability from era to era. This variability in time we cannot escape if we would, and it is not beyond the bounds of possibility that we may be able to face this inevitable change with full understanding and deal with it rationally. No society has yet achieved self-conscious and critical analysis of its own normalities and attempted rationally to deal with its own social process of creating new normalities within its next generation. But the fact that it is unachieved is not therefore proof of its impossibility. It is a faint indication of how momentous it could be in human society.

There is another major factor in the cultural conditioning of abnormality. From the material that is available at the present time it seems a lesser factor than the one we have discussed. Nevertheless, disregard of its importance has led to many misconceptions. The particular forms of behavior to which unstable individuals of any group are liable are many of them matters of cultural patterning like any other behavior. It is for this obvious reason that the epidemic disorders of one continent or era are often rare or unreported from other parts of the world or other periods of history.

The baldest evidences of cultural patterning in the behavior of unstable individuals is in trance phenomena. The use to which such proclivities are put, the form their manifestations take, the things that are seen and felt in trance, are all culturally controlled. The tranced individual may come back with communications from the dead describing the minutiae of life in the hereafter, or he may visit the world of the unborn, or get information about lost objects in the camp, or experience cosmic unity, or acquire a life-long guardian spirit, or get information about coming events. Even in trance the individual holds strictly to the rules and expectations of his culture, and his experience is as locally patterned as a marriage rite or an economic exchange.

The conformity of trance experience to the expectations of waking life is well recognized. Now that we are no longer confused by the attempt to ascribe supernormal validity to the one or the other, and realize how trance experience bodies forth the preoccupations of the experiencing individual, the cultural patterning in ecstasy has become an accepted tenet.

But the matter does not end here. It is not only what is seen in trance experience that has clear-cut geographical and temporal distribution. It is equally true of forms of behavior which are affected by certain unstable individuals in any group. It is one of the prime difficulties in the use of such unprecise and casual information as we possess about the behavior of the unstable in different cultures, that the material does not correspond to data from our own society. It has even been thought that such definite types of instability as Arctic hysteria and the Malay running-amok were racial diseases. But we know at least, in spite of the lack of good psychiatric accounts, that these phenomena do not coincide with racial distributions. Moreover, the same problem is quite as striking in cases where there is no possibility of a racial correlation. Running amok has been described as alike in symptoms and alike in the treatment accorded it by the rest of the group from such different parts of the world as Melanesia and Tierra del Fuego.

The racial explanation is also ruled out of court in those instances of epidemic mania which are characteristic of our own cultural background. The dancing mania that filled the streets of Europe with compulsively dancing men, women, and children in mediaeval times is recognized as an extreme instance of suggestibility in our own racial group.

These behaviors are capable of controlled elaboration that is often carried to great lengths. Unstable individuals in one culture achieve characteristic forms that may be excessively rare or absent in another, and this is very marked where social value has been attached to one form or another. Thus when some form of borderline behavior has been associated in any society with the shaman and he is a person of authority and influence, it is this particular indicated seizure to which he will be liable at every demonstration. Among the Shasta of California, as we have seen, and among many other tribes in various parts of the world, some form of cataleptic seizure is the passport to shamanism and must constantly accompany its practice. In other regions it is automatic vision or audition. In other societies behavior is perhaps closest to what we cover by the term hystero-epilepsy. In Siberia all the familiar characteristics of our spiritualistic seances are required for every performance of the shaman. In all these cases the particular experience that is thus socially chosen receives considerable elaboration and is usually patterned in detail according to local standards. That is, each culture, though it chooses quite narrowly in the great field of borderline experiences, without difficulty imposes its selected type upon certain of its individuals. The particular behavior of an unstable individual in these instances is not the single and inevitable mode in which his abnormality could express itself. He has taken up a traditionally conditioned pattern of behavior in this as in any other field. Conversely, in every society, our own included, there are forms of instability that are out of fashion. They are not at the present time at least being presented for imitation to the enormously suggestible individuals who constitute in any society a considerable group of the abnormals. It seems clear that this is no matter of the nature of sanity, or even of a biological, inherited tendency in a local group, but quite simply an affair of social patterning.

The problem of understanding abnormal human behavior in any absolute sense independent of cultural factors is still far in the future. The categories of borderline behavior which we derive from the study of the neuroses and psychoses of our civilization are categories of prevailing local types of instability. They give much information about the stresses and strains of Western civilization, but no final picture of inevitable human behavior. Any conclusions about such behavior must await the collection by trained observers of psychiatric data from other cultures. Since no adequate work of the kind has been done at the present time, it is impossible to say what core of definition of abnormality may be found valid from the comparative material. It is as it is in ethics: all our local conventions of moral behavior and of immoral are without absolute validity, and yet it is quite possible that a modicum of what is considered right and what wrong could be disentangled that is shared by the whole human race. When data are available in psychiatry, this minimum definition of abnormal human tendencies will be probably quite unlike our culturally conditioned, highly elaborated psychoses such as those that are described, for instance, under the terms of schizophrenia and manic-depressive.

34. THE IMPLICATIONS OF CULTURE CHANGE

FOR PERSONALITY DEVELOPMENT *

As in other disciplines, new subjects of study are sometimes merged and increase in depth with cross-fertilization and the addition of novel methods. The next selection weds the fields of acculturation and personality/culture.

In our current thinking about the development of human personality there is a tendency to discuss the effects of culture change—whether that change be between generations, or between the former and present environment, as though it were an interruption, however frequent, in normal development. Case histories note faithfully that one or other of the parents or spouses were immigrants, that the family has moved many times, or there was a shift from a rural environment to an urban. Allowances are made for these factors as one might make allowance for a physical handicap or the results of a railroad accident.

The assumption implicit in the case history is that the normal course of a human life would be cast under conditions where all the ancestors had lived for several generations in the same place, where social change as registered in the living habits of two successive generations was slow enough to be easily assimilable by adults, and where young people would

* Margaret Mead, "The Implications of Culture Change for Personality Development," *The American Journal of Orthopsychiatry*, Vol. 17 (1947), pp. 633–646. Reprinted by permission of the author and publisher.

If any one person symbolizes anthropology to the general public it is Margaret Mead (b. 1901) who is Curator of Ethnology at the American Museum of Natural History and Adjunct Professor of Anthropology at Columbia University. Few anthropologists have spent so much time in the field: some of her studies have been carried out in Samoa, the Admiralty Islands (Manus), New Guinea and Bali. Her interests are varied, as a partial list of her publications will reveal: *Coming of Age in Samoa* (1928), *Growing Up In New Guinea* (1930), *The Changing Culture of an Indian Tribe* (1932), *Kinship in the Admiralty Islands* (1934), *Male and Female* (1949), *New Lives for Old* (1956), and *An Anthropologist at Work* (1959).

in turn grow up to marry others of almost exactly the same background. This implicit model, derived as it is from the statistically more frequent types of family life in earlier centuries, has such important implications for education and therapy that it seems worthwhile to do two things: 1) to examine it in reality and not as a construct. That can only be done through field material on primitive or very isolated folk populations, so as to bring into relief the construct quality of the model with which we deal today. 2) To challenge the validity of the model for present-day thinking, and suggest an alternative formulation which seems closer to the observed facts of modern life.

When we examine personality development in a homogeneous, slowly changing culture we find certain outstanding characteristics. Every individual in the human environment will carry the same cultural assumption; both he who observes the social forms gladly, and he who flouts and ignores them; the man who is admitted to the ceremony, and the woman who is excluded; the chief who sets his foot on the slave's neck, and the slave who kneels to receive the stepping foot. If the child is influenced more by the phrasing of one parent than of the other, because of some temperamental identification or accident of upbringing, he will still make a choice that is completely encompassed within his culture.

In a polygamous culture the wife who accepts her co-wife and the wife who rejects her co-wife, both act on a common premise that polygamy is a way in which marriage is normally organized. The gentleness of a grandmother may be contrasted with rough handling, or even cruel practical joking on the part of the grandfather, but the grandmother's gentleness allows for and in a sense contains the joking of the grandfather. She can be gentler because his harshness will prevent her grandson from being too softened by her behavior. He can be harsh because the solace of her gentleness can be relied upon.

The knee baby may be weaned with great suddenness and apparent lack of care because an earlier period has been, as it were, included in the weaning process. The child has learned that suddenness is not necessarily cruelty, or that all periods of deprivation are followed by periods of indulgence, or that whenever he has been the victim, he has in turn been able to retaliate. The single act, or special treatment accorded the child at one period—at teething, weaning, or in learning sphincter control—does not stand alone to traumatize or provide some life-long obsessive pattern.

Adults and older children, within whose personality the culturally distinctive learning sequence has been integrated, are able to impart simultaneously the place of the present bit of learning in a longer sequence, that which the child has already experienced and the part which is to come. The trembling hand of old age, as it strokes a child's feverish skin, contains in it a promise not only of the bearableness of illness, but also of the bearableness of death itself, or of the unbearableness of both.

I do not mean to indicate that because a culture is homogeneous and very slowly changing, this means that growing up within it is necessarily a smooth, painless, or untraumatic process. However traumatic or frustrating the life experience is, it can nevertheless be presented to each growing individual as *viable*, and to that extent bearable. The demands made in traditional Japanese culture on the child and on every individual in the society may seem on inspection to go beyond the limits of human tolerance. Yet Japanese culture has survived and provided philosophical and aesthetic statements of life which made life significant and meaningful, if not pleasant, to those who were born within it.

This *simultaneity of impact* is carried not only by the behavior of each individual with whom the child comes in contact, but is also mediated by ritual, drama, and the arts. The shape of a pot, the design on the temple door, the pattern of the courtyard, the form of the bed, the grave posts or the funeral urn, the dancer's headdress and the clown's mask, are again reinforcements and whole statements of the same pattern which the child himself is experiencing serially.

Significant contrasts can be drawn between the course of personality development in which children are majorly reared by grandparents who have almost completed the cycle of life, by parents who stand at the maximum point of contrast with the child, or by older children, themselves but recently emerged from the state in which their younger charges now are. Even though differences in emphasis of this sort, or the comparable differences when the nurse is of a different class, or because of the intervention of the boarding school, may act as determinative factors in the distinctive differences between cultures, it is seldom an all or none matter. Children are not reared entirely by children, entirely by parents, or entirely by nurses. Many different people of different ages and both sexes, different temperaments and contrasting kinship positions, play counterpuntal roles in the life of the growing child.

Two further characteristics of growing up in a homogeneous, slowly changing society may be described as the effective *prefiguring of future experience* and *reinforcement and consolidation of past experience*. As soon as the child is able to assimilate the behavior of those about him, he sees older children living out the next steps in his own emerging life pattern, sees the dying and the dead completing it. On the other hand he sees the child at the mother's breast suckled as he was suckled, soothed or scolded in the same words which were so recently used to him. His own infancy—with its uncontrolled outbursts of anger, unmanageable fears, unregulated excretion, and exorbitant hungers and thirsts—does not remain as the same kind of partly repressed, partly remembered record of ignominy and licentiousness with which clinical pictures in our type of society make us so familiar.

Again and again the individual memory, so treacherous, so subject to distortion, is corrected and quieted by the child's experiences as a spectator of many other similar situations, which other babies are living through just as he is emerging from that stage himself. As a five- to ten-year-old he observes the differently loaded behavior of early childhood from a quite different set of preoccupations.

At adolescence, the reassurance provided by such repetition is available when the rapidity of physical changes within the body revives some of the early childhood patterns, or as the mother awaits the birth of her first baby, or the father anticipates parenthood. When extreme old age again brings early childhood experience dangerously or temptingly close to consciousness, infants are still present to scream and tauten their bodies like a bent bow, to defecate in anger, to pound the breast, or cling to it for comfort too long. Man lives through these events, which loom so conspicuously in his own overinflated memory, and comes out a quite usual person, neither a great criminal nor a great hero.

When an individual grows up in a homogeneous slowly changing culture, the older he grows, the surer he grows, and the better acquainted he becomes with the form which other peoples' behavior will take. Behavior can become automatic; for example, as those who drive motor cars in only one city can let more of their driving behavior sink below the level of consciousness. When to turn right and when to turn left, who should enter a door first and who second, who must be seated first, who will help themselves first from the common dish, when the ceremony will really begin, how much error to allow on any calculation, when people mean what they say and when their speech is only ceremonial self-deprecation or shrewd bargaining—all these the child learns as he grows.

As old age approaches and the immediate memory dims, the past is a reliable guide to the present, and the old grandfather threads his way with assurance through the most intricate social situation. Whether the culture is one in which consciousness is valued or deprecated, whether all of life flows smoothly or parts of it are designed to contrast sharply, there are nevertheless wide areas in which the freedom to act habitually lessens fatigue, makes motor behavior more economical, and provides a steady compensation for the decrease in spontaneity and zest which usually accompanies the aging process.

If we consider carefully these real characteristics of life in a homogeneous society, it becomes immediately apparent that these conditions are true for such a limited number of our population today that those few are placed in a position so deviant that it becomes a liability through its unusualness. The carefully fitted together internally coherent sequences of behavior and the implications for learning of their presence in the behavior of others, the prefiguration of the future and the consolidation of the past, or finally, the increase in automatic behavior and sureness with age—all these are missing. The rapidity of social change alone during the last few decades has, for most people, eliminated all of these features. Each person who approaches an infant is likely to approach it with behavior which embodies sequences to which the child will not otherwise be exposed. The behavior of the adults is discrepant and confused because of the breaks in continuity in their own upbringing.

The growing child sees old people sicken (although seldom allowed to see them die) and fail in a way congruent with *their* past. Children only a few years younger than himself are reared along entirely different lines —they are rocked where he was put firmly in his cradle; fed on self-demand where he was kept to schedule, given a pacifier where he was denied one, or the reverse. Instead of being able to develop more and more automatic behavior, he must learn to be increasingly on the alert for lights that turn off differently, lavatories with a different flushing system, games which have the same names but are played with different rules, etc. Far more important, on the social level, he meets ever-changing standards of manners and morals, shifting criteria of refusal and acceptance. There is no chance for relaxation, for, even as he becomes adept and in part accustomed to the ways of his adult contemporaries, his own children begin to display new forms of behavior to which he has no clues. By the time grandchildren arrive, the gap is so great that many grandparents are refusing even to try to bridge it.

Seen in this light, it will be recognized that the normal expectancy today is for a type of personality development with different characteristics, and that there is urgent need to define these characteristics and integrate them into our systematic expectations of human beings. Since our systematic knowledge of personality formation in homogeneous societies far outstrips our knowledge of the process or even of the effects of heterogeneity and social change, the next step must be to indicate some of the problems involved; that is, to alert the research worker and begin to clarify the task of the educator and therapist.

We may begin with the type of case in which an individual reared in *one homogeneous culture enters, as an adult, a quite different culture.* By this I mean such contrasts as between an Italian village and the city of Detroit, or between a Puerto Rican village and an American factory, or correspondingly when a member of western Euro-American culture goes to live permanently in an isolated part of the Arctic, or in a Southeast Asian jungle. In this case the individual has already a coherent personality, nurtured under the conditions which we have already described. (The Italian villager or the Puerto Rican will have come from a more coherent background then the member of a modern urbanized culture, but it is still possible to find living individuals in England or Germany who grew up within a culture which was still relatively homogeneous and not yet completely disrupted by unassimilated change.) It will be useful to indicate here some of the types of adjustment which may occur.

The immigrant may keep intact his cultural picture of the world, his cultural ideas of hierarchy or order of the way in which events "naturally" occur, and merely accept from his environment concrete information and points of references. He will learn the address of a restaurant, how to read the menu, what a meal will cost and how much of a tip to give. The significance of the restaurant itself—as a place where men go to be away from their women folk, where one takes one's whole family on a holiday, as a place where one takes a mistress but never a wife, where one drinks alone in a curtained booth—will retain its original configurational meaning for him. When he goes there he will experience the sense of irresponsible masculinity, the pater familias role, the sense of pleasant sin, or rather repellent sin for which restaurant life stood in his original culture. He may learn the names of many restaurants, their street numbers and days of closing, but each item remains simply a concrete, more or less imperfect substitution of a foreign element in an unaltered scheme. He may marry a wife from the new culture, and only perceive her behavior at the points where it can be interpreted in terms of his own conception of the wife and mother role. If from her cultural background she expects him to carve the roast, while he comes from a culture in which one honors the man by never letting him serve a spoonful of peas or even ask for the salt, her behavior will symbolize lack of respect to him to the end of his days.

We see an interesting illustration of the relationship between the substitution of such concrete and historical bits of a preexisting pattern as contrasted with the substitution of new patterns in the phenomenon known as "tropical memory." After several years in a completely alien environment, where the physical environment, the food, the tempo, the very premises of life are different, the occidental often finds that he has forgotten most of the proper names which were completely available to him in his western life. Practically every item in his former life which would have been spelled in English with a capital letter disappears, while the life which they stood for is remembered perfectly clearly. Conversations on one's return to the old scene after several years absence have an extraordinary quality. There is conversation of the respective merits of two actors whose names are forgotten, of a play, the name lost, at two theatres, once familiar and now designated as "that theater near the center of town with the very wide single balcony." As each of these fantastic conversations, studded with omitted proper names goes on, the names begin to come back and, after a few weeks in the home environment, again become parts of the ordinary memory store. It will take much research to describe this process which gives the impression of a different "setting" of the human organism on a concrete historical level on the one hand, and the cultural pattern level on the other.

A second type of conflict occurs when the immigrant or colonist attempts to establish a new pattern by trying to alter his expectations and standards to fit into the new society. Here a variety of effects may be seen. His previous cultural experience may become almost inaccessible, even to the point where a language spoken until adulthood appears to be forgotten, so intense is his acceptance of the new and the need for blocking out the "interference" of the old. If the individual later leaves the new culture and returns to the old, a similar type of apparent loss of memory may occur. In this type of "culture contact adjustment," the individual does not fit the two cultures together, but puts, as it were, the whole of his personality in a position to learn the new culture. What this means in terms of psychosomatic cost, we have as yet no method of assaying.

Even a relatively homogeneous culture may utilize such sharp contrasts in the course of the developmental sequence that a related type of forgetting may occur and some items be almost completely removed from memory availability. In tracing personality development under such circumstances, there is, I believe, adequate data to show that these intervals of extreme contrast in the life history, although sinking below the level of availability, are part of the personality structure of the individual. It is possible that some of these contrasts, whether in structure of situation within the life history in a homogeneous culture, or between two cultures, each learned at a different period of life, may be found to have a variety of systematic and identifiable effects. In some cases they may be part of a vertical structure, and an essential part of it; in others, mere horizontal supplements to the rest of life in which the "years I spent in Paris" are regarded essentially as duplications of years spent learning and enjoying another culture. They may also play into a more abstract definition of life in which the individual who has shared intensely in two contrasting cultures, may include contrasts in culture in his widened gestalt. In the case of children, exposed serially to two cultures, some scattered evidence suggests that the premises of the earlier may persist as distortions of perception into later experience, so that years later errors in syntax or reasoning may be traced to the earlier and "forgotten" cultural experience.

Another order of complication occurs when the split between the old and the new culture is made, not as a split between the conceptual and the concrete, or completely in time and attention, but instead as between different areas of life, such as home and work, family life and public life, etc. Materials on immigrant families provide abundant illustrations of these various splits, of groups who live in enclaves where the native language is still spoken and the whole pattern of living conforms to the original culture. Leaving it daily for the working world, they speak the language of that outside world, handle the currency, fill out the forms, and meet the work expectations of the new culture. Where such a split is made, the older conceptual framework in which home and work had their own significance is likely to survive to invest the culture of the "working world" with the glamor or drudgery assigned to work, versus home life, in the older culture. Where the living habits of the new culture are taken over for everyday life, but festival patterns of the old cultures are invoked for weddings, funerals, and all high holidays, the new culture becomes invested with the aura of the ordinary; the old keeps a nostalgia-invoking quality.

A still different type of split occurs with the need to adjust to the new culture through the person of a relative or spouse, as when an immigrant boy comes to live with a highly acculturated uncle, or a recently arrived immigrant marries a girl who is thoroughly representative of the new culture. Whatever patterned significance the particular relationship had, if a wife was seen as comfort or responsibility, a mentor and curber of errant impulses, or a partner in indulgence, becomes the conceptual form in which the new culture is perceived and assimilated.

Changes in status as an immigrant moves from one country to another may also deliver such a shock that the perception of the new culture contains a sharp gradient, or sharp discontinuities as a major element. The shock may be so great that no systematic perception of the new culture is ever achieved or a systematic distortion may result.

I have discussed first the type of change which occurs when an individual is reared in one culture, and migrates to the second culture in which he establishes a relationship of some duration. These are the dramatic situations, easy to delineate, extremely conspicuous and familiar in the American scene. Lesser types of migration, especially from rural to urban life, or from class to class, present the same features in less dramatic form.

In generation change, we can find the analogue of the individual who keeps his original cultural orientation and merely adjusts superficially to the new culture. Those who live in the past, while transacting their everyday business on a contemporary level, are familiar figures in societies which combine rapid change with class mobility. An adjustment may be "frozen" at an earlier level by identification with parents whose way of life belonged to another generation, because the individual, now adult, cannot live at the same class level or in the same way they did. Without models for his new life, he may make only the most superficial adjustment, and his values and patterns of human relationships may be completely referred to the past. Conversely, we have the type of adjustment in which the individual "migrates" into the next generation, assumes the manners and attitudes of the child generation, often suppressing completely all the values of his own generation. The present trend in American life to keep the mother perennially young is tending to standardize this type of generation displacement. It is developing compensatory or defensive reactions on the part of the young as they attempt to distinguish themselves—the real inhabitants of adolescence in 1947—from the invading forty-year-olds.

Fragmented types of development may occur as the growing child patterns his conscience on some member of the older generation, and shapes his ideal of himself upon the expressed day dreams of some other member who belongs to a different generation or possibly to both a different generation and a different original culture. Serious distortions occur when the mechanisms of inter-generation behavior, whatever that may be, break down. This occurs when an epidemic selectively kills off the grandparent generation, which happened in many parts of the South Seas in World War I, or where a work or war pattern takes the young men during the years when they would have been models or disciplinarians of their younger brothers, or buffers between the younger and the older. Memory distortions as severe as those which cover a change from one culture to another may occur, as the elders retrospectively falsify their own past behavior either to make it conform to the demands which *their* parents implanted in them as children, or to the world of their children to which they do not belong. Both types of distortion create difficulties, as both violate the original consistencies of the real behavior and make it possible either to perpetuate an increasingly untenable behavioral ideal of imputed past conservatism, or to obscure the possible difficulties and contradictions involved in some new experimental step being taken by the adolescent generation. Thus a parent insisting that his youth conformed to the highest standards, rather than admitting he often failed to conform and paid heavily in anxiety or guilt, will introduce a disorienting factor into the child's adjustment. Likewise, the over-complacent parent who takes advantage of loosening standards to live out vicariously some license which was not permitted in his own youth, may equally cast a shadow of sin over some adolescent practice which would otherwise have its own workable ethics.

There remain to consider those types of generation contrast which occur with cumulative, rapidly accelerating change such as the world has experienced in the last two or three hundred years. A new set of contrasts become conspicuous. The previous generation seems surer because of having been reared under more homogeneous conditions which are gone, and the contemporary generation is both up to date and unsure.

Culture change aggravates the effects of oscillatory changes between the members of different generations within the same family, as when an indulgent mother spoils and over-protects a daughter, who then makes heavy demands on *her* daughter. She, in turn, schooled to self-denying service, becomes an indulgent mother. It is probable also that those trends within single family structure in which there is some deep instability, will have a greater tendency to become cumulative and result in disaster during a period of rapid accelerating change.

It should furthermore be recognized that the types of contrast due to contrast of culture and those due to contrast between generations are of course interwoven in every possible way, with the culture contrast being at least superficially easier to describe.

Both types of contrast—those introduced by migration of individuals between cultures, and those introduced by a rapidity of change which places the members of succeeding generations who do not migrate in very strongly contrasted position—may be described as primary effects of cultural change. The disorganizations they produce have a kind of clarity of outline which may be attributed to the existing degrees of homogeneity in the cultures or generation behavior patterns involved. We face in the present day world a form of personality which reflects these primary contrasts, at a second and third remove in the children and grandchildren of those whose personalities have been subjected to pressures and changes of the order which has been described. Where the first generation of sharp culture contact, between different cultures or between different periods of rapid cultural change, manifested the various types of amnesia, distortion, and confusion between different perceptions of cultural and historical reality, the second generation shows the effects of having been reared among individuals who were in various degrees representative of the first type.

This second stage of manifestation of extremely rapid change combined with increasing mobility of peoples so that both temporal and local roots are gone, is becoming the expected personality type for the world. This is so provided the breakdown of European feudal institutions on the one hand and of Oriental agrarian societies on the other, proceed piecemeal under various unrelated auspices rather than under the auspices of any group powerful enough to handle their own orthodoxy as a homogeneity which must be accepted. Although data are lacking, it is probable that such a purposive westernization or modernization of a society, under the guidance of a self-consistent ideology, will produce merely another example of primary culture contact. In North and South America, in

Western Europe, and in Britain the war has loosened the old locality ties which preserved some cultural and local orientation in the face of great technological change. We may therefore expect to find as the emerging type of personality the child who has been reared among persons who have themselves been subjected to profound cultural and historical disorientation. The same is true of all those parts of the orient where modernization and the importation of western ideas is unaccompanied by power sufficient to regularize and integrate the change. This power did exist in nineteenth century Japan, so that Japanese culture maintained its cultural integrity through industrial revolution, as Britain had done earlier.

In this group of partially disoriented and partially reoriented persons, certain characteristic forms of behavior may be examined systematically in their effect on the children who grow up under their influence. Among them may be found: 1) a nostalgia for a homogeneous and internally consistent view of life which becomes an available focus for various forms of religious and political propaganda offering a unitary solution of all problems; 2) a disturbance between memories of the past and expectations of the future; 3) internal discrepancies in habits of disciplining children, conducting domestic relations, and managing work contacts; 4) disturbed and inconsistent images of their children's future; 5) unevennesses in grasp of the contemporary culture in which they live, ranging from formal literacy without any real ability to handle reading as a tool, to isolated professional patterns of behavior thoroughly discrepant with the rest of their habits of living. It is necessary to add to this picture that in most instances no single pair of parents will show the same pattern. Teachers, friends, and relatives will show other variants, so that to the internal contradictions and inconsistencies existing in each rearing adult, must be added the whole set of intricate relationships among a group of such adults.

As it was possible to describe the characteristics of personality development within a homogeneous, slowly changing society, when members of such societies were subjected to sharp and prolonged exposures to other cultures or to very rapid technological change, so it should also be possible to begin to describe the characteristics of this group who show the secondary effects of the spatial and temporal disturbances of modern times. This secondary effect has been described by Charles Eastman (son of a Sioux Indian mother and a father who was part Sioux, part Caucasian) who lived as a boy the life of his grandparents, and as an adult, the life of an educated modern American.

As a child I understood how to give, I have forgotten this grace since I became civilized. I lived the natural life, whereas I now live the artificial. Any pretty pebble was valuable to me then; every growing tree an object of reverence. Now

I worship with the white man before a painted landscape whose value is estimated in dollars! Thus the Indian is reconstructed, as the *natural rocks are
ground to powder and made into artificial blocks* which may be built into the
walls of modern society.

Here speaks the representative of the primary stage who already sees
the young in the next stage where values are no longer multiple and in-
commensurate but estimated in dollars; that is, estimated *on a single scale.*

The capacity to organize experience in terms of a cultural reality
inherent in growing up in a homogeneous culture, is lost among the
children of those who have themselves undergone the first impact of
change. As a result perceived experience becomes *atomized* into units
which have no structural relationship to a whole that can no longer be
perceived. The shape of the blocks themselves is seen as arbitrary in
contrast to the "natural rocks," those whose form was not imposed upon
an aggregation of meaningless units.

Individuals reared in this secondary stage develop an approach to
life which Erikson has called "tentative" and I have described as "situational". Erikson has pointed out that the modern American, who is perhaps the best studied example of this modern type of human being, must
be able to be *sedentary* as well as *migratory.* His tentativeness must
cover not only a range of situations but a range which actually involves
polarization.

A fourth characteristic of this personality type may be described as a
tendency to fragment, unsystematically, the counterpart within personality development of the tendency to perceive the world atomistically.
This lack of coherence, this tendency toward fragmentation under
strain provides an opening for propagandist movements offering a
coherent view of life just as the nostalgia of the primary stage presents an
opening to such movements.

Meanwhile modern American culture has developed a variety of therapeutic and educational measures designed to protect and strengthen the
individuals who are exposed to this terrific cultural strain, especially
during childhood. Conspicuous among these socially self-corrective devices are: 1) emphasis on a new type of child rearing which takes "self-
demand" (the child's own individual physiological rhythm) as the framework for habit formation; 2) the progressive education movement with
its philosophy of letting the child strike its own pace; 3) types of social
case work and psychiatry which stress the need for helping the individual
work out his own problems and achieve a new integration. These methods
may be seen in historical perspective as the efforts of a disoriented society to develop human beings who will be strong enough to survive and
participate constructively in creating new cultural forms which will again
restore some order to human life.

Kepes has described the modern artist as fasting from the indigestibility of the visual forms of this muddled modern world and turning entirely to inner experience as the only reliable contemporary guide. Movements which turn to "inner rhythms" may be expected to develop in almost every field of life during this period of unprecedented strain which now faces the human race. They need not be seen as a final rejection of cultural form or traditional, ethical, or aesthetic discipline, but rather as a blessed expedient, imaginatively devised, for the present human emergency.

35. A CRITIQUE OF CULTURE-
PERSONALITY WRITINGS *

The furor roused within the discipline by culture and personality
studies is similar in heat, if not light, to the controversies raised by
culturology, cultural evolutionism and psycholinguistics. Some
anthropologists, Leslie White for example, decry some of these studies as
reactionary debasements of the science of culture. Others pinpoint certain
assumptions and methods and concentrate their fire on them. This
selection, written by two sociologists, is a good example of this latter
category of criticism.

T HIS PAPER is concerned with an analysis and criticism of what
have come to be known as "culture and personality" writing, including
among others the work of Benedict, Mead, Gorer, Kluckhohn, DuBois,
Linton, La Barre, Erikson, and Kardiner. The scholars who have contributed to this movement have a common general orientation although
some differences of opinion and emphasis exist. One wing of the movement includes psychoanalytically trained persons like Fromm, Erikson,
and Kardiner. Another wing, represented by a writer like Benedict, places
the main emphasis upon descriptions of cultural configurations and personality types, but puts relatively little emphasis upon genetic explanations or on psychoanalytic concepts. Most of the writers fall between

* A. R. Lindesmith and Anselm Strauss, "A Critique of Culture-Personality Writings," *American Sociological Review*, Vol. 15 (1950), pp. 587–600. Reprinted with
permission of the authors and the publisher.

Alfred R. Lindesmith (b. 1905) is Professor of Sociology at the University of
Indiana. He is the author of *Opiate Addiction* (1947) and co-author, with Anselm
Strauss, of *Social Psychology* (1950, 1957).

Anselm L. Strauss (b. 1916) is Professor of Sociology at the University of Chicago.
In addition to his co-authorship of *Social Psychology*, he is editor of *The Social Psychology of George Herbert Mead* (1956).

the extremes, using a sprinkling of psychoanalytic terminology, sometimes in combination with ideas derived from other areas.

The interdisciplinary nature of this approach is often stressed but it is, in actual fact, sharply limited. For example, the theory and research of most psychologists, social psychologists, and sociologists who are concerned with personality and psychological processes, are virtually unaffected by the culture-personality writings. Conversely, in the latter there is rarely any reference to the research of social psychologists or psychologists other than clinicians and psychiatrists of Freudian persuasion, and almost no references to the writings of foreign psychologists.

The major preoccupations of the culture-personality writers are: (a) the description and psychological characterization of cultural configurations and the delineation of personality types associated with them, and (b) the explanation of given personality types as products of cultural influences and especially of interpersonal relations in early childhood. We shall discuss each of these major interests in turn.

CULTURAL CONFIGURATION AND
MODAL PERSONALITY POINT OF VIEW

The traditional method of ethnology emphasized the exhaustive description of primitive societies with relatively little emphasis upon psychological characterization as such or upon the total configuration or gestalt. The emphasis was rather upon specific modes of behavior in definitely delineated situations and upon the "psychological" features mainly as exhibited in the overt behavior and verbalization of the natives. The change in viewpoint initiated by the culture-personality school is well indicated by Kroeber's comment: "As late as 1915 the very word 'personality' still carried overtones chiefly of piquancy, unpredictability, intellectual daring. . . ." Influenced by conceptions borrowed from Gestalt psychology and psychoanalysis, and by Sapir's early stress on the need to study the individuals in a society, some ethnologists have attempted to characterize societies in psychological terms as functioning wholes or configurations. The observer seeks to characterize what may be called the "essence" of the culture in psychological terms, i. e., the people's view of the world and of human relations. Such characterization of peoples and nations is not a totally new enterprise. Long before the rise of modern anthropology, writers and scholars attempted the same sort of description of what was called the "genius" or "ethos" of a people. As Kroeber notes: "More than eighteen hundred years ago Tacitus gave to posterity one of the masterpieces of this genre in his analysis of German custom and character."

Following logically from this emphasis on cultural configurations is the idea that given cultural configurations have their counterparts in the individuals of each society. Given cultures produce one or more types of personality designated by such terms as "modal personality," "basic personality structure," "character structure," and so on.

In arriving at their characterization of cultures and personality types the investigators rely upon conventional ethnological techniques and data, but seek to go beyond them by utilizing them in combination with studies of individuals. Much attention is paid to interpersonal relations, childhood training, projective and objective tests, and sometimes even to photographing people in specified situations.

The investigator immerses himself in a given society as far as the barriers of language, time, available informants, and his own personality permit. From the welter of data he arrives at his characterizations through acts of abstraction, selection, and synthesis. Some characterizations are made vicariously, the writer utilizing materials collected by others, supplemented usually by interviews with emigrants.

The investigators do not describe very clearly or in detail how given characterizations are arrived at. Stress is placed upon offering the reader a mass of data concerning those aspects of behavior which are the focus of the characterizations.

It should be noted that anthropologists often view the culture-personality approach as something in the nature of a fad, although it is generally conceded that it offers interesting and potentially significant knowledge. In terms of total output, culture-personality writings constitute only a small portion of anthropological writings. Current popularity of the point of view is attested by Kroeber who remarks: "Personality is the slogan of the moment . . . the prospect may look dire to those who are interested in culture as such. But with experience one learns that these waves go much as they come."

The works of the culture-personality writers, widely read outside of academic circles, offer a valuable antidote to provincialism and ethnocentrism. The implications of the cultural relativity principle have not by any means been fully taken into account either by social scientists or by the general public. The point, no doubt, needs to be hammered home as these writers are doing. Their works amply demonstrate the enormous range of variation in the organization of societies and human responses. The criticisms which follow are not intended in any way to detract from this substantial accomplishment.

CRITICISM

Oversimplification and the homogeneity postulate. The attempt to make psychological characterizations of cultures "may be regarded as attempted short-hand translation of the more general patterns of a culture." This procedure raises questions having to do with selectivity, neglect of inconsistent data, proof of assertions, and the possibility of corroboration by other investigators. No one, of course, questions the existence of gross differences between cultures. The question is rather that of the scientific precision of specific characterizations and the methods of obtaining them.

Anthropologists have questioned the accuracy of the boiling-down process when carried too far. Benedict, for example, was criticized for describing Zuni, Kwakiutl, and Dobu peoples too simply. In short, one notes that the number of questions that are raised concerning any characterization tends to increase with the number of investigators familiar with the society. The question was raised whether many nonliterate societies might not be characterized more profitably in terms of multiple patterns or "themes." A similar point has been made with respect to the numbers of personality types within given societies. The earlier culture-personality writings often understressed or ignored individuals who did not conform to the personality type assumed as typical of the culture. This explaining-away or ignoring of negative evidence has given way to

. . . the study of the *range* of personalities in a society. . . . Characteristic personality sub-types may develop from the differing situations of the life of persons who play different roles in a given group.

This trend toward studying the "range of personalities" and of multiple themes within a culture, if carried out to its logical limits, implies a radical revision of the original ideas, as we shall show later. It represents a healthy tendency to move toward more limited and specific problems which can be handled by the established techniques of analysis and proof, rather than dealing with the impossible task of handling entire cultures in one fell swoop, as "wholes." A good many of the questions now being raised will no longer be pertinent when the tendency described by Herskovits is carried further. When this is done, however, stricter standards of proof will have to be met, and many other theories besides the neo-Freudian will have to be taken into account. The dangers inherent in gestalt descriptions of societies are graphically brought out by culture-personality efforts to describe complex modern societies. Any social scientist who seeks to characterize a modern nation, even in a whole volume, to say nothing of a few pages, has to handle a host of detailed problems and meet a number of exacting requirements. These are so numerous and so complex that to one not imbued with the culture-personality fervor the task looks impossible. These problems and requirements have to do with such matters as sampling, statistical distributions, regional differences, migration, ethnic differences, social classes, diverse group affiliations, standards, social change, culture conflict, and enormous bodies of literature and historical materials. One may admire the boldness of the attempts to make broad general characterizations of such peoples as the Americans, Japanese, and Germans, but one must view the results and methods of proof with a generous measure of skepticism. The same strictures apply with even greater force to attempts to characterize Western character and culture in general.

The applications of culture-personality methods to modern societies—especially the American, with which we are reasonably well acquainted—have fared so badly at the hands of competent critics that one wonders along with Bierstedt whether the effect has not been "to stimulate the growth of skepticism concerning the information which anthropologists have given us about nonliterate peoples."

Undoubtedly the heterogeneity of modern nations, as many of the writers themselves have pointed out, offers a considerable obstacle to the application of present configurational methods. It is hoped, however, that after the techniques have been perfected in the study of simpler, more "homogeneous" societies they may be extended successfully to more complex groups. A more fundamental question must, however, be raised concerning the general validity of the homogeneity assumption itself, even as applied to the larger groupings of non-literate peoples. One suspects, as Bernard has said, that too much attention is being paid to "the blond Swede."

Psychic Entities vs. Behavior. The homogeneity-configuration postulates savor strongly of Aristotelian conceptions of "essence" and "accident." The "essences" (configuration, basic personality structures) are given high status in the realm of "being," whereas the behaviors which "express" these essences are of an inferior status. Even though the behavior may vary from one individual to the next, and from one generation to the next, it is thought of as an emanation or manifestation of the same essence. Current recognition of a range of personality types and of multiple configurations within a single society is an effort to deal with negative evidence and deviations often ignored by earlier writers, but the accident-essence framework is still retained since the number of essences is merely increased. The range idea also has the effect of making it doubly difficult, if not impossible, to prove that the generalizations reached are either true or false.

There is a tendency in these investigations to deduce psychic entities from overt behavior in specific situations, and then to explain the overt behavior in terms of these reifications. There is a search for something like the "real inner personality" or "authentic individual" conceived as something apart from behavior. The inner reality thus becomes a force which manifests itself in the behavior from which it is inferred. Linton explicitly states this position:

The nature and even the presence of psychic needs are only to be deduced from the behavior to which they give rise. . . .

Personality will be taken to mean 'the organized aggregate of psychological processes and states pertaining to the individual.' [This definition] rules out the overt behavior resulting from the operation of these processes and states, although it is only from such behavior that their nature and even existence can be deduced. . . .

In general, all the individuals who occupy a given position in the structure of a particular society will respond to many situations in very much the same way. . . . Until the psychologist knows what the norms of behavior imposed by a particular society are, and can discount them as indicators of personality, he will be unable to penetrate behind the facade of social conformity and cultural conformity to reach the authentic individual.

What is meant by "authentic individual"? Do not cultural roles and internalized norms connected with them (e. g., sex roles) influence the "authentic individual"?

The search for the "real motives," the "deep inner core," the "authentic individual," conceived as something separate from behavior leads to circularity of proof and immunity to negative evidence. Thus, if there is no available evidence that ascribed reactions actually take place, it can always be assumed that they are "unconscious" reactions. If the persons seem to have no knowledge of them, or deny the imputed motives, or give other interpretations of their behavior, these objections are easily disposed of by calling them "rationalizations" or by pointing out that, after all, the people are not usually aware of the premises of their culture which as motivations underlie their daily conduct.

A gross example of this procedure is provided by G. Roheim, who argues with regard to knowledge of procreation among primitives, that:

If we see, on the one hand, that the Arunta deny knowing anything of the matter, and on the other that they have beliefs and rites that are only explicable on the assumption that such knowledge exists somewhere and makes itself felt in their psychic system, we shall say that they are unconscious of their own instinctive knowledge of procreation and that the concepts that enter consciousness are symbolic substitutes of a physiological account of the process of procreation.

The above may be dismissed as an extreme psychoanalytic fantasy, but, with some differences, the same technique of calling on unconscious ideas when the evidence fails, or is disputable, is widespread. Thus Benedict in her book on the Japanese says that: "In this task of analysis the court of authority is not necessarily Tanaka San, the Japanese 'anybody.' For Tanaka San does not make his assumptions explicit, and interpretations written for Americans will undoubtedly seem to him unduly labored."

Such a procedure allows the interpretive framework of the investigator to persist undisturbed in the face of negative evidence and criticisms, even from intelligent and trained members of the group being characterized.

Trait psychology lends itself very readily to the use of reified psychic elements to explain behavior of which these traits are, in reality, merely names. Thus, when aggressive behavior is explained in terms of a "fund of aggression," or of a "trait of aggressiveness," this amounts to saying that behavior is aggressive because it is aggressive. These traits are often not self-evident, and at the beginning of his research the investigator often is uncertain of the "meaning" of specific acts. The "meanings" that are finally found are thus the investigator's inferences from behavioral data. The final psychological characterizations often leave this behavioral or situational basis of the inferred psychic elements or traits out of consideration.

Confusion of Fact and Interpretation. The terms that are used in these characterizations are inevitably taken from Western psychological vocabularies, and inevitably lead the reader to think of the people according to the Western models with which he is familiar. A description of the psychological responses of people within the behavioral context of the society does not run into the same dangers of unchecked inference. In this regard a remark of Titiev's, a Southwest specialist, is pertinent:

> Dr. Thompson . . . exhibits an unfortunate tendency to distort various items taken from literature. A girlish pursuit game somewhat comparable to follow-the-leader, is magnified into a faithful portrayal of "the guidance role of the mother and the difficult and centripetal life course of the Hopi girl."

Titiev's criticism may be extended to many culture-personality inferences. Thus, whenever it is postulated that a given people have a given trait such as "aggressiveness," "passivity," "withdrawnness," "impulsiveness," as part of their "basic personality structure," it is easy to take the unwarranted step of regarding specific behavior as a manifestation or effect of the given trait. Conclusions of this type are buttressed not so much by evidential proof as by the piling up of illustrations which are unlikely to convince anyone who is not already sold on the underlying ideology.

No one is likely to quarrel seriously with characterizations of a people when these descriptions are couched in objective behavioral terms, as in conventional ethnological accounts. But when ethnologists interpret the "meanings" of behavior in psychological terms, it becomes exceedingly difficult for the reader to separate facts from interpretations. An interesting comment bearing on this point was made by the Murphys in a review of Mead-Bateson's *Balinese Character.* They conclude that "in spite of the photographic record, the study still shows some lack of systematic framework, the lack of sharp distinction between hypotheses and fact."

The extensive use of photographs in the Mead-Bateson book made it possible for the reviewers to question some of the authors' interpretations. The reviewers go on to say that the photographs allow the reader to observe incidents in the backgrounds of the pictures which raise questions about matters in the foregrounds. They add that "as a device for cultural study this has very important advantages over one which presents data and interpretations so intertwined that they are impossible to handle independently."

The necessity for presenting "data" and "interpretations" separately becomes greater the more remote and inaccessible the culture. The closer a society is to us and the more that is known about it, the easier it becomes to dispute interpretations of it. One wonders what would happen to the various characterizations of psychologically remote societies if the natives, as well as the investigator's own colleagues who happen to have some knowledge of the society, were able to answer back! We know what happened when the "natives" read the Mead and Gorer material on the United States.

Two interesting incidents that bear upon this point may be cited. Herskovits writes that "Li, a Chinese anthropologist, whose own physical traits made him inconspicuous among the Indians [Zuni], found them, as people, to be quite different from the picture of themselves they had presented to white students." Li spent a mere two and one-half months of moderately intimate participation in Zuni life—the Zuni being among the most studied and most characterized non-literate peoples in the world. Another relevant case is that of the anthropologist Peter Buck, of Maori descent, who called into question some of the fundamental interpretations of Maori character and culture made by the Beagleholes.

The recent tendencies to present more documentation of conclusions is certainly a step in the right direction since it allows the reader to form some opinions of his own. This documentation usually consists of auto-biographies and test results. The utilization of these materials has, however, raised additional questions. For example, there is the question of sampling that arises when autobiographies are gathered. DuBois' study of the Alorese employs this method and illustrates the problem very well. H. Powdermaker suggests that the autobiographies do not represent Alorese modal character because DuBois was apparently able to interview only relatively unsuccessful Alorese, "those who did not approximate the goals of their culture." She also raises the question of the influence of the investigator upon the interview situation. "We know of no society where people will talk about their private inner feelings upon request [and for pay], and in response to questions from a relative stranger at regular periods each day." The use of autobiographical documents is of course desirable but does not in itself prove anything. The critical reader is not convinced that the persons used in obtaining the documents constitute a representative sample, or that the documents cannot be interpreted in a variety of ways.

The claim that projectives and other tests may be used to validate analyses made by other ethnological methods must be qualified by noting that test results are not self-explanatory, but must themselves be interpreted like other data. The tests are certainly useful, but they are not an open-sesame to the truth. All of them were devised and validated by Western investigators operating within the confines of Western culture, and even within that culture their significance is a matter of controversy. This is especially true of the projectives. The discrepancies between Kardiner's interpretations of Alorese character and Overholzer's inferences from Rorschach results raise some doubts about the use of projectives in culture-personality research.

The use of tests may prove to be misleading by suggesting an illusory precision and definitiveness. This is especially true when the usual statistical precautions are not followed. Thus, in a review of the *Children of the People*, M. Kuhn remarks:

. . . a defect is the failure of the researchers, after espousing the use of quantitative methods, to apply even the minimum sampling standards, such as tests of representativeness, adequacy, and statistical significance of difference which are required by these methods.

An idea of the inadequacy of some of the interpretations of the tests may be obtained from the fact that in *The Hopi Way* conclusions about Hopi animism are based on the answers to a single question! And this is done in spite of the extensive controversial literature on methods of testing animism in children. As other examples, Powdermaker notes that the thirty-seven Alorese who took DuBois' Rorschach test were unidentified and probably unrepresentative, and Titiev questions how the Hopi way, "which is a subtle, complex, and mature outlook on life, can be properly interpreted or clarified on the basis of tests administered to 190 school children, of whom no less than 45 per cent were 10 years of age or younger."

The Operation of Western Biases. The use of projective tests points up one of the fundamental and pervasive weaknesses of many of the interpretations of non-Western peoples; namely, that Western biases must inevitably find expression in the inferences made about the psychological characteristics of given peoples. As R. Benedict has said:

No man ever looks at the world with pristine eyes. He sees it edited by a definite set of customs and institutions and ways of thinking. Even in his philosophical probings he cannot go behind these stereotypes; his very concept of the true and the false will still have reference to his particular traditional customs.

Herskovits makes a similar point. *"Judgments are based on experience, and experience is interpreted by each individual in terms of his own enculturation."* (Italics his.)

Anthropologists constantly warn their readers against Western biases, and quite rightly. They are generally aware that these biases can, and perhaps must, unwittingly influence their own research. This warning has not been taken into account in anything like its full implications by culture-personality writers. Admittedly the problem of describing non-Western peoples without including one's own biases in the account is a difficult undertaking. One cannot help but feel that many conclusions reached about non-Western character structures and their genesis should have been couched in much more tentative and cautious terms. This is especially relevant to characterizations which seek to get at "inner psychic realities" and their origins.

A comment from Li, whose short participant-observer residence among the Zuni we have previously mentioned, portrays vividly the culture-personality writer's difficulties:

We find another one-sided statement on . . . the problem of interpretation of Zuni life. Avoidance of leadership in social life is a corollary of the lack of personal feelings in religion. If one is not interested in vision quest . . . what is more natural than the supposition that leadership among men is not desired. But here is just a case in which the premise is correct enough while the conclusion does not necessarily follow. Dr. Benedict reports that a Zuni is afraid of becoming "a leader of his people" lest he should "likely be persecuted for sorcery," and that he would be "only interested in a game that a number can play with even chances" for "an outstanding runner spoils the game." The basic fallacy seems to lie in *the tendency to reason with the logical implications of one's own culture.* [Our italics.] In the competitive Western world where one is brought up to assume that the world is made for his exploitation, and where if one does not push ahead, one is surely pushed behind, it is certainly logical that lack of personal acquisitiveness implies the denial of leadership.

One of the aspects of anthropological thinking which tends to neutralize the wholesome emphasis on cultural variability and the dangers of ethnocentric bias, is the out-of-hand dismissal of the hypothesis that intellectual processes may vary in different societies and even within different groups within the same society. This is part of the reaction against the writings of some scholars like Levy-Bruhl, who have attempted to give brief, simple characterizations of primitive thought in general. Linton perhaps summarizes a fairly usual position when he asserts categorically:

CULTURAL ANTHROPOLOGY

As far as we can ascertain, the intellectual processes themselves are the same for all normal human beings in all times and places. At least individuals who begin with the same premises always seem to arrive at the same conclusions.

Linton has inconsistently assailed his own view by elsewhere describing language as "a tool for thinking" (note the characteristic dualism which separates language behavior from thinking behavior by animistically designating the former as a tool of the latter); and asserting that "concepts which are an integral part of all linguistic forms have a subtle influence upon individuals' ways of thinking. The concepts are even more compulsive because they are totally unconscious." His primary criticism of linguistics appears to be that it has ignored this problem of how linguistic forms condition different ways of thinking.

Since virtually all readers of characterizations of non-literate peoples are themselves Westerners, unacquainted with the peoples in question, there are few competent critics to point out any but the most flagrant instances of the influence of Western "projective systems" on the ethnologists' accounts. It is, for example, relatively easy to detect La Barre's wartime pro-democratic feeling in his unsympathetic account of Japanese "compulsive" character, and it is easy to agree with J. Honigmann that Kardiner has placed a rather gross evaluation upon Alorese "narrowness" and "unfitness for cooperation"; and one may readily agree with Kroeber's statement that DuBois' characterization of the Alorese:

. . . seems one-sidedly repellant. . . . The appraising observer comes from a culture that values internalization, conscience, reliance, scruple, courage, consistency of feeling and relations, dignity, and achievement, qualities that are under-developed in Alor. Hence the picture is black.

The detection of more subtle biases awaits the scrutiny of other trained observers—especially natives and cultural hybrids—and the development of more objective techniques of evaluation. Thomas and Znaniecki's *Polish Peasant* might be taken as a suggested model in that one of the authors was a native Pole.

Kroeber, having the Western bias in mind, has suggested that although some of the characterizations of non-Western peoples are undoubtedly partially correct, there is not at present any way of distinguishing what is valid from what reflects merely "personalized reactions." He even suggests that the basic assumptions of culture-personality studies may be unwarranted since "the categories of psychological characterization developed among Occidentals for Occidentals break down, tend to lose their meaning when applied to Asiatics." He suggests that comparative studies of Western societies may be a necessary preliminary to valid configurational and personality studies of non-Western peoples. D. Haring's caution on drawing conclusions about Japanese character might well be extended to all works in this field:

. . . those who do such research should spend years, not months, in Japan. The writer "learned all the answers" in his first year in Japan. The next six years taught him that practically all of those answers were misleading or false. Perhaps another seven years would have indicated the wisdom of saying nothing at all.

DEVELOPMENT OF MODAL OR BASIC PERSONALITY POINT OF VIEW

In culture-personality writings, personality is conceived largely as the product of interpersonal relationships in childhood. Various degrees of emphasis are placed upon different types of experience. The more psychoanalytically-oriented writers, such as Gorer, Roheim, Kardiner, La Barre, and Erikson, stress the earliest years as the most crucial; whereas others, like Thompson, Kluckhohn, Goldfrank, Mead, and Benedict place considerable emphasis upon later experiences. Some of the genetic explanations employ a straight neo-Freudian terminology, and most of them use at least a few psychoanalytic concepts. Virtually the only hypotheses which are generally regarded as worthy of checking are the modified Freudian ones. A. I. Hallowell gives the rationale for this tendency:

This problem [personality] could not be appreciated by either anthropologists or students of human psychology until a working hypothesis about the nature of human personality as a structural whole had been developed. Neither academic psychologists nor psychiatrists of a generation ago had much to offer. It is here that psychoanalysis enters the picture.

There has been some recent attention paid to the possible applicability of learning theories in this field, but in general the work of social psychologists and the mass of critical material on Freudian concepts are ignored.

CRITICISM

Effects of Infant Experience Are Undemonstrated. The lack of attention to alternative hypotheses and the neglect of criticism and negative evidence concerning various aspects of psychoanalytic theory give the culture-personality writings the characteristics of illustration and documentation of a point of view already assumed to be true. The principal problem merely seems to be to show how the view may be extended to other cultures and perhaps modified in minor ways in the process.

A point of view that looms very large in these writings is the one that emphasizes the predominant character-forming efficacy of the infant disciplines: bowel and bladder training, nursing, weaning, mothering, restraint of motion, punishment, amount and kinds of frustration, and so on. Thus, La Barre virtually ascribes the main features of Japanese personality to the rigid bowel training of infants; C. Kluckhohn and O. Mowrer state that too precipitous training of the child in weaning, cleanliness, sex taboos, and aggression control lays the groundwork for "obsessive ambition" and "severe competitive behavior" in adults. E. Erikson carries this type of explanation to an absurd limit:

> The Yurok child . . . is weaned early and abruptly, before the full development of the biting stage, and after having been discouraged from feeling too comfortable with his mother. This expulsion may well contribute to the Yurok character a residue of potential nostalgia which consequently finds its institutionalized form in the Yurok's ability to cry while he prays in order to gain influence over the food-sending powers behind the visible world. . . . The Yurok, in order to be sure of his food supply, feels it necessary to appear hallucinatory, helpless, and nostalgic, and . . . to deny that he has teeth or that his teeth can hurt anybody.

The general unproved assumption lying behind this type of interpretation is expressed as follows by Erikson:

> We hold that a child absorbs through his needy senses the cultural modalities of what happens in, to, and around him long before he is provided with a vocabulary. . . . Adults . . . selectively accelerate and inhibit the sensual maturation of body orifices and surfaces, and they encourage and restrict the gradual expansion of sensory, muscular, and intellectual mastery. In doing so, they systematically though unconsciously establish in the infant's nervous system the basic grammar of their culture's patterns.

H. Orlansky, in an excellent recent paper, has critically evaluated the data and assertions bearing on the question of the influence of infant care on personality development. He has shown that there is no body of evidence to support assertions like those given above. Some of his main points may be summarized as follows: (a) various writers attribute different and contradictory effects to the same or similar childhood experiences; (b) the alleged influences of given infant disciplines or types of experience on personality have not been proven within our own society, to say nothing of others; (c) the method of "proving" that early infancy is of primary importance is shot through with anthropomorphism and unsupported assumptions; and (d) post-infantile childhood experiences are probably of more vital importance in shaping personality than the prelingual ones.

Most psychologists and social scientists agree that there is a special significance attached to first or early learning. There is good evidence for this assumption. What we do not know, and are unable to discover from the culture-personality writings, is what precisely it is that is learned in early infancy and what its exact significance may be for later training. As D. O. Hebb tersely remarks: "In such matters, our ignorance is virtually complete."

Ineffectual Attempts to Salvage Infantile Determination. In an attempt to bring post-infantile experiences into the picture and to salvage remnants of the original doctrine it is commonly asserted (a) if post-infantile experiences tend to reinforce the personality trends established in infancy, then the resulting adult traits will conform to the infantile pattern; however, (b) if later experiences run counter to earlier ones the resulting adult character may be something not predictable from infantile experiences alone.

Thus E. Beaglehole distinguishes between the "primary character structure" formed in infancy and "secondary character structure" formed later if later experiences do not reinforce the earlier ones. Similarly, Kluckhohn and Mowrer assert that:

> It should be emphasized that, like biological heredity, infant experiences, while placing certain constraints upon personality, give mainly potentialities. . . . Whether these potentialities become actualized or not, or the extent to which they become actualized, depends upon later social and other conditions which structure the individual's experience.

Kardiner makes the same point when he notes concerning the effects of infantile experiences: "The . . . question that arises is whether these attitudes need remain permanent. They need not, if other factors are introduced into the child's life which would tend to counteract them. However, if they are not counteracted, they tend to continue."

These statements raise serious methodological problems that are not dealt with adequately, if at all, in this literature. A verifiable theory is one which can be proved to be right, and this implies that conceivably it might be proved wrong by exceptional cases. The latter possibility is not allowed for in the doctrine since, as Kluckhohn and Mowrer state:

> Substantially the same personality trait may be caused by different patterns of childhood experience. . . . The same basic discipline or event in early life may result in quite different personality trends, depending upon the juxtaposition of various other disciplines, the problems which individuals in each particular society have to meet, and, always, the differing biological equipment of different individuals.

Thus, whatever happens, the theory is confirmed in a heads-I-win-tails-you-lose procedure. Orlansky has made a similar point in speaking of infantile disciplines:

. . . the same childhood experience is arbitrarily read as having one significance for personality formation in one society and the opposite significance in
another. . . .

The concept of causation which we are criticizing might be called
"proof by juxtaposition." Using this method, culture-personality writers
describe two sets of phenomena widely separated in time, and assert a
causal relation. The *post hoc* nature of this reasoning is clearly exemplified
by Kardiner's own account:

It is well nigh impossible to tell in advance what particular elaborations will
take place in a given culture of such a basic pattern. However, once we are told
by the Rorschach that certain end results can be identified, it is a relatively
easy matter to reconcile them with the more basic traits.

This *post hoc* method apparently does sometimes have its difficulties, for,
as Kardiner tells us: "I feel somewhat ashamed to confess that some of
the main points in Alorese personality did not become clear to me until
four years after I originally got to know the material."

Some writers stress not only that culture shapes personality, but also
that personality affects culture. Though the latter assertion is not of
concern in this paper, it may be noted that the same sort of *post hoc*
reasoning is used. Thus DuBois suggests that institutions and child
training techniques should be regarded as interdependent variables, and
advances the thesis that institutions should be altered indirectly through
changes in child-rearing practices.

In an excess of enthusiasm, Gorer carries the *post hoc* method to an
all-time high when he offers twentieth-century urban middle-class fads
in child training as the basis for the American form of government
established in the eighteenth century.

Anthropomorphism.   Culture-personality explanations of the development and fixation of personality in early infancy and childhood are
pervaded by anthropomorphism, as Orlansky has amply shown. The main
reasons for this appear to be (a) that little direct study of infants or
children is undertaken to determine whether the reactions attributed to
them actually occur, and (b) it is assumed that the reaction of infants to
a given type of experience "must be" of a certain character without any
effort to prove that such is the case, and (c) the dualistic procedure,
which postulates psychic "processes and states" as forces or "first causes"
that produce behavior, invites the investigator to attribute motives and
reactions which appear reasonable or plausible to him. The following
quotation nicely illustrates the last two of these points:

To the white child, whose feedings and other routines are rigidly scheduled,
the mother or nurse *must appear incalculable.* He finds that there are rules of
behavior which are above and beyond his needs or wishes. No matter how hard

he cries, he does not get his bottle until the clock says he should. *He must de-velop a feeling that each individual is alone in life.*

To the Navaho baby, on the other hand, other persons *must appear warmer and more dependable,* for every time he cries, something is done for him. . . . [Our italics.]

What is "Basic"? Everyone will agree that persons in adult life change occupations, learn new skills, change their status, and so on. It will be admitted that such changes involve personality alterations of some kind. What objective grounds are there for stating that such changes are or are not "basic"?

The idea that basic personality patterns are established in the first couple of years of life or in pre-adolescent childhood involves the assumption that personality does not change, or changes only in minor ways, in response to later experiences and cultural influences. This view of the matter involves a considerable commitment on an issue that must still be regarded as unsettled, and requires that some kind of objective statement about the so-called "basic" elements of the personality be made. It may be pointed out that if personality is conceived as a system of responses arising in a cultural matrix, the individual lives his entire life within such a matrix and is never independent of it. Why, then, unless one assumes that learning and the organization of responses takes place only in childhood, should later experiences be largely ruled out? Most of the culture-personality studies by their very emphases are only partially situationally oriented—that is, with respect to childhood—and take the relative insignificance of later experience for granted. Though this assumption appears to be generally plausible to most social scientists, it is nevertheless necessary to show empirically which response systems change readily and which do not, and under what conditions.

Indirect vs. Direct Learning. The belief that personality patterns are fixed unconsciously and early involves a corollary assumption that these patterns cannot be directly taught, or that they can be taught later only if the childhood training has been favorable. The latter argument is another heads-I-win-tails-you-lose proposition; the former argument rests upon an invidious comparison of different types of behavior, some being judged as more basic than others without specification of the grounds for these conclusions. At times the argument assumes a purely circular form: those patterns which come first are most important because they are the earliest ones.

In reports of research on non-literate peoples considerable data are of course given on direct teaching, but in the interpretation of the deeper meaning of the data and in offering genetic explanations of personality there is a clear tendency to stress the major influence of indirect and unconscious learning. For example, the Beagleholes explain the free spending habits of the Maori in terms of childhood frustrations. The fundamental motive operating here is said to be the "buying of love" which the individual is afraid of losing because of the impact of certain childhood experiences. Peter Buck denies this interpretation, suggesting that patterns of handling money are directly taught—a point that is also made by B. Mishkin.

The Beaglehole interpretation is rendered untenable anyhow by the fact that, regardless of types of childhood training, most non-literate peoples were resistant to the introduction of European economic practices and ideas.

Though this particular interpretation by the Beagleholes is more obviously vulnerable than others of like character, it is, nevertheless, a good example of the emphasis on cumbersome and unverifiable theories of indirect learning where much simpler explanations are available. Admittedly the hypothesis of direct learning is not always applicable, but whenever it is, it is attractive by contrast in its simplicity and verifiability. The predilection for indirect explanations no doubt stems from stresses placed upon "unconscious" processes, upon emotional aspects of interpersonal relations, and upon the deep, hidden, inner reality called "personality." We agree with Linton who says:

. . . how far is the personality formed by these factors which operate on the child without the child really understanding what is happening, and how far is it formed by actual instruction? I think this is a question we have not solved at all at the present time.

SUMMARY AND SUGGESTIONS

The bulk of this paper has been concerned with negative criticisms, raised by us and others, concerning the conclusions, evidence, methods, and general conceptual framework offered and used by culture-personality writers. These criticisms seem to us to indicate quite clearly that available evidence offered by the writers in support of their conclusions is inadequate and does not justify their conclusions. Positive generalizations made in this area are generally based upon unwarranted confidence in rather loose unscientific methods of interpreting data, and upon a relatively uncritical acceptance of a particular conceptual scheme.

Research on the psychological responses of non-Western people needs to be made more specific and concrete. Culture-personality writers have, on the whole, tended to avoid this kind of limited investigation for a number of reasons having to do with the danger of viewing a given segment of behavior out of its cultural context. The emphasis upon cultural configurations was in part a reaction against such segmental interpretations. Moreover, ethnologists have not been concerned with specific psychological problems because they have been urgently concerned with gathering descriptive materials about non-literate societies before they vanished or were distorted by Western influences.

In his role as a psychologist the anthropologist needs to integrate his work as a careful ethnologist with a large body of psychological theory and research, including the non-clinical. The study of limited, specific, and verifiable propositions does not necessarily run counter to the ethnologist's insistence that a culture must be understood as a whole before specific psychological studies are undertaken. The cultures best suited for these purposes should be those concerning which a considerable amount of ethnological material is available. Such investigations would be valuable, not only as correctives of certain ethnocentric tendencies in psychological theorizing, but should also make constructive theoretical contributions on specific issues. Aside from the obvious benefits accruing to anthropology from this "gearing-in," another advantageous effect might be to arouse much more interest in anthropological work on the part of the great majority of psychologists and social psychologists.

A concern with more concretely limited and traditionally emphasized psychological problems would broaden the culture-personality ethnologist's range of choice of conceptual schemes and hypotheses. As it is now, the substantial choice is between no psychology at all and a brand of neo-Freudianism. The emphasis should not be on committing oneself to one school of thought or another, but of checking all rival hypotheses on specific problems by accepted scientific procedure.

Postscripts

Edward tylor, whose studies helped establish modern anthropology and whose view of culture appears earlier in these pages (see No. II:1), closed his two-volume work on *Primitive Culture* (1877) with a pessimistic view of the future. He feared that the future would bring a return of traditionalism and conformity and was depressed at the thought that the great thinkers of his time would become sources of authority—their hypotheses dogma, and their methods of free inquiry taboo. Yet Tylor believed that, though reaction was inevitable, it might be possible to experience it at a relatively high level of cultural development, thereby vitiating some of the effects of decline. In this regard he saw the science of culture as "a reformer's science" which could enable men to "move onward with clear view."

The shades of opinion to be discovered among contemporary anthropologists resemble those in the general intellectual community. It is therefore impossible to represent it with but a few statements. In closing the book with two anthropological *obiter dicta*, it is not the intention to place the weight of the science behind either of these views or their common aspects, but simply to provoke the reader to his own reflections on the meaning of our times in the context of a million years of culture.

36. MAN'S CONTROL OVER CIVILIZATION: AN ANTHROPOCENTRIC ILLUSION *

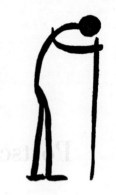

. . . numerous survivals of the anthropocentric bias still remain and here [in sociology], as elsewhere, they bar the way to science. It displeases man to renounce the unlimited power over the social order he has so long attributed to himself; and on the other hand, it seems to him that, if collective forces really exist, he is necessarily obliged to submit to them without being able to modify them. This makes him inclined to deny their existence. In vain have repeated experiences taught him that this omnipotence, the illusion of which he complacently entertains, has always been a cause of weakness in him; that his power over things really began only when he recognized that they have a nature of their own, and resigned himself to learning this nature from them. Rejected by all other sciences, this deplorable prejudice stubbornly maintains itself in sociology. Nothing is more urgent than to liberate our science from it, and this is the principal purpose of our efforts.
                                                                —EMILE DURKHEIM.

. . . it appears like a grandiose dream to think of controlling according to the will of man the course of social evolution.
                                                                —WM. F. OGBURN.

T̲HE BELIEF that man controls his civilization is widespread and deeply rooted. Customs and institutions, tools and machines, science, art, and philosophy are but man's creations and are therefore here only to do his bidding. It lies within man's power, therefore, to chart his course as he pleases, to mold civilization to his desires and needs. At least so he fondly believes.

* Leslie A. White, "Man's Control Over Civilization: An Anthropocentric Illusion," *The Scientific Monthly*, Vol. 66 (1948), pp. 235–247. Reprinted by permission of the author and publisher.

Thus we find a distinguished British scientist, the late Sir James Jeans, assuring us that

We no longer believe that human destiny is a plaything for spirits, good and evil, or for the machinations of the Devil. There is nothing to prevent our making the earth a paradise again—except ourselves. The scientific age has dawned, and we recognize that man himself is the master of his fate, the captain of his soul. He controls the course of his ship, and so, of course, is free to navigate it into fair waters or foul, or even to run it on the rocks.

Mr. Stanley Field, president of the Chicago Natural History Museum, appeals to anthropologists in espousing free will:

But if we listen to the anthropologists, who can scientifically demonstrate that it is not color of skin, or type of hair or features, or difference of religion, that creates problems between peoples, but factors for which man is responsible and which he can control or change if he will, then we shall at least come within sight of that better world which we now realize we must achieve if we are not finally to perish as victims of our own perversity.

Professor Lewis G. Westgate tells us that man can "take the problem of his future in hand and solve it. . . . The mind that can weigh the infinitely distant stars . . . track down the minute carriers of disease . . . dig the Panama Canal . . . can solve its social problems when and if it decides to do so."

It would seem that the salvation of an earlier era has become the social reconstruction of today: we can achieve it if we will; if we fail, it is because of our "perversity."

When, however, we look for examples of man's control over culture, we begin first to wonder, then to doubt. We shall not begin our inquiry by asking if two world wars in one generation are evidence of planning or perversity, or whether Germany and Japan were crushed and Soviet Russia made dominant in Eurasia in accordance with a farsighted plan or as a result of blindness and folly. We shall start with something much more modest. During the past century we have witnessed attempts to control tiny and relatively insignificant segments of our culture, such as spelling, the calendar, and the system of weights and measures, to name but a few. There have been repeated and heroic attempts to simplify spelling and make it more rational, to devise a more rational calendar, and to adopt an ordered system of weights and measures instead of the cumbersome, illogical agglomeration of folk measurements we now use. But what successes can we point to? Reform in spelling has been negligible. We have succeeded to a considerable extent but not wholly in eliminating the *u* from such words as *honor*. But to do away with silent letters, such as the *b* in *lamb*, is too big a mountain for us to move. And such spellings and pronunciations as *rough, cough, dough,* and *through* are much too strong to yield to our puny efforts. It usually takes a great political and social upheaval to effect a significant change in spelling or a calendrical system as the French and Bolshevik revolutions have made clear. And as for the metric system, it has found a place among the little band of esoterics in science, but yards, ounces, rods, pints, and furlongs still serve—awkwardly and inefficiently—the layman.

We begin to wonder. If we are not able to perform such tiny and insignificant feats as eliminating the *b* from *lamb,* or modifying our calendar, how can we hope to construct a new social order on a worldwide scale?

Let us look about us further. Men and women are forever contending with fashions. Man perennially rebels against his attire. It is often uncomfortable, injurious to the health at times, and, some men think, the ordinary costume is unaesthetic, the formal attire ridiculous. But what can he do? He must wear his coat and tie no matter how hot the weather. He is not permitted to wear pink or blue shoes. And as for "evening clothes"—he must submit to them or stay home. Man's vaunted control over civilization is not particularly conspicuous in this sector.

But if man is helpless, woman is an abject slave, in the grip of fashion. She must submit to any change, no matter how fantastic or ugly. To be sure, she may not realize that the new designs are fantastic and ugly at the time; "the latest style" can becloud a woman's judgment. But one has only to browse through an album of old snapshots to realize that beauty, grace, and charm do not dominate the course of fashion.

And as for women's skirts! First they are short; then they are long. A distinguished anthropologist, Professor A. L. Kroeber, of the University of California, has made a very interesting and revealing study of the dimensions of women's dresses over a considerable period of time. He found that "the basic dimensions of modern European feminine dress alternate with fair regularity between maxima and minima which in most cases average about fifty years apart so that the full-wave length of their periodicity is around a century." The rhythms are regular and uniform. Women have nothing to say about it. Even the designers and creators must conform to the curve of change. We find no control by man—or woman—here, only an inexorable and impersonal trend. When a maximum point on the curve is reached, the trend is reversed and skirts lengthen or shorten as the case may be. Women are helpless; they can do nothing but follow the trend. When the curve ascends they must shorten their dresses; when it descends, they must lengthen them. It may seem remarkable that a great class of citizens who cannot even control the dimensions of their own skirts will nevertheless organize themselves into clubs to administer the affairs of the world. We shall return to this point later.

Few men would undertake to repair an automobile or a radio without some understanding of its mechanism. We tend more and more nowadays to leave medicine and surgery to those who know how. Knowledge and skill are required even to make good pies or home brew. But in matters of society and culture everyone feels qualified to analyze, diagnose, and prescribe. It is one of the premises of democracy that not only do the people rule, but they have the requisite knowledge and understanding to do it effectively. In matters political, one man's view is as good as another's.

When, however, we examine the knowledge and understanding with which the affairs of the nation are administered, we begin again to wonder. We find the most august authorities espousing different and even contradictory views on such subjects as inflation, the function of labor leaders, the divorce rate, the popularity of crooners, and so on. This is a picture of the anarchy of ignorance.

When we turn from matters of national proportions, such as the cause of inflation, to lesser problems, we are not always reassured. Does capital punishment diminish the number of murders? Does the use of alcohol affect the divorce rate? Why do people keep dogs? They are noisy, dirty, unhealthful, useless, and expensive. To say that they are kept because people like them is merely to phrase the problem in a different form. Why don't they "like" raccoons? They are cute, cleanly in their habits, and very amiable.

The fact is we don't really know very much about the civilization we live in. Let us take one of the simplest and most elementary questions imaginable: Why does our society prohibit polygamy? Other societies permit plural mates, and Western Europe once did also. But now we feel very strongly about it. We will put a man in a prison for years if he takes unto himself more than one wife at one time. His wives may be perfectly satisfied with the arrangement and he may have injured no one. Yet we put him in gaol. Why? Why not have one more wife and one less schoolmarm? There are, to be sure, ready answers to these questions: polygamy is "wrong," "immoral," "undemocratic," etc. But practices are not prohibited because they are "wrong"; they are wrong because they have been prohibited. It is not wrong to buy and sell whisky now; it was while the Eighteenth Amendment was on the books. And as for democracy, we permit a man to have two yachts if he can afford them, why not two wives?

I know of no really adequate answer to this question in such literature of social science as I am acquainted with. As a matter of fact, the question is very seldom raised. I have looked for it in a great number of treatises on sociology and anthropology written during the past quarter century without finding it. Some social scientists of the latter half of the nineteenth century tried to explain the prohibition of polygamy, but we cannot accept their conclusions.

The fact is we are ignorant. We do not know the solution to such an elementary problem as singular or plural mates. And in our day, we have not reached the point of asking such questions, to say nothing of answering them. As Archibald MacLeish has said, "We know all the answers, but we have not yet asked the questions." Over half a century ago the great French savant, Emile Durkheim, commented upon the immaturity of social science as follows:

> In the present state of the science we really do not even know what are the principal social institutions, such as the state, or the family; what is the right of property or contract. . . . We are almost completely ignorant of the factors on which they depend . . . ; we are scarcely beginning to shed even a glimmer of light on some of these points. Yet one has only to glance through the works on sociology to see how rare is the appreciation of this ignorance and these difficulties.

Despite the progress that has been made since *The Rules of Sociological Method* was written, this statement has a certain relevance today. If the science of society and civilization is still so immature as to be unable to solve such a tiny and elementary problem as the prohibition of polygamy, where are the knowledge and understanding requisite to planning a new social system, to constructing a new world order? One would not expect a savage craftsman, whose best tools are made of chipped flint, to design and build a locomotive.

Let us have a look at this civilization man thinks he controls. The first thing we notice is its antiquity. There is no part of it, whether it be technology, institutions, science, or philosophy, that does not have its roots in the remote past. The lens of the new 200-inch telescope, for example, is made of glass. Glass emerged from the manufacture of faïence in ancient Egypt, which in turn originated apparently as a by-product of burning bricks and pottery, which followed the use of sun-dried brick and, earlier, mud daubs of Neolithic, or even Paleolithic, huts. The United Nations can be traced back to primitive tribal councils and beyond. Modern mathematics goes back to counting on one's fingers, and so on. Culture is as old as man himself. It had its beginnings a million-odd years ago when man first started to use articulate speech, and it has continued and developed to the present day. Culture is a continuous, cumulative, and progressive affair.

Everyone—every individual, every generation, every group—has, since the very earliest period of human history, been born into a culture, a civilization, of some sort. It might be simple, crude, and meager, or it might be highly developed. But all cultures, whatever their respective degrees of development, have technologies (tools, machines), social systems (customs, institutions), beliefs (lore, philosophy, science), and forms of art. This means that when a baby is born into a cultural milieu, he will be influenced by it. As a matter of fact, his culture will determine how he will think, feel, and act. It will determine what language he will speak, what clothes if any he will wear, what gods he will believe in, and how he will marry, select and prepare his foods, treat the sick, and dispose of the dead. What else *could* one do but react to the culture that surrounds him from birth to death? No people makes its own culture; it inherits it ready-made from its ancestors or borrows it from its neighbors.

It is easy enough for man to believe that he has made his culture, each generation contributing its share, and that it is he who controls and directs its course through the ages. Does he not chip the arrowheads and stone axes, build carts and dynamos, coin money and spend it, elect presidents and depose kings, compose symphonies and carve statues, worship gods and wage war? But one cannot always rely upon the obvious. It was once obvious that the earth remained stationary while the sun moved; anyone could see that for himself. We are now approaching a point in modern thought where we are beginning to suspect that it is not man who controls culture but the other way around. The feat of Copernicus in dispelling the geocentric illusion more than four hundred years ago is being duplicated in our day by the culturologist who is dissipating the illusion that man controls his culture.

Although it is man who chips arrowheads, composes symphonies, etc., we cannot explain culture merely by saying that "man produced it." There is not a single question that we would want to ask about culture that can be answered by saying, "Man did thus and so." We want to know why culture developed as it did; why it assumed a great variety of forms while preserving at the same time a certain uniformity; why the rate of cultural change has accelerated. We want to know why some cultures have money and slaves and others do not; why some have trial by jury, others ordeal by magic; why some have kings, others chiefs or presidents; why some use milk, others loathe it; why some permit, others prohibit, polygamy. To explain all these things by saying, "Man wanted them that way," is of course absurd. A device that explains everything explains nothing.

Before we go very far, we discover that we must disregard man entirely in our efforts to explain cultural growth and cultural differences —in short, culture or civilization as a whole. Man may be regarded as a constant so far as cultural change is concerned. Man is one species, and, despite differences of skin, eye, and hair color, shape of head, lips, and nose, stature, etc., which after all are superficial, he is highly uniform in such fundamental features as brain, bone, muscle, glands, and sense organs. And he has undergone no appreciable evolutionary change during the past 50,000 years at least. We may, therefore, regard man as a constant, both with regard to the races extant today and with regard to his ancestors during the past tens of thousands of years. Man has a certain structure and certain functions; he has certain desires and needs. These are related to culture, of course, but only in a *general*, not a specific, way. We may say that culture as a whole serves the needs of man as a species. But this does not and cannot help us at all when we try to account for the variations of specific cultures. You cannot explain variables by appeal to a constant. You cannot explain the vast range of cultural variation by invoking man, a biological constant. In England in A.D. 1500 there was one type of culture; in Japan, another. Neither culture can be explained in terms of the physical type associated with it. Culture underwent change in England between A.D. 1500 and 1900, as it did in Japan. But these changes cannot be explained by pointing to the inhabitants in each case; they did not change. Plainly, we cannot explain cultures in terms of Man.

Nor can cultural differences be explained in terms of environment. Quite apart from the difficulty of accounting for differences in musical styles, forms of writing, codes of etiquette, rules of marriage, mortuary rites, etc., in terms of environment, we soon discover that even economic, industrial, and social systems cannot be so explained. The environment of central Europe so far as climate, flora, fauna, topography, and mineral resources are concerned has remained constant for centuries. The culture of the region, however, has varied enormously. Here again we see the fallacy of explaining the variable by appeal to a constant.

If, then, we cannot explain cultures in terms of race or physical type, or in terms of psychological processes, and if appeal to environment is equally futile, how *are* they to be accounted for and made intelligible to us?

There seems to be only one answer left, and that is fairly plain—after one becomes used to it, at least. Culture must be explained in terms of culture. As we have already noted, culture is a continuum. Each trait or organization of traits, each stage of development, grows out of an earlier cultural situation. The steam engine can be traced back to the origins of metallurgy and fire. International cartels have grown out of all the processes of exchange and distribution since the Old Stone Age and before. Our science, philosophy, religion, and art have developed out of earlier forms. Culture is a vast stream of tools, utensils, customs, and beliefs that are constantly interacting with one another, creating new combinations and syntheses. New elements are added constantly to the stream; obsolete traits drop out. The culture of today is but the cross section of this stream at the present moment, the resultant of the age-old process of interaction, selection, rejection, and accumulation that has preceded us. And the culture of tomorrow will be but the culture of today plus one more day's growth. The numerical coefficient of today's culture may be said to be 365,000,000 (i.e., a million years of days); that of tomorrow, 365,000,000 + 1. The culture of the present was determined by the past, and the culture of the future will be but a continuation of the trend of the present. Thus in a very real sense, *culture makes itself.* At least, if one wishes to explain culture scientifically, he must proceed *as if* culture made itself, *as if* man had nothing to do with the determination of its course or content. Man must *be* there, of course, to make the existence of the culture process possible. But the nature and behavior of the process itself is self-determined. It rests upon its own principles; it is governed by its own laws.

Thus, culture makes man what he is and at the same time makes itself. An Eskimo, Bantu, Tibetan, Swede, or American is what he is, he thinks, feels, and acts as he does because his culture influences—"stimulates"—him in such a way as to evoke these responses. The Eskimo or American has had no part in producing the culture into which he was thrust at birth. It was already there; he could not escape it; he could do nothing but react to it, and that on its own terms. The English language, the Christian religion, our political institutions, our mills, mines, factories, railroads, telephones, armies, navies, race tracks, dance halls, and all the other thousands of things that comprise our civilization are here in existence today. They have weight, mass, and momentum. They cannot be made to disappear by waving a wand, nor can their structure and behavior be altered by an act of will. We must come to terms with them as we find them today. And they will be tomorrow what their trend of development in the past dictates. We can only trot along with them, hoping to keep up.

Man has long cherished the illusion of omnipotence. It is flattering and comforting to his ego. In days gone by, man has believed that he could control the weather; countless primitive peoples have had rituals for making rain, stilling high winds, or averting storms. Many have had ceremonies by means of which the course of the sun in the heavens could be "controlled." With the advance of science, however, man's faith in his omnipotence has diminished. But he still believes that he can control his civilization.

The philosophy of science—of cause-and-effect relationships, of determinism—has been firmly established in the study of physical phenomena. It is well entrenched in the biological field also. Psychology may have demonstrated the operation of the principle of cause and effect, of determinism, in mental processes, and may have dispelled the notion of free will for the *individual*. But social science is still so immature as to permit one to find refuge in a collective free will. As Professor A. L. Kroeber has recently observed:

I suspect that the resistence [to the thesis of cultural determinism] goes back to the common and deeply implanted assumption that our wills are free. As this assumption has had to yield ground elsewhere, it has taken refuge in the collective, social, and historical sphere. Since the chemists, physiologists, and psychologists have unlimbered their artillery, the personal freedom of the will is thankless terrain to maintain. Culture they have not yet attacked; so that becomes a refuge. Whatever the degree to which we have ceased to assert being free agents as individuals, in the social realm we can still claim to shape our destinies. The theologian is piping pretty small, but the social reformer very loud. We are renouncing the kingdom of heaven, but going to establish a near-millennium on earth. Our personal wills may be determined, but by collectivizing them we can still have social freedom.

Primitive man could believe that he could control the weather only because he was ignorant; he knew virtually nothing of meteorology. And today it is only our profound and comprehensive ignorance of the nature of culture that makes it possible for us to believe that we direct and control it. As man's knowledge and understanding grew in meteorology, his illusion of power and control was dissipated. And as our understanding of culture increases, our illusion of control will languish and disappear. As Durkheim once observed, "As far as social facts are concerned, we still have the mentality of primitives."

Needless to say, this is not the view taken by many today who look to science for our salvation. Far from expecting belief in our ability to control to diminish with the advance of social science, many people expect just the reverse. It has become the fashion these days to declare that if only our social sciences were as advanced as the physical sciences, then we could control our culture as we now control the physical forces of nature. The following quotation from a letter published in *Science* is a conservative statement of this point of view:

For if, by employing the scientific method, men can come to understand and control the atom, there is reasonable likelihood that they can in the same way learn to understand and control human group behavior. . . . It is quite within reasonable probability that social science can provide these techniques [i.e., for "keeping the peace"] if it is given anything like the amount of support afforded to physical science in developing the atomic bomb.

The premise underlying this view is unsound. It assumes that wars are caused, or at least made possible, by ignorance and the lack of social control that goes with ignorance. It assumes that, given understanding through generous grants of funds to social scientists, wars could be prevented—the "peace could be kept." The lack of understanding and realism displayed here is pathetic. The instinct of self-preservation of a society that subsidized atom-bomb inventors rather than social scientists holding views such as these is a sure one. Wars are not caused by ignorance, nor can "the peace be kept" by the findings of social scientists. Wars are struggles between social organisms—called *nations*—for survival; struggles for the possession and use of the resources of the earth; for fertile fields; coal, oil, and iron deposits; for uranium mines; for seaports and waterways; for markets and trade routes; for military bases. No amount of understanding will alter or remove the basis of this struggle, any more than an understanding of the ocean's tides will diminish or terminate their flow.

But the fallacy of assuming that we can increase and perfect our control over civilization through social science is even more egregious than we have indicated. To call upon science, the essence of which is acceptance of the principles of cause and effect and determinism, to support a philosophy of free will is fairly close to the height of absurdity. Verily, Science has become the modern magic! The belief that man could work his will upon nature and man alike *if only he had the right formulas* once flourished in primitive society as magic. It is still with us today, but we now call it science.

No amount of development of the social sciences would increase or perfect man's control over civilization by one iota. In the man-culture system, man is the dependent, culture the independent, variable. What man thinks, feels, and does is determined by his culture. And culture behaves in accordance with its own laws. A mature development of social science would only make this fact clear.

The philosophy of free will and omnipotence is rampant in the field of education. "Educators," high-school principals, commencement orators, and others never seem to tire of telling the world that its salvation lies in education. Naturally, one does not expect meat packers to preach vegetarianism, and it is reasonable for educators to advocate schooling and to urge the support of schools and colleges. But one could wish that they would place their propaganda on a somewhat higher intellectual plane; after all, one expects more of educators than of vendors of soap and cigarettes. The fact is, however, that the appeals and claims of educators are seldom more realistic than soap and cigarette ads. Education will no more cure the ills of society than cigarette X will soothe the nerves, or soap Y beautify the hands, of the user. As a matter of fact, the premise upon which the educator's claim rests is, if anything, less sound than the premise of the advertisements, for these are at least relevant, whether sound or unsound, whereas the educator's premise is hardly even relevant. The soap or cigarette will certainly have *some* effect upon the user. But education does not, strictly speaking, have an effect upon culture at all; *it is a part of it*. Education, whether formalized in the classroom or informal in the course of everyday living, *is one of the processes of culture:* it is the means of transmitting culture from one individual, one group, or one generation, to another. Being a process *within* the system that is culture, it is therefore fallacious to think of it as acting upon culture from the outside. It is not people who control their culture through education; it is rather the other way around: *education is what culture is doing to people,* namely, equipping them with ideas, beliefs, ideals, codes of conduct, tools, utensils, machines, etc. —in short, determining how they shall think, feel, and behave.

The position taken here will of course be vigorously denied and opposed. People do not give up their illusions easily. As the distinguished anthropologist, A. L. Kroeber, has put it:

> Our minds instinctively resist the first shock of the recognition of a thing [cultural determinism] so intimately woven into us and yet so far above and so uncontrollable by our wills. We feel driven to deny its reality, to deny even the validity of dealing with it as an entity; just as men at large have long and bitterly resented admitting the existence of purely automatic forces and system in the realm that underlies and carries and makes possible the existence of our personalities: the realm of nature.

A common reaction—verbal reflex—to the theory of cultural determinism is to brand it "fatalistic" or "defeatist." The choice of these words is significant. Why is it that, when one employs the principle of cause and effect in the realm of physical and chemical phenomena, no one cries "fatalism," but the instant one applies it to human cultural phenomena this accusation leaps forth? Why is it that an admission of our inability to control the weather brings forth no charge of "defeatism," whereas this reproach is promptly leveled against anyone who recognizes man's inability to control the course of civilization?

The reason is fairly plain. "Fatalism" implies free will; "defeatism," omnipotence. When atoms, cells, or tissues behave in accordance with their nature and properties, no one calls it fatalistic because no one expects freedom of choice and action of them. But when one asserts that cultural phenomena have a nature of their own and consequently must behave in terms of their nature, the response is not an acceptance of the principle of cause and effect but a charge of "fatalism."

> To many educated minds [the great English anthropologist, E. B. Tylor, wrote many years ago], there seems something presumptuous and repulsive in the view that the history of mankind is part and parcel of the history of nature, that our thoughts, wills, and actions accord with laws as definite as those which

govern the motion of waves, the combination of acids and bases, and the growth of plants. . . . If law is anywhere it is everywhere.

We have combined "a scientific realism, based on mechanism," says Alfred North Whitehead, with "an unwavering belief in the world of men and of the higher animals as being composed of *self-determining organisms*" (emphasis ours). He feels that this "radical inconsistency" is responsible for "much that is half-hearted and wavering in our civilization. It . . . enfeebles . . . [thought] by reason of the inconsistency lurking in the background."

Implicit in the charge of "fatalism" and "defeatism" is the further notion of refutation. To brand a view "fatalistic" is, to many minds, to call it false as well. "Cultural determinism is fatalistic and therefore false," is about the way the reasoning would go if it were made explicit. "How can determinism exist?" is the question that is implied but unspoken. "Determinism is unthinkable." And so it is to one possessed by a philosophy of free will. We find this point of view rather well expressed by Lawrence K. Frank in a recent article, "What is Social Order?"

Perhaps the major obstacle we face today, therefore, is this essentially defeatist tradition expressed in the various conceptions of social order described earlier, as above and beyond all human control. . . . In this situation, therefore, we can and we must find the courage to view social order as that which must be achieved by man himself.

Of course man can "find the courage" to view social order as something "that must be achieved by himself." It does not take courage to do this, however; what is required is ignorance and hope. "Must find the courage," "must be achieved by man himself," is hardly the language of science. It is, rather, exhortation and rhetoric—of a type with which we have long been familiar: "if we will but purpose in our hearts. . . ."

No doubt the first to question man's control over the weather, the first to claim that the winds will blow, the rain and snow fall, the seasons come and go, in accordance with their own nature rather than in obedience to man's wish and will expressed in spell and ritual, were accused of "fatalism" and "defeatism," if, indeed, they were not dealt with more harshly. But, in time, we have come to accept our impotence in this regard and to become reconciled to it. If it be argued that man cannot control the weather because that is a part of the external world, whereas culture, being man-made, is subject to his control, it must be pointed out that the exact opposite is the case. It is precisely in the realm of the external world that man's control is possible. He can harness the energies of rivers, fuels, and atoms because he, as one of the forces of nature, lies *outside* their respective systems and can therefore act upon them. But man, as an animal organism, as a species, lies *within* the man-culture system, and there he is the dependent, not the independent, variable; his behavior is merely the function of his culture, not its determinant. Both theoretically and practically, therefore, it is possible for man to exert more control over the weather than over culture, for he can exert *some* control over the former even now (dispel fog on airfields) and he may increase this control in the future. But he exerts no control whatever over his culture, and theoretically there is no possibility of his ever doing so.

The usual reactions to this manifesto of cultural determinism are as unwarranted as are the assumptions of free will, from which, of course, these responses flow. After expostulating on the theme of "fatalism" and "defeatism," the conventional protest goes on to demand: "What is the use then of our efforts? Why should we try to do anything to improve our lot if we have no control over our culture? Why not just sit back and let the evolutionary process take care of everything? Of what use could a science of culture possibly be to us if control lies beyond our grasp? What good is an understanding of culture if there is nothing we can do about it?"

These questions are naive and betray a lack of understanding of what the cultural determinist—the culturologist—is trying to say. The determinist does not assert that man is irrelevant to the culture process. He knows full well that the contrary is the case; that man is an absolute prerequisite to it; that without man there could be no culture. He realizes very clearly the essential role that man plays in the system that is man-and-culture. What the culturologist contends is that in this system the human organism is not the determinant; that the behavior of the culture process cannot be explained in terms of this organism but only in terms of the culture itself; that the growth and changes among the Indo-European languages, for example, cannot be accounted for in terms of man's nerves, muscles, senses, or organs of speech; or in terms of his hopes, needs, fears, or imagination. Language must be explained in terms of language.

But to turn to some of the specific questions with which dissatisfaction with the philosophy of determinism is expressed: In the first place, we cannot "just sit back" and let the evolutionary process take care of all our problems. While we live we are confronted by our culture and we must come to terms with it. Even just sitting back, incubating a case of dementia praecox, is "doing something about it." So is committing suicide; as a matter of fact, suicide rates for various societies provide excellent indexes of cultural determinism. In some societies, the rate is high; in others, suicide is virtually nonexistent. This is not because suicide determinants are more abundant in the chromosomes of some

populations than of others. It is due to the fact that the cultural determinants vary: hara-kiri is something that a culture does to an organism
that, of its own nature, tends to persevere in that form of motion we call
"life." It is obvious that we cannot avoid reacting to our culture.

To assume that the process of cultural evolution will take care of
everything without effort on our part is of course absurd, and constitutes
no part of the determinist's philosophy. Of course we must exert ourselves while we live, we cannot do otherwise. But the question is not
"Who does the work, ourselves or cultural evolution?" It is obvious that
the energy is expended by or through human beings. The question is,
*What determines the nature, the form and content of this expression
of energy in the culture process, the human organism or the extrasomatic
culture?* The answer is of course fairly obvious—after a small amount
of reflection. Let us consider two groups of human organisms, A and B.
Group A raises taro, catches fish, carves wood, makes no pottery, speaks
a Polynesian language, has chiefs but no currency, is nonliterate, drinks
kava, is greatly concerned with genealogy, and so on. Group B mines
coal and iron, speaks Welsh, imports its food from the outside, uses
money, is literate, drinks ale, etc. Now the question is, Why does each
group behave as it does? Is it that one group of organisms possesses traits
or characteristics—genes, instincts, or psychological tendencies—that
cause them to drink kava rather than ale? This is, of course, ridiculous;
the one group of organisms is fundamentally like the other biologically.
It is obvious that each group of organisms behaves as it does because
each is reacting to a particular set of cultural stimuli. It is obvious also
that a consideration of the human organism is totally irrelevant to the
question. Why is one group stimulated by one set of stimuli rather than
by another? This is a cultural historical question, not a biological or
psychological one. So, one is not so silly as to say, "Why should we mine
coal or catch fish? Let our culture do it." The question is not Who mines
the coal? but What is the determinant of this behavior? And, the culturologist points out the obvious: the culture is the determinant.

The reaction of many sincere, altruistic and conscientious people, upon
being told that it is not they who control their culture and direct its
course, is "Why then should we try to do good, to better our lot and that
of mankind?" We have answered this question in part already. In the
first place one cannot avoid trying to do something. As long as one
accepts life and is willing to continue with it, he must exert himself.
"Trying" is merely the name we give to the effort exerted in the process
of living. To strive for this or that, therefore, is inseparable from our
lives. But *what* one strives for and *how* his effort is expressed is determined by his culture. For example, the goal of one people may be
eternal life in heaven, for which their terrestrial existence is but a prep-

aration. The goal of another might be the good life "here below." One group may deny the reality of sickness; another may admit its existence and try to combat it. One group may use charms and incantations; another, clinics and laboratories. Whatever the goal and whatever the means employed to reach it are matters determined by the culture of the group.

But, it should be pointed out with emphasis, this is not a philosophy of defeatism or hopelessness by any means. Least of all does it declare that one's efforts do not count. The fact that one's efforts to stamp out tuberculosis are culturally determined in no way minimizes the effort or the result. A life saved is a life saved. A letter written to a congressman has an *effect,* too, no matter what kind or how much. A resolution on world affairs passed by a woman's club has a real function in society, although it may be a very different one from that imagined by the good ladies. The question we raise is not one of the value of effort or whether effort has consequences. Human effort is just as real as anything in the realm of the geologist. And effort is followed by consequences, just as effect follows cause in physics or geology. Living human beings cannot help but exert themselves, and everything they do counts for something in one way or another. Far from wishing to deny or ignore this, we wish to emphasize it. But this is not the question raised by the culturologist, the cultural determinist. What he claims is not that it is futile to try because what one does counts for nought, but that what one does, how he does it, and the end and purpose for which it is done is culturally determined, is determined by the culture of the group rather than by the free will of the individual or of the group. More than that, what a person or group desires is determined or at least defined by the culture, not by them. What constitutes the "good life" for any people is always culturally defined.

From the cultural determinist's point of view, human beings are merely the instruments through which cultures express themselves. A physician, saving lives each day, is an instrument through which certain cultural forces express themselves; if they were not there or if they were different, the organism in question would not be practicing medicine, or he would practice it in a different way. The gangster, evangelist, revolutionist, reformer, policeman, impoverished beggar, wealthy parasite, teacher, soldier, and shaman are likewise instruments of cultural action and expression; each is a type of primate organism grasped and wielded by a certain set of culture traits. It is only the inveterate habit of thinking anthropocentrically that makes this point of view seem strange or ridiculous.

But, granting that what we do counts even though it is culturally determined, of what use is it to develop a science of culture if we cannot control civilization or direct its course? We have a science of pathology in order to combat disease, sciences of physics and chemistry to control the external world. But if we do not control our culture and cannot ever hope to control it, of what use would a science of culture be? We might begin our reply to this question by asking, Of what value is it to know the temperature of a star a million light-years away? Questions such as these betray a limited understanding of science. Science is not primarily a matter of control in the sense of harnessing rivers with hydroelectric plants or constructing uranium piles. Science is a means of adjustment; control is but one aspect of adjustment. Man finds himself in a universe to which he must adjust if he is to continue to live in it. Mythology and science are means of adjustment; they are interpretations of the world in terms of which man behaves. There is, of course, a vast difference in terms of adjustment between a philosophy that interprets stars as a flock of snowbirds lost in the sky and one that measures their masses, distances, dimensions, and temperatures. This difference is a very practical one, too, in terms of the contribution that each philosophy makes to the security of life.

Our ancestors once thought they could control the weather, as contemporary savages still do. They finally outgrew this illusion, even going so far as to outgrow calling the new view "fatalistic" and "defeatist." But we do not think a knowledge and an understanding of weather and climate useless. On the contrary, we are devoting more time and money to meterorology now than ever before. Here again we see the situation in terms of adjustment rather than *control*. We may not be able to control the weather, but adjust to it we must. And knowledge and understanding make for more effective and satisfying adjustments. It would be advantageous if we *could* control the weather. But if we cannot, then weather prediction is the next best thing. And for prediction we must have knowledge and understanding.

So it is with culture. We cannot control its course, but we can learn to predict it. As a matter of fact, we make predictions all the time, and many of them are quite accurate: wheat production, traffic fatalities, freight carloadings, births, exhaustion of oil reserves, and many other matters are already within the reach of limited but nevertheless valuable prediction. If our ability to predict were greatly increased by the development and maturation of a science of culture, the possibilities of a rational, effective, and humane adjustment between man and culture and between one cultural segment and another would be increased accordingly. If, for example, a science of culture could demonstrate that the trend of social evolution is toward larger political groupings, then the chances of making the futile attempt to restore or maintain the independence of small nations would be lessened. If the trend of cultural evolution is away from private property and free enterprise, why strive to perpetuate them? If it could be shown that international wars will continue as long as independent, sovereign nations exist, then certain delusions now popular would find less nourishment and support. The fact is that culture has been evolving as an unconscious, blind, bloody, brutal, tropismatic process so far. It has not yet reached the point where intelligence, self-consciousness, and understanding are very conspicuous. Our ignorance is still deep-rooted and widespread. We do not understand even some of the most elementary things—the prohibition of polygamy, for example. In short, we are so ignorant that we can still believe that it is we who make our culture and control its course.

This ignorance is not surprising, however. It has not been very long since we gave up burning witches, cudgeling hysterics to drive out demons, and other savage practices. Even in technology, which tends to outstrip the social and ideological sectors, we have surpassed the savage at two points—fire making and the use of the bow and arrow—only within the past century or two. Chemical matches are but a little more than a century old, and within the past hundred years the bow and arrow was used in bison hunting on the American plains in preference to the best firearms available at the time. It was only yesterday, culturologically speaking, that a small portion of mankind began to emerge from a condition of savagery. For most of his career thus far man has subsisted wholly upon wild foods; less than 2 percent of human history, as a matter of fact, has elapsed since the origin of agriculture. Other significant indexes: some 0.7 percent of culture history since the beginning of metallurgy, 0.35 percent since the first alphabet, 0.033 percent since Galileo, 0.009 percent since the publication of Darwin's The Origin of Species, and only 0.002 percent since William Jennings Bryan and the Scopes trial. A mature, urbane, and rational civilization is not to be achieved in a mere million years from the anthropoid level.

It should be made clear that, if an adequate understanding should come about as a consequence of a science of culture, it would not have been "us" who achieved it but our culture. In the interaction of elements in the culture process, those traits less effective in providing adequate adjustment in terms of understanding and control are gradually relinquished and replaced by more effective traits. Thus, bronze axes replace stone axes, ikons and spells give way to laboratories and clinics, and, finally, a science of human culture begins to challenge the primitive philosophy of omnipotence and free will. The new science will of course have to prove its superiority over the older view, just as astronomy, chemistry, and medicine have in other sectors of experience. The success of science— the philosophy of materialism, of cause and effect, of determinism— in the physical and biological sectors of experience encourages us greatly in the belief that this point of view and these techniques of interpretation will prove effective in the social sphere also.

Our role in this process is a modest one. Neither as groups nor as individuals do we have a choice of roles or of fates. Swedes are born into their culture just as Zulus, Tibetans, and Yankees are born into theirs. And each individual is thrust by birth into some particular place in the "magnetic field" of his culture, there to be molded by the particular organization of cultural influences that play upon him. Thus, he may have the belief that typhoid exists only in the mind, or is caused by witches or bacilli, thrust upon him—or "into his mind." He may be endowed with a belief in personal immortality, the efficacy of prayer, or the periodic law of Mendelyeev. He may be inspired to preach the only true faith to the heathen in distant lands, or to wear out his life in a genetics laboratory, or to believe that "only saps work." To be sure, the response of the human organism to cultural stimulation will vary with the quality of the organism. Some will be silk purses; others, sow's ears. The order in which an organism undergoes experiences is important too; the influence of events $a, b, c,$ will not be the same as $a, c, b.$ An experience will have one effect at fifteen; quite another at fifty. There is room, therefore, for almost infinite variety of permutation and combination in the experience of individual organisms.

Man discovers his place in the cosmos slowly and accepts it with extreme reluctance. Time was when his solid earth was planted in the center, the sun and stars spread upon the vault of heaven, and men and gods together acted out the drama of life and death. It was all so compact, so familiar, so secure. Then it was that man, like God, could cry, "Let there be light," and there was light. Like God, too, man was "omnipotent," if, however, to a lesser degree. With his magic formulas, his spells, prayers, charms, and rituals, mighty man could control the weather, the seasons, and even enlist the gods in the service of man. Now it is different. Man finds himself but one of innumerable animal species crawling about on an insignificant planetary speck, fighting, feeding, breeding, dying. Once the child of God, he now finds himself an ex-ape. But he has acquired a new faculty, one unknown among all other species: articulate speech. As a consequence of this, a new way of life has been developed: culture. But this culture, this mass of extrasomatic tools, institutions, and philosophies, has a life and laws of its own. Man is just beginning to understand this.

Man is wholly at the mercy of external forces, astronomic and geologic. As a matter of fact, it is rather disconcerting to think of how narrow is the margin within which man lives. Change the temperature, velocity, rainfall, or atmosphere of the earth but a little and life would cease. It is a curious and, from a cosmic viewpoint, momentary, concatenation of circumstances that has made life possible. Man did long rebel against his dependence upon these outside forces; to be wholly at their mercy was unendurable. As a matter of fact, man has employed his precious and unique gift of speech more to deny the facts of his existence than to improve upon them. But a certain portion of the human race has come at last to accept our dependence upon nature and to try to make the most of it.

And so it is with culture. Belief in our omnipotence has, as Durkheim says, always been a source of weakness to us. But we are now discovering the true nature of culture and we can in time reconcile ourselves to this extrasomatic order as we have to the astronomic, geologic, and meteorologic orders. To give up magic and mythology, which promised much but yielded nothing—nothing but the soothing comfort of illusion— was a painful experience. But to receive and accept science and a technology that promises less but achieves a great deal is to reach a goal most men are loathe to lose. We may believe that knowledge and understanding of culture will make for a more satisfactory life, just as these traits have been of value in physics and biology. To be sure, understanding culture will not, as we have argued here, alter its course or change the "fate" that it has in store for us, any more than understanding the weather or the tides will change them. But as long as man remains an inquiring primate he will crave understanding. And a growing Science of Culture will provide him with it.

37. TALK WITH A STRANGER *

O NE DAY last month as I sat on an old bench near my house on the outskirts of Chicago, a stranger appeared and sat down beside me.

"Do you mind if I join you?" he asked. "There is some information I want very much to get. But perhaps I interrupt your thoughts?"

I told him that my thoughts were at the moment not much—I had been trying to think of an address I was to give to some college students.

He asked me what I would say to them.

"Give them good advice," I replied. "That is the usual thing to do."

"About what?" He seemed really interested.

"I don't quite know," was my answer, "but the usual thing is to tell them about the importance of the free mind and the privilege they enjoy in getting an education. And that sort of thing. You know—exhort them and commend them and encourage them."

"If you can advise them," said the stranger, "perhaps you can advise me."

I remembered that he had said he wanted information. My first thought had been that he would ask me about what kind of dogfood I bought for my dog—you know, market research—or that perhaps he was making a political canvass of our neighborhood. But his first question showed me that these guesses were very wrong.

"I wish you would explain to me about this war that I hear is going on—the war that is now cold and might get hot. Are you people at war with each other?"

That didn't seem to me the way to put it. I started to explain. "The Russians want to conquer everybody, by propaganda if they can and by force if they have to. So they make monstrous weapons that threaten us and that force us to make monstrous weapons to threaten them. We have some bombs big enough to kill millions of people that we carry around

* Robert Redfield, "Talk with a Stranger," An Occasional Paper on the Free Society (New York: The Fund for the Republic, 1958). Reprinted by permission of the author and The Fund for the Republic.

567

in airplanes in case the Russians begin to drop bombs on us. For the Russians have bombs just as big, and now they are learning how to shoot them over to us with rockets or maybe pretty soon from space-ships circling overhead. So of course there is a kind of war—two sides all ready to shoot at each other."

He didn't say anything for a while. He seemed to be thinking. Then he said, "Tell me, do you yourself know anything about war?"

"Well, yes." I tried to sound modest. "I had some personal connection with a war in 1917 and I saw something of another one in the 1940's."

"And this cold war you speak of," he continued, "when it becomes hot, when the monster bombs are dropped, will it be like those old wars you knew?"

At once I understood that it would be quite different. But I found it hard to get out the words that would describe the new thing we were calling war. I thought of the sober estimates of scientific advisors to our President that if the bombs are set off, whether by design or by accident, about sixty million Americans would be killed, our greater cities would be reduced to ruin, and the survivors—in whatever appalling chaos they might find themselves—as well as their children and children's children would be poisoned and distorted to an extent impossible to predict. I thought of this and knew that the provincial little massacre I witnessed on the Aisne River in 1917 was something else again. I thought, but I could say little.

"No, it would be a new kind of experience," I said.

"Then," said the stranger, "it should have a different name. Not 'war.' 'Mutual suicide,' perhaps. Or maybe I should put it down that you people are getting ready for your own partial extermination. Is that it?"

I felt I was becoming confused. And a little annoyed with my visitor. I didn't like the way he kept saying "you people." What did he mean by "you people"? I asked him that in so many words.

"Oh," he said, "you people—you, and Khrushchev and the young college people you are going to talk to and John Foster Dulles and the boys down at the corner in Brooklyn and those fishermen drawing up their nets on the Malabar coast."

He did talk in a strange way. Where had he come from? I tried to get our conversation back into easier paths.

"Do *you* come from India?" I asked.

"No," he said, "no. I come from farther away than that."

He sat silent and I tried to get a good look at him. But although he sat close to me on the bench, I could not see him well because the sun was setting just behind him. It was he who took up the conversation. "I suppose you people want to go on living?"

I said that most of us did.

"Then," he said, "I suppose you people are doing what you can to prevent this thing that you call a war but would not be a war but a kind of suicide?"

"We are doing what we can," I replied. "In this country we are spending more money for missiles and maybe we can get the Europeans to put our missiles on their land nearer to the Russians and maybe we can build space-ships before the Russians do and so get the drop on them that way. We have been working pretty hard to make our weapons as big as or bigger than the Russians' weapons. You know we were the first to kill people with atomic bombs and we were the first to make bombs one thousand times bigger than the little ones that killed only about seventy-five thousand people apiece in Japan. We had to make the very big bombs because if we hadn't the Russians would have made them first and then we wouldn't have had security. Neither side wants to start a war when it is clear that the starter would be destroyed also. Of course it is true that the Russians made the very big bombs too and now they are going after space and the moon and we have to go after these things too. Two-thirds of the national budget for next year will be used for military purposes of one kind or another. So we *are* trying to prevent it from happening."

He made a gesture of interruption. "You go too fast," he said. "I can't quite follow. You say you Americans are doing these things for security? And you Russians are doing these things too?"

You Russians! He addressed *me* as "you Russians"! I took him up. "I can't speak for the Russians," I said. "We can't trust the Russians."

"Why not?" he asked. "Don't they want to live too? And can't you trust their common interest with you in continuing to live? It seems to me quite a basis for getting together on some arrangement not to shoot at each other. Two men with firebrands in a room of explosives share one very immediate common interest. But there is something else in what you just said that puzzles me. I think you told me that you went ahead with making more monstrous weapons in order to have security. Tell me, now that you have the thousand-times-bigger bombs, do you feel more secure?"

My impatience had subsided, and, besides, I saw that he had a point or two. I tried to answer his question honestly.

"No," I said, "I don't really feel more secure now than before we had the hydrogen bomb. For at least two reasons. The destruction that could be done now is very much greater—all civilization could be blown to bits. And also, so many countries are getting the weapons and their management is getting so difficult and complicated that the decisions whether or not to fire a missile or drop a bomb must be left to many different people—base commanders, airplane pilots and so on—so that the chance that the first big explosion might occur through a misunder-standing or a rash act grows greater and greater. We might more and more easily have a catastrophe by a sort of inevitable accident. No, I don't feel more secure."

He was thoughtful. Then he spoke again. "I shouldn't express an opinion. But I can say I am confused. You seem to be telling me that you are working hard to prevent this mutual suicide by making bigger and bigger weapons to shoot at each other, and that the more you make, the more likely they will go off of themselves. It is like piling more and more explosives into this room with the two waving firebrands. It seems a strange way to seek security."

Again there was a silence. Then he asked me if I thought that the young college people would continue to choose the same way to security when they took over matters. I told him that I could not predict as to that.

"They might find some other way," he said. "They might call the thing that you are trying to prevent not war but mutual destruction. They might become less bellicose about that struggle that is now going on between some of you and others of you. They might talk less about how each wants to destroy the other and fears to be destroyed by the other and talk more with each other about your common interests—in keeping alive, in keeping down the cost of threatening each other. They might even move some of the explosives out of the room—what difference would that make to mutual security if each can destroy the other several times over with the explosives that are left? They might even stamp out the firebrands and walk away from the explosives.

"These young people don't *have* to do just what you have been doing," he continued. "They will do better. They are more experienced than you."

"*Less* experienced, I think you mean," said I.

"No, I mean more experienced. They start knowing not only what you know but also what you did—which is more than you knew when you started. So they are a more experienced people than you. And I suppose I am at liberty to believe that you people learn by experience? That you do things better as you go along?"

"Yes," said I. "That is progress. Progress is something we all believe in. Or maybe used to believe in. There seem to be doubts now about progress. Progress, it appears, is not going forward step by step, or leap by leap, to the better and better. It seems to me like going ahead and backward at one and the same time, by the same effort of movement. Or like—"

"Like what?" he asked.

"Like a strange dream in which one opens door after door down a corridor with a light at the end of it only to find that each door opened makes the light brighter and the darkness darker. There is more light all the time: the antibiotics and the good music that comes out of my loudspeaker and the old slums torn down. And there is also more darkness: people living longer to suffer from other diseases, and many wasted hours in front of the TV, and the new slums growing up around the overcrowded cities. Progress seems to me very untrustworthy. She can't just be believed in. She has somehow to be managed."

"You are becoming eloquent," he said. "If I may say so without offense, eloquence is like progress—bright and shining, but untrustworthy. Let us try again to understand the problem of how to go forward without going backward, to let new light shine undarkened. May I ask how you people are doing with space control?"

"Not much—yet," I said. "We have put some satellites into orbit and our President proposed that space be controlled internationally—an interplanetary police force, some day—"

He interrupted. "You misunderstand me. I referred not to interplanetary space—which by the way seems to me a very poor place to be—but to space right here, on your own planet, where you people live. How are you people doing with respect to control of your own terrestrial space?"

I remembered a piece I had been reading by Paul H. Sears about how badly we had been doing, and I recalled some facts about occupation of terrestrial space. So I began at once to provide the stranger with information about the topic he had just raised.

"The population of our planet is increasing at a rate of about 40,000,000 a year. By 1987, when college students of today are putting their children through college, at the present rate of growth there will be about six and a half billion people. The world will then be more than twice as crowded as it is now. China will have a population of five billion people in a hundred years if the present rate of growth continues. Indeed, stranger, if your wish was to get to know us, you have come at a favorable time, for about twenty per cent of all the people who ever lived are alive now. But more important than this great number of us is the fact that the rate of increase overcomes much of the advantages we think we give ourselves by modern medicine and technology. The Egyptians are probably poorer than ever because there are so many more of them. Most of the increase that India has achieved by better technology and planning is no real increase at all because medicine and hygiene have caused the number of people who eat the food to increase as rapidly as the food has."

"You do indeed go forward backward toward a darkened light," said he. "However," he continued, "you don't look so badly off right around here—on this American patch of your terrestrial space."

"We are very proud, we Americans, of our standard of living. I will give you another statistic. It is estimated that with present technology this planet of ours could support, with the standard of living enjoyed by Americans, less than one-third of the people who are now on it. So some of us are doing pretty well. And we shall probably do better. Gunnar Myrdal says that on this earth the rich nations are getting richer. Of course he also says that the poor ones are getting poorer."

"That does not sound like a very desirable arrangement," went on the stranger. "It must cause some hard feelings. And I suppose you people who are Americans do pretty well by making and consuming things? Don't you ever use up any of the things you need for getting along better?"

I had still another statistic for him. "The people of my nation, with about seven per cent of the world's population, are now absorbing about sixty per cent of the world's minerals—mostly irreplaceable. We are indeed great consumers. We consume raw materials, use up water so it sometimes has to be rationed in cities, pollute air and rivers with waste products, and almost take pride in the piles of junked automobiles. It all goes to make the American standard of living the highest on earth. Now that I understand that it is the control of terrestrial space in which you are interested, I can say that we overrun it rather than control it."

He was silent and thoughtful. "What is that great wall of earth over there?" he suddenly asked. I followed the line of his gaze.

"That is a superhighway under construction. It will get more people around places faster."

"It certainly overruns space," he remarked. This time I did not say what was on my mind—that industry and highways take out of agricultural use about a million acres of American land yearly, and Sears' prediction that the agricultural surpluses that are now so troublesome will be only a memory twenty years from now. Instead I said that Chicago was growing very fast and needed better transportation.

"You are indeed an odd people," he said. "In your efforts to get security from war you make yourselves more and more insecure; in your efforts to get a good life, you rather mess up much of the life you are busy improving. This is indeed a darkened light."

The sun had set now and the twilight made that wall of earth loom larger against the amber sky. My mind, perhaps tired by the effort to explain how things are on this earth, relaxed into reminiscence, into dreamy consideration of times past. I said something like this to the stranger.

"Where that superhighway runs, there used to be a cornfield. In June the unfolding leaves made a neat, fresh carpet there—nine acres of it.

In August one walked slowly between the rows of stalks, taller than one's head. When we went into the corn on very hot nights and stood still and listened, we used to tell ourselves that we heard the corn growing. And over there farther, there was a piece of aboriginal prairie that had never been broken by the plow. Only native plants grew there, prairie dock and tickseed, downy phlox and bluegrass. And up there where there are so many houses, the oaks stood very old and tall, and I used to find yellow adder's tongue growing beneath some of them.

"Do you know what I miss? I am thinking just now, although the season of the year is not appropriate, that I miss very much the sound of the whetstone on the scythe—a good, clean sound. Oh, and many other things I miss—the voice of the bobwhite, the flight of the red-headed woodpecker as he flashed along the dirt road to fling himself like a painted dart against a telephone pole. And I miss the fields filled with shooting stars. And the clang and rattle of the windmill when the vanes swung around in a shift of breeze, and the puddles of water at the well where the wasps came in summer.

"Excuse me," I said. "This must bore you. Older people tend to look back on things that are gone and were good to them. If now you were talking to a young person, he would not have on his mind these changes that are losses to me. It is a great and necessary thing about young people that they look forward with a confidence unshaken by such regrets. It is a good thing that some things are unremembered as the generations pass. Really you should be talking to the young people. Why don't you go to some college town and talk to young people?"

He told me that he might do just that. I could see that indeed he was growing tired of me. Neither of us spoke for a time and in the growing dusk I thought I could see him looking through the pages of a notebook.

"Young people," he said. "I do have some notes on the topic. I have been looking into some of the authorities you have on young people, at least young people who are Americans. The matter has been investigated by *The Nation*, David Riesman, William Whyte, Alan Harrington, and others. I have here a summary of the results of research on this subject. Yes, here it is: 'American young people are uncommitted and other-directed; they have no heroes and few illusions; they seek security and togetherness; they want only to find places in the slots of employment and safe advancement; after comfortable years in college they become organization men and succumb slowly to creeping contentment.'"

His words stirred me to a disagreement, even resentment, that I could not at once express. Was this true of our young people? I wanted to argue the matter with him but could not find the words. But my resentment was growing. Somehow I felt that the view of us people that he was developing was incomplete. He saw us, but in a queer, unnatural light, a light from firebrands and neon signs. It was true, and yet it was not true. Or not all the truth, and my resentment was directed also at myself, for had I not been telling him things, true things yet not all the truth, about us? Somehow I had responded to him in such a way as to help him to form this true yet not quite true view of us. I wanted to turn upon him, to make *him* say something, make some observations that I could contradict. He had risen and I saw he was about to leave me.

"Stranger," I said, "before you go won't you tell me what your impressions are, on the whole, thinking over what you know about us, all of us here?"

When he did speak his words were only one more question. "How do *you* know all these things you have been telling me, about war and space control and the multiplication of people and so on?"

"I read things," I said, "and then we have many studies of these matters. And commissions and reports and committees and conferences."

"I see," he said. "You have commissions and reports and conferences. Tell me, did you ever have a conference on the good life?"

"On what?"

"On the good life. On what a good life would be for all you people. Just in case you stamp out the firebrands and go on living with yourselves. A conference as to what would be a good life, for everybody, given the limitations of earth and space and the nature, whatever it is, of all of you."

"It seems a large subject. And not too definite. How would such a conference be organized?"

"I think I could make some suggestions," said the stranger. "I could propose a tentative agenda. The topics could be formulated for group discussion in the form of a list of questions. Like this:

ITEM ONE: Do you want more and more people existing together somehow or do you want not quite so many people living well?

ITEM TWO: What is growth—is it getting bigger or getting better?

ITEM THREE: What is a good standard of living, more things to consume or better things to appreciate and discriminate? This third item on the agenda would require much subdivision and consideration of particular subtopics. You could appoint a subcommittee for each subtopic, you know. For example, Subtopic 37, Production and Consumption, Subsubtopic 49, division b, 3: Do you want to buy the car of tomorrow today only to find that tomorrow it is already the car of yesterday and you are expected to buy another? And so on. Oh, it could be quite an agenda.

ITEM FOUR: What is the right relation of man to the cosmos? Again, a subtopic: Which is the better use of the moon: to hit it with a rocket or just to look at it?

ITEM FIVE: Where are the frontiers of human enterprise? That item could be put in different ways, for example: Should people build and pioneer always outward or sometimes inward?

He must have seen that I still looked puzzled. So he tried again. "Item Five could be put more concretely," he said. "Like this: To take risks, make adventures, create and add to human life, is it necessary to climb a mountain or build a space-ship, or could one also adventure and create within a limited world? Find new good things within the limits of earth-space, production and consumption? Exercise restraints to free one's self for the making of new things for enjoyment, improved experience, wiser and finer judgments? Where is freedom? In always doing more and more or in doing fewer things to do them better? That, of course, amounts to asking if the very abundance of material goods may not result in a loss of freedom."

I was trying to take this in. "It would certainly be a difficult conference to organize," I said. "And it would make some people very uneasy. It seems to ask questions that are somehow, where I live, not quite the sort of question to ask. And so different from what is discussed at the conferences that I do go to! Those conferences are concerned with how to do things. Your conference would be concerned with why one should do them at all. And with what is good to do and why."

"Just so," he said. "And now I say goodbye. It has been nice knowing you people. You *are* odd, and, from what I have seen of you, pretty mixed up. But I wish you well. Goodbye."

He was gone, and I have not seen him since. But what he said is much in my mind. It troubles me a good deal. Somehow the conversation was unsatisfactory. I didn't like being asked so many questions. And such questions! As an anthropologist, I am used to being the one who asks the questions; I find out about other people. With this stranger I felt that somehow I had caught hold of the wrong end of the stick. And I felt that I had held up my end badly. I hadn't said things about us that he ought to know, if he really wanted to understand us. Ever since he went away my mind has been full of what is called "staircase wit"—those clever or right things you didn't say and wish you had as you go down the stairway jamming your hat on your head and getting angrier and angrier with yourself.

I had told him truly things that indeed show that mankind is confused. I could not deny that we are in a terrible predicament. It had to be admitted that we waste our substance and threaten ourselves with a perhaps ultimate destruction. It is so that at least locally, here in America, we are inclined to trust too much in technology to get us out of trouble, pretty complacent about ourselves, and unwilling to look the human tragedy in the face. So much of the worst about us he had got out of me with his unexpected questions. If you come to us, just like that, from somewhere outside of our human affairs, we do appear a mixed-up lot of people leading a totteringly precarious existence, and doing much that is both stupid and base. And yet that is not all that is true and important about us. What had I failed to say?

As I turned it over in my mind and struggled to understand my dissatisfaction with the interview, one clarifying thought came to me. So far as I could tell, the stranger had found out nothing about our past. He had asked about us now, what we were doing now, what we are like now. Can a stranger come really to understand a man by asking some questions about his present situation only? I might meet a man at a moment of crisis, when his affairs were confused and his very existence endangered; learning this about him I might conclude: This is a hopeless incompetent on his way to immediate destruction through his own folly. But, if I had the story of his life, if I saw how he had acted in other crises, if I came to know not only his present predicament but his character, I might change my judgment of him and his prospects; I might come to see that in spite of his current mistakes he had managed to deal with earlier difficulties and, perhaps, had shown that he did indeed learn by experience; that he had been growing, adding to his capacities, making some judgments more wisely than he had been able to at an earlier stage in his career. So, I thought, it was with this interviewing stranger: he showed no knowledge of the human career; he gave no indication that he had looked into the story of the collective human life from the days of the cave man to today. I just wished I had kept him with me long enough to take him to a performance of Thornton Wilder's play, *The Skin of Our Teeth*.

I began to say to myself some of the things I should have said to him. A phrase came into my mind, a phrase used by Albert Camus when he replied not long ago to some questions put to him by another French novelist. The phrase was, "the spirit matures." Yes, it does. Our human career is growing up. Though our follies continue and our dangers increase, it is also true that if not century by century then millenium by millenium we grow more worth saving. We learn to put some bad things behind us and we make new good things that we could not make before. Slavery and legal torture are no longer respectable. We learn to write books, and good books! The cave man could not give us the Platonic dialogues. Once there was no Bach, no Tolstoi and no Einstein, and then, after the spirit had further matured, there were these men. That stranger, coming to us at one moment, could not know these things.

Yes, I went on saying to myself and as it were to him: On the whole we people are busy making a living, keeping house, and avoiding boredom. We might seem to be so many ants, living and dying one after another

in an eternal, changeless anthill. But it is not so. Over and beyond the
eating and the sleeping, the mere living and dying one after another, the
spirit adds, invents, creates what is better than what was before. Other
words spoken by Camus came to me and I imagined myself saying them
to the stranger. It was plain that he had thought us a pretty poor lot. But
I wished that I had spoken as Camus spoke; then I would have caused
him, I thought, to pay "homage to the miserable, magnificent life we live."

How badly I had replied, or how I had not replied at all, to his remarks
about the young people of America! He had been led to form a judgment that they are complacent seekers of a mean society. I thought of
the replies I should have made. I should have doubted that this is the
full truth about them. There are so many of them, and among the many
are some, I might have said, who will take the risks of being truly themselves, who will speak and act for the common good though it be to their
own injury. There have always been such, and there will be such again.
I should also have said that the people of a generation change, become
something different from what they were, as they grow older and as the
terrible demands of the human predicament press upon them. The young
people of today will be a different kind of people. Now we are all in a
condition of shock from abrupt realization of the human predicament.
But these young people of today will later have borne with the shock, and
will have found the strength to deal with the predicament.

And then I should have recognized my own limited, parochial mind in
responding, with silent resentment, to his succinct report on American
youth. American young people so described are not all of us. We people
are composed of many kinds, and each kind has its virtues and its weaknesses. If Americans are complacent and shelter themselves with an un-
considered optimism, others of us are basely cynical, and still others of us
are more resolute in confronting tragedy. If, in my own country, there is
an aversion from or denial of suffering, some others of us have seen the
necessary part of suffering in the maturing of the human spirit. Dostoevsky
wrote it, and it is heard in the great music of Beethoven. We are many, of
many kinds, and though today each kind tends to think of itself and for
itself, one may venture to recognize a growing tendency, as yet small, for
the different strains of the common humanity to affect one another, and
perhaps one day to develop a mankind whose best men and women speak
not for just one kind of us, here in America, or somewhere else, but for
all of us.

And then I had responded badly to the stranger's easy lumping of all
mankind into one kind of thing. I had resented his calling me "you Russians." I should not have resented it; I should have thought about how
I can and do speak also for Russians, and yet cannot and do not always
speak for them. I am one with them because they and I are human, be-

cause we live and love and work and laugh and feel tender or unhappy as do all men. They and I share this earth and whatever annexes to it come about in outer space; and we share the responsibility of making it a decent place to live for us all. Further, Americans are like Russians in particular respects in which others—say the people of India or the South Sea Islanders—are not like Russians or Americans. We both like to make big things; both look for material results and probably make too much of technology; both have a class of managers to run most of their affairs. In these respects we join in a common effort to give the growth of mankind a bias, a bent toward one side that may not, in the very long judgment of human kind, prove to be a wise deflection.

On the other hand, we who are Americans are different from the Russians in ways that place upon us special responsibilities, that give us, in these respects, the larger share of power and duty to extricate us all from the predicament. We mean this difference when we say that we are free, and they are not. We are a people all of whom have some power and responsibility to think and speak and act as to what ought to be changed, as to what measures to take, as to what new lines of effort to pursue to avoid the mutual suicide and to work upon the good life. The Russians today, the common, ordinary, on-the-street Russians, cannot stand up and say, "This we do is wrong. The right lies there." But we, in America, can. In this we *are* different; here I can speak only for a Russian who is silenced and perhaps waiting; but we in America have made a society in which differences and dissensions are the very stuff of public life. Every one of us can, if he will, speak, strive, persuade, decry, and insist. So, though we on this earth are, in the stranger's words, "we people," we are a diversity within our unity, and to each kind falls the responsibility to make strong, to put to work for all on earth the virtue and the power special to his own kind.

I thought I might have said these things and then I thought of the immediate peril to us all, the threat, the still-increasing threat, of an ultimate destruction. In answering his questions about the peril, I had told the truth; I could not, in the second thoughts, imagine myself denying that peril. I had to admit that the growth of the human spirit might, by destruction, come to an end. It could end in nuclear violence; it could end in abasement to a nihilism of values, a tyranny of doctrine, police power, or material things. What a fragile thing is human spirit! So threatened are we that a stranger might well conclude his investigations of us with a judgment that we are neither able to save ourselves nor worth saving.

And again I found my mind imagining that he had not spoken with me but with some stronger and wiser one of us. I thought once more of the words of Camus: "We suffocate and we survive; we think we will die of grief and life triumphs . . . Anyway, we have no choice . . . wherever we are and to the best of our abilities we must do what has to be done so that everyone can live together once again." "The very fact that atomic warfare would make the future meaningless gives us back our freedom of action." These things he said. And he said, "We have nothing to lose—except everything. So let's go forward . . . If we fail, it will be better to have taken our stand at the side of those who want to live rather than with those who destroy."

What words! As I remembered them, I wanted to recall the stranger so that he could hear them. Those words were spoken from the maturing human spirit. It will speak, like that, from this one or that, no matter how great the peril. We are indeed an odd people, but odd in ways that I fear the stranger did not fully understand. We are a thrust upward amid dangers and darknesses of our own making. We have no promise from the universe that we shall survive. We live for the growing of the human spirit, and in spite of all, we strive toward that growth, up to the last moment of possibility.

38. ANTHROPOLOGY AS A CAREER [*]

1. TRAINING

Professional anthropologists usually need an advanced degree. They must obtain the bachelor's degree after four years of college, and then the master's or doctor's degree after several years of graduate work. A master's degree is received after one or usually two or more years of graduate work. The doctorate, which is normally necessary for the better positions, usually requires at least four years' work beyond the bachelor's degree.

It is possible to acquire all one's anthropological training in graduate work, after undergraduate study with a major in an entirely unrelated field. However, the student who determines his objective early can get valuable training and experience while he is in college and even earlier.

The international languages of science are English, French, German, and, increasingly, also Russian. Important advances in knowledge may be made known in any of these languages. For this reason, a reading knowledge of two foreign languages is usually required for the doctor's (Ph.D.) degree; normally these are French and German, but Russian promises to be more and more acceptable instead of one of these. A linguist seeking a Ph.D. in a department of linguistics, rather than in a department of anthropology, may need Latin, Greek, and Sanskrit as well as French and German. Depending on their areal specialties, anthropologists must often use other languages in addition to French and German. Fieldwork may require speaking knowledge of another language, and even if this is not the case, important published sources are often in other languages. For these reasons, knowledge of Spanish is necessary for work in Latin America and is helpful in the study of United States

[*] William C. Sturtevant, "Anthropology as a Career," (Washington, D.C.: Smithsonian Institution, 1958), pp. 8–14. (This is the second part of the same pamphlet from which selection No. I:2 comes.) Reprinted by permission of the author and the Smithsonian Institution.

Indians, particularly those of the West, Southwest, and Southeast; Portuguese is necessary for work in Brazil and parts of Africa; Dutch and Indonesian are required for study of the peoples of Indonesia; Danish is an advantage in Eskimo studies, etc. Knowledge of languages is thus very important for an anthropologist, and the student can save time and effort by beginning their study as early as possible.

The basic groundwork for formal anthropological training can be laid in the college preparatory course in high school. In addition to languages, the high-school student should take English composition, since a large proportion of the anthropologist's research time is spent in writing reports on the results of his studies. Mathematics, at least through algebra, should be taken as the basis for later training in statistics. Courses in geography and history will prove beneficial. Some competence in typing, photography, sketching, and simple surveying is advantageous and can be gained at this stage in the student's education.

The use which the high-school student makes of his spare time and vacations can be equally as important as his formal studies—provided, of course, that he does well enough in school to meet requirements for college entrance. Many of the Boy Scout merit-badge subjects are examples: camping, cooking, Indian lore, first aid, photography, surveying, botany, zoology, bird study, geology, astronomy, basketry, pottery, and textiles. Many of the Girl Scout activities and programs are also appropriate. Experience in camping will be found particularly useful.

Many areas have local amateur archeological societies which engage in excavations and have regular meetings. Participation in these activities is valuable for any prospective anthropologist, regardless of his principal interest within the field. If there is a museum nearby which has anthropological collections, the student will find repeated visits interesting and useful. Museums often accept volunteer help by high-school students. This type of work is very good training, as many anthropologists find museum experience valuable, and the young student may get an opportunity to handle specimens and to get informal training and advice from practicing anthropologists.

If there is a nearby Indian reservation or community, frequent visits by the young student will give both interesting and valuable experience. He can get to know Indians as people and also become familiar with conditions of life in an Indian community. Reading the published literature on the tribe and examining local collections of their artifacts will give background for talks with Indian acquaintances. The student should learn to keep notes on his findings and investigations.

In college, an undergraduate major in anthropology is often advantageous, but not absolutely necessary. Almost all State universities, and many other colleges, offer some undergraduate instruction in anthropology. A choice among several possible colleges may be made in several ways. A trip to the nearest university or large museum to talk with a professional anthropologist about one's special interest and problems is a good idea. The student can get some idea of the adequacy of the undergraduate anthropology training in the college being considered by inquiring about its graduate program: most colleges that offer a master's degree or doctorate in anthropology also have good undergraduate programs.

If the college selected has an undergraduate major program in anthropology, the student should consult the adviser for the anthropology department when he enters into his freshman year, even if the regulations do not require this. Ordinarily a student must spend a year or two on general studies before formal enrollment in a major subject; the anthropology adviser can help in planning the program during this period to give the best foundation for the future major.

In the college program, the nonanthropology courses taken (and the major, if the college lacks an anthropology department) will partly depend on the student's interest within anthropology. Languages, especially French and German, should be taken by any student who expects to continue in anthropology. For physical anthropology, courses in general zoology, genetics, embryology, comparative anatomy, physiology, ecology, vertebrate paleontology, and biological statistics should be included if possible. For archeology, courses in such fields as geology, history, the history of art, elementary surveying, paleontology, statistics, zoology, comparative anatomy, and climatology will be useful. For ethnology, courses in sociology, linguistics, psychology, economics, history, general zoology, botany, statistics, geography, art, and musicology are advantageous. For linguistics, as many languages as possible, psychology, history, mathematics, and logic may be mentioned. A course or two in English composition will not be wasted, regardless of the future specialization.

Several universities have summer field schools, where training in archeology is given by participation in excavations under expert supervision. Many anthropologists have gotten useful training by attending such summer sessions, at their own or another university, while they were undergraduate students.

It is sometimes an advantage to take a few undergraduate courses in anthropology but to have an undergraduate major in one of the subjects related to anthropology, waiting until graduate work before concentrating in the field. There is often considerable duplication between undergraduate and graduate anthropology courses; the increase in interdisciplinary studies also makes such collateral training profitable. On the other hand, anthropology is an excellent major for the student who wants a liberal arts education ending in a bachelor's (B.A.) degree, and people with such training have made valuable contributions by pursuing anthropological research as a spare-time activity in later years. A few applied anthropology jobs are open to those with only a B.A., with a major in anthropology.

It is almost always advisable to change to another university after completing undergraduate work, since different teachers will increase the range of the student's knowledge. Choice of a graduate school is very important, for one's future job depends on the training received there and on the standing of the faculty in the school chosen. If the college attended for undergraduate work lacks an anthropology department, it is worth traveling to the nearest university that has such a department in order to get advice sometime during the senior year. An effort should be made to find somone in one's own special field of interest to discuss the problem with. Faculties change, and it is important to get up-to-date information.

Graduate training in anthropology takes longer than that in many other fields, since the student is usually required to spend several months to a year doing fieldwork, after his first year or two of classwork. The thesis for the doctoral degree is then written on the investigations conducted during this fieldwork. Very few students receive a Ph.D. after only three years of graduate work; many take four, five, or more years.

There are some 1,000 to 1,500 professional anthropologists in the United States today; most of them teach in universities. There are a few teaching in junior colleges, and a very few in private secondary schools. Large universities often have separate departments of anthropology whose faculties teach only anthropology. However, many universities combine sociology and anthropology in a single department; anthropologists in these schools, and some who hold positions in departments of sociology, may teach some sociology courses as well as anthropology courses. For this reason, some training in sociology is often advantageous in gaining a university teaching position.

The other major field of employment for anthropologists is in museums. Most large museums and some smaller ones have anthropological collections and hire trained anthropologists as curators of these materials. Many such museums, however, are connected with universities, and their curatorial staffs usually also hold teaching appointments in the university department of anthropology, devoting part time to museum duties and part time to teaching. Most museum anthropologists are archeologists, who usually find museum collections more necessary to their research than do ethnologists. In recent years there has been a shortage of ethnologists with museum training and experience to fill curatorial positions in ethnology. The student of ethnology who is interested in artifacts will thus find it advantageous to gain museum experience during his schooling and should try to select for his graduate work a university having an associated museum with anthropological holdings.

There are a few other types of positions open to anthropologists. There are one or two hundred such jobs in the following U. S. Government agencies: Smithsonian Institution; National Park Service; Trust Territory of the Pacific Islands; Department of Health, Education, and Welfare; Department of Justice; Department of State; Department of Defense; Library of Congress; Government of American Samoa; National Science Foundation; Veterans Administration; Extension Service of the Department of Agriculture; Bureau of the Census; Immigration Service; and the Bureau of Indian Affairs.

Other organizations that have hired a few anthropologists include some independent research organizations; a few philanthropic foundations; some hospitals, particularly mental hospitals; state and local health departments; the United Nations (especially UNESCO); some industrial and advertising companies; a few businesses with interests abroad; and law firms working on Indian claims cases. These jobs, however, are not numerous. Television, radio, documentary movies, and related concerns are sources of at least part-time employment for a few trained anthropologists.

An anthropologist almost always obtains his first job through the university department in which he receives his advanced degree. News of job openings is received by the university faculties, and they consider it an obligation to place their students in their first positions. Subsequent jobs are received as the professional's reputation in his field becomes known, particularly through his publications.

The financial rewards for anthropologists are not great, considering the time and cost of the training involved. Annual salaries range from about $4,000 to $5,000 for a new Ph.D. to about $15,000 for a few who have been in the field for many years. Fieldwork is not usually financed from such salaries but is paid for by the institution employing the anthropologist, or by grants of funds by philanthropic and scientific foundations. No one should go into anthropology in the expectation of large economic rewards. The rewards are of another nature: job security is relatively great, and the researcher gets his major satisfaction from earning his living at what he most enjoys doing.

2. UNIVERSITIES

Any selected list of universities offering training in anthropology rapidly gets out of date, since expansion of departments and of their topical coverage is continuous, and since the special opportunities at well-established departments change as older faculty members retire and are replaced by young men with different interests, or as a faculty member moves to a different university to accept a job at a higher rank. The prospective student should therefore write to several universities for the latest catalogs and compare their course offerings.

All State universities (except Vermont) offer training in anthropology. Several of them have outstanding departments in the field, while others are less specialized in anthropology. Those with the largest departments include the State universities of Arizona, California (both Berkeley and Los Angeles), Colorado, Indiana, Michigan, New Mexico, North Carolina, Ohio, Oklahoma, Oregon, Texas, Washington, and Wisconsin. Other universities and colleges that offer undergraduate training in anthropology include the following (those with the larger departments of anthropology are starred):

American University, Washington, D. C.
Atlanta University, Atlanta, Ga.
Barnard College, New York, N. Y.
Beloit College, Beloit, Wis.
Bennington College, Bennington, Vt.
Boston University, Boston, Mass.
Brandeis University, Waltham, Mass.
Brigham Young University, Provo, Utah
Brooklyn College, Brooklyn, N. Y.
Brown University, Providence, R. I.
Bryn Mawr College, Bryn Mawr, Pa.
University of Buffalo, Buffalo, N. Y.
Catholic University of America, Washington, D. C.
*University of Chicago, Chicago, Ill.
City College, New York, N. Y.
Colgate University, Hamilton, N. Y.
*Columbia University, New York, N. Y.
Connecticut College for Women, New London, Conn.
*Cornell University, Ithaca, N. Y.
Dartmouth College, Hanover, N. H.
University of Denver, Denver, Colo.
Dropsie College, Philadelphia, Pa.
Duke University, Durham, N. C.
Emory University, Atlanta, Ga.
Fordham University, New York, N. Y.
Hamilton College, Clinton, N. Y.
Hartford Seminary Foundation, Hartford, Conn.
*Harvard University, Cambridge, Mass.
Hobart College, Geneva, N. Y.

Hofstra College, Hempstead, L. I., N. Y.
Howard University, Washington, D. C.
Hunter College, New York, N. Y.
University of Miami, Coral Gables, Fla.
New York University, New York, N. Y.
*Northwestern University, Evanston, Ill.
*University of Pennsylvania, Philadelphia, Pa.
Princeton University, Princeton, N. J.
University of Puerto Rico
Queens College, Flushing, N. Y.
Radcliffe College, Cambridge, Mass.
Reed College, Portland, Oreg.
St. Lawrence University, Canton, N. Y.
University of Southern California, Los Angeles, Calif.
Smith College, Northampton, Mass.
Southern Illinois University, Carbondale, Ill.
Stanford University, Stanford, Calif.
Syracuse University, Syracuse, N. Y.
Tufts University, Medford, Mass.
Tulane University, New Orleans, La.
Vanderbilt University, Nashville, Tenn.
Vassar College, Poughkeepsie, N. Y.
Washington University, St. Louis, Mo.
Wayne University, Detroit, Mich.
Wellesley College, Wellesley, Mass.
Western Reserve University, Cleveland, Ohio
Wheaton College, Wheaton, Ill.
*Yale University, New Haven, Conn.

In Canada, undergraduate training in anthropology is offered at the University of British Columbia, Université Laval, McGill University, and the University of Toronto.

Glossary

adze: a cutting tool. It is like an axe but its cutting edge is perpendicular to the plane of its movement (where the cutting edge of an axe is parallel to the plane of its movement.)

affect: a quality of interpersonal relations; basically, interaction which emotionally rouses one or more of the participants.

affinal: by marriage (same as Morgan's affineal).

age-area hypothesis: the theory that, other things being equal, the culture trait with the widest distribution is the oldest. While this theory and its several corollaries have provided many interesting insights, they are not to be applied at face value.

age-set: a social group composed of persons of a certain age and generally of the same sex. Also known as an age-grade.

Apollonian: referring to cultures which are said to encourage placid and emotionally restrained behavior on the part of their members.

Aryan: properly used (as by Morgan) the term refers to speakers of any of the Indoeuropean languages.

Aurignacian: a widespread stone industry of diverse facies occurring in Upper Pleistocene times.

ayllu: the local kin group of the Quechua-speaking people of the Andes, including the Inca. The precise nature of the Inca ayllu is still uncertain.

bilaterality: the tracing of descent without partiality either to the maternal or paternal line.

catalepsy: an attack or seizure in which an individual becomes rigid and speechless.

catallactic: for the purpose of exchange.

catarrhines: the Old World monkeys.

cicisbei: male admirers of married women.

clan: a group of persons united by claimed but not necessarily demonstrable descent from a common ancestor. Though stipulated, the descent is strictly unilineal.

collateral: referring to relationship through horizontal or sidewise links. Ego's "uncles," "aunts," "cousins," etc. are his collateral relatives.

588

composition: the property which is paid to an injured or aggrieved party in order to settle ("compose") a dispute or feud.

conjugal: having to do with marriage.

consanguine: "of the same blood," i.e., pertaining to a genetic relationship.

corm: a subterranean stem. Certain plants are grown from cuttings from underground portions of their stems rather than from seed.

covert: hidden or secret. With reference to culture it means that which is not quite on the verbally recognized level. People may act according to rules which they perceive dimly, if at all.

cross-cousin: a cousin related through intermediate persons of two different sexes. Thus the children of your mother's brother(s) and your father's sister(s) are your cross-cousins.

Dionysian: referring to cultures which are said to encourage great emotionalism and extremes of activity in their members.

disintegration: in culture, to lose consistency and harmony in the interaction of the institutions constituting the fabric of daily life.

ego: "I"; the stated point of reference from which analyses of kinship begin.

empirical: on the basis of experience.

endogamy: a socially enforced requirement that marriages take place between persons who are both members of some defined group such as a kin, local or religious group.

Erse: pertaining to the Celtic languages.

ethnocentrism: the use of the values of one's own culture as a standard against which all others are invidiously compared.

etiology: the cause of a disease or sickness.

exogamy: a socially enforced requirement that marriages take place between persons who are not both members of some defined group such as a kinship or local group.

exoteric: that which is openly known and not secret, as opposed to esoteric.

extended family: any family which includes more members than the *nuclear family* (which see). There are many possible types of extended family.

famille particulariste: the *nuclear family* (which see).

famille souche: the "stem" family, which consists of parents, *one* married child and spouse, and the children of this younger couple. Unmarried children of the grandparents may also be in this family but they move out on marriage.

father-right: pertaining to patrilineally oriented systems of descent.

genealogical: through the means of a genealogy or family tree.

heuristic: for the purpose of furthering knowledge.

holistic: taking a complete view. With reference to culture, including all aspects of the phenomenon rather than selected portions.

iconography: the representation of things through the media of graphic and plastic arts.

integration: to act or function as a whole; specifically, in culture, the consistent and harmonious interaction of institutions.

kindred: a kinship aggregate based on the principle of bilateral descent.

Kula: the ceremonial exchange system found in a certain part of Melanesia. Necklaces (*soulava*) move in one prevailing direction, while bracelets (*mwali*) move in the other.

levirate: the practice whereby a widow is taken as wife by her deceased husband's brother.

lineage: a group of persons united by genealogically demonstrable common unilinear descent and having a minimum span of three generations.

lineal: referring to a relative by direct connection such as a grandparent, parent, sibling, child or grandchild.

loess: soil composed of tiny air- or water-borne grains of dirt.

Magdalenian: a widespread stone industry occurring in Upper Pleistocene times.

mana: a Malayo-Polynesian word referring to a supernatural power which is believed to pervade the universe.

matriarchal: a word often misused to mean "matrilineal." Actually, the word should be used only to refer to situations in which women control the political power of a society.

matriclan: (matrilineal clan) a clan based upon descent traced exclusively through females.

matrilineage: (matrilineal lineage) a lineage based upon descent traced exclusively through females.

matrilocality: term widely but loosely used to signify the post-marital residence of a husband and wife with the relatives of the wife.

mechanical solidarity: a concept developed by Durkheim relating to the way in which social groups interact. Mechanical solidarity refers to the interaction of groups which are strictly equivalent in membership and function. (See *organic solidarity.*)

megalomania: a delusional system centering about the conviction of one's personal greatness. Delusions of grandeur.

mise en scène: setting the stage; in the context of this book *mise en scène* means preparing a background.

moiety: a half, that is, one of two groups into which a society is organized. Generally, membership is assigned on the basis of descent.

mores: socially sanctioned behavioral norms, infractions of which are taken quite seriously by the community.

morphology: the form or structure of a thing or organism or the study of that form or structure. All branches of anthropology study morphology: physical anthropology studies the morphology of man and his ancestors; linguistics studies the form of sounds and words and the structure of grammars; cultural anthropology studies the morphology of society, the form of whole cultures, etc.

mother-right: pertaining to matrilineally oriented systems of descent.

nuclear family: the family which consists of one set of parents and their unmarried children and no other relatives.

oestrus: a state of sexual desire; used of animals with a definite mating season or cycle.

organic solidarity: like *mechanical solidarity* (q.v.) a concept developed by Durkheim. Organic solidarity refers to the interaction of divergent groups whose memberships and functions are dissimilar and unequal.

paleontology: the study of the remains of extinct and ancient life as revealed in the geological record.

palimpsest: a parchment or canvas or other surface on which something has been written or painted, erased, and used again.

parallel cousin: cousins related through intermediate relatives both of which intermediates are of the same sex. Thus the children of both your mother's sister(s) and your father's brother(s) are your parallel cousins.

paranoia: a psychotic state characterized by delusions of persecution.

parfleche: a leather envelope used by Plains Indians to carry food, tobacco, etc.

patriarchal: referring to the vesting of political power in the hands of males acting as the heads of large domestic units.

patriclan: (patrilineal clan) a clan based upon descent traced exclusively through males.

patrikin: one's relatives on the father's side. Differs from patrilineage or patriclan in at least one of two ways: (a) includes both paternal and maternal relatives of father; (b) if only the former are included, they lack functional group organization.

patrilineage: (patrilineal lineage) a lineage based upon descent traced exclusively through males.

patrilocality: term widely but loosely used to signify the post-marital residence of a husband and wife with the relatives of the husband.

phratry: a group of clans basing their unity upon a myth of ultimate common ancestry.

phylogenetic: relating to the evolution of a species or order of life as opposed to *ontogenetic,* relating to the development of an individual.

platyrrhines: the Ceboidea, or New World monkeys.

polyandry: a condition of marriage in which a woman has two or more husbands at the same time.

polychrome: of many colors.

polygyny: a condition of marriage in which a man has two or more wives at the same time.

prosimian: an animal with the evolutionary rank of an early primate, for example, a lemur or tarsier.

sanctions: reactions of the community to acts of behavior. Sanctions may be positive or premial, reinforcing certain actions, or they may be negative or punitive, punishing actions which are deemed bad.

sementary society: a society composed of a number of corelative segments, generally equivalent kinship groups.

Semitic: a family of related languages including Arabic, Hebrew, etc.

socialization: the education of a child in the behavioral norms of his society.

Solutrean: a stone industry of Europe in Late Pleistocene times.

sub-culture: a significant though not autonomous sector of a larger culture. A sub-culture is distinguished from the larger culture by regular differences in behavioral norms and institutions. Sub-cultures may form on the basis of class differences, regional differences, etc.

sumptuary law: a law regarding consumption. Generally, a prohibition on the wearing or using of certain things except by persons of high or otherwise specified status.

superorganic: see p. 332.

Tamilian: L. H. Morgan's word for the people speaking Dravidian languages, i.e., Tamil, Malayalam, Canarese, etc.

taxonomy: classification, especially on the basis of natural relationships.

transference: a term borrowed from psychoanalysis. In its context in this book it signifies the complete identification of an ethnographer with his informant and the consequent loss of objectivity by the ethnographer.

tumpline: a line, generally of cloth, worn about the forehead and used to add support to objects being carried on the back and shoulders. Usually associated with women.

Turanian: a term, now becoming obsolete, referring narrowly to speakers of Turkic languages and, broadly, to speakers of any of the Ural-Altaic languages.

unilineal descent: the tracing of kinship through intervening relatives who are always of the same sex, i.e., a line of descent traced exclusively through males or exclusively through females.

Uralian: referring to the Uralic family of languages which includes Hungarian, Finnish, Cheremis, etc.

Würm: name given in Europe to the fourth (and last) great glaciation of the Pleistocene.

Correlation of This Book
with Representative Texts

Beals, Ralph L. and Harry Hoijer, *An Introduction to Anthropology*, Macmillan, 1953

Chapter Nos.	Related selections in *Readings in Anthropology*	Chapter Nos.	Related selections in *Readings in Anthropology*
1	I:1–3	12	II:8–11
2	I:4, 5, 7	13	II:5, 12–19
3	I:8	14	II:5, 12–19
4	I:9, 10	15	II:20, 21
5	I:4–7	16	II:27–30
6	I:9–11	17	I:14–20
7	I:12, 13	18	II:30–32
8	I:15; II:1, 2, 5	19	II:4, 33–35
9	I:25, 26	20	I:35; II:1, 6, 7, 9, 36
10	I:28–33	21	II:22–26, 37
11	. .		

Beals, Ralph L. and Harry Hoijer, *An Introduction to Anthropology*, 2nd ed., Macmillan, 1959

Chapter Nos.	Related selections in *Readings in Anthropology*	Chapter Nos.	Related selections in *Readings in Anthropology*
1	I:1–3	13	II:10, 11
2	I:4, 5, 7	14	II:5, 12–19
3	I:4–7; 21–34	15	II:5, 12–19
4	I:8	16	II:20, 21
5	I:9–13	17	II:27–30
6	I:9–13	18	I:14–20
7	I:9–13	19	II:30–32
8	I:15; II:1, 2, 5	20	II:33–35
9	I:21–34; II:6–9	21	I:35; II:1, 6, 7, 9, 36
10	I:21–34; II:6–9	22	II:22–26, 37
11	I:21–34; II:6–9		
12	I:21–34; II:6–9		

Hoebel, E. Adamson, *Man in the Primitive World*, 2nd ed., McGraw-Hill, 1958

Chapter Nos.	Related selections in *Readings in Anthropology*	Chapter Nos.	Related selections in *Readings in Anthropology*
1	I:1–3	19	II:17–19; II:5
2	⎫	20	II:15, 16
3	⎬ I:4, 5, 7, 25 ⎫	21	· ·
4	⎭ ⎪	22	· ·
5	I:4, 6 ⎪	23	· ·
6	I:21–27; II:30 ⎬ I:14	24	II:23
7	I:28–35 ⎪	25	⎫ II:9, 10
8	I:8–11 ⎪	26	⎭
9	I:12, 13 ⎪	27	⎫
10	I:15; II:1, 2 ⎭	28	⎬ II:20, 21
11	⎫	29	⎭
12	⎬ II:6, 8–10	30	⎫ II:27–29
13	⎪	31	⎭
14	⎭	32	I:15, 19, 20
15	II:30, 31	33	II:33–35
16	⎫	34	II:6, 7, 25, 26, 36
17	⎬ II:12–14	35	I:17, 35; II:1, 23, 36
18	⎭		

Turney-High, Harry Holbert, *General Anthropology*, Thomas Y. Crowell Co., 1949

Chapter Nos.	Related selections in *Readings in Anthropology*	Chapter Nos.	Related selections in *Readings in Anthropology*
1	I:1–3	13	· ·
2	I:4–7, 14	14	· ·
3	I:8–13	15	· ·
4	II:1, 2, 15	16	· ·
5	⎫ I:21–26	17	I:15–20
6	⎭	18	⎫ II:6, 8, 9
7	⎫ I:28–32	19	⎭
8	⎭	20	II:12–19; II:5
9	⎫ I:33, 35	21	II:20–23
10	⎭	22	II:10, 11
11	I:27	23	II:27–30
12	I:34		

Herskovits, Melville J., *Man and His Works*, Alfred A. Knopf, 1949

Chapter Nos.	Related selections in *Readings in Anthropology*	Chapter Nos.	Related selections in *Readings in Anthropology*
1	II:1–3	20	II:18, 20–23
2	II:1	21	II:27–29
3	II:5	22	
4	II:33	23	II:30, 31
5	II:29, 33	24	II:27, 28
6	II:3, 4	25	II:32
7	I:4–7	26	I:15–20
8	I:21–32	27	I:17, 35; II:1, 9, 17, 23, 36
9	I:8–13	28	II:22, 25
10	II:6, 7	29	. .
11	II:2	30	I:35
12	II:2	31	II:25
13	II:33	32	II:33
14	II:17	33	. .
15	II:2	34	. .
16	II:8, 9	35	II:6, 7
17	II:10, 11	36	II:36
18	II:12–19	37	. .
19	II:1, 28, 34	38	II:26, 37

Herskovits, Melville J., *Cultural Anthropology*, Alfred A. Knopf, 1955

Chapter Nos.	Related selections in *Readings in Anthropology*	Chapter Nos.	Related selections in *Readings in Anthropology*
1	I:1–3	15	I:15–20
2	I:4–7	16	II:1
3	I:21–32	17	II:5
4	I:8–11	18	II:33
5	I:12, 13	19	II:28, 29, 33
6	II:6, 7	20	II:3, 4
7	II:2	21	II:2
8	II:8, 9	22	II:17, 33
9	II:10, 11	23	I:17, 35; II:1, 9, 17, 23, 36
10	II:12–19	24	II:22, 25
11	II:18, 20–23	25	II:25
12	II:27–29	26	II:33
13	II:30, 31	27	. .
14	II:27, 28, 32	28	I:35; II:6, 7, 36

Titiev, Mischa, *The Science of Man,* Henry Holt & Co., 1954

Chapter Nos.	Related selections in *Readings in Anthropology*	Chapter Nos.	Related selections in *Readings in Anthropology*
1	I:1–3	15	I:33, 35
2	..	16	I:27
3	..	17	I:34
4	I:4, 5, 7	18	I:35; II:9
5	I:4, 5, 7, 25	19	II:1, 3–5
6	I:4–7	20	II:2, 33
7	I:8–13	21	II:6, 7
8	I:14	22	II:12–23
9	I:15, 25; II:12	23	II:27–29
10	I:21–24	24	I:15–20; II:30–32
11	I:25–26	25	II:33–35
12	I:25–26	26	II:24, 26
13	I:28–32	27	II:25, 36, 37
14	I:33, 35		

Titiev, Mischa, *Introduction to Cultural Anthropology,* Henry Holt & Co., 1959

Chapter Nos.	Related selections in *Readings in Anthropology*	Chapter Nos.	Related selections in *Readings in Anthropology*
1	I:1, 2	11	II:2, 6, 23
2	..	12	II:12–19
3	I:4–14	13	II:20–22
4	I:15	14	II:33–35
5	I:25, 26, 27	15	II:27–29
6	I:28–32	16	II:27–29
7	I:33, 34	17	I:15–20
8	I:35; II:25	18	II:30–32
9	II:1–5	19	..
10	II:6, 7	20	II:25, 26, 36, 37

Keesing, Felix M., *The Science of Custom,* Rinehart and Co., 1958

Chapter Nos.	Related selections in *Readings in Anthropology*	Chapter Nos.	Related selections in *Readings in Anthropology*
1	I:1–3, 14; II:1, 4, 5, 38	10	II:5, 12–19, 22–24
2	I:1; II:1, 2, 5, 22, 23	11	II:5, 20, 21
3	I:4–14	12	II:21, 28
4	I:21–35	13	II:27–29
5	II:6, 7	14	II:30–32
6	I:35; II:1, 5, 9, 17, 18, 23	15	I:15–20
7	II:2	16	I:35; II:22, 25, 26, 36
8	II:8, 9	17	II:26, 36, 37
9	II:10, 11, 17		

Firth, Raymond, *Human Types,* Thomas Nelson & Sons, 1956, Mentor Books, 1958

Chapter Nos.	Related selections in *Readings in Anthropology*	Chapter Nos.	Related selections in *Readings in Anthropology*
1	I:8–13	5	II:5, 17, 20, 21
2	II:6, 7	6	II:27–29
3	II:8–11, 17	7	II:1, 22–26, 33–37
4	II:5, 12–19, 22–24		

Kroeber, A. L., *Anthropology,* Harcourt, Brace and Company, 1948

Chapter Nos.	Related selections in *Readings in Anthropology*	Chapter Nos.	Related selections in *Readings in Anthropology*
1	I:1–13	9	. .
2	I:15	10	II:25
3	I:4–6	11–14	. .
4	I:8–11	15	II:33–35
5	I:12, 13	16	I:21–26
6	I:15–20	17	I:28–33; 35
7	II:1, 2, 23	18	I:27, 34
8	II:2	19	I:36, 37

Kluckhohn, Clyde, *Mirror for Man,* Whittlesey House, McGraw-Hill, 1949; Premier Books, Fawcett-Wills, 1957

Chapter Nos.	Related selections in *Readings in Anthropology*	Chapter Nos.	Related selections in *Readings in Anthropology*
1	I:1–3	6	I:15–20
2	II:1–5	7	II:33–35
3	I:21–24	8	II:23–26
4	I:14, 4–7	9	II:36, 37
5	I:8–13		

Harry L. Shapiro (ed.), *Man, Culture, and Society,* Oxford University Press, 1956

Chapter Nos.	Related selections in *Readings in Anthropology*	Chapter Nos.	Related selections in *Readings in Anthropology*
1	I:4–8, 11	9	I:15–20
2	I:21, 22, 24	10	. .
3	I:25, 26	11	II:25, 36
4	I:28–32	12	II:12–14
5	I:33, 35	13	II:15–24
6	I:27, 34, 35	14	II:27–29
7	II:1, 2; I:15	15	II:8–11
8	. .	16	II:5, 11, 23

Honigmann, John J., *The World of Man*, Harper & Brothers, 1959

Section Nos.	Related selections in *Readings in Anthropology*	Section Nos.	Related selections in *Readings in Anthropology*
1	I:1, 2; II:38	23	
2	I:15; II:1, 2	24	
3	I:3; II:1	25	II:12–19, 23
4	I:21–24	26	
5		27	
6		28	
7	II:3–6	29	II:20, 21, 28
8		30	
9	II:1, 2, 5	31	II:27–29
10	II:7, 22, 24, 33	32	I:15–20
11	. .	33	II:33–35
12		34	
13		35	
14		36	
15	I:15, 17, 18, 34;	37	II:27–29
16	II:6, 17, 25, 34, 36, 37	38	
17		39	
18		40	
19	II:2	41	I:25, 26, 28–33, 35
20		42	
21	II:8–11	43	I:27, 34
22		44	
		45	I:4–14
		46	

INSTRUCTOR'S MANUAL

THE POWER TO PERSUADE

A Rhetoric and Reader for Argumentative Writing

Second Edition

Sally De Witt Spurgin

Southern Methodist University

PRENTICE HALL
Englewood Cliffs, New Jersey 07632

© 1989 by **PRENTICE-HALL, INC.**
A Division of Simon & Schuster
Englewood Cliffs, N.J. 07632

10 9 8 7 6 5 4 3 2 1

ISBN 0-13-688623-X
Printed in the United States of America

Contents

Introduction

While this Instructor's Guide is written with the needs and uncertainties of the beginning instructor in mind, I hope that it may prove useful in small ways to the experienced instructor as well. What I have done in these pages is to share the experiences I have had teaching argumentation and effective writing to freshmen and sophomores in college. I include suggestions for supplementing the material in *The Power to Persuade*; ideas for directing class discussion of issues raised in the text and in the readings; warnings about the pits I have fallen into myself and how to avoid them; ways of organizing a one-semester course using *The Power to Persuade*; and possible responses to the exercises and questions in the text. Chapter notes include brief biographical notes on the authors of readings and (in several instances) a sample analysis of one reading, focusing on the chapter's emphases. In addition, the selected references for each chapter, listed at the end of the textbook, are highly recommended to the beginning rhetoric instructor.

The study of argumentation helps students appreciate the role of rhetoric in *their* worlds, the worlds beyond books of literature, where making a sale, justifying a policy, reassuring a client, trying to understand a colleague's criticisms, finding a solution to a problem and convincing the boss to implement it, and many other such activities put both knowledge and persuasiveness to the test on a daily basis. Students both need and (either immediately or eventually) appreciate the skills they develop or hone in writing and analyzing arguments. After all, as Jim W. Corder notes in his *Uses of Rhetoric* (Lippincott, 1971), "[W]hile we have great long shelves of books on the strategies and styles of poetry, we have little to show us how language works in modes of discourse we are almost constantly exposed to" (9). Argumentation is one such mode of discourse, and perhaps the most prevalent, as the range of readings in *The Power to Persuade* indicates.

I hope that you and your students will enjoy using *The Power to Persuade*. So that future editions of the textbook and this Guide may benefit from your experience in working with them, I would greatly appreciate your comments and suggestions, which can be sent to either of the following addresses.

c/o College Editorial	Department of English
Prentice Hall	Southern Methodist University
Englewood Cliffs, NJ 07632	Dallas, TX 75275

Permission is hereby given for instructors using *The Power to Persuade* to reproduce—for classroom use only—material included in this Guide.

Suggestions for Organizing Syllabus

A fifteen-week rhetoric course using *The Power to Persuade* might be organized in several ways, depending on the instructor's aims for the course. Obviously, you can follow the book straight through, giving more time to the longer or more complex chapters (such as "Revising" or "Deductive Reasoning") and less time to the shorter chapters with simpler concerns (such as the introductory chapter or "Definition"). But you may find other emphases or orders suit your preferences and your particular students' needs. For instance, if you are teaching this material in the second semester of a two-semester writing course, you may need less time for the chapters on invention and revision. If you prefer not to teach the documented essay in this course, you will omit parts of Chapter 4. If you wish to emphasize inductive and deductive reasoning from the beginning of the term, you will want to use Chapters 7, 8, and 9 early—perhaps even before the chapters on the writing process.

If chapters are not followed in the order given, a few questions may appear to have been begged on occasion and some questions at the end of readings will not be appropriate until other chapters have been read. The instructor should supplement other questions if desired.

Three possible ways of organizing the course are suggested below.

	(A)	(B)	(C)
Week 1	Chapter 1	Chapter 1	Chapter 1
Week 2	Chapter 7	Chapter 2	Chapters 2 & 3
Week 3	Chapter 7	Chapter 2	Chapters 5 & 6
Week 4	Chapter 8	Chapter 3	Chapter 4
Week 5	Chapter 8	Chapter 5	Chapter 4
Week 6	Chapter 8	Chapter 5	Chapter 7
Week 7	Chapter 9	Chapter 6	Chapter 7
Week 8	Chapter 2	Chapter 7	Chapter 8
Week 9	Chapter 3	Chapter 7	Chapter 8
Week 10	Chapter 5	Chapter 8	Chapter 8
Week 11	Chapter 5	Chapter 8	Chapter 9

	(A)	(B)	(C)
Week 12	Chapter 6	Chapter 9	Chapter 9
Week 13	Chapter 4	Chapter 4	Chapter 10
Week 14	Chapter 4	Chapters 4 & 10	Chapter 10
Week 15	Chapter 10	Chapters 4 & 10	Chapter 10

• Outline (A) may be appropriate for the instructor who intends to focus on inductive and deductive reasoning throughout the semester and who plans to teach formal reasoning skills before assigning full essays.

• Outline (B) is designed for the instructor who plans to teach a formal research paper at the end of the semester and who prefers to defer discussion of the uses of outside source material until that point. The instructor who prefers to omit outside source material entirely might choose to follow this arrangement, omitting Chapter 4 altogether except perhaps for Hayakawa's "Reports, Inferences, Judgments" (which works well with Chapter 7, "Inductive Reasoning"). In that case, readings from Chapter 10 or additional class workshops would easily take up the slack in this outline.

• Outline (C) is designed for the instructor whose students need little review of invention and revision.

Because *The Power to Persuade* contains some forty-five readings, the course can be adapted to the individual instructor's preferences. You may prefer to spend one day on text and two on readings each week; two days on text and one on readings; or one day on text, one on readings, and one on class editing and writing workshops (in which students read and comment on each other's writing-in-progress).

1

Argument and Persuasion

The aim of this chapter is, first, to acquaint students with the aims of argumentation and the vocabulary we will use in describing and assessing it; and, second, to demonstrate the pervasiveness of argument in everyday life. Toward those ends, you may find it helpful to ask students to bring to class examples of newspaper editorials, charitable solicitations, magazine essays, and their own textbooks from other courses, with arguments marked for the class's assessment. Ask them also to make a point of noticing arguments put forward in casual conversations that they overhear or take part in. An argument journal is a useful means of encouraging students to take notice of arguments in many such contexts. In a notebook students record each day examples of arguments they read or hear. These may be cut-and-pasted or written out, but each should be properly documented as to source (providing an opportunity to familiarize students with the requirements of citing sources as explained in Chapter 4).

Students need to be able to identify premises and conclusions before going any further in the study of argument. Once they are able to do so confidently, they should be able as well to distinguish between conclusions to major arguments and conclusions to arguments that seem to be offered in support of the more important points. In this way, students can become accustomed to identifying the thesis (conclusion to the principal argument) of a piece of writing. Even advanced composition students can have trouble identifying theses immediately, particularly if they are implicit or stated somewhere other than in the last sentence of the first paragraph.

Important topics for classroom discussion of the material in this chapter include (1) the ethics of argument and the role of argument in the pursuit of understanding; (2) the rhetorical context of argument—writer, reader, and purpose; (3) what constitutes an arguable assertion; (4) the problems posed by rationalization and differing *a priori* beliefs; (5) the role assumptions play in our reasoning; (6) the relative appeals of

5

logic, emotion, and *ethos*; and (7) the importance of language choices in persuasion.

EXERCISES

Exercise 1–1

1. I'm serving Watergate cake for dessert.
2. I will plan to be out of town that day. (*accordingly*)
3. It seems likely that the situation in Jordan is not resolvable by Western intervention. (*consequently*)
4. Margaret must dislike the color red.
5. [Spiders] can't be insects. (*so*)
6. Every college ... needs a career-counseling office. (*therefore*)

Exercise 1–2

A. Numbers 2, 3, 6, and 18 are not arguments. Further relationships need to be stated or implied in order to create arguments. Item 2 is simply an assertion. Item 6 might puzzle some students: It is only a statement, but what it reports is based on an argument made by those who opposed Bork's nomination. And Item 18 is again simply a statement.

Item 3 offers a good illustration of personal idiosyncracy masquerading as argument. It's worth giving a little class time to discussing this kind of problem. Much breath has been wasted trying to "reason" people out of their personal tastes and preferences!

Students may find item 14 a little difficult, since they may not yet have the vocabulary or conceptual training to recognize an enthymeme with an implicit conclusion. Just ask, "So what relationship is Downing trying to draw here?" (It is that dependency can lead to self-hatred.)

B. The unstated assumptions (premises) in the list are as follows:

1. People who cheat at Monopoly can't be trusted.
4. Apartment houses give rise to traffic, pollution, and the deterioration of yards and gardens.
5. No one who is capable of rational thought and of making himself or herself understood is a poor thinker.
7. Several assumptions here: What is more likely to kill is more dangerous. Fires are more likely to kill people than burglars are. Burglar bars prevent people from escaping fires.
10. Therefore, the more that is given, the more poverty will increase.

11. Republican administrations create or worsen unemployment and inflation.
12. Democrats are liberal and free-spending.
14. Therefore, dependency can lead to self-hatred.
15. Studying biology will give English majors an understanding of organic structure.
16. Several assumptions here: The first person to do a thing should get credit for it. Credit for an invention should not be limited to a single person when two or more people actually developed it. People need not work together in order to share credit for something they have in common.
20. Washing dishes is worth doing.

The other arguments have explicit premises. Among them, some confusion may still arise. While we won't discuss formal fallacies just yet, some students may be puzzled by Wilson's comment in 9. He is guilty of the fallacy of division (in effect introducing an extra term, because idealistic countries are not the same class as idealistic individuals), believing that what is true of the whole must be true of each part. The argument could be restated as follows: All idealistic countries are [synonymous with] America. I am idealistic. Therefore I am an American.

Don't worry too much if students find additional unstated assumptions (Toulmin's "backing") even for arguments with all premises expressed. They don't yet have a formal understanding of the syllogistic argument, after all. I'd be inclined to applaud them for recognizing the deeper and sometimes *a priori* assumptions in even straightforward arguments.

C. 2. Because the Vikings beat Columbus to America, authors really should put more emphasis on that Nordic accomplishment in American history books.
   3. No, I won't go to the concert. Symphony orchestra concerts do not have the relevance to life today that television does, and people really need to spend their time on what's relevant to their interests and needs. So I'm going to stay home and watch TV.
   6. Should he be named to the Supreme Court, Judge Robert Bork's concept of judicial restraint might tend to undermine the advances that have been made in civil rights matters. To undermine those advances would be undesirable. Therefore, Judge Bork should not be named to the Supreme Court.
(This is roughly the argument that Item 6 alludes to but does not itself put forth.)

18. Because space shuttle cabins are properly and securely designed, and oxygen can be supplied without cumbersome space suits, in the future shuttle astronauts will wear simple overalls as long as they remain inside the vehicle.

Exercise 1-3

First conclusion (paragraph topic, although emphasis is to be on humankind, not animals): "Sex and reproduction are natural and nonproblematic for all animals except Man." Supporting premises: the following examples of sex among animals and sexual tensions among humans (inductive support). Additional conclusion (restatement of paragraph topic): "Sex is ... simple and straightforward for animals, [and] painful for the rest of us."

Premise: "We have entered the world of good and evil." Notice that "Nothing could be simpler" and "We have entered the world of good and evil" are asserted but not themselves argued. The final argument depends on some shared *a priori* beliefs—that, for instance, this is indeed "a world of good and evil."

Exercise 1-4

Not all of these terms are defined in the chapter—some must be looked up in the index or a dictionary—but students need to recognize, in order to avoid confusion later, that these words have precise meanings in argument.

argument: a reasoned consideration of an idea in the pursuit of understanding and truth, usually with the further aim of persuasion

persuasion: the act of "win[ning]" over (someone) to a course of action by reasoning or inducement" (*American Heritage Dictionary*)

persuade: to affect attitude or behavior through any means

convince: to affect understanding as well as behavior through reason (Recall the old ditty, "The man convinced against his will/Is of the same opinion still." *Persuaded* is what is meant here, but *convinced* fits both meter and irony better.)

fallacy: logical error in reasoning

lie: untrue statement

premise: supporting statement giving evidence or reason

conclusion: assertion supported by premises

ethical appeal: the persuasive quality of the arguer's character; often generated in written arguments through plenty of illustrations and examples and a moderate tone with touches of self-deprecating humor—not to mention a fluid and appropriately emphatic style *emotional appeal:* the persuasive quality of appeals to empathy, fear, and other emotions in the reader

assumption: something not directly stated that extends the meaning of what *is* stated

qualification: limits the extent of what is stated

Exercise 1–5

Here students have an early opportunity to write a simple argument. In addition to discussing what elements make each in fact an argument, the class may find it illuminating to identify the appeals their paragraphs make and how successful they anticipate those appeals would be. Since these arguments will be no longer than a page, you might reproduce a few samples (overhead transparencies work particularly well) for students to comment on.

READINGS

Debbie Sapp, "What So Proudly We Hailed?" (Student Essay)

This essay is included with the aim of making students comfortable with the idea of writing argument. Argument need not be ponderous or even profound to be both successful and engaging. Student response to the essay may be mixed; some readers will be put off by what they perceive to be either flippancy of tone or triviality of content. A discussion of tone and the writer's degree of success in reaching her reader will get students to begin thinking about rhetorical contexts. As to the content, discuss the effect that Sapp's offering a solution has on the argument as a whole. She complains, but she does more than *just* complain. Discuss, too, the tactics Sapp employs to engage our interest in her introduction, and the means she employs to conclude without simply restating her thesis. Her effective transitions between ideas and between paragraphs are worth noting as well.

Ask students to suggest another "pet peeve" topic for discussion: What kinds of arguments could be advanced concerning it? How might such arguments be made both convincing and interesting? Students will begin to appreciate what Sapp has done when they attempt a similar effort.

Analysis of the Essay Debbie Sapp has written an entertaining variation on a tired topic: "my pet peeve." However, at first it looks like the usual pet of this species. The controlling idea, or thesis, of her essay is that the national anthem of the United States is unsatisfactory and should be changed; she states this thesis in the last sentence of her introductory paragraph. Luckily for us, Sapp has considered her audience in planning her argument. Aware that her topic has great potential for dullness and is not likely to fascinate her readers—initially, the members of her rhetoric class—she engages our interest and attention by the mock-defiance of her introduction: "I am not a Communist." Throughout the essay her tone is never more than half-serious, yet she is careful to balance the light touch with some telling points.

Sapp has three primary reasons for her objections to the "Star-Spangled Banner," and each of these reasons becomes the topic of a paragraph. First, the song is difficult to sing; few people can reach the high notes comfortably. Second, the lyrics celebrate a single battle in which the United States defeated Great Britain: Our national anthem insults our closest ally. And finally, half the people who sing the song do not understand what they are singing in the first place. Sapp develops each of these points with examples drawn from the lyrics and from experiences her readers can identify with, such as standing next to someone who *can* hit the high notes. And she makes her transitions from point to point smooth and natural. The first paragraph concerns the music, for example, and the second paragraph prepares us for the transition to another idea with its declaration that "a national anthem is more than just music." The discussion of the lyrics moves from its subject matter, in paragraph 3, to its difficulty, in the transitional first two sentences of paragraph 4.

The writer has considered her readers well. We respond with a smile of recognition to the points she makes; even if exaggerated for effect, they cannot be entirely refuted. Lest we find her merely petulant, however, she does more than criticize: She offers a solution to the problem she has identified. We can replace the current anthem with a better one, perhaps even a new one. To support the idea of change, the writer draws an analogy that begins seriously and ends lightly: Black Americans were emancipated, women were given the vote, and now, by the same token, vocal cords need their freedom, too.

Possible Responses to the Questions

1(a) The thesis conclusion is that "there are plenty of reasons and a good number of alternatives that would justify a change [in the song designated the U.S. national anthem]." The supporting premises are:

Few people can sing the whole range of "The Star-Spangled Banner."

The SSB inappropriately commemorates a single battle with England.

The vocabulary of the SSB is somewhat obscure and unintelligible.

Among the appropriate alternatives to the SSB are "America the Beautiful," "My Country, 'Tis of Thee," and "Grand Old Flag."

(b) For example, in paragraph 1: "I am angry *because* ...." In paragraph 4: "It must be powerful poetry *because* ...." In paragraph 6: "... and

Canada; *for* at least ....." Students may notice that Sapp uses fewer such markers than we might expect.

2. National anthems should be democratic in themselves: songs with simple tunes and lyrics and wide appeal. A buried *a priori* idea that some students may note is that practicality is more important than tradition.

3. Sapp seems to believe that we won't be truly put off—but rather, intrigued—by her denouncement in the first sentence. She figures we are more likely to be bored than priggish, more responsive to humor than passion (on this subject). She assumes we are fellow American citizens who attend football games, don't sing particularly well, and bear England no grudges.

4. My own response is strongest to the ethical appeal—I have almost a stronger sense of the writer than of the argument. (I have never met this student, by the way; she wrote the essay for a colleague and she and I have communicated only by letter.) The emphasis may not be appropriate in a serious attempt to bring about a change; but frankly, it had a rather different purpose. As the first essay of the semester, it was designed chiefly to win over the instructor. Most essays with that aim fail abysmally; this one, because it does consider the issue and the wider (classroom) audience as well, succeeds rather well.

William F. Buckley, Jr., "Why Don't We Complain?"

(1925–   ) A prominent conservative political commentator known both for his essays (published frequently in *The Atlantic, Harper's,* and other periodicals) and, more recently, for his novels. He is editor-in-chief of *National Review* and hosts a PBS program, *Firing Line,* on which he interviews public figures.

1. Implicit thesis: "Americans should not be so hesitant to assert themselves, to complain about what needs redress or remedy." The two parts of Buckley's thesis are that Americans *are* hesitant to complain (a point that he several times declares in so many words) and that they should not be. He devotes this essay to giving evidence of the former (chiefly his own experiences, such as on the train and in the movie theatre) and reasons for the latter (e.g., "When our voices are finally mute, ... we shall have become automatons, incapable of feeling"—paragraph 22).

2. Buckley does seem to regard complaint in something like the way that we have defined *argument*—an assertion backed up by reasons. He advocates fault-finding argument, not mere whining. Buckley here

gives complaining the stature of a gesture for patriotism and the American Way.

3. The example of Buckley's experience in the Vermont ski shop does indeed undermine his thesis, but does so deliberately. Buckley concedes that our complaints can make us look churlish when we don't understand circumstances fully. His humor prevents the ski-shop example from rebounding against him: "I looked up manfully—into a score of man-eating eyes. I put the experience down as a reversal" (paragraph 17).

4. Buckley's sense of irony and his low-keyed humor are evident throughout the essay. For example, "we sweated, but we did not moan" in paragraph 1; the "gauntlet of eighty sweating American freemen" in 2; the observations that "I did not have the manliness to order her to take the milk back, but instead settled for a cowardly sulk," in 11; or the wry comment quoted above from 17. The anecdotal quality of Buckley's illustrations is achieved in part through his use of conversation and his casual contractions ("It isn't just the commuters," 4) and simple transitions ("But notice that no one did," 8). Ask students to discuss whether the serious arguments in paragraphs 19–22 are convincing or melodramatic in this context.

ADDITIONAL SUGGESTIONS FOR WRITING OR DISCUSSION

1. As antidotes to common misconceptions about argument, put on library reserve James Harvey Robinson's *The Mind in the Making* (Harper, 1921) and Marya Mannes's *But Will It Sell?* (Lippincott, 1964). Ask students to read the essays mentioned in the "Suggestions for Writing and Further Discussion." The essays serve to dispel erroneous notions that our own beliefs are always founded on reason and sound analysis (Robinson) or that judgments and values are all merely "relative" (Mannes).

2. Oscar Wilde's Lord Henry says, in *The Picture of Dorian Gray*, "I never approve, or disapprove, of anything now. It is an absurd attitude to take towards life. We are not sent into the world to air our moral prejudices. I never take any notice of what common people say, and I never interfere with what charming people do." Let discussion of this statement, so unintentionally ironic on Lord Henry's part, generate possible theses for an essay on the impossibility of not judging—and perhaps on the responsibilities entailed or the biases revealed in making judgments.

3. Additional exercises or possible quiz on identifying conclusions and premises:

Of course you gained weight. You eat Oreo cookies all day long. [conclusion stated first]

Violin music is soothing, and all soothing things are healthful. Therefore, violin music is heathful. [conclusion last]

"When nurse Genene Jones was on duty in a San Antonio hospital, babies had mysterious emergencies and sometimes died. Then she moved to a Kerrville clinic, and the awful pattern began again."—Peter Elkind, "The Death Shift," *Texas Monthly*, Aug. 1983, 106 [conclusion implicit]

Platinum is more valuable than gold, so it follows that more people would want jewelry made of platinum than would want jewelry made of gold. [conclusion last]

Beginning this year, no student may enter the School of Business without having earned at least a C+ average during the freshman year. The problem is, all freshmen students with C+ averages (or better) have signed up for the Schools of Engineering, Humanities and Sciences, and Fine Arts for the coming year. So it looks as if no continuing students at the university will enter the School of Business this year. [conclusion last]

4. Have students examine the most recent State of the Union message or another political speech and discuss the logical, emotional, and ethical appeals therein.

5. In some future edition of this text, when my editor will let it run somewhat longer, I plan to include a wonderful essay which I will in the meantime recommend to you as a first-rate way to either begin or end the course. The essay is William G. Perry, Jr.'s "Examsmanship and the Liberal Arts" (Members of the Harvard Faculty, *Examining in Harvard College: A Collection of Essays*, Harvard UP, 1963). While dated in some of its details, "Examsmanship" remains always fresh and vital in its message to both students and teachers. It is about grades and getting by; but it is also (and not at all incidentally) about the power and importance of the ability to reason.

2

Creating Arguments

The primary aims of this chapter are twofold: first, to show students that argument takes place in a context and not in a void, and that considering the second and third elements of the context—the reader and the reason for addressing the reader—will help them generate both content and the first element of the rhetorical context, the persona. The writer who considers the issues and considers the reader will find what needs to be said—the argument's content—and how best to present it, and in so doing will create a credible and persuasive persona. This is, therefore, a chapter on invention, on creating and developing arguments that meet the reader's needs according to the writer's purpose.

Second, this chapter aims to help students with specific suggestions for generating a thesis and rough plan for their written arguments. You won't find here any discussions of "brainstorming" or "looping" tactics or others of the more fashionable invention strategies—not that your humble author discounts their worth, but only that she cannot see how a textbook can usefully teach them. An instructor equipped with an overhead projector can do far more, and this book does not attempt to duplicate such efforts with sketches—either verbal or pictorial. Instead, this chapter concentrates on three class-tested strategies that enable students to generate a thesis for an assigned writing project. (Some of the more freewheeling strategies work better, it seems to me, for those occasions when one is simply told to write *something* about *anything*— but I betray my prejudices!)

The chapter may be adapted to the instructor's personal style in teaching invention. Should its presentation of these three strategies— considering topical questions, finding and resolving contradictions, and developing enthymemes—strike you as too prescriptive, you may prefer to use only the first part of the chapter (on the rhetorical contexts in which arguments occur). But novice writers often are grateful for specific guidelines such as these—and they are included at the urging of many instructors. My own experience has been that they generate, not stifle, creative thinking. Both my students and I have had greatest success with the second strategy, finding and resolving contradictions. Some colleagues have been more satisfied with the papers generated from the enthymemic strategy. But should time permit you to discuss only one strategy, the list of topical questions is the easiest to cover quickly.

EXERCISES

Exercise 2–1

This exercise provides an opportunity to talk about bias and stereotyping. When some students share their lists, do any others frown or shake their heads in protest? What characteristics of the group do people seem to have ignored? Ask each student to add one personal characteristic or interest (an academic major, a home town, a hobby, etc.) that was not included in the general list: Do any additional patterns emerge?

Exercise 2–2

A. Some additional possible topics:
    Prayer in public schools
    American relations with Israel (or Jordan, Panama, Nicaragua, etc.)
    Mandatory draft registration
    Police roadblocks to check for drunken drivers
    Required courses
    Writing on the blackboard a number of responses to one of the suggested subjects can help students who had trouble with this assignment see the possibilities for developing a subject in a number of different ways. Discuss the thesis sentences that emerge: Are they restricted, complete, and interesting? The paper that lacks a promising preliminary thesis is doomed to trouble; it is well worth taking the time at this point to discuss thesis-writing in some detail.

B. This part of the exercise is intended to reinforce for students just how important it is to consider the reader in finding something to say about a given subject. This analysis might seem to contradict the chapter's claim that an effective persona comes out of rather than precedes other considerations. But it is not necessarily unethical and manipulative to think for a moment about how one wishes to sound to one's reader. Doing so, as long as sound does not become more important than sense, can enable the writer to anticipate reader response as well as reader needs.

C. The theses generated here might prove suitable for further development in essays. Have the class evaluate and discuss several (you might collect their homework and put three or four anonymous examples on the board).

Exercise 2-3

A. For example:

1. Judges should remain above the political fray, and yet at most levels they must participate in partisan politics in order to be elected. Is a judge supposed to be the best legal mind available AND the best campaign organizer and fundraiser?

2. Is it an inherent right in a representative democracy that nearly every person who is to have some control over his or her fellows should be elected by them? Should this be true of judges? If so, why are some judges elected and some appointed?

3. For governors and presidents to appoint all judges would mean that the electorate would not have to make uninformed decisions about the fairness and judicial expertise of candidates, but it might make the process even more susceptible to other abuses—such as the repayment of political favors.

4. So, apparently, there is no way to insure the democratic placement of truly qualified individuals in the judiciary. Or is there?

Exercise 2-4

A. "Injured hikers" concerns a question of policy and thus would lead to an argument with only two terms: Those who are aware of hiking's risks should pay for the cost of their own rescues. But why? We don't have a real argument until some premise addresses that question.

"Hiking permit fees" concerns a question of influence. As the examples stand, this is the most workable thesis and the best structured enthymeme of the lot.

"The lives of injured hikers" concerns a question of value. People who are careless are worth less than other people?? How does one support such a claim?

"Requiring injured hikers" concerns a question of influence. It includes a number of assumptions, some quite questionable, and too many terms.

"Hikers get injured" concerns a question of influence, but only two terms: injured hikers and risk-takers. No argumentative structure as yet.

READINGS

Student Draft, "Group Discussions Are Beneficial"

Although this piece was published in our campus newspaper, I call it a draft because it is one—and a first draft at that, showing all the jumps in thought and shifts in direction first drafts are prone to. And it shows the dangers of writing without a clear sense of purpose or a regard for audience (the writer antagonizes everybody, students as well as professors)—and consequently, writing without a thesis. But it shows as well all the potential first drafts can hold. Had the writer gone back over this material after a short interval, he might have determined which of his three ideas would bear development into a coherent argument.

1. Our author here shows only his clear sense that the semester, the school year, and his job on *The Daily Campus* are drawing to a close. And that he is in a hurry.

2. There are actually three main points: (1) "Many Americans come to expect their answers quickly," and college students are no exception; (2) "College has become too much memorization and not enough thinking"; and (3) "Discussion groups are the best way to learn." These are not linked into a single coherent thesis. How about dropping the first point and trying, "Both professors and students are to blame for the fact that students leave college without the creative and analytical skills they need most." (The "because" clause, or premises, could point to the emphasis on rote memorization and lecturing rather than on study and discussion.) Or focus on the first point with something like "Americans want a quick fix for every problem, but college is not designed to offer that." The essay would then resolve a contradiction (between what colleges were established to do and what we expect of them) through definition (what colleges are intended to do). In that case the second and third points might be dropped or used only as illustrations.

3. Suggestions are given in 2, above.

4. This is the flip side of question 3. The answers will depend on the thesis each student decides on. But in any event some concepts need defining. The notion of "discussion groups" in paragraph 12 is one such concept—which the writer seems to think means only learning "the opinions of [his] peers."

5. There are many gaps. For example, the reference to "the Ward Cleaver effect" is incomprehensible in paragraph 2 (and becomes only slightly clearer two paragraphs later). And how do we get from one hour a day of studying, in paragraph 5, to "Therein lies the problem: College has

become too much memorization and not enough thinking," in paragraph 6? (A muddle not helped by the curious predication of that sentence!)

6. The editor didn't help matters with the title—which, in addition to its blandness, leads the reader to expect an emphasis that does not arise until the next-to-last paragraph. You can have some fun with a class discussion of alternative titles. I'm partial to "Maximize? Memorize!" Or how about "Calling Ward Cleaver!"

Linda Chavez, "Pay Equity Is Unfair to Women"

At the time this essay was written (1985), Linda Chavez was staff director of the U.S. Commission on Civil Rights. Before joining the commission in November 1983 she was an assistant to Albert Shanker, president of the American Federation of Teachers.

—*Fortune*, 4 Mar. 1985, 16

In discussing this essay, you may wish (in anticipation of the next chapter) to call students' attention to the use of definition in Chavez's persuasive strategy (e.g., "comparable worth," "pay equity," equation of "traditionally female jobs" with "jobs with benefits for women"). In paragraphs 5 and 6 Chavez talks about the wage gap between men and women—but notice the *logical* gap in the assumption that women *choose* jobs in lower paying fields. And why should "professional" women make less than "professional" men in the same field with the same education, training, and so forth? *Do* working mothers get those "other benefits" alluded to in paragraph 6 in exchange for their lower paying jobs? Then, too, there is a problem in paragraph 9: Higher pay to fewer workers for the same total work *does* work out to higher productivity for higher pay. If a job can be done away with, was it a needed job or a makework job?

1. Students probably will point to the dramatic assertion in paragraph 2: "[I]n the long run all women will lose." Perhaps Chavez makes this point early to get readers' attention—but then the title does that first. Some students may think that the thesis is the rhetorical (and question-begging) question at the end of paragraph 2: "Why, then, have so many otherwise sensible people endorsed comparable worth?" But the paragraphs that follow *don't* exactly follow. Neither point is argued very clearly or convincingly. The "women will lose" point disappears just after being made, only to re-emerge in the last three paragraphs. The trouble with this essay is that it, like the student draft in this chapter, lacks the focus a coherently developed thesis would provide. (See question 5 for a potentially workable thesis enthymeme that could unify much of this material.)

2. Probably (since she begins and ends with it) Chavez intends the "all women will lose" idea to be her thesis. If so, her supporting points

are that (1) pay equity advocates have "mimick[ed] the strategy of the civil rights movement" (paragraph 3); (2) "the courts have held that government ought to remedy any disparities" among different groups of people" (4—which contains several tenuously related points); (3) women work at different jobs than men do (para. 5); (4) women work at those different jobs because they are willing to "take less pay to get other benefits" (para. 6)—and so on. These do not clearly lead to or support the presumed thesis. Even the last several paragraphs, which do relate to the "thesis," offer only assertions, except for paragraphs 9 and 10. But paragraph 9 still assumes that women want to be secretaries, and paragraph 10 is vague about just what Australia's "variation of comparable worth" is—making comparisons and assessment difficult.

3. Some unsupported value statements or assumptions:

   "But in the long run all women will lose." (2—and 8, and 11. As the Bellman said to the Snark, "What I've told you three times is true"?)

   "Earnings clearly play only a partial role in women's *decision* to work in a limited number of jobs." (6; emphasis added)

   A woman who takes a job with less pay does get other benefits—is not penalized for taking off time for childbirth, etc. (6)

   "The fact that women continue to seek employment primarily in low-paying, female-dominated jobs . . . does not suggest to comparable worth advocates that the non-monetary benefits of certain jobs may have appeal." (7)

4. These are mostly identified in 2, above. Chavez thinks most of the disparities comparable worth advocates point to are only apparent, but that the contradictions she finds in their position are real.

5. Although Chavez does not develop this argument fully, here is the thesis that she could have and perhaps should have developed. The major premise is easily granted (it is in fact almost a definition). The minor premise needs to be proven (and this draft does not do so). Then, the conclusion would work. *Then*, the concluding paragraph could advance a value statement:

   What leads to fewer jobs with benefits for women is bad for women. (an easily granted value statement)
   Comparable worth leads to fewer jobs with benefits for women. (proven in the "new" essay)
   Therefore, comparable worth is bad for women. (a now-inescapable value statement)

6. Yes, obviously, she is trying to do too much. The thesis she could have developed is the argument of paragraph 9. The new thesis assertion could be expressed as "Far from helping women, comparable worth leads to fewer jobs with benefits for women."

ADDITIONAL SUGGESTIONS FOR
WRITING OR DISCUSSION

Here are some possible assignments that can expand the discussion of the persona a successful writer creates through considering purpose and audience to arrive at a workable thesis.

1. Ask students to find signed newspaper and magazine articles and reprinted public statements that comment on some single, specified recent event or crisis. For example, in 1987 one stimulus for widespread comment was commercial airline safety in the aftermath of several crashes; others were the revelations of unbecoming behavior by political candidates Gary Hart and Joseph Biden and by television evangelists Jim Bakker and Jimmy Swaggart. Collect the clippings and duplicate brief arguments by journalists and observers and quoted comments by the principals and others involved in the event or its aftermath. In a class meeting, ask students to discuss the personas of the various writers or speakers: How knowledgeable do they seem? How fair? How well do they express themselves? Ask students also to identify what seems to be the intended audience for each, and the apparent purposes the writers individually hope to achieve through their arguments. Students will notice the range of responses and voices: Ask them to discuss what clues, if any, help us decide whom to believe.

2. Give students a sense of writing for real audiences (since we the instructors are not quite "real" people to them!) by asking them to write a letter on a subject of current and personal interest to a politician or bureaucrat or to the editor of the campus or local newspaper—and actually mail it. Discuss what differences would be likely in letters on the same topic—say, a controversial bill before Congress—addressed to the legislator sponsoring the bill and to a newspaper. Ask: Should there be any difference? Is it dishonest to express an idea differently to different audiences?

3. If possible, invite a criminal trial lawyer to discuss jury selection methods with the students. Trial lawyers have to be experts in audience analysis, but students may find disturbing the stereotyping lawyers pragmatically engage in.

4. Some kinds of written communication have as their aim chiefly the expression of emotion—congratulations, sympathy, welcome, thanks. In such cases sensitivity to the particular reader and the creation of a warm persona are of utmost importance. And such writing assignments can be among the most difficult kinds of writing to do really well. I once had occasion to write a note to a college friend just after her brother had shot the president of the United States. I had to write

another to a friend who had given birth to a brain-damaged child, and to still another whose only child had died. On happier occasions, I have written notes of welcome and invitation to visitors from Spain and from England, and congratulations to friends upon their earning Ph.D.'s. Some years ago I wrote hundreds of thank-you notes for wedding gifts, and took pains to make each one different (you never know when people will compare notes!). Such letters and notes are among the most frequent kinds of writing we do in the "real" world where few people write essays. Give students some hypothetical contexts for which to write notes of thanks, congratulation, sympathy, and the like. Discuss the results, particularly the temptation to use underlinings, exclamation marks, vague adjectives, and weak intensifiers like *so* rather than saying anything specific or meaningful.

5. Ask students to discuss the epigraph that heads this chapter.

3

Using Definition in Argument

Argument begins here—and sometimes ends here. Clear definition of the issue at hand in a given argument, and of supporting concepts and terms, is essential both to the clarity of argument and to the arguer's control of the rhetorical context in which he or she argues. But students are sometimes unsure how to define key terms or how to decide what must be defined and what need not be. This chapter provides explanation, examples, and guidelines for using definition in argument. It also discusses the power of argument: Ask students to answer the question following the quotation from Thomas Szasz. Can it be that "the struggle for definition is veritably the struggle for life itself"?

If your students are keeping an argument notebook, ask them to begin looking for persuasive definitions (*persuasive* in the sense defined by Irving Copi in the text). To help the students spot such definitions, discuss the excerpts from Sindler (the Bakke reverse discrimination suit) and Copi (the mock-letter on abortion) and share with them several examples from current periodicals and books. Even cartoons—especially political cartoons—can provide examples. And if any of your students are debaters or have debated competitively in the past, ask them to explain to the class the crucial function definition plays in debate.

But with all this emphasis on the power of definition, students need to be reminded that definitions of words and terms are not intrinsic but contractual. Logician Wesley C. Salmon describes the concept in this way: "Offering a definition is like making a proposal. One may accept it or reject it, but the proposal, itself, is not true or false" (*Logic*, 2nd ed., Prentice, 1975, 122). This might be a good point at which to discuss reification (see also "Additional Suggestions for Writing or Discussion" 2, below).

EXERCISES

Exercise 3–1

A few observations:

It isn't as important that students "get the labels right" as that they get a sense of the wide range of what can serve as definition—and that they learn to recognize when a definition is being stipulated rather than simply reported.

This chapter omits definition by enumeration of parts because it usually can be subsumed into the genus-plus-differentiae category: "*Monopoly* consists of a board, cards, playing pieces (and so on)" offers the differentiae without naming the genus (games). I have also omitted the label of "negative definitions" (what a thing is *not*) because the category of "contrast" covers most such definitions.

Definitions by comparison—certainly metaphorical comparisons, but also literal ones—are inherently stipulative.

1. Reportive; combined methods: genus (metal soleplates) plus differentia (bearing sharp teeth) and conditions for use (to be strapped to hiking shoes and to grip ice)

2. Stipulative; synonyms (substance . . . evidence . . . .)

3. Stipulative; genus (faculty of discernment) plus diff. (means of persuasion)

4. Stipulative; combined methods: conditions for use (must seem better than competitors) and contrast (does not explain all facts)

5. This one is hard. There are two definitions here, but I am never concerned if students overlook the fact that *information* is defined (by examples). I just remind them that definition doesn't always appear in "X is Y" form. *Knowledge* is defined by combined methods: contrast (unlike information, knowledge is "orderly and cumulative"), conditions for use ("the province of books" doesn't so much tell us what knowledge is as where we can apply the term), and synonym (knowledge is "the enduring treasure of our whole human past"). The definition is stipulative.

6. Stipulative; symbolic examples

7. Principally reportive (expands what a dictionary might say) with stipulative elements in its analogy and the judgment implicit in "not simply"; comparison and contrast (like income tax; not simply evaluation process) and genus (ways of providing incentives) plus differentia (for certain intellectual behavior)

8. Stipulative; combined methods: genus (mechanism) plus diff. (makes religion nonreligion) and examples (Marxism, democracy, utopianism, human rights)

9. Reportive; genus (city or town or village) plus diff. (at least 2,500 residents). But notice Hacker's disapproving tone. By saying "city or *town* or *village*" instead of "municipality," isn't he implying some absurdity in the Census Bureau's designation? Who ever heard of an urban village?

10. Reportive; genus plus differentiae

11. Stipulative; contrast (not a sport) and genus (spectacle). Notice the lack of differentiae, however.

12. Reportive; genus plus differentiae

13. Stipulative; synonym

14. Stipulative; genus (absolute squares of wave functions) plus diff. (that cannot be normalized)

15. Reportive; genus (divorce) plus diff. (after which the couple continues to live together). Some students will insist this definition is stipulative. But ask them to think a minute about the nature of a definition in a game show question. It *has* to be reportive, even if reportive of a slang or colloquial expression.

16. Stipulative because metaphorical and because it limits what can be called definition to "genus plus differentiae." This is itself a genus (dialectical animal) plus diff. (with body and soul) definition.

Exercise 3-2

1. This is pretty good although the last dependent clause is unduly narrow: Crampons are useful in other circumstances as well. Letter carriers sometimes use them in icy weather, for example.

2. This is not a bad definition by synonym, considering the abstract nature of the term defined.

3. Can rhetoric be a faculty? Dreadful puns come to mind. This is not an entirely clear definition in any event: "discerning in every case" of what? Is one only to *discern* the "available means of persuasion," or to use them?

4. This is a partial definition; we still don't know just what a paradigm is (and in fact one problem with Kuhn's book is the number of different ways in which the author uses the term).

5. The definition of *information* is clear but partial (limited to examples of the kinds dispersed in print). The definition of *knowledge* is vague—perhaps necessarily so, given the broadness of the category. And, of course, it is not *only* the province of books, as Sidey might have us believe.

6. Like many definitions by example, the symbols of wealth are here too few to provide more than a suggestion—ironic at that—of what the term *success* means.

7. This definition offers a literal analogy, and an engaging if incomplete one: We don't learn in this sentence just how grading is "a way of providing incentives for various sorts of intellectual behavior" or just what kinds of incentives or sorts of behavior are intended. Therefore, we must fault the definition for inexactness if it is intended to stand

alone (it isn't, of course, in the essay from which it was plucked) and also intended to inform. Notice that a simple definition by synonym is included (albeit negatively) within the larger definition: Grading is an evaluation process.

8. While this is a fascinating definition, like many stipulative definitions its purpose is more to influence readers' attitudes than to clarify a term.

9. This is a precise definition, but it defines a term much more broadly than people ordinarily use it.

10. OK

11. While perhaps more true—at the professional level—than the definition in 10, this is too vague to really explain the term.

12. OK

13. Clear enough, but of course incomplete.

14. OK within its field, but too technical (wave function?) for those who are not students of physics.

15. OK

16. The metaphor confuses things a bit, particularly as the comparison is not parallel in the way that readers today would expect (should be body/genus and soul/difference, not difference/soul).

Exercise 3-3

Caution students to look up the words before defining them; *enormity* does not mean *enormousness*, for example.

READINGS

Tom Wolfe, "The Right Stuff"

(1931–   ) The quintessential New Journalist, Wolfe has authored many books in addition to *The Right Stuff*, most recently the novel *The Bonfire of the Vanities*. Wolfe has described New Journalism as "the use by people writing nonfiction of techniques which heretofore had been thought of as confined to the novel or to the short story, to create in one form both the kind of objective reality of journalism and the subjective reality that people have always gone to the novel for" (*Contemporary Authors*, New Revision Series, vol. 9).

1. Since Wolfe announces that the quality he here sets out to define is "ineffable" (paragraph 2), we might well expect him to get at it by example and by indirection. And so he does. But to try a one-sentence definition: The "right stuff" is the bravery, the manliness, of *repeated*

risk-taking in a meaningful cause (paragraph 2). The right stuff is what the Chosen Few have that gets them through military flight training; and so Wolfe takes us through the flight training program and into the very psyches of the men in training. The extended definition makes real and almost terrifying what the single sentence cannot hope to give shape and meaning to.

2. It is both a persuasive definition and an implicit argument. We have all the premises—the examples, the supporting anecdotes—but the conclusion is left to us: Is the "right stuff" a good thing or a dangerous phenomenon, or neither? This question should elicit considerable class discussion. (Insist that students ground their conclusions in specific references to the text.)

3. Paragraph 5 is a good example of Wolfe's flamboyance. Students should observe that the paragraph moves in and out of the flight trainee's consciousness and from calm observation to near-hysteria.

4. Most students like this excerpt, but you will probably find that some emphatically do not. In talking with friends who have read the book, I have noticed that most of the men liked *The Right Stuff* and many of the women claimed not to. That difference in response may stem from the book's relentlessly macho, male perspective. But I, for one, was fascinated by Wolfe's ability to bring the space program to life; to give it a real, human shape; even to take me inside the fighter pilots' minds in an uncannily convincing way. Tell students that elsewhere in the book the author takes us inside the mind of a monkey-cosmonaut, and even those who are unimpressed by this excerpt may be sufficiently intrigued to want to read more.

Archibald MacLeish, "Ars Poetica"

(1892–1982)   Poet and several-time winner of the Pulitzer Prize in poetry and in drama (the latter for *J. B.: A Play in Verse*, 1959). MacLeish wrote an Academy Award-winning screenplay for *The Eleanor Roosevelt Story*, 1966. Professor of poetry and creative writing at Harvard University, MacLeish first taught constitutional law at that institution, in 1919, and had a public service career that included the position of Librarian of Congress (1939–44) and Assistant Secretary of State (1944–45).

1. The thesis is most directly stated in the last two lines: "A poem should not mean/But be." The poet's argument is that a poem is not supposed to offer arguments.

2. "A poem should be solid and silent on the page . . . ." The definitions lose almost all of their mellifluous beauty, but they gain something, too: The reader has to really pay attention to what the words mean, what the poem says. Such paraphrases can be a valuable tool for close

reading and can remedy the student's lament that a given poem doesn't seem to mean anything in particular.

3. We don't ordinarily read poetry expecting to be convinced of its argument, and we don't expect modern poetry to be didactic. Certainly it is more than enough that poetry show us the world afresh. But poems can and do persuade, and some put forth arguments. Ask students to discuss MacLeish's assertions here, and then read them the following from Emerson's "The Poet" (*Essays, Second Series*):

> For it is not meters, but meter-making argument that makes a poem—a thought so passionate and alive that like the spirit of a plant or an animal it has an architecture of its own, and adorns nature with a new thing.

When students bring in (or add to their argument notebooks) examples of poems with persuasive aims, it may be helpful to first discuss the qualities of "good" poetry so that the class has an agreed-upon definition on which to base their judgments. The definition need not be a sophisticated one at this point; the mere act of attempting to create one provides an instructive case in point of both the need for and the problems inherent in definition.

Joan Didion, "On Morality"

(1934–) Contributing editor, *National Review*, columnist, and freelance writer. Among Didion's works is *Slouching Towards Bethlehem* (1968), a collection of essays from which "On Morality" is taken.

This essay can be difficult for students, but it is well worth tackling if you are prepared for some initial confusion. A possible essay topic given below—Additional Suggestions for Writing or Discussion #3—gives some suggestions for helping students better understand what Didion is arguing. Since many of them will disagree with her, the discussion that follows can be both fascinating and fierce.

1. Didion isn't so much interested in giving us a definition of morality (though she does that, after a fashion) as in showing us what she considers to be dangerous about the concept when we let it become more than a basic human contract that we will not, for example, leave dead bodies to the hungry coyotes. To Didion, morality is a primitive social code (paragraphs 4 and 5), and when we attempt to make it more than that—when we try to impose our personal conscience (8) on others—we move toward "the monstrous perversion to which any human idea can come" (7). Personal conscience is *not* morality as Didion defines the term.

2. After discussing question 1, students who feel that Didion hasn't really defined *morality*—because she does not sound like a dictionary in so doing—will probably understand better how argument-by-definition works in this essay. Do ask them to identify the thesis of the essay; some may have understood her argument without understanding how definition figures in it. Didion's thesis here concerns not so much the denotation of the word *morality* as the implications of the concept. That thesis might be most succinctly expressed by combining the first sentence of paragraph 8 with the first sentence of paragraph 9: None of us has the right to impose our personal conscience on another, for "we have no way of knowing—beyond that fundamental loyalty to the social code—what is 'right' and what is 'wrong,' what is 'good' and what is 'evil.' " Didion titles the essay "On Morality" because she is troubled that we use the word broadly and misleadingly, when *expediency* or *desire* would more accurately describe our motives. The ultimate implications of what troubles Didion are expressed in paragraph 7 and the last two sentences of the essay.

   Didion's definition of *morality* is stipulative in that she restricts the word to a very narrow meaning. It is also intended to persuade. Students' attempts to define the word should generate some interesting discussion; they may find it hard to reach consensus on a definition.

3. "Wagon-train morality" is the most primitive, basic elements of the social code—all the social code that was sometimes possible among pioneers going westward against the grain of civilization. We will bury the dead; we will not eat our own blood kin.

4. First, Didion thinks people use the word when they really mean something else (see paragraph 9). Second, she regards "claim[ing] the primacy of personal conscience"—personal morality—as "arrogant" (paragraph 7). Third, she considers such "moral" claims dangerous. (Ask students what *it* refers to in the last sentence of paragraph 7.)

ADDITIONAL SUGGESTIONS FOR WRITING OR DISCUSSION

1. Definition on a broad scale is used by publicity agents and campaign managers to shape public opinion of public figures. A movie actor with a boring image is redefined as exciting and sexy by carefully planted gossip and photographs taken with attractive and well-known people. A candidate with an unappealing image is redefined with no less care. Ask students to find examples of public figures who seem to have been "redefined." One such figure was Richard M. Nixon, whose "Checkers Speech" is included in the readings for Chapter 9.

You might wish to use that speech in conjunction with this chapter as a study in successful redefinition, then look at it again when you come to the study of fallacies.

The various *Selling of the President* books and Dan Nimmo's *The Political Persuaders: The Techniques of Modern Election Campaigns* (Prentice-Hall, 1970) offer apt analyses of image definition in politics. See, as well, Irving R. Rein's *Rudy's Red Wagon: Communication Strategies in Contemporary Society* (Scott, Foresman, 1972) for a fascinating discussion of the Nixon campaign strategists' "redefinition" of their candidate for the 1968 presidential race. They were working for a candidate whose "public image . . . was that of a petty, vindictive loser," and who, in his televised debate with John Kennedy in 1960 had looked "like a black-jawed enforcer for the Mafia, or like a high-pressured used-car salesman with a five-o'clock shadow" (page 26). Their redefinition was successful long enough for their candidate to win both election and re-election.

2. Ask students to consider the power of words. Not only the definitions we offer but the very words we choose affect both the meaning and reception of what we say. The word is not the thing, but we act sometimes as if it were. If you wish to expand the discussion of words and meaning, you might ask students to read Susanne Langer's "Signs and Symbols," a frequently anthologized section of her long essay "The Lord of Creation" (*Fortune*, January 1944), or "The Language of Prejudice" in Gordon Allport's *The Nature of Prejudice* (Addison-Wesley, 1979). See also Neil Postman's discussion of reification in *Crazy Talk, Stupid Talk* (Delacourt, 1976), especially page 142. I suggest the following as a possible topic for subsequent discussion or writing:

   If words are not things, and reifying them is fallacious, then why are women bothered by the use of the masculine pronoun for generic reference? And why are members of minority groups, including the handicapped, bothered by labels applied to them, such as "my crippled friend" or "my Chicano neighbor"?

3. My colleague Dennis Foster developed the following assignment to use after discussing the readings in this chapter:

   In our discussion of "The Right Stuff," we saw the difficulty of assigning a positive meaning (i.e., one with a solid content) to the idea of "manhood," the right stuff. We know pretty clearly what Wolfe's idea is, though manhood turns out to be more a matter of situation than "truth"—and it turns out to be a label that is none too flattering at that. Didion has a similar problem in "On Morality" insofar as she discusses an idea that she thinks has no content, no absolute truth: it is "hollow."

For this essay you are to analyze Didion's argument for an audience that (like many in our class) finds "On Morality" difficult to fully comprehend. You need not answer all the following questions in your essay, but think about them.

- What is the problem Didion sees with the word *morality*? What does she think the word means? What does she say other people think?
- What do Didion's examples tell us about what she calls the "social code"? How does a social code differ from a moral code?
- Why does Didion tell us so much about the insanity possible in the desert? What is she saying about sanity and its relation to the voice of conscience?
- Why can't Didion talk about morality "in some abstract way"? What happens when she attempts to?
- Notice the number of times examples in this essay use a negative phrasing, like the "thou shalt not." How do negatives function in defining an idea?
- Finally, notice how these questions ask you to think about morality in relation to exclusion.

4

Research and the Uses of Evidence

Because finding, evaluating, and incorporating evidence is so integral a part of successful written argument, this chapter is included to offer guidelines for students undertaking to support their arguments with evidence beyond their own immediate experience. Students should find help here in locating and using secondary material for their documented essays, both for this course and others. This chapter is not intended to replace a research handbook, however; space prohibits any attempt to do again what has been done well elsewhere. So one assumption of this text is that students have access to a good grammar and research handbook. If the "research paper" (as distinguished from the shorter and often less formal documented essay) is to be an integral part of the course, I would suggest that the material in this chapter be supplemented with information from a research handbook such as Lester's *Writing Research Papers* (5th ed., Scott Foresman, 1987) or (for additional help with the mechanics of citation) the *MLA Handbook for Writers of Research Papers* (3rd ed., MLA, 1988).

With the aim in mind of not duplicating the efforts of complete research handbooks, Chapter 4 lists basic sources in a variety of fields about which undergraduate students are likely to write papers, but according to the frequency of updating rather than according to field. (Listings are alphabetical within each period of time.) I am not aware of any handbook that emphasizes which indexes and bibliographic references are most likely to be up-to-date for current subjects, yet students in many fields often need the latest possible information. For this reason, also, the chapter indicates some of the many computer database sources that may be drawn upon for current information and recent articles.

One thing most handbooks fail to do is to inspire any enthusiasm in students for the act of research. That is undoubtedly because students come to college having been taught The Research Paper as the worst form of drudgery: one hundred notecards required; a twenty-five page minimum length with at least twenty footnotes and at least thirty

31

sources, ten of which must be periodicals and ten of which must be books. (The specifications may vary, but the effect on students is universally the same.) These jaded souls will laugh cynically at the naïveté of the chapter epigraph from Pavlov: *passion* in research? While there are no magic cures for such an attitude, a few ways to combat it include:

- Giving students a degree of freedom in picking topics. In order to avoid being presented with a paper written by a student's friend the year before, I do require students to choose from *my* list of topics, but I give them a wide selection, such as that shown at the end of Chapter 4. In addition, I change the list of topics every time I assign documented essays. (This is not a time-consuming project if one does as my colleague Virginia Oram suggests: Throughout the year, she keeps a running list in her own notebook of interesting questions that come up in the news and in what she reads and sees.)

- Encouraging students to look on research as a means of discovery, not as a rehashing of other people's words. Ask them to try to see what others may not have observed in their subject, to ferret out the little-known rather than skimming off the obvious. Demand—for this course, particularly—that they find an argumentative edge to their subject.

- Assigning documented essays of manageable length—say, seven to ten typed pages—before or instead of assigning projects of massive length. Give the students a taste for research before drowning them in it. No butt of malmsey, this.

- Allowing some flexibility in the way materials are gathered, as long as careful record-keeping of sources and scrupulous distinctions between what is quoted and what is summarized or paraphrased are observed. However orderly notecards may be, they are just not congenial to some people's styles of collecting and assimilating information.

Especially if you do not plan to emphasize research in your course, but do wish to make students appreciate the importance of sources, you might want to begin your class discussion of this chapter with the following passage:

The first rule for understanding the human condition is that men live in second-hand worlds. They are aware of much more than they have personally experienced; and their own experience is always indirect. The quality of their lives is determined by meanings they have received from others. Everyone lives in a world of such meanings. No man stands alone directly confronting a world of solid fact. No such world is available. The closest men come to it is when they are infants or when they become insane: then, in a terrifying scene of meaningless events and senseless confusion, they are often seized with the panic of near-total insecurity. But in their everyday life they do not experience a world of solid fact; their experience itself is selected by stereotyped meanings and shaped by ready-made interpretations. Their images of the world, and of themselves, are given to them by crowds of witnesses they have never met and never shall meet.

Yet for every man these images—provided by strangers and dead men—are the very basis of his life as a human being.
—C. Wright Mills, *Power, Politics, and People*
(New York: Ballantine, 1963), 405

EXERCISES

Exercise 4–1

1. Here the writer will need both material available in books and journals a year or more old, and material as current as possible.

2. Issues of justice are timeless. Current information is not necessary, but, since the issue has been recently in the news, current information may be plentiful to illustrate the principles argued.

3. As I write, OPEC is meeting again, its unity and its member countries' fortunes on the wane. Very current information would be helpful here.

4. The writer's own experience and that of friends will suffice here. Such information is likely to be quite current, but to require no library source material at all (unless one is undertaking a sociological survey).

5. Again, a relatively timeless issue.

6. Research into AIDS has been given major emphasis in recent years and, while no cure is yet in sight, results of tests and experiments are reported frequently. Absolutely up-to-the-minute information is essential for a paper on this topic to be accurate. Computerized information retrieval services would be a writer's best resource.

7. Material a year or more old in books, journals, and newspapers would be appropriate and useful, but current information (for this topic, that would mean articles, essays, or speeches written within the past year) would be critical as well in order to support the predictive element of this topic.

Exercise 4–2

1. Example. The source is likely to be accurate and fair. The evidence is historical, secondary, unbiased, and anomalous within either the class of business people or that of millionaires at the turn of the century.

2. Testimony (judgment). The source is likely to be accurate. The evidence is a judgment dated by two decades (but that is not a significant problem as impressionism is not today a popular trend in opera). Being a judgment, the statement is necessarily both primary and biased. It is impossible to say whether or not it is typical of the kind of judgments offered by this source.

3. Testimony (judgment). I am the source of this observation, and its content reveals me to be a suspect source. No reasonable person

would draw present conclusions about the internal politics of a country based on a short visit more than fifteen years ago. The evidence is primary but outdated and biased.

4. Identification presented as common knowledge. The statement could be checked by referring to a dictionary of mythology.

5. Statistical data. The source is likely to be accurate and fair, but it is dated. If Lamorisse worked on a film after 1974, the evidence would be inaccurate. The evidence, then, is outdated, secondary, and unbiased.

6. Identification presented as common knowledge. The statement could be checked for accuracy in any basic chemistry book or encyclopedia.

7. Testimony (judgment). The source here is fictitious, so the evidence is no evidence at all. If we assume that Professor Slocum and his college are real, then a professor of mechanical engineering would be a source we would likely trust. On some questions we might prefer to check Mr. Slocum's academic credentials, but common sense tells us this assertion is a reasonable one. Any old bridge should be checked regularly for structural defects that might occur after years of wear and tear.

8. Statistical data. The source is generally regarded as accurate and fair, but we could better assess the fairness of *this* conclusion if we knew just how the question was worded and just what size and type of sampling the pollsters used. The source is fairly recent, but if used to support an argument about attitudes regarding abortion today, a poll taken within the last year would be more persuasive.

9. Identification presented as common knowledge. The statement could be checked in a good unabridged dictionary.

10. Statistical data. The source is generally regarded as a reliable one, but the information here is historical, not recent. It cannot be used to support an argument about attitudes today.

11. Examples. The source is reliable. The examples may or may not be representative of the poet's love of bizarre titles. More examples are needed if the evidence is to be offered as supporting any such claim.

12. Examples offered as common knowledge. The statement could be checked in a *current* almanac.

13. Example. The source is not likely to be as accurate and scholarly as some others in this list. The student would do better to look up the subject in a comprehensive encyclopedia or dictionary. Because the evidence is historical, a source would not have to be particularly recent to be authoritative.

14. Statistics presented as common knowledge. Statistics *never* should be assumed to be common knowledge.

15. Testimony. I'd look for corroboration elsewhere (under "Trollope"

in a good encyclopedia), just in case Galbraith's memory is mistaken or he is stretching a point to make a point. Economists are not automatic experts in literary (or postal) trivia.

16. Statistical data. The Census is a reliable source for such statistics, and we have no reason to doubt Hacker's accuracy (we feel even more comfortable about it when we look up his book and note that it was published by Oxford UP).

Exercise 4–3

For example:

1. Fraternities promote elitism—social, sexist, and racist—on this campus.
2. Salaries for state representatives in Virginia should be raised so that honest people of modest income could better afford to participate in our state government.
3. Economics is the most useful major a prospective business manager could elect.
4. Video games are bad for children's physical health: They emit small doses of potentially harmful radiation; they create eyestrain; they exercise only the fingers.
5. Soccer, not football, is the truly democratic sport. (Support by examples of physical requirements, cost of equipment, playing time.)
6. Both for their own best interests and the public's, law schools should cut back on the numbers of students they graduate each year.
7. Snowmobiles should be banned as recreational vehicles.
8. A winter in New Zealand offers more than a refuge from the icy Northern Hemisphere; it offers another world altogether.
9. Abortion in cases of rape, incest, danger to the mother's health, and malformation of the fetus should remain legal during the first trimester of pregnancy.
10. Because of the privileges that enable the wealthy to avoid paying much income tax, a flat, no-exemption income tax would stand to increase tax revenue while reducing the bureaucracy now needed to administer and enforce tax laws.

READINGS

S. I. Hayakawa, "Reports, Inferences, Judgments"

(1906–   ) A semanticist and author (or editor) of many works, Hayakawa is best known for the book from which this excerpt is taken (*Language in Thought and Action*), for his presidency of San Francisco State

36   Instructor's Edition

College (remembered for quelling student riots during the turbulent late 60s), and for his subsequent tenure as U.S. Senator from California, from 1976–82. Since his retirement from the Senate, Hayakawa has devoted much of his energy to a campaign to make English the official language of the United States.

As useful as I find this excerpt from *Language in Thought and Action* (4th ed.), the distinctions between inferences and judgments are not (and, I think, cannot be) as clear-cut as Hayakawa suggests they are. Judgments color what is inferred and even what is reported (by selection or omission of detail). But this excerpt makes clear that statements offered as evidence are of different kinds and merits—and such awareness is crucial to effective written argument and to evaluation of arguments.

1. This is deductive reasoning from the unstated assumption that all who have calloused hands must be manual laborers. The assumption itself may have been arrived at inductively if the person making it knows many people with calloused hands, all of whom are also manual laborers.

2. No. All arguments rely on inference, and most, on judgment as well.

3. No. If you see many examples of books published by a particular publisher, and you notice that all the books have blue covers, you may reach an inductive conclusion that the next book you see from that publisher will also have a blue cover. No particular judgment is implicit in that observation alone.

4. Judgments, once articulated, acquire a kind of sanctity and self-evident quality in our minds. We automatically stop refining and qualifying our ideas, and seek only to make what we observe fit the judgment we have made. If to think is to search for understanding, judgments effectively stop that process. The implications of this problem for writers are that judgments, if arrived at prematurely, result in underdeveloped arguments and begged questions. We may also be blinded to what needs revision and rethinking.

Mark Alsop, "The Problem of Bias in Television News Reporting" (Student Essay)

Although Mark Alsop's documented essay is included primarily as an example of a paper using sources and following the revised MLA method of documentation, you may find the subject he discusses to be of interest in connection with the concerns of this chapter, for television is a principal source of information for most of us. Ask students if they agree or disagree with his observations or with his sources he cites (they should note that, for an essay about an ongoing problem, some of the sources are dated—one book goes back some fifteen years). Call to their attention that Alsop attempts to offer a solution to the problem he sees: Do they find that device makes his argument more effective, his persona more pleasing?

ADDITIONAL SUGGESTIONS FOR WRITING OR DISCUSSION

1. Give students practice in incorporating quotations effectively into their own arguments by supplying them with a thought-provoking quotation (along with its source) to use in a paragraph of original argument. (I like to offer surprising or outrageous statements from public figures currently in the news.) Remind them always to incorporate quotations grammatically, to give them a context beyond the students' own paragraphs, and to comment on them. Direct quotations never should be offered as being self-evident: If they are remarkable enough to warrant mention, they will need clarification or reaction from the writers using them. These reminders may help students to resist using quotations merely as filler.

2. Ask students to bring to class examples from what they have read recently of arguments invoking statistics as support for or proof of conclusions. Evaluate the writers' use of statistics.

3. Ask students to watch the national news broadcasts one evening, with members of the class assigned to cover different networks: ABC, CBS, NBC, and perhaps CNN. This assignment works best in small groups, in which one student times the length of stories; one keeps track of the order stories are presented, who reports on them, and what point of view gets the "last word"; and two or three take notes on the content of stories and whether or not they include interviews, film footage, charts and diagrams, or other presentations. Have students put their data on the blackboard and see what conclusions, if any, can be drawn. Are the networks more consistent or less so than Alsop and his sources found them to be?

4. My colleague Carolyn Channell has used the following assignment to allow students to explore the differences in what constitutes a "fact" in the different disciplines:

> Write a paper in which you use two courses that you have taken in college to illustrate the point that different disciplines create knowledge in different ways. Pick courses from two disciplines and ask yourself these questions as you work toward a thesis:
>
> • What is considered acceptable evidence or facts?
> • What problems does the discipline attempt to solve? What questions does it attempt to answer?

- To what extent are its methods an attempt to achieve perfect objectivity? To what extent does it admit subjectivity into its methods?

- To what extent does objectivity or subjectivity enter into its standards for reporting its knowledge to others in the discipline?

- What can you say about the standards and methods for passing the knowledge on to students and for teaching the students to think and write in this discipline?

5. To underscore the importance of evaluating statistics carefully, you might share with students the following items that appeared in *The Dallas Times Herald* on 5 October 1987 (A7), written by reporter Bob Drummond:

"Driving is safer than flying—right?"

An often repeated maxim is that it is safer to fly than to drive. As recently retired Federal Aviation Administration chief Donald Engen put it last June: "it is more dangerous to drive from your house to the airport than it is to fly from Chicago to Los Angeles." But that claim depends on the statistic used to support it.

The traditional backing for the planes-are-safer argument relies on the often-cited measure of safety as the rate of deaths "per passenger-mile"—a method in which a 100-mile flight in a plane carrying 150 people counts for 15,000 passenger-miles, while a 100-mile drive in a car carrying two people counts for 200 passenger-miles. Using passenger-miles as the standard, scheduled airline fatalities were 0.06 per 100 million passenger-miles between 1973 and 1982, while cars had a rate of 2 per 100 million passenger-miles—which makes air travel seem 33 times as safe.

But some critics argue that a truer standard for accident risks measures the chances that an individual car or plane will be involved in a fatal accident. Under a method of deaths per vehicle-mile, a car and a plane both get equal credit for 100 miles on a 100-mile trip. Using that standard, cars—with a rate of 2.2 deaths per 100 million vehicle-miles between 1976 and 1985—appear more than twice as safe as scheduled major and commuter airlines, which had a fatality rate of 4.8 per 100 million vehicle-miles during the same period. Excluding commuter airlines, the major carriers still had a rate of 3.9 deaths per 100 million miles during that period, substantially higher than that for automobiles.

"Statistics on air safety sometimes deceiving"

While debate rages over aviation safety, concerned fliers still are soothed with a mass of statistics showing that, for all the publicity about the occasional catastrophe, flying is still a remarkably safe form of travel. But statistics can be molded and massaged in a number of ways. And, in aviation safety, some of the reassuring claims are based on statistics that don't always give the full picture. As reported in a U.S. Department of Transportation publication, last year saw "more than 394 million passengers [travel] 302 billion miles on the major scheduled U.S. carriers without a single fatality."

That sentence, however, carries a number of inconspicuous qualifying statements:

* Remove the word "passengers" from that phrase and the death toll rises from zero to one. While not actually aboard a major airline flight, an occupant of a small plane was killed in an accident with an airliner on the ground at the airport in Tampa, Fla.

* Take out the word "scheduled"—to include charters and some cargo flights that are lumped in with major airlines in government record keeping—and the 1986 fatality total becomes four.

* Erase the word "major," to include deaths on commuter flights, and the total 1986 death toll for commercial flights of all types skyrockets to 72.

5

Revising

Students tend to underestimate the devastation incoherence and even faulty grammar can wreak on their persuasive aims in writing. They feel a little like Eliza in Shaw's *Pygmalion:* "I don't want to talk grammar. I want to talk like a lady." The aim of this chapter is to offer a corrective of sorts to that attitude, to emphasize the real relation between effective writing and persuasion—between the competence of writers' prose and the personas their readers respond to. Its emphasis, therefore, is on improving clarity and coherence through revision, a crucial part of the ongoing writing process. First, the chapter offers suggestions for rounding off an argument with an effective introduction and conclusion and filling in gaps in the main argument. These large-scale concerns are grouped together under the heading of "macro-revision." As I mention in the text, apparently disproportionate space is given over to discussion and examples of introductions and conclusions—but that is in response to many requests from both colleagues and students. It always helps to see examples. The second main focus is on "micro-revision," that is, strengthening development, coherence, and clarity within paragraphs and individual sentences.

Due both to the purposes of this text and to lack of space, this chapter makes no attempt to substitute for a good handbook of grammar and usage. The only grammatical element discussed in detail, therefore, is sentence logic or *predication,* a thorny problem for many students and one that is both overlooked by many handbooks and directly related to this text's emphasis on making sense logically.

One good way to make students receptive to the relationship between coherent, grammatical prose and persuasion is to offer the testimony of people who will judge their writing and their work in the future—business employers, graduate school admission officers, and the like. See, for example, Maxine Hairston's survey of educated persons' responses to assorted grammatical gaffes in her *Successful Writing* (2nd ed., Norton, 1986).

And, second, call to students' attention the significant differences in meaning that result from the use or omission of simple punctuation marks, as is so ably and delightfully demonstrated in Maxwell Nurnberg's *Questions You Always Wanted to Ask about English but were afraid to raise your hand** (Pocket Books, 1972). For example, students should recognize the difference between "The butler called the guests' names" and "The butler called the guests names." In 1983, the Florida Legislature and a number of organizations, such as the Boy Scouts, discovered how costly an inadvertent comma can be:

The measure ... says exemptions [from paying sales tax] can be granted to groups with an Internal Revenue Code exemption and to "other non-profit organizations, whose sole and primary purpose" is to provide various social services.
    The revenue department argues that the comma after the word "organizations" means that even groups with IRA exemptions must have as their sole purpose the furnishing of social services. Ms. Margolis, a North Miami Democrat, charges that the House committee drafted its changes sloppily and inadvertently added a comma that altered the intent of the legislation.
    —*The Dallas Morning News*, 12 June 1983, 27A

And if a comma can be that important, how much more important a logical organization of ideas and the clear, coherent expression of them must be to persuasive prose.

EXERCISES

Exercise 5–1

The assignment for this essay required students to think about the narrator and clerk in "Bartleby the Scrivener" in light of their recent study of Bentham (in an interdisciplinary course for freshmen). The student writers' aim was to see whether "Bartleby" might shed some light on some of the tenets and problems of utilitarianism—or, perhaps, vice versa. They were instructed to consider the class their audience, an audience somewhat familiar with the material but inclined to oversimplify both the concept of utilitarianism and the Melville story. Your students may be familiar with both or neither; if the latter, they will see the defects in the paragraphs all the more readily.

The paragraphs reprinted in the text were sample introductory paragraphs from first drafts (submitted as finished drafts, I regret to add).

*A brief reference for student writers who are not using a comprehensive handbook such as Guth's *New English Handbook* or Troyka's *Simon and Schuster Handbook* is Blanche Ellsworth's *English Simplified*, 5th edition (Harper & Row, 1985), a 32-page pamphlet that covers with surprising completeness the basic rules of grammar, punctuation, mechanics, and spelling.

The first introductory paragraph is choppy and boring, and the apparent "thesis" makes no point. It does offer a helpful definition but also the misleading impression that utilitarianism is discussed in the Melville story (and the curious impression that utilitarianism can "state" something). The second paragraph starts out promisingly but bogs down as it gets to the last two sentences. Ask students to discuss why (it's as if the student suddenly remembers, "formal essay," and becomes pompous). The third paragraph is boring because it is underdeveloped (remind students that two-sentence paragraphs in drafts should be flagged for close scrutiny) and offers a "so what?" idea for development. The fourth is focused and almost interesting. This writer brings in the notion of utilitarianism a bit further on in the essay, keeping the readers' attention on the story. But this paragraph, too, needs a rewrite to help readers see why we should regard the last sentence as an idea central to understanding the story.

Students invariably will settle on either paragraph #2 or #4 as the most promising. It's worth a little class time to discuss the strengths and weaknesses of the two. In the discussion, students often decide that #2 has a more pleasing style and #4 holds more promise for a workable thesis.

Exercise 5–2

The responses will of course vary with the student populations and college locations (mass transit in Miami will be a problem more familiar to students at the University of Miami, Florida, then to those at Miami University of Ohio). Some *possible* responses:

> *Extensive exposition would be needed:* commodities trading, the relative merits of *WordPerfect* and Microsoft *Word*, the Nicaraguan economy, the "theory of everything"

> *Brief exposition would suffice:* deer hunting, the requirements at this college for a liberal arts or an engineering degree, African photo safaris, the psychological needs reflected in slang usage among high school students

> *Exposition might be omitted:* writing letters of complaint to landlords, fraternity grade requirements at this college, ethics in argumentation (for an audience of *this class* only), the enduring appeal of the game of Monopoly

More disagreement is likely to arise over the third category than the others. It will become apparent to the students that it is not often possible to assume an audience's complete familiarity with a subject; *some* exposition is usually required.

Exercise 5–3

One tentative ordering:

- Obscenity is a nebulous concept.
  Add: It is difficult to define.
- What is obscene to one person may be art to another.
- Juries have difficulty reaching verdicts in obscenity cases.
- It might be more useful to promote ethics education than to pass vague and probably unenforceable legislation.

Possible deletions:

- Obscenity can have violent overtones.
- Students in a mass media class couldn't decide what was obscene.

Exercise 5–4

The *WordPerfect* thesis will require relatively little refutation if the audience is mostly comprised of people who do not own computers or do not use them much for writing. If they do, however, considerable refutation may be needed. People get very attached to their word processing programs and will defend them passionately. A point-by-point refutation comparing *WordPerfect*'s user support system to those of other companies might work best.

The fear-over-photos thesis will require little refutation unless the essay attempts to play on readers' fears to an audience well-educated about AIDS, or adopts a sarcastic tone to an audience of conservationists and animal lovers—or affluent North Americans. The refutation could go either before or after the writer's own arguments.

The *Monopoly* thesis sounds likely to be tongue-in-cheek. If it isn't, the essay may require extensive refutation, for people are likely to regard playing *Monopoly* as a harmless pastime. The refutation should be put first in that case.

Exercise 5–5

1. *Weaknesses:* "in conclusion"; "this essay has demonstrated"; ends with another's words (but rather effective ones!)

   Strengths: last sentence makes a telling point, humorously and memorably

2. *Weaknesses:* insults reader in failed attempt to be humorous; lacks coherence between first and second sentence

   Strengths: parallelism in last sentence (sorry, that's the best I could come up with)

3. *Weaknesses:* unwieldy first sentence

   Strengths: succinct conclusion; effective rhetorical question

4. *Weaknesses:* fails to make broader application of personal thesis to reader; second sentence is poorly predicated; last sentence belabors the paragraph's (and essay's) point; tends to use too many sentence openers

   Strengths: clever; reminds reader of key points and illustrations (the Smilodon) without being heavyhanded about it

5. *Weaknesses:* an additional illustration might have added interest and a pleasing balance in the paragraph (sorry, that's the worst I could come up with)

   Strengths: sums up well; gives a final illustration; epigrammatic last sentence

You may or may not decide to mention to your students the fact that the last three paragraphs were all written by the same student. They have rather different "voices." #3 is a bit ponderous in tone; #4 is clever but "I-centered"; and #5 is serious but not self-important. The student's varied attitudes toward the subjects and assignments give rise to the different voices of his arguments.

Exercise 5–6

A possible revision, with changes and additions underlined:

Garlic gets bad press (for causing bad breath) that it does not deserve. This problem must have arisen because people do not know enough about garlic. Garlic, a member of the lily family and cousin to the onion, has been grown in the Mediterranean basin since ancient times. Dioscorides, a first-century Greek physician, believed that garlic could cleanse the body of toxins, restore energy, and increase male virility. In the centuries since, it has been claimed as a cure for everything from dandruff to athlete's foot. During World War I, children wore garlic around their necks to ward off the dreaded Spanish influenza, while British soldiers used sphagnum moss soaked in garlic juice to dress wounds when hospital gauze ran out. In Mexico, garlic soup is even today a folk remedy for digestive problems and intestinal parasites. Garlic may not have all the powers people have attributed to it over the years, but it does taste good—and who cares about a little bad breath?

Exercise 5–7

A possible revision, with changes and additions underlined:

As we grow older, many of us begin to realize just how absurd it is to set the specific age of sixty-five for mandatory retirement. Why, if we must have mandatory retirement at all, must it occur at that particular age, rather than forty-nine or seventy-two? We do not suddenly grow incapable of competent work on any one birthday. So what is the significance of age sixty-five? The truth is that during the German worker revolts of the late nineteenth century, Bismarck's advisors determined that setting mandatory retirement at sixty-five would pacify most of the workers, for few people even lived to that age. In effect, the then-new mandatory retirement law meant that most people could work their entire adult lives. Today, the average lifespan has increased markedly, but the same retirement age is still the rule at most companies. Employers persist in following the tradition Bismarck established, but not the spririt of that tradition.

Exercise 5–8

The original version of the paragraph:

We do not choose to be born. We do not choose our parents. We do not choose our historical epoch, or the country of our birth, or the immediate circumstances of our upbringing. We do not, most of us, choose to die; nor do we choose the time or conditions of our death. But within all this realm of choicelessness, we do choose how we shall live: courageously or in cowardice, honorably or dishonorably, with purpose or in drift. We decide what is important and what is trivial in life. We decide that what makes us significant is either what we do or what we refuse to do. But no matter how indifferent the universe may be to our choices and decisions, these choices and decisions are ours to make. We decide. We choose. And as we decide and choose, so are our lives formed. In the end, forming our own destiny is what ambition is about.

Exercise 5–9

When you discuss transitions, it's a good idea to remind students that *also* is a weak connector, especially between paragraphs.

Some possible revisions of the paragraphs, with transitions and changed punctuation (in combined clauses) underlined:

1. After fighting the mountain for another eight hours, I managed to pass the other climbers, reaching the peak of Fremont first. But as I took my final step to the summit, I realized that Mount Fremont had won the battle after all: I did not feel the glory I had anticipated feeling. Instead, I felt uncomfortable, as if I had invaded a sacred place. The mammoth mountains and their ring of clouds were serenely oblivious of my accomplishment. Indeed, the vastness of all I could see made me feel as inconsequential as the little pikas squeaking defiance at me from the rocks and boulders.

2. All students should study abroad at some point in their academic career, for the contact with a foreign culture, even one similar to our own, provides a remedy for American insularity. We tend to think that the world revolves around the United States—as provincial in our own way as the people of the Middle Ages who believed the sun and planets revolved around the earth. Study abroad remedies this provincialism. It makes history, geography, and political science come to life for students, and at the same time makes us appreciate our own country and the freedom and conveniences it offers. It promotes understanding among peoples of different cultures and beliefs. In all these ways, study abroad offers the most efficient and memorable way to complete a liberal education.

Exercise 5–10

1. However implies contrast and qualification; what the student means is something like for one thing or for example. And the study of three foreign languages is not an example of the variety of students from many countries; it is in keeping with the international atmosphere. Accordingly means in keeping with [what I have just said], while the student means something more like in no way did Sweetly Prep foster.... Finally, the last sentence commits one sin in not summing up the actual content of the paragraph, and another in announcing some sort of logical consequence (in therefore) that cannot possibly exist in this paragraph.

2. (a) "Prep schools offer a student the opportunity to get to know students from all over [the world]"; (b) the rigorous course of study at prep schools; (c) the living conditions at one prep school.

3. With the two topics identified in question 2 and the three additional topics identified above in the answer to 2, students have at least five possible topics on which to write a paragraph. Discuss which could be made to work together in a single essay. Ask students to come up with a thesis sentence for such an essay.

Exercise 5–11

Discuss the different ways in which students developed paragraphs with real content from the topic, "Freshmen in college probably should not attempt to declare a major." Read several paragraphs aloud (or mimeograph them) and ask students to notice which paragraphs support the topic coherently, with specific reasons and concrete detail.

Exercise 5–12

1. Mr. Pomeroy, Ambassador to Malingua, ambassador, diplomat, government employee, citizen, worker, person

2. *Roe* v. *Wade*, legal decisions on abortion, laws, controversial issues
3. lives, exists, is
4. Jane Jones, computer technician, woman, person, female
5. Boeing 747, airplane, aircraft, transport vehicle, machine

Exercise 5–13

1. Students should observe that *acquiesce* and *go along with* connote greater reluctance than does *agree*, while *endorse* connotes greater enthusiasm. To *support* denotes more active agreement than does *favor*, which implies but the nod of one's head.
2. Of this group of words, *idea* may be the most favorable in connotation. Ideas can be right. *Theories* and *hypotheses* may also be respectable because of their "scientific" associations, but they are still speculative. As is, of course, *speculation*, but here we have lost the aura of the laboratory. And a *conjecture* is a guess only, little better than a *wild guess*. Wild guesses are usually wrong, or "just lucky."
3. *Ok* and *acceptable* express more reserved approval than do *commendable* or *desirable*. *Advantageous* and *beneficial* imply that someone will gain by what is so described, with the former word perhaps the stronger in that implication. If something is *essential*, it is necessary, but it may offer no particular advantage.
4. A *criminal*, *crook*, or *parolee* have all violated the law, but the parolee must have been legally convicted of crime, while the other two may have been. That notwithstanding, *parolee* is a slightly less pejorative term than the other two. A *felon* may or may not be in prison at the moment, but has been convicted of a felony. *Prisoner* is a word that can even convey sympathy for the person so described, while *jailbird* conveys only the writer's condemnation of that person.
5. If a person refuses to say something we want him to say, we might condemn his *cowardice*. More charitably, we might concede his *reticence* or *diffidence* regarding public speaking. If he seems not to think that he should speak, we recognize his *reluctance*; if he seems undecided, we call it *uncertainty*. But if we are relieved and even glad that he keeps silent, we may well call his behavior *diplomacy*.

Exercise 5–14

A sample revision:

Movie reviewers really do not do much good. They see a lot of free movies, praise the ones they like, and pan the ones they dislike. What value have those opinions for the rest of us? Reviewers' tastes are no better than anyone else's, and they rarely agree even with each other. Gene Shalit panned _____ last week while the local reviewer, Bobbie Wygant, praised its "moving account of a mother's attempt to keep her family together after her husband's murder." This week, no one has agreed whether _____ is a "must-see" movie or one destined to sink into a well-deserved oblivion. The real merits of movies inevitably give way to the reviewers' personal prejudices and immediate state of mind—even, I suspect, to the temperature in the theatre and the amount of padding in the seat cushions—when they write their pronouncements for our edification.

Exercise 5–15

Some possible versions:

1. Next summer I will be a lifeguard at a girls' camp.
2. His ambition was to climb Mt. Everest.
3. Janie was eager to get started.
4. Your ability will not help you get the job.
5. The cases currently before the Honor Council include those involving Ralph Lawrence and Peter Cardin.
6. Not only did she steal pages from a library book, but in doing so she denied others access to the material.
7. Edward is only a clerk because he cannot get along with his superiors.
8. Stopping in Memphis and changing planes enables us to save fifty dollars on the airfare.
9. The near-tragedy involving little Jessica McClure, who fell into a well in October 1987, shows why all inactive wells should be capped.
10. The stock market's volatility led Avery to put most of his money into bonds.

Exercise 5–16

Student paragraph revisions should reflect their awareness that television does not *reflect* a bad effect—it *has had* one. And it is the lure of lucrative television contracts, not television *per se*, that *tempts* (not makes) colleges to recruit illegally. A second bad effect *has been* (not *shows*) increased inconvenience for players and fans in that games are arranged to fit television schedules, so they may be played at odd hours of the day or night. Limited television coverage *means* (not *is why*) that minor sports are likely to be neglected.

READINGS

Kathy Taylor, "Conformity and Nonconformity: The Prices Paid for Each" (Student Draft)

Suggestion: Ask students to read the rough draft and answer the questions following it BEFORE reading the final version of the essay.

1. "We contrasted with the other cliques in many ways, and ... we ultimately benefited from our various differences." "In many ways" and "various differences" are clues that the thesis is not focused or well-defined. And the paper that follows doesn't seem to show very clearly the benefits of being in the "outcast" group, as the thesis leads us to expect. A possible revision, based on this draft: "Strangely enough, our outcast status changed as we went through high school; it finally became almost 'in' to be 'out.'"

2. The student writer cannot quite decide what her subject is or what her attitude is toward it. Paragraphs 2 and 3 describe the metamorphosis of campus opinion toward the writer's circle of friends; paragraph 4 explores and exposes both the sham of that group's behavior and the character-building benefits that went with it. Paragraph 5 attempts to moralize in a way that the more tentative, but more honest, paragraph 4 does not prepare us for. The essay does not coherently support the thesis, but then, the thesis is not coherent—yet.

3. For one thing, the bizarre mixed metaphor "we drowned ourselves in a search for higher meaning" is contradictory; nor can one "throw" oneself "into a facade of superiority" without winding up with a terrific metaphorical headache. For another, most of the fourth paragraph comes near to contradicting most of the third. And finally, the last paragraph's celebration of individuality contradicts nearly all of the rest of the argument.

4. The "etc." in the first paragraph needs to be replaced with specific examples. Some examples of "the endless social customs of school life" would add life to the second paragraph. The reader needs a more concrete idea of what about the writer's group seemed "peculiar" to the others, or what later came to be admired by them (paragraph 3). The last paragraph is totally impersonal in its generalizations, and needs additional detail to make it interesting.

5. (a) Eliminate "I think." (paragraph 1, twice)
   (b) Combine "... in defiance .... also in retaliation ...." (paragraph 2)
   (c) "Looked down upon condescendingly" (3) is redundant, as is
   (d) "Peculiar, weird, odd" (3). Two would do.

6. Paragraph 2: "Tired of being misfits, we retaliated by forming our own anti-group group and refusing to acknowledge the endless social customs of school life."

   Paragraph 3: "The other groups at first looked down on us, regarding us as peculiar, even weird."

   Paragraph 3: "They even began to see some worth in our attempts and to admire us for what they considered our uniqueness—a worth and a uniqueness we didn't quite believe in ourselves."

Paragraph 4: "Our revolt was a defensive tactic, for we clung together mainly for the support and comfort no one else had been willing to offer us."

7. Shift in pronoun reference is a recurring problem, particularly in the first paragraph. Some sentences (for example, the last) are convoluted in syntax.

8. The title is not appropriate. It suggests a balance of emphasis between the subjects of conformity and nonconformity, and a further emphasis on the costs (not necessarily the benefits) of each. The conformists are given little attention in the paper that follows this title. And the nonconformists are shown to be conformists of a sort themselves. The student author is discovering her subject and her attitude toward it only as she writes: This is "writing as discovery" in the truest sense. She never quite resolves her ambiguous feelings about her high school experience, but the next draft will show how much she has learned about her subject in the process of writing and revising the essay. The change in title will be significant as well: Alert students to take note of it.

Kathy Taylor, "Nonconformity: The Price and the Payoff" (Student Essay)

1. Some students will point to the greater fluidity of the prose, the polishing of the transitions and smoothing out of bumpy clauses. And some will applaud the greater use of concrete supporting detail, little things like titles and A-line skirts that make us believe it is all real. But the most important *substantive* change is pointed to by the title: The author now knows where her real focus lies, and she is examining it more carefully, more consciously, more creatively. She knows that she wants to talk about both the price her group paid for their eccentricities and the benefits they derived thereby. She is not able to "resolve" the question of whether price or payoff was greater, but her honesty is believable in a way that a more pat and tidy conclusion could not be.

2. The answers here will depend, of course, on student responses to the questions following the rough draft. Ask students if Taylor's thesis is complete enough in the final draft. Does it lean too heavily toward the "benefits" of nonconformity when much of what follows cannot be described in quite that way?

3. The persona here is more appealing than that in the first draft, if only because it speaks more articulately. Some students may believe that Taylor succumbs to self-pity ("but I, for one, secretly would have loved to sit in the football stadium ...."), but most will find her honesty refreshing (it is hard, after all, to admit that you were a nobody in school) and unself-pitying.

ADDITIONAL SUGGESTIONS FOR
WRITING OR DISCUSSION

1. If you haven't already done so, this is a good point at which to introduce class editing of essays. Because our students often do not regard us as "real" people, the papers they write for us are likely to sound stilted and artificial—"teacher" papers. I combat that tendency by requiring students to bring a rough draft of each paper to class a meeting or two before the paper is due. Students exchange papers and edit them quickly for specific strengths and weaknesses, filling out a short editing sheet in the process. (The questions on the editing sheet will vary according to our course emphases of the moment, but I always ask for an evaluation of the thesis.) The editing sheets and rough draft are returned to the writer for his or her use in revising, and both are submitted along with the final version of the paper. The purpose of the editing sessions is to help the students become aware of an audience beyond the instructor and more adept at spotting problems in their own papers as they revise. Many instructors use some kind of peer editing of papers; I have found it to be an indispensable teaching resource.

2. A common but always useful exercise in understanding paragraph coherence is to take a paragraph of five or six sentences from some well-written piece (perhaps one of the readings in this book), scramble the order of sentences, and distribute the "new" version to students, who then try to reconstruct the original ordering. Finally, compare versions and discuss the various elements that signal connections and coherence.

3. As the letter to my friend Allan Bilbo shows, business letters require skill in persuasive, articulate writing that some writers never master. (That letter, by the way, is authentic: I changed only Allan's address and the name of the lake.) Ask students to write a business letter for a hypothetical situation such as the following:

You are applying to a "Study Abroad" program sponsored by another college. Write a cover letter to one of your professors, asking her or him to fill out the accompanying—lengthy!—recommendation forms.

You ordered some chino slacks from a mail order firm, and wore them several times. According to the label, the slacks could be washed in cold water, but dry cleaning was preferable. You washed them, and they shrank. Write a letter to the mail order firm, with the aim of getting another pair of pants or your money back.

As secretary of the campus chapter of Young Politicians, you have invited a prominent member of the House of Representatives to speak to your group when he visits your city. He has accepted. However, his usual speaking fee is about double what your group can afford. Write to the Representative and ask for a fifty percent reduction in the fee.

If your students are using a comprehensive handbook, it will include a section on writing business letters. If not, a brief review of the conventions—and a brief warning not to succumb to conventional archaisms—may be in order.

4. A former student of mine shared with me a memo she received (when she was working as a sophomore "advisor" in a freshman dorm) from the Office of Residence Life. It begins:

LOCK-OUTS

The Problem

The problem of student residents locking themselves out of their rooms can reach proportions which impact staff morale and availability to fulfill job responsibilities of a more important nature. Even though letting students into their rooms is a necessary service, approaches to the provision of this service should be taken which minimize undue incidents of this nature.

The decision of what plan of action should be followed to minimize lock-outs is a community decision similar in nature to the decisions on quiet hours and visitation. Although the lock-out infraction is perhaps more directly inconveniencing to the staff than to the residents at large, it is important that staff educate residents to understand the principle that when time is spent in such a non-productive way as opening "lock-out" doors significant reduction in other staff services and programs results.

Procedure for Determining Response to Lock-Outs

The procedure to be followed in determining the approach to lock-outs is as follows:

(But I won't burden you with the procedure. Share this memo with students when you discuss clarity and concision—let them cut it down to size and down to plain English.)

6. In additon to teaching undergraduates, I teach first-year law students. Here are a few gems from legal-writing class that you might ask your students to improve:

To intensify matters, the organization was made up of Mr. Laurence's peers, law students now, but members of the bar in the future. We must consider whether we would want a colleague with such interior motives in our midst.

This kind of conduct is clearly disapproved of at our College of Law, and demonstrates a lack of good moral character on the student's part which is so essential in the legal profession.

Cardin was found guilty of submitting a paper in a constitutional law seminar, which had some of the same ideas and exact quotations from his sister's paper.

6

The Power of Style

Students in first- or second-year rhetoric classes rarely think of themselves as having a writing "style" (and, frankly, some of them have none as yet). To them, "style" means "writing the way the professor likes," and they devote considerable energy to the doomed enterprise of discovering just what that is: "You like long sentences? OK, I'll give you long sentences." To combat this attitude, and to help students whose style is still essentially unformed, studying specific elements of style can prove surprisingly helpful. A style study demystifies and makes more attainable what some students think is possible only for professional writers: not merely the ability to write sentences and paragraphs, but the ability to write with *style*.

The most effective preparation for polishing style—or acquiring some—is to read a great deal and to love words. Many of our students do neither. Yet they can be shown what is characteristic about the way they put words together; and when they become conscious of the patterns of their prose, they have taken the first step toward getting control of their writing. A simple and purely mechanical assessment of some features of style, as described in the first pages of the chapter, helps students see that comments about style are not pulled out of thin air. As early in the study of this chapter as possible, have students undertake such an analysis of a passage of their own writing. Ask them to describe their own writing style in terms of what they discover, and also to indicate any changes they intend to work on in revising future essays. For example, some students will notice that their sentences tend to be all the same length, or to begin all in the same way. Others may observe that they rarely use complex sentence structure to show subordinate relationships of ideas. Still others may note that they favor *to be* verbs and long, abstract nouns. Follow up this study with another one on a later paper to see whether the students' style is developing as they intended.

If students are keeping an argument journal, ask them to begin looking for paragraphs (preferably, but not necessarily, argumentative) that they particularly enjoy the *sound* of, regardless of their feelings about the arguments. That distinction in itself can become a topic for class discussion: Sound and sense do seem to go together. We often find jarring to the ear what annoys the mind. Ask students how often, in doing the assignment, they disliked the style of something they found objectionable in content. Then ask them if occasionally the way an argument was expressed made them respond to it more favorably than they expected to.

EXERCISES

Exercise 6–1

This is a challenging exercise, and students will do best with it if you work through the process for A and part of B in class for *one* of the three paragraphs. In this way they will better understand what to do with the other two and will enjoy more success with the experiment. Woolf is the most daunting; I usually work with her passage in class. The paragraphs were chosen, by the way, in part for their different styles but also in part for what they have to say about reason and writing.

Exercise 6–2

This exercise reminds students that style is woven into the very fiber of the rhetorical context of purpose, audience, and persona. It reinforces some of the key concepts not only of this chapter but also of Chapters 2 and 5.

Exercise 6–3

A. I'd suggest using this as an ungraded exercise (but, if your students are anything like most of mine, I also suggest not mentioning that until afterward). It is useful for students to be aware of figures of speech, but less important that they get all the labels right.
   1. anaphora
   2. pun
   3. metaphor
   4. anastrophe
   5. paradox
   6. overstatement (hyperbole)
   7. irony and parallelism
   8. simile
   9. rhetorical question
   10. antithesis
   11. pun
   12. climax and parallelism

13. irony
14. ellipsis
15. understatement (litotes)
16. metaphor (and pun on "Stephanie"'s frosted hair)
17. overstatement (hyperbole)
18. metaphor
19. climax and antithesis
20. metaphor

B. Imitation is an old-fashioned exercise—but a splendid way of giving students a feel for the various rhythms of well-written prose. Identifying figures of speech by name, as part A requires, is really no more than a way of calling to students' attention some of the ways language works. But imitating the rhythm of sentences they like can have an impact on their own sense of style, and that is more important than a game of "Name That Trope."

Exercise 6–4

This is a fun exercise but takes a while to do well. You may find that you get more thoughtful and proficient work from your students if you let them select three or four of the concepts for which to develop metaphors, rather than requiring them to work with all ten.

Exercise 6–5

Paragraph 1 (which is also the first paragraph in the editorial) is more effective than Paragraph 2 in its use of metaphor. "Enveloped by a miasma" and "vaporous bog" work well together and aptly create an image of foggy confusion. Paragraph 2 (which is the sixth of nine paragraphs) creates an awkwardly visual image of a "vast" funnel full of opinions and people, with the president at the bottom. How is someone supposed to act decisively, as the paragraph asserts, at the bottom of a funnel? And how does one become a "winner" in a funnel? All this reader sees here is the president clogging up an outlet through which things (opinions and people?) are supposed to drain. Or should we envision Dorothy and Toto? No, that doesn't quite work, either.

Exercise 6–6

One possible paragraph drawn from this material:

Imprisoning white-collar criminals is senseless. It does nothing to improve either the criminals or the society they have offended; it merely wastes the prisoners' abilities—which could be put to profitable use by the state—and society's money. It fails to rehabilitate the prisoners or to repay the victims of their crimes. A better solution, since most white-collar crimes involve money, not guns, would be prison externships under close supervision. After all, people who are guilty of writing hot checks or embezzling money are no great threat to the physical safety of others. They should be compelled to do work that brings income to the state, serving in government facilities or in private ones, such as factories and hospitals, under state government contracts. From that income, the state should reimburse the victims to the extent such reimbursement is possible.

Exercise 6–7

One effective way to use this exercise is to have students bring the original letters to class, then have all the students work in class on improving the style of one of the letters. This can be done individually or in small groups. If you use small groups, you might mimeograph their final versions for the whole class to assess at the next class meeting.

Exercise 6–8

This exercise works best if you require students to create a dominant impression without actually labeling the room (apartment, etc.) as "shabby," "messy," or what-have-you. I'd reserve the option of imitating a famous writer's style for advanced comp or honors students unless you have a particularly well-read group in need of a challenge.

READINGS

William James, "War and Reason"

(1842–1910)   An American psychologist and philosopher who led the movement known as pragmatism, James was originally trained as an M.D. at Harvard. He was the elder brother of the novelist Henry James.

Analysis of the Essay   This essay, printed in *The Atlantic* in 1904, is the text of the speech William James gave in Boston on the last day of the World's Peace Congress, October 7 of that year. At the time, Japan was at war with Russia, but the rest of the world maintained an uneasy peace. That peace might be forever maintained was the fervent hope of most of the Congress's delegates, and no less that of James. Unblinkingly realistic, however, James sees little chance that reason might win out over the warlike tendencies he regards as innate in the human heart. "The plain truth is that people *want* war," he asserts, and he gives a convincing argument to support that declaration. James's point is that the world does not run on reason but on "prejudices, partialities, cupidities, and excitements." And of all sources of excitement, war—or even the thought or anticipation of war—is the greatest. It has even been, James acknowledges, the source of countless accomplishments (though he counters that notion with the unknown achievements that might have been realized had mortal energies not been focused so much on war). In the contest for human energy and attention, war will always win out over reason—so the best thing to do, James concludes, is to leave open the possibility of war for the enthusiasts, but always to work, day by day, to defer its actuality. We cannot end war by fiat, but perhaps we can hold it forever at bay.

James's dream is not one that could be realized overnight, he makes clear. To put advocates of peace in positions of world leadership and "to educate the editors and statesmen to responsibility" is an aim that, if it could be managed at all, could be managed only over several decades. And in the meantime, what? World wars and regional wars—James would not live to see them, but he would not have been much surprised. The power of reason mounts only by slow accretion; the power of emotion is immediate and immense.

The power of James's own essay is as much emotional as it is logical. Since the original audience had no text to follow, James uses repetition skillfully to help the hearers follow his line of thought easily; we who read the essay benefit no less. In the first paragraph, for example, James makes clear the contrast between reason and emotion with the repetition of key words such as *philosopher, rational, animal, reason,* and *excitements.* James's sentences are balanced and parallel in structure; he prevents their becoming lifeless and stiff by using informal connectives (*but*) and parenthetical elements ("there is not a man in this room, I suppose, who doesn't buy both an evening and a morning paper, and first of all pounce on the war column"). He employs irony, as in the statement that "wars have been, especially for non-combatants, the supremely thrilling excitement." (The view from the trenches is likely to be less exhilarating.) And he offers a little joke on his own profession, drawing an analogy between the function of philosophers and that of statistics.

James grounds the weightless abstractions of "apologists and idealizers" and "our actual civilization" in concrete examples: "historians in their studies, and clergymen in their pulpits"; Japan, England, and Venezuela. And he fleshes out pale abstractions with apt and beautiful metaphors: Reason is the sand-bank against which the sea of emotions beats; the sand-bank is weaker than the tides but grows patiently and forever. A world without the most emotional of states, war, would be to most people "a stagnant summer afternoon of a world." For such people, war is "God's court of justice" or even "a sacrament . . . [of] mystical blood-payment." And in a startling metaphor, James draws an analogy between war and love—an analogy that forms the support for his proposed solution to the problem of war. The solution he proffers is, metaphorically, "preventive medicine, not . . . radical cure." He engages our imagination with a view of a world in which military officers sit idle, and dream of what might have been.

Possible Responses to the Questions

1. James's diction can be characterized as polysyllabic and abstract, using metaphor to clarify the abstractions with concrete analogies. (The analysis above has more to say about James's use of metaphor.) As to his sentence structure, it is more often simple or compound than complex, and relatively few of his sentence openers are dependent clauses. His sentences are marked, as noted in the question, by parenthetical elements, and vary widely in their length, from some as short as four words ("It is a sacrament"—paragraph 6) to others as long as forty-nine or more ("But sand-banks . . . intermittent"—paragraph 1). Most of his sentences, however, are not especially lengthy: James compensates for his lofty subject and lofty vocabulary with sentences that are usually twenty words or fewer.

   The subordination of ideas is found in parenthetical asides more than in grammatical subordination; and the effect of those asides is to make us feel that he is really speaking to us, thinking through and qualifying his assertions as he considers them.

2. Well, perhaps for a cynical age *startling* is too strong a word; we may be more accustomed to linking love and combat than we ought to be. But the connection James draws between love and war is a subtle and precise one that we may not have thought of: both war and love have a necessarily *intermittent* quality; they are too intense to consume our attention all of the time without consuming us in the process.

3. James's idea is thought-provoking. It is unusual enough to generate student response, not only about its feasibility, but about its insight into human nature. Implementing his plan, however, requires "putting peace-men into power" and "seiz[ing] every pretext, however small, for arbitration methods"—and James doesn't quite tell us how we are to accomplish *that*.

Lewis Lapham, "Sculptures in Snow"

(1935–   ) Editor of *Harper's*, 1971–81, and author of numerous articles and a collection of essays, *Fortune's Child*.

1. Before students will be able to comment on the quotations offered here, they will have to understand them. Ask them to think carefully about what Lapham *means* before they either challenge or agree with him.

2. For example:

   Metaphor: Paragraphs 3–6 offer a series of noteworthy metaphors. Lapham also brings to life cliches and buried metaphors: ". . . it never has much trouble drumming up friends, applause, sympathetic exigesis, and a band" (14).

Parallelism: "resolution, ingenuity, punctuality" (6); "its pessimism, its cynicism, its unwillingness" (7); series of rhetorical questions in (11); "the surgeon and the labor leader, the ballerina and the stock-car driver" (20).

Sentence length: widely varied (see question 3, below)

Vocabulary: ranges from the colloquial to the erudite, with emphasis on the latter; depends also on educated reader familiar with such diverse personages as Pallas Athene, Balzac, and Dorothy Parker.

3. The first three sentences are long and lofty; the fourth's short, down-to-earth simplicity—"This is silly"—bursts the bubble of inflated rhetoric and wrong thinking that the first three sentences mock.

ADDITIONAL SUGGESTIONS FOR WRITING OR DISCUSSION

1. In addition to the writing and analytical exercises suggested earlier, consider photocopying two or three well-written student essays on the same topic that argue roughly the same point. (Anticipating this assignment, you might set some aside earlier in the semester.) Ask students to make a comparative style analysis of those essays. If you prefer to use professional examples, try William F. Buckley, Jr.'s "Capital Punishment" and H. L. Mencken's "The Penalty of Death" for two examples of essays that argue much the same point in markedly different styles. You'll find the first essay in Buckley's *Execution Eve and Other Contemporary Ballads* (Putnam, 1975) and the second in Mencken's *A Mencken Chrestomathy* (Knopf, 1926).

2. As a bit of stylistic detective work, give students four passages, three by one writer and a fourth by a different writer. Ask them to pick out the paragraph by the different writer and explain the grounds for their judgment.

3. Ask students to find examples of particularly appealing and effective metaphors and bring them—in context—to class for discussion.

4. Have students rewrite a single paragraph four different ways:

    (a) using extended metaphor

    (b) using short sentences with varied structure

    (c) using long sentences with varied structure

    (d) using parallel structure and ellipsis (and antithesis, if appropriate)

5. Martin Luther King, Jr.'s "Letter from Birmingham Jail" (in Chapter 10) provides fine models for imitating sentence patterns.

6. The following is one of the style analysis guidesheets I developed for my students to use in analyzing a paragraph or two of their own prose. I usually let them select a passage from a paper they are pleased with, or else one they plan to revise.

STYLE ANALYSIS OF A PASSAGE

I. General impressions after a close re-reading: Do you sound the way you wanted to? Does the paragraph develop a single—and interesting—point fully and coherently? What is the tone (serious, humorous, stilted, etc.)? Does the passage seem articulate and grammatical?

II. WORDS

Describe the diction in terms we discussed in class. (Refer to Chapter 6 and your class notes.)

Are word choices precise?

Does the level of diction seem consistent (or varied for effect, not unconsciously) and appropriate to the audience and occasion?

Did you use any metaphors? What?

III. SENTENCES

Count the number of words in each sentence in the passage. List the numbers, and then the average number of words per sentence overall. Does the length of sentences vary? Is the average length much below—or over—twenty? Comment.

How many sentences does the paragraph (or each paragraph, if more than one is under consideration) contain? Does it strike you as particularly long or short? Comment.

Identify the structures (grammatical and functional) of the sentences. Do you find variety? What kind of sentence structure do you use most often?

Identify any schemes in the passage: parallel structure, antithesis, etc.

IV. COHERENCE

Assuming that all the sentences in each paragraph are directly related to the topic of the paragraph, are those sentences arranged in the most logical order? If not, comment.

Do you vary your sentence openers? Are transitions logical? Do you use any transitions in addition to these: *however, therefore, yet, so, and, but*? Identify any others.

7
Inductive Reasoning

I suspect there is no such thing as a purely "inductive" essay or a purely "deductive" one. Induction and deduction are not so much patterns of organization as processes of thought, and rarely do we find either in isolation. So the aim of this chapter and the next is not to introduce students to the writing and analysis of "inductive essays" and "deductive essays," but to show them ways of making sense in their thinking and in their writing. We make sense in reasoning by drawing inferences out of statements (the concern of Chapter 8) or by looking beyond statements to what further implications can be drawn from the evidence they contain (our concern here). Accordingly, in a chapter on inductive reasoning we center our attention on the latter kinds of processes: the accumulation of data and the drawing of conclusions about additional data of the same sort; the examination of sequential incidents for the possibility of causal relationships; and the examination of analogous phenomena for the possibility of additional, significant similarities. Induction, as noted in the first section of the chapter, is centered on the concrete; but it always moves beyond what lies before us.

The emphasis on the concrete, on data to support the claims we make, makes it appropriate at this point in the course to consider how to find, evaluate, and use source material. Chapter 4 can be taught together with, as well as prior to, Chapter 7 if you want your students to use outside resources on a regular basis. If you prefer to wait to the end of the semester and use Chapter 4 in conjunction with a research assignment, Chapter 7 can work adequately alone. However, in that case students will be limited to what they know out of their own experience as a source of "evidence" to support the claims they make. I have tried it both ways, and my experience has been that classes having trouble with the basic concepts of inductive and deductive reasoning do not need any additional complications at this point, while advanced composition students welcome the freedom to use secondary material. Most of the writing suggestions at the end of the chapter do not require the use of any material beyond the student's own experience and knowledge.

In keeping with the emphases of the chapter, the readings have been chosen for their use of analogy, causal reasoning, and examples (the Syfers essay is a notable example of the latter). In some cases, writers build implicit theses through the accumulation of evidence and analogy, not stating the thesis idea until the very end of the essay (the Ward essay, for instance). This organizational pattern is the closest to what we might call an "inductive essay." Students may wish to try their hand at writing such an essay; when done well, the essay with a deferred thesis statement builds reader interest as it goes along. But writers must be cautioned to have their thesis idea well in mind—I suggest that they write it down and tape it to the wall in front of them as they write—or the essay is likely to meander.

Exercise 7–1

Harris's argument is highly persuasive and likely to elicit discussion—and dissention—about the nature of his analogies. There are two related major analogies: Earth is like a spaceship, and earth is like a sealed room. The spaceship analogy is literal in many respects; the sealed room analogy, while closer to our everyday experience, is metaphorical. Harris does jump back and forth from one to the other: Paragraphs 1, 3, and 5 employ the sealed room analogy; and paragraphs 2, 3, and 7, the spaceship analogy. A minor literal analogy is that between the "thin layer of air surrounding the earth" (paragraph 5) and "materials ... [and] water." Students may notice that the spaceship is compared to a living creature in the last sentence—a problematic anthropomorphism.

Exercise 7–2

1. Literal analogy. No conclusion is explicit here, but the conclusion we are meant to draw is clear: This situation is inequitable. The point of similarity (the wages earned) is strong; the points of dissimilarity (notably, the education of the groups compared) are even stronger. The persuasive point of this analogy depends as much on the dissimilarities as on the similarities.

2. Metaphorical analogy (and the worst sort of cliché).

3. Literal analogy. The parallels are strong and the writer does not try to force them to "prove" the inevitable demise of most computer manufacturers. However, the implicit conclusion suggested is just that.

4. Literal analogy. The parallels with different sorts of special interest groups are strong.

5. Literal analogy. The parallels between cheating on academic work and cheating on income taxes are indeed strong, but not for the second reason cited. People who cheat on academic work hurt themselves most; people who cheat on taxes hurt their fellow citizens—who must take up the slack—most. Both activities are reprehensible, and both, as the argument states, are common.

6. Literal analogy: "Gravitation is to God as electricity is to man." The letter writer's point is that God and gravitation are not mutually exclusive—that gravitation is God's mechanism for keeping the planets in their course—and so to say that the planets "are kept in their course by God" is not to deny gravity, any more than to say that "London [is] lit by man" is to deny the existence of electricity.

7. Literal analogy, with close points of resemblance as far as it goes. The conclusion is a bit strong for the extent of the similarities, however: "Aspertame may well prove to be ..." might be safer.

8. Metaphorical analogy with close-to-literal points of connection. Teacher and guide (and textbook and guidebook) are literally similar; lab course and foreign country are metaphorically analogous here. Strong points of resemblance.

9. Metaphorical analogy, and an effective one: clear and memorable.

10. Metaphorical analogy. Television is not a substance to be ingested or smoked. Nor is it physically addictive as alcohol can be (and as some argue marijuana can be). But all three can be psychologically habit-forming. Schrank draws a literal parallel among the *effects* television, alcohol, and marijuana can have.

Exercise 7–3

1. "Must have" is too strong. The possibility of additional causes is great. Not acceptable.

2. The parallels among the accidents are strong, simple coincidence is unlikely, and the conclusion is not overstated. Acceptable causal reasoning.

3. Perhaps I underestimate the power of television, but I would find this claim acceptable only with supporting evidence (Gallup polls, perhaps) and/or a modified assertion: *possibly* rather than *probably*. Not acceptable causal reasoning as it appears here.

4. The possibility of coincidence has been carefully eliminated, and the conclusion refrains from overstatement. Acceptable.

5. Amusing and effective causal reasoning. Now I know why I love to go to the beach. But if we are going to be logical, we cannot call Galbraith's reasons both necessary and sufficient to explain the attraction of the beach. Not logically acceptable.

6. Post hoc reasoning: neither necessary nor sufficient cause. Not acceptable.

7. Post hoc reasoning: not a sufficient cause. Not acceptable.

8. The suggested cause of Mr. Mims's symptoms is reasonable, for other possible causes have been ruled out. While still not guaranteed, the conclusion is acceptable.

9. The concession in the first clause helps make this an acceptable argument. The cause Simon cites is not entirely sufficient, as he concedes, but he makes a good case for its necessarily leading to a lack of emphasis on foreign language study in the U. S.

10. Post hoc reasoning: neither necessary nor sufficient cause. Pure coincidence, of course.

Exercise 7–4

Even if your students are not familiar with Petrarchan conventions of courtly love, they are bound to be impressed with Kennedy's argument from examples. The touches of humor reinforce his argument: This is no monster to be feared.

Exercise 7–5

A. The responses will vary according to the students' own biases (the sorts of things that seem "self-evident" to each of them). For example, the student who regards the Communist Party as a force of evil on earth will not think the point difficult to prove or one requiring much evidence for support. And the student who hates cats will probably feel that a great deal of evidence and examples must be mustered to make a case for the selfish creatures.

B. Again, responses will vary. Call to students' attention the changes in their *own* lists (from A) as well as the differences among classmates' lists.

C. For example, students might come up with something like the following potential thesis statements for statement 9:

1. A day at the circus can bring out the nine-year-old buried within the most jaded adult.

2. Circus performers are real-life Peter Pans; they never have to grow up.

3. The circus offers a junk food lover a few hours of unequalled delight.

Or for the opposite viewpoint:

1. Circuses are showcases of institutionalized cruelty to animals.

2. Circuses are not only dirty—but dangerous.

3. Circus performers are exploited individuals—migrant workers in bright costumes.

READINGS

Albert Z. Carr, "Is Business Bluffing Ethical?"

(1902–1971)   Writer of both fiction and nonfiction, a contributor to magazines such as *Saturday Evening Post, Harper's Bazaar,* and *Life,* and author of several films and television plays. The range of Carr's interests is illustrated by a sampling of his books: *How to Attract Good Luck and Make the Most of It in Your Daily Life* (1952), *A Matter of Life and Death: How Wars Get Started or Are Prevented* (1966), *The Girl with the Glorious Genes* (1968), and *Business as a Game* (1968).

1. According to Carr, "business bluffing" is like poker in that both are "game strategy" (paragraph 2) not bound by the rules of "private morality." Both employ a use of falsehood better described as "bluffing" because "it is understood on all sides that the truth is not expected to be spoken" (3). Both "have a large element of chance" (5), and "in both games ultimate victory requires intimate knowledge of the rules, insight into the psychology of the other players, a bold front, a considerable amount of self-discipline, and the ability to respond swiftly and effectively to opportunities provided by chance" (5). And so on throughout the essay; Carr is nothing if not thorough in his development of the analogy.

   What Carr refuses to acknowledge is that business and poker are alike in only superficial ways. Business is *not* a game; rules of "private morality" do apply in business if they apply anywhere. Carr's argument finally breaks down in paragraph 11, where he admits that he doesn't really believe in ethics at all; when people speak of being ethical in business, he claims, "it is a self-serving calculation in disguise."

2. Students will notice that "bluffing" is Carr's euphemism for "lying and cheating." But in the field of business, Carr believes, all lying and cheating short of "malicious" lying and actually breaking the law is OK, as he argues in paragraph 10.

3. You might challenge Carr's definitions, claiming that honesty is not situational, and that the rules of the "game" of life are exactly what Carr dismisses: private morality. You might accuse him of waffling in paragraph 15, which advises the business person not to be ruthless and to be ruthless ("bluff hard") all in the same breath, and says that the business person need not be treacherous but need cultivate the *appearance* of honesty.

It might prove easier to refute Carr's thesis to a rhetoric class than to a marketing class. The experiment would be interesting, but the results might prove discouraging. If students feel that they would have to modify their argument substantively in addressing the different audiences, discuss their reasons. Is their impulse simply a consideration of their audience's differing interests, or a case of arguing what is likely to "sell"? I have found in discussing "Business Bluffing" that an alarming number of students believe that if the end is good, any means to it is justifiable. This essay offers an opportunity to discuss the ethics of persuasion in some depth. Joan Didion's "On Morality" (Chapter 2) can provide a useful counterpoint to some parts of Carr's argument. Ask students whether Didion and Carr share the same ideas about morality and ethics.

4. Student response here will vary, but in any event it should stimulate renewed debate among class members. Some students will add the argument that one's first responsibility is to provide for one's family, whatever that end requires.

5. That Carr regards his audience as entirely composed of business people is fair enough; he was writing for the *Harvard Business Review*. That he regards his audience as entirely male is regrettably plain: He speaks only of business*men*. Students should note that Carr's illustrations are all aggressively masculine in their connotations, from the Wild West to poker itself.

   Students who are business majors or are working in business will find the issues Carr raises to be real and troubling ones, whether they agree with him or disagree. Those with no interest in business may claim the argument has nothing to do with them—but of course it has. Because all of us use the goods and services business generates, all of us are affected by the honesty or unscrupulousness of people who run those businesses.

Judy Syfers, "Why I Want a Wife"

Syfers wrote this essay for the inaugural issue of *Ms.* magazine, Spring 1972. No longer married, she now lives and works in San Francisco.

1. This essay speaks first to married women; by implication, to married men; and less immediately, to other adults. If students are not female, they may feel (mistakenly) that they are not part of the intended audience; if they are not married or contemplating marriage, they may be put off by the essay. If they are put off, ask them whether or not theirs may be a "Scarlett O'Hara" response: "I'll think about it tomorrow." A person need not be married or have been married in order to judge the essay fairly, but should have some familiarity with married people—perhaps parents or friends.

2. Virtually all of the issues Syfers raised in the early seventies remain issues in the late eighties. Wives work and still find that they, not their husbands, are expected to miss work when children are sick. Only the last point may have changed, for when husbands have completed their educations, many no longer want their wives to quit their jobs: Most families want two incomes.

3. Syfers offers many particulars to support her ironic conclusion: Anybody, including a woman, could use a wife as *wife* is defined here. The examples are convincing; objections to Syfer's argument are likely to be based on preconceptions about male and female roles.

4. Syfers begins by identifying herself as a wife, and then shows how she came to think about the attractiveness of having a wife by recounting a visit from a divorced male friend who was looking for one. She organizes her points by describing first how a wife can simplify looking after one's children (paragraph 3), looking after one's personal needs (4), and taking care of one's social life (6) and sexual needs (7). There is, of course, more to her thesis than the surface declaration. The message really is "Husbands use their wives, never appreciating all that women do to make life happier for their ungrateful husbands."

5. Student response to Syfers's persona is likely to range widely. Some will find her witty and amusing; others will think her bitter. Some will feel sorry for her; some will accuse her of self-pity. After they sort out the degree to which their own reactions to the subject have colored the writer's persona for them, many will acknowledge that the irony of a woman's expressing a desire for a wife is a clever and effective means of making a serious point about the role of married women. Syfers's persuasive aim is to make us look at the incredible complexity of what is often a thankless job.

Andrew Ward, "The Trouble with Architects"

(1946–   ) Writer whose works (essays and short fiction) have appeared in such magazines as *Atlantic Monthly*, *Horizon*, and *American Heritage*. Ward has also written several books, including *The Premature Memoirs of Andrew Ward*. Chiefly a humorist, Ward believes "that laughter, at least the laughter that comes with recognition, is our surest barometer of truth."

1. The short narrative introducing this essay draws us in even if we don't think we want to know anything about architects. It does indeed illustrate Ward's point that the architects of modern skyscrapers have lost the human scale in their work.

2. Ward's thesis is, as stated just above, that architects have lost the human scale in their works. Their skyscrapers can be appreciated

properly only by people in airplanes, or by birds. Ward's support for this thesis consists of descriptions of the models of proposed buildings (showing how artificial is the perspective the models offer) and other specific examples, such as the difference in the appearance of Cornwall, Connecticut from the air and on the ground.

3. Paragraph 1: "a mean woman with an X-Acto knife," "the enforced veneration for the firm's presiding genius"

   Paragraph 4: "the Olympian perspective of a god, an angel, a chairman of the board"

   Paragraph 6: "and stooping down does not come naturally to your upper-echelon corporate exec," "the little everyday defects that have no place in a meeting where traffic flow patterns, image, and executive toiletry are up for discussion"

   And so on.

   We who otherwise might have been uninterested in Ward's argument stay interested because of his wry, low-keyed humor. It adds to his persuasiveness, rather than detracting from his argument.

4. The best refutation would take the form of specific award-winning design, accompanied perhaps by a discussion of the ways in which modern skyscrapers take *more* heed of their occupants' comforts than did the old buildings of stone and mortar. Then, too, skyscrapers permit more people to be accommodated in increasingly limited space on increasingly valuable property.

NOTE: A few words of identification may be in order here. Albert Speer (paragraph 5) was the official architect (and later the second most powerful man in Hitler's inner circle) of Nazi Germany. His buildings are massive neoclassic structures. Harold Geneen (11) is one of those Olympians to whom Ward refers, the former chairman of the board of ITT. And Asher Benjamin (13) was an American architect and writer (1773–1845) famed for the graceful symmetry of his late colonial design.

Edwin Arlington Robinson, "How Annandale Went Out"

(1865–1935) An American poet, Robinson is noted for short character studies in poetry. He received the Pulitzer Prize three times for volumes of his poetry. Students may be interested to learn that the "Richard Corey" they know in song is taken from the famous Robinson poem of the same name.

1. Annandale was the friend and patient of the narrator (line 3).
2. The narrator is a physician (line 3).

3. The narrator is defending his act of euthanasia.

4. The narrator's defense is that his friend was terminally ill and facing excruciating pain (7-8).

5. The speaker first refers to Annandale as *it* (10), speaking of the wreck of a man, no longer fully alive; but in line 4 he uses the pronoun *him* to speak of Annandale.

6. The "apparatus" is the friend's body, which the speaker describes in mechanical terms in order to distance himself from it emotionally. What he kills is not his friend but the "apparatus" of his diseased body.

7. The "slight kind of engine" is either a gun or a hypodermic needle for making a lethal injection. The former is more accurately described in these terms, but the latter is a more likely choice for a physician committing a mercy killing.

8. The speaker has done the deed out of *love* for his friend, whose suffering he cannot bear to prolong.

ADDITIONAL SUGGESTIONS FOR WRITING OR DISCUSSION

1. It is a good idea to talk about the kinds of conclusions we can draw from the different inductive reasoning processes. As a quiz of students' comprehension of the differences, ask the following questions (taken from George W. Ziegelmueller and Charles A. Dause, *Argumentation: Inquiry and Advocacy*, Prentice-Hall, 1975):

   • Why does an argument by example not reach conclusions of explanation?

   • Why does an argument by analogy not reach conclusions of explanation?

   • Why does an argument by causal correlation not reach conclusions of essence or existence? (109)

2. Ask students to discuss the following assertion in Irving Copi's *Introduction to Logic*, 6th ed. (Macmillan, 1982): "If an effect is specified with sufficient precision, the apparent plurality of causes tends to disappear" (411).

3. Ask students to consider Wesley Salmon's observation (in *Logic*, 2nd ed., Prentice, 1973, 17) that *no arguments about future events would be possible without induction.*

4. Give students a list of topics and ask them to come up with analogues, both metaphorical and literal, for purposes they may invent. For ex-

ample, you might ask them to find analogues that would help a reader better understand:

the experience of skydiving
the theory of relativity
what a younger brother is like
the significance of the national debt
the value of Halloween
the allure of junk mail

8

Deductive Reasoning

The most frightening experience I had in my first year as a graduate teaching fellow came when I was handed Edward P. J. Corbett's *Classical Rhetoric for the Modern Student* (2nd ed.) and was informed that I would be teaching syllogisms. That I am today a convert to the value of teaching students to recognize enthymemes and reconstruct syllogisms in order to analyze reasoning is a tribute both to Professor Corbett's splendid text and to my bright, hard-working students in that first class, who were determined to learn something whether I could teach it or not. Since this brief guide is directed primarily to beginning instructors, many of whom have been trained in literature rather than rhetoric and argumentation, I hope the following suggestions will prove helpful.

Syllogisms are out of favor these days in many academic circles, for they strike some rhetoricians as contrived, formulaic, and unreal—entirely unsuited to the current emphasis on "process" over "product" and writing as "discovery." But as I hope the rest of this text makes clear, the study of formal argumentative principles is intended to further, not to stifle, the aims of creativity and discovery in writing. For it to achieve that aim, we need only abandon the notion that there is such a thing as a purely deductive essay—a set formula into which a writer plugs statements.

Syllogisms are analytic tools with which to evaluate enthymemic argument, so that we as writers can determine in a conscious and deliberate way what about our own or others' arguments is or isn't making sense. Only if we are capable of that kind of analysis can we do anything more than react instinctively to argument: "That sounds wrong; I don't know why, it just does." Your best students will be able to say "why," more or less specifically, without studying formal argumentative principles and logical fallacies. Your other students will not. It is to them that this material is most specifically directed. Syllogisms are training wheels for the critical thinker; two years from now, students who master the principles of syllogistic reasoning probably will not be able to reel off the six rules for validity in categorical reasoning, but their study of those rules and the logical principles they represent will have made them more able critical thinkers. And better thinkers make for better writers.

One byproduct of studying deduction is that students become more aware of the relationships between ideas and even between parts of sentences. And, indeed, a useful starting point in teaching this chapter is to analyze what different statements mean and how they may complement or contradict each other. First, discuss the concept of distribution (see text, "Distribution of Terms") and have students practice transforming sentences into two-term propositions (Exercise 8-1). *Make sure students have grasped the concept of distribution of terms before going on, for it is essential to all that follows.* I suggest spending at least one class meeting on distribution.

Next, discuss the four kinds of two-term propositions among which we will find relationships in arguments: the universal affirmative (A-proposition), the universal negative (E-proposition), the particular affirmative (I-proposition), and the particular negative (O-proposition). These particular letters were originally assigned by logicians to the four propositions simply as a mnemonic device: A and I, for the affirmative propositions, are the first two vowels in the Latin word meaning "I affirm"—*affirmo*—and E and O, for the negative propositions, are the vowels in the Latin word meaning "I deny"—*nego*. I do not ordinarily teach the square of opposition as such, but some of my colleagues use it and endorse it so enthusiastically that I include it here (not, however, in the text proper) as a teaching aid you may find helpful. The square of opposition shows the possible relationships among the four kinds of propositions.

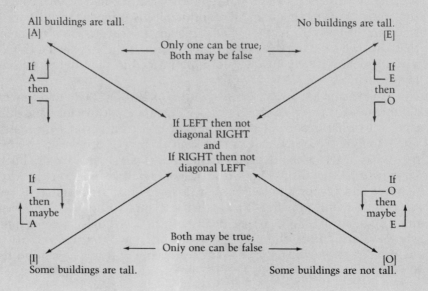

The square of opposition can help students grasp what kinds of statements are logically compatible with each other and what kinds are not. If it is true that some buildings are tall, for example, it naturally follows that we cannot claim no buildings are tall. Caution students not to dismiss these relationships as self-evident, for they are not always as obvious when we are talking about philosophical and political issues as they are when we are talking about buildings.

The following pointers should help students deal with statements that appear in various disguises:*

(1) **ALL . . . ARE NOT . . . .** (AVOID this form.)

Remedy (a): **If the word** *not* **modifies the entire statement, change the wording to** *no* **or** *none* **(universal negative).**

Remedy (b): **If the** *not* **modifies the** *all,* **change the wording to** *some* **(particular negative).**

Examples: All of the pigs are not fat.

(a) None of the pigs are fat creatures.   (universal neg.)

(b) Some of the pigs are not fat creatures.   (part. neg.)

(2) **"ONLY"**   (Treat as universal affirmative—but which term is subject?)

Remedy: **To determine which term is the subject term, remember that** *the term following "only" is the predicate term.*

Example: Only patriots deserve well of their country.
Convert to universal affirmative form: All _____ are _____ .

Step 1:   **Find the subject noun and predicate noun:** *patriots* follows *only* and is therefore the predicate.
The subject noun, then, must be what is left over.
All _____ are patriots.
What is left over is "deserve well of their country."

Step 2:   **Add a noun to make this the subject:**
All *people who deserve well of their country* are *patriots.*

(3) **"THE ONLY"**   (Treat as universal affirmative—but which term is subject?)

Remedy: **To determine which term is the subject term, remember that** *the term following "the only" is the subject term.*

*My colleague Lyssa Bossay has kindly permitted me to reprint here a handout she uses for her own students in this course.

Example: The only ones who failed were those who were careless. Convert to universal affirmative form: All _____ are _____.

Step 1:   **Find the subject noun and the predicate noun.** "Ones who failed" follows "the only" and is therefore the subject:

All *ones who failed* were _____.
What is left over, then, must be the predicate. "Those who were careless" is left over and must be the predicate.

Step 2:   **Reconstruct the proposition:**
All *ones who failed* were *those who were careless.*

Step 3:   **To clean it up a bit, you might want to rephrase it as:**
All people who failed were people who were careless.

(4) **"ALL . . . BUT"** (Treat as universal affirmative—but which term is subject and which is predicate?)

Remedy: **Negate the term following *but* and make it the subject term.**

Example: All but the important cases were reviewed by the jury.

Step 1:   **Convert to universal affirmative: All _____ are _____.**
Find the subject and predicate. The noun following *but* is "the important cases." Negated, it becomes "the non-important cases" or "the unimportant cases."
After the term is negated, it becomes the subject:
All *the unimportant cases* were _____.

Step 2:   **The leftover becomes the predicate:**
All *the unimportant cases* were [*cases*] *reviewed by the jury.*

(5) **"NONE BUT"** (Treat as universal affirmative, and follow same procedure as for (2): **Treat *none but* just as you would *only*.**)

(6) **SINGULAR PROPOSITIONS** (Treat as universal affirmatives by adding *all*.)

Examples: John is a bright boy.
All John is a bright boy.

Science is the curse of the human race.
All science is the curse of the human race.

This close look at sentences almost always has positive effects on the way students use words. They begin to think about what *meaning* sentences express. Some students even seem to use fewer cliches and mixed metaphors after learning to make two-term propositions out of complex sentences—a process that compels them to look closely at what a sentence says and how the subject and predicate terms are related. Faulty predication (discussed in Chapter 5) becomes somewhat less a problem in their writing.

The next step is to begin working with simple categorical syllogisms already set out in valid form for the students' analysis. Students often are puzzled by the whole notion of the syllogism at this point, and I attempt to address that issue at some length at the beginning of Chapter 8 and again in "Testing Validity: The Syllogism." The syllogism is simply a naked argument with all the verbal trappings that can disguise it removed. It is a model for analyzing the logical relationships among statements, the way people connect their ideas and observations: the *form* of argument. *Make sure students understand the difference between validity and truth and can pick out major, minor, and middle terms before proceeding further.* Students should become familiar with the six rules for judging validity and should be able to supply conclusions for syllogisms (see Exercise 8-3). At this point they will begin to see why the concept of distribution is important, for we must consider *all* of the class that constitutes the linking ("middle") term before we can logically deduce a relationship between the major and minor terms.

So that students will better understand the logic underlying the six rules for validity, I include a discussion of the formal fallacies—that is, what goes wrong when a syllogistic argument does not meet one or more of the requirements for validity (see "Formal Fallacies" in text).

The usual form in which deductive reasoning occurs in written argument is as *enthymemes*, elliptical arguments with all three terms present but a premise or even conclusion left implicit rather than stated outright. If you taught the enthymemic thesis in Chapter 2, your students are already familiar with the uses of enthymemes for invention; in Chapter 8 we focus on logical analysis of enthymemic arguments. The second distinctive feature of most enthymemes is that they express probability rather than certainty. Here Stephen Toulmin's emphasis on qualifiers (see "The Limitations of Logic: Toulmin's Corrective" in text) will help students judge the consistency of quantitative modifiers in enthymemic arguments. We work with truly universal affirmative and negative statements (*All* x are y; *no* m are n) in studying syllogisms because they make the concept of distribution easier to grasp; but since we cannot always speak with assurance about *all* the members of a class, we can treat the statement "Most liberal senators favor Medicare" as if it were distributed, as long as the conclusion expresses no greater degree of certainty.

Thus, the enthymeme "Jordan probably favors Medicare, since she is a liberal senator" is rhetorically valid. The syllogism we would work out for the argument goes as follows:

Most liberal senators favor Medicare.	(implicit premise)
Jordan is a liberal senator.	(stated premise)
Jordan probably favors Medicare.	(stated conclusion)

The enthymeme "Jordan must favor Medicare because most liberal senators do" is rhetorically invalid, on the other hand, if the implicit premise is meant to be "Jordan is a liberal senator." (Note the ambiguity in the argument: The implicit premise also could be "Jordan always favors what most liberal senators favor." In that case, the enthymeme is valid. The two statements do not have precisely the same meaning. The ambiguity should be resolved by the context in which the argument appears; if it isn't, the arguer must express himself or herself more clearly.)

The main initial difficulty students have with enthymemes is determining the three terms of an argument. And the best way of resolving that problem, as indicated in the text, is to look for the conclusions. The ability to distinguish a conclusion from a premise is no trivial skill in itself for writers. Students who can do it begin to notice in their own essay drafts the points at which they make unsupported assertions. Once they can identify conclusions confidently, they need only apply the already-mastered skill of reducing sentences to two-term propositions in order to determine the minor term (subject term in the conclusion) and the major term (predicate term in the conclusion). They then have little difficulty recognizing the term linking major and minor terms as the middle term.

Whether or not students are keeping an argument notebook, what they are studying becomes more real for them if you ask them to look for enthymemes in what they read, write, and hear, and to bring examples to class for discussion. If you are teaching this material for the first time, however, you may wish to take up their examples at the end of one class, duplicate some of the more interesting ones, and discuss them at the beginning of the next class. Poor writing and illogic in arguments—such as are commonly found in letters to newspapers—sometimes warrant a little study and headscratching, and that can be done more easily without twenty pairs of eyes looking at you expectantly.

Hypothetical and alternative arguments are structurally simple and generally pose no great problems to teach. Only two points run counter to "common sense" logic, and some students will not grasp them immediately:

1. The two fallacies of hypothetical reasoning.
2. The fallacy of affirming an alternative.

These may require some additional discussion. One way to help students understand the hypothetical fallacies is to pick a hypothesis that demonstrates a *causal* relationship, such as "If it doesn't rain all summer, the crops will die" or "If you loan a friend money, you will lose a friend." Students can grasp the fallacies of affirming the consequent or denying the antecedent in such arguments: a fungus or insect problem also could destroy crops; the friend's death or a quarrel could end a friendship. (By the way, the close and complementary relationship of deduction to induction is apparent in such examples.) With regard to the problem of affirming an alternative, students must accept the fact that *or* can imply *and*.

EXERCISES

Exercise 8–1

1. Subject undistributed; predicate undistributed
2. Subject distributed; predicate undistributed
3. Subject undistributed; predicate distributed
4. Subject distributed; predicate undistributed
5. Subject undistributed; predicate distributed
6. Subject distributed; predicate undistributed
7. "Circumstantial evidence [is material that] has merit in courts of law." Subject distributed; predicate undistributed
8. Subject distributed; predicate distributed
9. Subject undistributed; predicate distributed
10. "Most Americans [are people who] can recite the Pledge of Allegiance." Subject undistributed; predicate undistributed

Exercise 8–2

1. Invalid (The middle term, "creatures that multiply rapidly," is undistributed.)
2. Valid
3. Invalid (too many terms: *Catholic* and *catholic* do not signify the same class)
4. Valid
5. Valid (The conclusion should be rephrased for analysis: "Some frozen yogurt is among the things I will not eat." Caution students that the "not" here does not deny the predicate term, but is *part* of the predicate term: "things I will not eat.")
6. Invalid (Middle term, *Democrats*, is not distributed.)

7. Valid

8. Invalid (There are four terms: "stiff, mandatory penalties," "things that reduce crime," "drunk driving," and "crimes.")

9. Invalid (Both premises are negative; no conclusion is possible.)

10. Valid

11. Invalid (middle term undistributed)

12. Valid

13. Valid

14. Invalid (middle term undistributed)

15. Valid

Exercise 8–3

1. No A are C.

2. Some frogs cannot break the spell.

3. Senator Smithers is not contemptible.

4. If the first premise is taken to mean "No A are B," the correct conclusion is "No A are C." If the first premise is taken to mean "Some A are not B," the correct conclusion is "Some A are not C." Refer students to the footnote in the section on "Distribution of Terms."

5. Cardiopulmonary resuscitation is a skill people should know.

6. "A person" (the speaker) should major in sociology.

7. "A person" (their daughter) should major in pre-med.

8. Pit bulls should be destroyed.

9. Chemists should change their occupations.

10. Some people feel depressed on Thanksgiving.

Exercise 8–4

1. Valid

2. Invalid: middle term not distributed

3. Invalid: term distributed in conclusion but not in premise

4. Invalid: four terms (two different things meant by "altered states of mind")

5. Valid

Exercise 8–5

1. **Stated premise, rephrased:** All who deserve scholarships have financial need. **Implied premise:** Stewart has no financial need. **Stated conclusion:** Stewart does not deserve a scholarship. **Terms:** those who deserve scholarships, financial need, Stewart

2. **Stated premise, rephrased:** Liver is a thing children hate to eat. **Implied premise:** Things children hate to eat are not things children should be forced to eat. **Stated conclusion:** Children shouldn't be forced to eat liver. **Terms:** liver, things children hate to eat, things children are forced to eat

3. **Implied premise:** All who make Phi Beta Kappa are people assured of success in life. **Stated premise:** Cynthia has made Phi Beta Kappa. **Stated conclusion:** Cynthia is assured of success in life. **Terms:** all who make Phi Beta Kappa, people assured of success in life, Cynthia

4. **Stated premise:** All lying is wrong [or in other words, something you shouldn't do]. **Implied premise:** To tell your roommate that you like those lavender bedspreads would be lying. **Stated conclusion:** To tell your roommate that you like those lavender bedspreads would be wrong [that is, something you shouldn't do]. **Terms:** lying, things that are wrong [things that you shouldn't do], telling your roommate that you like those lavender bedspreads

5. **Implied premise:** The language spoken by the greatest number of people should be the language of international trade and diplomacy. **Stated premise:** Chinese is the language spoken by the greatest number of people. **Stated conclusion:** Chinese should be the language of international trade and diplomacy.

6. **Implied premise:** Knowledge can be taught. **Stated premise:** Virtue is a kind of knowledge. **Stated conclusion:** Virtue can be taught. **Terms:** Virtue, knowledge, things that can be taught

7. • Sports generate competitiveness. (Stated premise, restated)
   • Competitiveness leads to aggressive behavior in children.

   (Stated premise)

   • Sports generate aggressive behavior in children.
   (Implied conclusion of first argument; implied premise of second)
   • All activities that generate aggressive behavior in children are activities children should not participate in. (Stated premise)
   • Sports are activities children should not participate in.

   (Stated conclusion)

Exercise 8-6

1. "Possibly" would be safer than "probably." Robert may have attended Purdue only for a time (not graduated), or a relative may have done so, or Robert may have simply bought a sticker in the campus bookstore.

2. OK

3. "Know" is a little too strong. "Reasonably sure" would be better.

4. "Slim chance" is unreasonably tentative. "Good possibility" would be fair under the circumstances.
5. If a majority or a large plurality of the population is indeed jobless, as the implied premise here indicates, the conclusion is OK.
6. The conclusion is overstated. "Runs the risk of" would be better.
7. The conclusion reasonably could be stronger: "is almost certainly."

Exercise 8-7

Some examples:

1. If we abolish the right of private ownership of land, abolish monopoly, make the world partners in production, partners in the good things of life, then we will abolish crime and criminals (implicit: because it is inequities among people's situations that lead to crime).
2. Nobody would steal if he could get something of his own some easier way. (Implicit: People can't get something of their own any easier way. Therefore, they do steal.)
3. There should be no jails [because] they do not accomplish what they pretend to accomplish.
4. Jails do not promote equality, so jails should be abolished. ("The only way to cure these conditions is by equality. There should be no jails.")
5. If you would wipe [jails] out there would be no more criminals than now because [jails] terrorize nobody [that is, do not function as deterrents to crime].

Exercise 8-8

1. Invalid: denies antecedent
2. Valid
3. Invalid: denies antecedent
4. Invalid: affirms an alternative
5. Invalid: denies antecedent
6. Valid
7. Invalid: affirms an alternative
8. Invalid: denies antecedent
9. Valid
10. *Minor premise:* Schizophrenia probably will turn out to have a biochemical cause and cure. *Conclusion:* Schizophrenia in that event will no longer be one of the diseases for which a person would be involuntarily committed. (Valid—and implicit in Szasz's argument)
11. Valid (Minor premise—"The report is late"—is implicit.)

12. Valid
13. *Minor premise*: We (the ancient Egyptians) do preserve both the body and a sculptured image of it. *Conclusion*: Our immortality is assured. (Valid)
14. Valid
15. Valid

READINGS

Barbara Tuchman, "Should We Abolish the Presidency?"

(1912–   ) Tuchman is a historian (author of *A Distant Mirror, The March of Folly*, and other best-selling works) who always considers her audience: "Historians who put in everything plus countless footnotes aren't thinking of their readers. Subsequently [sic], they're not readable" (*Contemporary Authors*, New Revised Series, vol. 3).

1. Much of Tuchman's essay is argument from definition. She argues what the presidency is intended to be and how it presently does not fulfill that definition. She offers an extended definition of the nature and functions of the cabinet government she proposes.
2. The presidency should not be administered by dictatorial people. Individuals tend to be dictatorial.
   Therefore, the presidency should not be administered by individuals.
3. The first reason is stated in paragraphs 4 and 5: The presidency is no longer balanced in power and prestige by the Congress, a condition for which the people of the United States are responsible. The argument is deductive. It could be expressed syllogistically as follows.

The problems of the presidency are a result of Congress's failure to act independently—to function as a check on the presidency.

(Tuchman offers inductive backing for the statement that Congress has failed.)

The failure of the Congress is a result of the voters' failure [to elect responsible representatives].

Therefore, the problems of the presidency are a "failure of the people [voters]."   (Implicit conclusion)

The second reason is stated in paragraph 6: The presidency is in trouble because an individual Chief Executive "forms policy as a reflection of his personality and ego needs." This argument, too, is deductive.

The president's image is readily transmittable to millions of people.

What is readily transmittable to millions is powerful.

Therefore, the president's image is powerful.

*

What is powerful tends to take precedence in a person's concerns.

The president's image is powerful.

(conclusion of first argument)

Therefore, the president's image tends to take precedence in his or her concerns.

And an important assumption underlies these arguments:

People to whom image is most important tend to make wrong decisions.

4. Tuchman's argument is that quick decisions are not limited to individual decisions—and that no president makes individual decisions in times of crisis, anyway. Tuchman here uses the word *invalid* in the logical sense, "wrongly reasoned."

Arthur C. Clarke, "We'll Never Conquer Space"

(1917–   ) British writer noted particularly for his books and articles on scientific subjects and for his science fiction (including: *2001: A Space Odyssey*). Clarke has lived in recent years in Sri Lanka, where he continues to write and to engage in underwater exploration and photography.

1. What is permanently separated from the earth cannot be conquered. Space is permanently separated from the earth [by time]. Therefore, space cannot be conquered.
   The argument is sound if we accept Clarke's definition of *conquer* and his assertion that time cannot be conquered (see paragraph 14).
2. Other terms restricted in meaning include *conversation* (paragraph 12), "time barrier" (14), *colonies* (28). Certainly, however, everything in the argument hinges on the definition of *conquer*, so Clarke devotes several paragraphs to his restricted definition.
3. This question should generate some controversy if students really stop to think about its implications.

Arthur Conan Doyle, "The Tell-Tale Hat"

(1859–1930) Scottish physician and author best-known for his creation of the arch-detective, Sherlock Holmes, in "A Study in Scarlet" (1887). While Doyle wrote four mystery novels and more than fifty short stories about Holmes, he would have preferred to see his literary reputation rest upon his historical novels or his scholarly works (such as *The British Campaigns in Europe*, 1912).

1. No wife who will allow her husband to go out with a week's accumulation of dust upon his hat is a wife who loves her husband. This man's wife has allowed him to go out in such a state. Therefore, this man's wife no longer loves him.

   This argument depends in part on an assumption that only wives have the responsibility of brushing hats: All who have the responsibility of brushing hats are wives.

2. For example:

   (a) All who have large heads have large brains.
   The owner of this hat has a large head.
   Therefore, the owner of this hat has a large brain.

   (b) All men who wear old hats have no other hats to wear.
   This man is wearing an old hat.
   Therefore, this man has no other hats to wear.

   (c) All who buy expensive hats are well-to-do people at the time.
   The owner of this hat bought an expensive one.
   Therefore, the owner of this hat was a well-to-do person at the time.

   (d) All who have just one old hat are people in financial straits.
   The owner of this hat has just one old hat. [See conclusion (b).]
   Therefore, the owner of this hat is in financial straits.

   (e) A person who does not replace the broken elastic of a hat-securer is a person who lacks foresight.
   All who lack foresight suffer from moral retrogression.
   Therefore, a person who does not replace the broken elastic of a hat-securer suffers from moral retrogression.

Expressed as they are above, Holmes's syllogisms are valid, but their unsoundness is revealed. When we set out Holmes's arguments as valid syllogisms, the unqualified generalization (*dicto simpliciter*) of each of their major premises is revealed (*"All* people with but one hat must be impoverished"?); and if we restrict the scope of the premises to something that is tenable (*"Many* people with no more than one hat are financially distressed"), the syllogism is no longer valid. Valid deduction requires that the middle term be distributed and that the strength of the conclusion cannot be greater than the premises—that a term may not be distributed in the conclusion if it was not distributed in a premise.

Eugene Ionesco, "The Logic Lesson, or My Cat Socrates"

(1912–   )   Native of Romania, but now a French citizen, Ionesco is a playwright of renown who has received awards in France, Italy, Monaco,

Austria, Israel, and other countries. When he received the Jerusalem Prize in 1973, for the total body of his work, Ionesco's play *Rhinoceros* was singled out as being "one of the great demonstrations against totalitarianism."

1. Undistributed middle term
2. Two syllogisms can be reconstructed here, for Jean makes both an observation about Berenger's present state and a prediction about his future.

   All who exist are thinkers.
   Berenger is not a thinker.
   Therefore, Berenger does not exist.

   If you think, you exist.
   Think, Berenger.
   Then, you will exist.

3. It is circular reasoning, and equivocates the meaning of *natural* to boot.

Anonymous, "Sonnet for a Philosopher"

1. Certainly logic is limited, but then, it does not claim to do all that the speaker of the poem says it does. The objections are well-founded to the extent that logic removes the blood and passion from human experience, and experience ceases to be human when that happens.
2. No. "War is Hell" means war is *a part of* hell. So we cannot say that war and hell have nothing to do with each other, that "Hell is not War." What the speaker is objecting to is, more accurately, grammar. Grammatically, the predicate term is taken to be larger than the subject term—even if actually such is not the case.

ADDITIONAL SUGGESTIONS FOR WRITING OR DISCUSSION

1. The following enthymemes for student analysis could be used as a quiz or for additional practice in reconstructing syllogisms. The last two are difficult; allow plenty of time to work them out.

   (a) If we regard activity as being in itself a good, then we must count all snobberies are good; for all provoke activity.
   —Aldous Huxley, "Selected Snobberies"

   (All things that provoke activity are good.
   Snobberies provoke activity.
   Therefore, snobberies are good.)

(b) Forks had been invented by the time Henry VIII reigned, so all the legends of his eating with his hands are untrue. (Implicit: If people have forks, they will use them. Henry VIII had access to forks; therefore, he must have used them.)

(c) Heard in court:

"If you hadn't been there, the accident wouldn't have happened."
"No, of course not."
"So you admit it was your fault."
—E. R. Emmet, *Handbook of Logic: The Use of Reason* (Littlefield, Adams, 1979), 170

(What happens because you are present always is caused by you.)

(d) From rest and sleep, which but thy [Death's] pictures be, Much pleasure; then from thee much more must flow, . . .
—John Donne, "Death Be Not Proud"

(Restated:
What is but a picture of something else must be less intense than it.
Rest and sleep are but a picture of Death.
Therefore, rest and sleep are less intense than death.
SO,
If rest and sleep give pleasure, then Death must give greater pleasure.
Rest and sleep do give pleasure.
Therefore, Death does indeed give even greater pleasure.)

(e) "What flows into you from the myth is not truth but reality (truth is always *about* something, but reality is that *about which* truth is), and, therefore, every myth becomes the father of innumerable truths on the abstract level."
—C. S. Lewis, "Myth Became Fact"
(*Note*: Working out a syllogism from this sentence becomes an exercise in close reading. Doing so, we become aware that Lewis does not mean to imply that truth has nothing to do with myth, but rather that what we experience from myth is more immediate than, and greater than, abstract truth. Through myth, he claims, we understand reality. Understanding reality, we understand "innumerable truths." So,

Reality is contained in myth.

Truth is part of reality.
Therefore, truth is contained in myth.

We see that Lewis argues here that myth is all-encompassing.)

2. Ask students to look closely at the assumptions underlying arguments they encounter in everday contexts: magazine articles, advertisements, overheard conversations. Even closer at hand are the readings in other chapters in *The Power to Persuade*. Ask students to look again—with the more specific logical criteria set forth in Chapter 8— at the arguments in the readings for Chapters 1 and 2, for instance, or the student essay in Chapter 5 ("Nonconformity: The Price and the Payoff"). Have them look for enthymemes and reconstruct syllogisms from the enthymemes, noticing particularly the implicit premises or conclusions. Ask: Do the implicit premises tend to be factually or logically weaker than what is stated? Do they sometimes reveal a writer's *a priori* beliefs?

3. Have students examine the logic of their own enthymemes in an essay written either earlier in the semester or for a previous course. Ask them what changes, if any, they might now make in their arguments or the way those arguments are expressed.

4. Now that your students have studied both induction and deduction, ask them to discuss whether or not they understand/agree with the following assertions:

"[A]ll inference is deductive and . . . what passes as induction is either disguised deduction or more or less methodical guesswork."
—Morris R. Cohen, *A Preface to Logic*
(Holt, Rinehart, 1965, 32–33)

"In actual fact, then, the difference between *rhetorical* induction and deduction is that induction establishes the general on the basis of examples, while deduction establishes the general on the basis of dialectic; furthermore, the two processes are usually inseparable in any given argument."
—W. Ross Winterowd, *Rhetoric: A Synthesis*
(Holt, Rinehart, 1968, 23)

9
Fallacies

Students who struggled and strained to master the concepts of deductive reasoning in Chapter 8 will find Chapter 9 a pleasant relief, for somehow problems in other people's reasoning tend to be more obvious and amusing—or annoying—than flaws in one's own reasoning. Chapter 9 also will reinforce the principles of the previous chapters in ways that may make problematic concepts fall into place: The student who can't quite grasp the logical problem of an undistributed middle term often has no problem discerning the unfairness of guilt-by-association, for example.

This chapter covers but a few of the dozens of fallacies that logicians have identified over the centuries, but I have tried to include a good sampling of the most typical kinds. Given the many names a single fallacy may answer to, you will find that I have occasionally referred to a fallacy by a name other than the one you prefer—but differences of that sort are minor as long as the students grasp the concept involved. For that reason, I do not require my own students to "label" fallacies in class discussions and on tests, as long as they do what is far more important: explain the factual or reasoning problem involved. I do point out to them—appealing to their self-interest—that such labels provide a useful shorthand and save time.

This chapter several times brings up the issue of ethics in argument. The aim of your course and this book is *not* to train clever and deceitful manipulators, but don't we run that risk in teaching students about foul as well as fair means of persuasion? The issue warrants some discussion in class. I believe the actual result of studying Chapter 9 and its readings is more likely to be increased skepticism toward the arguments students read and hear—a heightened awareness of fallacies that may well send students on logical witch-hunts, so that they see fallacies in *everything* they read. Students should be warned against this response as they work exercises and read essays.

EXERCISES

Exercise 9–1

1. Counterattack (tu quoque)
2. Appeal to pity
3. Equivocation (two senses of *rhetoric*)
4. Post hoc
5. Begging the question (circular reasoning)
6. Equivocation
7. Bandwagon (more countries recognize PLO); loaded phrases
8. Oversimplification
9. Post hoc
10. Lack of contrary evidence
11. False dilemma (black or white)
12. False analogy
13. Fallacious appeal to authority
14. Ad populum appeal (and holiness by association)
15. False analogy
16. Personal attack (ad hominem) and trivial objections
17. Lack of contrary evidence (also known as the appeal to ignorance)
18. Post hoc
19. Argument from definition—not fallacious
20. A potpourri of fallacies here: fallacious use of unattributed statistics; overgeneralization; false dilemma (either people watch TV all day or they work); loaded phrases; post hoc (in claimed relationship between idle TV-watching and social programs).
21. Another potpourri (including complex question), but the most malodorous element is a "tu quoque" attack (see "Personal Attack" in text): The government purports to fight drug addiction while subsidizing the "dangerous drug . . . at the top of the list," tobacco.
22. Oversimplification and personal attack
23. False dilemma (black or white): Mr. Swanigan argues that he has only two alternatives, scavenging or a life of crime.
24. Hypothesis contrary to fact (described more fully in "Love Is a Fallacy")
25. False dilemma (black or white)

Exercise 9–2

These opinion essays were published in *USA Today*, September 14, 1984 (14A+). Miss America, Vanessa Williams, had just been forced to relinquish her title after it was disclosed that she had posed for nude photographs (which were then published in *Penthouse* magazine). Some fallacies in the Morgan piece:

- Lots of **name-calling** (ad hominem)
- **Oversimplification** ("they all send the same message" and "beauty pageants are simply the flip side of the pornographic coin")
- **Appeals to popular sentiments** (while attacking just such fallacious appeals to popular sentiments by those Morgan criticizes)
- **Post hoc** (pageants are a substantial factor in the continued discrimination against women)
- **Guilt-by-association** ("*Penthouse* and the pageant—they're a marriage made in heaven, and they deserve each other."

Some fallacies in the Marks place:

- More **name-calling** ("ridiculous," "shows gross ignorance," etc.)
- **Equivocation** ("it's the young women who exploit the Miss America pageant")
- **Affirms an antecedent** ("If young women in swimsuits are sexist, then thousands of women on America's beaches are sexist.")
- **Exaggeration** ("If the critics had their way, we'd have to close every beach in America.")
- **Shifts ground** ("Physical fitness, poise under trying conditions—I would hardly regard those things as sexist.")
- **Post hoc** (implication that being in the pageant led to careers for "tens of thousands of young women")

Exercise 9–3

I have had students undertake this study with newspapers of widely varying quality (from the *New York Times*, *Washington Post*, and the like to assorted small-circulation weeklies). I then have asked them to compare their results. While no sweeping generalizations can be made, surprising consistency within individual publications has been sometimes noted. Letters to one newspaper in one sampling, for example, relied heavily on analogy. Another seemed to attract ad populum appeals and ad hominem attacks. Another, appeals to authority (some legitimate authority, some not). Still another, with a national readership, drew letter-writers who are themselves nationally known authorities on the subjects on which they wrote. These writers frequently cited statistics to support strongly deductive arguments.

Exercise 9-4

What makes this exercise challenging is the requirement that the point of view and conclusion of the original letter must be maintained in the revision. You may want to advise students to select a letter that supports a conclusion with which they agree, although they may not agree with the way the writer reaches that conclusion. If they select a letter with which they disagree, however, they will have the even more interesting challenge of constructing a reasonable case for what they regard as an unreasonable conclusion. In that case, they will be more likely to spot fallacies in the argument they construct—fallacies they must try to eliminate.

READINGS

Richard M. Nixon, The "Checkers" Speech

(1913–   )   Thirty-seventh president of the United States and only president to resign from office before completion of term. Trained as an attorney, Nixon began his political career in 1947 as a U.S. Representative from California. While the Watergate scandal and his forced resignation from office will be forever associated with his presidency, Nixon is also considered one of the outstanding presidents in foreign policy matters. One of his accomplishments in that area was the renewal of relations with mainland China.

Analysis of the Essay   Richard M. Nixon's address to the nation on September 23, 1952, was one of the most immediately and overwhelmingly successful speeches in the American politics of this century. Here was a man cornered, accused of graft, about to be dropped from the Republican ticket: Within hours after the delivery of what has been known ever since as the "Checkers" speech, he was triumphantly restored to favor and trust, and went on with Dwight Eisenhower to victory in the November election. The speech was persuasive indeed, but, examined in the cold light of a post-Watergate day, we might wonder why. Hindsight makes us wise; the evasions, the appeals to pity and to popular prejudices all seem obvious now.

The speech is carefully organized. Nixon describes the charge innocuously ("that I, Senator Nixon, took $18,000 from a group of supporters") and offers three hypothetical premises that would have made accepting that gift "morally wrong" (he dismisses out of hand any possibility that it might have been legally wrong, despite the Freudian slip in the sixth paragraph—a few sentences that were deleted from the version he had published later). In arguing from these premises, Nixon constructs formally fallacious arguments that deny the antecedent in every case. For example,

If any of that $18,000 went to Senator Nixon for my personal use, [taking] it was morally wrong.
None of the $18,000 went to Senator Nixon for my personal use.
Therefore, [taking] it was not morally wrong.

Nixon then offers "a complete financial history" as proof that he did not "fake this thing," that he took no money in cash for his own personal use. The history is neither complete nor is it altogether financial: It begins, in David Copperfield fashion, "I was born in 1913" and goes on to tell the rags-to-Republican story of Nixon's life. He does not go so far as to tell us that he walked seven miles through the snow to school, but we get the idea. The "complete financial history" centers on ad populum and ad misericordiam appeals. The appeals to popular attitudes include digressions on "the best thing that ever happened to me" (marrying Pat Ryan), his service in World War II ("I guess I'm entitled to a couple of battle stars"), and the fact that after the war all his savings were in Government bonds. The appeals to pity—which served also to identify Nixon with many of his hearers—include emphasis on his family's poverty and on his and his wife's financial struggles in their early married life. He speaks of having saved for several years to buy a house. He talks of his family's modest circumstances even at present.

Quite a few numbers are offered in the speech, but nowhere is Nixon's total income for any year given. Nowhere does he declare that he has mentioned *all* sources and amounts of income. Whether or not some evidence has been suppressed we can only speculate, but the fact that Nixon relies on the lack of contrary evidence to prove his case is certain. He describes his assets briefly, noting that Pat has no fur coat (an appeal to popular attitudes, for most of the women in the audience did not own fur coats, either, and an appeal to the pity of those who did). The implied argument is: "If I had taken $18,000 for my personal use, Pat would have a fur coat." The hypothetical syllogism is valid (Pat did *not* have a fur coat), but the hypothesis itself is suspect.

Nixon seems confident that his audience is sympathetic; if they have been uneasy about the allegations, he intimates, surely their uneasiness has resulted from an "honest misunderstanding" and not from the only other possible source, lies and "smears." In a black-or-white disjunctive fallacy, Nixon identifies only those two possible kinds of opposition to his taking the $18,000. Similarly, he postulates only two kinds of people: honest, patriotic Americans like himself and Dwight Eisenhower; and "the crooks and the Communists" and a vaguely specified "they" (as in, "regardless of what they say about it") who oppose the patriots.

But the fallacy that has given this speech its unofficial title is a wonderful exaggeration of Nixon's own honesty and the pettiness of those who have "smeared" him. This "straw man" takes the form of a cocker spaniel puppy given by a supporter to Nixon's young daughters—a personal gift, Nixon announces in mock defiance, that he *will* keep because of his little girls' attachment to it, and damn the consequences. Little Checkers has long since departed this life, but he has been immortalized in the history of American politics. What awful person would even suggest that a puppy should be torn from the arms of his six-year-old mistress? "They" must be terrible people indeed.

The portion of the speech that is not here reprinted consists of several fallacious arguments. After a few verbal detours to attack the chairman of the Democratic National Committee as an elitist and to remind the audience of Nixon's own defense of our nation's honor against the treason of Alger Hiss, Nixon returns to the topic of campaign contributions. He reads a heart-rending letter from an impoverished young woman with a baby in her arms and a husband fighting in Korea, a letter in which the woman expresses her confidence in "great Americans like you" and encloses a ten-dollar check for Nixon's campaign. Here is a contribution that Nixon will cherish but will not take: "Folks, it's a check for $10, and it's one that I will never cash." What is his point here? That he will take money only from the well-to-do? Interestingly, this part of the speech is silently deleted from the Nixon-approved version published in Bela Kornitzer's *The Real Nixon* in 1960.

Throughout the speech Nixon makes veiled ad hominem attacks on the current administration: "Why can't we have prosperity and an honest government in Washington, D.C., at the same time?" (a loaded question) and "those who have corrupted the government" (a begged question). One paragraph near the close of the speech is remarkable for its total lack of logic: the circular argument that "I [won't] quit because I'm not a quitter" and the irrelevant premises of "Pat's not a quitter . . . [because] her name was Patricia Ryan and she was born on St. Patrick's Day, and you know the Irish never quit." The last clause here is additionally a begged question ("everybody knows") and an overgeneralization. And the conclusion itself is a rousing mix of ad populum and ad hominem appeals.

The entire speech is a red herring, luring the audience away from the scent of a more crucial issue than Nixon's personal life, an issue that is briefly brought up and then dismissed in a couple of sentences. Who are the contributors of the $18,000, and what, if anything, are they to receive in return for their contributions? Nixon's assurance that they have received no favors in the past does not preclude favors in the future from a potential president of the Senate and vice-president of the United States. For that matter, Mrs. Nixon's lack of a fur coat does not prove that Nixon did not use any of the money for personal ends. And this scrupulous honesty in disclosing the gift of a cocker spaniel does not prove that he might not keep secret larger and more valuable gifts.

In short, the speech offers inadequate grounds and plenty of slanted and irrelevant "evidence" for accepting its conclusions. It is fallacious and may even be untrue. But in 1952 it was tremendously successful. Letters and telegrams flooded the Republican National Committee headquarters, and Nixon rode the crest into Washington in the November elections. But after more than thirty-five years, we are certain that we are more informed and cynical than the voters of 1952; we would not be susceptible to fallacious appeals as our parents and grandparents were. I wonder if we are safe in that assumption.

Possible Responses to Questions

1. Insofar as defensive arguments attempt to redefine terms and shift ground, considerable similarity in the speeches is possible. Appeals to popular values will be apparent in both cases as well—but the popular values appealed to may be different. Discuss in class what similarities and differences are apparent in the popular values appealed to.

2. None, really. But since Nixon offers Pat Nixon's cloth coat as tacit "evidence" of the honesty that has kept him poor, we might well feel invited to conclude that a fur coat would be tacit evidence of dishonesty that has made him rich. But then we would be guilty of denying the antecedent:

   If Pat Nixon does not have a fur coat, Richard Nixon isn't getting rich through graft and corruption.
   Now, Pat Nixon does have a fur coat.
   Therefore, Richard Nixon has gotten rich through graft and corruption.

3. Fallacy of exaggeration. Nixon creates a "straw man" by implying that Mitchell's statement that a person should be able to afford to be in the Senate (at an adequate but not extravagant salary) had meant that Mitchell thought the Senate should be limited to *rich* men.

4. He has indeed shifted ground. From a man on the defensive he has become a noble crusader against the oppressive and unpatriotic individuals who would prevent the election of Dwight Eisenhower (and, of course, himself).

T. J. Stone, "Lies, Fallacies, and Santa Claus" (Student Essay)

1. The last sentence does not actually contradict the first eight paragraphs of Stone's essay, for those paragraphs lay the groundwork for a thesis with which it is entirely consistent: "Do not do away with

Santa Claus or presents or Christmas trees—simply do away with the lies and evasions."

2. Santa Claus is usually regarded as a harmless bit of make-believe, or "the spirit of giving," and students may not ever have given the tradition any thought. Some may defend it without being able to give any reasons; others, more cynical, may reject out of hand any such "pointless" customs. As to the question of telling children lies, surely there are some things ("Your uncle was an ax-murderer"?) that a small child may not be able to deal with emotionally, and other things ("Christmas is the religious celebration of the earthly incarnation of God's Son; accordingly, those of the Christian faith exchange gifts to symbolize the great Gift God sent humankind") that a child may not be able to grasp intellectually.

   After students have discussed the question at suitable length, ask them whether or not the question itself is an example of equivocation: Is the tradition of Santa Claus really a "lie," in the usual sense?

3. This is an extension of the previous question, leading students to think about the conclusion they reached regarding telling children "lies" of the Santa-Claus sort. If they reach different conclusions for, say, the Easter bunny, the inconsistency of their positions should be challenged.

Jeffrey Schrank, "The Language of Advertising Claims"

(1944–   ) Writer among whose numerous books are *Understanding Mass Media* (National Textbook, 1976) and *Snap, Crackle, and Popular Taste* (Dell, 1977). Schrank's major interests are education and the impact of the media on both education and popular culture.

1. Schrank does not fully explain how advertising works on the subconscious. He has nothing to say about the "psychological hooks . . . of symbols, color, and imagery." He chooses instead to limit his analysis to the texts of advertisements, to show how ads make us think they are saying more than—or something other than—what they are saying. To that extent he is convincing, and he supports his claims with many examples as inductive premises.

2. They are empty or fallacious because they advertise products that are identical competing products—or because they advertise products with little real value. Examples of parity products advertised today may include shampoos, computer diskettes, disposable shaving razors, to name but a few. Students should locate specific advertisements as examples.

3. The "we're different and unique" claim: depending on context, can

be either an appeal to snobbery or an appeal to popular values (the popular value of individuality).

The "water is wet" claim: a counterpart to trivial objections—trivial support.

The "so what" claim and the vague claim: usually beg the question.

The endorsement or testimonial: very often, fallacious appeal to authority.

The "compliment the consumer" claim: sometimes, snob appeal; sometimes, a pleasant opposite to the personal attack—here, the personal praise that has no more to do with the issue at hand than a personal attack does.

Fallacious claims not previously discussed:

The weasel claim
The unfinished claim (incomplete comparison)

4. One advertising appeal that Schrank does not discuss is the threat. Often veiled, the threat is nonetheless a potent sales tactic: Don't buy your child our computer, and she will grow up to be a ditchdigger. Don't buy our dental floss, and you'll be wearing dentures before you know it. Use our cold cream—or watch wrinkles crease your face. Another advertising appeal that Schrank doesn't do much with is snob appeal.

Examples of Advertisements

The advertisements on these pages show the variety of appeals typical in magazines. Your students will probably find one or two particularly attractive and one or two much less so. Lest students become hypercritical after reading Schrank's essay—which would have us believe that almost all advertisements are somehow duplicitous—I have deliberately included a couple that do not emphasize fallacious appeals. The Heineken ad, for example, relies on appealing photography and a low-key bandwagon appeal.

1. A correct estimation of the target audience and what will appeal to it is crucial to the success of any advertisement—and an important consideration as well in the writing of a persuasive essay. Have students discuss in specific detail what makes them feel that they are or are not part of the target audience for each advertisement, and what elements of each ad appeal to or offend them.

2. It might be a good idea to ask students to examine one general-interest

magazine and one special-interest magazine and compare the kinds of ads and kinds of appeals made. Or they might look at advertisements in magazines directed primarily toward male readers (*Esquire*, *GQ*, *Sports Illustrated*) and compare them to those in magazines like *Mademoiselle* or *Vogue*. Ads for the same product or same kind of product make interesting comparisons: What makes the stereo ads in *Time* different from those in *Stereo Review*? What about the cigarette ads in *GQ* as opposed to those in *Glamour*?

3. Some requests for donations, even from reputable and highly worthy organizations, rely almost shamelessly on appeals to pity, popular sentiments, or fear. You are likely to receive more of these than your students do; if you save your "junk mail" for a few weeks prior to the study of fallacies, you no doubt will have many examples for the students to analyze.

4. Here is a little dose of reality that will prepare your students in small measure for the shock that awaits them if they do not yet own their own homes or condominiums. The exercise could lead to an entire essay describing the visit and the almost inevitable letdown—if, that is, students limit themselves to "affordable" houses. The class may be able to compile a quick "homebuyers' glossary of real estate terms": What do "charming cottage," "marvelous possibilities in this three-bedroom home," and "tree-shaded back yard" *really* mean?

Max Shulman, "Love Is a Fallacy"

(1919–   ) Humorist and author of novels, plays, and screenplays. Shulman's Dobie Gillis character (the narrator of "Love Is a Fallacy") became the hero of a popular television program, *The Many Loves of Dobie Gillis*, 1959–62. About the importance of research for effective humor, Shulman says, "Facts are essential to comedy. Recognizable facts and verifiable details give the appearance of reality you need to make comedy stand up."

1. Shulman's tone is, of course, tongue-in-cheek. You may be startled at the number of students who fail to grasp that, however, or who meekly accept the pronouncement that "Love Is a Fallacy" is an essay:
   All essays are written messages that develop an argument, cite instances, and reach a conclusion.
   "Love Is a Fallacy" is a written message that does all these things.
   Therefore, "Love Is a Fallacy" is an essay.

   The logical problem is that the middle term is undistributed. The "argument" fails to account for all of the class of "written messages that develop an argument, cite instances, and reach a conclusion," even if we accept his declaration that all essays do these three things.

2. Love is a "fallacy" only if we conclude that all nonlogical, nonrational mental processes are fallacious. Dobie Gillis undoubtedly concludes that love is fallacious because it can't be inspired by logic.

3. The fallacy of dicto simpliciter is overgeneralization—drawing a conclusion about an entire group out of particular premises. Poisoning the well is the fallacy of personal attack. "Hypothesis contrary to fact" appears to be a fallacy we have not dealt with, but what makes it structurally fallacious is that it necessarily results in the fallacy of denying the antecedent. A fallacy we have not discussed elsewhere (except in the Square of Opposition in this Guide) is contradictory premises.

4. Yes. Shouting is a form of threat, persuasive but not convincing.

5. Students often say that the humor in the story, along with the vivid examples with which Dobie illustrates his explanation, make the fallacies particularly memorable.

ADDITIONAL SUGGESTIONS FOR WRITING OR DISCUSSION

1. Some additional examples of fallacies to use as a quiz or for discussion:

"In civilized society, personal merit will not serve you so much as money will. Sir, you may make the experiment. Go into the street and give one man a lecture on morality, and another a shilling, and see which will respect you most."

—Samuel Johnson (**hasty generalization**)

"If you are getting the worst of it in an argument with a literary man, always attack his style. That'll touch him if nothing else will."

—J. A. Spender
(What is fallacious about this advice?—**personal attack**)

"Paris is devine [sic]. I mean Dorothy and I got to Paris yesterday, and it really is devine. Because the French are devine."

—Anita Loos (**circular reasoning**)

"Who says I am not under the special protection of God?"

—Adolf Hitler, after an attack on his life, 20 July 1944
(**shifting burden of proof**)

"If only I had known [that my discoveries would make the atom bomb possible], I should have become a watchmaker."

—Albert Einstein (**hypothesis contrary to fact**)

"Thank you for stocking cotton ironing board covers. I have been married for 23 years, so I know they are the best."

—Letter written to the Vermont Country Store
and printed in one of its catalogs

(A **non sequitur**, though some might also deem it a **fallacious appeal to**

authority: Does being married for 23 years automatically make a person an authority on ironing board covers?)

2. A colleague, Michael Simms, shared with me the following assignment he has used variously as an in-class exercise and as a written exam.

* * *

Analyze the following arguments for validity and soundness. Your analysis should demonstrate all of the principles of effective writing as well as sound reasoning.

Dear Mr. Simms:

I do not deserve a "D" in this course for the following reasons:

1) A number of personal problems have kept me from doing my best work. My parents are getting a divorce. My brother has been arrested and I have to be a witness in his embezzlement trial. My roommate is mentally ill and has driven me crazy as well this semester. Please take these hardships into consideration when determining my grade.

2) I have never missed a class, have always participated in discussions, have completed all the assigned homework, and have turned my essays in on time. This diligence should count for something, surely. Furthermore, you said that if we missed more than three classes our grades would be lowered. Since I never missed a class, I do not deserve to have my grade lowered.

3) Being a student is my job. People are usually paid for their work at a job based on the number of hours they put in. I have put in many hours at my studies, and I deserve to be paid with a commensurate grade, don't I?

4) I am a member of the XYZ fraternity. The ZITS, as we are known, have a reputation for being outstanding scholars. Furthermore, everyone in my family has always made high grades. Being both a ZIT and a member of such an academically outstanding family, I must be a better student than you are giving me credit for being.

5) You have often said that what is important is not the grade we make but what we get out of the course. If this is true, then why not give away high grades?

6) I am sorry to have to say it, but frankly, this semester you have not done the job I expected from a professor privileged to teach here. The evidence is clear enough: Had you done a better job, I would have scored a higher grade. You were more interested in the book you are writing than in your students.

7) I don't know if you were aware of this, but my father is on the Board of Trustees of this college.

Since you are a reasonable and intelligent man, I am sure you will take all these factors into account and review my grade with them in mind. I have enjoyed your course; you really have a great sense of humor!

Sincerely,

Manny Pullate

3. Ask students to evaluate the reasoning (both the writer's and the pharmacist's) in the following letter to Dear Abby printed on 13 Apr. 1984:

Dear Abby: My 16-year-old son is taking Tegretol for seizures. While filling his weekly medicine container, I noticed that some of the pills looked different. I took the pills back to the drugstore and found out that half of them were penicillin!

The pharmacist said she had used a machine to count the pills, and while filling my prescription for Tegretol, she had some penicillin pills sitting next to it, and she got the penicillin by mistake and mixed those pills up with the Tegretol. (They look very much alike.)

She told me I wasn't the first person that happened to. After that, the drugstore got rid of the counting machine. Fortunately no harm was done to my son.

What I'm saying Abby, is . . . warn your readers to watch their pills!

10

Readings for Further Discussion

These readings are included to use as you see fit. You may choose to use some or all of them for students' analysis and response at the end of the course, or you may prefer to use them in conjunction with earlier chapters. Some possible contexts in which you may find them useful follow.

Fran Lebowitz, "When Smoke Gets in Your Eyes . . . Shut Them"

(1951?–   ) Writer of humor and satire whose essays have appeared in a number of magazines and in two collections, *Metropolitan Life* (1978) and *Social Studies* (1981).

Chapter 2: Creating Arguments
(Have students identify Lebowitz's thesis and supporting points. Ask them to describe her persona and how she creates it.)

Chapter 6: The Power of Style
(What is distinctive about the style of this essay? What makes it so?)

Chapter 9: Fallacies
(Ask students to identify fallacies.)

Rhoda Nichter, "A Question of Rights"

(1926–   ) An antismoking activist, Nichter is the founder and President of Greater New York Council Against Public Smoking and allied organizations. She calls her *Yes, I Do Mind if You Smoke!* (Ashley Books, 1978), from which this short essay is drawn, a "humorous survival guide for nonsmokers" (*Contemporary Authors*, vol. 81–84).

Chapter 1: Argument and Persuasion
(Use as an example of a very short argument.)

Chapter 5: Revising
(Have students revise this argument to improve transitions and paragraphing.)

Robert E. Coulson, "Let's Not Get Out the Vote"

(1924–   ) Attorney and author of books about law for the general reading audience. Among Coulson's works are *How to Stay Out of Court* (1968) and *Business Arbitration: What You Need to Know* (1980).

Chapter 1:   Argument and Persuasion
(Use as a model of short argument.)

Alan Wertheimer, "For Compulsory Voting"

Chapter 1:   Argument and Persuasion
(Use with Coulson as a model of short argument for analysis.)

Chapter 8:   Deductive Reasoning
(Reconstruct syllogisms from the enthymemes here and evaluate them.)

Ethics Committee of the American Fertility Society, "The Rationale for Surrogate Motherhood"

Chapter 1:   Argument and Persuasion
(Examine the language both for evidence of slanting and/or scrupulous attempts to avoid slanting. Consider what might be the *a priori* convictions of an organization devoted to helping infertile couples.)

Chapter 3:   Using Definition in Argument
(Find and evaluate the numerous definitions in the essay. Discuss: To what extent does the whole argument turn on definition?)

Chapter 5:   Revising
(Discuss the organization of the essay. In what ways does its arrangement advance its thesis?)

William E. May, "Surrogate Motherhood: An Ethical Dilemma"

(1928–   ) Christian ethicist, father of seven children, and professor of moral theology at Catholic University of America, Washington, D.C. May is the author of numerous works; the range of his concerns is indicated by some of their titles: *Human Existence, Medicine, and Ethics* (1977), *Sex, Marriage, and Chastity* (ed., 1981), *Studies in Natural Law* (forthcoming).

Chapter 3:   Using Definition in Argument
(Use together with previous essay to examine differences in definitions that are central to the issue of surrogacy.)

Chapter 5:   Revising
(Why does May place his refutation where he does?)

Chapter 6:   The Power of Style
(Contrast the style of this essay with that of the American

Fertility Society argument. Discuss how purpose and intended *ethos* affect style.)

Chapter 8: Deductive Reasoning
            (Evaluate the enthymemes.)

Irving Kristol, "Pornography, Obscenity, and the Case for Censorship

(1920–   ) Founder (1965) and editor of *Public Interest* quarterly and Henry R. Luce Professor of Urban Values (since 1969) at New York University. Kristol is the author or editor of five books and a contributor to periodicals such as *Harper's, Atlantic Monthly, Fortune,* and to *The New York Times* and *Wall Street Journal.*

Chapter 3: Using Definition in Argument
            (Notice how key terms are defined. Are the definitions fair?)

Chapter 8: Deductive Reasoning
            (Reconstruct syllogisms from Kristol's argument and evaluate them.)

Chapter 9: Fallacies
            (Identify fallacies, both those committed and those exposed.)

Eli M. Oboler, "Defending Intellectual Freedom"

(1915–1983) Librarian (University of Chicago and Idaho State University) and author of books on censorship and freedom of expression. Oboler received the Robert Downs Award for Intellectual Freedom in appreciation for his work in opposing censorship.

Chapter 4: Research and the Uses of Evidence
            (Use as an example of citing evidence from an outside source. Remind students that Oboler is quoting from a longer version of the Kristol essay included here.)

William J. Bennett, "We Need Routine Testing for AIDS"

Secretary of Education in the Reagan administration.

Chapter 5: Revising
            (Use as an example of point-by-point refutation. Discuss: Does Bennett do well to choose this tactic?)
            (Evaluate use of analogy to support argument.)

Arthur S. Leonard, "AIDS: The Legal Epidemic"

Professor at the New York School of Law (New York City) and author of a legal issues column for the *New York Native,* a gay weekly.

Chapter 2: Creating Arguments
            (Use to illustrate the enthymemic thesis.)

Chapter 5:   Revising
             (Discuss: Why is exposition so important to an argument on
             this subject? Is Leonard's exposition sufficient and clear?)

Clarence Darrow, "Why I Am an Agnostic"*

(1857–1938)   American lawyer famed as defense counsel in a number of
controversial trials, including that of Socialist leader Eugene V.
Debs (for conspiracy in the Railroad Union case, 1894) and that of John Thomas
Scopes (for teaching evolution in Dayton, Tennessee, 1925). Author of
many articles and several books, including *Crime, Its Cause and Treatment*.

Chapter 3:   Using Definition in Argument
             (How does Darrow use definition to create and develop his
             argument? What are his key definitions? Evaluate them ac-
             cording to the standards described in Chapter 3.)
Chapter 9:   Fallacies
             (Ask students to read and comment on Darrow's arguments
             before revealing their reliance on fallacies. Try to draw out
             their awareness gradually. See possible questions and re-
             sponses in the addendum below.)

C. S. Lewis, "What Are We to Make of Jesus Christ?"

(1898–1963)   British professor of medieval literature at Oxford and, after
1954, Cambridge University. Author of more than thirty books, ranging
from literary criticism to science fiction to Christian apologetics to children's fiction, Lewis is best remembered today for his writings on religious subjects. The most popular of these has been *The Screwtape Letters*, a satire comprised of letters of advice from an old devil to a young
devil.

Chapter 2:   Creating Arguments
             (Use this essay as an example of an argument that is developed
             out of the attempt to resolve a contradiction.)
Chapter 8:   Deductive Reasoning

Caroline Bird, "The Case for Equality"

(1915–   )   A feminist commentator on contemporary issues, Bird is
best known for *Born Female* (rev. ed. 1970), *Everything a Woman Needs
to Know to Get Paid What She's Worth* (1973), and *The Case Against
College* (1975).

---

*The Darrow and Lewis essays were included within chapter readings in the first
edition. The questions and possible responses from the first edition are included at the end
of this section.

Chapter 3: Using Definition in Argument
(What definitions are at the heart of this essay?)
Chapter 8: Deductive Reasoning
(Examine the hypothetical arguments.)
Chapter 9: Fallacies
(Identify fallacies, both those committed and those exposed.)

William J. Byron, S. J., "Paid Homemaking: An Idea in Search of a Policy"

(1927–   ) A Jesuit priest and University of Scranton (Pennsylvania) administrator, Byron's interests range from economic and ethical theory to contemporary social issues. Byron has written essays and articles in a number of collections and periodicals, among them, *America, Commonweal,* and *Today.*

Members of the Birmingham Clergy, "A Call for Unity"

Chapter 2: Creating Arguments
(Describe the collective persona of these writers and what elements create it.)
Chapter 3: Using Definition in Argument
(Identify the key issues of definition here.)
Chapter 6: The Power of Style
(Describe the specific elements. Compare to King's style.)

Martin Luther King, Jr., "Letter from Birmingham Jail"

(1929–1968) Baptist minister and leader of the civil rights movement in the United States in the 1950s and 1960s. King was awarded the Nobel Peace Prize in 1964 for his work and his advocacy of nonviolent resistence in the struggle for racial equality. In developing his own principles of justice, King was influenced by the work and philosophy of India's Mahatma Gandhi. Among his several books is *Why We Can't Wait* (1964), which contains the text of his famed "Letter from Birmingham Jail."

Chapter 2: Creating Arguments
(Describe the author's persona and what specific elements create it.)
Chapter 3: Using Definition in Argument
(Identify the key issues of definition here.)
Chapter 5: Revising
(Outline the essay to study how King has organized his argument.)
Chapter 6: The Power of Style
(Describe the specific elements. What figures of speech predominate? Compare to John Kennedy's style in his Inaugural Address. What similarities can be found?)
Chapter 8: Deductive Reasoning
(Evaluate the enthymemes.)

Rami Khouri, "Sharing the Land and the Legacy"

An editor of the *Jordan Times* and Jordan correspondent for several news organizations in the United States and Great Britain, Khouri is a New York-born Palestinian.

Chapter 2: Creating Arguments
(Use as an example of an argument that develops its thesis out of the attempt to resolve a contradiction.)

Chapter 4: Research and the Uses of Evidence
(Evaluate the evidence Khouri offers as inductive support of his argument.)

Chapter 6: The Power of Style
(Use together with the next essay, contrasting this rather colorless prose with the memorable style of Benvenisti's.)

Meron Benvenisti, "Maps of Revenge"

(1934–   ) A lifelong, politically active resident of Jerusalem (including a tenure as city councillor and deputy mayor from 1969–78), Benvenisti has been a free-lance writer, primarily on the subject of his country and city, since 1979, and director of the West Bank Data Base Project since 1983.

Chapter 6: The Power of Style
(Discuss the importance of the map imagery as a way of understanding the Middle East dilemma.)

Chapter 7: Inductive Reasoning
(Use to illustrate argument from examples)

ADDENDUM

Former In-Text Questions for Darrow Essay

1. You probably know the name of Clarence Darrow, the eminent attorney famous for his participation in the Scopes Trial (the historic trial centering on the issue of teaching the theory of evolution in schools) and for his writing on many subjects. To what extent does the distinguished reputation of the writer predispose you favorably toward his arguments even before you read them? Discuss.

2. Darrow defines *agnostic* in his first paragraph. Does he restrict the definition in any way? Compare his definition with that given in a dictionary. Comment on any differences you find.

3. Put the following enthymemes (from paragraph 1) into syllogistic form and evaluate their soundness.

   Anyone who thinks is an agnostic about something, otherwise he must believe that he is possessed of all knowledge. And the proper place for such a person is in the madhouse or the home for the feeble-minded.

4. How does Darrow organize his argument, and what is his primary conclusion?

5. Identify four precepts Darrow calls both Christian and fallacious. Do you agree or not? Comment. If you do not agree with Darrow, how would you answer him?

6. Does Darrow commit any fallacies himself? If so, give examples and explain why they are fallacious.

7. In paragraph 6 Darrow argues against the existence of the soul. The topic of the paragraph may be summarized as an enthymeme: "All bodies are made by the multiplication of cells, so the body cannot have a soul." Reconstruct this enthymeme as a syllogism. What is the implicit underlying premise? Is the argument sound? Explain.

8. What underlying assumptions about the structure and composition of books support Darrow's enthymemic argument about the Bible in paragraph 8? Would Darrow call an anthology a book?

9. Evaluate the following alternative enthymeme from paragraph 12: "In all prophecies facts are made to suit the prophecy, or the prophecy was made after the facts, or the events have no relation to the prophecy." What names have we given these three kinds of fallacy? Are Darrow's alternatives the only ones possible? Comment.

10. Comment on the persona Darrow creates within this essay. How well does it correspond with his public persona?

The lessons this essay has to teach are most effective if you assign the essay without much advance comment other than a reminder that its author was a renowned attorney, social reformer, and writer, whose best-known trial was the Scopes "monkey" trial of 1925. You might also mention that he is writing here to expose what he regards as the fallacy of Christianity. And he is persuasive, particularly on the basis of his ethical appeal. But (and this I would suggest not telling the students, as to do so before they read the essay begs the question) his argument, rather than being couched in reasonable and convincing terms, is itself fallacious from beginning to end. Most students, even just after studying fallacies, fail to see the fallacies on a first reading. They are too awed by the persona of the famous lawyer. The questions following the essay should gradually elicit a more critical appraisal of the essay.

Possible Responses to the Questions

1. As noted above, the distinguished reputation of the writer goes far to predispose the reader to accept his arguments. Even the student who disagrees with Darrow's conclusions may mumble something to the effect that "I don't agree with him, but I can't really answer

his arguments." And the student who does agree with him may do so uncritically, all because of the writer's strong ethical appeal.

2. Darrow defines *agnostic* as "one who doubts or disbelieves the main tenets of the Christian faith." Under that problematic definition, of course, a devout Jew or Muslim is an agnostic. The usual meaning of agnostic is one who "does not deny God but denies the possibility of knowing Him" (*American Heritage Dictionary*).

3. Either people are agnostic or they believe they are possessed of all knowledge.

All who think are people who know they are not possessed of all knowledge.

Therefore, all who think are agnostic.

All who believe they are possessed of all knowledge are people who belong in the madhouse.
Non-agnostics are people who believe they are possessed of all knowledge.
Therefore, non-agnostics are people who belong in the madhouse.

The syllogisms are valid but the truth of the major premise in each can be challenged. The first is a black or white fallacy: Many people consider themselves neither agnostic nor omniscient. The second argument's major premise can be accepted only if the first one is true, for Darrow's has defined the class "all who believe they are possessed of all knowledge" *very* broadly.

4. Darrow organizes his essay according to the order of the points he sets forth in paragraph 2: He first challenges the belief in God; second, the belief in immortality (the soul); and third, the belief in "a supernatural book" (the Bible). By far the greatest part of his argument centers on his challenge of the Bible and the miracles and prophecies it recounts. His main conclusion is that "the fear of God [Christianity, in his argument] is the death of wisdom" (paragraph 23).

5. Some of the precepts Darrow challenges include:

(a) belief in God (paragraph 3)

(b) the divine origin of the universe (4–5)

(c) the existence of the soul (6)

(d) the Bible and its divine inspiration (8–9, 13)

(e) miracles and prophecies (10–12, 15–18, 20)

(f) God's creation of the human race (14)

(g) the miraculous conception of Jesus (19)

The biggest problem with his challenges is that they are themselves blatantly and gratuitously fallacious, full of ad hominem attacks, straw men, and begged questions ("You can't believe in God unless you believe in the kind of God I tell you to—an anthropomorphic God. You can't believe in *anything* you can't visualize.")

6. Darrow strews fallacies about so casually that he insults his readers' intelligence, regardless of whether they disagree with him or agree. For example (in addition to fallacies identified in questions 2 and 3, above):

   (a) The "three basic tenets" Darrow ascribes to Christians are held by other religions as well; and Darrow omits the *one* tenet that is distinctively Christian: a belief in Jesus Christ as the Son of God who died for the sins of humankind and rose from the dead. Darrow distorts through oversimplification and omission—the fallacy of the partial truth.

   (b) "They carry no such implication because no one has any knowledge or experience of someone having made these natural objects which everywhere abound," (4). This is the fallacy of "lack of evidence to the contrary"—the appeal to ignorance. "What we don't know isn't so."

   (c) "Not one scrap of evidence exists to prove any such impossible thing" (7). Loaded phrase (begging the question) and shifting burden of proof—"I don't have to prove my point of view; you must prove yours."

   (d) "There is no such book" as the Bible because it is made up of sixty-six books. See question 8, below.

   (e) Paragraph 9 contains a circular argument about violations of natural laws.

7. All things made by the multiplication of cells are things that cannot have a soul.

   Bodies are made by the multiplication of cells.

   Therefore, bodies are things that cannot have a soul.

   The implicit premise argues that nothing with a biological basis can be more than, greater than, or substantively different from its source. Any biochemist would find this statement puzzling. The implicit premise is by no means self-evident or proven, so the argument begs its central question.

8. Darrow's enthymeme here argues that no volume comprised of independent units (particularly if those units were written over a long period of time or by a number of different authors, and even more

particularly if those authors have different opinions and points of view) can be called a "book." He assumes, we must conclude, that to be called a "book" a volume should be a single work by a single author expressing a single point of view. This definition necessarily excludes anthologies and collections.

9. All three involve causal relationships, but not quite the same fallacy.

"Facts are made to suit the prophecy": distortion (of the facts) through exaggeration or oversimpification

"Prophecy was made after the facts": a deliberate lie

"The events have no relation to the prophecy": post hoc fallacy

Darrow's alternatives are not the only ones possible. Sometimes insightful people prophesy things that do come about: economic recessions, improved or deteriorating relations between countries, and the like. So there must be at least one other possible alternative: The prophecy comes not from "hearing voices" but from astute analysis of conditions and accurate prediction of consequences.

10. The persona Darrow creates depends on how carefully we read his argument. On a quick reading, we may think we have before us the relentlessly logical, hard-hitting, famed attorney we have read about in history books. On a closer reading, we may decide that Darrow has so little regard for his hearers' and readers' intelligence that he has indulged in sloppy reasoning and careless fallacies.

Former In-Text Questions for Lewis Essay

1. Express the core argument as a disjunctive syllogism. Lewis argues that "there is no half-way house"; that the two alternatives he presents are the only ones possible. What support does he offer for his premises? Evaluate his evidence and reasoning.

2. Has Lewis overlooked any possible alternatives for "what we are to make of Jesus Christ"? If so, what are they?

3. What is the "appalling claim" that Lewis declares Jesus made? What is appalling about it?

4. Lewis says that "it is very necessary to get the story [of the Resurrection] clear." How, if at all, does his argument in paragraph 6 support his thesis? Express the argument in paragraph 6 as a syllogism. Is it valid?

5. Because religious questions concern matters that people hold *a priori*—outside of and beyond the realm of logic—we are often advised not to attempt argument on such questions. Of course, we do not always heed that advice but, with Lewis and Clarence Darrow, plunge in

where the proverbial angels develop cold feet. While we must grant that arguments about religion necessarily will contain premises the truth of which some readers will question, what does Lewis show us about ways to offer reasonable arguments in support of our *a priori* convictions?

6. What kind of persona does Lewis project in this essay? What particular features of his tone, examples, vocabulary, and so on create this voice? Discuss your sense of Lewis's persona with classmates who either strongly agree or strongly disagree with Lewis's own convictions. What differences do you find, if any? Try to determine how much of your and their reactions is response to Lewis's persona, how much response to the subject of his essay.

Possible Responses to the Questions

1. Jesus Christ was "either God or a complete lunatic." (paragraph 3) He was not a complete lunatic. (paragraph 1) Therefore, he was—is—God.

   The support Lewis offers is to take the widespread acknowledgment that Jesus was a great moral teacher and challenge its truth given any terms other than his divinity. First, Jesus claimed to be God and went about telling people he forgave their sins. Second, Jesus's followers were devout Jews to whom the idea of multiple gods was abhorrent, so they would not have been eager to manufacture the notion that Jesus was a god unless evidence compelled them. Third, the stories about Jesus are not likely to be legends because they are radically different in content and style from legends of that time.

   Students' evaluation of Lewis's reasoning is likely to be colored by their own *a priori* notions. Discuss the extent to which their *a priori* beliefs, and even your own, interfere (either favorably or unfavorably) with reasonable evaluation of Lewis's arguments. Remembering that the aim of argument is to find truth, not merely to defend or attack positions, they may find it helpful to write down the points at which they particularly applaud or condemn Lewis's assertions, and to examine the reasoning therein on strictly logical grounds (taking as "givens" Lewis's *a priori* belief system).

2. Other possibilities have been advanced by theologians and philosophers, including the possibility that Christ's claims were symbolic rather than literal.

3. The "appalling claim" (paragraph 2) is the claim to be God. Lewis calls it appalling because, if it is not true, it is either sacrilegious or megalomaniacal.

4. The argument in paragraph 6 is related to Lewis's thesis in that it

discusses the event on which all else hangs: the Resurrection. Lewis is insistent that the event happened. (Again, he argues that it was an account so unexpected in its form that Jesus's followers, who might have manufactured a story about ghost-survival, were hardly likely to have made up such a tall tale as a bodily resurrection.) Therefore, his main concern here is not to prove the *event* of the Resurrection but to make clear the *nature* of the Ressurection: "a totally new mode of being."

> The Resurrection was either ghost-survival or a totally new mode of being that defeats death.
>
> The Resurrection was not an example of ghost-survival.
>
> Therefore, in the Resurrection, Christ defeated death.

The alternative syllogism is valid: the minor premise denies one alternative, and the conclusion affirms the other.

5. One thing Lewis shows us is the rhetorical strength of the alternative deductive argument. If we can find alternatives that represent the likely or tenable positions on a subject, and then show how all but one of the alternatives proves inadequate or mistaken, we can make a persuasive case for our position, even when arguing *a priori* issues.

6. Differing responses to Lewis's persona may well stem from the readers' own differing beliefs. Agnostics may claim he is smug. Some Christians may say he is simplistic, and others may assert that he is reasonable and persuasive. Require *all* responses to this question to be supported by examples from the text, and the differences in perception will grow somewhat fewer.